EPIGRAPHIA ZEYLANICA

BEING

LITHIC AND OTHER INSCRIPTIONS OF CEYLON

EPIGRAPHIA ZEYLANICA

BEING

LITHIC AND OTHER INSCRIPTIONS OF CEYLON

EDITED AND TRANSLATED BY

DON MARTINO DE ZILVA WICKREMASINGHE

IN FOUR VOLUMES
1904-1934

Vol. II
1912 - 1927

GYAN

Published by

Gyan Publishing House
5, Ansari Road
Daryaganj, New Delhi-110002
Phone: 011-47034999, 9811692060
E-mail: books@gyanbooks.com

Distribution Network
gyanbooks.com
India, USA, Canada, UK, Australia, France

ISBN : 978-81-212-3351-4 (Set)
ISBN : 978-81-212-4988-1 (PB)
First Published, 1928

2nd Impression 2020

Printed at: Gyan Press, Delhi.

ARCHAEOLOGICAL SURVEY OF CEYLON

EPIGRAPHIA ZEYLANICA

BEING

LITHIC AND OTHER INSCRIPTIONS OF CEYLON

EDITED AND TRANSLATED

BY

DON MARTINO DE ZILVA WICKREMASINGHE, Hon. M.A. (Oxon.)

EPIGRAPHIST TO THE CEYLON GOVERNMENT

READER IN TAMIL AND TELUGU IN THE UNIVERSITY OF LONDON

LECTURER IN SINHALESE AND HEAD OF THE DRAVIDIAN DEPARTMENT

AT THE LONDON SCHOOL OF ORIENTAL STUDIES

Vol. II

1912–1927

LONDON

PUBLISHED FOR THE GOVERNMENT OF CEYLON BY HUMPHREY MILFORD

OXFORD UNIVERSITY PRESS, AMEN HOUSE, E.C.

1928

THIS VOLUME IS DEDICATED

TO

HARRY CHARLES PURVIS BELL,

C.C.S. (RETIRED)

AS A SMALL TRIBUTE OF RECOGNITION OF HIS EMINENT SERVICES TO CEYLON EPIGRAPHICAL AND HISTORICAL STUDIES

PREFACE

In presenting this volume of the *Epigraphia Zeylanica* to the public, the Editor has to express his regret at the delay that there has been in its production owing to various unavoidable circumstances. Foremost among them is the difficulty of the task which the Editor had to perform singlehanded in the midst of University duties and his anxiety to obtain the best possible results, regardless of all personal inconveniences resulting from postponement of publication. The delay would have continued, had it not been arrested by the present Archaeological Commissioner of Ceylon in supplying the Editor with the material needed for the last part of the present volume. The Editor hopes that the same spirit of co-operation in research work will be continued in the future to enable him to produce the *Epigraphia Zeylanica* regularly in a style commensurate with the expenditure that is being incurred thereon by the Government of Ceylon.

The Editor wishes to avail himself of this opportunity to express his profound indebtedness to Professor A. B. Keith for the final revision of his work. The Ceylon Government is indeed fortunate in receiving the free assistance of an eminent scholar of Professor Keith's world-wide reputation.

The Editor has, moreover, taken the liberty to dedicate this volume to his erstwhile chief, Mr. H. C. P. Bell, as a small token of gratitude for his services in the cause of Ceylon epigraphy by having initiated the publication of the *Epigraphia Zeylanica* some thirty years ago, as stated in the preface to the first volume.

Finally the Editor's thanks are also due to the Oxford University Press for bestowing their usual care in the production of this volume. His indebtedness to various scholars who have generously given him the benefit of their knowledge will be found duly acknowledged in the body of the work.

The Index being a continuation of that appended to Vol. I includes all the words and proper names in the two volumes.

DON MARTINO DE ZILVA WICKREMASINGHE.

London School of Oriental Studies,

June, 1928.

CONTENTS

LIST OF PLATES

THIS VOLUME IS DEDICATED

TO

HARRY CHARLES PURVIS BELL,

C.C.S. (RETIRED)

AS A SMALL TRIBUTE OF RECOGNITION OF HIS EMINENT SERVICES TO CEYLON EPIGRAPHICAL AND HISTORICAL STUDIES

LIST OF PLATES

SYSTEM OF TRANSLITERATION

Devanāgarī	Sinhala	Tamil	Roman
अ	අ	அ	a
आ	ආ	ஆ	ā
—	ඇ	—	ä
—	ඈ	—	ǟ
इ	ඉ	இ	i
ई	ඊ or ඊ	ஈ or ஈ	ī
उ	උ	உ	u
ऊ	ඌ	ஊ .	ū
ऋ	ඍ	—	ṛ
ॠ	ඎ	—	ṝ
ऌ	ඏ	—	ḷ
ॡ	ඐ	—	ḹ
—	එ	எ	e
ए	ඒ	ஏ	ē
ऐ	ඓ	ஐ	ai
—	ඔ	ஒ	o
ओ	ඕ	ஓ	ō
औ	ඖ	ஔ	au
क	ක	க	ka
ख	ඛ	—	kha
ग	ග	க (medial)	ga
घ	ඝ	—	gha
ङ	ඞ	ங	ṅa
च	ච	ச	ca
छ	ඡ	—	cha
ज	ජ	ஜ, ச	ja
झ	ඣ	—	jha
ञ	ඤ	ஞ	ña
ट	ට	ட (when doubled ட்)	ṭa
ठ	ඨ	—	ṭha
ड	ඩ	ட	ḍa
ढ	ඪ	—	ḍha
ण	ණ	ண	ṇa
त	ත	த	ta
थ	ථ	—	tha
द	ද	த (medial)	da
ध	ධ	—	dha
न	න	ந	na
प	ප	ப	pa
फ	ඵ	—	pha
ब	බ	ப (medial)	ba
भ	භ	—	bha
म	ම	ம or [illegible]	ma
य	ය	ய	ya
र	ර	ர	ra
ल	ල	ல	la
व	ව	வ	va
—	—	ழ	ḻa
—	—	ள	ḷa
—	—	ற	ṟa
—	—	ன	ṉa
श	ශ	ச	śa and ça
ष	ෂ	ஷ	ṣa
स	ස	ச or ஸ	sa
ह	හ	க or ஹ	ha
ळ	ළ	—	ḷa
ं (anusvāra)	ං	—	ṁ
ँ (anunāsika)	c (?)	—	˘ ˘
ः (visarga)	ඃ	—	ḥ
ऽ (avagraha)	—	—	'

ABBREVIATIONS

A. = Apabhraṁśa.

Abh. = Abhidhānappadīpikā, edited by Waskaḍuwe Subhūti. Colombo, 1865.

A. I. C. = Ancient Inscriptions in Ceylon. By Dr. E. Müller. 2 vols. London. 1883.

Am. = Amāwatura, edited by H. Jayatilaka. Colombo, 1885–86.

AMg. = Ardha-Māgadhī.

Arch. Surv. = Archaeological Survey.

A. S. C. = Archaelogical Survey of Ceylon.

A. S. S. I. = Archaeological Survey of Southern India.

A. S. W. I. = Archaeological Survey of Western India.

Bt. = Bell's Text.

C.B.R.A.S. = Ceylon Branch of the Royal Asiatic Society.

C. I. I. or Corp. Inscript. Ind. = Corpus Inscriptionum Indicarum.

Comp. Gram. = A Comparative Grammar of the Modern Aryan Languages of India. By John Beames. 3 vols. London, 1872–79.

Dh. = Dhammapada (Fausböll's edition. 1885).

Dv. = Dīpavaṁsa.

E. I. or Ep. Ind. = Epigraphia Indica.

E. S. = Etymologie des Singhalesischen, von Wilhelm Geiger. München, 1897.

E. Z. or Ep. Zeyl. = Epigraphia Zeylanica.

Gram. = Grammar or Grammatik.

Hc. = Hēmacandra.

Ind. Ant. = Indian Antiquary.

J. or Journ. = Journal.

Jay. = H. Jayatilaka's Elu-Akārādiya. Colombo, 1893.

JM. = Jaina-Māhārāṣṭrī. JŚ. = Jaina-Śaurasēnī.

Lit. = literally.

L. S. S. = Litteratur und Sprache der Singhalesen, von Wilhelm Geiger. Strassburg, 1900.

M. = Māhārāṣṭrī. Mg. = Māgadhī.

Mp. = Müller's plate. Mt. = Müller's text.

Mv. = Mahāvaṁsa. Mv. Ṭ. = Mahāvaṁsa Ṭikā.

M. W. Dict. = Sir Monier Monier-Williams' Sanskrit Dictionary. Oxford, 1899.

Nām. = Nāmāvaliya.

Or. Soc. = Oriental Society.

P. = Pāli. p. = page. par. = paragraph.

Piyum. = Piyummala.

p. p. p. = past participle passive. Pkt. = Prākrit.

R.A.S. = Royal Asiatic Society.

Ruvan. = Ruvanmala.

Ś. = Śaurasēnī.

S. B. E. = Sacred Books of the East, edited by F. Max Müller.

Sinh. = Sinhalese. Skt. = Sanskrit.

T. = George Turnour.

W. = L. C. Wijēsiṇha, translator of the Mahāvamsa.

Z. D. M. G. = Zeitschrift der Deutschen Morgenländischen Gesellschaft.

ADDITIONS AND AMENDMENTS

[H=suggested by Mr. A. M. Hocart, the present Archaeological Commissioner of Ceylon.
B=suggested by Mr. H. C. P. Bell, the late Archaeological Commissioner of Ceylon.]

Page 2, line 13, *read* 'Kassapa IV (891–908 A.D.)'; line 28, 'Udaya I (880–891 A.D.)'.

4, Kirigallāva, Pillar-inscription. Lines D 10 and 12. A *daṇḍa* used as a punctuation mark. This is noteworthy. (H).

6, line 11, *read* 'Udaya I (880–891 A.D.)'.

7, Noccipotāna, Pillar-inscription. The syllables *nne* and *ssā* written thus: ෙනනා and සසා. This way of writing conjunct consonants is not usual in the records of this period (H).

— do. L. A. 6, *Gelgamu,* the archaic form of the modern name of *Galegama*, the neighbouring village (B).

9, paragraph 5. With the *birudas* Abhā Salamevan and Siri Saṅg-bo used alternately by the Sinhalese kings of the ninth and tenth centuries, compare the similar usage of the titles Rājakeçarivarman and Parakeçarivarman by the Coḷas, and Māṟavarman and Jaṭilavarman by the Pāṇḍyas (H).

9, paragraph 3, *read* 'Kassapa IV (891–908 A.D.).'

9, paragraph 5, *read* 'the kings of the ninth and tenth centuries in order, Sena I (826–846 A.D.); Sena II (846–880 A.D.); Udaya I (880–891 A.D.); Kassapa IV (891–908 A.D.); Kassapa V (908–918 A.D.); Dappula IV (918 A.D.)'.

10, line 1, *read* 'Dappula V (918–930 A.D.)'.

10, line 3, *read* 'Mahinda IV (954–970 A.D.)'.

10, line 6, *read* 'to the latter half of the ninth century and the tenth century A.D.'.

10, line 11, *read* 'Kassapa IV (891–908 A.D.)'.

12, Tim̆biri-väva, Pillar-inscription. Side B. lines 22–24, read *Soḷi Tundi ber no-koḷavanu isā,* 'Coḷiyans and Toṇḍiyans shall not (be permitted to) have tom-toms beaten'. (B.)

14, paragraph 3, *read* 'Udaya I (880–891 A.D.)'; 'Kassapa IV (891–908 A.D.)'.

15, line 3, *read* 'Udaya I (880–891 A.D.'; 'Kassapa IV (891–908 A.D.)'.

16, Nāgama, Pillar-inscription. Side A, l. 12. The occurrence of the form of *ṇ* [illegible] side-by-side with the later and more common form ණ is worthy of remark. (H.)

20, lines 9–10, *read* 'Kassapa IV (891–908 A.D.)'.

22, lines 1–2, *read* 'Kassapa IV (891–908 A.D.)'.

22, line 3, *read* '902'.

27, line 21, *read* 'Kassapa V (908–918 A.D.)'.

28, line 1, *read* 'Mahāsena (334–361 A.D.)'.

28, line 3, *read* 'Kaniṭṭha Tissa (226–244 A.D.)'.

28, lines 5–6, *read* 'Aggabodhi IV (651–667 A.D.)'.

28, lines 7–8, *read* 'Vijaya Bāhu I (1058–1114 A.D.)'.

28, line 9, *read* '1137–1153 A.D.'.

28, line 12, *read* '1187–1196 A.D.'.

28, Mäḍirigiriya Pillar-inscription. A replica of this pillar has been found by Mr. Harry Storey and published in the *Ceylon Antiquary* (vol. x, pp. 67–87) by Mr. H. C. P. Bell. (H.)

Page 30, Mādirigiriya Pillar-inscription. Side A, line 7, *read* Madhurā. (B.)

32, line 5, *read* 'Madhurā-dunu'. Note 5, *read* 'Madhurā-dunu' 'who conquered Madhura'. (B.)

35, lines 4–5, *read* 'Kassapa V (908–918 A.D.)'.

35, lines 4–5, *read* '(908–918 A.D.)'.

38, *Väl-gattan*. Could this be equivalent to Sanskrit *vetradhāra*? (H.)

39, line 2, *read* '(908–918 A.D.)'.

40, line 2, *read* '(908–918 A.D.)'.

44, paragraph 2, *read* 'Dappula V (918–930 A.D.)'.

45, lines 3–4, *read* 'Dappula V (918–930 A.D.)'.

45, line 8, *read* 'Sena II (846–880 A.D.)'.

45, lines 21–22, *read* 'Aggabodhi I (564–597 A.D.)'.

48, Ātavīragollāan Pillar-inscription. Side C, lines 23–25, read *Tuṇḍi Soḷiyä gasan no vadnā isā* (B).

49, line 4, *read* 'Toṇḍi and Coḷa noosers shall not enter' (B).

50, With *yamuguru-gattan*, compare *dāṇḍika* occurring in the Nālandā copper plate of Devapāladeva (*Ep. Ind.*, xvii, p. 325). (H.)

50, lines 1–2, *read* 'Mahinda IV (954–970 A.D.)'.

50, line 24, *read* 'Sena II (846–880 A.D.)'.

51, line 10, *read* 'Dappula V (918–930 A.D.)'.

51, line 11, *read* 'Ramukkaṇḍu'. (H.)

51, line 16, *read* 'Mahinda IV (954–970 A.D.).

54, Rajamāligāva Pillar-inscription. Side B, lines 24–26, read *Tuṇḍi Soḷi gasan no vadnā hoṭ isā.* (B.)

56, line 11, *read* 'Toṇḍi and Coḷa noosers shall not enter', *for* 'Tuṇḍise shall not secretly enter'. (B.)

59, lines 19–20, *read* 'Sena IV (950–953 A.D.)'.

64, lines 13–14, *read* 'Mahinda IV (954–970 A.D.)'.

64, lines 22–23, *read* 'Mahinda IV (954–970 A.D.)'.

68. Raṁbāva Slab-inscription. Translation of line 28. *Demahak* may perhaps mean two *māshas*. For the use of the word *māsha*, as a measure of capacity, see Alutväva Pillar-inscription. In this case (*sati*)*n lahasuyen* ought to be taken as the name of a standard measure as the Rājakeçari-Nāḷi occurring in Coḷa inscriptions. (H.)

71, paragraph 2. In connexion with the discussion of the two names Ruvanväli and Ruvanmäli, see Geiger, *L. S. S.*, p. 48, where, with reference to the rule that the letters *m* and *v* are interchangeable in certain words, the Professor quotes this very example. (H.)

72, line 1, read *kartṛ*. (H.)

93, Häṭa-dāgē Wall-inscripton, line 4, read *rājayan* for *rājadhāni*; line 10 *boho* for *bogo*; line 17, *visaṁburu-vala-da* for *pisaṁburu-valu-da*.

101, line 4, read *Āyasmanta*.

105, Galpota Inscription, A, line 8. The form *kurūra* for Skt. *krūra* is worthy of note. (H.)

106, do. do. B, line 10, read *devunuvara*.

107, do. do. B, line 18, read *rajadaruvanhā guṇen mitra*.

109, do. do. C, line 23, read *genäda*.

118, do. do. A, line 23. The word *devadāna* has been translated 'offerings to Gods' This word, perhaps, is here used in its technical meaning as 'lands dedicated for the service of gods' in which sense it is of frequent occurrence in Indian Inscriptions. (H.)

Page 129, Kalā-krīḍā-vinoda-gal-āsana-inscription, line 3 *yācakayanaṭ* is an archaism. (H.)

141, Rankot-dāgaba Pillar-inscription. Side D, line 16, read *dig-vi-*.

171, Prīti-dānaka-maṇḍapa Inscription, l. 35. A possible reading instead of Mahapuṭupaya is Mahavuṭuvaya. If the latter reading is adopted, the place could be identified as Mahātittha, the well-known seaport of Ceylon in olden days. (H.)

196, line 1, read *Suddhodana*. (H.)

202, Aṁbagamuva Rock-inscription. This rock is in St. Clive Estate, Nawalapitiya.

217, note 3. It is possible that *ihi* is a variant of *ehi*. By the influence of the final *i* the initial vowel may be changed. In this case the phrase *ihi dā vaňdanaṭa* may be translated 'to worship the relics (by being) there'. (H.)

223, note 1. Another possible reading is *kaňga-koṇḍa-paṭṭaṇama* equivalent to Kaṅgai-koṇḍa-paṭṭaṇam. This place was, in all probability, a port in the Coḷa country named after Rājendra-Coḷa I who, we know, bore the Surname Kaṅgai-koṇḍa. (H.)

224, l, 28. Instead of රජකළ, I prefer the reading ර[ා]ජකළ. In the translation the corresponding change would be 'should they make them belonging to royalty', i.e. 'confiscate them'. (H.)

235, In connexion with the Ānanlandāva Slab-inscription, it may be interesting to notice that a Tamil slab-inscription from Vāhalkaḍa opens with the identical words, and belongs to the same guild of merchants. Judging from Mr. Bell's eye-copy the stone seems to have been badly preserved. No estampage is available. (H.)

241, Potgul Vehera Inscription, lines 20–22. The reading *dutiyaṁ yā aggataṁ gatā* which is clear on the stone, does not accord with the metre. (H.). It accords wtth the metre when *yā aggataṁ*, are taken and pronounced as *yā 'ggataṁ*. [Editor.]

EPIGRAPHIA ZEYLANICA

No. 1. KIRIGALLÂVA PILLAR-INSCRIPTION

KIRIGALLÂVA is a hamlet in Kaḍawat Kōrale, about twenty miles north-north-east of Anurādhapura.

The inscribed pillar was discovered[1] by Mr. H. C. P. Bell in 1892. It is about 5 ft. high and 9½ in. square. Each of the first three sides contains fifteen lines of writing within ruled spaces, the fourth has twelve lines ending with the figures of a crow and a dog[2].

The letters, one to two inches in size, are very well preserved. They represent the alphabet of the tenth century, but their type is a mixture of that of Kiribat-vehera and of Moragoḍa pillars[3]. As in the former and in the records of Kassapa V, Dappula V, and some of Mahinda IV, the two vertical strokes of the letters *a*, *r*, and the medial vowel *u* are written separately so that their lower ends do not meet.

This is a later type[4], while the akṣaras *ka*, *ma*, *ya*, and *la* have the older forms occurring in the Moragoḍa, Īripinniyāva, and Raṁbāva pillars[5]. Judging from the form of script taken as a whole, the date of our record must be earlier than the Kiribat-vehera, but later than that of Īripinniyāva, and this would fall within the period covering the reigns of Udaya I and Kassapa IV (*circa* 952–980 A.D.).

As regards **orthography**, attention may be drawn to the forms *mekāppară* for *mey-kāppar*[6] and *melāsīn* for *melāṭsīn*, *melākṣīn*, *melātsīn* and *melăttī* in other lithic records[7]. *Perălăkkan* and *dunumaṇḍlan* are fresh additions to the list of obscure technical terms such as *perenăṭṭiyam*, *melāṭsīn*, etc., occurring in Ceylon inscriptions. The expression *abhiṣēka dī* (side D, line 2), which obviously

---

[1] See *A. S. C. Annual Report* for 1892, p. 9.

[2] See accompanying facsimile (Plate 1).

[3] Cf. Vol. I, Plates 20 and 26 with the present one.

[4] *Ibid.*, p. 242.

[5] *Ibid.*, Plates 21, 22, and 26.

[6] *Ibid.*, p. 154, note 2, p. 164, note 5, and pp. 245, 251.

[7] See Index to Vol. I for references, and below, p. 20.

stands for *pärähär dī*[1], shows that the ceremony of granting immunities and setting up pillars of Council Warranty may have involved some form of consecration, such as anointing (*abhisēka*)[2].

The subject-matter is the granting of the usual immunities to a village called **Itnaru-gama** in **Amgam-kuḷiya** by decree of His Majesty **Abhā Salamevan** in Council in the second year of his reign. The State Officials who carried out the order were (a) **Maṇitilā Kiliyem** and (b) **Gaṅguḷhusu Ag-boyim** of the family of Mekāppar-Vädārum[3] **Vadurā**[4], and (c) **Kavasilāṅg Gavayim** of the family of the Chief Secretary **Araksama Kasbā**. Nothing is known about these three officers except that, as the first two were descendants of Mekāppar-Vädārum Vadurā, they must have been related to Ataragalu Kottā and Mulavaḍā Sakarā who set up the *aṭṭāṇi* pillar at Moragoḍa in the sixteenth year of Kassapa IV (963–980 A. D.). The Chief Secretary Araksama Kasbā may perhaps be identified with the minister Dāru Kassapa, a contemporary of Vajira (Sinh. *Vadurā*)[5], also a minister of Sēna I.

As to the names of places in the record, we see from the Vēvälkäṭiya slab[6] that Amgam-kuḷiya was a district in the Northern Quarter; but the village Itnaru-gama in it is not mentioned as the property of a temple or other public institution as is usually the case. This is interesting, for it raises the question whether immunities such as those stated in the present inscription used to be granted to private lands also or not. For two other similar grants, see the Noccipotāna and the Nāgama pillars dealt with below (Nos. 2 and 4).

We have stated that palaeographically the **date** of our inscription must be fixed in the reign of Udaya I or of his successor Kassapa IV, but in view of the important information contained in the Tiṁbirivāva pillar[7] as to the *biruda* title of Udaya I being Abhā Salamevan[8], while that of his brother and successor, Kassapa IV, was Siri Saṅg-bo, we are inclined to attribute the authorship of the present record to Udaya I (952–963 A. D.). And as the inscription is dated on the tenth day of the first fortnight of *Äsela* (June–July) in the second regnal year, it must have been set up some twenty-five years before the Moragoḍa pillar, ten years before the Tiṁbirivāva one, or about eight months after the Raṁbāva and Īripinniyāva pillars.

---

[1] See the Moragoḍa pillar, side D, line 15 (Vol. I, No. 17).

[2] Cf. *Abhiṣēkayen daru* in the Buddhannehäla pillar (Vol. I, p. 192).

[3] Regarding this title, see Vol. I, p. 193.

[4] See Vol. I, p. 202.

[5] *Ibid.*, p. 202.

[6] *Ibid.*, p. 243.

[7] See below, pp. 9–10.

[8] Regarding the title Abhā Salamevan, see Vol. I, p. 165.

TEXT.

A.

1 අභා සලමෙ
2 වන් මපුර්
3 මූකා සත් නැ
4 ගූ දෙවන හ
5 වුරුදු යෙහි
6 ඇසෙළු පුර
7 දස පක් ද
8 වස් මෙකාපප
9 රු වැදෑරුම්
10 වදුරු වරු
11 වන මණික්
12 ලැ කිලිගෙම්
13 ග[1]ගුල්ගුසු
14 අග්බොයිම්
15 මහලෙ අර

B.

1 ක්සම ක
2 ස්බා වරින්
3 ආ (කවසිලා)
4 ග් ගවයිම්
5 ඇප් මෙතුවා
6 ක් දෙනමො එ
7 ක්සෙවැ වත්
8 ගිමියන් එ
9 ක්තැන්සම්
10 යෙන් වදෑලෙ
11 සින් අම්ග
12 මකුළිගෙහි
13 ආවූ (ඉත්න)
14 (රූ) ගමට් දු
15 නුමඬලන්

C.

1 (කුළී) මෙලාසින්
2 මඟ්දිව පෙ
3 දිව නො වද්
4 නා කොට් රත්[2]
5 කොල්කැම්ය
6 න් පෙරලැක්
7 සින් සෙ .. .. ..
8 රුවනෑ වැස්
9 සන් පෙරනා
10 ටපියම් නො ව
11 ද්නා කොට් ගැ
12 ල් හොන් වැරි
13 යන් නො නග
14 තු කොට් වත්
15 ගිමියන් ව .

D.

1 දැලෙසින් මෙ
2 අභිෂෙක දි
3 අත්තා-ණීක
4 ණු ගිඤ්වූම
5 හ මෙයට් වැ
6 දැ ආ(ශු) ඊ
7 ලැ(ඝ)නා කළ
8 කොනෙකුන් ඇ
9 ත දෙස් .. ..
10 .. කරනු | ක
11 වුඩු බලූ
12 වනු | සිකි

---

1 'හඟුල්' යිද කියවිය හැකියි

2 'රද්' වෙනුවට

TRANSCRIPT.

A.

1 **Abhā Salame-**
2 **-van** Mapur-
3 -mukā sat nä-
4 -ňgū devana ha-
5 -vurudu yehi
6 Äseḷä pura
7 dasa pak da-
8 -vas Mekāppa-
9 -rä-Vädārum
10 **Vadurā**-varä
11 vana **Maṇiti-**
12 **-lā Kiliyem**
13 **Gaňguḷhusu**[1]
14 **Ag-boyim**
15 Mahale **Ara-**

B.

1 **-ksama Ka-**
2 **-sbā**-varin
3 ā (**Kavasilā-**)
4 **-ňg Gavayim**
5 äp metuvā-
6 -k denamo e-
7 -k-se-vä vat-
8 -himiyan e-
9 -k-tän-sami-
10 -yen vadāḷe-
11 -yin **Amga-**
12 **-m-kuḷiyehi**
13 āvū (**Itna-**)
14 (**-ru**)-gamaṭ du-
15 -numaňḍlan

C.

1 (kulī) melāsīn
2 maňg-diva pe-
3 -diva no vad-
4 -nā koṭ rat-[2]
5 -kol-kämiya-
6 -n peräläk-
7 -kan se .. .. ..
8 -ruvanā väs-
9 -san peranā-
10 -ṭṭiyam no va-
11 -dnā koṭ gä-
12 -l gon väri-
13 -yan no naňga-
14 -nu koṭ vat-
15 -himiyan va-

D.

1 -dāḷeyin me
2 abhiṣēka dī
3 attāṇi-ka-
4 -ṇu hind-vūma-
5 -ha meyaṭ vä-
6 -dä ā(jňā) u-
7 -lä(gha)nā kaḷa
8 kenekun ä-
9 -ta des- .. ..
10 .. karanu | ka-
11 -vuḍu balu
12 vanu | siddhi

---

[1] This may also be read *Haňguḷhusu*.

[2] For *raa-*.

Kirigallǟva Pillar-inscription.

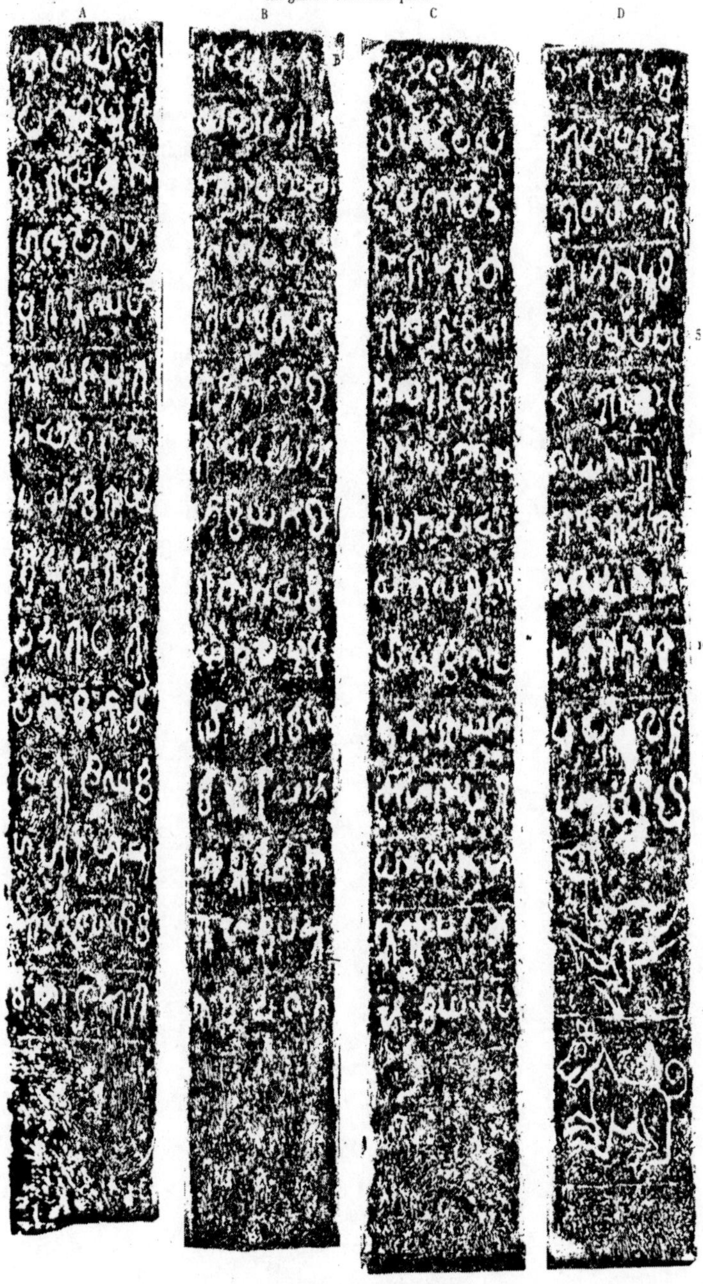

From an ink-impression supplied by the Archaeological Commissioner, Ceylon.

Scale about 2 inches to 1 foot.

TRANSLATION.

On the tenth day of the waxing moon of [the month of] *Äseḷa* (June–July) in the second year after the raising of the canopy of dominion by his Majesty **Abhā Salamevan.**

Whereas it was [so] decreed by His Majesty[1] in Council, we all of us, namely, **Maṇitilā Kiliyem** and **Gaṅguḷhusu Ag-boyim** [both][2] of the family of Mekāppar-Vädārum **Vadurā,** and **Kavasilāṅg Gavayim** of the family of the Chief Secretary **Araksama**[3] **Kasbā,** have conjointly and with due inaugural ceremonies[4] granted [the following immunities] to the village **Itnaru-gama** in the district of **Amgam-kuḷiya** :—*Dunumaṇḍlan*[5], *kulī*, *melāsī*[6], tramps and vagrants shall not enter; servants of the royal family, *perälākkan*, inhabitants holding two kinds of services[7], and *peranāṭṭiyam* shall not enter; and carts, oxen, and labourers shall not be appropriated.

[To this effect] we have set up this pillar of Council Warranty by Order of His Majesty.

Should any person enter this [village] and transgress the enactments, let him be . . . . let him be a dog or a crow [in his future birth. May there be] prosperity.

No. 2. NOCCIPOTĀNA PILLAR-INSCRIPTION

THIS pillar lies at a spot called Noccipotāna, about one and a half miles from Galegamạ in Egoḍapattuva in the Tamankaḍuva district, some sixty miles south-east of Anurādhapura. It measures about 5 ft. by 1 ft. 2 in. square. The inscription is clearly engraved on three of its sides, horizontally ruled for the purpose. Sides A and B contain nineteen lines each, and C eight lines.

---

[1] *Vat-himiyan* (B, lines 7–8). See Vol. I, p. 199, note 1, and p. 206, note 2.

[2] The relative participle *vana* may qualify Maṇitilā Kiliyem only. In this case the family name will not be applicable to the second named officer.

[3] See below, p. 32, note 10. [4] *Abhiṣēka dī* (D, line 2). [5] See below, p. 27.

[6] Same as *Melātti* or *-ṭsī*. This passage may also be translated 'the hired labourers and the *melāsīs* (foreign mercenaries?) of the archery department'.

[7] Cf. *Deruvänä ḍekamtän vässan* in the Vessagiri record, l. 25 (Vol. I, p. 37, note 7, and p. 207, note 3).

It was in a state of good preservation when the Archaeological Commissioner examined it on September 24, 1897.

The **akṣaras**, which are about 1¼ to 2½ in. in size, belong to the alphabet of the tenth century, but they are distinctly older in type than those in the records of Kassapa V. The letters *a*, *k*, *m*, *y*, *r*, and *l*, resemble most the forms found in the Kirigallāva, the Nāgama, the Kukurumahan-damana, and the Moragoḍa pillars. The inscription may, therefore, palaeographically be ascribed either to Udaya I or Kassapa IV; but in view of the statement in the Tiṁbirivāva pillar (below, p. 9) as to the *biruda* title of Udaya I being Abhā Salamevan, while that of Kassapa IV was Siri Saṅg-bo, we are justified in identifying **Abhā Salamevan** of our record with Udaya I (952–963 A. D.).

The **date** of the edict being the ninth year of the reign of this monarch, that is to say, about 961 A. D., it is seven years later than that of Kirigallāva.

The **subject** of this Council Warranty is devoid of historical interest, except that here we come across another grant of immunities to a land apparently unassigned to a religious or public institution, and similar in character to the two *attāṇi* pillars at Kirigallāva and Nāgama. As to the four officials instrumental in proclaiming the Council Warranty, the family of Pāṇḍi-rad Dāpuḷa is mentioned also in the Kiribat-vehera and the Mäḍirigiriya pillar-inscriptions[1] of Kassapa IV and Kassapa V respectively, while a certain **Nilavasa Mandiyā** figures also in the Ayitigevāva edict of Kassapa V about twenty-four years later[2].

TEXT.

A.

1 ශ්‍රී අ(භා) සලමෙව
2 න් මපුර්මූකා (න)ව ව
3 නෙහ වැපැ අව ස
4 නවක් දවස් (මුගු
5 නෙළු)වගමැ (වලර)
6 (කා)හෙල්ගමු දියවත්
7 (ග)ම්සගි අන්තා
8 ණිකණු ගිඤ් වත්
9 නව් වදලෙයින් ආ
10 සභායෙ නිලවස
11 මඳියා ඉසා මහකා
12 (බුඝසාදු මිතු) ඉසා
13 පාඬිරද් දපුළ ව
14 ඨ මෙය්කාප්පර් දු
15 වි මහනු(ගු)ණය(ා)
16 ඉසා ගලුකැගැල
17 මායා ඇතුළ්වැ මෙතු
18 වාක් සම්දරුවන්වි
19 සින් මෙ ගමට් මග්

---

[1] Side A, lines 8 and 9 (Vol. I, p. 159), and below, p. 27.

[2] See below, p. 35.

Noccipotāna Pillar-inscription.

A B C

From an ink-impression supplied by the Archaeological Commissioner, Ceylon.

Scale about 1½ inches to 1 foot.

B.

1 (දිව් පියදිව් මෙ
2 ලාට්සි පෙරෙලැක්
3 කාන් නො වද්නා ඉ
4 සා රට්ලදු පස්ල)
5 දුවන් නො (වද්නා)
6 ඉසා පියො වදාර
7 නුවන් නො වද්නා
8 ඉසා දෙරුවනා දෙ
9 කම්තන් නො වද්
10 නා ඉසා ගැල් ගො
11 න් වැරි මිවන් නෙ[ා]
12 ගන්නා ඉසා ග
13 ඦ් කඬට් වැරි නො
14 ගන්න[ා] ඉසා පෙරෙ
15 නාට්ටියම් නො ව
16 ද්නා ඉසා අභය
17 සඳහ වනුවන්
18 නො ගන්නා ඉසා
19 නො රැක්කමනා කෙ

C.

1 නකුන් ගැමින්
2 පිටත් කරවා ග
3 නුන් මිසැ ගම්
4 වැදැ නො ගන්නා කො
5 ට් මෙ ගම්හි අන්
6 තාණ්කණු හිඳුව[ා]
7 විදාළෙයින් මෙ පෙ
8 රැහැර් දෙනු ලදී

TRANSCRIPT.

A.

1 Śrī **A**(**bhā**) **Salameva**-
2 -**n** Mapurmukā (na)va va-
3 -nne Väpä ava sa-
4 -tavak davas (**Muṅgu**-
5 -**neḷu**)**va-gamä** (**Valara**-)
6 (-**ka**-)**heḷ-gamu** diya van
7 (ga)misahi attā-
8 -ṇi-kaṇu hind-van-
9 -naṭ vadāḷeyin ā
10 sabhāye **Nila-vasa**
11 **Madiyā** isā **Maha-Ka**-
12 (-**bussālu Mitu**) isā
13 **Pāṅḍirad Dāpuḷa-va**-
14 -rä Meykāppar **Du**-
15 -**ṭ Maha-nu**(**gu**)**ṇay**(**ā**)
16 isā **Galukāhäla**
17 **Māyā** ätuḷ-vä metu-
18 -vāk samdaruvan-vi-
19 -sin me gamaṭ maṅg-

B.

1 (-div piya-div me-
2 -lāṭsi pereläk-
3 -kan no vadnā i-
4 -sā raṭ-ladu pas-la-)
5 -duvan no (vadnā)
6 isā piyo-vadāra-
7 -nuvan no vadnā
8 isā deruvanā de-
9 -kam-tan no vad-
10 -nā isā gäl go-
11 -n väri mivan no
12 gannā isā ga-
13 -ṅg kaṅḍaṭ väri no
14 gann[ā] isā pere-
15 -nāṭṭiyam no va-
16 -dnā isā abhaya
17 sandaha vanuvan
18 no gannā isā
19 no räkkamanā ke-

C.

1 -nakun gämin
2 piṭat karavā ga-
3 -nut misä gam
4 vädä no gannā ko-
5 -ṭ me gamhi at-
6 -tāṇi-kaṇu hind-v[ā
7 vadāḷeyin me pe-
8 -rähär denu ladī

TRANSLATION.

Hail! On the seventh day of the waning moon of [the month of] *Väp* (September–October) in the ninth[1] year [of the reign] of His Majesty **Abhā Salamevan.**

Whereas it was decreed that a pillar of Council Warranty[2] should be set up at the upper end of the village[3] **Muṅguneḷuva-gama**, irrigated by the waters of **Valaraka Heḷ-gama**, all these Officers of State, Members of the Council, namely, **Nila-vasa Madiyā**[4], **Maha-Ka(bussālu Mitu)**[5], Meykāppar **Duṭ-maha-nuguṇayā**[6] of the family of **Pāṇḍi-rad Dāpuḷa**, and **Galukāhäla Māyā**, have come and set up in the aforesaid village the pillar of Council Warranty, granting by Order the [following] immunities to the village :—

Tramps and vagrants, *melāṭsi*, and *pereläkkan* shall not enter; district headmen, and keepers[7] of (district) records shall not enter; enforcers of customary rules shall not enter; holders [of the management] of two places of business shall not enter; carts, oxen, labourers, and buffaloes shall not be appropriated; labourers shall not be impressed for river-work[8]; *perenāṭṭiyam* shall not enter; those who have come for asylum shall not be arrested; should there be any undeserving of protection, they shall be taken after they have been made to quit the village, but shall not be arrested by [officers] entering the village.

---

[1] 'Second year', according to Mr. Bell (*A. S. C. Annual Report* for 1897, p. 11).

[2] *Attāṇi-kaṇu*, side A, lines 7–8.

[3] *Gamisahi* (A, line 7). This passage may also be rendered 'at Gamisa in the village Muṅguneḷuva-gama'.

[4] This may mean 'Madiyā of the family of Nīla'. Cf. *Nila-mahā-yōdhayā*, a name of one of the warriors of Gaja Bāhu I, according to the Rājāvaliya. *Vasa* is apparently a substitute for *vara* usually found in tenth-century records. Cf. *Piritti-radun-dā-vasä* in the Bilibāva pillar, below, p. 42.

[5] *Mitu*=P. *mitta*.

[6] This is a curious name. Literally it means 'the wicked-great-vicious-one'; possibly a nickname. Cf. *Duṭṭha-Gāmaṇi* 'Gāmaṇī, the wicked', *Vaṅkanāsika Tissa* 'Tissa, the crooked-nosed'.

[7] Dr. Müller also thinks that the above interpretation of *pas-laduvan* is better than any of the earlier renderings (*J. R. A. S.* for 1912, p. 516).

[8] *Gaṅg-kaṇḍaḷ väri no gannā* (B, lines 12–14).

No. 3. TIMBIRIVÄVA PILLAR-INSCRIPTION

TIMBIRIVÄVA is a small village in the Pahala Kälägam Tulāna of Vilacciya Kōrale, about twenty-three miles to the west-south-west of Anurādhapura.

The inscribed pillar here is one of those examined by the Archaeological Commissioner (Mr. H. C. P. Bell) between 1898 and 1900[1]. It measures about 5½ ft. x 10 in. x 9 in., and the writing which covers the first three sides and half of the fourth is in some parts very much worn, as may be seen from the accompanying facsimile (Plate 3). Side A contains twenty-five lines; B, probably twenty-eight, of which the last four lines and portions of lines 9, 10, 15, and 24 are illegible; C, about twenty-five lines, of which the first three and the last five are wholly illegible; while D seems to have only eight lines, the last two of these being illegible, and the first and sixth partially so.

The **akṣaras**, one to three inches in size, belong to the alphabet of the tenth century A. D., and closely resemble the type of the letters in the Moragoḍa pillar[2] of the sixteenth year of Kassapa IV (963–980 A. D.).

The style of the **language**, too, is in agreement with this record, the first twelve lines in both being almost the same word for word. There is, therefore, no doubt that **Kasub Siri Saṅg-bo**, described in both as the brother of **Udā Abhā**, the conqueror of **Ruhuṇa** and **Mala-maṇḍulu**, is one and the same person, namely, Kassapa IV, as stated above on p. 201 of Vol. I.

The present record gives the *biruda* title of **Udā** (Udaya I) as **Abhā Salamevan.** This information is important, as it, added to what we already know from other sources, enables us to make the inference that the kings of this period followed a certain method in the use of the *birudas Salamevan* and *Siri Saṅg-bo.* No one king seems to have used both the titles; and if one was known as *Salamevan*, his successor was called *Siri Saṅg-bo*, and *vice versa.* To take the kings of the tenth century in order, Sēna I (*circa* 897–917 A. D.) had the *biruda* name *Salamevan*[3]; Sēna II (917–952 A. D.), *Siri Saṅg-bo*[4]; Udaya I (952–963 A. D.), *Salamevan*[5]; Kassapa IV (963–980 A. D.), *Siri Saṅg-bo*[6]; Kassapa V (980–990 A. D.), *Salamevan*[7]; Dappula IV (990 A. D.), probably *Siri Saṅg-bo*, though

[1] *A. S. C. Annual Report* for 1900, p. 12. Inscription, No. 83.
[2] Vol. I, No. 17.
[3] P. *Silāmēghavaṇṇa.* In *Mv.* l. 43, *Silāmēghō.*
[4] Vol. I, pp. 24 and 42.
[5] The present inscription.
[6] Vol. I, p. 201, and the present record.
[7] *Ibid.*, p. 42.

we have no certain evidence of the fact; and Dappula V (990–1002 A.D.), *Salamevan*[1]. So far as we know, there is only one exception to this rule. In the inscriptions of Mahinda IV (1026–1042 A.D.) his father is described both as *Abhā Salamevan* and *Siri Sang-bo*[2]. If the above inference is correct, then it follows that the records which must, for palaeographical reasons, be assigned to the middle period of the tenth century A.D., and which bear the name of Abhā Salamevan—the inscriptions, for instance, at Īripinniyāva[3], Rambāva[3], Kirigallāva[4], and Noccipotāna[4]—should be ascribed to Udaya I rather than to Kassapa IV.

The **date** of our record being the first regnal year of **Kasub Siri Sang-bo** or Kassapa IV (963–980 A.D.), it is thirteen years earlier than the Kiribat-vehera pillar, and fifteen years earlier than the Moragoḍa one.

The **contents** deal with the immunities granted to the village **Mibäḷi-gama** attached to the **Māḍbiyan-pirivena**[5]. One of the privileges worth drawing attention to is that fines exacted from the villagers should not be appropriated by the State, but should be delivered over to the pirivena.

No one of the three officials who set up the *aṭṭāṇi* pillar is known to history. The ancestor of the first one, namely, Mekāppar-Vädārum **Vidurangu-nā Nimulā**, may, however, be either identical with or related to Mekāppar-Vädārum **Viduragu** (or **Vijuragu**), the ancestor of Mekāppar **Sangpahim** and **Kaḍusu Vadurim** of the Buddhannehäla pillar[6].

TEXT.

A.

1 (සිරි ලක්දි
2 ව්හි පිහිටි)
3 සිරිපිඬ ය
4 ස ඉසිරි රැහු
5 ණුදනවූ ම(ල)ම
6 ඹුලු තමහට්
7 පිරිබො කළ **ඔකා**
8 **අභා සලමෙව**
9 **න්** මහරද්හු සො
10 හොවුර් **කසුබ්**
11 **සිරිසඟ්බො**
12 මපුර්මූකා පල
13 මූ වස්නෙහි
14 වෙසැගැ පුර
15 දසපක් දව
16 ස් වදැලෙසි
17 න් ආ මෙකාප්
18 පර් වැදැරුම්
19 **විදුර(ගු)නා**

[1] Vol. I, p. 24. [2] *Ibid.*, p. 213. [3] Vol. I, Nos. 12–13. [4] Vol. II, Nos. 1–2.
[5] Probably *Māṭambiya*. See *Mv.* xlvi. 19. [6] Vol. I, No. 16.

20 හිමුලා වරු
21 මෙකාප්පර් (ද)
22 ම(ක්නනි) ස
23 කිම ඉසා මෙ
24 කාප්පර් (හෑ)
25 (නෑ කොඩ)සි

B.

1 ම ඉසා ම
2 හාලෙ නිමු
3 ල් මියිඤුරක්
4 සමණියන් ව
5 රු කුඩසලා
6 නා(මු[1] දෙ)පිම
7 ඉසා ඇප්
8 මෙතුවාක් දෙ
9 නාමො ව
10 .. (සැනි) අ
11 වූ (නඩිරවණි)
12 මාඩබියන්
13 පිරිවෙන් (බ)
14 ද් (ඕබැළි)ගම
15 ව .. .. දුනුම්බූ
16 ලූ මෙලාත්ති
17 නො වද්නා කො
18 ට් ඉසා ම
19 ගිව පියගි
20 ව නො වද්නා
21 කොට් ඉසා
22 (සොලී පාඩී) ..
23 ම්බූර් නො කො
24 .. .. වනු ඉසා
25 .. ..
26 .. ..
27 .. ..
28 .. ..

C.

1 .. ..
2 .. ..
3 .. ..
4 වැරියන් නො
5 ගත්නා කොට්
6 ඉසා කිරි ගෙ
7 (රි) ගැල් (මිවු)න්
8 නො ගත්නා
9 ඉසා දෙකම්
10 තැන් දෙරුව
11 නෑ නො වද්නා
12 ඉසා පෙරෙ
13 (ලැක්කන් වත්)
14 හැමැගි (සිට)
15 තිරු කොට් ග
16 ත් අඩ රද්කොල
17 ව් නො ගෙනෑ පි
18 රිවෙනට් දේ(නු)
19 ඉසා වදෑළෙයි
20 න් අ රත්කොල්[2]
21 [සම්දරුවමො ?]
22 .. ..
23 .. ..
24 .. ..
25 .. ..

D.

1 (සිම්) .. .. ..
2 මෙ පෙරුහ
3 ර් දි මෙ අත්
4 තාණී කඤු
5 හි(ඤ්වූම්)
6 (හයි) .. ..
7 .. ..
8 .. ..

---

1 'නාවූ' සීද කියවිය හැකියි

2 'රද්කොල්' වෙනුවට

TRANSCRIPT.

A.

1 (Siri Lak-di-
2 -vhi pihiṭi)
3 siri-piḍ ya-
4 -sa isiri Ruhu-
5 -ṇu-danavuMa(la-)ma-
6 -ňḍulu tamahaṭ
7 piribo kaḷa **Udā**
8 **Abhā Salameva-**
9 **-n** maharad-hu so-
10 -hovur **Kasub**
11 **Siri Saṅg-bo**
12 Mapurmuka paḷa-
13 -mu vannehi
14 Vesaga pura
15 dasa-pak dava-
16 -s vadāleyi-
17 -n ā Mekāp-
18 -par-Vädārum
19 **Vidura(ňgu-)nā**
20 **Nimulā**-varä
21 Mekappar (**Da-**)
22 **-mi**(**nnani**) **Sa-**
23 **-kim** isā Me-
24 -kāppar (**Hā-**)
25 (**-tä Koňda**)**yi-**

B.

1 **-m** isā Ma-
2 -hā-le **Nimu-**
3 **-l Mihind-arak-**
4 **-samaṇan-va-**
5 -rä **Kuňḍasalā**
6 **Nā(ṭ[1]u-de)ṭim**
7 isā äp
8 metuvāk de-
9 -namo va .. .. ..
10 .. (säni) ā-
11 -vū (**Naḍ-raṭ-hi**)
12 **Māḍbiyan-**
13 **piriven** (ba-)
14 -d (**Mibäḷi-**)**gama-**
15 -ṭ .. .. **dunumaḍu-**
16 -lu meḷätti
17 no vadna ko-
18 -ṭ isā ma-
19 -ňgiva piyangi-
20 -va no vadnā
21 koṭ isā
22 (Solī Pāňdi) ..
23 -mbur no ko
24 .. .. vanu isā
25 .. ..
26 .. ..
27 .. ..
28 .. ..

C.

1 .. ..
2 .. ..
3 .. ..
4 väriyan no
5 gannā koṭ
6 isā kiri ge-
7 (-ri) gäl (mivu)n
8 no gannā

---

[1] This can also be read *Nävu-*.

Timbirivāva Pillar-inscription.

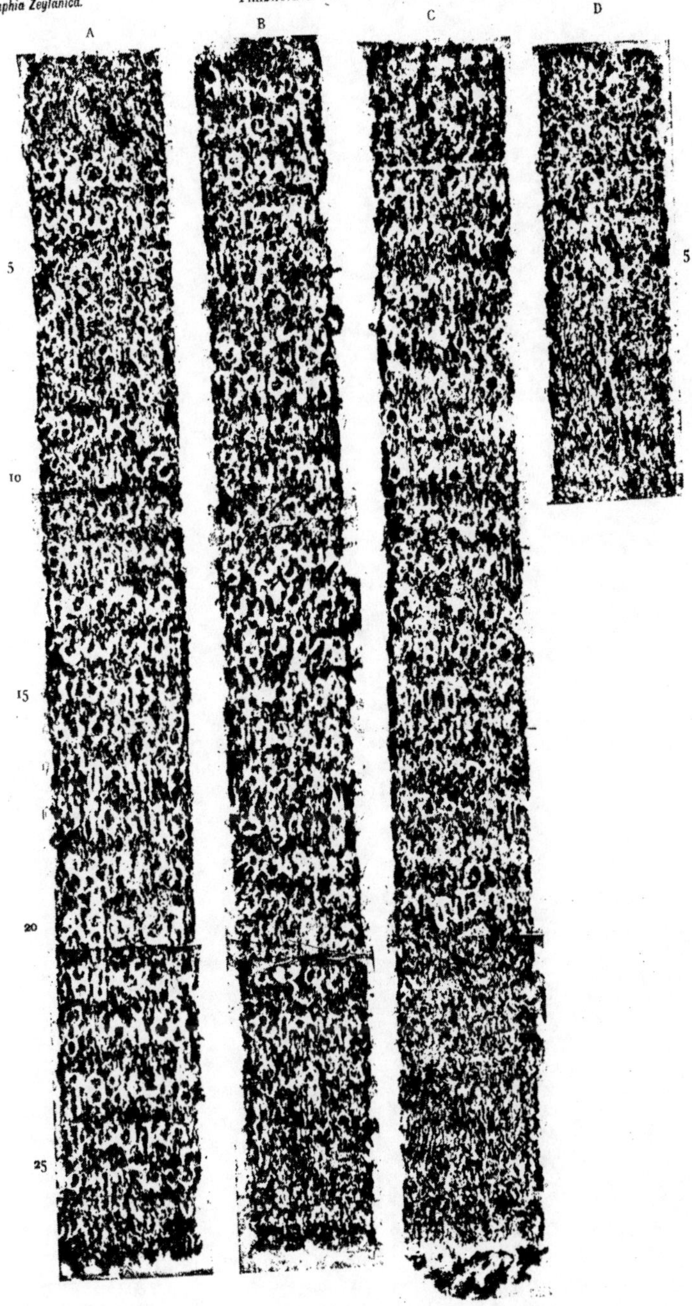

From an ink-impression supplied by the Archaeological Commissioner, Ceylon.

Scale about 1½ inches to 1 foot.

9 isā de-kam-
10 -tän deruva-
11 -nā no vadnā
12 isā pere-
13 (-läkkan van)
14 gämähi (siṭa)
15 tirā koṭ ga-
16 -t daḍ rad-kola-
17 -ṭ no genä pi-
18 -rivenaṭ de(nu)
19 isā vadāḷeyi-
20 -n ā rat-kol-[1]
21 [-samdaruvamo ?]
22 .. ..
23 .. ..
24 .. ..
25 .. ..

D.

1 (-yim) .. .. ..
2 me perāha-
3 -r dī me at-
4 -tāṇi-kaṇu
5 hi(nd-vūm-)
6 (-hayi) .. ..
7 .. ..
8 .. ..

TRANSLATION.

On the tenth day of the waxing moon of [the month of] *Vesąk* (April–May) in the first year of [the reign of] His Majesty **Kasub Siri Saṅg-bo**[2], brother of the great king **Udā Abhā Salamevan**[3], who secured for himself the possession of the Ruhuṇu Province and the Mala[4] District and [the enjoyment] of the combined wealth, glory, and prosperity that prevailed[5] in the beautiful Island of Laṅkā.

Whereas it was [so] decreed[6], we all of us, namely, Mekāppar **(Da)mi(nnani) Sakim** and Mekāppar **(Hāta Koṅḍa)yim** [both] of the family of Mekāppar-Vädā-rum[7] **Vidura(ṅgu)-nā**[8] **Nimulā**, and **Kuṅḍasalā Nā(ṭu-de)ṭim** of the family of the Chief Secretary **Nimul Mihind-arak-samaṇan**, have come.

And whereas it was [so] decreed concerning the village **Mibäḷi-gama** attached to the **Māḍbiyan-pirivena** at **(Naḍraṭ)** in . . . . . . we, Officers of State, have come . . . . and granted these immunities, viz.—

. . . . . *dunumaḍulu* and *melātti* shall not enter [this village]; tramps and vagrants shall not enter; Solī Pāṇḍi . . . . . shall not . . . . . ; labourers shall not

[1] For *rad-kol-*.

[2] P. *Kassapa Siri Saṅghabōdhi.*

[3] P. *Udaya Abhaya Silāmēghavaṇṇa.*

[4] *Mala* stands for *Malaya* 'the hilly country': Tamil, *malāi* 'hill'.

[5] *Pihiṭi.* This may either be the p.p.p. of *pihiṭanavā*, or the name of the northern division of the Island. See Vol. I, p. 206, note 1.

[6] *Vadāḷeyin.* See Vol. I, p. 206, note 2.

[7] Regarding this official title, see Vol. I, p. 193.

[8] P. *Vajiragga* (or *Vajiraṁga*) *Nāyaka* (or *Nātha*).

be appropriated; milch cows, carts[1], and buffaloes shall not be appropriated; managers of two places of business[2] shall not enter; the fines which had been exacted after making due inquiry[3] in the village (entered by *pereläkkan*) shall not be appropriated by the State, but shall be handed over to the *pariveṇa*.

And [to this effect] we have set up this pillar of Council Warranty . . . . . .

No. 4. NĀGAMA PILLAR-INSCRIPTION

NĀGAMA is at present a 'Moor' village in Nāgampaha Kōrale, about twenty-five miles south of Anurādhapura. The inscribed pillar, measuring about 4½ ft. by 8½ in. square, stands now in the premises of the Mosque. Its top is broken off. Mr. H. C. P. Bell, the Archaeological Commissioner, examined it in 1895[4]. The writing covers all its four sides, twenty-one lines on each, including the two top lines that are missing.

The **akṣaras**, one to two inches in size, are well incised within horizontally-ruled spaces. These represent the alphabet of the tenth century A. D. The letters *a*, *k*, *r*, and the medial vowel *u*, have open lower ends. These, as well as *m*, *y*, *l*, etc., closely resemble the type of the characters in the Kirigallāva, the Noccipotāna, and the Moragoḍa pillars of Udaya I (952–963 A. D.) and Kassapa IV (963–980 A. D.). On palaeographic grounds we have no hesitation in ascribing this grant to Kassapa IV, especially as all the records we know of his successor Kassapa V show a distinctly later form of script. A comparison of the letter *k* alone in the inscriptions of the two kings affords sufficient proof. The only other king to whom this record may palaeographically be assigned is Udaya I; but its contents are against such a supposition. **Udā Mahāpāṇanvahanse** mentioned therein was most probably the brother[5] and sub-king of Sēna II, who succeeded him as **Udaya I**. And it is highly improbable that he would speak of himself merely as *Mahāpā* without any

---

[1] *Gäl-mivun* may also mean 'cart-buffaloes'.

[2] *Dekamtän deruvanā.* We are still in the dark as to the true signification of this technical term. See Vol. I, p. 207, note 3.

[3] *Tirā koṭ* = Skt. *sthira-kṛtvā* lit. 'having made certain'.

[4] His report runs:—'**Negama.** Pillar-inscription of the 10th century, dated in the 7th year of some king whose name is lost with the top of the stone. This village is now occupied by Moors, and the pillar has been set up within the precincts of the Mosque.'—*A. S. C. Annual Report* for 1895, p. 5.

[5] See the genealogical table in Vol. I, p. 184.

qualifying phrase. Besides, the chronicles of this period make no reference **to** any other Udā Mahāpā.

If the above identification of the king with Kassapa IV (963–980 A. D.) be correct, the date of the record being the seventh year of his reign, it is six years later than the Tiṁbiriväva pillar, and nine years earlier than the Moragoḍa one.

The **language** is, as is usual, similar in style to other tenth-century pillar edicts. We may, however, draw attention to the honorific term *vahanse* occurring in A, line 8. This is the earliest instance of its use in inscriptions so far as we know at present[1]. The expression *hasin pamaṇu koṭ* shows that in the tenth century A. D. seals were affixed to documents conveying lands[2].

As to **orthography**, note the forms *mahā-pā* and *mahayā, Ag-boy-ārakṣa-maṇan* for *Ag-boy-arak-samaṇan*, probably through the engraver's ignorance of its correct **etymology**[3], *rat-kol* for *rad-kol,* and *melätti* for the more common *melätsi.*

The contents of the record deal with the grant of the usual immunities **to Koḷayunugama**, a village which had been given by **Udā Mahāpā** to one **(Ki)tambavä Mahayā**[4] as *pamaṇu* or 'descendible' property. As a rule, *aṭṭāṇi* pillars of this kind were set up in lands belonging to temples or other public institutions. But in the present instance, as well as in the two cases at Kirigalläva and Noccipotāna, the immunities were granted apparently to private lands, unless, of course, these were so well known as temple lands, that special reference to this fact in the inscriptions was considered unnecessary. As to **Udā Mahāpā**, we have already identified him with king Udaya I. He must have been *mahāpā*[4] of Sēna II when he made the grant of land to **Kitambavä**, who was afterwards, that is at the date of the inscription, a *mahayā* under Kassapa IV. Nothing, however, of this minister or of those State Officials who set up the pillar can be gleaned from the chronicles, although some of their titles and names, such as *Mekäppar-Vädārum*, *Mugayin* (P. *Moggallāna*), *Kiliṅg*, *Mahāle*, *Kuṇḍasalā*, etc., are familiar enough to us from other inscriptions. The *Maha-piḷima-ge* referred to in the record is, no doubt, identical with the historic building mentioned in line 45 of the Jētavanārāma slab[5] (No. 2) of Mahinda IV.

---

[1] See Vol. I, p. 114. [2] *Ibid.*, p. 102, note 5. [3] See below, p. 32, note 10.

[4] P. *Mahādipāda* (Sinh. *Mahāpā*, *Mahapā*, *Māpā*, or *Mahayā*) is a title often applied to a *yuva-rāja*, 'heir-apparent' to the throne. See Vol. I, p. 187, note 6. Cf. also Skt. *mahā-pātra* 'a prime minister', 'a large bowl' (Vol. I, p. 106, note 16). Udaya succeeded Mahinda to the office of sub-king in the thirty-third year of Sēna's reign. *Mv.* li. 63.

[5] Vol. I, p. 236.

TEXT.

A.

1 [සිරිසඟ්
2 බො මපුර්]
3 මූකා සත්ව
4 ත්තෙ පොසො
5 නැ පුර දස ව
6 ක් දවස් ළද
7 මහාපාණ
8 න්වහන්සෙ
9 මහයා (කි)ත[1]
10 මබවැහව්
11 හසින් ප
12 මණු කොට් ව
13 දළ තණ බි
14 මිහි අවූ කො
15 (ළසුනු) නැමැ
16 අත්තාණි ක
17 ණු ගිසද්වත්
18 නව් ආ මෙකා
19 ප්පර් වැදූ
20 රුම් මුගසින්
21 (ම)ණු වරු වත්

B.

1 .. ..
2 .. ..
3 .. [කි]ලි(ග්) ග
4 [ව]සිම (ඉ)සා
5 මහාලෙ අග්
6 බොයාරක්ෂ
7 මණන්[2] වරු ව
8 න් කුඩසලා
9 අග්බොසිම
10 ඉසා මෙ තුවා
11 ක් දෙනමො එක්
12 තැන්සම්යෙ
13 න් වදාලෙසින්
14 මෙ ගමට් වැරි
15 පෙරෙනාව්ටූ
16 නො වද්නා කො
17 ට් ඉසා ගැල්
18 ගොත් මීවූන් නො
19 ගන්නා කොට්
20 ඉසා මගිව
21 (පෙගි)ව නො ..

C.

1 .. ..
2 .. ..
3 .. .. (වත්) .. ..
4 .. නො වද්නා (කො)
5 ට් ඉසා මිහීකො
6 වා මෙ ගම වත්
7 නො ගන්නා කො(ට්)
8 ඉසා රත්කොල්[3]
9 කැමියත් නො ව
10 ද්නා කොට් ඉ
11 සා මෙලාත්නි
12 නො වද්නා කො
13 ට් ඉසා මෙ ග
14 මට් අභය
15 තුරු බගිපි
16 වෙහෙරු ම
17 (හපිළිමගෙ)
18 (ගි .. ණැ)හ

---

1. 'කාත' යිද කියවිය හැකිසි
2. 'අග්බොයරක්සමණන්' විය යුතුයි
3. 'රද්කොල්' වෙනුවට

Nāgama Pillar-inscription.

From an ink-impression supplied by the Archaeological Commissioner, Ceylon.

Scale about 2¼ inches to 1 foot.

19 ට .. .. .. තෙ
20 ල් බ(දු)හවුරුදු
21 පතා සඤු ..

D.

1 .. ..
2 .. ..
3 (හැ) දන්වා .. ..
4 වෙහෙරකැමි(ය)
5 නට් කියා ස
6 හා ගෙනැ වෙ බ
7 (දු දී වළඤ)නු කො
8 ට් ඉසා වදාළෙ
9 [සින්] අත්තාණි
10 කණු ගිඤ්ව
11 න්නට් ආ පෙ
12 රෙ කී මෙනුවාක්
13 දෙනමො මෙ ග
14 මට් අභය
15 සඤ්ගා අත්
16 නාණි කණු පෙ
17 රුහැර් දුන්ම
18 හසි මෙයට්
19 උ(ල)ග්නා කළ කෙ
20 නෙකුන් ඇත ක
21 වුඩු බලූ වනුයි

TRANSCRIPT.

A.

1 [**Siri Saṅg-**
2 **-bo** Mapur-]
3 -mukā sat-va-
4 -nne Poso-
5 -nä pura dasa-va-
6 -k davas **Udā**
7 Mahāpāṇa-
8 -n-vahanse
9 Mahayā (**Ki**)**ta-**[1]
10 **-mbavähaṭ**
11 hasin pa-
12 -maṇu koṭ va-
13 -dāḷa Taṇa-bi-
14 -mhi āvū **Ko-**
15 (**-ḷayunu-**)gämä
16 attāṇi-ka-
17 -ṇu hindvan-
18 -naṭ ā Mekā-
19 -ppar-Vädā-
20 -rum **Mugayin**
21 (**Ma**)**ṇu**-varä van

B.

1 .. ..
2 .. ..
3 .. [**Ki**]li(ṅg) **Ga-**
4 [**-va**]**yim** (i)sā
5 Mahāle **Ag-**
6 **-boyārakṣa-**
7 **-maṇan** [2]-varä va-
8 -n **Kuṇḍasalā-**
9 **Ag-boyim**
10 isā me tuvā-
11 -k denamo ek-
12 -tän-samiye-

---

[1] This may also be read *Kāta-*.

[2] Read *Ag-boy-araksamaṇan.*

13 -n vadāḷeyin
14 me gamaṭ väri
15 perenāṭṭu
16 no vadnā ko-
17 -ṭ isā gäl
18 gon mivun no
19 gannā koṭ
20 isā maṅgiva
21 (pegi)va no ..

C.

1 .. ..
2 .. ..
3 .. .. (van) .. ..
4 .. no vadnā (ko-)
5 -ṭ isā minī-ko-
6 -ṭā me gama van
7 no gannā ko(ṭ)
8 isā rat-kol-[1]
9 kämiyan no va-
10 -dnā koṭ i-
11 -sā melātti
12 no vadnā ko-
13 -ṭ isā me ga-
14 -maṭ **Abhaya-**
15 **-turā Bagiri-**
16 **veherä** ma-
17 (-ha-piḷima-ge-)
18 (-hi .. ṇā)-ha-
19 -ṭ .. .. .. te-
20 -l ba(du) havurudu
21 patā sandu ..

D.

1 .. ..
2 .. ..
3 (-hä) daṇvā .. ..
4 vehera-kämi(ya)-
5 -naṭ kiyā sa-
6 -hā genä me ba-
7 (-du dī vaḷanda)nu ko-
8 -ṭ isā vadā(ḷe-)
9 [-yin] attāṇi-
10 kaṇu hind-va-
11 -nnaṭ ā pe-
12 -re kī metuvāk
13 denamo me ga-
14 -maṭ abhaya
15 sand-hā at-
16 -tāṇi-kaṇu pe-
17 -rähär dunma-
18 -hayi meyaṭ
19 u(la)ṅgnā kaḷa ke-
20 -nekun äta ka-
21 -vuḍu balu vanuyi

TRANSLATION.

[Hail !] On the tenth day of the waxing moon of [the month of] *Poson* (May–June) in the seventh year [of the reign] of His Majesty [**Siri Saṅg-bo**].

Whereas it was [so] decreed by the Supreme Council[2], we all of us, namely, ... of the family of Mekāppar-Vädārum **Mugayin (Ma)ṇu, [Ki]li(ṅg) Gavayim** . . . . . . , and **Kuṇḍasalā Ag-boyim** of the family of the Chief

---

[1] For *rad-kol-*.

[2] *Ek-tän-samiyen vadāḷeyin* (B, lines 11–13), same as *val-himiyan ek-tän-samiyen vadāḷeyin* (in the Kirigallāva pillar, B, lines 7–11, above p. 4). See also below, p. 32 note 6, p. 37 note 5, and Vol. I, p. 206 note 2.

Secretary **Ag-boy Araksamaṇan**, have come to set up a pillar of Council Warranty in respect of the village **Ko(ḷayunu)** in the district of **Taṇa-bima**[1], which His Highness **Udā Mahāpā**[2] had assigned with [his own] seal as a *pamaṇu*[3] land to **Mahayā**[2] **Kitambavä**.

And whereas we all the aforesaid persons have come by Order to set up the pillar of Council Warranty [to the effect that] labourers, and *perenāṭṭu*, shall not enter this village; carts, oxen, and buffaloes shall not be appropriated; tramps and vagrants [shall not enter]; . . . . shall not enter; those who have entered this village after committing murder shall not be arrested; servants of the royal family shall not enter; and *melātti* shall not enter; to this village . . . . for (the performer of *pūṇā* (?) service) in the great image-house[4] at **Abhayaturā Bagirivehera**[5] a yearly (rent) for oil . . . . . . and that after informing the monastery servants and with their assistance after paying this rent, the village shall be enjoyed . . . . . ., we have granted the immunities [contained] in the pillar of Council Warranty to this village so that it might be a sanctuary.

Whoever transgresses this [edict] shall be born a crow or a dog [in his future birth].

No. 5. KUKURUMAHAN-DAMANA PILLAR-INSCRIPTION

THIS pillar was discovered by the Archaeological Commissioner (Mr. H. C. P. Bell) whilst exploring the ruins in Moragolla Wanni in September, 1896[6]. It measures 6 ft. by 11 in. by 8 in. approximately, and

---

[1] Lit. 'grass land'.

[2] See above, p. 15, note 4.

[3] *Pamaṇu* or *pamuṇu*. Same as modern *pravēṇi*, P. *pavēṇi*, 'a descendible grant' of land. See above, Vol. I, pp. 117, 130, 182 note 1, 240 note 1, and 250 note 7.

[4] *Maha-piḷimage*. Cf. *mañgul-mahasala-piḷimagehi pūṇā kämiyak* in the Mihintale tablet, B, line 41 (Vol. I, p. 96), and Jētavanārāma slab (2) of Mahinda IV, line 45 (*Ibid.*, p. 236).

[5] P. *Abhayuttara Abhayagiri-vihāra. Ibid.*, p. 216.

[6] Mr. Bell refers to the discovery in his diary as follows:—

'**Sangaranparatti-oya**.—September 14. Push on eight miles through sandy country, thorn, and *nelu*, across three or four *pitali* (now dry) along a probable ancient "Yoda-ęla" (called by the guides simply *agala* "moat") to the Sangaranparatti-oya, the term by which the Taláwé-ęla is known as it approaches the sea. Camp in the river-bed at Deviyanne-vela-mankaṇḍiya.

'**Kukurumahan-damana**.—After some days' search in the trackless jungles find an inscribed

was found lying almost embedded in the ground at Kukurumahan-damana, some thirty miles west-north-west of Anurādhapura. The inscription is boldly engraved on a somewhat rough surface. Sides A and B contain 22 lines each, C 25 lines, and D 4 lines with the figures of sun and moon above and those of a crow and a dog below.

The **akṣaras**, one to two inches in size, represent the alphabet of the tenth century A.D. Their type, like that of the Kirigallāva pillar (above, No. 1), is a mixture of old and new forms. They, however, resemble most the characters in the Moragoḍa pillar of the sixteenth year of Kassapa IV (963–980 A.D.)[1]. It will be seen that the two vertical strokes of *a*, *r*, and the medial vowel *u* meet at their lower ends as in the Īripinniyāva pillar[2], while in the Moragoḍa pillar both the closed and open forms occur. See remarks on this point above, Vol. I, p. 242. As regards the akṣara *ya*, we see that from the very earliest times two types were in use in the Brāhmī alphabet. One was evidently formed by commencing with the left or right limb (most probably the former) and drawing the style or pen up the central vertical line. Then after thickening its top a little the pen is brought down to make the other side limb as in [illegible]. In the other type the vertical line was written first and the bottom curve afterwards[3] as in [illegible]. That these two ways of forming *ya* prevailed in Ceylon in the tenth century A.D. may be inferred from the two types of this character occurring in the lithic records. The form [illegible] in the Kirigallāva pillar[4] and in the slab of Kassapa V[5] near the 'stone canopy' in Anurādhapura, as well as the modern ය is the development of the first method, whilst the type [illegible] in the Īripinniyāva[6] pillar and in the present one is that of the second.

The **language** is the same in style as that of other pillar records of the tenth century. Most of the words and phrases are more or less common to all of them. We need, therefore, draw attention only to the less usual form *melātti*, and to the two names *arākkan* and *perelākkan* which occur also in the Kirigallāva, Bilibāva, Noccipotāna, and Āṭavīragollāva pillars (Nos. 1, 2, 8, and 9).

---

pillar, spoken of by hunters, at Kukurumahan-damana, near the left bank of the Sangaranparatti-oya. Elephants had thrown down the pillar, and trampled it into the ground. The inscription runs to all four sides, and the pillar further has sun, moon, dog, and crow emblems cut on it. It is dated in the eleventh year of King Siri Sang Bo (Sena I). One small ruin near.'

[1] Compare the accompanying facsimile with Plate 26 of Vol. I.

[2] See Vol. I, Plate 21.

[3] See also Bühler's remarks in *Indische Palaeographie*, p. 36, and those of mine in Vol. I, p. 14.

[4] See above, Plate 1.

[5] See Vol. I, Plate 12.

[6] See Vol. I, Plate 21.

The **subject** of the inscription is a grant of certain immunities by king **Siri Saṅg-bo** and his Council in respect of **Kereḷā-gama**, a village belonging to the hospital built by the Commander-in-Chief **Sēna** opposite the nunnery called **Mahindārāma** on the High Street of the Inner City [of Anurādhapura].

The five State Officials who set up the *attāṇi* pillar proclaiming the mandate of His Majesty in Council are not known to us from other sources; but the Commander-in-Chief **Sēna** is clearly no other than **Ilaṅga Sēna**, the *sēnā-pati* of the army of Kassapa IV. The pillar-inscription at Ayitigeväva[1] places this identification beyond doubt, for there we read that the nunnery Tissārāma, the building of which is ascribed in the *Mahāvaṁsa* (ch. lii. 24) to Ilaṅga Sēna, was erected by the Commander-in-Chief Sēna. The chronicle speaks of him as a prince of the royal family, and gives a detailed account of his charitable acts. Besides the Tissārāma nunnery which he built for the sisters (*bhikkunīs*) whom he appointed to have the care of the Maricavaṭṭi Thūpa and the Great Bōdhi-tree, he erected several religious edifices such as the Dhammārāma, Kassapa Sēna, Hadayuṇha, and Samuddagiri. He also established hospitals (*vejja-sālā*) at Anurādhapura and Poḷonnaruva for the prevention of pestilential diseases, as well as dispensaries (*bhēsajja-gēha*) in divers places in the capital. To these institutions he granted fruitful lands and gardens with keepers. The present inscription records the building of another hospital which is not mentioned in the *Mahāvaṁsa* account. The location of this hospital in close proximity to the *Mihind-aram* (P. *Mahindārāma*) nunnery suggests that it was either meant for the exclusive use of the nuns or that these devotees, like the nursing sisters of the present day, attended on the patients, succouring the sick being a *veyyāvaccaṁ* (Sinh. *vatāvat*), one of the ten meritorious acts which Buddhism imposes upon its votaries[2].

The High Street *Maṅgul-maha-veya* of the Inner City is also referred to in the slab-inscription of Kassapa V[3], near the 'stone canopy' at Anurādhapura, as the locality where this king established royal hospitals (*raj-ved-hal*) and thus allayed the fear of diseases.

From the foregoing palaeographical and historical data it appears certain

[1] See below, p. 35.

[2] For the ten meritorious acts, see Childers' *Pāli Dictionary* s.v. *puñño*. The *Kāvyasēkhara* (ix verses 40–41) enumerates twelve.

[3] See Vol. I, No. 4.

that king **Siri Saṅg-bo** of the present record is identical with **Kassapa IV** (963–980 A.D.) of the *Mahāvaṁsa.* And as the inscription is dated in the eleventh year of his reign, the pillar may have been set up in 974 A.D. or thereabouts. The date of the Moragoḍa pillar being the sixteenth year of the same king, it is later than the present one by about five years.

TEXT.

	A.		B.
1	**සිරි සඟ්බො**	1	**මැ(ණි)න් ග**
2	මපුර්මුකා	2	**මු (ළදගි) ඉ**
3	එකලොස් ව	3	**සා නිකා වැ**
4	ත්නෙ මැඬින්	4	**ළි සෙනු ඉ**
5	දිනැ පුර වි	5	**සා මහකු**
6	සෙනි දවස්	6	**බුස්සා(ළු)**
7	**සෙන් සෙනෙවි**	7	**මිතු ඉසා (රි)**
8	**රදුණින්** ඇ	8	(ගැ)ව රද්සි[3]
9	තුළ් නුවරැ ම	9	වූ වරැ මෙකා
10	තුල් මහවෙ	10	ප්පර් (න)මු[4]
11	යැ **මිහිඳ් අ**	11	ඩැ නිලා ඉ
12	**රම්** මෙහෙණි	12	සා (දිගිවි)[5]
13	වර් පෙරෙට් (කැරූ)	13	**(ළිකණ්ණා)**
14	වෙද්හලැ බ	14	ඇතුළ්වැ
15	ද් පැ(ළැ)පසැ	15	මෙනුවාක්
16	(වලපූ[1]) තිමැ අ	16	සම්දරැ
17	**වූ (කො)රෙළැගැම**[2]	17	වන්විසි
18	සිමා පහණ්	18	න් මෙ ගම්
19	අත්තාණිකණු	19	වි පියො ව
20	ගිඳ්වත්නට්	20	දුරනූව
21	වදැළෙසින්	21	න් නො වද්
22	සභායෙන් අ	22	නා කොට් ඉ

[1] 'වල්වූ' යිද කියවිය හැකිසි

[2] 'වෙණුළැගැම්' යිද කියවිය හැකිසි

[3] 'රිගැවෙරද්සිවූ' යිද කියවිය හැකිසි

[4] 'රමු' යිද කියවිය හැකිසි

[5] 'දියපිළිකණ්ණා' යිද කියවිය හැකිසි

Kukurumahan-damana Pillar-inscription.

A B C D

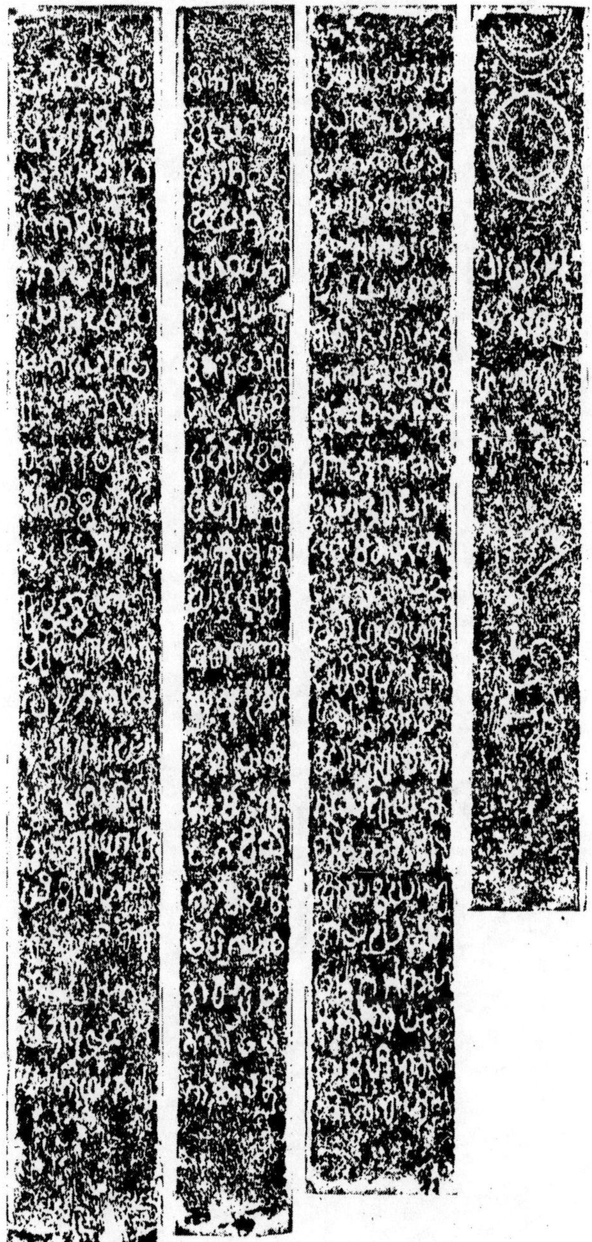

From an ink-impression supplied by the Archaeological Commissioner, Ceylon.

Scale about 1½ inches to 1 foot.

C.

1 සා රව්ලදු ප
2 ස්ලදුවන් නො
3 වද්නා කොට් ඉ
4 සා රද්කොල්කැ
5 මියන් නො වද්[1]කො
6 ට් ඉසා මෙලා
7 ත්හින් නො වද්
8 නා කොට් ඉසා ම
9 සිව පියගිව
10 නො වද්නා කොට්
11 ඉසා දෙරුවනෑ
12 දෙකම්තැන් නො
13 වද්නා කොට් ඉ
14 සා ගැල් ගොන්
15 වැරි මීවුන් නො
16 ගන්නා කොට් ඉ
17 සා අරුක්ක
18 න් පෙරෙලැක්
19 කන් නො වද්නා
20 කොට් ඉසා අ
21 භය සඤ්හා
22 වත්නාන් නො ග
23 න්නා කොට් මෙ
24 ගැම්ගි අන්නා
25 ණීකණ්ඩු ගිඤ්

D.

1 වා වදාළෙ
2 පින් මෙ පැ
3 රුහැර් දෙ
4 නු ලදි ව

TRANSCRIPT.

A.

1 **Siri Saṅg-bo**
2 Mapurmukā
3 ekaḷos va-
4 -nne Mändin-
5 -dinä pura vi-
6 -seni davas
7 **Sen Senevi-**
8 **radāṇan** ä-
9 -tuḷ-nuvarä Ma-
10 -ṅgul maha-ve-
11 -yä **Mihind-a-**
12 **-ram** meheṇi-
13 -var pereṭ (kärū)
14 ved-halä ba-
15 -d pä(ḷä-)pasä
16 (valapu-[2]) bimä ā-
17 -vū **(Ke)reḷā-gāma**[3]
18 sīmā-pahaṇ
19 attāṇi-kaṇu
20 hind-vannaṭ
21 vadāḷeyin
22 sabhāyen ā

B.

1 **Mä(ṇi)n-ga-**
2 **-mu (Udahi)** i-
3 -sā **Nika-vä-**
4 **-li Senu** i-
5 -sā **Maha-Ku-**
6 **-bussā(lu)**
7 **Mitu** isā **(Ri-)**
8 (-ṅgā-)va **Rad-si-**[4]

---

1 'වද්නා' වියයුතුයි

2 This may also be read *valvū-*.

3 This may also be read *Veṇuḷā-gāma*.

4 This may also be read *Rigäve Rad-sivu* or *Rigā-Varad-sivu*.

9 **-vu-**vaṛä Mekā-
10 -ppar (**Na**)**mu-**[1]
11 **-ḍā Nilā** i-
12 -sā (**Digivi-**)[2]
13 (**-li-Kaṇṇā**)
14 ätuḷ-vä
15 metuvāk
16 samdaru-
17 -van-visi-
18 -n me gama-
19 -ṭ piyo-va-
20 -dāranuva-
21 -n no vad-
22 -nā koṭ i-

C.

1 -sā raṭ-ladu pa-
2 -s-laduvan no
3 vadnā koṭ i-
4 -sā rad-kol-kä-
5 -miyan no vad[3]ko-
6 -ṭ isā melā-
7 -ttin no vad-
8 -nā koṭ isā ma-
9 -ṅgiva piyagiva
10 no vadnā koṭ
11 isā deruvanā
12 dekam-tän no
13 vadnā koṭ i-
14 -sā gäl gon
15 väri mīvun no
16 gannā koṭ i-
17 -sā aräkka-
18 -n pereläk-
19 -kan no vadnā
20 koṭ isā a-
21 -bhaya sand-hā
22 vannan no ga-
23 -nnā koṭ me
24 gämhi attā-
25 -ṇi-kaṇu hind-

D.

1 -vā vadāḷe-
2 -yin me pä-
3 -rähär de-
4 -nu ladi ව

TRANSLATION.

On the fifth day of the waxing moon of [the month of] *Mändindina* (Feb.–March) in the eleventh year of [the reign of] His Majesty **Siri Saṅg-bo.**

Whereas it was decreed that boundary stones[4] and a pillar of Council Warranty[5] should be set up in the village of **Kereḷā**[6]**-gäma** situated in the district of **Valapu**[7] in the Western Quarter, which (village) was attached to

---

[1] This may also be read *Ramuḍā.*

[2] This may also be read *Diyapili Kaṇṇā.*

[3] Read *vadnā.*

[4] *Sīmā-pahaṇ* (A, line 18).

[5] *Attāṇi-kaṇu* (A, line 19).

[6] Or *Veṇulā.*

[7] If the reading *valvū bimā* is adopted, the translation should run 'in the forest tract in the Western Quarter'.

the hospital[1] built by the Commander-in-Chief **Sen** in front of the **Mihind-aram**[2] nunnery on the High Street **Mañgul-maha-veya**[3] of the Inner City[4], all these Officers of State, namely, **Mä(ṇi)ngamu (Udahi), Nikaväli Senu, Maha-Kubussā(lu) Mitu,** Mekāppar (**Na**)**muḍā**[5] **Nilā** and (**Digivili**[6]-**Kaṇṇā**) [both] of the family of **Riñgäva**[7] **Rad-sivu**, have come from the Council[8] and have set up in this village a pillar of Council Warranty, granting by Order the following immunities :—Enforcers of customary laws[9] shall not enter this village; headmen of districts and keepers of district records shall not enter; servants of the royal family shall not enter; *melätti* shall not enter; tramps and vagrants shall not enter; holders [of the management] of two places of business[10] shall not enter; carts, oxen, labourers, buffaloes shall not be appropriated; *aräkkan*[11] and *pereläkkan*[11] shall not enter; those who have come for refuge shall not be arrested.

No. 6. MÄḌIRIGIRIYA PILLAR-INSCRIPTION

IN the course of exploring the ruins of Mäḍirigiriya, more correctly Mäḍiligiriya[12], in Tamankaḍuva, about forty-six miles east-south-east of Anurādhapura, the Archaeological Commissioner (Mr. H. C. P. Bell) discovered the present pillar-inscription of Kassapa V (980–990 A. D.) in August 1897.

---

[1] *Ved-hala*, P. *vejja-sālā* (*Mv.* lii. 25) in contradistinction to *behet-ge* (P. *bhēsajja-gēha*) 'dispensary' (*Ibid.*, 27). Cf. also *Tumbarab-behed-ge* (P. *Thūpārāma-bhēsajja-gēha*) in the Kiribat-vehera pillar, side B, lines 4–6 (Vol. I, No. 11).

[2] P. *Mahinda-ārāma.*

[3] P. *Maṅgala-mahā-vīthi*, 'the auspicious high street.'

[4] *Ätul-nuvara* (A, lines 8–9).

[5] Or *Ramuḍā.*

[6] Or *Diyapili.*

[7] Or *Rigäve Rad-sivu* or *Rigā Varad-sivu.*

[8] *Sabhāyen ā* (A, line 22), lit. 'who have come from the Council'.

[9] *Piyo-vadāranuvan* (B, lines 19–21). The above is only a tentative interpretation. See Vol. I, p. 207, note 1.

[10] *Deruvanā de-kam-tän.* See Index to Vol. I for references.

[11] See above, pp. 1 and 20.

[12] See side B, line 7, of the pillar-inscription. Mr. Bell's description of the site is as follows:—

'This most picturesque site lies in the very heart of the forest, six miles from Divulaṇkaḍawala, the nearest village.

'Mẹdirigiriya is an extensive rock outcrop, not very high, bifurcated by jungle into two stretches side by side. There are ample remains on one rock—*sīmā pahura* (boundaries), a fair-sized *dāgaba*, cave, pillared ruin, and inscribed pillar of "*Abhaya Salamewan*" (Kasyapa V), third year.

'But the gem of Mẹdirigiriya is its "*Waṭa-dā-gé.*" This beautiful shrine stands on the highest point

Since then another inscription on a slab, measuring 5 ft. 3 in. by 3 ft. 3 in., has come to light. Mr. D. A. L. Perera, the Head Draughtsman of the Archaeological Survey, found it in October, 1907, lying at a distance of about 100 yards south-east of the so-called *Vaṭa-dāgē*. It is engraved in 44 lines of writing in small Sinhalese script of the eleventh century A. D., but the letters are so worn that the two ink-estampages before me do not admit of a reading good enough for publication. So much of the text as has been made out shows that it is a *samvatā-pahaṇa* 'edictal stone' containing rules for the management of the hospital [1] attached to the monastery. Here and there we read interesting terms, such as *ved-hal-kämiyan*, 'employees of the hospital,' *ved-hal-dasun*, 'serfs of the hospital,' *ved-sam-daruvan*, 'State physicians,' *ved-hal-bad-gam-bim*, 'villages and lands attached to the hospital,' *ved-hal-bad-kuḍīn*, 'tenants attached to the hospital.' Had this record been legible, it would have doubtless given much valuable information concerning public hospitals to which the Ceylon chronicles make frequent but scanty references.

The inscription on the pillar (6 ft. by 12½ in. square) is, on the other hand, in fairly good preservation. It covers all the four sides, A, B, and C having 26 lines of writing, and D 17 lines with the figures of a crow and a dog below two others of which one looks like that of a *vaṭā-pata*, 'Buddhist monk's fan,' while the other, according to Mr. Bell, represents a sickle.

The **akṣaras** belong to the alphabet of the tenth and early eleventh centuries A. D. Their size varies from one to one and a half inches each, and their type is practically the same as that of the slab records of Kassapa V and Dappula V with the exception of *ma*, which retains here, as it does even in some later records, the 'archaistic' form. Compare Plates 8 and 12 of Vol. I with the accompanying facsimile.

---

of the rock surrounded, like its known prototype at Polonnáruwa, by a slab wall carved with surface ornament, and three concentric rows of graceful columns (sixty-eight in all) of the type seen at Thúpáráma and Laṇkáráma, Anurádhapura. The inner and second row of pillars bear single lions and pilasters on their capitals, the outermost posturing *ganas* (dwarfs). In height this row of columns is but 9 ft. 9 in., while the two inner rows reach 16 ft. All are octagonal, and all are unbroken, save four; but several have lost their spreading capitals. Within the circle of pillars, seated on an *ásanaya*, is a Buddha in stone; probably one of four, cardinally placed, with their backs to a small central dágaba. The design on the stone slab wall encircling the dágaba and columns is the "Buddhist-railing" pattern, in this differing from the flowered ornamentation of the Polonnáruwa *Waṭa-dá-gé*.'—*A. S. C. Annual Report* for 1897, p. 7.

[1] The ruin marked A in Mr. Perera's report is probably the site of the hospital (*ved-hala*) referred to in the two inscriptions. See *A. S. C. Annual Report* for 1907, pp. 30–32.

The **language** is the same in style as that of Kiribat-vehera, Īripinniyāva, **and** other tenth-century inscriptions of the kind.

The **contents** tell us that king **Abhā Salamevan** was a son of **Mayurā-dunu Siri Saṅg-boy** by the twice-anointed queen, and that, under a decree of his Supreme Council, in the third year of his sovereignty, three Officers of State, namely, (a) Mekäppar **Asaholu Mihindu**, of the family of **Paṇḍi-rad Dāpuḷu**, (b) **Sumeragamu Sātā**, probably of the same family, and (c) **Kuṇḍasalā Kit**, of the family of the Chief Secretary **Kasbā Araksamaṇa**, came and granted certain immunities in respect of the land within the four boundaries of **Mäḍiligiri-Ätveher**[1]**-Piyan-gala** in **Rantisā** in the district of **Bidervatu-kuḷiya**. The nature of the privileges agrees in the main with other similar records of the period. There occur, however, some new words and expressions in addition to those already familiar to us, of which the full signification is not very clear. They are ***dunu**-maḍula*, probably 'those belonging to the archery department,' ***dunuvā**-balat*[2], 'captains of the bowmen,' *velä-yut-pas-denā*, 'the five engaged in the supervision of fields' (?), and *sändive de-utu-kiri*.

The order that 'dead goats and fowls' should be given to the hospital attached to the Vihāra shows that animal food was allowed in these Buddhist institutions under certain restrictions. Obviously the regulation refers to animals killed by accidents.

The present record undoubtedly belongs to Kassapa V (980–990 A. D.), and is only three years earlier than this king's inscription near the 'stone canopy' in Anurādhapura[3]. Both the documents agree not only in the type of the script but also in the historical facts that he bore the *biruda* title **Abhā Salamevan**[4], that he was the son of **Siri Saṅg-boy** (Sēna II) by a twice-anointed queen[5], and that he took an interest in the establishment of hospitals. The title *Mayurā-dunu* applied to his father has not been found elsewhere. It may either be the birth-place of **Siri Saṅg-boy** (Sēna II) or may have reference to a traditional ancestry.

Of the places mentioned in our inscription, **Rantisā** may be identified with

---

[1] *Ät-vehera* and *Piyan-gala*. Judging from the context where these two names occur in the inscription of Kassapa V near the 'stone canopy' (Vol. I, No. 4), and in the Mihintale tablets of Mahinda IV (*Ibid.*, No. 7), it seems that they are terms applied to certain important buildings of a monastery set apart for a special purpose.

[2] See below, p. 33, note 4.

[3] Vol. I, No. 4.

[4] *Ibid.*, p. 24.

[5] *Ibid.*, p. 42.

Suvaṇṇa Tissa, a tank built by king Mahāsēna[1] (*circa* 325–352 A.D.) and repaired by Parākrama Bāhu I (1153–1186 A.D.)[2], and **Mäḍili-giri** with **Maṇḍala-giri** (or °**girika**). Here Kaniṭṭha Tissa (*circa* 223–241 A.D.)[3] constructed an *upōsatha* house[4]. 'The Malaya Rājā[5], a man of exceeding great wealth, built a relic-house' during the reign of Aggabōdhi IV (*circa* 721–737 A.D.). Sēna II or Siri Saṅg-boy of the present record dedicated some of his own possessions for the support of the Maṇḍalagiri-vihāra[6]. Vijaya Bāhu I (*circa* 1055–1110 A.D.) made repairs to it[7], while king Gaja Bāhu II (1133–1153 A.D.), during the strife between Parākrama Bāhu and Māṇābharaṇa, 'went up to the Vihāra Maṇḍalagiri and made a solemn declaration there[8],' saying, 'I have given the king's country to king Parakkama[9].' King Kīrti Niśśaṅka Malla (1188–1197 A.D.) in his inscription at Śiva Dēvālaya in Poḷonnaruva refers to this Vihāra as one repaired by him.

As regards the State Officials who gave effect to the mandate of the King in Council nothing is known. The expression *Pāňḍi-rad Dāpuḷu-varin ā* corresponds with *Pāňḍi-rad Dāpuḷa-varä* in the Kiribat-vehera pillar[10]. The use of *varin ā* for *varä* or *varä van* clearly proves that *vara* stands for the termination *gē* in modern family names, as pointed out at page 193 of the first volume. *Asaholu*, *Sumergamu*, and *Kuňḍasalā* are probably names of the birth-places of the respective officials. The last name *Kuňḍasalā* occurs in other lithic records, and from its position in the series of titles of a personage there seems to be no doubt that it is the name of a place[11].

TEXT

A.

1 ඔකාවසින් බ
2 ව (ජීයොරා) සිරි ල
3 ක්දිවව් තලාවින්
4 වූ සිරබර් සිරිප
5 ඞ තමා යෙසෙන්
6 දම්බ්දිව්තල එක්
7 හෙළි කොට් මසුරණ්
8 'දුනු සිරි සඟ්බො
9 ය් මහරද්හු දෙ
10 තිසෙව්හු දැ ඈ
11 හා සලමෙවන් ම

---

[1] See *Pūjāvaliya*, extract, p. 23. [2] *Mv.* lxxix. 33. [3] According to Prof. Geig.

[4] *Mv.* xxxvi. 17. [5] *Mv.* xlvi. 29. [6] *Mv.* li. 75. [7] *Mv.* lx. 59.

[8] Probably in Piyangala temple. See above, p. 27, note 1, and cf. *palana-gala* in the Perumäiyaṇ-kuḷam rock-inscription (Vol. I, p. 71).

[9] *Mv.* lxxi. 4. [10] See Vol. I, p. 160.

[11] *Ibid.*, pp. 166, 169, 171, 175, and 245.

12 පූර්මූකා තුක්වත්
13 [නෙ] .. .. [අ]
14 [ව] විසෙ:නිය[ැ එ]
15 ක්නැත්සම්[යෙ]
16 න් වදූලෙසි[න්]
17 සාඞ්රද් දූපු[එ]
18 [වරි]න් ආ මෙ[කා]
19 [ප්පර්] අස[1][ගො]
20 ලූ ඞකිඥ ඉ[සා]
21 සූමෙරගමු [සා]
22 නා ඉසා මහා(ලෙ)
23 කාස්බාරක්ස
24 මණක් වරින් ආ
25 කුඩසලා කිත්
26 ඉසා ඇප් මෙිනු

18 වැරියත් ගම්
19 ගොෟත් ගැල් හිවූ
20 න් නො නගනු ඉසා
21 දූනුවාබලත් රට්
22 ලදූ පස්ලද්දන් වැ
23 දැ ඉසිර් නො කර
24 නු ඉසා වෙලැයුත්
25 පස්දෙනා නො වද්
26 නා ඉසා මග්දිව

B.

1 වාක් රද්කොල් ස
2 ම්දරුවමො වදූ
3 ලෙසින් අවූද්
4 කිදෙර්වතුෟනු
5 ළිසෙකි ආවූ ර
6 ත්නිසැයෙ ගි පි[2]
7 ටි මැඞිලිගිරි
8 ඇත්වෙහෙර් පිය
9 න්ගලැ සතර් සි
10 මායෙත් ඇතුල්වූ
11 තාක් තැනට් දෙරු
12 වනැ දෙකම්තැන්
13 නො වද්නා ඉ[සා]
14 පෙරෙනාටිය(ම්)
15 නො වද්නා ඉසා දූ
16 නුම්බූල මෙලාත්
17 නි නො වද්නා ඉසා

C.

1 පියදිව නො වද්
2 නා ඉසා (සැඤීවෙ[3])
3 (දෙ) උනු කිර් කිලි
4 සාල් කිලිබත් නො
5 නගනු ඉසා (කොටා)
6 වත් ගැම්න් පිටත්
7 කරවා ගනුත් මිසැ
8 ගම් වැදැ නො ගත්
9 නා ඉසා වෙද්හල්
10 වැස්සත් ගම් වැදැ
11 ඇ .. .. .. නො
12 කරනු ඉසා වෙලැ
13 යුත් සම්දරුවත්
14 ගමට් වැදැ රට් ..
15 නො ගත්නා ඉසා [ම]
16 ළ එළු කුකුළත් වෙ
17 හෙර් වෙද්හලට්
18 බහා ලනු කොට් එ
19 ක්නැත්සමියෙත්
20 වැ(ඤැ) වදූලෙසින් සා
21 ඞිරද් දූපුළුවරි
22 න් ආ මෙකාප්පර්

---

[1] 'අය' සීද කියවිය හැකිසි
[2] 'රත්නිසැයෙ පිගිටි' විය යුතුසි (හතරවෙනි පැත්තේ පස්වෙනි පෙළ බලනු)
[3] 'සැණිපෙ' සීද කියවිය හැකිසි

23 අස[1]හොලු මිහිඳු
24 ඉසා සුමෙර්ගමු
25 සාතා ඉසා මහා
26 ලෙ කස්බාරක්ස

D.

1 මණන්වරින් අ කු
2 ඩසලා කිත් ඇතු
3 ළුවැ බිදෙර්වතුකුළි
4 යෙහි ආවූ රන්ති
5 සැයෙ පිහිටි මැඩි
6 ලිගිරිඑවෙහෙර් පිය
7 ක්ගලැ සතර් සීමා
8 යෙන් ඇතුළුවූතාක්
9 තැනට් වදාළෙයින් අ
10 වුද් රද්කොල්සම්දරු
11 වමො මෙ අත්තාණි
12 පෙර්හැර් දුන්මහ
13 .. ..
14 [උල]ගහනා කළ
15 [කො]නොක් කවුඩු බලු
16 වාහයි ආරො
17 ගය සිඞි

TRANSCRIPT.

A.

1 Okā-vasin ba-
2 -ṭ (jiyorā) siri La-
3 -k-divaṭ talā-ṭik-
4 vū siri-bar siri-pi-
5 -ḍ tamā yesen
6 Damb-div-tala ek-
7 heḷi koṭ **Mayurā-**
8 **-dunu Siri Saṅg-bo-**
9 **-y** maha-rad-hu de-
10 -bisevhu dā **A-**
11 **-bhā Salamevan** ma-
12 -purmukā tun-van-
13 [-ne] .. .. [a-]
14 [-va] viseniy[ä e-]
15 -k-tän-sami[ye-]
16 -n vadāḷeyi[n]
17 **Pāṅḍi-rad Dāpu**[ḷu]-
18 [vari]n ā Me[kā-]
19 [-ppar] **Asa**[ho-][2]
20 **-lu Mihindu** i[sā]
21 **Sumeragamu** [Sā-]
22 **-tā** isā Mahā(le)
23 **Kasbā-rak-sa-**
24 -**maṇan**-varin ā
25 **Fuṅḍasalā Kit**
26 isā äp metu-

B.

1 -vāk rad-kol-sa-
2 -m-daruvamo vadā-
3 -ḷeyin avud
4 **Bider-vatu-ku-**
5 **-ḷiyehi** āvū **Ra-**
6 **-n-tisāye** hi pi[3]-
7 -ṭi **Mäḍiligiri-**
8 **Ätveher-Piya-**

---

[1] 'අය' සිද කියවිය හැකියි

[2] This may also be read *Ayaholu*.

[3] Read *Rantisāye pihiṭi* as in D, lines 4–5.

Mādirigiriya Pillar-inscription.

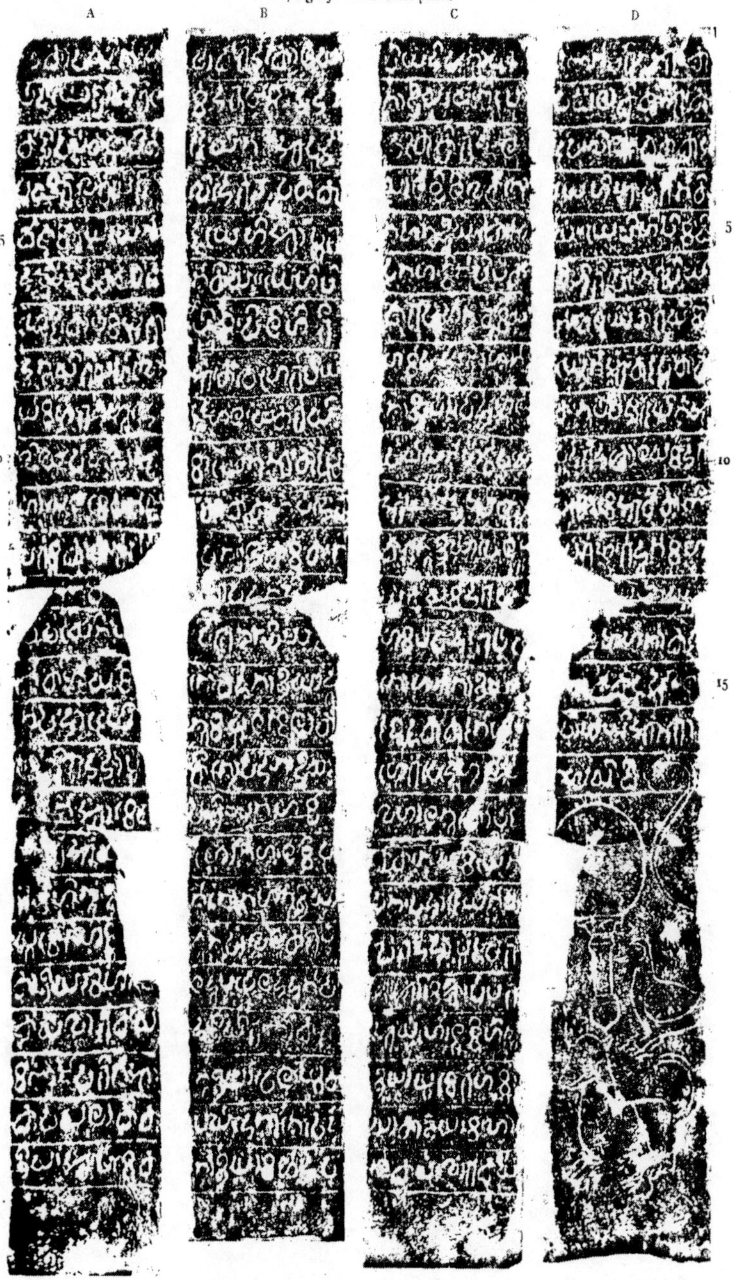

From an ink-impression supplied by the Archaeological Commissioner, Ceylon.

Scale about 1¼ inches to 1 foot.

9 **-n-galä** satar sī-
10 -māyen ätuḷ-vū-
11 tāk-tänaṭ deru-
12 -vanā dekam-tän
13 no vadnā i[sā]
14 perenāṭṭiya(m)
15 no vadnā isā du-
16 -numaḍula melāt-
17 -tī no vadnā isā
18 väriyan gam
19 gon gäl mivu-
20 -n no naṅganu isā
21 dunuvā-balat raṭ-
22 -ladu pas-laddan vä-
23 -dä isir no kara-
24 -nu isā velä-yut
25 pas-denā no vad-
26 -nā isā maṅg-diva

C.

1 piya-diva no vad-
2 -nā isā (sändive[1])
3 (de)-utu-kiri bili-
4 sāl bili-bat no
5 naṅganu isā (koṭā)
6 van gämin piṭat
7 karavā ganut misä
8 gam vädä no gan-
9 -nā isā ved-hal
10 vässan gam vädä
11 ä .. .. .. no
12 karanu isā velä-
13 -yut sam-daruvan
14 gamaṭ vädä raṭ ..
15 no gannā isā [ma-]
16 -ḷa eḷu kukuḷan ve-
17 -her ved-halaṭ
18 bahā lanu koṭ e-
19 -k-tän-samiyen
20 vä(ndä) vadāḷeyin **Pā-**
21 **-ṇḍi-rad Dāpuḷu**-vari-
22 -n ā Mekāppar
23 **Asaholu[2] Mihindu**
24 isā **Sumergamu**
25 **Sātā** isā Mahā-
26 -le **Kasbā-raksa-**

D.

1 **-maṇan**-varin ā **Ku-**
2 **-ṇḍasalā Kit** ätu-
3 -ḷa-vä **Bider-vatu-kuḷi-**
4 **-yehi** āvū **Ran-ti-**
5 **-sāye** pihiṭi **Mäḍi-**
6 **-li-giri-veher-Piya-**
7 **-n-galä** satar sīmā-
8 -yen ätuḷa-vū-tāk-
9 tänaṭ vadāḷeyin a-
10 -vud rad-kol-samdaru-
11 -vamo me attāṇi
12 perhär dunmaha
13 .. ..
14 [ula]ṅg-hanā kaḷa
15 [ke]nek kavuḍu balu-
16 -vāhayi āro-
17 -gya siddhi

---

[1] This may also be read *säṇipe*.

[2] This may also be read *Ayaholu*.

TRANSLATION.

On the fifth day of the waning moon [of the month of . . . . .], in the third year [of the reign] of His Majesty **Abhā Salamevan** who is [like unto] a *tilaka*[1] mark [of adornment] to the . . . .[2] prosperous island of Laṅkā, an embodiment[3] of good fortune and majesty, a descendant of the Okkāka dynasty, and who was born of the twice-anointed queen[4] unto the great king **Mayurādunu**[5] **Siri Saṅg-boy**, illuminating the whole of Dambadiva with his glory.

Whereas it was [so] decreed by the Supreme Council[6], we, all of us, Officers of State, namely, Mekāppar **Asaholu Mihindu** of the family[7] of **Pāṇḍi-rad Dāpuḷa**, and **Sumeragamu Sātā**[8] and **Kuṇḍasalā Kit** of the family of Mahāle[9] **Kasbā Araksamaṇa**[10], have come.

And whereas, touching the area included within the four boundaries of **Mädiligiri-Ätveher-Piyan-gala** situated in **Rantisā** in the district of **Bidervatu-kuḷiya**, it was graciously decreed by the Supreme Council that holders (?)

---

[1] *Siri Lak-divaṭ talā-ṭik-vū* (A, lines 2–4). Cf. *Lak-poḷo-mehe-sanaṭ talā-ṭik-bandu* in the Vessagiri record of Mahinda IV (Vol. I, p. 34, note 6) and *raj-kulaṭ talā-ṭik* in the slab of Kassapa V (*Ibid.*, p. 47, transcript, line 12).

[2] *Jiyorā.* This reading being doubtful, no attempt is made to give it an interpretation.

[3] *Siri-piḍ.* See Vol. I, p. 204, transcript, line 3. Cf. also the expressions *kaṇḍā piṇḍā* and *piṇḍ koṭ* (*Ibid.*, p. 236, transcript, lines 41 and 49).

[4] *De-bisevhu dā.* Cf. *de-bisevä jā* (*Ibid.*, p. 50, note 17).

[5] *Mayurā-dunu*, 'born of the Mayurā (pea-hen).' I have not come across this epithet elsewhere. Could it be in any way connected with the popular legend given in the *Rājaratnākara*, which traces the ancestry of a Sinhalese dynasty to a princess Mayurāvatī, born of a pea-hen, and married to one of the princes who escorted the branch of the Sacred Bōdhi-tree to Ceylon in the reign of Dēvānampiya Tissa (247–207 B.C.)?

[6] *Eklän-samiyen vadāḷeyin.* See Vol. I, p. 206, note 2, and above, p. 18, note 2.

[7] *Varin ā*, lit. 'descended from the family'. See the suggested explanation of the expression *vaṛä van* in Vol. I, pp. 193–194.

[8] Most probably of the same family.

[9] P. *mahā-lēkhaka*, 'chief secretary.'

[10] The Pāli equivalent of this seems to be *ārakkha-samaṇa* (Skt. *ārakṣa-śramaṇa*), but as the form *arak-sama* also occurs (e.g. in the Kirigallāva pillar, above, No. 1) it is possible that it is a derivative of P. *ārakkha-sama*, the final syllable *ṇa* being one of the forms of the honorific suffix *āṇa* so common in Sinhalese. See the *Sidatsaṅgarā*, ch. iv. *Araksama* is most probably the older form of *arakmehe* or *arak-mē*, *sama* becoming *mehe* by metathesis and the qualitative change of the vowel *a* (cf. *śramaṇa*, *samaṇa*, **hamaṇa*, *mahaṇa*, and *kadalī*, *kehel*). According to the *Pūjāvaliya*, *arakmē-nā* was a title conferred upon one of the princes who brought the Sacred Bōdhi-tree over to Ceylon from India. Though the etymology of *araksamaṇa* is thus fairly certain, the duties attached to the office are obscure. Possibly it was merely an honorary title. *Kasbā* = P. *Kassapa.*

of [the management of] two places of business[1] shall not enter; *perenäṭṭiyam* shall not enter; *dunumaḍula melätti*[2] shall not enter; labourers, village oxen, carts, and buffaloes[3] shall not be appropriated; officers of bowmen[4], heads of districts or keepers of (district) record books shall not enter and exercise authority[5]; the five superintendents of fields[6] shall not enter; tramps[7] and vagrants shall not enter; .... milk[8], gifts of raw or boiled rice shall not be appropriated; those who having committed homicide[9] come [into the village for refuge] shall only be arrested after they have been made to quit the village, but no [official] shall enter the village and arrest them. Inmates of the hospital shall not enter the village and commit ......; agricultural officials[10] shall not enter the village and appropriate .... (Dead?) goats and fowls shall be assigned to the hospital of the Vihāra.

We [the said] State Officials, namely, Mekāppar **Asaholu Mihindu** of the family of **Paṇḍi-rad Dāpuḷa**, and **Sumergamu Sātā**[11] and **Kuṇḍasalā Kit** of the family of Mahāle **Kasbā Araksamaṇa**, have come by Order and granted this Council Warrant of immunity to the area included within the four boundaries of **Mäḍiligiri-veher-Piyan-gala** situated in **Rantisā** in the district of **Bidervatu-kuḷiya.**

Whoever shall transgress this [edict] shall be crows and dogs [in their future birth. May there be] Health and Prosperity!

---

[1] *Deruvanā dekamtän.* See Vol. I, p. 207, note 3.

[2] This may mean '*melätti* of the archery department'.

[3] *Gäl-gon* and *gäl-mivun* may also mean 'draught-oxen' and 'draught-buffaloes'.

[4] *Dunuvā-balat*, 'archers' officers.' *Dunuvā*, probably from Skt. *dhanurvat* or *dhanurbhṛt*, occurs in the *Guttila* as in *vidinaḷa Budun maṅgadī* | *dunuvāyan yedī.* So also in connexion with the same incident in the *Saddharma-ratnāvali.* See Mudaliyar W. F. Guṇawardhana's scholarly edition of the *Guttila*, pp. 34–35.

Balat=P. *balattha.* See Vol. I, p. 190, note 2. The reading *dunu pābalayan* in the Moragoḍa pillar (Vol. I, No. 17, C, line 10) should be altered to *dunuvā-balatun.*

[5] *Isir*=Skt. *īśvara*, P. *issara.* See Vol. I, p. 92, transcript, line 19.

[6] *Velā-yut pas-denā* (B, line 24) and *velā-yut sam-daruvan* (C, lines 12–13) are obviously officials, but no reference to them has been found elsewhere that would give one an idea as to the nature of their duties. See also below, p. 43, note 9.

[7] *Maṅg-diva piya-diva*, evidently synonyms for *maṅg-giva* and *piya-giva*, for both the forms do not occur in the same inscription. See Vol. I, p. 171, note 1. The interpretation of *maṅg-diva* (Skt. *mārga-jīva*) as 'highway robbers' does not seem to suit the context here.

[8] *Sändive de-utu-kiri* (C, lines 2–3). This expression occurs also in the Bilibāva pillar, below, p. 39. Its signification is not clear.

[9] *Koḷā* for *minī koḷā.* See Vol. I, p. 47, transcript, line 24; p. 171, note 3, and p. 249, note 5.

[10] *Velā-yut samdaruvan.* See above, note 6.

[11] Most probably of the same family.

No. 7. AYITIGEVÄVA PILLAR-INSCRIPTION

AYITIGEVÄVA is a small hamlet in Kum̆bukväva Tulāna in the Kuñcuṭṭu Kōrale, about twenty-five miles north-north-east of Anurādhapura. The pillar was examined by the Archaeological Commissioner (Mr. H. C. P. Bell)[1] and myself in 1892. All its four sides are inscribed on. Side A contains eighteen lines of writing, with the figure of a *vaṭāpata* carved in relief below; B, twenty lines, followed by the figure of a dog; C, seventeen lines, with a symbol which, according to Mr. Bell, represents a sickle; and D, ten lines, with the emblems of sun, moon, and a crow.

The **letters** are well engraved, and are about one to two inches in size. They represent the alphabet of the latter half of the tenth century A. D. and in type resemble mostly those in the Mäḍirigiriya pillar[2] of Kassapa V. In both these records the letter *m* retains its 'archaistic' form, while in regard to *a*, *r*, and the medial vowel *u*, the present pillar differs from the other in the use of the older type with closed lower ends.

The **language** is the same in style as that of other *aṭṭāṇi* pillars of the period; but there occur in this inscription several hitherto unknown technical expressions of which the real meaning is at present obscure. These are (*saba*)*rā kǟbäli*, *suamburā* (*paddalā*) *kǟbäli*, *seṇa*, *tol*-(or *kol*-)*päṭṭin*, *väl*-(or *päl*-)*gattan*[3].

The **subject-matter** is a grant of the usual immunities to a certain plot of ground, five *payalas* in extent, belonging to **Tisaram** (P. *Tissārāma*) nunnery built on the 'Auspicious High Street' (*Mañgul Maha-veya*) by the Commander-in-Chief Sēna.

---

[1] His report runs:—'**Ayitigevewa.**—A well-preserved pillar, still standing, with an inscription of sixty-five lines: figures of dog and crow and symbols cut in relief below. The letters are mostly well incised. The record belongs to the fifth year of "Abhá Salamewan."

'Near are remains of the brickwork and some pillars of the ancient viháré, in front of which has been erected a small modern temple (Kandyan type) on stumps of broken columns of the old shrine. Lying prone at the site of the ancient viháré was found the trunk, armless and footless, of a standing Buddha; and close by, the head in excellent preservation. The joggle-holes in the neck, hands, and ankles of the trunk and in the head proved that the feet and other members had (as usual with these standing images) been separately carved and attached. The circular pedestal with the feet block was unearthed amid the brick *debris* in its original position. With infinite labour the statue was set up *in situ*. It stands 9 ft. 6 in. from head to pedestal.'—*A. S. C. Annual Report* for 1892, pp. 6–7.

[2] Compare the accompanying facsimile with Plate 6 of this volume.

[3] Cf. *dǟli-gattan* in the Äṭavīragollǟva pillar, side C, line 15 (below, p. 49, note 1). The reading *väl*- or *päl*- is clear in the present pillar, side C, lines 12–13.

The **date** is the fifth year of **Abhā Salamevan.** Some of the historical facts referred to in this record occur as well in the Kukurumahan-damana pillar[1] of the eleventh year of the reign of Siri Saṅg-bo (Kassapa IV). On palaeographic grounds alone we must assign the present inscription to Kassapa V (*circa* 980–990 A. D.); it is, therefore, later than the Mäḍirigiriya pillar by two years, and earlier than the slab near the 'stone canopy'[2] at Anurādhapura by one year.

As to the personages mentioned in the inscription, we know now for certain by comparing the *Mahāvaṁsa* account (ch. lii. 24) with the present record and the Kukurumahan-damana pillar that the Commander-in-Chief **Sēna** is identical with **Ilaṅga Sēna**, the *sēnā-pati* of the army of Kassapa IV. The State Official, **Nilą-vąsä Mandiyā**, or a namesake of his, figures also in the Noccipotāna grant[3]. The two ministers **Ataragalu-Kottā** and **Mulavaḍā-Sakarā**, who took part in the inauguration ceremony of the Moragoḍa pillar-edict, must have been related to **Mekäppar Namiḍā(rili)** and **Tisā Senu** of our record, as they all have the same family name of **Senevirad Vadurā.**

TEXT.

A.

1 අභාසලමෙව
2 ස් මපුර්මුකා ප
3 ස් වත්නෙ අ
4 සෙළු පුර දස
5 වැකැ වදළ එ
6 ක්තැන්සම්
7 යෙන් සභායෙ
8 න් අ (නි)ලව
9 සැ මඬියා[4] ඉ
10 සා (තුඹුවස්)[5]
11 කැමි සෙනු (ඉසා)
12 සෙනෙවිරද් වදු
13 රැ වරැ මෙකාප්
14 පර් නමිඩැ(රිලි)
15 ඉසා තිසැ සෙ
16 නු ඇතුළ් වැ මෙ
17 තුවාක් සම්ද
18 රුවන්විසින්

B.

1 සෙන් සෙනෙවි
2 රදළුණ්ස් මගු
3 ල් මහවෙසැ
4 කැරු තිසරම්
5 මෙහෙණිවර්
6 බද් ලොහොදු
7 විලැ කුළිසෙහි
8 අවු (දෙ)මෙළි
9 න් (හෙපිහයි)
10 න්[6] බහාලු (සබ)
11 රැ කැබැලි පු

[1] Above, No. 5. [2] Vol. I, No. 4. [3] Above, p. (

[4] 'මනියා' සිද කියවිය හැකිසි [5] 'තුඹුපය' සිද කියවිය

[6] 'හෙපිවාසින්' සිද කියවිය හැකිසි

12 අම්බුරැ (පද්ද
13 ලැ)[1] කැබැලී ඈ
14 තුළ්වැ එක් ප
15 ශල් (සෙණක්)
16 ඈතුළවූ සු
17 අම්බුරැ පස්
18 පයලට් රට්
19 ලදූ පස්ලදූ
20 වත් නො වද්

10 කොල් සම්ද
11 රුවන් තොල්[2]
12 පාවටින් වැ[3]
13 ල් ගත්තත්
14 නො වද්නා ඉ
15 සා මගිව පිය
16 ගිව නැල් ගොත්
17 මිවුන් වැරියන්

C.

1 නා ඉසා කුලී
2 මෙලාවිසී නො
3 වද්නා ඉසා
4 දෙරුවනෑ දෙ
5 කම්තැන් පෙ
6 රෙ̣නාවිපිය
7 නො වද්නා ඉ
8 සා පියො ව
9 දුරනුවන් රද්

D.

1 නො ගන්නා ඉසා
2 කොටා වත්න
3 ත් නො ගන්තා
4 කොට් සම්ද
5 රුවන්විසින්
6 අත්තාණි කණු
7 ගිඤ්වා මෙ ප
8 ස් පයලට් මෙ
9 සෙ පැරහැර්
10 දෙනු ලදී

TRANSCRIPT.

A.

1 **Abhā Salameva-**
2 **-n** Mapurmukā pa-
3 -s vanne A-
4 -seḷä pura dasa-
5 -väkä vadāḷa e-
6 -k-tän-sami-
7 -yen sabhāye-
8 -n ä **(Ni)la-va-**
9 **-sä Mandiyā**[4] i-
10 -sā (**Tuḍu-vas**)[5]
11 **Kämi Senu** (isā)
12 **Senevirad Vadu-**
13 **-rā**-varä Mekāp-
14 -par **Namiḍā(rili)**
15 isā **Tisā Se-**
16 **-nu** ätuḷ-vä me-
17 -tuvāk sam-da-
18 -ruvan-visin

B.

1 **Sen Senevi-**
2 **-radāṇan Maṅgu-**
3 **-l Maha-veyä**

---

[1] 'වළදලැ' සිද කියවිය හැකිසි
[2] 'කොල්' සිද කියවිය හැකිසි
[3] 'පැ' සිද කියවිය හැකිසි
[4] This may also be read *Maniyā*.
[5] This may also be read *Kuḍupaya*.

Ayitigevāva Pillar-inscription.

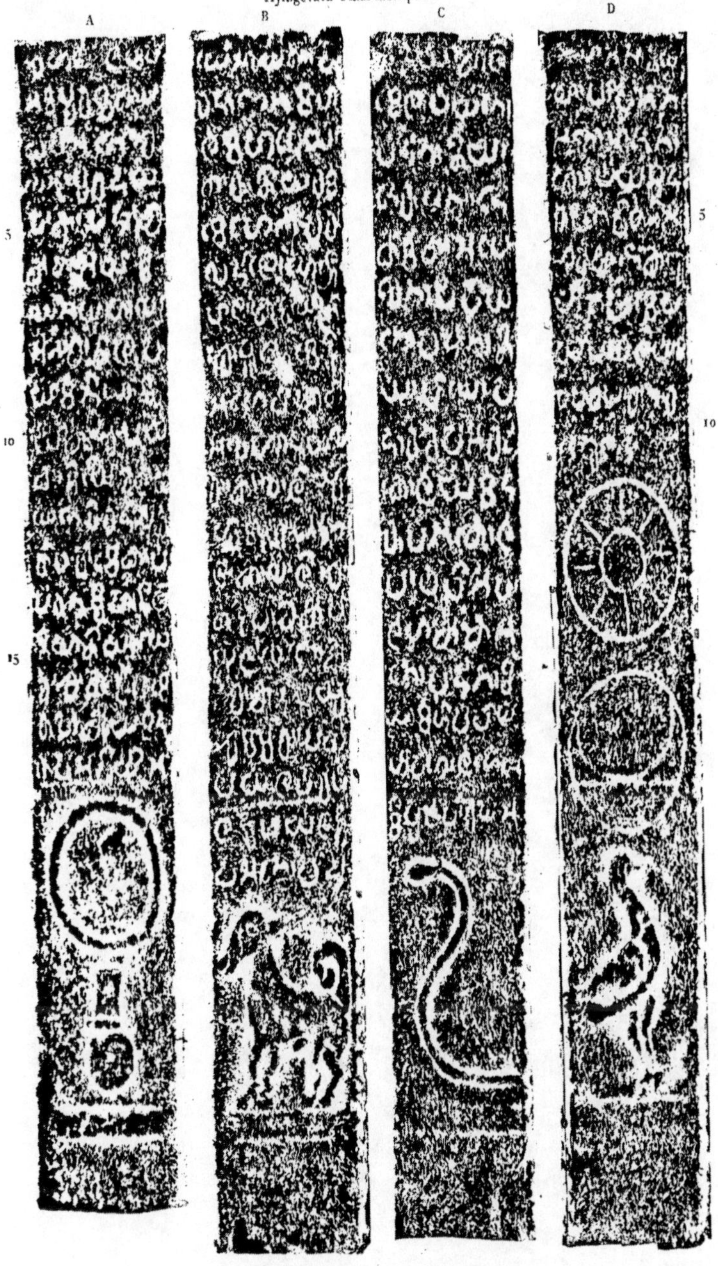

From an ink-impression supplied by the Archaeological Commissioner, Ceylon.

Scale about 1⅜ inches to 1 foot.

4 kärū **Tisaram**
5 meheṇivar
6 bad **Loholu-**
7 **-vilä kuḷiyehi**
8 āvū (De)meḷi-
9 -n (-heṭihayi-)
10 -n [1] bahālū (saba-)
11 -rā kābäli su-
12 -amburā (padda-
13 -lä) [2] kābäli ä-
14 -tuḷ-vä ek pa-
15 -yal (seṇak)
16 ätuḷa-vū su-
17 amburā **pas**
18 **payalaṭ** **raṭ-**
19 ladu pas-ladu-
20 -van no vad-

C.

1 -nā isā kulī
2 melāṭsī no
3 vadnā isā
4 deruvanā de-
5 kam-tän pe-
6 -renāṭṭiya
7 no vadnā i-
8 -sā piyo-va-
9 -dāranuvan rad-
10 -kol-sam-da-
11 -ruvan tol-[3]
12 -pāṭṭin vä-[4]
13 -l-gattan
14 no vadnā i-
15 -sā maṅgiva piya-
16 -giva gäl gon
17 mīvun väriyan

D.

1 no gannā isā
2 koṭā vanna-
3 -n no gannā
4 koṭ sam-da-
5 -ruvan-visin
6 attāṇi-kaṇu
7 hind-vā me pa-
8 -s payalaṭ me-
9 -se pärahär
10 denu ḷadi

TRANSLATION.

On the tenth day of the waxing moon in [the month of] *Aseḷa* (June–July) in the fifth year of His Majesty **Abhā Salamevan.**

Whereas it was [so] decreed by the Supreme Council[5], all these Officers of State, namely, **Nilavasä Mandiyā, (Tuḍu-vas) Kämi Senu**[6], Mekāppar **Namiḍā(rili)** of the family of **Senevirad Vadurā**, and **Tisā Senu**[7], have come from the Council. And, touching the five *payalas* of *suamburā* (field) including [the plot of ground of] one *payala* and one *seṇa* made up of *sabarā* allotments and *suamburā* (*paddalä*) allotments, [which land was] set apart from

---

[1] This may also be read *heṭivāsin*.

[2] This may also be read *kol-*.

[3] This may also be read *vaḷadalā*.

[4] This may also be read *pä-*.

[5] *Vadāla ek-tän-samiyen* (A, lines 5–7), same as *vat-himiyan ek-tän-samiyen vadāḷeyin* (in Kirigalläva pillar, B, lines 7–11, above p. 4). See also above, p. 18, note 2, p. 32, note 6, and Vol. I, p. 206, note 2.

[6] Or *Kuḍupas-kämi Senu* or *Tuḍu-paya-kämi Senu*.

[7] Probably of the same family.

(De)meḷin(heṭihaya) situated in the district of **Loholuvilä kuḷiya**, and attached to the **Tisaram**[1] nunnery built on the 'Auspicious High Street' (*Mañgul Maha-veya*) by the Commander-in-Chief **Sēna**, [the following immunities were granted :—]

District headmen, and keepers of district records shall not enter; coolies and *melāṭsī* shall not enter; holders [of the management] of two places of business, and *perenāṭṭiya*[2] shall not enter; enforcers of customary laws, members of the royal family[3], *tolpāṭṭin*[4] and *väl-gattan*[5] shall not enter; tramps and vagrants [shall not enter]; carts, oxen, buffaloes, and labourers shall not be appropriated; those who have come [for refuge] after committing murder shall not be arrested[6].

To this effect the State Officials have set up the pillar of Council Warranty and granted the immunities to the aforesaid five *payalas* [sowing extent of land].

No. 8. BILIBĀVA PILLAR-INSCRIPTION

WHILST exploring the ancient sites in Vilacciya Kōrale in 1896, the Archaeological Commissioner (Mr. H. C. P. Bell) came upon this pillar[7] (6 ft. by 1 ft. square) at Bilibāva in Ihala Kälāgam Tulāna, about fifteen miles to the south-west of Anurādhapura. Three of its sides are inscribed on, A containing 27 lines, B 31, and C 22, followed by the figures of a dog and a crow. Those of sun, moon, and *vaṭāpata* (Buddhist monk's fan) mentioned by Mr. Bell must be on the fourth side. To judge from the two estampages before me, the letters do not appear to have been deeply engraved on a properly prepared surface.

The **akṣaras**, 1 to $1\frac{1}{2}$ in. in size, belong to the alphabet of the latter half of the tenth century. They resemble most the type of letters in the Buddha-

---

[1] P. *Tissārāma.* See *Mv.* lii. 24.

[2] Not *perenāṭṭiyam* as in other records.

[3] *Raj-kol-sam-daruvan* means also in a wider sense 'officers of state'.

[4] Or *kolpāṭṭin.*

[5] Or *päl-gattan.* See above, p. 34, note 3. These are unknown technical terms. Their meaning is at present obscure.

[6] See in this connexion the Noccipotāna edict, above, p. 8.

[7] Mr. Bell describes it as follows :—

'**Bilibewa.**—Inscribed square pillar—perhaps the handsomest yet discovered in the Island—in excellent preservation. Crowned with a carved *kalasa*, or round vase, the writing covers three sides; and there are in addition sunk figures of sun, moon, *watahapota*, dog and crow—all emblematic. The inscription is very clear. It belongs to the seventh year of "Abhá Salamevan" (Kassapa V, 929–939), son of "Siri Sang Bo" and "the twice-crowned queen."'—*A. S. C. Annual Report*, 1896, p. 5.

nnehäla pillar of the third year of Abhā Salamevan [1]. This king has already been identified with Kassapa V (980-990 A.D.). The present record confirms the identification both palaeographically and historically. As it is **dated** in the seventh year of his reign, it is four years later than the Buddhannehäla inscription, and one year later than the Anurādhapura slab-inscription of Kassapa V [2], though some letters, such as *a*, *k*, *m*, and *r* in the present pillar, are more archaic in type than those of the slab.

The **language** is the same in style as that of other tenth-century records familiar to us, the first nineteen lines of the text agreeing, word for word, with lines 1-16 and 22-24 of side A of the Elleväva pillar [3] of Dappula V, half-brother [4] of Kassapa V. Attention may, however, be drawn to the technical expression *ek-tän-samiyen vändä vadāḷeyin avud* (B, lines 11-13) which occurs in most of the inscriptions of this period, but with some variation or other, e.g. *vadāḷa ek-tän-samiyen ā* [5], *vadāḷeyin* [6], *vadāḷeyin ā* [7], *vadāḷein avud* [8], *vadāḷen avud* [9], *vadāḷeyin sabhāyen ā* [10], *vadāḷa ek-tän-samiyen sabhāyen ā* [11], *vat-himiyan ek-tän-samiyen vadāḷeyin* [12], and *vändä vadāḷeyin* [13].

In ordinary speech *vändä* (P. *vanditvā*) means 'having worshipped' with closed palms placed on the forehead. Whether it means this here or not it is difficult to say. It is, however, interesting to note that this form of showing respect is observed even to-day amongst Sinhalese country folk in conversing with a superior. Possibly members of the King's Council used the same formality in giving their assent to the proposed decrees. The expressions *vela-yut pas-denā* (B, lines 29-30), *pereläkkan* (C, lines 1-2), and (*sändive*) *de-utu-kiri* (C, lines 5-6) are still unintelligible.

The **contents** give us the usual particulars of a grant of immunities to **Mahagāpiyova**, a village in the district of **Pirivatu** in the Southern Quarter, dedicated to the **Kasub-Senevirad-pirivena** [14] which **Sak-Senevi Saṅgalnāvan** had built in the Mahāvihāra.

---

[1] See Vol. I, p. 192.

[2] *Ibid.*, No. 4.

[3] *A. S. C. Seventh Progress Report*, 1891, p. 45; *A. I. C.*, No. 116.

[4] See the genealogical table in Vol. I, p. 184.

[5] Vessagiri slab, No. 2, line 32 (Vol. I, p. 34).

[6] Kiribat-vehera pillar A, lines 7-8 (*Ibid.*, p. 159), Mäḍirigiriya, A, line 16 (above, p. 30).

[7] Īripinniyāva pillar D, lines 8-9 (*Ibid.*, p. 169), and Noccipotāna pillar A, line 9 (above, p. 7).

[8] Raṁbāva pillar D, lines 7-8 (*Ibid.*, p. 174).

[9] Īripinniyāva, D, lines 26-27.

[10] Kukurumahan-damana, A, lines 21-22 (above, p. 23).

[11] Ayitigeväva, A, lines 5-7 (above, p. 36).

[12] Kirigallāva, B, lines 7-11 (above, p. 4).

[13] Alutväva, A, lines 6-7.

[14] P. *Kassapa-Sēnāpatirāja-pariveṇa.*

The king **Abhā Salamevan**, of our record is, as stated above, identical with Kassapa V (980–990 A.D.), the inscriptional notices of his parents being in agreement with those of the chronicles[1]. **Sak-Senevi**[2] was his son, and the **Kasub-Senevirad-pirivena** may be the building referred to in the *Mahāvaṁsa*[3] as the 'delightful *parivēṇa* which he called after his own name, and gave it unto the Thēriya [i.e. the Mahāvihāra] brethren with lands'. If this be the case, the full name of the son of Kassapa V must have been **Kasub Sak-Senevi Saṅgalnāvan.**

The five State Officials who took part in the grant are not known to us from other sources. The name **Budim**, however, occurs in the Ellevāva pillar.

TEXT.

A.

1 සිරිබර් කැ
2 න් කුල කොත්
3 ඔකාවස් ප
4 රපුරෙන් බ
5 ව් ලක්දිව්
6 පොළොයොන් ප
7 රපුරෙන් හි
8 මිවු **සිරි** ස
9 **ගබො** මහර
10 ද්නු සත් නැ
11 ගු නව වන
12 හවුරුදුයෙ
13 හි පාඬිරව්
14 පැහැර් දිය
15 කිත්ති ලද්
16 මහරද්නු
17 (ද)රු දෙබිසෙ
18 වැදූ **අභා ස**
19 **ලමෙවන්** මපු
20 රුමුකා සත්
21 වන්නෙය් දු
22 රුත්තෙ අව
23 විසෙනි දව
24 **ස් පිරිත්නි**
25 **රද් කශ්බා**
26 වර් වන මෙ
27 කාප්පර් **දෙ**

B.

1 .. ..
2 **කරගම් සෙනි**[4]
3 **ම්** ඉසා **ඇකැ** (ශ)
4 **සැසිම්** ඉසා **ස**
5 **ඤ් පිරිත්නි** ර
6 **දුන්** දෑ වසැ ස
7 හායෙන් ආ **බැමැ**
8 **බුදිම්** ඉසා මෙ
9 හි මැ **නිමුලිම්**[5]
10 ඉසා මෙතුවාක් දෙ
11 නමො එක්තැන්ස
12 මියෙන් වැඳෑ වද,
13 ළෙසින් අවුද් මන
14 වෙහෙර් **සක්සෙ**

---

[1] See Mr. Bell's notes on the Ellevāva pillar (*A. S. C. Seventh Progress Report*, 1891, p. 45), and above, Vol. I, p. 192.

[2] P. *Sakka-Sēnāpati*.

[3] Ch. lii. 61–62.

[4] 'සෙඤි' සීද කියවිය හැකියි

[5] 'නිමිලිම්' සීද කියවිය හැකියි

Bilibāva Pillar-inscription.

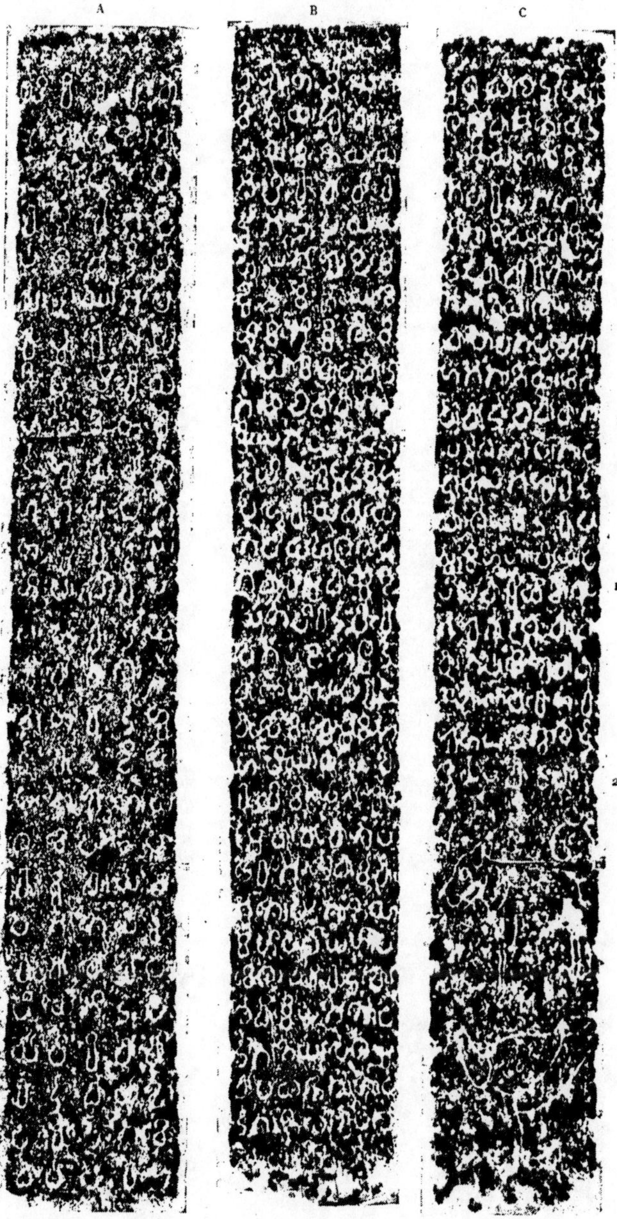

From an ink-impression supplied by the Archaeological Commissioner, Ceylon.

Scale about 1¾ inches to 1 foot.

15 **හෙව් සගල්නාව**
16 **ස්** කැරවූ **කසුබ්**
17 **සෙනෙවිරද්පිරි**
18 **වෙනව්** බහාලූ ද
19 කුණ් පසැ **පිරිව**
20 **තුඹිමැ** ආවූ **මහ**
21 **ගැපිගොවැ** සත
22 ර් සීමායෙන් ඇතු
23 ළ්වූතාක්තැනට්
24 දෙරුවනැ දෙකම්තැ
25 න් නො වද්නා ඉසා
26 ඹගිව පියගිව
27 මෙලා(විසි) රද්කො
28 ල් කැමියන් නො ව
29 ද්නා ඉසා වෙලඳු
30 ත් පස්දෙනා නො ව
31 ද්නා ඉසා රවිල

C.

1 දු පස්ලදු පෙරෙ
2 ලැක්කන් නො වද්
3 නා ඉසා ගැල් මිවූ
4 න් වැරියන් නො ග
5 න්නා ඉසා (සැඬිවෙ)[1]
6 දෙ උතුකිරි නො ග
7 න්නා ඉසා මෙයට්
8 කොටා වන් වැදැ නො
9 ගන්නා ඉසා මෙතු
10 වාක් දැ එක්තැන්
11 සම්යෙන් වැඳැ ව
12 දෑළෙසින් ආ රද්
13 කොල් සම්දරුව
14 මො **මහගැපිගොව**
15 **ව්** සතර සීමායෙ
16 න් ඇතුළ්වූතාක්
17 තැනට් මෙ අත්තා
18 ණීක(ණු) පැරැහැර්
19 අභය දෙනුලදි
20 මෙයට් (අනියා) ..
21 .. [කවුඩු] බලු .. ..
22 .. ..

TRANSCRIPT.

A.

1 Siri-barä Kä-
2 -t kula kot
3 Okāvas pa-
4 -rapuren ba-
5 -ṭ Lak-div-
6 poḷoyon pa-
7 -rapuren hi-
8 -mivū **Siri Sa-**
9 **-ňg-bo** Maha-ra-
10 -d-hu sat nä-
11 -ňgū nava vana
12 havuruduye-
13 -hi Pāňḍi-raṭ
14 pähärä diya-
15 kitti-lad
16 maha-rad-hu
17 (da)ru de-bise-
18 -vä-dā **Abhā Sa-**
19 **-lamevan** Mapu-
20 -rumukā sat-
21 -vanney du-
22 -rutte ava
23 viseni dava-
24 -s **Piritti-**
25 **-rad Kasbā-**
26 varä vana me-
27 -käppar **De-**

[1] 'සැණිවෙ' යිද කියවිය හැකියි

B.

1 .. ..
2 **Karāgam Seni-**[1]
3 **-m** isā **Ātä (Ya-)**
4 **-säyim** isā **Sa-**
5 **-nd Piritti-ra-**
6 **-dun** dā vasä sa-
7 -bhāyen ā **Bämä**
8 **Budim** isā me-
9 -hi mä **Nimulim**[2]
10 isā metuvāk de-
11 -namo ek-tän-sa-
12 -miyen vändä vadā-
13 -ḷeyin avud Maha-
14 -veherä **Sak-Se-**
15 **-nevi Saṅgal-nāva-**
16 **-n** kärāvū **Kasub-**
17 **Senevirad-piri-**
18 **-venaṭ** bahālū da-
19 -kuṇ pasä **Piri-va-**
20 **-tu-bimä** āvū **Maha-**
21 **-gä-piyovä** sata-
22 -r sīmāyen ätu-
23 -ḷ-vū-tāk-tänaṭ
24 deruvanā dekam-tä-
25 -n no vadnā isā
26 maṅgiva piyaṅgiva
27 melā(ṭsi) rad-ko-
28 -l-kämiyan no va-
29 -dnā isā vela-yu-
30 -t pas-denā no va-
31 -dnā isā raṭ-la-

C.

1 -du pas-ladu pere-
2 -läkkan no vad-
3 -nā isā gäl mivu-
4 -n väriyan no ga-
5 -nnā isā (sändive)[3]
6 de-utu-kiri no ga-
7 -nnā isā meyaṭ
8 koṭā van vädā no
9 gannā isā metu-
10 -vāk dā ek-tän-
11 -samiyen vändä va-
12 -dāḷeyin ā rad-
13 kol-samdaruva-
14 -mo **Mahagāpiyova-**
15 -ṭ satara sīmāye-
16 -n ätuḷ-vū-tāk-
17 tänaṭ me attā-
18 -ṇi-ka(ṇu) pärähär
19 abhaya denu-ladi
20 meyaṭ (aniyā) ..
21 .. [kavuḍu] balu .. ..
22 .. ..

TRANSLATION.

On the fifth day of the waning moon of [the month of] *Durutu* (Dec.–Jan.) in the seventh year of (the reign of) His Majesty **Abhā Salamevan,** born of the 'twice-anointed queen'[4], and son of the great king who won the fame of victory by conquering the Pāṇḍya country[5] in the ninth year after

---

[1] This may also be read *Sendi.*

[2] This may also be read *Nimilim.*

[3] This may also be read *säṇive.*

[4] *Debisevä-dā.* See above, pp. 27 and 32, note 4.

[5] See Ellevāva pillar A, lines 1–22 (*A. S. C. Seventh Progress Report*, 1891, p. 45).

the raising of the canopy of dominion by the great king **Siri Saṅg-bo**, descended from the Okkāka dynasty, the pinnacle of the illustrious Kṣatriya race, and lord, by lineal succession of kings, of the Island of Laṅkā[1].

Whereas it was graciously [so] decreed by the Supreme Council, we, all of us, namely, Mekāppar **De** ..... of the family of **Piritti-rad Kasbā**[2] ...... **Karāgam Senim**[3], **Ätä (Ya)säyim, Bämä Budim**, a member of the Council, of the family of **Sand Piritti-rad**[4], and **Nimulim**[5] of the same family, have come.

And whereas concerning the area included within the four boundaries of **Mahagāpiyova** situated in the district of **Pirivatu**[6] in the Southern Quarter—(which land was) dedicated to the **Kasub-Senevirad-pirivena**, built by **Sak-Senevi Saṅgalnāvan** in the **Mahāvihāra**, the following immunities[7] were graciously granted by the Supreme Council:—Holders [of the management] of two places of business[8] shall not enter; tramps, vagrants, *melāṭsi* and servants of the royal family shall not enter; the five agricultural (?) officials[9] shall not enter; district headmen and keepers of [district] records and *perelākkan* shall not enter; carts, buffaloes, and labourers shall not be appropriated; (*sändive*) *de-utu*[10] milk shall not be appropriated; those who have come here after committing murder[11] shall not be arrested [by Officers] entering (the village).

We the (aforesaid) State Officials have come, and by this pillar of Council Warranty granted these immunities and right of asylum in respect of the area included within the four boundaries of **Mahagāpiyova**.

Whoever (does injustice) to this [enactment shall be born] a crow or a dog [in his future birth].

---

[1] *Lak-div-poḷoyon-parapuren himi.* See Vol. I, p. 248, note 7.

[2] *Piritti-rad* may be a corruption of Skt. *pṛthvī-rāja* through Tamil *pirutivi°*. *Kasbā* = Skt. *kāśyapa, kacchapa*; P. *kassapa, kacchapa.* Cf. Sinh. *käsup, kasup, käsubu, kasub,* and *käsbă.*

[3] Or *Sendim.*

[4] Probably for Skt. *Candra-pṛthvī-rāja.*

[5] Or *Nimilim.*

[6] Cf. *Pirivatuguṇa mahalā* in the *Daḷadāpūjāvaliya* (ed. 1893), p. 35.

[7] *Metuvāk dā ek-tän-samiyen vändä vadāḷeyin* (C, lines 9–12), lit. 'Since all these matters were graciously declared by the Supreme Council' (i.e. His Majesty in Council).

[8] *Deruvanā dekamtän*, B, line 24.

[9] *Vela-yut pas-denā*, B, lines 29–30. See also above, p. 33, note 6.

[10] This term occurs also in the Mäḍirigiriya inscription above, pp. 27 and 33, note 8.

[11] *koṭā* (C, line 8) for *minī koṭā* 'having committed murder'. See Vol. I, pp. 47, 169, 174, 205, 247, and 249, note 5.

No. 9. ĀṬAVĪRAGOLLĀVA PILLAR-INSCRIPTION

THIS pillar, measuring about 5½ ft. by 11 in. square, lies on a side of the *pin-pāra*, the village-road of Äṭavīragollāva, about eleven miles from Maḍawacci in Kaḍawat Kōrale. It is inscribed on all its four sides, but owing to the splitting of the stone at the top several lines on sides A and D are obliterated. Judging from the height of the pillar, side A may have contained more than eighteen lines, or else the space above the writing must have borne a Buddhist emblem. Side B has twenty-eight lines; C, twenty-five, surmounted by a figure of the sun; and D, seventeen, with figures of a crow, a dog, a Buddhist monk's fan (*vaṭāpata*), and a so-called sickle. The inscription was first read by Dr. Goldschmidt [1]. Dr. Müller published a rough transcript, with a translation of the first side only, in 1883 [2]. The Archaeological Commissioner (Mr. H. C. P. Bell) re-examined it in 1890 [3].

The **characters**, half to one and a half inches in size, belong to the alphabet of the last quarter of the tenth century A. D. In type they resemble, more or less, the letters in the Puliyaṉkuḷam slab of Udā Mahayā [4], dated the twelfth year of Dappula V (991–1003 A. D.).

The **language** is in keeping with the style of other similar records of the period. The text on side A agrees with that on side A of the Ellevāva [5] and of the foregoing Bilibāva pillars almost word for word. Attention may also be drawn to the use of *van* in B, lines 13 and 18, and *varä* in line 22, instead of the fuller and more familiar form *varä van*. Among the various classes of people prohibited from entering the protected village are some names of obscure meaning, and not of frequent occurrence in inscriptions. These are *ulavāḍu*, *aräkkan*, *peraläkkan*, *dunuvā-balatun* (captains of bowmen ?), *däli-gattan* (net-men ?), (*y*)*amuṅguru-gatuvan* (mace-men ?), and *tuṅḍise*.

The **contents** tell us that king **Abhā Siri Saṅg-bo** ransacked the Pāṇḍya country, and obtained a victory in the ninth year of his reign, that his son was **Abhā Salamevan**, and that in the tenth year [6] of this king's sovereignty, the immunities mentioned in the record were granted to the village **Velangama** belonging to the **Sirisaṅgbo-rad-pirivena**, and an *attāṇi* pillar was set up to

---

[1] See *Ceylon Sessional Papers*, No. XI of 1876, p. 9.

[2] *A. I. C.*, No. 117.

[3] *A. S. C. Annual Report* for 1890, p. 8.

[4] *E. Z.*, Vol. I, No. 15.

[5] *A. I. C.*, No. 116; *A. S. C. Seventh Progress Report*, 1891, p. 45.

[6] Owing to the text being damaged here, the exact day and the name of the lunar month cannot be made out.

that effect by the three Officials, Mekāppar **Tambu[ruga]mu Kitim, Ki(liṅg)-bo Sa(ki)m**, and **Ku(ṇḍa)salā (Siṅgim)**.

King **Abhā Salamevan** has already been identified with Dappula V (991–1003 A. D.). The Ellevāva pillar, which has the same introduction as the present one, calls him **Abhā Salamevan Dāpuḷa**, while the Vessagiri[1] slab, No. 1, gives his full name as **Buddas Abahay Salamevan Dāpuḷa**[2]. His father **Abhā Siri Saṅg-bo**, or more fully **Buddas Siri Saṅg-boy Abahay**, has also been identified with Sēna II (917–952 A. D.)[3]. The Ellevāva, the Bilibāva, and the present pillars refer to the successful campaign carried out by his generals in the Pāṇḍya country, so graphically described in the *Mahāvaṁsa*[4]. Other epigraphical documents afford us the information that Sēna II had at least two wives, namely, the twice-anointed queen **Saṅghā**, called **Saṅg Baṇḍay** in the slab-inscription[5] near the 'stone canopy', and the sub-queen **Dēvā Rājñī**, mentioned in the Vessagiri record. Kassapa V or Abhā Salamevan of the Bilibāva pillar was the son by the former queen, while Dappula V or Abhā Salamevan of the present pillar was the son by the latter[6].

The date of the present record, as well as the one at Ellevāva, being the tenth year of Dappula's reign, both these are about eight years later than his Vessagiri slab[6] and two years earlier than the Puliyaṉ-kuḷam slab of Udā Mahayā[7].

The **Sirisaṅgbo-rad-pirivena** referred to on side B, lines 4–5, may be identified with the **Sirisaṅghabōdhi-parivēṇa** built by Aggabōdhi I (*circa* 615–649 A. D.)[8].

TEXT.

A.

1 .. ..
2 .. .. .. (ව) ශ්‍රී ..
3 .. .. ය .. ..
4 .. ..
5 .. .. .. වී ඔක[ාව]
6 [ස් රද් ප]රපුරෙ[න්]
7 [බට ල]ක්දිව් පෙ[ා]
8 [ලොයො]න් පරපු[රෙ]
9 [න් හි]මිවූ අ[භා සි]
10 [රි ස]ඟ්බො මහර
11 [ද්නු] තුමා සත් ලැ
12 [ගූ] නව වන හවූ
13 [රැදු]යෙහි පාඬිරට
14 [පැ]හැරැ දිය ලද් ම
15 [හ]රද්නු දරැ අභා
16 සලමෙවන් මහ
17 [ර]ද්නු තුමා සත් ලැ
18 [ගූ] දසවන හවූ

[1] *E. Z.*, Vol. I, pp. 23–24.
[2] P. *Buddhadāsa Abhaya Silāmēghavaṇṇa Dappula.*
[3] *A. S. C. Seventh Progress Report*, 1891, p. 43; *E. Z.*, Vol. I, pp. 24, 42, and 184.
[4] Ch. li, vv. 27–47.
[5] *E. Z.*, Vol. I, No. 4.
[6] *Ibid.*, No. 2. iii (1).
[7] *Ibid.*, No. 15.
[8] *Mv.* xlii. 10–11.

B.

1 රුදුයෙහි .. .. ..
2 පස්හි .. ..
3 ස බිමැ දෙනා[වෙ]
4 හෙරු සිරිස[ග්]
5 බොරද්සිරි[වෙණ්]
6 බද් වෙලන්[ගැ]
7 මැ අත්තා[ණි කණ්‍ඩු]
8 හිඤ්වා දෙවා [ව]
9 දළ එක්(තැ)[න්]
10 සම්යෙන් [මෙකා]
11 ප්පර්වැදූරු[ම්]
12 තලා අරක්[නා වැ]
13 දූරුම් වත් [මෙකා]
14 ප්පර් තම්බු[රුග]
15 මු කිතිම් ඉ[සා මෙ]
16 කාප්පර් ති .. [වෙ]
17 හෙරු සිහිම් .. ..
18 නා වත් කි(ලිග්)
19 බො ස(කි)ම්[1] ඉසා
20 මහාලෙ (බමරක්)
21 කස්බාරක්ස
22 මණක්වරු කු(ඩ)
23 සලා (සිහිම්) ..
24 ඇතුළුවැ ඇප් [මෙ]
25 තුවාක් දෙනමො [එ]
26 ක්සෙවැ [මෙ ගම්වි]
27 මයිව් (පෙදිව) කු
28 ලී මෙලා(ත්සි) රද්කො

C.

1 ල් කැමියන් නො [ව]
2 ද්නා කොට් ඉසා උ
3 ලවාබූ පෙරෙනා
4 වපියම් නො වද්නා [ඉ]
5 සා රට්ලදූ පස්
6 ලද්දන් නො වද්
7 නා ඉසා දෙරුව
8 නෑ දෙකම්තැන් නො
9 වද්නා ඉසා අරක්
10 කත් පෙර(ලැ)ක්ක
11 න් නො වද්නා ඉසා
12 දූනු(වා)බලතුන්
13 නො වද්නා ඉසා
14 පියොවදූරන්න
15 න් (දැලි)ගත්තන්
16 (ය)මුගුරු (ග)තුව
17 න් නො වද්නා ඉ
18 සා කිරිගෙරි ග
19 ම්ගොන් නො ගත්
20 නා ඉසා ගැල් ම්
21 වුන් වැරියන් වැ
22 රි සාල් නො ගත්
23 නා ඉසා තුඩි(සෙ)
24 .. .. (නො)
25 වද්නා ඉසා (රි)

D.

1 .. ..
2 .. .. .. ගම්වි ..
3 .. .. .. (වාල) .. ..
4 .. .. .. සා වදෑ[ළ]
5 [එක්තැ]න්ස[මි]
6 [යෙන්] ආ මෙතු[වා]
7 [ක් දෙ]නමො
8 .. ..
9 .. ..
10 .. ආබූතාක් .. ..
11 .. .. .. වා මෙ අත්
12 තාණ් කණ්‍ඩු ..
13 .. ..
14 (ආනෑ පවත්)
15 නා කොට් මෙ අ
16 ත්තාණි පෙරු
17 හැර දෙනු ලදි

[1] ‘සතිම්’ සීද කියවිය හැකිසි

Āṭavīragollǣva Pillar-inscription.

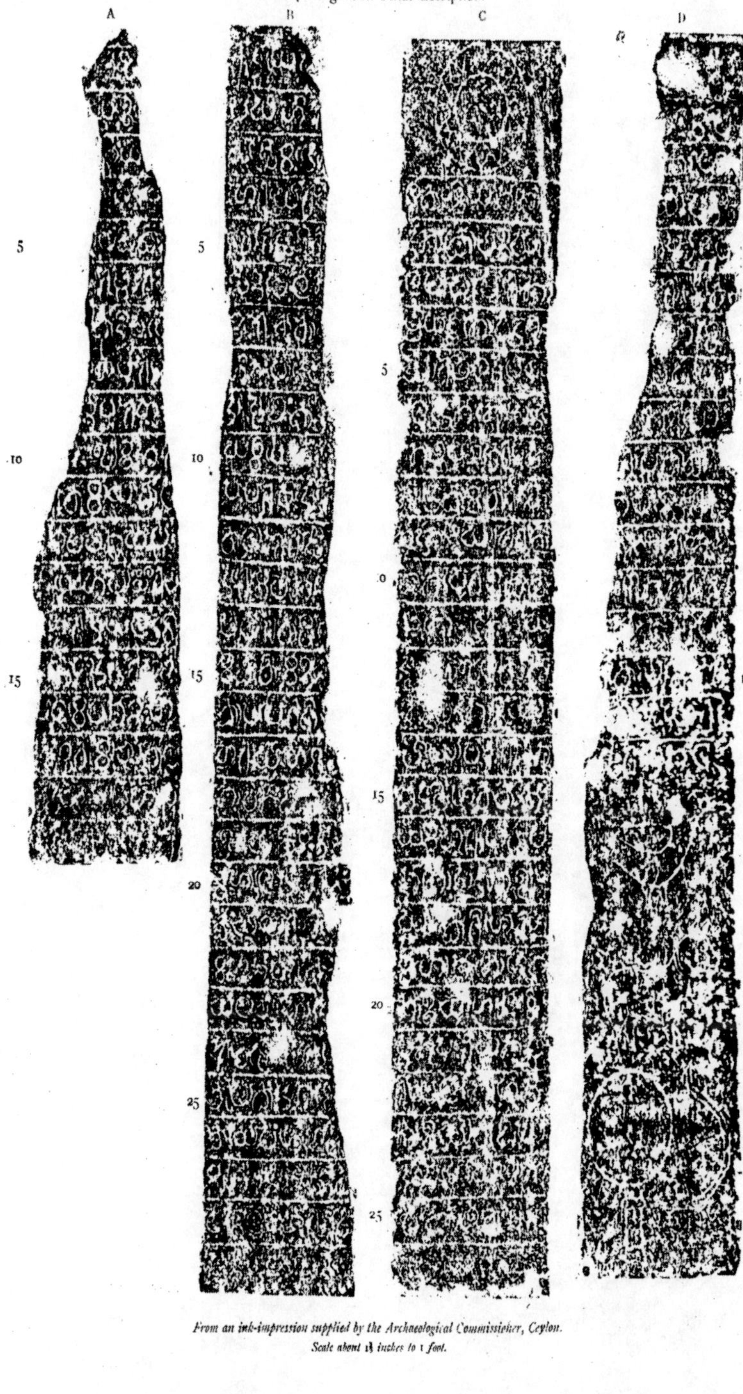

From an ink-impression supplied by the Archaeological Commissioner, Ceylon.

Scale about 1¾ inches to 1 foot.

TRANSCRIPT.

A.

1 .. ..
2 .. .. .. (va) i ..
3 .. .. ya .. ..
4 .. ..
5 .. .. .. ṭ Ok[ā-va-]
6 [-s rad pa]rapure[n]
7 [baṭ La]k-div p[o-]
8 [-ḷoyo]n parapu[re-]
9 [-n hi]mi-vū **A**[**bhā Si-**]
10 [**-ri Sa**]**ṅgbo** Mahara-
11 [-d-hu] tumā **sat lä-**
12 [-ṅgū] nava **vana** havu-
13 [-rudu-]yehi Pāṇḍi-raṭ
14 [pä]härä diya lad ma-
15 [-ha]rad-hu daru **Abhā**
16 **Salamevan** maha-
17 [ra]d-hu tumā sat lä-
18 [-ṅgū] dasa-vana havu-

B.

1 -ruduyehi .. .. ..
2 pashi .. ..
3 **-sa** bimä **Denā-[ve-]**
4 **-herä Sirisa[ṅg-]**
5 **-bo-rad-piri[ven]**
6 bad **Velan-**[**gä-**]
7 **-mä** attā[ṇi-kaṇu]
8 hindvā devā [va-]
9 -dāḷa ek-(tä)[n-]
10 samiyen [Me-kā-]
11 -ppar-Vädāru[m]
12 **Talā Aräk-[nā Vä-]**
13 **-dārum** van [Mekā-]
14 -ppar **Tambu[ru-ga-]**
15 **-mu Kitim** i[sā Me-]
16 -kāppar **Ti** .. [**-ve-**]
17 **-herä Siṅgim** .. ..
18 **-nā** van **Ki**(**liṅg-**)
19 **-bo Sa**(**ki**)**m**[1] isā
20 Mahāle (**Vaṭarak**)
21 **Kasbāraksa-**
22 **-maṇan-**varä **Ku**(**ṅda-**)
23 **-salā** (**Siṅgim**) ..
24 ätuḷu-vä äp [me-]
25 -tuvāk denamo [e-]
26 -k-se-vä [me gamaṭ]
27 magiv (pediv) ku-
28 -lī melā(tsī) rad-ko-

C.

1 -l-kämiyan no [va-]
2 -dnā koṭ isā u-
3 -lavāḍu perenā-
4 -ṭṭiyam no vadnā [i-]
5 -sā raṭ-ladu pas-
6 -laddan no vad-
7 -nā isā deruva-
8 -nā dekam-tän no
9 vadnā isā aräk-
10 -kan pera(lä)kka-
11 -n no vadnā isā
12 dunu(vā)-balatun
13 no vadnā isā
14 piyo-vadāranna-
15 -n (däli-)gattan
16 (ya)muṅguru-(ga)tuva-
17 -n no vadnā i-

---

[1] This may also be read *Satim.*

18 -sā kiri-geri ga-
19 -m-gon no gan-
20 -nā isā gäl mi-
21 -vun väriyan vä-
22 -ri sāl no gan-
23 -nā isā tuṇḍi(se)
24 .. .. (no)
25 vadnā isā (ri-)

D.

1 .. ..
2 .. .. .. gamaṭ ..
3 .. .. .. (vāla) .. ..
4 .. .. .. sā vadā[ḷa]
5 [ek-tä]n-sa[mi-]
6 [-yen] ā metu[vā-]
7 [-k de]namo ..
8 .. ..
9 .. ..
10 .. āvūtāk .. ..
11 .. .. .. vā me at-
12 tāṇi-kaṇu ..
13 .. ..
14 (ānā pavat-)
15 -nā koṭ me a-
16 -ttāṇi perä-
17 -hära denu ladi

TRANSLATION.

. . . . . . in the tenth year since the elevation of the canopy of dominion by His Majesty **Abhā Salamevan**, son of the great king who obtained victory by ransacking the Pāṇḍya country in the ninth year after the raising of the canopy of dominion [by him, to wit] the great king **Abhā Siri Saṅg-bo**, lord, by hereditary succession of kings, of the Island of Laṅkā, descended from the line of kings of the Okkāka dynasty . . . . . .

Whereas it was decreed by the Supreme Council that a pillar of Council Warranty should be set up in the village **Velan-gama** attached to the **Siri-saṅgbo-rad-pirivena** [1] of Denā-vehera [2], [and situated] in the district . . . . . ., we all of us together, namely, Mekāppar **Tambu[ruga]mu Kitim** of [the family of] Mekāppar-Vädārum **Talā Aräk[nā Vä]dārum, Ki(liṅg-)bo Sa(ki)m** [3] of [the family of] Mekāppar **Ti .. [ve]herä Siṅgim . . . . nā**, and **Kuṇḍasalā (Siṅgim)** of the family of the Chief Secretary (**Vaṭarak**) **Kasbāraksamaṇa**, have come by Order of the Supreme Council [to grant the following immunities to this village] :—

Tramps, vagrants, coolies, *melātsī*, and servants of the royal family shall not enter this village; *ulavāḍu* [4] and *perenāṭṭiyam* shall not enter; district headmen and keepers of district records shall not enter; the managers of two places of business shall not enter; *arākkan* [5] and *peralākkan* shall not enter; officers

---

[1] P. *Sirisaṅghabōdhi-rāja-pariveṇa.* [2] P. *Jētavana-vihāra.* [3] Or *Satim.*
[4] See above, Vol. I, p. 199, note 12. [5] See above, p. 20.

of bowmen shall not enter; enforcers of customary laws, *däli-gattan*[1] and (*ya*)*muṅguru*-(*ga*)*tuvan*[2] shall not enter; milch cows and village oxen shall not be appropriated; carts, buffaloes, labourers, or rice belonging to labourers shall not be appropriated; *tundise*[3] . . . . . . shall not enter . . . . . .

And we all of us [have set up] this pillar of Council Warranty, and [thus] instituting these rules, granted these Council immunities.

No. 10. POḶONNARUVA: RAJA-MĀḶIGĀVA PILLAR-INSCRIPTION OF MAHINDA IV

THIS **quadrangular pillar, measuring** about 6 ft. by 9½ in. by 8 in., was discovered[4] at the site of the so-called Raja-māḷigāva[5] (royal palace) which stands within the Citadel at Poḷonnaruva[6]. It now lies on the premises of the Archaeological Commissioner at Tōpa-väva.

The inscription is engraved on the first three sides of the pillar between parallel lines. Side A contains 40 lines, B 42, and C 36.

The **akṣaras,** which are from ½ to 1¼ in. in size, belong to the alphabet of the early eleventh century A. D. The letters *a*, *r*, and the medial vowel *u* have open lower ends. These, as well as most of the others, closely resemble the

---

[1] Probably 'bird-catchers': *däli* is no doubt a derivative of Skt. *jālikā* 'a net', and *gattan* 'by those who take', from *gattā*, pret. of *gannavā* (Skt. √*gṛh*). Cf. also Sinh. *däl*, *dälu* (Skt. *jāla* or *jālikā*) 'a coat of mail'. *Nāmāvaliya*, v. 198, and *Ruvanmala*, v. 349.

[2] Probably men armed with clubs for hunting purposes: *ya* (Skt. *ayas*) 'iron', *muṅguru* for *muguru*, P. *muggara*, Skt. *mudgara* 'a club', and *gatuvan*, another form of *gattan*. In both instances the oblique stem of the plural is used for the instrumental; the nominative being *gatuvō* and *gattō* respectively.

[3] See Vol. I, p. 199.

[4] See *A. S. C. Annual Report*, 1905, p. 40, inscription No. 31. In a note at the bottom of p. 6 Mr. Bell refers to a portion of an inscription of the tenth century which came to light on the back of a cap-stone of the basement of this building, near its north-west corner. This is obviously another inscription.

[5] In his detailed description of the plan and architecture of this ruin, Mr. Bell says: 'This beautiful building, fashioned in stone with its bold lion-guarded staircase, is, among Buddhistic stone ruins of Poḷonnaruwa, second only in elegance and profusion of sculpture to the unique Waṭa-dá-gé. In design the "Raja Máligáwa" is almost an exact replica, on the slightly smaller scale, of that, wonderfully close approximation to the classical *basilica*—the "Council Chamber" on the Promontory.' *Op. cit.*, p. 3.

[6] See plan of Poḷonnaruva ruins facing p. 84, below.

type of the characters in the Vēvälkäṭiya slab of Mahinda IV (*circa* 1026–1042 A. D.[1]).

The style of the **language** too bears out this age, the introductory portion agreeing nearly word for word with the first three lines of the two long slab-records of this king at Jētavanārāma in Anurādhapura[2]. As in many of the earlier pillar-records of the present kind, there occur here also the technical terms, *tuḍise, aräkkan, pereläkkan* written also *piraläkkam*[3], *vel-vässan, vel-kämiyan, väriyan, perenāṭṭu, deruvanā dekam-tän, yamuṅguru* (*veli*) *gattan, dunuvā* and *balatun*, of any of which the exact meaning is still not quite clear. Attention may also be drawn to the expression *Lakdiv-poḷo-nava-yona-parapuren kimi* which occurs also in the *Nāmbākaḍa pillar*[4], but not in any other record yet come to light. For an explanation of this phrase, see Vol. I, p. 248, note 7.

The **date** of the inscription is the tenth day of the first half of the lunar month of *Navan* (Jan.–Feb.) in the eighth regnal year of king **Siri Saṅg-bo.** As in most of his other records, Mahinda IV is mentioned here by his *biruda* only. His parents' names are also given as king **Abhā Salamevan** and queen **Dev Gon**, without any information whatsoever which might lead to their identification[5].

The **subject** is the granting of immunities to a village called **Kiṇigama** belonging to **Kuḷu-Tisa-rad-maha-vehera**[6] of the Mahāvihāra Nikāya, and situated in the Eastern Quarter. This monastery both from its geographical position and the etymology of its name may be identified with the **Kūṭa-Tissa-Vihāra** mentioned in the *Mahāvaṁsa*[7] as one of the vihāras richly endowed by king Sēna II (917–952 A. D.).

The State Officials who carried out the order of the King in Council were (*a*) . . . ., (*b*) *Mekāppar-Vädārum* **Koḷombä Budim**, (*c*) *Mekāppar* **Niṭtarā Agboyim**, all of the family of **Bamba Senevi Lokanāthan**, (*d*) **Mevan-(miṇi) Kiliṅg-gam Kiliṅg Sātim** of the family of **Kiliṅg Dimbulā Nāvan**, and (*e*) **Kuṇḍasalā Vat-kämi Mihindim** of the family of **Ramuk Kuṇḍasalā Nāvan**, together with (*f*) **Perevari Budu** who had come with instructions from (**Nuvara-gala**) **Sen Senevi-rada** to make a grant of the trees and shrubs in any tract of land in this village of Kiṇigama that is irrigated by the **Great Canal.**

---

[1] See accompanying facsimile (Plate 10).
[2] See Vol. I, Nos. 19 and 20.
[3] See side B, line 28, and C, lines 18–19.
[4] *A. S. C. Seventh Progress Report*, p. 66.
[5] For a discussion on this point, see Vol. I, pp. 213–214.
[6] P. *Kūṭa-Tissa-rāja-mahā-vihāra.* Sinh. *kuḷu* = Skt. P. *kūṭa.* Pkt. *kūḍa.* See *E. S.*, p. 26 *s. v.*
[7] Ch. li. 75.

Of these officials nothing definite is known to us from other sources. The first three, however, may have been related to **Sabā-vaḍunnā Raksayim**, **Valuvaṇisäsākayim** and **Kaliṅgu Ambā Kitla-deṭim** referred to in this king's Vessagiri inscription (side A) set up about a year and a half later than the present one, because they all bear the family name **Bam̃ba Senevi Lokanāthan**. As to **Sen Senevi-rada** mentioned in line 25, side C, he is no doubt identical with the general **Sēna** whose victory over Vallabha's forces is recorded in the *Mahāvaṁsa* [1] and is also referred to in Mahinda's inscriptions at Vessagiri and Jētavanārāma [2]. With the names of the fourth and the fifth officials (B, lines 10–16), compare **Kiliṅgbo Sakim** (or **Satim**) in the Äṭavīragollāva pillar [3] of Dappula V (991–1003 A. D.) and **Mahale Ramuk-kan̆du Vadurā Raksamanan-varā vana Kuḍasalā Vata-kämi-nilā** in the Elleväva pillar [4] of the same king. These names may refer to identical persons or at least to men closely related to one another. If this be the case, it will give support to the probability that Dappula V or his predecessor and half-brother Kassapa V was the father of Mahinda IV (1026–1042 A. D.) as advanced elsewhere [5].

TEXT.

A.

1 (ස්වස්ති ශ්‍රී)
2 සිරිවත්
3 අපිරියන්
4 ගුණමුළින් උතු
5 රත්වැ මුළු දඹ
6 දිව්හි අන් කැත්
7 කුල පාමිලි[6] කල ඔ
8 කාවස් රදපරපුරෙ
9 න් හිමි කැත්උසබ්
10 නට් අග්මෙහෙසුන්
11 වූ ලක්දිව්පොළොනව
12 යොන පරපුරෙන් හිමි
13 **අභා සලමෙවන්** ම
14 හරද්හට් එමැ කුලෙ
15 න් සමදැ **දෙව් ගොන්**
16 කිසො රඇනැ කුසැ
17 ඉපැදැ ඇපා මහ
18 යා සිරි මිඤැ පිළි
19 වෙළ්සෙ රඇ පැමි
20 ණ් දස අග්හි පැ
21 හිරි යසතෙදින් ර
22 ද්කරන **සිරි සඟ්**
23 **බො** මහරදනු නු(මා)
24 සත් ලැගු අටවන
25 හවුරුදුයෙහි තව
26 යැ සඳ පෙරෙ අඩ
27 මස්හි දසපක් දව
28 **ස් මහවෙහෙර න**

---

[1] Ch. liv. 12–16.
[2] See Vol. I, pp. 30 and 215.
[3] Side B, lines 18–19 (above, p. 47).
[4] *A. S. C. Seventh Progress Report*, p. 45.
[5] Vol. I, pp. 79, 213–214.
[6] 'පැමිලි' සීදු කියවිය හැකිසි

29 සාගි බද් පැඳුම් ප
30 ස්ගි (කුළු)[1]තිසරද්
31 මහවෙහෙර් ආවූ
32 කිණි[2]ගම දග[3] දරගි
33 වෙහෙර කිණි[2]ගැමැ
34 කුලී මෙලාත්නි හ(රූ)
35 අත්තාණිකණු ගි
36 නුවන්නට් වදාළ එ
37 ක්තැන්සම්යෙන්
38 ආ බමබ සෙනෙවි
39 (ලොක)නාථන් වරූ (ව)
40 [න්] .. ..

B.

1 .. .. [මෙ]
2 කාප්පර්(වැදෑරු)
3 ම් කොළොම්බැ (බූ)
4 දිම ඉසා මෙකා
5 ප්පර් (නිවිනරූ[4]
6 අග්)බොයිම
7 ඉසා කිලිග් (දි
8 මබුලා)නාවන් ව
9 (රත්) මෙවන්(මිණි)[5]
10 (කි)ලිග්ගම කි(ලි)
11 ග් සාතිම ඉසා
12 (ර)මුන් කු(ඩස)
13 (ලා)නාවන් වරූ (ව)
14 (න්) කුඩසලා ව
15 ත්කැම් මිහිඳි
16 ම ඇතුළුවැ ඇප්
17 මෙතුවාක් දෙන
18 මො එක්සෙවැ පැ
19 දුම් පස්ගි ආවූ
20 තිසමහවෙහෙරූ
21 බද් කිණිගැමැ
22 මෙ ගැම් සතර සී
23 මායෙන් ඇතුළත්
24 වූ තාක්තැනට් තු
25 (ඩිසෙ රහසින් නො)
26 වද්නා (කොට්) ඉසා
27 දෙමෙළ්කිණිගම් ල
28 ද් පිර(ලැ)ක්ක(ම්[6] මෙ)
29 ගමට් වැදැ කුලී මෙ
30 ලාත්නි ද(ඩු මුර)
31 බූ මගිව පෙදිව
32 නො ගන්නා කොට්
33 ඉසා මගඇළින්
34 දිය වන් තාක් තැ
35 න(ට කුළින)[7] වත්
36 නට් (හසුලා)න
37 (ට්) ගන්නා දිය
38 .. .. දූ වෙල්වැස්
39 සාත් වෙල්කැම්
40 යන් නො වලකනු
41 ඉසා ඇළ(ට් පෙරෙ)[8]
42 .. ..

C.

1 (ආ වැරියන් මිස)
2 (අ)සෙළි(න්)[9] ගමට් වැ
3 දැ වැරියන් නො ග
4 න්නා ඉසා පෙ(රෙනා)

---

1 'කුලා' යිද කියවිය හැකියි
2 'කාණ' යිද කියවිය හැකියි
3 'දහ' යිද කියවිය හැකියි
4 'නිවිහිරූ' යිද කියවිය හැකියි
5 'මෙව්න මණි' යිද කියවිය හැකියි
6 'පිරපක්කම්' යිද කියවිය හැකියි
7 'පකුළිනු' යිද කියවිය හැකියි
8 'වැව් දි' යිද කියවිය හැකියි
9 'ඇසළින්' යිද කියවිය හැකියි

5 (විටු) නො වද්නා ඉ
6 සා වෙල්වැස්ස
7 න් ගමවි වැදැ ත
8 ලන් දුළුපන් නො ක
9 පනු ඉසා ගමවි
10 වැදැ මිවුන් ගැල්
11 ගොන් නො ගන්
12 නා ඉසා (කොටා)
13 මරා මෙ ගම් ව
14 න ගැමින් පිට
15 ත් කරවා ගනු
16 ත් මිසැ නමවි
17 නො වද්නා ඉ(සා)
18 අරැක්ඛන් පෙ
19 රේලැක්ඛත් දෙ
20 රුවනැ දෙකම්තැ
21 න් යමුගුරු(වෙලි)
22 ගත්තන් දුනුවා
23 බලතුන් නො වද්
24 නා ඉසා **නුව(රග)**
25 **(ල) සෙස් සෙනෙවි**
26 **(ර)දුන්** (කම්)ගිම්
27 (යෙ)න් මෙ ගමැ ම
28 හඇළින් දිය ව
29 ද්නා තාක් කැමැ(ත්)
30 තැනවි ගසු[1]ගැ(ස්)
31 දෙන්නවි ආ **පෙරෙ(ව)**
32 **(සි බුදු)** ඇතුළුවැ මෙ
33 නුවාක් දෙනාවිසි
34 න් වදෑලෙසින් මෙ
35 අත්තාණ්කාණ්ඩු සි
36 ර(ලාභ) දෙනු ලදී

TRANSCRIPT.

A.

1 (Svasti śrī)
2 sirivat
3 apiriyat
4 guṇa-muḷin utu-
5 -rat-vä muḷu Damb-
6 divhi an Kät-
7 kula pāmili[2]-kaḷa O-
8 -kā-vas rada-parapure-
9 -n himi Kät-usab-
10 -naṭ ag-mehesun-
11 vū Lakdiv-poḷo-nava-
12 -yona parapuren himi
13 **Abhā Salamevan** ma-
14 -ha-rad-haṭ emä kule-
15 -n sama-dā **Dev Gon**
16 biso rädänä kusä
17 ipädä āpā maha-
18 -yā siri vindä piḷi-
19 -veḷ-se rädä pämi-
20 -ṇa dasa at-hi pä-
21 -tiri yasa-tedin ra-
22 -d-karana **Siri Saňg-**
23 **-bo** maha-radahu tu(mā)
24 sat läňgū aṭa-vana
25 havuruduyehi nava-
26 -yä sanda pere aḍ-
27 mashi dasa-pak dava-
28 -s **Maha-veherä Na-**
29 **-kāhi** bad pädum pa-
30 -shi (**Kuḷu**)[3]-**Tisa-rad-**

---

[1] 'ගසු' සිද කියවිය හැකිසි

[2] This may also be read *pämili*.

[3] This may also be read *Kuḷā*.

31 **mahaveher** āvū
32 **Kiṇi**[1]**-gama Daga**[2] **darahi**
33 **vehera Kiṇi**[1]**gämä**
34 kulī melätti har(ä)
35 attāṇi-kaṇu hi-
36 -nduvannaṭ vadāḷa e-
37 -k-tän-samiyen
38 ā **Bamba Senevi**
39 (**Loka**)**nāthan** varä (va-)
40 [-n] .. ..

B.

1 .. .. [Me-]
2 -kāppar-(Vädāru-)
3 -m **Koḷombä** (**Bu-**)
4 **-dim** isā Mekā-
5 -ppar (**Niṭṭarā**[3]
6 **Ag**)**boyim**
7 isā **Kiliṅg** (**Di-**
8 **-mbuḷā-**)**nāvan** va-
9 (-ran) **Mevan**-(**Miṇi**)[4]
10 (**Ki**)**liṅg-gam Ki**(**li-**)
11 **-ṅg Sätim** isā
12 (**Ra**)**muk Ku**(**ṅḍasa-**)
13 (**-lā**)**nāvan** varä (va-)
14 (-n) **Kuṅḍasalā Va-**
15 **-t-kämi Mihindi-**
16 -m ätuḷuvä äp
17 metuvāk dena-
18 -mo ekse-vä pä-
19 -dum pashi āvū
20 **Tisa-maha-veherä**
21 bad **Kiṇi-gämä**
22 me gäm satara sī-
23 -māyen ätuḷat-
24 vū tāk-tänaṭ tu-
25 (-ṅḍise rahasin no)
26 vadnā (koṭ) isā
27 **Demeḷ-Kiṇigam** la-
28 -d pira(lä)kka(m[5] me)
29 gamaṭ vädä kulī me-
30 -lätti da(ṅḍu mura-)
31 -ṅḍu maṅgiva pediva
32 no gannā koṭ
33 isā Maha-äḷin
34 diya van tāk tä-
35 -na(ṭa kuḷita)[6] vat-
36 -taṭ (hasu-lā)na-
37 (-ṭ) gannā diya
38 .. .. du vel-väs-
39 -san vel-kämi-
40 -yan no valakanu
41 isā äḷa(ṭ pere)[7]
42 .. ..

C.

1 (ā väriyan misa)
2 (a)seḷi(n)[8] gamaṭ vä-
3 -dä väriyan no ga-
4 -nnā isā pe(renā-)
5 (-ṭṭu) no vadnā i-
6 -sā velvässa-
7 -n gamaṭ vädä ta-
8 -lan puḷupan no ka-
9 -panu isā gamaṭ
10 vädä mivun gäl
11 gon no gan-
12 -nā isā (koṭā)

---

[1] This may also be read *Kaṇa* or *Kiṇa*.
[2] This may also be read *Dah.*
[3] This may also be read *Niṭṭirā.*
[4] This may also be read *Mevn.*
[5] This may also be read *pirapakkam.*
[6] This may also be read *pakuḷi.*
[7] This may also be read *väv di.*
[8] This may also be read *äsaḷin.*

Poḷonnaruva: Raja-māḷigāva Pillar-Inscription.

A B C

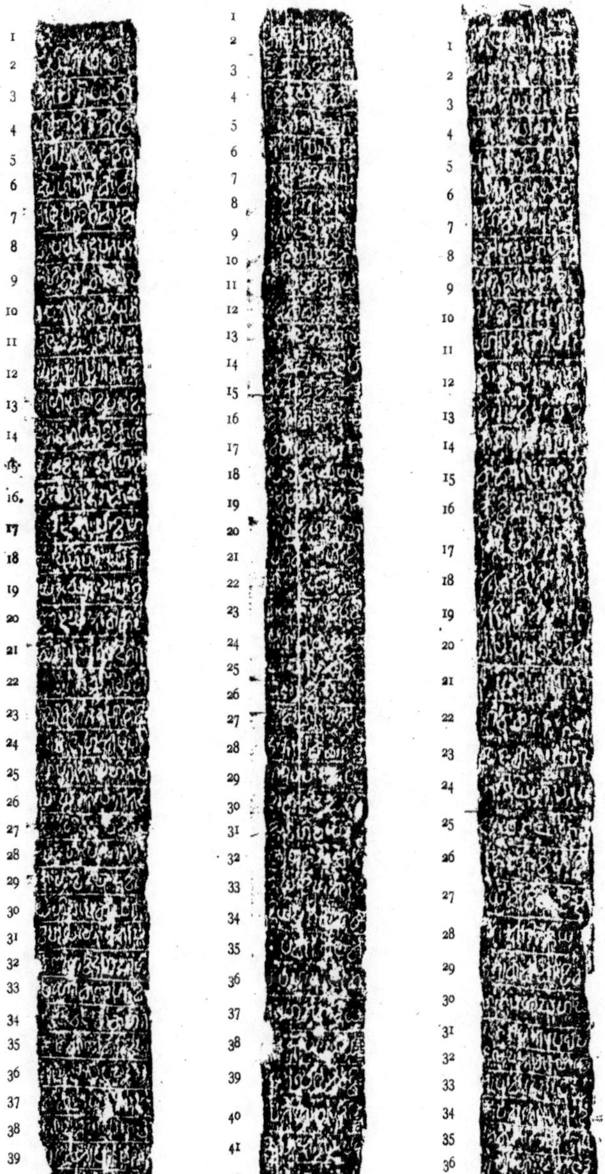

Scale about 1½ inches to 1 foot.

mpression supplied by '' *Commissione,*

13 marā me gam va-
14 -na gämin piṭa-
15 -t karavā ganu-
16 -t misä gamaṭ
17 no vadnā i(sā)
18 aräkkan pe-
19 -reläkkan de-
20 -ruvanā de-kam-tä-
21 -n ya-muṅguru-(veli-)
22 gattan dunuvā-
23 balatun no vad-
24 -nā isā **Nuva(ra-ga-)**
25 (-la) **Sen Senevi-**
26 (**ra**)**dun** (kam)-himi-
27 (-ye)n me gamä Ma-
28 -ha-äḷin diya va-
29 -dnā tāk kämä(t)
30 tänaṭ gasu'-gä(s)
31 dennaṭ ā **Pere(va-)**
32 (**-ri Budu**) ätuḷuvä me-
33 tuvāk denā-visi-
34 -n vadāḷeyin me
35 attāṇi-kaṇu si-
36 -ri-(lābha) denu ladi

TRANSLATION.

Hail! Prosperity! The great king **Siri Saṅg-bo** was born unto the great king **Abhā Salamevan**, lord by lineal succession of the lords of the soil of the Island of Laṅkā which has become [as it were] the chief queen[2] unto the Kṣatriya princes descended from the royal line of the Okkāka dynasty, which, overflowing with an assemblage of boundless and benignant virtues[3], has caused other Kṣatriya dynasties of the whole of Jambudvīpa to render it homage[4]: [he was born] of the womb of the anointed queen **Dev Gon** of equal birth and descent. After enjoying the dignities of Governor and Chief Governor[5] he in due course became king.

On the tenth day of the first half of the [lunar] month of *Navan* (Jan.–Feb.) in the eighth year since the raising of the canopy of dominion by this great king **Siri Saṅg-bo** who now rules with the effulgence of his glory spread in [all] the ten directions[6].

Whereas it was decreed by His Majesty in Council that a pillar of Council Warranty excluding coolies and *melātṭī* be set up in the village **Kiṇigama**

---

[1] This may also be read *has-ugäs.*

[2] *Kat-usabnat ag-mehesun vū Lak-div-poḷa-nava-yona-parapuren himi.* This phrase may also be rendered 'lord, by hereditary succession, of the soil of the Island of Laṅkā, [which is like unto] a young maiden that has [always] been [as it were] the chief queen unto the Kṣatriya princes'. See Vol. I, p. 248, note 7.

[3] See Vol. I, p. 224, note 3.

[4] *Ibid.*, note 4.

[5] Or 'heir-apparent'. See above, p. 15, note 4.

[6] Dasa-at = Skt. *daśa-hasta* same as *daśa-diśā*.

attached to the monastery at **Kiṇigama Dagadara** in the Eastern Quarter, which [monastery] belongs to the great monastery **Kuḷu-Tisa-rad-maha-vehera** [1] of the Mahāvihāra Nikāya [2], we all of us, namely . . . ., *Mekäppar-Vädärum* **Koḷombä Budim,** *Mekāppar* (**Niṭṭarā Ag**)**boyim** [all] of the family of **Bamba Senevi Lokanāthan, Mevan-miṇi** [3] **Kiliṅg-gam Kiliṅg Sātim** of the family of **Kiliṅg Dimbuḷā-nāvan** and **Kuṅḍasalā Vat-kämi Mihindim** of the family of (**Ra**)**muk Ku**(**ṅḍasalā**)-**nāvan** have come and conjointly [instituted the following rules] in respect of the area included within the four boundaries of this village **Kiṇigama** in the Eastern Quarter, attached to the **Tisa-maha-vehera** [4] :—

Tuṇḍise [5] shall not secretly enter; the *piralākkam* [6] who have received [for their use] the village **Demeḷ** [7] **Kiṇigam** shall not enter the village (Kiṇigama) and take away [8] the coolies, the *melātti, daṇḍu* (club-men ?), *muraṇḍu* (strong-willed men ?), *maṅgiva* [9] and *pediva* [9] ; *vel-vässan* (field-inhabitants) and *vel-kämiyan* (field-workers) shall not obstruct (the distribution of) water received (for the cultivation of) the garden (appertaining to ?) the land irrigated by the Great Canal; (except labourers who have come) . . . . . to the Canal, none from the neighbourhood shall enter the village and take away *väriyan* (labourers); *perenāṭṭu* shall not enter; *vel-vässan* (field-inhabitants) shall not enter the village and cut down palmyra and coco-nut trees; they shall not enter the village and take away buffaloes, carts, and oxen [10]; those who have entered the village after committing murder [11] shall be arrested after causing them to quit the village, but [officers] shall not enter the village [and arrest them]; *arākkan, perelākkan, deruvanā dekam-tān, ya-muṅ*[12]*guru-*(*veli-*)[13]*-gattan*[14] (mace and spear-bearers), *dunuvā-balatun* [15] (officers of bowmen) shall not enter.

---

[1] P. *Kūṭa-Tissa-rāja-mahā-vihāra.* [2] That is the Thēriya-nikāya, the orthodox Buddhist sect.

[3] Probably P. *Mēghavaṇṇa-Maṇi.*

[4] That is the **Kuḷu-Tisa-rad-maha-vehera** referred to on side A, lines 30–31.

[5] The reading here being doubtful, I am not sure of the above interpretation.

[6] Probably same as *perelākkan.* [7] Demeḷ = Tamiḷ. [8] Probably impress for service.

[9] These two terms, derived as they probably are from Skt. *mārga-jīva* and *pāda-jīva*, have hitherto been rendered 'tramps and vagrants' (above, p. 33, and Vol. I, p. 171, notes 1, 2). But this rendering does not seem to suit the context here. Could they be the names of two classes of errand-men or carriers, or is the verb *gannā* used here in the sense of arresting a criminal as on side C, line 15? In the latter case, the passage should be translated 'the *piralākkam* . . . . shall not enter the village (Kiṇigama) and arrest the coolies', &c. [10] Or 'cart-oxen'.

[11] *Koṭā marā* (C, lines 12–13.) Cf. *marā keḷuva* in the Vēvälkäṭiya slab (Vol. I, p. 249, note 5).

[12] Skt. *ayo-mudgara.*

[13] *Vel, vela,* a spear or lance. *Nāmāvaliya,* v. 207, *Piyummala,* p. 54, Jayatilaka's *Elu-Akārādiya,* p. 40. [14] See above, p. 49, notes 1–2. [15] See above, p. 33, note 4.

It being [thus] decreed, the high advantages[1] of this pillar of Council Warranty were granted by the [aforementioned] personages including **Perevari Budu** who had come (with instructions) from (**Nuvaragala**) **Sen Senevi-rad** to make a grant of the plants and shrubs[2] within so much of the land in this village that is irrigated by the Great Canal.

No. 11. MAYILAGASTOṬA PILLAR-INSCRIPTION

THIS quadrangular pillar, measuring about 6 ft. × 11 in. × 7 in., was discovered by Mr. J. H. Dawson, the Irrigation Officer at Mayilagastoṭa, a village about eight miles from Tissamahārāma in the Hambantoṭa district. Dr. P. Goldschmidt examined it and published a short account of it with a portion of the text in 1876[3]. The pillar was subsequently brought to the Colombo Museum where it now lies.

The inscription covers three sides of it, but that on the third side is not legible. The first two sides contain thirty-five lines each.

The letters belong to the alphabet of the tenth or early eleventh century A. D. Their size varies from $\frac{3}{4}$ to $1\frac{1}{4}$ in. each, and their type[4] is that of the Vessagiri slab of Mahinda IV[5].

The language too agrees with the style adopted in the shorter inscriptions of this king, and its phraseology is nearly the same as that of his pillar-inscription at Attanayāla-vihāra[6] in the same Hambantoṭa district.

---

[1] *Siri-lābha.*

[2] The clause *diya vadnā tāk kämä(l) tänaṭ (ga)su gä(s) dennaṭ ā Pere(va)ri Budu* is not quite clear to me. The above translation is offered tentatively.

[3] See *Ceylon Sessional Papers*, No. XI, 1876, pp. 7 and 9.

[4] See *E. Z.*, Vol. I, p. 242.

[5] Cf. the accompanying Plate with Plate 9 of Vol. I.

[6] Dr. Müller's report on this record runs: 'A little off the same road [from Udukiriwila to Ranna] at Attanayâla wihâra there is a pillar-inscription of more modern date, of which one side is tolerably well preserved. It bears the name of a king Sri Sang Bo, but as there are so many of this name (cf. Goldschmidt's *Report*, XI, p. 7) it is difficult to find the exact date of the inscription. At any rate it must belong to the tenth or eleventh century . . . .

'Nearly the same words, only connected with other names, occur in the inscription of Aepâ Mahinda at Mayilagastota, eight miles from Tissamahârâma, which is now in the Colombo Museum.' (*Ceylon Sessional Papers*, No. XXV, 1878, pp. 3–4.)

As mentioned before, the inscription was first read by Dr. Goldschmidt, and then by Dr. Müller who published a transcript and a translation of it with a short preliminary note in his *Ancient Inscriptions in Ceylon* (No. 120). The subjoined edition of the text has been carefully prepared with the aid of ink-impressions supplied by the Archaeological Commissioner (Mr. H. C. P. Bell). That it differs considerably from the former will be apparent on a comparison of the two versions and their English translations.

Both Goldschmidt and Müller found this record most useful in identifying **Mahinda IV** of the *Mahāvaṁsa* with **Siri Saṅg-boy Abahay** of the Mihintale tablets. Though this identification has now been found to be correct, yet the facts which they were able to adduce at the time were not sufficient to prove the identity of Mahinda IV, still less that of his parents[1]. The present reading of the inscription, however, gives the link which these scholars desired so much. I have elsewhere[2] stated reasons for supposing that Mahinda's father, the great king Abhā or Abahay Salamevan or Siri Saṅg-bo Abhā (or Abā), may have been either Dappula V or Kassapa V. This can now be settled definitely, for on side A, lines 12 to 16 of the record, there appear distinctly the names of king **Abhā Salamevan** and queen **Saṅg**[3] **Gon-biso** as those of the parents of **Mahinda.** The former is identical with **Kassapa V**[4], who bore this *biruda*, and the latter with his queen **Saṅghā**, the beautiful daughter of the sub-king (Mahinda)[5]. A confirmation of this relationship may be inferred from the statement in the *Mahāvaṁsa* (liii. 51 and liv. 48) that Mahinda IV's *mātula*, i.e. his mother's (namely Saṅghā's) brother (probably half-brother), was king Udaya III who died whilst engaged in re-building the palace called Maṇi, that the army of the Cōḷa king had destroyed with fire. Touching the children of the sub-king Mahinda (brother of king Sēna II) the *Mahāvaṁsa* (li. 15–18) says that by his principal

---

[1] See *E. Z.*, Vol. I, pp. 78–79.

[2] *Ibid.*, pp. 79, 213, and 214, and above, p. 51.

[3] Both Goldschmidt and Müller read this as *siṭi*, but in both the 'squeezes' before me the two akṣaras *sa* and *ṅg* are quite clear. The only doubtful point is whether we should take what looks like a curved line faintly engraved above *s* to be the sign of the medial vowel *i* and so read the character as *si* instead of *sa*. See the accompanying facsimile (Plate 11).

[4] With reference to my statement on p. 9 above, as to the alternate use of the *birudas Salamevan* and *Siri Saṅg-bo* by Ceylon kings, Mr. H. C. P. Bell has written to me to say that he gave me the 'tip' for this theory when I visited Ceylon in 1909. If this be the case and my memory has played me false, all credit is due to him for the suggestion. I may, however, add that I am now not quite so certain that the theory holds good in every case. We know that it does not in the case of Mahinda IV's father.

[5] See *Mv.* li. 15–18, and *E. Z.*, Vol. I, p. 184.

wife Tissā he had a daughter named Saṅghā who became queen of Kassapa V, and by his other wife Kittī he had one daughter and four sons of whom Kittaggabōdhi was the governor who raised a rebellion in Rōhaṇa (*l.c.* 94). About the other three sons the chronicle is silent, but from the Puliyaṉ-kuḷam slab-inscription[1] it appears certain that king Udaya II was one of them. The *Pūjāvaliya* says that king Sēna III was a brother of Udaya II. So he must be identical with the third son, and the fourth was obviously king Udaya III referred to as the *mātula* (maternal uncle) of Mahinda IV.

The accompanying genealogical table, which I have prepared from data derived from inscriptional and other sources, will enable the reader to form an idea as to how the Ceylon kings of the tenth, eleventh, and twelfth centuries A.D. were related to one another.

The **contents** of the present record **deal** with the dedication of certain **lands to Uḍa-Tisa-pirivena** situated near **Mahagama** on the left bank of **Kirind-ho** and with an enumeration of the immunities which usually form an important feature of such grants.

No **date** is given, but it is clear from the use of the title *āpā* that the grant was made when king Mahinda IV was a mere governor, before he was raised even to the rank of *māpā* (*mahayā*), or *yuva-rāja*, by Sēna IV (*circa* 1023–1026 A.D.). This would, therefore, be during the early part of Mahinda's career, probably when he was ruling Rōhaṇa, of which Mahāgāma mentioned in the record was the capital, and the Uḍa-Tisa-pirivena in question was close by.

The village which still bears the name Māgama or Mahagama lies on the left bank of the Māgama or Kirinde river (*Kiriňdu-hoya* or *-oya*), not far from the ruins of Tissamahārāma, north-east of Hambantoṭa. Moreover, in his interesting report on Tissamahārāma[2], Mr. H. Parker says that Uḍa Tihāwa (i.e. Uḍa-Tisa-väva) is well known at Tissamahārāma as the name of the upper part of Tissa tank and that it once formed a separate tank, the bund of which is now to be seen inside the present Tissa tank. The *pirivena*, he adds, may have stood between the adjacent river and the tank, as attested by the remains of some building which are reported to exist in the jungle to the west of the upper part of the Tissa tank. As to Dr. Müller's suggested identification[3] of Uḍa-Tisa-pirivena with Uddhakandaraka-vihāra built by Mahānāga[4] (*circa* 200 B.C.), definite proof is still wanting.

---

[1] *E. Z.*, Vol. I, No. 15.
[2] *C. B. R. A. S. Journal*, No. 27, 1884.
[3] *A. I. C.*, p. 57.
[4] *Mv.* xxii. 9.

Mr. Parker supports the suggestion on the ground that Uddha-kandara was in Rōhaṇa and that *Karinda* (Sinh. *Kirinda*) is probably a later form of *Kandara*[1].

TEXT.

A.

1 (ස්වස්ති ශ්‍රී)
2 සිරිවත් අපි
3 රියත් ගුණ මූ
4 (ළි)ත් උතුරත්වැ අ
5 න් කැත්කුල පාමි[2]
6 ලි කළ ඔකාවස්
7 පරපුරෙන් බට්
8 රද්පුරුමූවනට්
9 අග්මෙහෙසුන්
10 (වූ) ලක්දිව්පොළො
11 යොනපරපුරෙන්
12 හිමි සඟ්[3] ගොණ්
13 කිසො රද්න කුස්
14 හි (උපන්) අභා ස
15 ලමෙවන් මහරද්හු
16 උරෙහි දෑ කැතැ
17 කුල කොත් වියත්
18 දහම් නිය (පුත්)
19 ඈපා මිහිඳුහු
20 විසින් කිරිඤ්(හො)
21 (වම් තෙර්හි) මහ(ග)
22 (ම) උවනිසා පිහි
23 පි සිරි(බර) ම(හවෙ)
24 හෙර්නකාඝි (දම්)
25 රද් ප(ර)පුර් (වචිනු)
26 (පොවස්) තමා[4] (කැ)
27 (රූ උඩ) තිස පිරිවෙ
28 න් (සැහැවියට් ර)
29 (ද්පමණියෙන් කි)
30 මි (දෙවසි බූ)[5] .. ..
31 .. .. සම්ව
32 (ත්)පහ(ණ හිඤු)
33 (වා) .. .. (දුන්)
34 (තැනවි) මෙලාත්
35 සි (රද්)කොල්කැමි

B.

1 යත් නො
2 වද්නා ඉ
3 සා ගම්
4 ගොන් (රද)
5 (හරු)[6] කිලි
6 බත් ගැල්
7 මිවුන් වැ
8 රියත් නො
9 ගන්නා
10 ඉසා මගි
11 ව පියගි
12 ව නො වද්
13 නා ඉසා (දෑ)
14 වැඩමෙහි
15 මිස (මහ)
16 (හිමි)න් ඈ
17 තුළ(තැ) සි(ට)
18 (සනැසෙනු)

---

[1] See his *Report on Tissamahārāma*, p. 13.

[2] 'පැමිලි' සීද කියවිය හැකිපි

[3] 'සිඟ්' සීද කියවිය හැකිසි

[4] 'වෙවයඨා මා' සීද කියවිය හැකිසි

[5] 'ඈදහස් බූ' සීද කියවිය හැකිසි

[6] 'රළගරු' සීද කියවිය හැකිපි

Mayilagastota: Pillar-Inscription.

A

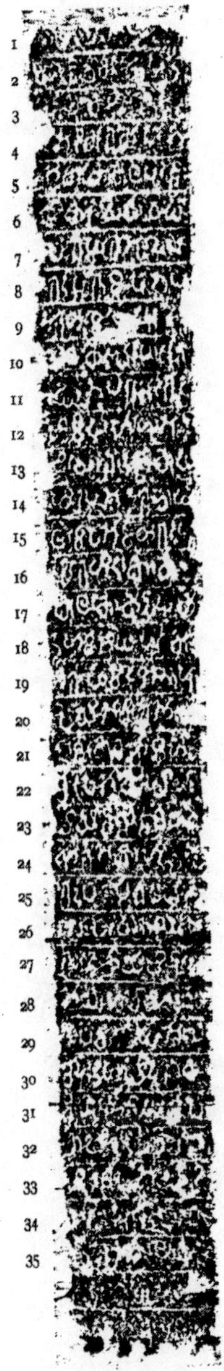

B

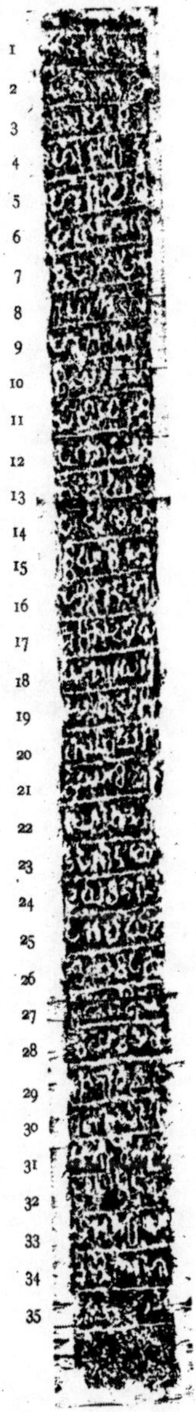

Scale about 1⅜ inches to 1 foot.

From an ink-impression supplied by the Archaeological Commissioner, Ceylon.

19 (සතුටින්)
20 නො (ගයනු)
21 ඉසා මෙ (වෙව)
22 (සථා) නො (වර)
23 ද්වා රද්කො
24 ල්සම්දරු
25 වන්විසින්
26 මෙ සම්වනා
27 රක්නා ඉසා
28 මෙ සම්වතා
29 (නො රක්නා කැ)
30 (මියනාවි) වර
31 (ද් අ) .. .. ..
32 .. .. (ඉ.. බැ)
33 වින් ඇපා
34 **මියිඇඟු**
35 .. ..

TRANSCRIPT.

A.

1 (Svasti śrī)
2 Sirivat api-
3 -riyat guṇa mu-
4 (-ḷi)n uturat-vä a-
5 -n Kät-kula pāmi-[1]
6 -li kaḷa Okā-vas-
7 parapuren baṭ
8 rad-purumuvanaṭ
9 ag-mehesun-
10 (vū) Lak-div-poḷo-
11 -yona-parapuren
12 himi **Sang**[2] **Gon**
13 biso rädna kus-
14 -hi (upan) **Abhā Sa-**
15 **-lamevan** maha-rad-hu
16 urehi dā Kätā-
17 kula kot viyat
18 daham niya (yut)
19 āpā **Mihinduhu-**
20 visin **Kirind-(ho)**[3]
21 (vam terhi[4]) **Maha-(ga-)**
22 (**-ma**) uvanisā pihi-
23 -ṭi siri(bara) **Ma(ha-ve-)**
24 **-her-nakāhi** (dam-)
25 rad pa(ra)pur (vaṭnu)[5]
26 (povas) tamā[6] (kä-)[7]
27 (-rū **Uḍa-**) **Tisa** pirive-
28 -n (sähävi-yaṭ ra-)[8]
29 (-d-pamaṇiyen[9] bi-)
30 -m (devayi bu)[10] .. ..
31 .. .. samva-
32 (-t-)paha(ṇa hindu-)
33 (-vā) .. .. (dun)
34 (tänaṭ)[11] melät-
35 -si (rad-)kol-kämi-

B.

1 -yan no
2 vadnā i-
3 -sā gam-
4 gon (rada-)

---

[1] This may also be read *pämili*.
[2] This may also be read *Sing*; Mt. *sili*.
[3] Mt. *karaṇḍ na*.
[4] Mt. *ulumhi mahana*.
[5] Mt. *vasnu*.
[6] This may also be read *pevas tamā* or *vevasthā mā*; Mt. *vavastamā*.
[7] Mt. *kärā*.
[8] This may also be read *-naṭ hevihiṭ ra-*; Mt. *sāhasi has*.
[9] Mt. *pamā yan ba-*.
[10] This may also be read *ā dahas bu*; Mt. *ma dayas nakā*.
[11] Mt. *vak*.

5 (haru)[1] bili
6 bat[2] gäl
7 mivun vä-
8 -riyan no
9 gannā
10 isā maṅgi-
11 -va piya-gi-
12 -va no vad-
13 -nā isā (dā-)
14 väḍmehi[3]
15 misa[4] (maha-)
16 (-himi)n ä-
17 -tuḷa(tä) si(ṭa)
18 (sanäsenu)
19 (satuṭin)
20 no (gayanu)[5]
21 isā me (veva-)[6]
22 (-sthā) no (vara-)[7]
23 -dvā rad-ko-
24 -l-sam-daru-
25 -van-visin
26 me samvatā
27 raknā isā
28 me samvatā[8]
29 (no raknā kä-)
30 (-miyanaṭ) vara-
31 (-d a) .. .. ..
32 .. .. (i.. bä-)
33 -vin āpā
34 **Mihinduhu**
35 .. ..

TRANSLATION.

Hail! Prosperity! The learned *āpā*[9] **Mihindu** endowed with a knowledge of the (Buddhist) doctrine[10], a pinnacle of the Kṣatriya race, being legitimately born unto the great king **Abhā Salamevan,** of the womb of the anointed queen **Saṅg Gon**; [as such] lord by hereditary succession of the lords of the soil of the Island of Laṅkā, which has been [as it were] the chief queen unto the royal chiefs[11] descended from the line of the Okkāka dynasty which abounds in a multitude of benignant and boundless virtues, and which has thereby caused other Kṣatriya dynasties to render it homage[12]:

The *āpā* Mihindu (having granted) lands out of crown property (for the

---

[1] This may also be read *raḷagaru*; Mt. *-hara*. [2] Mt. *bun*. [3] Mt. *davāsmehi*.
[4] Mt. *miyā*. [5] This may also be read *gasanu*; Mt. *no nasnā*. [6] Mt. *kana*.
[7] Mt. *yo ne para davā*. [8] Mt. *bisamvat*.
[9] See Vol. I, p. 187, note 6, and above, p. 15, note 4.
[10] *Daham-niya-yut*. This may also be rendered 'possessed of righteousness and justice' (Skt. *dharma-nyāya-yukta*). Prof. Geiger, however, suggests *naya* to be the Skt. equivalent of Sinh. *niyä* or *niya* (*E. S.*, p. 45).
[11] *Rad-purumuvanaṭ* instead of the more usual *Kät-usabnaṭ*. See Vol. I, p. 248, note 7. For the etymology of *purumuvan*, see *ibid.*, p. 26, note 1.
[12] *An Kät-kula pāmili kaḷa*. See Vol. I, p. 224, note 4.

up-keep ?)[1] of **Uḍa-Tisa-pirivena** which is situated near[2] **Mahagama**[3] on the left bank of **Kirind-ho**[4] and in which (he kept up the observance of the Buddhist sabbath[5] devolving upon [the members of the pupilary] succession of the Buddha) who belong to the illustrious Mahāvihāra sect, set up the edictal pillar [to the effect that] *melātsi*, and servants of the royal family shall not enter (the premises granted) . . . . . . that village oxen, rice set apart (for the royal household ?)[6], carts, buffaloes and labourers shall not be appropriated; that tramps and vagrants[7] shall not enter; that except on the occasion of a 'relic-procession' there shall be no musical entertainments[8] within the outer boundary[9]; that princes of the royal family shall not break these regulations, but shall perpetuate this edict; and that guilt (will accrue) to those employées who disregard this edict . . . . This being the (order), the *āpā* **Mihindu** . . . .

---

[1] **The** reading *hevihiṭ* may mean 'for tom-tom beating', same as *hēvisi* in modern Sinhalese.

[2] *Uraniā* (side A, line 22). See Vol. I, p. 35, note 8.

[3] P. *Mahāgāma*, modern Sinh. *Māgama*.

[4] P. *Karinda-sōta*, mod. Sinh. *Kiriňdu-oya*. Skt. *srōtas* = P. *sōta*, M. *sotta*, AMg. *soya*, Sinh. **soya*, *sō*, *hoya*, *hō*, and *oya*.

[5] *Po-* (or *pe-*)*vas* = P. *upōsatha-vāsa*. See Childers' *Pāli Dict.*, p. 535. As the text from line 23 to 33 is only partially legible, the above translation cannot be regarded as final. If we read *vävasthā* in line 26, the passage may be rendered 'and (in which he instituted) the regulations which have been observed by [members of the pupilary] succession of the Buddha (*Dam-rad*), who belong to the illustrious Mahāvihāra (the orthodox) sect'. Dr. Müller, on the other hand, gives the following totally different translation:—'having made the necessary repairings at the Mahāwihāra, caused priests to be ordained for the nikāyas at the Uḍa Tisa monastery' (*A. I. C.*, p. 115).

[6] Dr. Müller's rendering is 'that enemies shall not take away the villages, the cattle, the royal taxes, the revenue, the cart-buffaloes'.

[7] *Mañgiva piyagiva*. See above, p. 33, note 7.

[8] If *gasanu* be the correct reading, the translation would run 'there shall be no beating (of drums) for amusement'.

[9] The text here being only partially legible, the above translation is offered tentatively. Dr. Müller's version is quite different. It runs 'that daily the priests, including the high priest, shall not destroy life; that the officers of the royal family together with the queens shall not protect . . . . . All this was ordered by the aepā Mahinda'.

No. 12. RAMBĀVA SLAB-INSCRIPTION

RAMBĀVA is a well-known village in Kāňdā-kōrale at the junction of the two main roads from Anurādhapura and from Mihintale, about nine miles to the north-east of the former town. It should not be confounded with the village bearing the same name in Kuñcuṭṭu Kōrale, some twenty-five miles further, where lies the fine pillar-inscription of king Abhaya Salamevan (Udaya I) dealt with in Vol. I, article No. 13.

The present slab was discovered by the Archaeological Commissioner (Mr. H. C. P. Bell)[1] in 1892, while on tour during the second quarter of the year. It has since been brought into Anurādhapura.

The inscription covers a ruled surface of 4 ft. 7 in. by 2 ft. 6 in., and contains thirty-nine lines of writing more or less worn by the action of the weather.

The **letters** are on the average half to one inch in size, and closely resemble the type of the alphabet of the Vēvälkäṭiya slab[2] of Mahinda IV (*circa* 1026–1042 A.D.). The long *ē* in the word *vahansē* (line 27) of the present record, and the long *ō* in *yōna* in the Vēvälkäṭiya pillar clearly show that already in Mahinda's time the vertical *virāma* sign was in use to indicate a long vowel[3].

The **language** follows the style usually adopted in Mahinda's slab-inscriptions. The first six lines, moreover, and also several phrases in the body of the text, agree word for word with those in the two records[4] of this king at the so-called Jētavanārāma[5] in Anurādhapura.

The **date** is the tenth day of the bright half of the lunar month Väp (Sept.–Oct.) in the first regnal year of king Siri Saňg-bo Abhā (Mahinda IV, *circa* 1026–1042 A.D. or W. 975–991 A.D.).

In the foregoing article on the Mayilagastoṭa pillar I put together all the historical facts I could find bearing on the parentage of this king, with the result that it became almost evident that he must have been a son of king Kassapa V,

---

[1] His reference to it is as follows:—

'Rambewa.—Cleared the jungle round an inscribed slab in the jungle, a hundred yards south of the "Cooly Shelter" at Rambewa, and copied as much of the writing as is legible. The record almost certainly belongs to Mahinda IV (975–991 A.D.), though the name of the king has worn off the stone.' (*A.S.C. Annual Report*, 1892, p. 6.)

[2] Cf. the accompanying Plate with Plate 29 of Vol. I.

[3] See also Vol. I, p. 242.

[4] Vol. I, Nos. 19 and 20.

[5] i.e. The old Abhayagiri-vihāra.

who died according to the *Mahāvaṁsa* thirty-five years and seven months before Mahinda IV's accession to the throne. There arises now the question whether or not he is to be identified with Mahinda, the son of Kassapa, who successfully quelled a rebellion raised by Kittaggabōdhi in Rōhaṇa, and became the governor of that province, which he ruled during the reigns of Udaya I and Kassapa IV[1]. The inscriptional references[2] to Mahinda IV as conqueror of Rōhaṇa and restorer of religious monuments there, agreeing as they do with the *Mahāvaṁsa* account both of this king and of prince Mahinda, the son of Kassapa, go a great way to support the theory that they were one and the same person. As against this, must be taken into consideration the fact that Mahinda, the son of Kassapa, was old enough already in the reign of Udaya I[3] to lead a punitive expedition to Rōhaṇa, and that according to the *Mahāvaṁsa* reckoning Mahinda IV's accession to the sovereignty took place some sixty-three years later. So, if the two princes are identical, Mahinda IV must have been at least eighty years old when he became king, and ninety-six when he died. This is very improbable, and in view of the strong support from inscriptions in favour of the identity, I am inclined to fall back upon the theory that either the text of this portion of the *Mahāvaṁsa* as we have it at present is faulty, or its author got confused regarding the traditional dates of this period, and miscalculated the length of the reigns of some of the kings that preceded Mahinda IV, as I suggested on p. 157 of Vol. I[4] when discussing the Buddhist era in Ceylon.

The **contents** of the record deal with the grant of certain lands, with the immunities usually attached to such grants, to one **Kiliṅgu-rad Pirivat Häṁbuvan**, to be held by him and his descendants for the purpose of supplying oil to illuminate the stone image of the Buddha at the Sacred Bōdhi-tree. The statue is probably the one mentioned in the Jētavanārāma slab, No. 1, line 26[5].

Of the four ministers of Mahinda IV's Council who proclaimed this grant, **Kuḍasalā Vatkämi-deṭim** figures also in the Vessagiri grant of this king. The others are not known to us from other sources.

---

[1] *Mv.* li. 94–125 and lii. 4–10.

[2] See, for example, the present inscription, lines 12–13, and the Mayilagastoṭa pillar, side A, lines 19–28.

[3] See *Mv.* li. 99–102.

[4] Cf. in this connexion the important contribution to Sinhalese chronology by Professor Hultzsch, which appeared in the *R. A. S. Journal* for July, 1913.

[5] See Vol. I, pp. 219 and 228.

TEXT.

1 [ශ්‍රී] සිරිවත් අපිරියත් (ලොව් ඉසුත් ගුණ මුළින් උතුරත්)
2 (වැ මුළු) දඹදිව්(ගි) අත් කැත්කු(ල පාම්ලිකල ඔකාවස් රජ්පරපු)
3 රෙන් බට් කැ(න්උස)බ් **සිරිසඟ්බො අභා** [මහරජ්හට් එමැකුලෙන්]
4 සමදෑ **දෙව්ගොන්** කිසොරැජ්න කුසැ උපැදෑ (ඈපා මහයා සිරි)
5 විඳෑ පිළිවෙල්සෙ රදවැ (මිණිවුට්නෙන් පැහැයු) සිය මු(ඤ්නෙ)
6 න් ලොඋතුරා කිසෙව්නෙන් කිසෙස්වැ (නුමා) සිරින් (ලක්දිව්) පහ(යා)
7 .. ..
8 .. ..
9 .. ..
10 .. .. **අභයගිරිවෙ**
11 (**හෙර්)හි** මඟුල් මහසලපිළිම කුලදැති ඉඳුනිල් මිණි රුවනින්
12 ඇස් තබවා සිය විස්මෙත් දැනැ ගත් **රුහුණු** දනව්(යෙ)
13 (ගි **බො)ළතුලාවෙහෙරහි** (සුවත්මුවා) .. .. (මුනිඳුපිළිබි)
14 බි ක(රා සු)සිරසැ .. ..
15 යුත්නට් උවසර් වියත්නට් සඟ්රා දහම් .. .. යනට්
16 (සව්) මිතුරුනට් පිය(බස් වතුරු) .. .. (න්)නට් **පිරි** [කු]
17 (සල්) නමහට් එකත්සරු කළ **සිරිසඟ්බො අභා** මහරද්හු
18 නුමා සත් ලැගු පළමුවන හවුරුදුයෙහි (වැ)පැ සඳැ පුණ්ණු අ
19 ඩ මස්හි දස පක් දවස් **(කලණු)බිම්හි** ආවූ **(කිලිඳ්)**[1] **දෙ**
20 **ග්දරහි** ආවූ (**අසුන්පිපිනෙයි**)න් නුත් කිරියක් ඉ
21 සා මෙනුන් කිරියට් (වැළැදෙනු) පිටිකිම් (උ)යත් ඉසා මෙමැ (තිම්ණි)
22 ආවූ **කුව්වාවත්න** ඉසා පිස(ම්බු)ර්[2] දෙවියැලැ ආවූ **මොරෙ(ඹු)**
23 **මහසෙන්ගම්යෙ** කුම්බුරු ඉසා මෙහිමැ ආවූ (පළ බො) .. ..
24 **(ව[3])හුරු(පි)පි** (සම්හො)ග ගමු (සඟ්නට්) මෙයින් (හුනනා[4] හරැ) .. ..
25 .. .. මින් සිටි කුම්බුර් ඉසා මෙයට් (වැ)ළැදෙනු වතු
26 .. කිම් (මිවන්) ඇතුළත් කොට් මෙනුවාක් තැන් **මහවෙහෙරැ** මහ
27 බොගෙහි අවුණු සලපිළිම්බුදුන්වහන්සේ (ගෙ වැට් ද)
28 (ල්ව)නුවට් (සනි)න් ලහසුයෙන් හවුරුදු පතා දෙම්හක් තෙල්
29 (දෙනු) කොට් ඉසා මෙයට් වත් වියවුලක් ඇත **මහවෙහෙරැ**
30 අපිළිසරණ සඟුන් සාහා දෙනු කොට් ඉසා මෙනුවාක් තැන් **කිලිහුරද්**
31 **සිරිවන් හැඹුවන්** දරු මනුබුරු පිරි(වැල්ල)න් වළඳනු කොට් ඉසා (මෙ)
32 (යට්) දෙරුවනැ දෙකම්තැන් නො වද්නා ඉසා වැරි පෙරෙනාව්වූ කුලී මෙලාන්හි

---

[1] 'කැහිඳ්' සීද කියවිය හැකිසි

[2] 'විසම්බුර්' සීද කියවිය හැකිසි

[3] 'පහුරුපිටි' සීද කියවිය හැකිසි

[4] 'හුණා' හෝ 'ගණා' සීද කියවිය හැකිසි

Rambāva: Slab-Inscription.

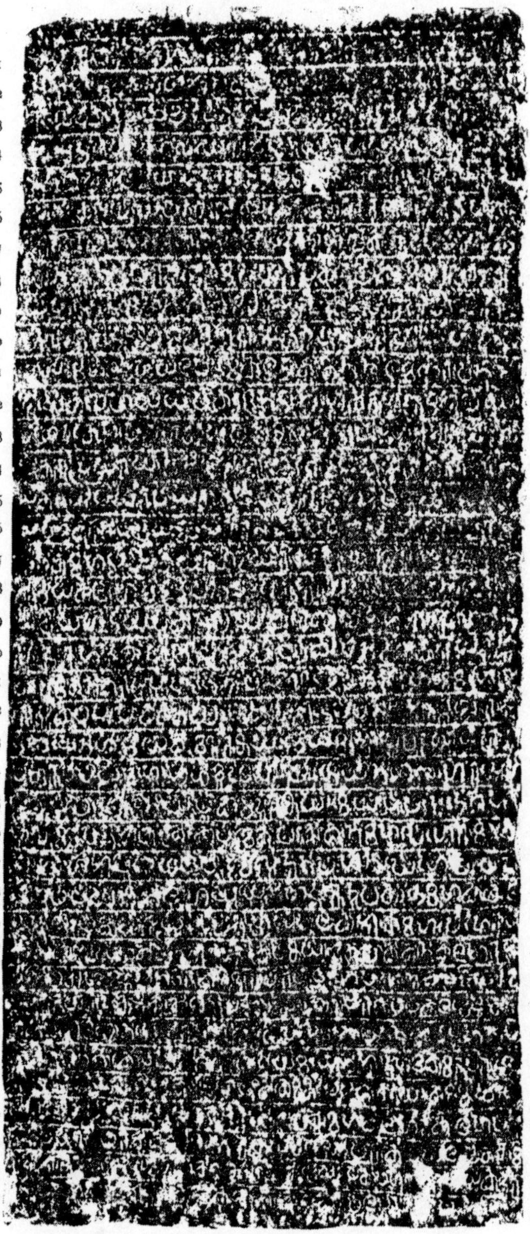

Scale about 2 inches to 1 foot.

From an ink-impression supplied by the Archaeological Commissioner, Ceylon.

33 .. .. .. ගම්ගොන් වෙහෙර්(කැම්) දුහුවා බලතුන් නො වද්නා කොට් (මෙගි කැබෑ)
34 (ලි නො) ගන්නා කොට් වදාළ එක්නැන් සම්යෙන් ආ **දුහල කුමරු**වර මෙ
35 (කාප්පර් වත්)කැම් **(අ)කුරෙළි ඈ(පු)ත්තෙම්** ඉසා **ඈත් සාතෙම්** ඉසා **ව**
36 .. .. **නිව්** .. .. **(නාවක්)**වර **මහකිළිග්ගම් කිළිගු වදු**
37 **(රා)** ඉසා **වටරක් සඟා අරක්සමණන්**වර **කුඩසලා වත්කැම්**
38 **(දෙපිම්)** ඈතුළුවැ අප් මෙනුවාක් දෙනාම්සින් මෙ සම්වතාපහණ්(අහ)ය කූ දෙනූ
39 [ලද්] .. මෙයට් අවුල් කළ කෙනෙක් කවුඩු බලු වූවාහයි

TRANSCRIPT.

1 [Śrī] sirivat apiriyat (lov ikut guṇa muḷin uturat-)
2 (vä muḷu) Damb-div(hi) an Kät-ku(la pāmili-kaḷa Okāvas raj-parapu-)
3 -ren baṭ Kä(t-usa)b **Siri-Saṅg-bo Abhā** [maharaj-haṭ emä-kulen]
4 sama-dā **Dev-Gon** biso-räjna kusä upädä (āpā mahayā siri)
5 vindä piḷivel-se rada-vä (miṇivuṭnen pähäyū) siya mu(ndne-)
6 -n[1] lo-uturā bisevnen bisesvä (tumā) sirin (Lakdiv) paha(yā)
7 .. ..
8 .. ..
9 .. ..
10 .. .. **Abhaya-giri-ve-**
11 **(-her)hi** maṅgul maha-sala-piḷima kula-däti indu-nil miṇi ruvanin
12 äs tabavā siya vikmen dänä gat **Ruhuṇu** danav(ye-)
13 (-hi **Bo)ḷatuḷā-veherahi** (suvan-muvā) .. .. (Munind-piḷibi-)
14 -b ka(rā su-)sirasä .. ..
15 yutnaṭ uvasar viyatnaṭ saṅgrā daham .. .. yanaṭ
16 (sav) miturunaṭ piya(bas vaturu) .. .. (-n)naṭ piri [ku-]
17 (-sal) tamahaṭ ekatsaru kaḷa **Siri-Saṅg-bo Abhā** maha-rad-hu
18 tumā sat läṅgu paḷamuvana havuruduyehi (Vä)pä sandä puṇu a-
19 -ḍ mas-hi dasa pak davas **(Kalaṇu)bimhi** āvū **(Kiḷind)**[2]**de-**
20 **-ṅgdarahi** āvū **(Asun-piṭi-teyi)n** tun kiriyak i-
21 -sā metun kiriyaṭ (väḷädenu) piṭibim (u)yan isā memä (bimhi)
22 āvū **Kuṭṭāvatta** isā pisa(mbu)r[3] de-viyälä āvū **Moro(ṇḍu)-**
23 **Mahasen-gamiye** kumburu isā mehimä āvū (paḷa bo) .. ..

---

[1] See Vol. I, p. 221, note 1.
[2] This may also be read *Kāhind*.
[3] This may also be read *visambur*.

24 (**Va**[1])**ñguru**-(pi)ṭi (sambho)ga gamu (saṅgnaṭ) meyin (hunnā[2] harä) .. ..
25 .. .. -min siṭi kumbur isā meyaṭ (vä)ḷädenu vatu
26 .. bim (mivan) ätuḷat koṭ metuvāk tän **Maha-veherä** maha-
27 ḅo-gehi avuṇu sala-piḷima-budun-vahansē (ge väṭi da-)
28 (-lva)nuvaṭ (sati)n lahasuyen havurudu patā de-mahak tel
29 (denu) koṭ isā meyaṭ van viyavulak äta **Maha-veherä**
30 apiḷisaraṇa saṅgun sāhā denu koṭ isā metuvāk tän **Kiliṅgu-rad**
31 **Pirivat Hämbuvan** daru manuburu piri(välla)n vaḷandanu koṭ isā (me-)
32 (-yaṭ) deruvanā dekamtän no vadnā isā väri perenäṭṭu kulī melätti
33 .. .. .. gam-gon veher-(kämi) dunuvā balatun no vadnā koṭ (mehi käbä-)
34 (-li no) gannā koṭ vadāḷa ektän samiyen ā **Duhala Kumaru**-varä Me-
35 (-käppar Vat)kämi (**A**)**kureḷi** (**Äpu**)**ttem** isā **Ät Sātem** isā **Va**
36 .. .. **niv** .. .. (**nāvan**)-varä **Mahakiliṅg-gam Kiliṅgu Vadu-**
37 (**-rā**) isā **Vaṭarak Saṅgā Araksamaṇan**-varä **Kuḍasalā Vatkämi-**
38 (**deṭim**) ätuḷuvä ap metuvāk denā-visin me samvatā-pahaṇ-(abha)ya-
-ku denu
39 [ladi] .. meyaṭ avul kaḷa kenek kavuḍu balu vūvāhayi

TRANSLATION.

[Lines 1–6.][8] Hail! The great king **Siri Saṅg-bo Abhā**[3] was born[4] unto [the great king] **Siri Saṅg-bo Abhā**, the Kṣatriya lord, descended from the royal line of the Okkāka dynasty, which, abounding in an assemblage of benignant, boundless and transcendental[5] virtues, has caused other Kṣatriya dynasties of the whole of Jambudvīpa to render it homage[6]: [he was born] of the womb of the anointed queen **Dev Gon**[7] of equal birth and descent. After enjoying (the dignities of governor and chief governor), he in due course became king, was anointed on his head, (resplendent with the bejewelled crown,) with the unction of world supremacy, and illumined the Island of Laṅkā with his glory.

[Lines 10–17.] He caused the eyes of the auspicious colossal stone-statue at **Abhayagiri-vihāra** to be set with brilliant sapphires of the first water

---

[1] This may also be read *Pañguru-piṭi*.

[2] This may also be read *huṇā* or *gaṇā*.

[3] See line 17.

[4] See Vol. I, p. 224, note 2.

[5] See *ibid.*, p. 224, note 3, and p. 237, note 5.

[6] *Pāmili*, see *ibid.*, p. 224, note 4.

[7] See above, p. 58.

[8] Probably of Mahinda Thēra. See Vol. I, p. 227, note 1, but cf. Mihintale tablets A, line 33, and B, line 41 (Vol. I, pp. 92 and 96).

[9] *Kula-däli-iñdu-nil-miṇi-ruvanin* = Skt. *kula-jātīndra-nīla-maṇi-ratnēna*.

At (**Bo**)**latuḷā-vehera** in the province of **Ruhuṇu,** conquered[1] by his own **valour**. he caused to be made a golden image of the Chief of Sages (Buddha) . . . . and on its sacred head . . . . kindly services to those engaged in . . . . patronage to the learned, floods of pleasant words to the righteous . . . . . . and to all friends. He made good deeds . . . . his own treasure.

[Lines 17–30.] Whereas in the first year since the elevation of the canopy (of dominion) by this great king **Siri Saṅg-bo Abhā**, on the tenth day of the bright half of the lunar month of *Väp* (Sept.–Oct.), it was declared by His Majesty in Council that from three *kiriyas*[2] [sowing-extent of land] at **Asun-piṭi-teya**[3] in **Kiḷind-deṅgdara** in the district[4] of **Kalaṇu**, together with the out-lying lands and orchards appertaining to these three *kiriyas*, as well as **Kuṭṭāvatta** in this district: from the fields with their produce in **Moroṅḍu-Mahasen-gamiya** in the two *viyalas*[5] of *pisambur*[6]: from the *sambhōga*[7] village **Vaṅgurupiṭi** together with the fields situated therein and gardens attached thereto, but exclusive of what is dedicated to the **Saṅgha**: from all these places there shall be supplied oil during two months every year at the rate of (a *lahas* measure a week) for the purpose of keeping alight the lamps[8] in the house[9] of the incomplete[10]

---

[1] *Dänä* also *däna*, *dana*, and *dina*, P. *jina*.

Cf. Alaḷava neta-kälum—lasa-gaman nil-upulan
kala-hasna *däna*-vū mā—tabā asadahu-lu ē nugiyō (*Kavsiḷumiṇa*, v. 556).

See also *E.S.*, p. 39, and Jay., p. 18.

[2] See Vol. I, p. 3, note 4.

[3] Cf. *uyan-teya* 'park-pond', *mahanel-teya* 'lotus-pond', in this king's Vessagiri inscription, line 19 (Vol. I, pp. 33 and 36).

[4] *Bim*, Skt. *bhūmi* 'ground', is used here apparently in the sense of a district or a large tract of land, cf. *taṇa-bimhi* in the Nāgama pillar, side A, line 13 (above, p. 17), and *valapu-bimä* in the Kukurumahandamana pillar, side A, line 16.

[5] See Vol. I, p. 119, note 1.

[6] Or *visambur*. The meaning of this agricultural term is at present not clear.

[7] See Vol. I, p. 8, note 1.

[8] *Väṭi*, pl., cf. *väṭiya*, P. *vaṭṭikā* 'a wick'.

[9] *Ge* (P. *gēha*) as a genitive suffix was not in common use until a later period. See *A.I.C.*, p. 19, and *L.S.S.*, pp. 61–62.

[10] *Avuṇu*. In the Jētavanārāma slab No. 1 (lines 25–26), probably of the eighth regnal year of this king Mahinda IV, mention is made of setting the eyes of this statue with rubies. The reading there also should be *avuṇ* instead of *apuṇ*. I am still inclined to derive it from P. *apuṇṇa*, Skt. *apūrṇa*, the image being incomplete without the eyes. The word *avuṇu* or *avaṇa*, however, is commonly used in Sinhalese literature as a derivative of P. and Pkt. *āpaṇa*, *āvaṇa*, 'a market'. If it is used in this sense here also, the above passage should run 'the stone-statue of the Lord Buddha at the market within [the precincts of] the house of the Sacred Bōdhi-tree in Mahāvihāra'. *Avuṇu* is also another form of *amuṇu* (P. *ammaṇa*), and the phrase *amuṇu* or *avuṇu baṅdinavā* means 'to construct dams' for diverting water for irrigation purposes. It is so used in the Galpota record of Niśśaṅka-Malla (*A.I.C.* 148 A, line 20). Both Müller and Geiger are, therefore, wrong in connecting it with *āpaṇa*.

stone-statue of the Lord Buddha at the house of the Sacred Bōdhi-tree in **Mahāvihāra**. Should there arise a dispute as regards these [regulations], the upright monks of the **Mahāvihāra** shall settle[1] it.

[Lines 30–39.] All these lands shall be enjoyed by **Kiliṅgu-rad Pirivat Hämbuvan,** his children, grandchildren, and their descendants. Into these [lands] there shall not enter *deruvanā dekam-tän*[2], *väri*, *perenāṭṭu*, *kulī*, *melātti* . . . . . . village oxen, temple-employées and officers of bowmen[3]. And no allotments[4] in these lands shall be taken.

We all of us, namely, *Mekāppar Vatkämi* **Akureḷi Äputtem** and **Ät Sātem** (both) of the family of **Duhala Kumaru**; **Mahakiliṅg-gam Kiliṅgu Vadurā** of the family of . . . . and **Kuḍasalā Vatkämi-deṭim** of the family of **Vaṭarak Saṅgā Araksamaṇan,** have come and granted these [aforesaid] immunities by means of a stone [slab] of Council Warranty.

Whoever commits infringement of this [edict] shall be [born] a crow or a dog [in the future birth].

No. 13. THE SLAB-INSCRIPTION OF KĪRTI-NIŚŚAṄKA-MALLA (1187–1196 A.D.) AT RUVANVÄLI-DĀGABA, ANURĀDHAPURA

NEAR the eastern altar of the Ruvanväli-dāgaba, and within a few yards of the statues, there stands erect this fine slab fixed in a bed of brick-work, and flanked by two monolithic pillars[5]. It was discovered in 1874 by Nāranviṭa Thēra, and it bears an inscription in excellent preservation, engraved on the side, smoothed and ruled for the purpose, and consisting of thirty-five lines, which cover a space of 3′ 14″ by 3′ 8″.

The **akṣaras** are about an inch in size on the average. They represent the type of the Sinhalese alphabet in use in the twelfth and thirteenth centuries.

---

[1] *Sāhā denu.* See the Puliyaṇkuḷam slab, line 44 (Vol. I, p. 187).

[2] For other references to these terms, see the Index at the end of each Volume. As regards *väri*, probably an agricultural labourer, compare the article on *vārakkuḍi* in Mr. Lewis' *Manual of the Vanni Districts*, Ceylon (ch. xix).

[3] See above, p. 33, note 4.

[4] *Kābāli.* See Vol. I, p. 37, note 5.

[5] For a good photograph of the slab, see Cave's *Ruined Cities of Ceylon*, Plate xvii.

The letter *r*, it may be noticed, is developed from the closed type of this character[1], and the *visarga* is indicated by a vertical stroke convexed to the left (ɩ), while the groups *ṁśa* and *rbba* are represented by the compound letters ංශ and ර්‍බ, which occur more frequently in later records.

The **orthography** is correct with the exception of a few irregularities, such as *pūrbba* (l. 5) for *pūrva*, *samurddha* (l. 9) for *samṛddha*, *akrata* (l. 35) for *akṛta*, *bya-* (l. 35) for *vya-*; the doubling of consonants in conjunction with a preceding *r*[2], as *lakṣair-d-dhanānām*, *pramāṇair-n-nirupama-racitām* (l. 34); and the unnecessary use of the *virāma* in consonantal groups instead of combined letters, especially when writing Sanskrit and Pāli words, e.g. පරම්පරා (l. 4), වස්තු (l. 7) for පරම්‍පරා, වස්‍තු, following no doubt the usage of Sinhalese orthography. The name of the dāgaba is given as *Ruvanväli* and *Ruvanmäli*. The former is the Sinhalese equivalent of P. *Ratanavāluka*[3], and the latter that of *Ratanamālika*[4]. Both these names were in common use in the twelfth century A.D., but before this period the dāgaba in question went by the appellations *Mahā-thūpa*, *Mahā-cetiya*, *Soṇṇa-mālī-*, *Hēma-mālī-*, *Hēma-mālika-*, and *Hēma-vāluka-cētiya*.

The **language** is Sanskritic Sinhalese with the exception of that of the last three lines, which contain a Sanskrit stanza in the beautiful *Sragdharā* metre. In phraseology and general style it approaches very much the modern literary form, and agrees so much with the other known inscriptions of **Kīrti-Niśśaṅka-Malla**, that I am inclined to attribute the authorship of all of them to one person. Sinhalese inscriptions often give the names of the officials or members of the *Curia regis* who were sent out with full powers to proclaim the mandate of the King in Council. In Indian records such an officer is technically called *dūtaka*[5], while the composer and the writer or engraver are respectively termed *kartṛ*[6] and *lēkhaka*[6]. Ceylon inscriptions make no mention of the last two classes of officials, and yet they must necessarily have been in existence. This leads to a consideration of the epithet **Śrī-Dhāman** mentioned in the

---

[1] See Vol. I, p. 242.

[2] This is the common rule in manuscripts and is, I believe, supported by grammarians.

[3] *Mv.* lxxvi. 105. Cf., however, *Ratanāvali-cētiya*, *ibid.*, lxxx. 20, lxxxvii. 65, and lxxxviii. 83.

[4] See *Rasavāhinī* (Colombo edition, 1893, p. 71). The *Dharmapradīpikā* (Colombo, 1886, p. 316) states that the *Ruvanmäli-dāgaba* is so-called owing to the fact that its relic-chamber is adorned with *ratna-mālā* 'necklaces of jewels'. See also the *Pūjāvaliya*, extract, p. 11.

[5] Fleet's *Gupta Inscriptions*, Index, *s. v.*

[6] *Ibid.*, *s. v.*

concluding Sanskrit stanza. Possibly it is the name of the composer (*katṛ*) of the present inscription [1], although the grammatical construction of the sentence points to it being only an attribute applied to king **Kīrti-Niśśaṅka-Malla** as 'the abode of prosperity'. See the translation on p. 83, below.

The special words occurring in our record and requiring notice are:—(*a*) *masuran* (ll. 7 and 25) 'gold *māsakas*', according to Prof. Rhys Davids [2], though a *masuran* coin is often used by Pāli and Sinhalese authors as an equivalent of a *kahāpaṇa* [3]; (*b*) *ridī-tiram* (l. 13) 'silver *tiram*', possibly the silver *drachma* of the Greeks, from Arabic *dirham* or Persian *diram* through some such Tamil form as *tiṟam* (திறம்) [4]; (*c*) *käti aḍa* [5] (l. 10) equivalent either to Skt. *kṣatriya+ardham*, P. *khattiya-aḍḍhaṁ* 'royal half', as Müller renders it, or to Skt. *karttrī+ardham* 'bill-hook share', most probably a technical term for a tax on grains raised on jungle-covered dry lands, the bill-hook (Sinh. *kätta*, pl. *käti*) being the weapon chiefly used in clearing the land of brushwood [6]; (*d*) *taliyan-tel* (l. 24), most probably *tala-tel* 'sesamum oil', as it is often used in temple worship [7].

As regards the **date**, I wish to draw attention to a slight error I made in my calculations on p. 123 of Vol. I. I stated there that the date of the accession

---

[1] Dr. A. B. Keith to whom I showed the stanza seemed also to think so at first sight.

[2] *Ancient Coins and Measures of Ceylon*, p. 23, note 2.

[3] Cf., for example, the passage 'ē vidi hīya genvā geṇa hīya kelin siṭuvā hī-pagiliya vasā *masuran* goḍak Phussa-dēvayanṭa deva', in the Sinhalese *Thūpavaṁsa* (Colombo ed., p. 143), with 'rājā laddha-jayo nagaraṁ āgantvā saraṁ anāpetvā puṁkhēna ujukaṁ ṭhapāpetvā taṁ pamāṇaṁ *kahāpaṇa-rāsiṁ* katvā Phussadēvassa adāsi' in the Pāli version (p. 51). Similarly in the *Rasavāhinī* (p. 70), '*kahā-paṇa-rāsiṁ* katvā Phussadēvassa adāsi.'

[4] The form occurring in Sanskrit inscriptions is *dramma*. See the Harṣa stone-inscription (*Ep. Ind.*, ii, No. 8), the Cambay Plates (*ibid.*, vii, No. 6) and the Siyadoni stone (*ibid.*, i, No. 21), where mention is made of coins *vigrahapāla-* (or *°pāliya-*) *dramma, vigrahapālasatka-dramma vigraha-tuṅgīya-dramma* and *pañciyaka-dramma*.

[5] Professors Rhys Davids and Müller read *käti aya*, but *aḍa* is quite clear on the two estampages before me.

[6] See Mr. S. M. Burrows' notes in *C.B.R.A.S.*, vol. x, p. 59, and compare the phrases *dukin karana sehen kaṭusara aya häma kalaṭamä no gannä niyäyen* and *käti aya keṭu kanaba aya manda vajra jīvikā heyin häma kalaṭama no gannā niyāyen* in the Galpota (l. 18) and the Daṁbulla (l. 9) inscriptions respectively (*A.I.E.*, Nos. 145 and 148). The reference is undoubtedly to the tax on *chena* produce. Mr. Dyke, writing in 1856, says 'in the district of Nuwarakalāwiya, as part of the old Kandyan territory, there is not any tax upon dry grain grown in the jungle land around the villages' (*Manual of the North Central Province*, p. 113).

[7] Cf. *mesēma satiyak taḷa-telin-ma pūjā keḷēya* (*Thūpavaṁsa*, p. 174).

of **Kīrti-Niśśaṅka-Malla** might be placed 'in the first half of 1188 A.D.' To be more precise, I should have said, 'in the third quarter of 1187 A.D.', for according to the *Mahāvaṁsa* he ascended the throne thirteen years and one day before the coronation of king Sāhasa-Malla, on the 23rd of August 1200 A.D.[1] Niśśaṅka-Malla's reign of nine years may, therefore, be reckoned from about September, 1187 A.D., to September, 1196 A.D.

In my article on this king's inscription at the Dambulla Vihāra[2] I put together all the information I could gather regarding his family and his activities as a beneficent ruler and as a restorer of religious monuments. The present record does not furnish any new facts, its **contents** being a general account of his various philanthropic and religious acts, mostly in Poḷonnaruva, his state visit to Anurādhapura in his fourth regnal year (between September, 1191 and September, 1192), the lavish manner in which he worshipped the Ruvanväli-dāgaba there, and the steps he took to restore the Mīrisaviṭiya and other vihāras. In lines 4 to 7 we are told that much of the lawlessness then prevailing was due to the oppressions[3] committed by Parākrama-Bāhu I. This might have been true, but yet Niśśaṅka-Malla would not have made a public statement of it, had he not belonged to the party of Kāliṅga princes at the Sinhalese Court, whose policy, as I pointed out elsewhere[4], was antagonistic to the aspirations of the nobles of the Govi-kula, whose leader was Parākrama-Bāhu I[5].

The *tulābhāra* or *tulā-puruṣa* gift mentioned in lines 11 to 14 is a common ceremony amongst Indian kings[6]. Mr. S. M. Burrows has drawn attention to a parallel even in England in the case of 'lady Rohese, the mother of Thomas à Becket, Archbishop of Canterbury, who was wont to weigh her

---

[1] See Vol. I, p. 123, note 4.

[2] *Ibid.*, No. 9.

[3] The *Mahāvaṁsa* (lxxiii, vv. 1–4) attributes to Parākrama-Bāhu I also quite a similar reference to the oppressions of past kings.

[4] Vol. I, p. 125.

[5] That Parākrama-Bāhu was full of national spirit is obvious from the incident recorded in *Mv.* lxxii. 134–137, which Wijēsiṇha renders 'the mighty hero bethought him that he would hold the festival of war, and shouted to his armour-bearer, saying, "bring hither to me a Sinhalese sword." And the armour-bearer understood it not, but brought a sword of Indian workmanship, saying it was a Sinhalese sword. But he cried out, saying, "say not to me that this is a sword of Sinhalese handiwork. . . . Lay this apart and bring me quickly a sword of Sinhalese handiwork." And when he had thus spoken, a fearful sword of Sinhalese handiwork was forthwith brought unto him.'

[6] See, for example, the Cambay Plates of Govinda IV (*Ep. Ind.*, vii, No. 6), the Raṅganātha inscription (*ibid.*, vi, No. 33), and the *Madras Journal of Literature and Science* for 1882–1894, p. 54.

son each year, on his birthday, against money, clothes and provisions, which she gave to the poor'[1].

In line 27 there is a curious allusion to a class of fowlers called **Kãmbodi**. King Niśśaṅka-Malla presented them with gold and cloth and whatever other kind of wealth they wished, and ordered them not to catch birds. Neither Rhys Davids nor Müller give any explanation whatsoever regarding them in their articles[2] on this inscription, while Mr. H. C. P. Bell identifies them with the Kāmbojian mercenaries who, he thinks, were employed by the Sinhalese kings at this period[3]. This identification is based, I believe, on the similarity of the two names, but it must be remembered that the Kāmbojians of Poḷonnaruva, whether they were monks, ambassadors, architects, or even mercenaries (as he surmises), must have been devout Buddhists. The inter-communication that existed between Cambodia and Ceylon during the eleventh, twelfth and thirteenth centuries, and that led to one of the gates of Poḷonnaruva being called **Kãmboja-vãsala** was more or less of a religious character; and I have so far not found a single allusion in the literary or inscriptional records of the Island pointing to the immigration of non-Buddhistic clans from Cambodia. Mr. Burrows was, therefore, quite right in wondering why the **Kãmbodin** of the present record, if they belonged to those who came over from Cambodia, should have been specially addicted to killing birds. And he was also on the right track in the solution of the problem, when he drew attention to a passage in Fergusson's *History of Indian and Eastern Architecture* supporting the local tradition that the Kāmbojians of Cambodia originally came from the north-west of India, and suggesting that Ceylon may have formed a half-way house[4]. In the Aśoka inscriptions[5] and in some of the other Indian records the **Kãmbojas** are almost always mentioned together with the **Yavanas** as if they were tribes dwelling in close proximity to one another. Kāmbojas inhabited the Kābul valley[6],

---

[1] See his interesting article entitled 'A Year's work at Poḷonnaruva' (*J.C.B.R.A.S.*, vol. x, p. 50).

[2] *J.R.A.S.*, vol. vii, p. 353 f., and *A.I.C.*, No. 145.

[3] *A.S.C. Annual Report*, 1903, p. 16, where in a foot-note he speaks of them as 'truculent soldiery, liable to get "out of hand", and needing to be appeased without stint, if we may read between the lines of Niśśaṅka Malla's inscription at Ruvanvęli Dágaba, Anurádhapura'. This is purely hypothetical.

[4] *J.C.B.R.A.S.*, vol. x, p. 65.

[5] Rock edicts V and XIII.

[6] Wilson places them in Afghanistan (*Vishṇu Purāṇa*, ii, p. 182). See also Bühler in *Ep. Ind.*, vol. i, p. 243. Foucher says that the Nepalese tradition makes Tibet the home of the Kāmbojas

while the Yavanas (Ionians), we know, were originally the Asiatic Greeks[1]. Both these names came in later times to be applied in a loose way to foreigners who came from the west or north-west. For example, we find four references to Yavanas in the *Mahāvaṁsa.* The first is in the compound word *yōnasabhāga-vatthu* (ch. x, v. 90 of Geiger's ed.). It is true that this is a doubtful case. Nevertheless, if the compiler of this portion of the *Mahāvaṁsa*, who probably lived in the sixth century A.D. (if not later), did really use this expression, he may have thought of the *Yavanas* as a class of foreigners for whose use king Paṇḍukābhaya (377–307 B.C.) set apart a piece of ground. Similarly the *Yavanas* mentioned in ch. xii, vv. 34 and 39 were most probably the foreign clans (not necessarily Greeks) on the north-west frontier of India, as suggested by Mr. V. A. Smith in speaking of those referred to in the Aśoka edicts (*Aśoka*, p. 132, note 2). The last reference is in connexion with an incident as late as the second half of the twelfth century A.D. We are told in ch. lxxvi, v. 268, that Yavanas were among the many communities that brought presents to General Laṅkāpura during his successful campaign in Southern India under Parākrama-Bāhu I (1153–1186 A.D.). They were undoubtedly Mussulman settlers who used to trade or were still trading all along the west coast from the Persian Gulf down to Ceylon, and possibly further east. They are called in Tamil *çōṉakar* (சோனகர்), no doubt from Pāli or Pkt. *yōnaka.* Their representatives in Ceylon bear the Sinhalese name *yonā* (pl. *yon* or *yonnu*), a derivative of P. *yōna*, or more likely *yōnaka.* Like them the Kāmbojas also may have entered India and Ceylon by land and sea, probably in pursuit of their trade in horses. The reference in the Vaṁśa Brāhmaṇa to a certain Kāmboja Aupamanyava as a pupil of Madragāra points, according to Prof. Macdonell and Dr. Keith[2], to 'a possible connexion of the Madras[3], or more probably the Uttara Madras, with the Kambojas, who probably had Iranian as well as Indian affinities'. The Kambohs of the present day in the NW. Provinces of India are

---

(*Iconographie bouddhique*, p. 134), while Langdon identifies them with 'the well-known Aramaic people Gambula, who appear in the annals of Asarhaddon 681–668 B.C. and are spoken of by the Arabic geographers in the Middle Ages. They were an important and powerful people who occupied the region east of the mouth of the Tigris along the Persian Gulf eastward towards Elam'.

[1] Yavana-deśa and Kambuja-deśa were also the names of states in the Eastern Peninsula. See Fergusson, *op. cit.*, vol. ii, p. 373, note 6.

[2] *Vedic Index*, *s.v.* Kamboja.

[3] 'The Madras mentioned in the Upaniṣad were, like the Kurus, probably settled somewhere in Kurukṣetra in the Madhyadeśa [of old India].' *Ibid.*, *s.v.* Madra.

supposed to be their descendants. Rājendra Lāla Mitra[1] calls them 'a turbulent, crafty, stiffnecked race, and, as such, more akin to Afghans than to any of the meek Hindu races of the plains of India'. Like the Yavanas of yore and the Yoṇnu or Ceylon Moors of the present day, the Kāmbojas also shaved their whole head[2], and references to Kāmboja horses as late as the twelfth century A.D. are not wanting in South Indian literature[3]. It is, therefore, not impossible that just as the Afghans of modern times, the Kāmbojas also may have come to Ceylon, probably as horse-dealers, and a colony of them may have settled permanently in Anurādhapura in company with the Yavanas when that city was in the zenith of its glory. They were, of course, not Buddhists, and, as such, it was not surprising that in the twelfth century A.D. their descendants, probably by Yavana or low-caste Sinhalese wives, having become poor, eked out an existence as fowlers, and were regarded as a special tribe of bird-catchers. I do not think they can be connected with those Buddhist monks, ambassadors and others who from time to time came over to Ceylon from Cambodia as a result of long friendly intercourse between the two Buddhist kingdoms.

Finally, a word or two about the present text and translation of the inscription. They have been prepared from the two ink-estampages supplied to me by the Archaeological Commissioner, and are quite independent of those already published by Professors Rhys Davids and Müller respectively in *J.R.A.S.*, vol. vii (1875), and in *A.I.C.*, as No. 145. Previous to these scholars, the Interpreter Mudaliyar of the Courts at Anurādhapura made for the first time a translation of the inscription, which he contributed to the *Ceylon Observer* for December 29, 1874. All of them, however, omitted to translate the Sanskrit stanza which, as I mentioned before, may possibly help us to settle the question of the authorship of all the inscriptions of king Kīrti-Niśśaṅka-Malla.

TEXT.

1 ශ්‍රීමත්වූ ත්‍යාග සත්‍ය ශෞර්‍ය්‍යාදිගුණගණයෙන් අසාධාරණවූ **ඔක්කාවස්**රජපරපු
2 රෙන් ආ **කාලිඟ චක්‍රවර්ත්ති**රාජවශයට තිලකායමානවූ **සිංහපුරයෙහි** ස
3 ජාතවූ **නිශ්ශංකමල්ල කාලිඟ පරක්‍රමබාහු** රජපාවහන්සෙ සවවශයට ප
4 රම්පරායාත ලංකාවිපයෙහි එක් සෙසත් කොටැ **මාලු පරාක්‍රමබාහු**වහන්සෙ පූ
5 ර්ව රජචරිත ඉක්මැ කළ අතිදඩ අවිනයෙන් පීඩිතවූ දිළිඳුවැ ගොස් සො
6 රකම් කොටැ ජීවත්වන බොහො ජනයා ජීවිතාශා හැරැ සොරකම් කරන්නෙ ධනා

[1] *Indo-Aryan*, vol. ii, p. 186.

[2] *M. W. Dict.*, s.v.

[3] See, for example, S. Krishṇaswāmi's *Ancient India*, p. 236. I am told that popular ballads regarding Kāmbojas exist to this day in the Telugu country.

7 ශාවෙන් වෙදසි රන් රිදී මසුරන් මුතු මැණික් වස්ත්‍රාභරණාදිවූ උන් උන් කැමැති
වස්තු හා

8 සරක් ගම් බිම් දී අභය දී සොරකම් හරවා සෙසු බොහො ජනයා ද ඒ ඒ
දුඃඛයෙන් ගලවා මෙසෙ

9 මැ විවිධවිචිත්‍රවස්තුදානයෙන් සනාථකොටැ මා දුන් දෙය ස්ථිරකොටැ තවද
වැඩියක් සමුඹව[1] ගතමනා

10 වේදසි අවුරුදු ගණිතකට අය හැරැ වදූරා තුන්රජයෙහිමැ හැමැ කලට කැති
අඩ හැරැ වදූරා මා ද

11 වසැ කාත් නො සිහා සුවසෙ විසුව මැනැවැයි පෙරැ රජදරුවන් නො
කළුවිරුලෙසෙකැ තුලාභාර නැගෙමී සිතා වදූ

12 රා උරෙහිදූ **වීරබාහු** මහපාණන්වහන්සෙ හා අගමෙසුන් **කාලිඟ සුභද්‍රා** බිසොවුන්
වහන්සෙ හා සහවොටුනු අබර

13 ණින් සැදී තමන්වහන්සෙ හා තුන්දෙනාවහන්සෙ තුලාභාර නැගී සත්රුවන්
හා ඇතළු[2] රිදී නිරම් හා අනන්ත කොටැ

14 රාජ ඊර්ෂියෙහි (නෙ)ස්වමින් මහාදානවෂීා පවත්වා තුන්රජයෙහි බොහොකොටැ
නිශ්ශංක නමින් සත්‍ර නංවා අන්න දාන ද නිරන්ත

15 රයෙන් පවත්වා සියලු දිළිඳුභය සොරභය කණ්ටකභය දුරුකොටැ ලක්දිව්
වාසීන් හැමැ දෙනා සුවපත්කොටැ ශා

16 සනයෙහි ද දුශ්ශීලයන් ද උත්කණ්ඨිතයන් ද පහනොවන්නේ ප්‍රත්‍යයලොභයෙන්
හා කටයුක්තෙහි භයින් බව දැ

17 නැ ශාසනය කිලුටු නො කොටැ සිවුරු හළවුන්ට කටයුතුදු නැතැ රන් පිළී
යකඩ බත් බිජුවට සරක් ආදිවූ දැ ද ලැ

18 බෙසි සම්මත කරවා වදූරා පුශිලවහන්සෙවරුන්දැට ද පළිබොධ නො වුව
මනා වේදසි ඔබගේ නෑවැදැයන්ට නො එ

19 ක් වස්තුයෙන් සග්‍රහ කොටැ සිවුපසයෙන් දානප්‍රවාහ පතුරුවා මෙසෙ ලොකය ද
ශාසනය ද සෙමෙහි තබා **පුලස්තිපුර**

20 **යෙහි** වැඩැවසනසෙයෙක් **රුවන්වැලි**දාගබ්වහන්සෙ දා වඳනා පිණිසැ සිපුරඟ
සෙනඟ පිරිවරා මහානුභාවයෙන්

21 තමන්වහන්සේට සතරවන්නෙහි නික්මැ දාගබ්වහන්සේ පෙනෙන ථානයෙහි
දිමැ වාහනයෙන් බැසැ ශ්‍රීපාදයෙන් **රු**

22 **වන්මැලි**මළුවට වැඩැ මළුවෙහි වැලි තවරන්නාසේ අනන්ත මුතු අතුටැ වැලිතලා
පිටැ නාන් කුසුම් පුදන්නාසෙ රන්

23 මල් රිදීමල් සත්රුවන් සිසාරා නිරතුරුකොටැ පුදා අනැගි පටකඩ පතාකායෙන්
දාගබට ආතපනිවාරණය කොටැ සිසා

24 රා නිරතුරුකොටැ කපුරු ගොඩ ගොඩකොටැ පහන් පුදා තලියන්තෙල්
සුවඳතෙල් ආදිවූ තෙලින් සතියක් පහන් පුදා

[1] 'සමෘඹව' වියයුතුයි

[2] 'ඇතුළු' වියයුතුයි

25 මෙසෙමැ කළුවැල් දුමින් සුවඳ මලින් පුද, සිවු දැ ගඳින් සිසාරා පිරිබඩ ගෙනැ සතලිස්ලක්‍ෂයක් මසුරනින් පූජා

26 කොටැ නුවරට හාත්පසින් සත් ගව්වක් පමණ තැනැ හැමැ සතුන් නො මැරිය ගැක්කැයි අභය දී බෙර ලවා දෙලොස්

27 මහ වෑ තැනැ මසුන්ට අභය දී කාම්බොදීන්ට රන් පිළී ආදිවූ කැමැති වස්තු දී පක්‍ෂීන් නො බඳන නියායෙන් ස

28 ම්මතකොටැ පක්‍ෂීන්ට අභය දී ප්‍රීතීන් ද, වඳනා වේලෙහි ඒහි බෞඩදෙවතාවන් ස්වාමීන් හා බණන්නා දුටු මිනිසුන්ගේ

29 ප්‍රීතිඝොෂණ අසා එවේලෙහි උපන් බුඩාලම්බන ප්‍රීතින් ලක්දිව්වාසීන්ට නැවැතැ හවුරුද්දකට අය හැර. එහි සි

30 ටි **ලොකේ අරක්මේනාවන්** අධිකාරකොටැ උන් ද පුද, **මිරිසවිටි** ආදිවූ විහාර කරවවයි අනන්ත වස්තු හා ඒ

31 සිය ගණන් (යාල) දී සිටුවා නුවර දෙවුනුවරක් සෙ පෙර පරිද්දෙන් සජ්ජිත කොටැ වදාළ නියා[1] ද මෙට සිතින් පූජා කල

32 නට බෞඩදෙවතාවන්ගෙන් මෙමැ ලෙසැ ආරක්‍ෂා ඇතිබව ද දැනැ මතුවන රජ දරුවනුදුවිසින් නුවර. විහාර

33 විහාරවාසීන් ලොකශාසන සනාථකොටැ රක්‍ෂා කටයුතු **ශ්‍රීධාමිනා රත්න ශෛලොපචිතිම්පිකාලෙ**

34 ශ්‍රෙයත ලක්‍ෂ්මීන්‍යනාං[2] චත්වාරිංශත්ප්‍රමාණෛර්හිරණ්‍යමරචිතාම් විඤ්ඤ සාමෙතුඃ ප්‍රමොදෛඃ [I] ප්‍රත්‍යක්‍ෂ(ශ්‍රෙය)

35 ච තෛ[3]කස්තුතිමකුත[4] තතඃ ප්‍රීතචිත්තො යමබ්දං ලංකානා**ථ...** බ[5]ය්‍යරචයදතරා**ශ්‍රීපරාක්‍රාන්තිබාහුඃ** [II]

TRANSCRIPT.

1 Śrīmat-vū tyāga satya śauryy-ādi-guṇa-gaṇayen asādhāraṇa-vū **Okā-vas-**raja-parapu-

2 -ren ā **Kāliṅga Cakravartti**-rājavaṁśayaṭa tilakāyamāna-vä **Siṁha-purayehi** sa-

3 ṁjāta[6]-vū **Niśśaṁka-Malla Kāliṅga Parākrama-Bāhu** raja-pā-vahanse sva-vaṁśayaṭa pa-

4 -ramparāyāta Laṁkā-dvīpayehi ek sesat koṭä **Mālu Parākrama-Bāhu-**vahanse pū-

5 -rbba[7] rāja-carita ikmä kaḷa ati-daṅḍa[8] avinayen pīḍita-vū diḷindu-vä gos so-

6 -rakam koṭä jīvatvana boho janayā jīvitāśā härä sorakam karanne dhan-ā-

---

[1] 'නියාවද මෙයට' වෙනුවටයි [2] 'නානාං' වියයුතුයි
[3] 'නෛ' වියයුතුයි [4] 'කෘත' වියයුතුයි [5] 'ව්‍ය' වියයුතුයි
[6] Mt. *sajāla.* [7] For *pūrva.* [8] Mt. *atidasa.*

Anurādhapura : Ruvanväli-dāgaba Slab-Inscription of Niśśaṅka-Malla.

Scale about 2½ inches to 1 foot.

From an ink-impression supplied by the Archaeological Commissioner, Ceylon.

7 -śāven vedayi ran ridī masuran mutu mäṇik vastr-ābharaṇ-ādi-vū un un kämäti vastu hā

8 sarak gam bim dī abhaya dī sorakam haravā sesu boho janayā da ē ē duḥkhayen[1] gaḷavā mese-

9 mä vividha-vicitra-vastu-dānayen sanātha-koṭä mā dun deya sthira-koṭä tavada väḍiyak samurddhava[2] gatamanā-[3]

10 -vēdayi avurudu gaṇanakaṭa aya härä vadārā tun-rajayehi-mä hämä kalaṭa käti-aḍa[4] härä vadārā mā da-

11 -vasä kāt no siṅgā suvase visuva mänäväyi perä raja-daruvan no kaḷa-virulesekä tulā-bhāra näṅgemī sitā vadā-

12 -ṛā urehidā **Vīra-Bāhu** mahapāṇan-vahanse hā aga-mesun **Kāliṅga Subhadrā** bisovun-vahanse hā saha-voṭunu abara-

13 -ṇin sädī taman-vahanse hā tun-denā-vahanse tulā-bhāra näṅgī sat-ruvan hā ätaḷu[5] ridī tiram hā ananta koṭä

14 rāja vīthiyehi (ne)svamin[6] mahā-dāna-varṣā pavatvā tun-rajayehi boho-koṭä **Niśśaṁka** namin satra naṁvā anna dāna da niranta-

15 -rayen pavatvā siyalu diḷindu-bhaya sora-bhaya kaṇṭaka-bhaya duru-koṭä Lak-div-vāsīn hämä denā suvapat-koṭä śā-

16 -sanayehi da duśśīlayan da utkaṇṭhitayan da paha-no-vannē pratyaya lobhayen hā kaṭayuktehi bhayin bava dä-

17 -nä śāsanaya kiluṭu no koṭä sivuru haḷavunṭa kaṭayutu-du nätä ran piḷī yakaḍa bat bijuvaṭa sarak ādivū dā da lä-

18 -beyi sammata karavā vadārā suśīla-vahanse-varundāṭa da palibodha no vuvamanā vēdayi obagē nāvädāyanṭa no e-

19 -k vastuyen saṅgraha koṭä sivu-pasayen dāna-pravāha paturuvā mese lokaya da śāsanaya da semehi tabā **Pulasti-pura-**

20 **-yehi** väḍä-vasana-seyek **Ruvanväli-**dāgab-vahanse dā vandanā piṇisä siyuraṅga senaṅga pirivarā mahānubhāvayen

21 taman-vahansēṭa sataravannehi nikmä dāgab-vahansē penena mānayehidī-mä vāhanayen bäsä śrī-pādayen **Ru-**

22 **vanmäli-**maḷuvaṭa väḍä maḷuvehi väli tavarannäsē ananta mutu atuṭä väli-talā piṭä nan kusum pudannäse ran-

23 mal ridī-mal sat-ruvan sisārä niraturu-koṭä pudā anäṅgi paṭakaḍa patākāyen dāgabaṭa ātapa-nivāraṇaya koṭä sisā-

---

[1] Mt. *dukkhayen.* [2] For *samṛddhava.* [3] Mt. *çalamanā.*
[4] Mt. *-aya.* [5] For *ätuḷu.* [6] Mt. *ne swāmin.*

24 -rā niraturu-koṭä kapuru goḍa goḍa-koṭä pahan pudā taliyan-tel suvanda-tel ādivū telin satiyak pahan pudā

25 mese-mä kaḷuväl dumin suvanda malin pudā sivu dā gandin sisārā piribaḍa genä satalis-lakṣayak masuranin pūjā-

26 koṭä nuvaraṭa hātpasin sat gavvak pamaṇa tänä hāmä satun no märiya häkkäyi abhaya dī bera lavā doḷos

27 maha vā tänä masunṭa abhaya dī *Kämbodīnṭa* ran piḷī ādi-vū käṃäti vastu dī pakṣīn no badana niyāyen sa-

28 -mmata-koṭä pakṣīnṭa abhaya dī prītīn dā vandanā vēlehi ēhi Bauddha-devatāvan svāmīn hā [1] baṇannā duṭu minisungē

29 prīti-ghoṣaṇā asā evēlehi upan Buddhā-lambana prītīn Lak-div-vāsīnṭa nävätä havuruddakaṭa aya härä ehi si-

30 -ṭi **Lokē Arakmēnāvan** adhikāra-koṭä un da pudā **Mirisaviṭi** ādi-vū vihāra karavavayi ananta vastu hā vī

31 siya gaṇan (yāḷa) dī siṭuvā nuvara devu-nuvarak se pera paridden sajjita-koṭä vadāḷa niyā da mēṭa sitin pūjā kaḷa-

32 -naṭa Bauddha-devatāvangen memä lesä ārakṣā äti-bava da dänä matuvana raja-daruvanudu-visin nuvarä vihāra

33 vihāra-vāsīn loka-śāsana sanātha-koṭä raksā kaṭa-yutu **Śrī-Dhāmnā Ratna-caitye** 'pacitim avikalai-

34 -r-yyena lakṣair-ddhanyanāṁ [2], catvāriṁśat-pramāṇair-nnirupama-**racitām** vīkṣya sāndraiḥ pramodaiḥ [1] pratyakṣa(ṇy-e-) [3]

35 -va t[4]aika-stutim akrata[5] tataḥ prīta-citto 'yam[6] abdaṁ, Laṁkān **Niśśaṁka-Mallo** b[7]yaracayad akarāṁ **Śrī-Parākrānti-Bāhuḥ** [II]

TRANSLATION.

[Lines 1–10.] The illustrious king, distinguished by [the possession of] a multitude of virtues, liberality, truthfulness, heroism, and the like, His Majesty **Niśśaṁka-Malla Kāliṅga Parākrama-Bāhu**, who was born in **Siṁhapura** as a *tilaka* ornament[8] to the royal dynasty of **Kāliṅga Cakravarti**, descended from the line of kings of the Okkāka family, brought the Island of Ceylon, his family's

---

[1] Mt. *saha mīnhā.*

[2] Read *dhanānāṁ.*

[3] As an amendment I would suggest *pratyakṣeṇ-aiva.*

[4] Read *naika.*

[5] For *akṛta.*

[6] Dr. Keith, with whom I discussed this stanza, thinks that it would perhaps be better to regard *yam* as a relative, and not as standing for *ayam.* See translation on p. 83, below.

[7] For *vyaracayad.*

[8] Cf. *Lak-polo-mehesanaṭ talā-ṭik bandu* in the Vessagiri slab (Vol. I, p. 32) and *Okā-raj-kulaṭ talā-ṭik* in Kassapa V's slab, line 12 (*ibid.*, p. 47), and also *Rāṣṭrakūṭa-kula-tilaka* (*Ep. Ind.*, vii, p. 217).

heritage, under one canopy of dominion. And [seeing that] many persons, oppressed by the excessive and illegal punishments inflicted by king **Parākrama-Bāhu, the Great**[1], in violation of the customs of former sovereigns, and being [thereby] impoverished, are eking out an existence by robbery, and [reflecting that] these men commit robberies, even at the risk of their lives, through their desire for wealth, he bestowed on them gifts of gold, silver, coins (*masuran*), pearls, precious stones, clothes, ornaments, and the like—[in fact] whatever [kind of] wealth each one desired, and also cattle, villages, and lands; and granting them security, he made them desist from stealing. He relieved a great number of other people also, each from his own misfortunes, and by similar manifold gifts of diverse kinds he gave them his patronage. Desiring that what he[2] had given should not only be maintained but also be increased, he graciously remitted taxes for several years, and abolished the taxes on *chena* cultivation[3] in the three kingdoms[4] [of Ceylon] for all time.

[Lines 10–20.] [Expressing the hope] 'may all live happily in my time without want' and resolving to mount the scale-pans as no former kings have ever done, His Majesty, together with his own legitimate son **Vīra-Bāhu**, the heir-apparent[5], and the chief queen **Kāliṅga Subhadrā**, three persons in all, wearing the crown and the other royal insignia, mounted the scale-pans and caused great showers of gifts to fall by throwing down[6] in the King's street unlimited quantity [of wealth], including the seven kinds of jewels and silver *tiram*[7]. In the three kingdoms he established very many alms-houses under the name of **Niśśaṁka** and maintained a continuous gift of food. Thus he dispelled all fear of poverty, fear of robbery, and fear of sedition[8], and brought happiness to all the inhabitants of the Island.

Perceiving that both those who lead impure lives, and those who are disappointed[9], do not leave the (Buddhist) Church through their greed for

---

[1] *Mālu*, contraction of *mahalu* (Skt. P. *mahallaka*), literally means 'old'. For other references to Parākrama-Bāhu I as *Mahalu P. B.*, see *Pūjāvaliya*, extract, p. 29, *Nikāyasaṅgraha*, p. 22, and *Rājaratnākara*, p. 39.

[2] The direct speech is used in the original.

[3] See above, p. 72.

[4] See Vol. I, p. 181, note 3.

[5] *Mahapāṇan-vahanse*. See above, p. 15, note 4, and *Nikāyasaṅgraha* (Engl. transl., p. 20, note 4).

[6] *Nesvamin*, pres. participle of a caus. verb perhaps connected with Skt. *neṣ* 'to go', or more likely with *nyas* 'to throw or lay down'. I have not come across the word before.

[7] See above, p. 72.

[8] *Kaṇṭaka*, any troublesome, seditious person who is, as it were, a thorn to the state and an enemy of order and good government.—*M. W. Dict.*

[9] Or 'those who are longing for [such impure life]', *utkaṇṭhitayan*, l. 16.

gain[1] and through fear of having duties [to perform to Government as laymen], he graciously proclaimed that those who disrobed themselves without defiling the Church would not only have no [such] duties to perform, but also they would receive gold, cloth, iron, food, seed-paddy, cattle, and such other things. Further, [desiring that] there should be no obstacle in the way of the reverend and virtuous monks, His Majesty bestowed much wealth on their relatives[2], and made an abundant stream of gifts of the 'four requisites' to flow [for the benefit of the monks themselves]. Having thus promoted the welfare of the State and the Church, he was residing in **Pulastipura.**

[Lines 20-29.] Then in the fourth year of his reign he proceeded in royal splendour, surrounded by his fourfold army, to worship the relics at **Ruvanväli-**dāgaba [in Anurādhapura]. As soon as he came in sight of the dāgaba, he alighted from his chariot and walked on his royal feet to the **Ruvanmäli** terrace. Then, as if he were sprinkling sand on the terrace, he scattered pearls, and as if he were offering various flowers on a bed of sand, he offered flowers of gold and silver and the seven kinds of gems placed so as to fill up the whole space around. He shut off the [sun's] rays from the dāgaba by [raising over it] flags of priceless silken cloth; he heaped up heaps of camphor all round with no intervening space and made an offering of their light; and for a week he offered lamps lit with oil such as *taliyan*[3] oil, scented oil, &c. Likewise he made offerings of the incense of *kaḷuväl*[4] and sweet-scented flowers, and he purified the whole place from the four kinds of odours and offered forty *lacs* of ***masuran*** (coins). Ordering by beat of drum that no animals should be killed within a radius of seven *gav*[5] from the city [of Anurādhapura], he gave security to animals. He gave security also to the fish in the twelve great tanks, and

---

[1] *Pratyaya* (P. *paccayo*), 'the priestly requisites', here used in a more general sense.

[2] Obviously to stop the corrupt practice of monks supporting their relatives out of church property. Cf. the Jētavanārāma Sanskrit inscription, line 12 (Vol. I, No. 1).

[3] Probably *tala-tel* (Skt. *tila-taila*) sesamum or gingelly oil.

[4] An odoriferous creeper (Clough). The Sinhalese glossaries give *agil*, *agaru*, and *dummilla* as synonyms.

[5] A *gavuva* or Sinhalese mile is equivalent to about three and a half English miles according to Clough, but see Rhys Davids *On the Ancient Coins and Measures of Ceylon*, p. 15 f., and Barnett, *Antiquities of India*, p. 217 f. The *Nava-nāmāvaliya* (vv. 75-76) and other glossaries give the Sinhalese lineal measures as follows:—

7 *ukā* = 1 *viyaṭa* (Skt. *vrīhi*, P. *vīhi* + Skt. *aṣṭi*, P. *aṭṭhi*, paddy-grain).
7 *viyaṭa* = 1 *añgala* (Skt. *aṅgula*, finger breadth).
12 *añgal* = 1 *viyata* (Skt. *vitasti*, P. *vidatthi*, span).

bestowing on *Kāmbodīn*[1] gold and cloth and whatever other kind of wealth they wished, he commanded them not to catch birds and so gave security to birds.

[Having done these acts of mercy], whilst His Majesty was engaged in worshipping the relics with great joy, the people, seeing the Buddhist *devas* holding converse with him, uttered shouts of joy. He heard the shouts, and from the joyous enthusiasm towards the Buddha, which then arose in him, he remitted to the people of Laṅkā taxes for another year.

[Lines 30-35.] Thereafter he placed in charge **Lokē Arakmēnā**[2], who was there present, and offered him also [to the Ruvanväli-dāgaba]. Enjoining on him to restore the **Mirisaviṭi** and other vihāras, he gave him unlimited wealth and hundreds of *yālas*[3] of paddy, and thus beautified the city [of Anurādhapura], as it was in former times, like the city of gods.

Seeing the manner [in which these meritorious works were accomplished] and the fact that the protection of the Buddhist *devas* is likewise vouchsafed to those who with sincere heart have made contributions to these [works], other kings in time to come should also protect and maintain the Vihāras in this city, as well as those who dwell in them, the Church and the State.

[The Sanskrit stanza.] [The people] having seen the reverence[4] paid by [the king], 'the abode of prosperity', to the **Ratna-caitya** (Ruvanväli-dāgaba) in a manner beyond comparison by means of [an outlay of] wealth amounting to full forty *lacs*, offered in ecstatic raptures many a praise [to him] in his very presence. Then this[5] [king] **Niśśaṁka-Malla Śrī-Parākrānti-Bāhu**, pleased at heart, made Laṅkā taxless for a year.

---

2 *viyat* = 1 *riyana* (Skt. *aratni*, *ratni*, P. *ratana*, cubit).
4 *riyan*[6] = 1 *baṁba* (Skt. *vyāma*, P. *byāma*, fathom).
7 *riyan* = 1 *yaṭa* (Skt. *yaṣṭi*, P. *yaṭṭhi*, rod).
20 *yaṭa* or 35 *baṁba* } = 1 *isiṁbu*, *isubu* or *isba* (P. *usabha*).
80 *isiṁbu* = 1 *gavuva* (P. *gāvuta*).
4 *gav* = 1 *yoduna* (P. *yōjana*).

[1] See above, p. 74.

[2] *Arak-mē-nā* an official title equivalent to 'Conservator-in-chief', of Monuments. Cf. the phrase *Jutindara-kumārayanṭa arak-mē-nā-tanaturu dī* 'having bestowed the office of *arak-mē-nā* on prince Jutindara' (*Pūjāvaliya*, extract, p. 15).

[3] See Vol. I, p. 103, note 11.

[4] *Apacitim nirupama-racitām* may also be rendered 'the expenditure incomparably incurred by [the king], the abode of prosperity'.

[5] Dr. Keith taking *yam* as a relative suggests the following interpretation of this passage:—

[The people &c.] 'offered in ecstatic raptures many a praise [to him] in his very presence in that year for the space of which the king Niśśaṁka-Malla Śrī-Parākrānti-Bāhu, pleased at heart, made Laṅkā free from tax'.

[6] According to *M. W. Dict.*, 5 *aratnis* = 1 *vyāma*.

No. 14. POḶONNARUVA: HÄṬA-DĀ-GĒ PORTICO SLAB-INSCRIPTION

THE so-called Häṭa-dā-gē[1], 'the Shrine of Sixty Relics', is the ruined vihāra marked No. 4 in the inset (B) of the accompanying plan of the Poḷonnaruva ruins, which has been reproduced here from the plans given in the Archaeological Commissioner's *Annual Reports* to enable the reader to form an idea as to the situation of the inscriptions dealt with in the following pages and the character of the ruins in which they are found.

In 1885, whilst removing the débris from this shrine, Mr. S. M. Burrows discovered three inscriptions[2], two in the shrine itself and one in the porch. The last is the present record. It is boldly engraved in twenty-three lines on the smoothed and ruled surface formed of two slabs fitted together edgeways, one above the other, on the right side of the passage through the portico[3].

The letters cover a quadrangular area of 5 ft. 3 in. by 3 ft. 8 in. of this surface. They are on the average one inch to one and a half in size. Their type is practically the same as that of Niśśaṅka-Malla's other inscriptions.

---

[1] Regarding the group of ruins to which this shrine belongs and by way of introduction to a detailed and lucid description of each separate building, Mr. H. C. P. Bell writes as follows:—'The cluster of ruins excavated during the season of 1903 is situated directly east of Tópávẹwa tank, and north of the Citadel and the isolated Hindú temple hitherto miscalled "*Daḷadá Máligáwa*". This is the most varied and important group at Poḷonnaruva. It comprises in all mọre than a dozen ruined structures, exhibiting different types of architecture, in which Aryan, Dravidian, Kambodian, and may be, Burmese, forms are mingled with bizarre, but pleasing, effect . . . . All these shrines stand upon a raised quadrangle, banked in rubble masonry, from 6 ft. to 10 ft. in height on the south and west with a batter varying from 1 in 2 to 1 in 3. This elevated temenos was formerly entered through porches on the west and east above staircases' (*A. S. C. Annual Report*, 1903, pp. 6–7).

[2] See his official report in *Ceylon Sessional Paper* X, 1886. Since then Mr. H. C. P. Bell has discovered a fourth (*A. S. C. Annual Report*, 1903, p. 13, foot-note).

[3] Mr. Bell's description of this porch runs:—'A portico, placed in the middle of its front, projected 4 ft. 2 in. from the wall line outside and half as much at the back. The few steps at the entrance were flanked by two pillars and a pair of solid shapely vases in stone, 2 ft. 6 in. high, and in diameter (now displaced from their square pedestals), with lotus bosses on top. A clear passage, 8 ft. 6 in. in length by 5 ft. 6 in. broad, gave admittance between the lofty inner walls of the portico. The four pillars at entrance and exit aided its roofing' (*op. cit.*, p. 11).

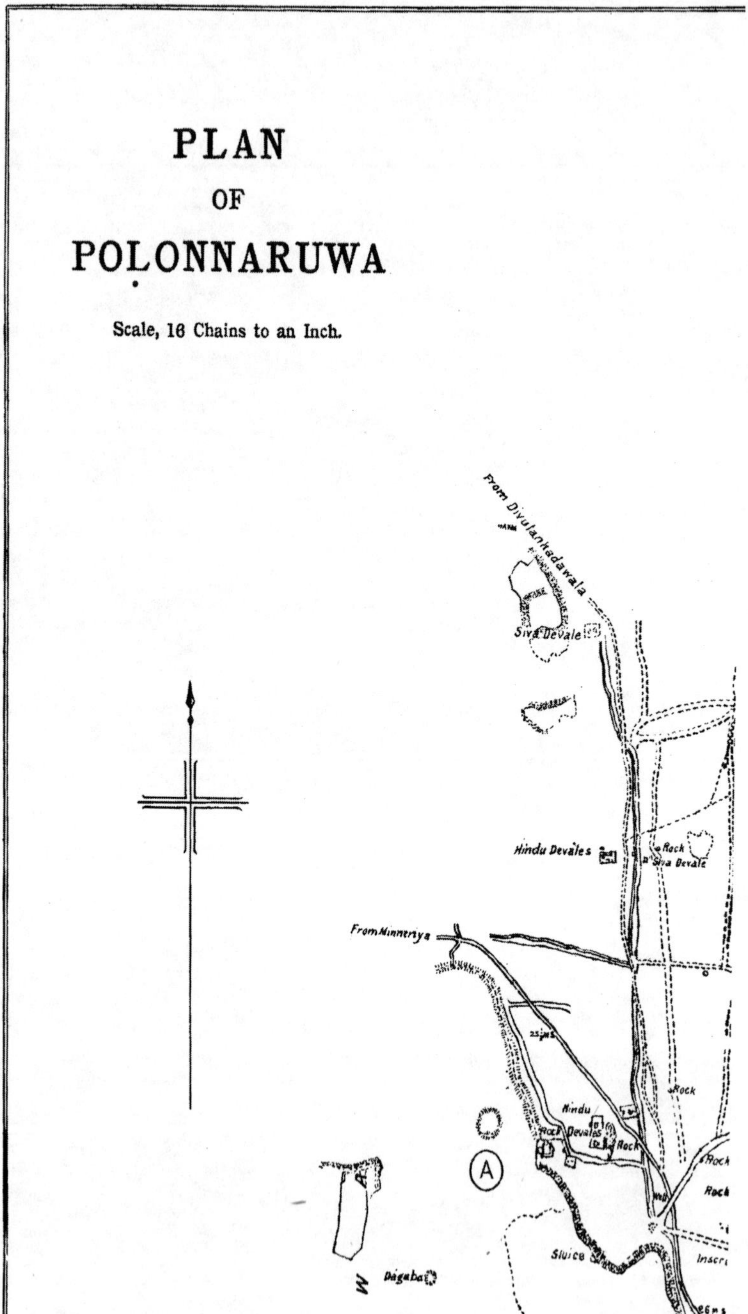
PLAN
OF
POLONNARUWA
Scale, 16 Chains to an Inch.
From Divulankadawala
Siva Devale
Hindu Devales
Rock
Siva Devale
From Minneriya
Rock
Hindu
Devales
Rock
Rock
A
Rock
Rock
Sluice
Dagaba
W

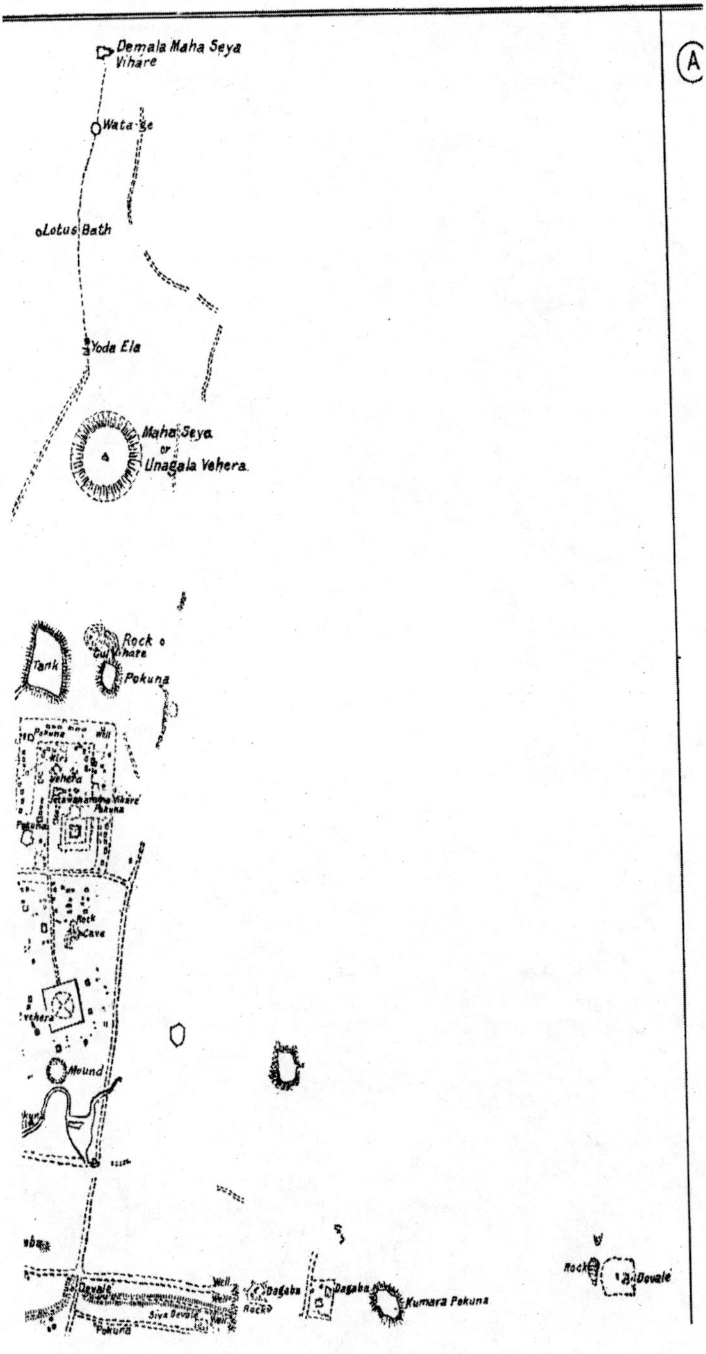
A
Demala Maha Seya
Vihare
Wata-ge
Lotus Bath
Yoda Ela
Maha Seya
or
Unagala Vehera
Rock
Gul Vihare
Tank
Pokuna
Jetawanarama Vihare
Pokuna
Rock
Cave
Vehera
Mound
Devale
Well
Siva Devale
Pokuna
Dagaba
Rock
Dagaba
Kumara Pokuna
Rock
Devale

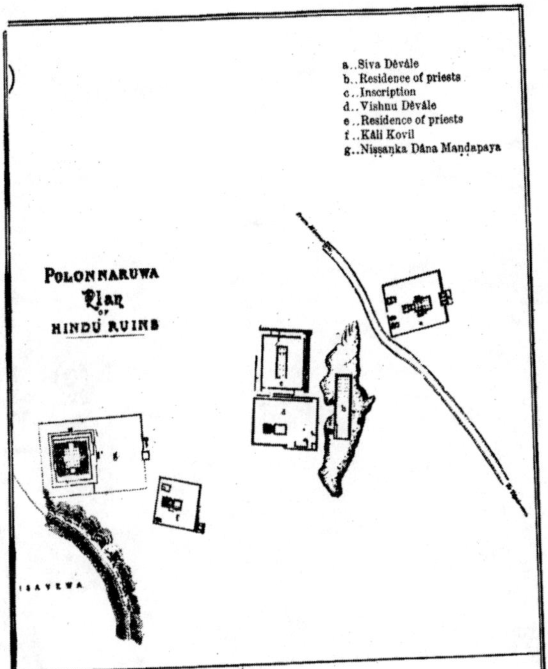
a..Siva Dêvâle
b..Residence of priests
c..Inscription
d..Vishnu Dêvâle
e..Residence of priests
f..Kâli Kovil
g..Nissanka Dâna Mandapaya
POLONNARUWA
Plan
OF
HINDU RUINS
ISAVEWA

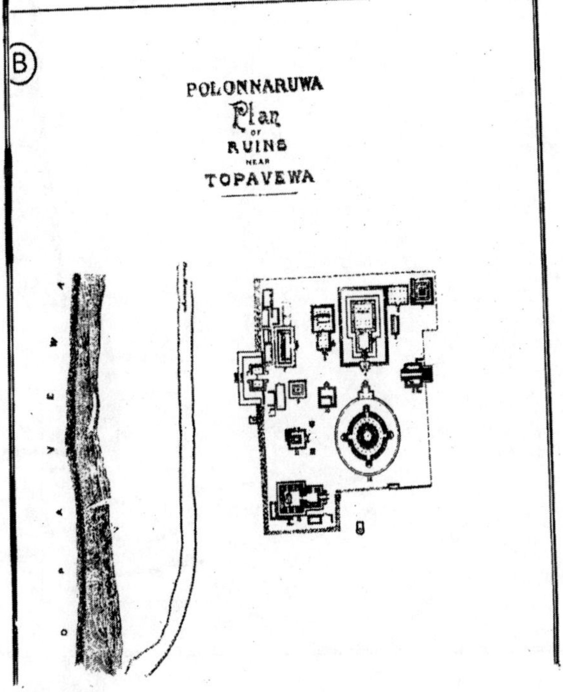
B
POLONNARUWA
Plan
OF
RUINS
NEAR
TOPAVEWA
TOPAVEWA

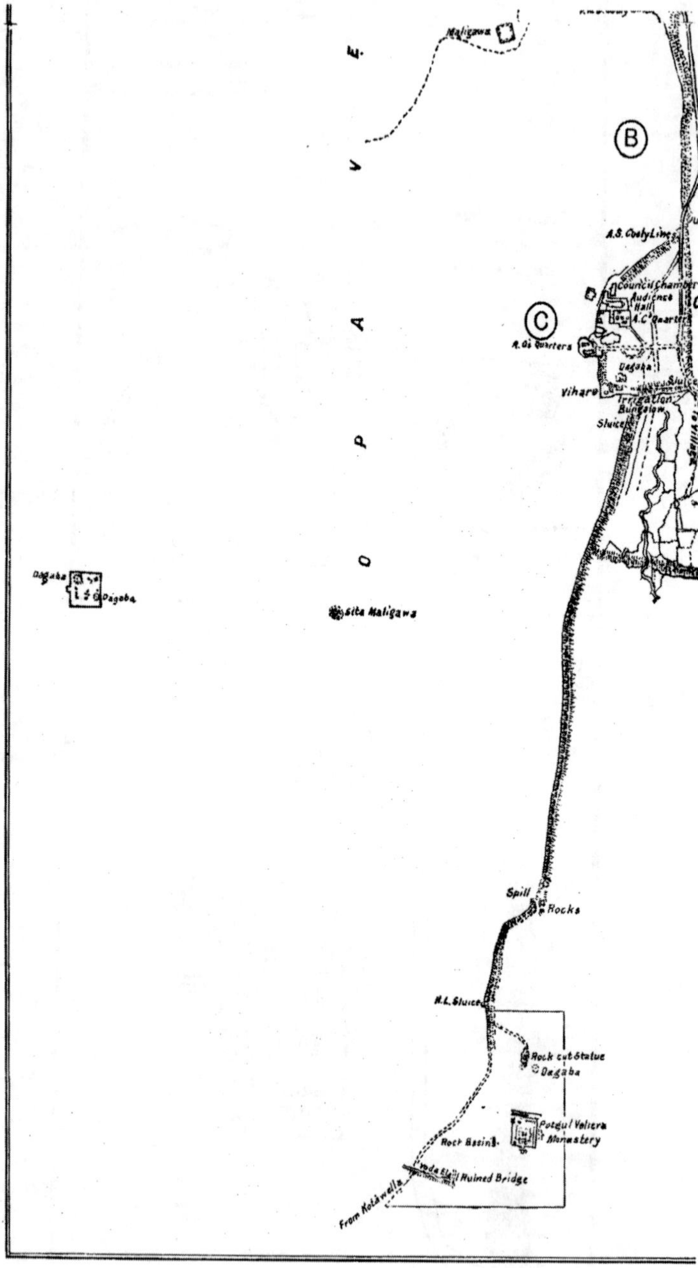
Maligawa
B
A.S. Cooly Lines
Council Chamber
Audience Hall
A.C. Quarters
C
A.G. Quarters
Dagaba
Vihare
Irrigation Bungalow
Sluice
Sluice
Dagaba
Dagaba
Site Maligawa
Spill
Rocks
R.L. Sluice
Rock cut Statue
Dagaba
Potgul Vehera Monastery
Rock Basin
Ruined Bridge
From Kotawella

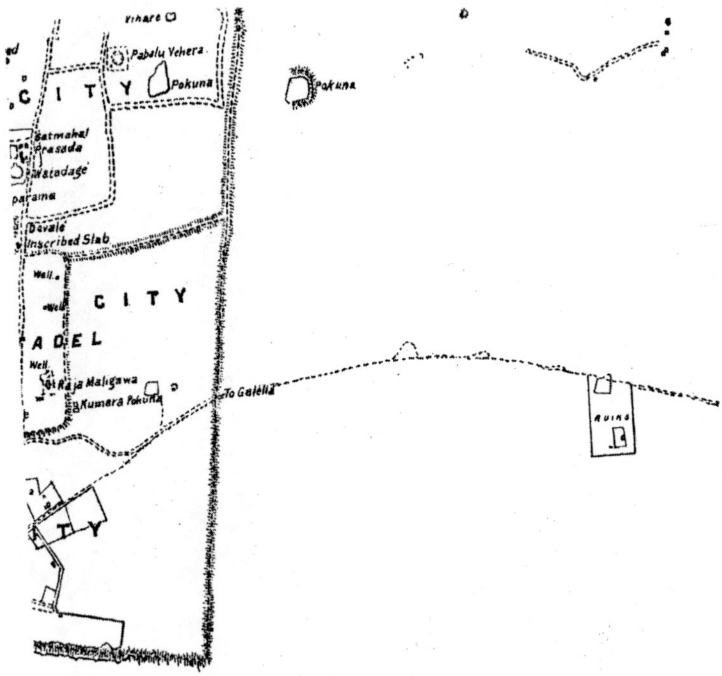

Vihare
Pabalu Vehera
Pokuna
CITY
Pokuna
Satmahal Prasada
Watadage
Devale
Inscribed Slab
Well
Well
CITY
Well
Raja Maligawa
Kumara Pokuna
To Galella
Ruins

9.. ... dapaya
10.. S...
11.. Shrine
12.. Watadage
13.. Thûpârâma

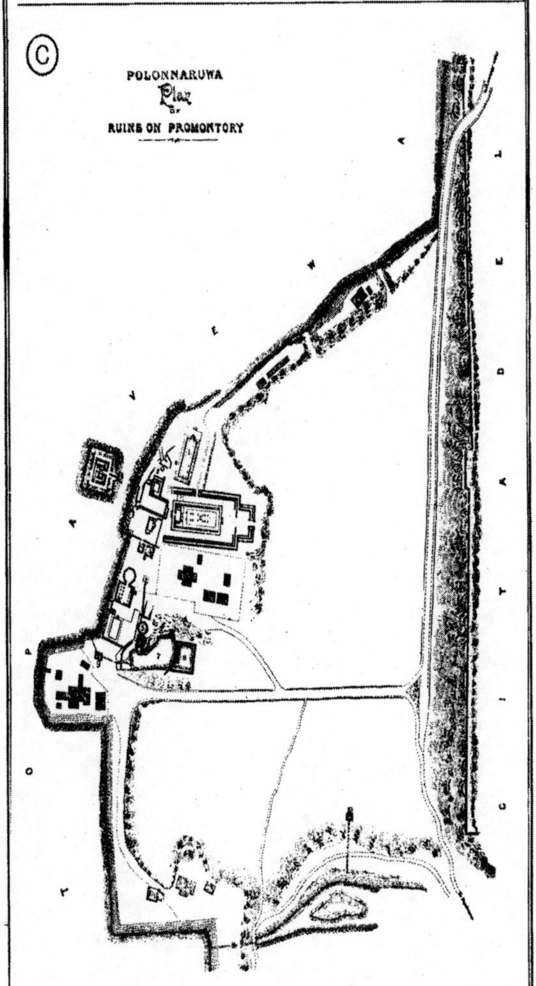

1.......... Council Chamber
2.......... Audience Hall
3.......... Pavilion
4.......... Mausoleum
5 & 6...... Baths
7 & 8...... Pokunu
9, 10 & 11.. Sluices
12.......... Vihare
13.......... Dagoba

So too are the **orthographical** peculiarities and the general style and phraseology of the **language**[1].

The inscription begins with a Sanskrit stanza in *triṣṭup śālinī* metre and ends in a Sinhalese quatrain, rather poor in composition. Both of these contain Niśśaṅka-Malla's appeal to future kings to protect and preserve the *Dharma.* The rest of the record mentions (*a*) king **Śrī Jaya-Gōpa** and queen **Pārvatī** as his parents, **Siṁhapura** in the Kaliṅga country as his birth-place, and the heir-apparent **Vīra-Bāhu** and princess **Sarvāṅga-Sundarī** as his children; (*b*) some of his administrative and charitable acts, such as the suppression of lawlessness, the remission of taxes for five years, the yearly distribution of gifts of value amongst the people, the granting of security of life to animals that live in forests and tanks, and his tours of inspection throughout the country; (*c*) his successful expedition to South India and the tribute he received from the Cōḷa and the Pāṇḍya kings; and finally (*d*) the building in stone of the **Vaṭa-geya** 'Rotunda', the **Niśśaṅka-latā-maṇḍapaya** 'Niśśaṅka flower-trail hall', and the **Niśśaṅka-daḷadā-geya** 'Niśśaṅka tooth-relic house', which Messrs. Burrows and Bell have identified with the ruins[2] marked Nos. 12, 9, and 4 of inset (B) in the accompanying plan.

---

[1] See above, p. 71.

[2] The following extracts from Mr. Bell's *Annual Report* for 1903 will enable the reader to form an idea of their structure:—

'There are three, and only three, ruined shrines built of stone within the quadrangle—the self-declared *Waṭa-dá-gé*, the *Niśśaṇ̥ka Latá Maṅḍapaya*, fixed by its architectural form and double record on slab and pillars, and the would be "Heṭa-dá-gé".

'This last fane can hardly, therefore, be other than the *Niśśaṇ̥ka Daḷadá-gé.* That the bombastic short-reigned monarch Niśśaṇka Malla must have laid claim to the original construction of several edifices erected by Parákrama Báhu the Great, dead less than a decade, is nearly certain (p. 13).

'Baldly the *Waṭa-dá-gé* may be thus outlined. Upon a circular *maḷuwa* or terrace, about 125 yards in circumference, stone-faced and paved throughout, with a rectangular bayed portico on the north, stood a structure, also circular and nearly 80 feet in diameter.

'The revetment of the basement displays moulded plinth, bowtell, and cornice, relieved by two broad vertical block bands, separated by a bold torus duplicated moulding. These dados bear figured panels in low relief—the lower, single lions *passant guardant;* the upper, *ganas* in every varying posture between pilasters with broad capitals.

'The surface of the coping forms a narrow gangway upon which rises a low screen of stone slabs, ornamented in flowered diaper pattern, joining up a ring of thirty-two short octagonal pillars with spreading capitals. Close behind this stone screen rose a high wall of brick. Within the brick wall, at the centre of a paved space, was built a small dágaba surrounded by two concentric rings of pillars similar to, but taller than, those on the basement gangway. The upper *maḷuwa* or platform of the

No date is given in the inscription. We know, however, from other sources that Kīrti-Niśśaṅka-Malla reigned from about September, 1187, to 1196 A.D. His record at the Ruvanväli-dāgaba (above, p. 73) tells us that he visited that shrine in his fourth regnal year (i.e. between September, 1191, and August, 1192), but in its glowing account of his doings no allusion whatsoever is made either to his tours of inspection in Ceylon or to his expedition to South India. From this we may infer that the present inscription, as well as others which expressly mention these two events of his reign, may have been set up after the fourth year, namely between 1192 and 1196 A.D.

In the preparation of the following text and translation I have utilized the two ink-estampages supplied to me by the Archaeological Commissioner (Mr. H. C. P. Bell). I have also consulted the transcript and translation which Mr. Burrows, who discovered the inscription, published for the first time in the *C.B.R.A.S. Journal* for 1887.

---

shrine, was reached from the four sides by granite staircases, of which the steps, balustrades, terminals, and moonstones are embellished with choice carved work.

'Facing the cardinal points opposite the doorways, were once four large granite Buddhas, seated upon moulded stone *áṣana*, besides twelve lesser images on pedestals of brick evenly ranged round the dágaba (p. 22).

'The *Niśśaṇka Latá Maṅdapaya* occupied an oblong space enclosed by a stone railing, which gives average measurements externally 34 ft. 3 in. east and west and 28 ft. 6 in. from north and south.

'There was but one entrance—on the east, between a pair of pillars planted immediately in front of the two posts at the middle of the parclose. Within the railing, leaving a paved way all round 4 ft. 10 in. wide, stood an open pavilion supported on eight sinuous columns, measuring (average) 20 ft. 9 in. lengthways east and west by 15 ft. 7 in. in breadth.

'*Niśśaṇka Latá Maṅdapaya*, or the "Niśśaṇka flower-trail hall", is, with the exception of the *Waṭa-dá-gé*, the choicest architectural monument left by king Niśśaṇka-Malla. The special purpose it served, which the slab inscription might have made clear if spared by Southern Indian invaders during their hold on Poḷonnaruwa, is problematical (pp. 18, 19).

'The *Niśśaṇka-daḷadá-gé* "the Niśśaṇka tooth-relic house" (if identical with the *Häṭa-dá-gé*) stood within a *peribolus*, or stone walled enclosure, covering an area about 40 yards north and south by 30 yards in breadth. There is but one means of entrance to the sacred precincts—through a portico in the south wall, from the open pathway uniting the West and East Porches of the quadrangular *maḷuwa*.

'The shrine measures 47 ft. each way, and is preceded by a *pronaos* or vestibule 30 ft. square' (pp. 11, 12).

TEXT.

1 ශ්‍රී: ධම්මසෙසායං සබ්බ[1]ලොකෙකමානඃශෙශ්‍රයො දෑයී සබ්බ[1]ද, රක්‍ෂණීයඃ [I]

2 භූපාලෙන්ද්‍ර, නාත්‍යවතෙ කිත්තිහෙතොර්භූයො භූයො **වීරනිශ්ශංකමල්ලඃ** [II]

3 ශ්‍රීමත් අනත් උතුම් ගුණගණෙන් ගිව් **ඔකාවස්**රජපරපුරෙහි වූ ආකාශවා

4 රි **කාලිඟ චක්‍රවර්ත්තීන්**වහන්සේ කුලෙනා **ශ්‍රී ජයගොප**රාජයන්වහන්සෙ නිසා **පාබ්බති** [2]

5 මහාදෙවීන්වහන්සෙ කුසෙන් **කලිඟරටැ සිංහපුරෙහි** ජාතවූ **සිරිසඟබො වීරරජ**

6 **නිශ්ශංක මල්ල අප්‍රති මල්ල කාලිඟ චක්‍රවර්ත්තීය්**වහන්සෙ රජ පිළිවෙළින් අභිෂෙක

7 ලදින් වොවූනු පැලැ(ඥැ ම)හරජනන් පත්වැ මුළු **ලක්දිව** නිෂ්කණ්ටක කොටැ පෙරැ

8 රජුන් නො බද අය ගෙනැ දුසළු කළ ලංකාවාසීන්ට පස් හවුරුද්දෙක අය හැරැ හ

9 දුරුදුපනා **පස්** තුලාභාරයක් (දී) නම් ගම් (වහල්) සරක් පමුණු පරපුරු රන් රුවන් වස්ත්‍රාභ

10 රණාදී බොහො වස්තු (දී සුවපතකරවා කැහිඅඩ හැම කලටමැ හැරැ වල් මඟ වැ තැනැ

11 ප්‍රාණීන්ට අභය දී තුන්රජය පැදැකුණු කොටැ සියලු ජලදුර්ග්ග ගිරිදුර්ග්ග වන

12 දුර්ග්ග පංකදුර්ග්ග හා ගම්තිම් බලා ලොකශාසන සමෘඬ[3] කොටැ යුඬාශායෙන් සියු

13 රඟ සෙනඟ පිරිවරා **දඹදිවු** වැඩැ වනවයුඬ සෙනායුඬ ඉල්වා නො ලදින් **චො**

14 **ඩ පාඬ්‍යාදි** රජදරුවන් වෙළඟෙනැ එවූ (රනැ) ඇ(ගිලි) හා රාජකන්‍යකාවන් හා පඩු

15 රු දැකැ ජයසතම්භ කරවා **ලක්දිවු** වැඩැ මෙලොවැ සතුරන් නැතිබැවින් පරලොසතු

16 රන් ජිනම්හයි සිතා (ස්වදෙශ) පරදෙශයෙහි බොහො සත්‍ර නංවා කප්රුක්සෙ සර

17 හා මහදන් පවත්වා දළදා පාත්‍ර ධාතූන්වහන්සෙට උරෙහි ද **වීරබාහු** මහපාණන්වහ

18 න්සෙ හා දූ **සර්ව්වා[4]ඟසුන්දරීන්**වහන්සේ හා පුදා දෙදෙනාවහන්සෙ ගළවනූ පිණිස(ැ ස)

19 නරන් දාගබක් කරවා ශිලාමය **චමංගය නිශ්ශංකලතාමණ්ඩපය නිශ්ශංක දළදාගෙ**

20 **ය** කරවා අනන්ත වස්තු පරිත්‍යාග කොටැ පූජාකරවා බොහො ගම්තිම් (වෙරවැස්සන්) පු

[1] 'සර්ව' වියයුතුයි [2] 'පාර්වති' වියයුතුයි

[3] 'සමෘඬ' වියයුතුයි [4] 'සර්වා' වියයුතුයි

21 දු වදුළ පරිද්දෙන් මනුවත රජදරුවනුදු රක්‍ෂා කරනු මැනවි දහම් නාමෙ මෙ මුළු ලො
22 සගන්නෙයැ[,] සිතා දෙලො සැපැත් අදරින් රක්නෙයැ[,] මනුවන රජවිරුත් මෙසෙ සගත්
23 නෙයැ[,] **කලිඟු ලකිඳු නිසකරජ** ගුණ (විඳුනෙයැ)

TRANSCRIPT.

1 Śrī: Dharmas so 'yaṁ sarbba[1]-lok-aika-mānyaś śreyo dāyī sarbba[1]-dā rakṣaṇīyaḥ [I]
2 bhūpālendrān yācate kīrtti-hetor-bbhūyo bhūyo **Vīra-Niśśaṁka-Mallaḥ** [II]
3 Śrīmat anat utum guṇa-gaṇen hivi **Okāvas**-raja-parapurehi vū ākāśa-cā-
4 -rī **Kāliṅga Cakravarttin**-vahansē kulen ā **Śrī-Jayagopa**-rājayan-vahanse nisā **Pārbbatī**[2]
5 mahā-devīn-vahanse kusen **Kaliṅga**-raṭā **Siṁha-purehi** jāta-vū **Siri-Saṅgabo Vīra-rāja**
6 **Niśśaṁka-Malla Aprati-Malla Kāliṅga Cakravarttīn**-vahanse raja piḷiveḷin abhiṣeka
7 ladin voṭunu pälä(ñdä ma)haraja-tan pat-vä muḷu **Lakdiva** niṣkaṇṭaka koṭä perä
8 rajun no bada aya genä dustha kaḷa Laṁkāvāsīnṭa pas havuruddeka aya härä ha-
9 -vurudu-patā pas tulābhārayak (dī) nam gam (vahal) sarak pamuṇu parapuru ran ruvan vastr-ābha-
10 -raṇ-ādī boho vastu dī suvapat-karavā käti-aḍa häma kalaṭa-mä härä val maha vā tänä
11 prāṇīnṭa abhaya dī tun-rajaya pädākuṇu koṭä siyalu jala-durgga giri-durgga vana-
12 durgga paṁka-durgga hā gam-bim balā loka-śāsana samraddha[3] koṭä yuddh-ā-
-śāyen siyu-
13 -raṅga senaṅga pirivarā **Dambadivu** väḍä dvandva-yuddha senā-yuddha ilvā no ladin Co-
14 -ḍa **Pāṇḍy-ādi** raja-daruvan veḷagenä evū (ranä) ä(ṅgüi) hā rāja-kanya-
-kāvan hā paṇḍu-

---

[1] Read *sarva*. [2] Read *Pārvatī*. [3] Read *samṛddha*.

Poḷonnaruva : Häṭa-dā-gē Portico Slab-Inscription.

Scale about 1⅛ inches to 1 foot.

From an ink-impression supplied by the Archaeological Commissioner, Ceylon.

15 -ru däkä jaya-stambha karavā **Lakdivu** väḍä melovä saturan näti-bävin para-lo-satu-

16 -ran jinamhayi sitā (svadeśa) paradeśayehi boho satra naṁvā kap-ruk-se sara-

17 -hā mahadan pavatvā daḷadā pātra dhātun-vahanseṭa urehi dā **Vīra-Bāhu** mahapāṇan-vaha-

18 -nse hā dū **Sarbbāñga**[1]**-sundarīn**-vahansē hā pudā de-denā-vahanse gaḷavanu piṇis(ä gha-)

19 -na-ran dāgabak karavā śilāmaya **Vaṭageya Niśśaṁka-latā-maṇḍapaya Niśśaṁka-daḷadāge-**

20 **-ya** karavā ananta vastu parityāga koṭä pūjākaravā boho gam-bim (vera-vässan) pu-

21 -dā vadāḷa paridden matuvana raja-daruvanudu rakṣā karanu mānavi daham name me muḷu lo

22 saganneyä[,] sitā delo säpät adarin rakneyä[,] matuvana rajavirun mese sagan-

23 -neyä[,] **Kaliñgu-Lakindu-Nisaka**-raja guṇa (vindaneyä)

TRANSLATION.

[Lines 1–2.] Hail! This *Dharma*, which gives happiness and which alone deserves to be honoured in[2] the whole world, should always be preserved. **Vīra-Niśśaṁka-Malla** makes this appeal over and over again to the Rulers of the earth in the name of [their] good fame.

[Lines 3–6.] In **Siṁhapura** in the country of **Kaliṅga** His Majesty **Siri-Saṅgabo Vīra-rāja Niśśaṁka-Malla Aprati-Malla Kāliṅga-Cakravarttī** was born of the womb of the great queen **Pārvatī** unto the king **Śrī-Jayagopa,** descended from the family of **Kāliṅga-Cakravarttin** who had the power of travelling through the air[3] and who belonged to the royal line of the Okkāka dynasty, exalted by [the possession of] an infinite assemblage of auspicious and sublime qualities.

[Lines 6–12.] [His Majesty] having in the due order of royal succession been anointed and crowned as the supreme king, freed the whole Island of Laṅkā from the thorns of lawlessness, and remitted taxes for five years for the benefit of the people of Laṅkā who had been distressed by the unjust exactions

---

[1] Read *Sarvāñga-*.

[2] Or 'by'.

[3] *Ākāśa-cārī.* This may be an honorific epithet (*biruda*) as suggested by Mr. Burrows.

of former kings. [Moreover] by giving [them] five *tulābhāras*[1] every year, and bestowing [on them] titles, lands, serfs, cattle, heritable lands, gold and gems, clothes and ornaments, and such [other kinds of] wealth in abundance, he made them prosperous. He abolished for all time taxes on *chena* cultivation[2] and gave security to animals that live in forests and large tanks[3]. He made tours throughout the three kingdoms[4], inspecting all lands and villages including the mountain and the forest fastnesses, as well as those places difficult of access owing to water and marshes[5]. [In this way] he promoted the welfare of the State and the Church.

[Lines 12–15.] Being desirous of martial contests, he proceeded to India[6] attended by his fourfold army and sought single combats or army contests. Finding none, and seeing [however] 'the golden fingers'[7], the royal maidens, and other tribute that were sent by the suppliant kings of **Coḍa, Pāṇḍi** and other countries, he raised columns of victory and returned to the Island of Laṅkā.

[Lines 15–23.] Then reflecting 'as there are no enemies in this world, we will conquer the enemies in the next', he established in his own country and in foreign lands many almshouses, and furnishing them like 'wish-conferring trees', he maintained almsgiving in abundance. To the venerated 'Tooth-relic' and the 'Bowl-relic' he offered his own son, the sub-king **Vīra-Bāhu** and his daughter **Sarvāṅga Sundarī**; and for the purpose of redeeming them he caused a dāgaba of solid gold to be made. He built of stone the **Vaṭageya** (the Rotunda), the **Niśśaṁka-latā-maṇḍapaya**, and the **Niśśaṁka Tooth-relic house**, and expended countless wealth in making offerings. He dedicated also many villages, lands, and serfs. In this wise may future kings also protect [the Dharma] It is indeed the Dharma that protects[8] this whole world. So thinking, earnestly secure the welfare of both the worlds. Let it be thus understood by future kings that these are the virtuous sentiments of king **Kaliṅgu-Lakindu-Nisaka**[9].

---

[1] See above, p. 73.

[2] *Käti-aḍa*. See above, p. 72.

[3] See also the foregoing inscription, lines 26–28.

[4] Namely Ruhuṇu, Māyā and Pihiṭi.

[5] For a repetition of this, see the Daṁbulla inscription, lines 12–13 (Vol. I, No. 9).

[6] *Daṁbadiva* (Skt. *Jambudvīpa*).

[7] I do not know what this expression really means. It occurs in the Galpota record (*A. I. C.*, No. 148) but Prof. Müller gives no translation of it. Mr. Burrows renders it by 'gold rings'.

[8] *Saganneyā*. This is a word new to me. I am inclined to connect it with Skt. *saṁ* + √*grah*.

[9] *Kāliṅga-Laṅkendra-Niśśaṁka*.

No. 15. POḶONNARUVA: HÄṬA-DĀ-GĒ VESTIBULE WALL-INSCRIPTION

THE front wall of the vestibule or *pro-naos* of the so-called Häṭa-dā-gē[1] which is probably identical with the Niśśaṅka-daḷadāgē mentioned in the foregoing inscription[2] was composed of a series of 'dressed slabs of all sizes fitted together dry, but so closely as to defy the inroads of vegetation. The plainness of this wall face is relieved most artistically by a double border, vertical as well as horizontal, of faintly incised carving—a band of *haṁsas* (swans) with another of leafy vignette'[3].

The inscription occupied a quadrangular area (about 3 ft. 4 in. by 6 ft.) of the outside face of this wall, on the right of the entrance. The accompanying facsimile (Plate 16) shows a portion of the ornamental border at the base and on the right side. The **akṣaras** which vary from one to one and a half inches in size are engraved in seventeen horizontal lines along ruled spacing of the smooth surface. The form of script and the peculiarities of **orthography** and **style** of composition of the record are practically the same as those of the foregoing slab.

The **contents**, however, give us some additional information regarding **Kirti-Niśśaṅka-Malla** (1187–1196 A.D.). He is here styled **Siṁhapureśvara Laṁkeśvara Kāliṅga-Cakravarti**, of which the first two *birudas* are not included in those mentioned on p. 124 of Vol. I. We are also told that he began his tours of inspection in the second year of his reign, and that he made journeys throughout Ceylon, including places difficult of approach, such as **Samanoḷa**[4] (Adam's Peak), in the course of which he corrected various administrative irregularities. He, moreover, fixed the distance of a *gavu*[5], and calling it a *Nissaṅka-gavu* he set up inscribed milestones in their proper places. His inscription at the Ruvanväli-dāgaba[6] which was incised in or after 1191 A.D. makes no mention of his tours to distant parts of the Island. It is, therefore,

[1] Ruin No. 4 in inset B of the plan of the Poḷonnaruva ruins facing p. 84, above.

[2] See above, p. 85.

[3] See *A. S. C. Annual Report*, 1903, p. 12.

[4] P. *Samanta-kūṭa*. It was on this sacred mountain that Vēdēha Thēra, the reputed author of the *Sidatsaṅgarā* and the *Rasavāhinī*, wrote in the thirteenth century A.D. a lyric poem in Pāli entitled *Samanta-kūṭa-vaṇṇanā*. See my *Catalogue of Sinhalese MSS. in the British Museum*, preface, p. xviii.

[5] See above, p. 82, note 6.

[6] Above, No. 13.

very probable that some, at least, of his journeys may have been undertaken after that date. And consequently the palaces and pavilions enumerated in lines 4 to 9 may have been built at a still later period, possibly after his return, as the context seems to indicate.

Reference is made in line 4 to a *māḷigāva* (palace) built by a former king in seven years and seven months. This was most likely one of Parākrama-Bāhu I's. If we may read between the lines, Niśśaṅka-Malla was evidently struck with the architectural beauty of the mansion, but was too proud to utilize it. So he built another of seven storeys (*sat-vana-māl-māḷigāva*), probably a poor imitation of it, in forty-five days. I am inclined to identify the former with the famous ruin called *sat-mahal-prāsādaya* [1] 'seven-storeyed palace'.

As regards the seven members of king Niśśaṅka-Malla's family, named in lines 12–15 as those who took part in the annual *tulābhāra* ceremony, we know from other records of his that **Kāliṅga-Subhadrā** was his chief queen, **Kalyāṇa** was his sub-queen, the **Mahapā** was his son **Vīra-Bāhu, Sarvāṅga-Sundarī** was his daughter, the minister **Vikrama-Bāhu** was one of his younger brothers, but nothing is known of Queen **Candrā** and Her Highness **Pārvatī** [2].

Mr. S. M. Burrows, who discovered this inscription in 1885, published a transcript and a translation of it in the *C.B.R.A.S. Journal* for 1887. These and the two 'squeezes' supplied by the Archaeological Commissioner have been utilized in the preparation of the following edition of the text and translation.

---

[1] See inset B of the plan of Poḷonnaruva ruins facing p. 84, above. The following extract from Mr. Bell's *Annual Report* for 1903, pp. 14–15, will give the reader an idea of the style of this remarkable building:—

'The present outlines of this brick-built structure show it as a square tower of six complete storeys and broken portions of a seventh, rising from a low basement, which measures 39 ft. 2 in. each way at ground level. Whilst each storey diminishes in lateral dimensions, the respective altitude follows a different system, whereby the elevation is made to vary at every third stage.

'The tower is still 53 ft. in height, and, if finished by some sort of pinnacle, may well have reached 60 ft. in all.

'The "*Sat-mahal Prásádaya*" is the sole edifice of its kind so far discovered in Ceylon . . . . . Fergusson considered it "one of the most perfect representations existing of the seven-storeyed temples of Assyria—a lineal descendant of the Birs Nimroud".'

[2] See Vol. I, p. 124.

TEXT.

1 ශ්‍රී සිංහවික්‍රම ඇති ශ්‍රී **සිංහපුරෙශ්වර ලංකෙශ්වර කාලිග චක්‍රවර්ත්තීන්වහන්සෙ** රජසිරි පැමිණි දෙවන

2 හවුරුදු පටන් ලංකාව සිසාරා ගම් නියම්ගම් රාජධානි ආදිවූ නො එක් ප්‍රසිද්ධ ස්ථානද ජලදුර්ග (පංකදුර්ග වනදුර්ග)

3 **සමනොල** ආදිවූ ගිරිදුර්ගද අනඹුලු පකාක්සෙ (බලා වදාරා) ගැනියක් නවරත්න පිරී කරඬුවක් ගෙනැයෙනමුත් තෙලෙ

4 කුමක්(දැයි) නො කියන නියායෙන් රාජ්‍යය නිෂ්කණ්ටක කොටැ සෙමෙහි තබා පූබ්බෙ[1] රාජධානි සත් හවුරුදු ස(ත්) මසෙකින් නැංවූ මාළිගා

5 බලා; වදාරා අපසෙවූ රජකෙනකුන් නැංවූ මාළිගාවෙ (ගිඤු වෙදයි) පන්සාලිස් දවසක් ඇතුළතැ සත්(වන)මාල්මාළි(ගා)

6 (වකුඩු නංවා පොර බලන පරිද්දෙන් අනර්ඝ මඩපයකුඩු නංවා ඇත්) පොර බලා (තර දූකැ) හාර ශාලාව ඇතුළුවූ තුන් (ආසනය)

7 (**කුඩු**) නංවා **මෙනි වාසල් පවුරු** ආදිවූ තැන්ද කරවා (සිලා[2]මය කොටැ තුන්) මඩපය **බොහො** කලක් පවත්නා නියායෙ

8 න් (කරවා **කාලිගොද්‍යානයද වෙළුවනයක්**සෙ) කරවා **කාලිග** වෙහි **කර්ණාට ගුර්ජර** ආදිවූ නො එක් දෙශයෙන් කිසොවරුන්

9 ගෙන්වා **අන්තඃපුරයෙහි** වෙනැ වෙනැමැ නො එක්ලෙස (මාළිගාද නංවා) බොහො සම්පත්ද දී වදාරා තුන්රජයෙහි නො එක් තැන්

10 හි මාළි(ගා)ද සත්‍රද නංවා අනන්ත යාචකයන්ට රන් රුවන් රිදී (වළඳී න .. .. ති) බොහො ධන දී වදාරා එ ඒ තෙනැ උයන්ද

11 ශිලාමය කොටැ **වීරසිංහාසනද** කරවා (නානාධිකරණයෙහි අන්‍යාය) නිවා රණය කොටැ මෙසේ තුන්රජය නොයෙක් පරිද්දෙන් බ

12 ලා (වදාරන කලැ ගො)වුද නියත කොටැ (නිශ්ශංකගො)වුයයි (මැම් ගිඤුවා) අකුරු කොටවා **කාලිග සුභද්‍රා** කිසවුන්වහන්සේ

13 හා **කල්‍යාණි** මහදෙවීන්වහන්සේ හා (**මහපා**)**ණන්**වහන්සේ හා **වික්‍රම**

14 **බාහු** ඈපාණන්වහන්සේ හා **චන්ද්‍රා**(කිසවුන්)වහන්සේ හා **පාබ්බතීන්**[3]වහන්සේ හා **සබ්බාග**[4] **සුන්දරීන්**වහන්සේ ඇතු

15 ළුවූ අටදෙනාවහන්සේ තුලාභාර නැඟී හවුරුදු පතා මෙලෙසැ දී පෙර නො බද අය ගෙනැ දුසස් කළ ලංකාවාසීන්ට රන් රුව

16 න් රිදී වළන් ආදිවූ බොහො සම්පත්ද දී වදාරා (දුබ්බී)විකා හෙයි(න් ව)ල් කොටා ගත් කෙත් අයද මහ වැ තැනින් .. .. ..

17 පිසඹුරුවතුද හැම කලටමැ නො ගන්නා .. ..

---

[1] 'පූර්වේ' වියයුතුයි

[2] 'ශිලාමය' වියයුතුයි

[3] 'පාර්වතීන්' වියයුතුයි

[4] 'සර්වාංග' වියයුතුයි

TRANSCRIPT.

1 Śrī siṁha-vikrama äti śrī **Siṁha-pureśvara Laṁkeśvara Kāliṅga Cakravarttīn-vahanse** raja-siri pämiṇi devana

2 havurudu paṭan Laṁkāva sisārā gam niyam-gam rājadhāni ādivū no ek prasiddha sthāna-da jala-durgga (paṁka-durgga vana-durgga)

3 **Samanoḷa** ādivū giri-durgga-da ataṁbulu pakak-se (balā vadārā) gāniyak nava-ratna pirī karaṇḍuvak genäyena-mut tele

4 kumak-(dāyi) no kiyana niyāyen rājyaya niṣkaṇṭaka koṭā semehi tabā pūrbbe [1] rājadhāni sat havurudu sa(t) masekin näṁvū māḷigā

5 balā vadārā apasevū raja-kenakun näṁvū māḷigāve (hindu vedayi) pansālis davasak ätuḷatā sat(vana)-māl-māḷi(gā-)

6 (-vakudu [2] naṁvā pora [3] balana paridden anargha maṇḍapayakudu naṁvā ät-) pora balā (tara däkä) hāra śālāva ätuḷuvū tun (āsanaya-)

7 (-kudu) naṁvā mehi vāsal pavuru ādivū tän-da karavā (silāmaya [4] koṭā tun) maṇḍapaya boho kalak pavatnā niyāye-

8 -n (karavā **Kāliṅgodyānaya**-da **Veḷuvanayak**-se) karavā **Kāliṅga Veṅgi Karṇṇāṭa Gurjjara** ādivū no ek deśayen bisovarun

9 genvā antaḥ-purayehi venä venä-mä no ek-lesa (māḷigā-da naṁvā) boho sampat-da dī vadārā tun-rajayehi no ek tän-

10 -hi māḷi(gā-)da satra-da naṁvā ananta yācakayanṭa ran ruvan ridī (vaḷan dī na .. .. ti) boho dhana dī vadārā e ē tenä uyan-da

11 śilāmaya koṭā **Vīrasiṁhāsana**-da karavā (nānā-dhikaraṇayehi anyāya) nivā- -raṇaya koṭā mesē tun-rajaya noyek paridden ba-

12 -lā (vadārana kalä go)vu-da niyata koṭā (Niśśaṁka-go)vu-yayi (ṭām hinduvā) akuru koṭavā **Kāliṅga Subhadrā** bisavun-vahansē

13 hā **Kalyāṇa** maha-devīn-vahansē hā (**Maha-pā-**)**ṇan**-vahansē hā **Vikrama-**

14 **Bāhu** āpāṇan-vahansē hā **Candrā**-(bisavun-)vahansē hā **Pārbbatīn** [5]-vahansē hā **Sārbbāṅga** [6] **Sundarīn**-vahansē ätu-

15 -ḷuvū aṭa-denā-vahansē tulā-bhāra näṅgī havurudu patā melesä dī pera no bada aya genä dustha kaḷa Laṁkāvāsīnṭa ran ruva-

16 -n ridī vaḷan ādivū boho sampat-da dī vadārā (dub-jī)vikā **heyi(n va)l koṭā gat** ket aya-da maha vā tänin .. .. ..

17 pisaṁburu-vatu-da häma kalaṭa-mä no gannā .. ..

---

[1] Read *pūrve*.

[2] The two estampages before me being defective just here, the words within round brackets in line 6 are copied from Mr. Burrows' transcript in *C.B.R.A.S. Journal* for 1887, p. 60.

[3] Mr. Bell reads *satara balana pā(sāda)ya anarghaṭayakudu naṁvā*. See *A. S. C. Annual Report*, 1903, p. 16.

[4] Read *śilāmaya* as in line 11.

[5] Read *Pārvatīn*.

[6] Read *Sarvāṅga*.

Poḷonnaruva: Häṭa-dā-gē Vestibule Wall-Inscription.

Scale about 1¼ inches to 1 foot.

From an ink-impression supplied by the Archaeological Commissioner, Ceylon.

TRANSLATION.

[Lines 1–4.] Hail! His Illustrious Majesty **Siṁhapureśvara Laṅkeśvara Kāliṅga-Cakravartī**, from the second year of his accession to the sovereignty, toured round Laṅkā, thoroughly inspecting, like a *nelli* fruit on the palm [of his hand], villages, market towns, capital towns, and many other localities of note, as well as those places difficult of access either on account of water, marshes, forests or mountains such as **Samanoḷa** (Adam's Peak). And he freed the kingdom from the thorns of lawlessness so thoroughly, that a woman might even carry a casket filled with the nine [kinds of] gems and not be asked, 'What is it?' Thus did he keep [Laṅkā] in a peaceful state[1].

[Lines 4–9.] Thereafter having beheld a palace which had been erected in the capital formerly in seven years and seven months, and thinking 'it befits us to sit only in a palace built by a king like ourselves', he erected within forty-five days a palace of seven storeys. He built also a magnificent *maṇḍapa* (pavilion) from which to watch fights, and he watched the elephant-fights (from it). Including the strong .... hall[2], he erected three thrones and furnished them with gates, ramparts, &c. He built of stone three *maṇḍapas* (pavilions) so that they might last a long time, and formed the **Kāliṅga Park** like another **Veḷuvana**[3]. He got him queens from various countries, such as **Kāliṅga, Veṅgi, Karṇāṭa, Gurjara**, &c., and building for them separate palaces of various kinds within the premises of the harem gave them much wealth.

[Lines 9–17.] In the three kingdoms he erected palaces and almshouses at several places; to numberless beggars he gave much treasure, such as gold, gems, silver vessels[4], &c., and at different places he formed parks and built of stone thrones (naming them) **Vīrasiṁhāsana.** He suppressed various administrative injustices. In the course of thus inspecting the three kingdoms in various ways he fixed [the distance of] a **gavu** and calling it a **Niśśaṅka-gavu,** he caused inscribed mile-posts to be set up [each in its place]. Thereafter His Majesty together with Queen **Kāliṅga Subhadrā**, the sub-queen **Kalyāṇa,**

---

[1] For a repetition of all this, see the Daṁbulla inscription, lines 12–14 (Vol. I, No. 9).

[2] *Tara dākä hāra śālāva* (line 6). The reading of the first three words is doubtful. Mr. Burrows' transcript gives *tarada kāhāra sālāva* which he renders 'banqueting hall'.

[3] *Vēḷuvanārāma* 'bamboo-grove monastery' is the name of the monastery presented by king Bimbisāra to Gotama Buddha.

[4] Cf. e kala kätiva geṇa giya *ran-vaḷan-da* piḷī sambaḍam ādivū sesu vastuva-da (*Thūpavaṁsa*, p. 144).

the sub-king [**Vīra-Bāhu**], the minister **Vikrama-Bāhu**, Queen **Candrā**, and Their Highnesses **Pārvatī** and **Sarvāṅga-Sundarī**—eight persons in all, ascended the scale-pan and in this manner made annual donations [of their weight of wealth]. To the inhabitants of Laṅkā who were impoverished by the inordinate taxes collected in former times, he gave gold, gems, silver vessels, and such other wealth in abundance. He abolished for all time the tax on lands cultivated by clearing the jungle[1] as this is a hard means of livelihood, as well as the *pisamburu-vatu*[2] . . . . from great tanks.

No. 16. POḶONNARUVA: HĀṬA-DĀ-GĒ INSIDE WALL-INSCRIPTION

THIS inscription was also brought to light in 1885 by Mr. S. M. Burrows, who published an incomplete transcript and translation in the *C.B.R.A.S. Journal* for 1887. Like the foregoing one, it is engraved on a series of slabs which were once built into the wall inside the shrine. The writing covers a quadrangular area, 4 ft. 1 in. by 1 ft. 6 in. of the smooth surface and consists of eight lines running along ruled spacing.

The **akṣaras** which vary from one inch to one and a half in size are precisely the same in type as those of other inscriptions of Niśśaṅka-Malla[3].

In respect of **orthography** or the **style** of composition, there is hardly anything that calls for notice. The record is a tactfully worded exhortation to Buddhist monks to exercise care in the selection of persons for admission to the priesthood and to desist from doing things contrary to the teachings of the Buddha. There is no doubt that the Buddhist monks of the time of Niśśaṅka-Malla were not all perfect, and he, like other kings before him, had occasion to assert his right as 'Defender of the Church' to put down corrupt practices.

TEXT.

1 ශ්‍රී සිරිසඟබො වීරරජ නිශංකමලල කාලිඟ පරක්‍රමබාහු චක්‍ර[වර්තීස්වහන්සේ]

2 සසුන් පස්වාදහස් පවත්නා සඳහා ශඞා[4] බුඩි පූඞ්ඞ[5]ගමවැ සුපිළි[පන් සංඝයා වහන්]

---

[1] See above, p. 72.
[2] See above, p. 69.
[3] See the accompanying Plate 17.
[4] 'ශ්‍රද්ධා' වියයුතුයි
[5] 'පූර්වා' වියයුතුයි

Poḷonnaruva: Häṭa-dā-gē Inside Wall-Inscription.

Scale about 2¼ inches to 1 foot.

From an ink-impression supplied by the Archaeological Commissioner, Ceylon.

3 සේ ධර්‍මවිනයවූ පරිද්දෙන් පුරන පිළිවෙත් ඇතද ශාසන රක්‍ෂාව ලක්දිවැ ර
4 ජුන් අයැති හෙයින් ශාසන රක්‍ෂාවට සුදුසු අවවාද මෙසෙ වදාරන සෙයෙකි අ(ත)
5 .. (දුන්) ආචාර්‍ය්‍ය උපාධ්‍යායවැ සිටිනා වහන්සේවරුන්දැ ශඨ කූට කෛරාටි
6 [ක] .. .. නුවණ නැති පාප සත්වයන්[1] නො විචාරා මහණ නො කටයුතු බුදුන් වදාළ ආ
7 .. .. තු (නො) මනාවක් නො කටයුතු ගුණ නැ(තිවැ) ගත් මහණවෙස් (තැවු) .. ..
8 .. .. යැ දුශ්ශීලවැ (පරා) පිළිබද් අහර වළඳනු නරකයෙහි .. ..

TRANSCRIPT.

1 Śrī **Siri-Saṅgabo Vīra-rāja Niśśaṁka-Malla Kāliṅga Parākrama-Bāhu Cakra**[**varttīn**-vahansē]
2 **sasun** pasvā-dahas pavatnā saṅdahā śarddhā[2] buddhi pūrbbaṅgama-vä[3] supiḷi[pan saṁghayā-vahan-]
3 -sē dharmma-vinaya-vū paridden purana piḷivet äta-da śāsana rakṣāva Lakdivä ra-
4 -jun ayäti heyin śāsana rakṣāvaṭa sudusu avavāda mese vadārana seyeki a(ta)
5 .. (dun) ācāryya upādhyāya-vä siṭinā vahansē-varun-dä śaṭha kūṭa kairāṭi
6 [ka] .. .. nuvaṇa näti pāpa satvayan[4] no vicārā mahaṇa no kaṭayutu Budun vadāḷa ā
7 .. .. tu (no) manāvak no kaṭayutu guṇa nä(ti-vä) gat mahaṇa-ves (tävu) .. ..
8 .. .. yä duśśīlavä (parā) piḷibad ahara vaḷandanu narakayehi .. ..

TRANSLATION.

Hail! His Majesty **Siri-Saṅgabo Vīra-rāja Niśśaṁka-Malla Kāliṅga Parākrama-Bāhu Cakravarttī**, with his mind filled with faith directed to the preservation of the religion for five thousand [years], inasmuch as the protection of the religion belongs to the kings of Ceylon, even though the pious members of the community perform their duties in accordance with the *Dharma* and the rules of discipline, was pleased to make the following exhortations conducive to

---

[1] 'සත්ත්වයන්' වියයුතුයි

[2] Read *śraddhā.*

[3] Read *pūrvāṅgama-vä.*

[4] Read *sattvayan.*

the preservation of the religion:—The venerable ones, who are in the position of . . . . teachers and spiritual preceptors, should not, without inquiry, robe foolish, sinful persons who are false and crafty. They should do no improper thing [contrary to] . . . . taught by the Buddha. The guise of a *śramaṇa* adopted without the virtues (of one) is . . . . [and] the partaking of food (belonging to another) while one leads an immoral life . . . . in hell.

No. 17. POḶONNARUVA: 'GALPOTA' SLAB-INSCRIPTION

CLOSE to the eastern outer wall of the so-called Häṭa-dā-gē mentioned above at page 84, and within a few yards south-west of that remarkable edifice known as the Sat-mahal-prāsādaya[1], there lies the oblong slab called *gal-pota*[2], 'stone-book', with its ends pointing north and south.

According to Mr. Bell[3], 'its exact measurements are: length, 26 ft. 10 in. down its axis; 26 ft. 7 in. at both edges; breadth 4 ft. 7 in., depth varying from 2 ft. 2 in. to 1 ft. 4 in. The upper surface of the slab was first smoothed, then framed and divided into three partitions by narrow fillets (1¼ to ¾ in.) horizontal and vertical, in imitation of the bare spaces on the palm leaves of *ola* manuscripts, in which holes are pierced at two convenient points for the uniting cord. Within these partitions (9 ft., 8 ft. 7 in., 8 ft. 8 in. in width) the record was carefully incised in sharply cut letters, in size 1¼ in., between ruled lines. Each partition is read by itself, the text running on from the first line at the top left-hand (south-west) corner of the stone slab. The inscription of seventy-two lines, containing more than 4,300 letters, is by far the longest known in Ceylon.

'The *galpota* was raised on a brick podium, measuring (average) 31 ft. 3 in. by 13 ft. 6 in., and sheltered by a canopy supported on ten pillars, 5 ft. in height

[1] Ruin No. 7 in inset B of the plan of Poḷonnaruva, facing p. 84. Fergusson, in his *History of Indian and Eastern Architecture* (ed. 1910, vol. i, p. 245), refers to this building as 'one of the most perfect representations existing of the seven-storeyed temples of Assyria'. For a description of it, with illustrations, see *A. S. C. Annual Report*, 1903, pp. 14–16.

[2] See site, No. 5 of inset B of the Poḷonnaruva plan. Sir Emerson Tennent, Messrs. Forbes, Fergusson, Burrows, and others have spoken of this gigantic monolith in their respective writings.

[3] *A. S. C. Annual Report*, 1903, p. 17.

Poḷonnaruva : 'Galpota' Slab-Inscription
(View from S. E.)

above the floor level. To bear the weight of so massive a slab the bottom was made to rest on "corduroy" under-pinning of short pillars laid flat, crossways.

'Both sides and ends of the slab are ornamented by double bands of *haṁsas*—two hundred and upwards in number[1]—moving from left to right. At the middle of each end is a seated figure of the goddess Lakṣmī holding flowers, upon which a pair of elephants, one on either side, pour water from a chatty—a frequent Indian motive and occurring in Ceylon elsewhere'[2].

The **letters** are very well preserved in the first two partitions, but in the third many of them have been so worn off as to render it impossible in some places to make out the words. As regards their type there is nothing to add to what has already been noticed in connexion with Niśśaṅka-Malla's inscriptions dealt with above[3]. The same may be said in respect of the **orthography** and the general style and phraseology of the **language** of the present record. The two forms *vēra* and *nirā* (in partition C, lines 2 and 7) are contractions of *vehera* (P. *vihāra*) and *niraya* (P. *naraka*). Note also should be taken of the use of the genitive in *-gē* as in *apage* and *rajakenakungē* (A, lines 14–15), the neuter plural in *-val* as in *vihāra-valā* (B, line 10) and the particle *-dī* affixed to nouns in the locative case for the sake of emphasis as *Rāmeśvarayehi-dī* (B, line 19). These **grammatical** forms occur rarely, if at all, in earlier inscriptions, though they are in common use in modern Sinhalese.

The **postscript** on the vertical face of the southern end, which covers the space below and on either side of the bas-relief[4], gives us the information that this stone was brought for the special purpose of engraving the present record from **Sāgiriya** (Mihintale) by the mighty men of Niśśaṅka-Malla under the leadership of **Adhikāra Toṭadanavu Mand-nāvan**[5]. We have thus a confirmation of the local tradition referred to by many a writer on Ceylon[6]. Major Forbes thought that in a situation abounding with rocks and quarries from which the Sinhalese could have riven masses of any size by means of wedges—a plan by which they procured pillars of great length—it was a matter of

---

[1] North, 9 top row, 6 bottom row; east, 45 top, 42 bottom; south, 8 top, 6 bottom; west, 40 top, 55 bottom—in all 211.

[2] See accompanying plates, Nos. 18 and 19.

[3] Vol. I, No. 9, and Vol. II, Nos. 13–16.

[4] See plate, No. 19.

[5] See below, p. 114, n. 4, for variant readings of this name.

[6] See, for instance, Tennent's *Ceylon* (vol. ii, p. 589), Pridham (ii. 550) and Forbes, *Eleven Years in Ceylon* (i. 420).

surprise that this weighty mass should have been thought worthy of being removed upwards of eighty miles; and it was still more wonderful how they found means to accomplish this feat. So Dr. Müller, when discussing this question in his *A.I.C.* (p. 66), put forward the ingenious suggestion that the original home of the slab was not *Sä-giri* but *Sī-giri* which is only about 15 miles distant, and that the engraver purposely incised *Sä-giri* instead of *Sī-giri* to give the record a more sacred character, *Sä-giri* being one of the oldest and most celebrated places of Buddhist worship[1]. This view does not seem to be very convincing, for if we once admit the ability of Niśśaṅka-Malla's men to remove such an enormous block of stone, the distance would hardly matter much, especially as the ground which they would have to cover is more or less flat. Nevertheless, Dr. Müller may be right for two reasons. First, on carefully examining the akṣara *sä* in the two estampages before me, I seem to notice marks of erasion of the *ī* vowel sign above the letter *s*, pointing to the probability that the engraver suddenly changed his mind and altered *ī* to *ä* before incising the next akṣara *gi*. Secondly, the postscript of the stone-seat[2] unearthed just outside the ruin of Niśśaṅka-Malla's Privy Council Chamber distinctly states that the slab for it was brought from Eṅdera-galla, probably the village now known as Eṅḍēru-gala[3], in the same district as the rock-fortress of Sī-giri, the distance between them being not more than five miles. This proves that quarries did exist in the Sī-giri district, from which Niśśaṅka-Malla had slabs brought to Poḷonnaruva to be used for his monuments.

As to **Adhikāra Toṭa-** [or **Koṭa-**]**danavu Mand-nāvan** who is stated to have conducted the operation, I am inclined to identify him with **Laṅkādhikāra Koṭadanavu Devalnāvan**[4] mentioned in the inscription[5] of **Kalyāṇavatī**, the dowager queen of our king **Niśśaṅka-Malla** as the nephew or son-in-law (*bäna*) of **Baṇḍārapota Pirivatu-bim**[6] **Vijayanāvan**, the minister who not

---

[1] Mr. Bell thinks that 'the sacred associations of Mihintalé-kanda, the great distance to be traversed, and the difficulties of transporting a block of granite so colossal, would doubtless stir the egregious vanity of that self-lauding monarch into this boastful *tour de force* merely to add special lustre to his name' (*A. S. C. Annual Report*, 1903, p. 17).

[2] See No. 21, below.

[3] See *A. S. C. Annual Report*, 1894, p. 8.

[4] Probably identical also with Dēvādhikāri who was sent to Valligāma by Āyasmanta, the chief of the army of Kalyāṇavatī, to build a vihāra there (*Mv.* lxxx. 38).

[5] See *J. C. B. R. A. S.*, 1882, pp. 181-182.

[6] See above, p. 42 B, lines 19-20, and p. 43, note 6.

only carefully guarded the treasures of Parākrama-Bāhu I and other princes, but also placed Kalyāṇavatī on the throne. Now this minister is called **Elaḷu Ābō Senevirat** (commander-in-chief) both in the *Pūjāvaliya* and in the *Rājāvaliya*, while the *Mahāvaṁsa* refers to him as **Ayasmanta** (Skt. *Āyuṣmat*) **Camūpati** (chief of the army) of the **Khandhāvara** family[1]. He seems, therefore, to have been known by several honorific titles. And judging from the similarity of these titles and from other circumstances he may, moreover, be identified with **Laṅkādhikāra Lolupälā Kuludūttävi Ābōnāvan,** called also **Lak-** (or **Lag-**) **Vijaya-Siṅgu Senevi Ābōnāvan,** or **Āyuṣmat,** or **Tāvurunāvan** in the Sāhasa-Malla's inscription and in the present one. According to the *Pūjāvaliya*, it was one **Tāvuru Senevirat,** probably this very general, who put Niśśaṅka-Malla's son **Vīra-Bāhu** to death—a fact not mentioned in the *Mahāvaṁsa*.

The **subject-matter** of the present inscription may be described in the words of Mr. Bell[2] as 'a blatant panegyric on the greatness of Niśśaṅka-Malla's mighty acts and munificence as assessed by himself', but, as will be seen presently, it was intended, like the contents of most of his other records, to serve a special purpose. In my article on this king's Dambulla record[3] I touched upon the political factors in force at the time of his accession to the throne. There were representatives of the Kāliṅga-vaṁsa to which the king himself belonged[4], of the Sinhalese Govi-kula who were adherents of Parākrama-Bāhu I, of the Pāṇḍya and probably also of the Cōḷa families, holding influential positions at the Sinhalese Court and elsewhere in the island. They were all perpetually intriguing for political supremacy, and Niśśaṅka-Malla must have felt the insecurity of his regal power, and more so of the claims of his dynasty to rule after him. This is clear from the fact that none of his successors was able to hold the sceptre for any length of time. They were either assassinated or deposed. So at the outset of Niśśaṅka-Malla's reign he found it necessary to adopt a plan of action by which he hoped to safeguard his interests. He had one of two courses open to him—either a policy of repression or of conciliation—and he wisely chose the latter which would have met with the success it deserved, had it not been for his open antagonism to the aspirations of the nobles of the Govi-kula.

---

[1] *Mv.* lxxx. 33–38. [2] *A.S.C. Annual Report*, 1903, p. 17.

[3] Vol. I, No. 9.

[4] See also Turnour's remarks on Niśśaṅka-Malla and his party in Forbes' *Eleven Years in Ceylon*, vol. ii, pp. 332–333.

Niśśaṅka-Malla's numerous inscriptions tell us how he pursued this policy. He took every opportunity to remind the people of the story of the Vijayan colonization of Ceylon as given in the *Dīpavaṁsa* (ch. ix. 1–31) and in the *Mahāvaṁsa* (ch. vii) and to impress upon them the theory that Vijaya was a prince of the **Kāliṅga-Cakravarti-kula** and that, therefore, the throne of Ceylon belonged only to this dynasty. He asserted, moreover, that the Kāliṅga princes alone were the defenders of the Buddhist Church, that their rule had always been for the benefit of their subjects, and that he himself assumed the sovereignty because it was incumbent on him to do so, as he was the rightful heir by hereditary succession. In this manner he justified his position and posed as a sovereign who held his authority entirely for the good of the community. He backed up these assertions by having his various administrative and charitable acts recorded in glowing terms not once but many times in inscriptions. The crowning point, however, of his conciliatory method is in his exhortation to his subjects in section C, where his theory of kingship is explained for their enlightenment. And it must indeed be said to his credit, whatever his motives might have been, that, so far as is known, no other king of Ceylon has ever attempted to win the confidence of the public in this manner and play the rôle of a political philosopher. If we analyse his ideas we see that they are Hinduistic, though strongly tempered with the cosmopolitan views of the Buddhists as regards the nature of society and the principles underlying social relations. He agrees with Manu [1] when he says that a king is a god in human form [2], but he goes against him in comparing 'an upright king' to a Buddha, for Manu believes in the natural inequality of man, while Buddha denies it and upholds the doctrine of the equality of man, agreeing in this respect with Seneca's theory that 'no one is in truth nobler than another,

---

[1] Ch. vii. 5, 7, and 8:

यस्मादेषां सुरेन्द्राणां मात्राभ्यो निर्मितो नृपः ।
तस्मादभिभवत्येष सर्वभूतानि तेजसा ॥ ५ ॥
सोऽग्निर्भवति वायुश्च सोऽर्कः सोमः स धर्मराट्
स कुबेरः स वरुणः स महेन्द्रः प्रभावतः ॥ ७ ॥
बालोऽपि नावमन्तव्यो मनुष्य इति भूमिपः
महती देवता ह्येषा नररूपेण तिष्ठति ॥ ८ ॥

[2] On this belief, see also Frazer's *Lectures on the Early History of the Kingship*, pp. 31–35, 128, 132, 280, and Figgis' *The Divine Right of Kings*, ch. ii.

except so far as his temper is more upright, his capacities better developed[1]'. Again, Niśśaṅka-Malla's advocacy of 'passive obedience' on the part of the people, and his reasons for it remind us of St. Paul's views on the subject as expressed in Rom. xiii. His contention as to hereditary right, his recognition of the elective principle within the limits of the royal family as was customary in Western Europe in the ninth century, his proposition that in the absence of a male heir, people should place on the throne a queen, or even a slipper[2] worn by a great king, to represent the sovereignty, and finally his appeal to the democracy to recognize the claims of the Kāliṅga dynasty and choose one of its members as their ruler—all these impress one with the rational character of Niśśaṅka-Malla's political theory.

The Sanskrit stanza in *triṣṭup śālinī* metre at the beginning of the inscription and the Sinhalese quatrain at the end are the same as those on the Häṭa-dā-gē portico slab[3]. And as to the rest of the contents, most of it, such as the names of Niśśaṅka-Malla's parents, queens and children, his charitable acts, tours of inspection, and the alleged victorious campaigns in Southern India, is already known to us from his other records published in this book. The statement, however, that he was born when 1700 years had elapsed since the arrival of Vijaya in Ceylon is an interesting bit of information as already alluded to by Dr. Fleet in his article 'On the Origin of the Buddhavarṣa[4]'. This date would give 1701 after Buddha (i.e. 1157 A.D.) as the year of Niśśaṅka-Malla's birth, if we follow the tradition that the Buddha's death is synchronous with the landing of Vijaya in Ceylon. Accordingly, Niśśaṅka-Malla must have been just thirty years old when he ascended the throne in 1187[5] and thirty-nine when he died.

It may perhaps serve a useful purpose to draw attention to Dr. Fleet's article mentioned above and state again that the *Buddha-varṣa* in use in Ceylon at this period is undoubtedly the one reckoned from 544 B.C., for the simple reason that it agrees with the details of the date given in the Poḷonnaruva inscription of King Sāhasa-Malla[6] who ascended the throne within a few years of Niśśaṅka-Malla's death. Mr. Seneviratna's contention[7] that the older reckoning

---

[1] Carlyle's *Mediaeval Political Theory in the West*, vol. i, p. 21.

[2] For the origin of this idea, see *Rāmāyaṇa*, ii. 112. I am indebted to Professor Keith for this reference.

[3] See above, No. 14.

[4] *J. R. A. S.*, 1909, pp. 329 and 332.

[5] See above, p. 73.

[6] See also *E. Z.*, vol. i, p. 123, note 4.

[7] Set forth with great enthusiasm and confidence in a paper read at a meeting of the members of the *C. B. R. A. S.*, on July 31, 1914.

from 483 B.C. remained in use up to the end of the fifteenth century does not therefore hold good. For reasons I have adduced elsewhere[1] I still adhere to the view that there was a confusion of dates in the tenth and eleventh centuries, and that by the end of the eleventh century[2] the Buddha-varṣa now current which would place the death of the Buddha in 544 B.C. became fairly established.

The present inscription, like others of Niśśaṅka-Malla, is not dated, but from the references to his public acts, religious and otherwise, it is quite apparent that he must have had it indited at about the close of his short but busy reign of nine years (1187–1196 A.D.).

The inscription was first translated by Mr. Armour in the Appendix to Turnour's *Epitome of the History of Ceylon*[3]. Dr. Müller's transcript and translation appeared in *A. I. C.* as No. 148. The present edition has been prepared independently of these from the two ink-estampages supplied by the Archaeological Commissioner of Ceylon. In this task Mr. D. B. Jayatilaka rendered me much help in the summer of 1912 and I avail myself of this opportunity to acknowledge my indebtedness to him.

TEXT.

A.

1 ශ්‍රී ධම්මාසොයං සබ්බ[4]ලොකෛකමානසශ්‍රෙයො දැයී සබ්බ[4]ද රක්‍ෂණීයඃ [।]
භූපාලෙන්ද්‍රානයාචතෙ කීර්ත්තිහෙතොර්භූයො භූයො **වීර නිශ්ශංක මල්ලඃ** [॥]
2 ශ්‍රීමත් අනත් උතුම් ගුණගෙණින් ගිම් ඔකාවස්රජපරපුරෙහි වූ ආකාශචාරී
කාලිඟචක්‍රවර්ත්තීන්වහන්සේකුලෙනා විජයරාජයන් බුදුන්ගේ නි
3 යොගයෙන් දෙවියන්විසින් අරගන්නාලදුවැ ලක්දිවූ බැසැ යක්‍ෂ පුළුයකොටැ
මනුෂ්‍යාවාස කළ එක්දහස් සත්සියක් හවුරුදු ගියකල්හි බුදු බොස
4 ත් සක්විත්තන් උපදනා උතුම් දඹදිව්හි **කාලිඟුරටැ සිංහපුරයෙහි** මෙමැ
රජපරපුරට තිලකයක් බඳු **ශ්‍රීජයගොප** රාජයන්වහන්සේ නිසා **පාර්වති**[5]
5 ඹහදෙවීන්වහන්සේකුසෙන් ඉපැදැ රජපෙරහරින් වැඩී තමන් යොනපරපුරෙන්
ගිම් ලක්දිවැ රජකරනුමැනැවැයි ලක්දිවැ කුලපෙ(වූ) මහරජුන් අ

---

[1] See above, p. 65.

[2] See also *J. R. A. S.*, 1912, p. 1113.

[3] Published in the *Ceylon Almanac* for 1834. For a reprint, see Forbes' *Eleven Years in Ceylon*, vol. ii, p. 343.

[4] 'සව්' වියයුතුයි

[5] 'පාර්වති' වියයුතුයි

6 යදමෙන් මහපෙරහරින් මෙ ලකට බැසැ ඇපාංගිමියා තනතුරු රජඉසුරු විඳිමින් ශස්ත්‍ර ශාස්ත්‍රාගම සකල කලා විද්‍යායේහි නිපු[ණුසෙ]වැ රජ පි

7 ළිවෙළින් අභිෂේක ලදින් වොටුනු පැලැඳැ මහරජතන් පත්වූ වොටුනු මඟුලෙහි අහස්කුස් පූරමින් ආ මහමෙකැලද කිපි බැ[ලූව] පමණෙකින් වි

8 සුරුවා බැව්[1] ලොවැස්සන් ඇසට නිපුණු අණසක් ඇති ක්‍රීඩාවනයෙහි ඉඳිරියට කකරා පිනූ කුරුරු සැඩ වැලසිනන අදු කැඩී සිය (පිළි)ත්නා සැමැගැ

9 පාපිට හෙළු මහා තද තෙද ඇති නිරුදකකතරෙහිද පැන් වුවමැනැවැයි සිතූ කෙණෙහිමැ අකාල මෙසයෙන් මහවතුරු පවත්බැවින් කැමැති තැනි

10 න් පැනූරනසිංහරාජවික්‍රම ඇති සමුද්‍රක්‍රීඩාවට **බැණ** වැඩි තැනැ අභිමුඛයෙහි පැනුණු මහපොළැගකු සම්පවූසෙ නපුරැයි පහවැ තොමැ නට

11 තුඳුස්ස දනයි වදළ බසට තමාමැ තමා ඩැහැ අදු පිඳුබැවින් අලංඝනීය ආදෙශ ඇති දුටු කෙණෙහිමැ සතුටුවැ කොවනාදකොටැ මඟුලැතු තමාමැ පිට දු

12 න්බැවින් දුටු මහාමගිමා ඇති **සිරිසඟබො කාලිඟ පරාක්‍රමබාහු වීරරාජ නිශ්ශංක මල්ල අප්‍රතිමල්ල** මහරජපාවහන්සෙ උදැගල් මුඳුන් ප

13 ත් හිරුහුසෙ සතුරඳුරු දුරුලා බහුජනයා මුවපිපුම් පුබුදුකොටැ අනත් රජසිරින් ශක්‍රදෙවෙන්‍ද්‍රයාසෙ සොම්ගුණෙන් [සු]පුන්සඳුහුසෙ ධීර

14 තායෙන් මෙරුවසෙ ගැඹුරුබැවින් සාගරයසෙ ක්ෂාන්තිගුණෙන් මහපොළොවසෙ ලොවැස්සන් පිනින් උපන් කප්රුකසෙ වැඩැසිටැ අපගෙ වශයට

15 පරපුරු මේ ලක්දිවුහි බහුජනයා අතුරෙකැ සමහර රජකෙනෙකුන්ගෙ දුර්නීතිවශයෙන් කුලාචාරධනයෙන් පිරිහුණු(සේ) [ව]නයි මහාකරුණ යෙන් ඔවු

16 න්ට කුලාචාර තබා දී පස්හවුරුද්දෙකැ අය හැරැ කෙත්වත් අය ගන්නාකලැ පෙරැ රජුඤවසැ වඩා ගන්නා අය හැරැ උත්තේ අමුණට එකමුණු තුන්පැළ හා ම

17 ඩරන් සාක හා මැදෙඳ අමුණට එකමුණු දෙපැළ හා මඩරන් සතරක හා පැස්සෙ අමුණට එකමුණු පැළ හා මඩරන් තුනක බැගින් ගනුත්මුත් වඩා නොගන්නා නියා

18 යෙන් හා දුකින් කරන සෙහෙන් කටුසර අය හැමැකලටමැ නොගන්නා නියායෙන් හා ව්‍යවස්ථා කොටැ කහවුණු තඹ ලොහො රන් රිදී මුතු මැණික් වස්ත්‍රාභර

19 ණාදි අනෙක ධන වෂ්ටියෙන් දිළිඳුගිම් නිවා දිවෙල් වහල් සරක් පමුණු පරපුරු රන්රිදී වළන් ගෙහිල ආදි බොහො සම්පත් තබා දී අමාත්‍යාදීන් ඇති

20 කොටැ තුන්රජයෙහි බොහො කල් අපවත් මහවැවු ඇළ අවුණු බඳවා එ එ රටැ සුභික්ෂකොටැ එහි සත්වයනට[2] අභයදැන දී විසමබුරු[3]වතද හැරැ

---

[1] 'විසුරුවූබැවින්' වියයුතුයි [2] 'සත්ත්වයනට' වියයුතුයි

[3] 'පිසමබුරු' සීදකියවියහැකියි

21 නොඑක් ජනපදයෙහි ධම්මාධිකරණ ලවා අන්‍යාය නිවාරණකොටැ සොරුන්නු සොරකම් කරන්නේ ධනාශායෙන් වෙදයි උන් උන් කැමැති වසතු දී චෞරභය

22 දුරුකොටැ වල්වැස්සන් පැල්වැස්සන් හැමැතැනම සාධා කණ්ටක ශොධනය කොටැ බුදුසස්නෙහිද නයවිනයවූ පරිද්දෙන් දුශ්ශීල කණ්ටක පහකොටැ ලො

23 ක-ශාසන නිෂ්කණ්ටකකොටැ සුශීල මහසගනට සිවුපසයෙන් උපස්ථානකොටැ හවුරුදු පතා මහණුවම් කරවා කඨිනදන දී දෙවදන දරුකුසලාන් මගකුසලා

24 න් පෙර පරිද්දෙන් තබා දී සස්නටද බොහො වැඩ සාධා දී ධම්මධර ශාසනධරයනට අනුරූප වූතති[1] දී ධම්මශාසනද පවත්වා මෙසේ ලො සසුන් වැඩ බොහො කල්

B.

1 පවත්නේ රාජවංශය නිසායැයි කලිඟුරට යවා සොමසූර්‍ය්‍යවංශ බොහො බිසොවරුන් ගෙන්වා උරෙහිද යුවරජතන් පත් **වීරබාහු** මහපාණන්

2 වහන්සේටද රාජ කන්‍යකාවන් ගෙන්වා රජකුලය මහත්කොටැ අග මෙහෙසුන් **කාලිඟ සුභද්‍රා මහදෙවින්වහන්සේ** හා **ගඟවංශ කල්‍යාණි මහ**

3 **දෙවින්වහන්සේ** හා සහවොටුනුරජබරණින් සැ(දී) උරෙහිද දරු **මහපාණන් වහන්සේ** හා දූ **සභිබාහ[2]සුභද්‍රින්වහන්සේ** හා එක්වැ තුලාභාර

4 නැඟී හවුරුදුපතා පස්තුලාභාරයක් බැගින් දී නවරත්නදානවර්ෂා පවත්වා නොඑක් දියින් රැස්වූ මහණ බමුණු කණ පිළී කුරු කුදුන් ආදිවූ දී

5 නානාථ ජනයන් සනාථකොටැ මෙසේ චතුසස(ග්‍ර)ගවසතුයෙන් ලොකශාසන සනහා සිත් ගත් බහුජනයා වෙනැ වෙනැ තමන් සිතැ ඇති සෙන

6 ග පක්ෂපාතකොටැ දිවි දී ගෙවම්හයි වෙළ ගන්නා පරිද්දෙන් ජනානුරජන ගුණයෙහි අගතන්පත්වැ දවසැ දවසැ දසපින්කිරියවත් පුරා

7 **සුලක්ඛිපුර** නමැති **කාලිඟකපුරයෙහි** වැඩැ වසනසෙයෙක් සවමඩල පරමඩලය චාරචක්ෂුසින් සතතයෙන් දකුතුදු අප ලක්දිව සෙ

8 මෙහි තුබූ පරිදි ප්‍රත්‍යක්ෂ කළ(මැනැවැ)යි සි(වු)රඟ සෙනඟ පිරිවරා ත්‍රිසිංහලයෙහි ගම් නියම්ගම් රාජධානි ජලදුර්ගග ගිරිදුර්ගග වනදුර්ගග පං

9 කදුර්ගග හා එක්කොටැ ක්‍රීඩාභවනයක්හිමෙන් ඇවිදැ බලා වදාරා ප්‍රත්‍යන්ත(වා)සි බහුජනයනු මහාදානවර්ෂායෙන් පිනවා තුන් රජයෙහි බැ

10 ලූ බැලූ **මියගුණු මහාවෙර**[3] **(ම)හගම [දෙමුනුවර?]කැ(ලැ)ණි** ආදිවූ ජරා විහාරවලැ නවකම්මාන්ත කරවා **දඹුලුලෙණැ** හොත් හුන් සිටි පිළිම දගබ[4] ර

11 න් ගාවා ලක්ෂයක් ධන වි(යද)ම්කොටැ (මහා)පූජා කරවා **අනුරාධපුරයෙ රු වන්මැලි**මහසැවහන්සේට සතිස්ලක්ෂයක් ධන වියදම්කොටැ පූජාකර

---

[1] 'වෘත්ති' වියයුතුයි

[2] 'සර්වාඞ්ග' වියයුතුයි

[3] 'මහවෙහෙර' වියයුතුයි

[4] 'දාගැප්' සීදකියවියහැකියි

12 වා ඒ පූජාවට සතුටු දෙවතා(වත්) .. .. ආශිබබ්ාද[1] කළ තැන (ග)ල්
දාගබක් කරවා එ එ තන්හි සදාචාර ශිලාලෙඛ කරවා මෙසේ සාරවූ
බුදුසසුන් පි

13 හිටි ලක්දිව පෙර දවසැ .. .. (ස) නපුරසි දැ(හැ)වැ **දඹදිවූ** (දිනීයපි)වැ
සියුරඟ සෙනඟ පිරිවරා තමන්වහන්සෙ **නිශශංකමල්ල** යනා

14 විරුදු ඇති බැවින් කිසිතැ(නකත්) සැකයක් නොකොටැ මහත් රාජානුභාවයෙන්
නිල්මිණි අ(සැ)ක්සේ නිසල්වූ මහමූහුදු තැර දඹදිවූ වැඩැ වඤ[2] යුඩ
සේනායුඩ

15 ඉල්වා දූතයන් හටයන් නගා යවා යුඩයට සැරහුණු කල්හි **ල(ශ්) විජයසිඟු සෙ
නෙවි කාවුරුනාවන්** දඹදිවූ සාඩා දෙන්නට මම්මැ පමිණිමි දන්වා යු

16 ඩයට නික්මුණු බව [දැකැ භය] පත්වූ **පාණ්ඩ්‍ය**රජ්ජුරුවන් හා මැණියන්විසින්
අප ජීවත්වන පමණ ග[මි දී රා]ජ්‍යය තමන්වහන්සේමැ ගෙනැ වදාළ
මැනැවැ

17 පි කියා වෙළ ගෙනැ (එවූ ර)නැඟිලි හා රාජකන්‍යකාවන් [හා හස්ත්‍යශ්වාදි ?]
නොඑක් පඬුරු හා **සොළී**රටින් මෙසේමැ එවූ බොහෝ පඬුරු නැමැති
ජලධාරයෙන් කොපා(ග්නි)

18 **තිවි ක[illegible] තෙල්ගුරු ගෞඩ කලිඟ ති[ලිඟ] ගු[ජ්ජර** ආදි] නොඑක් දෙශයේ
ගුණිතැමැති **රජදරුවන්හා** .. මිත්‍ර සන්ථානකොටැ නොකැමැත්තවුන්ට
තමන්වහන්සෙගෙ

19 ශෞය්‍යාතිශයෙන් භය එළවා එ එ රටින් කිසො[වරුන්හා] පඬුරු ගෙන්වා
රාමෙශ්වරයෙහිදී තුලාභාර නැඟී නොඑක් දෙශවාසීන්ට අනන්ත වස්තු ත්‍යාග
කොටැ එ

20 තන්හි බොහො කල් පවත්නා නියායෙන් ජයස්තම්භ කොටැ **නිශශංකේශ්වරයැ**
යන දෙවාලයක් නංවා ප්‍රතිමල්ලයක්හු නැතිබැවින් අපට අභය දී වදාළ

21 මැනැවැයි දඹදිවැ රජුන් කළ ආරධනායෙන් (වහල්) ගෙනැ එමැ සෙනඟ
පිරිවරා ලක්දිවූ වැඩැ මෙ ලොවැ සතුරන් නැති බැවින් පරලොවැ සතුරන්
දනම්හයි

22 සිතා ස්වදෙශ පරදෙශයෙහි නොඑක් තැනැ **නිශශංකදාන[ස]ත්‍රය** ඇතුළුවූ
නොඑක් දානසත්‍ර කරවා රන් රිදී වළන් ආදිවූ අනෙක අනුභව වස්තු

23 යෙන් කප්රුක්සෙ සරහා මහදන් පවත්වා දන් ගත් යාචකයන්ගේ
සන්තොෂොත්සව බලනු සඳහා **නිශශංකදානමණ්ඩපයැ** යන මණ්ඩපයකුදු කා

24 රවා දළදාපාත්‍රධාතූන්වහන්සේට ප්‍රතණුවන්වහන්සේ හා දියණියන්වහන්සෙ
හා පූදා සනරන්දාගබක් ඇතුළුවූ ධන පූදා ගළවා ශිලාමය

C.

1 **දළදාගෙය වටගෙය නිශ්ශංකලතාමණ්ඩපය** දෙරටූ පවුරු බැලූවන්ට සිත් සතුටුවන්
ස්වර්ගමොක්ෂවන නියායෙන් කරවා **ම**

---

[1] 'ආශිර්වාද' වියයුතුයි

[2] 'වඤුව' වියයුතුයි

2 හවෙර[1] දාගබ සාකොටැ උපකාරචෛත්‍යය කරවා රජගෙට උතුරුදිගැ අෂ්ඨ අත් **රුවන්මැලි**දාගබ්වහන්සේ කරවා සිසාරා දෙරටු

3 පවුරු සංඝාරාම කරවා ලොකශාසනය බොහොකල් පවත්නාසේ කොටැ තවද ලංකා[ද්වීපය සසුන්] පිහිටි වූ හෙයිනුදු උත්තම භූමි

4 යැ සත්වයො[2] උත්සිම ගුණ ඇත්තාහ අවවාද කියා රක්‍ෂාකළමැනැවැයි කරුණායෙන් අවවාද කිය(නුසෙයෙක්) [රජ]දරුවන් මනුෂ්‍යරූපයෙ

5 න් සිටියද නරදෙවතා හෙයින් දෙවියන්සේ දක්කැ යුතුයැ (මැඳහත්) රජුන් ලැබීම් බුදුන් ලැබීම් සේ [සැලකියැ යුතු]යැ රජදරුවො වරද

6 ට සුදුසු නිග්‍රහ කරනාහු ශරීරයෙහි රොගයකට වෙදහු කරන පිළියමක්සේ හිත සිතින් කර[නාහාහ අක]ට යුත්තෙන් වලකා

7 අපායෙහි නොහිය දෙනාහාහ කටයුත්තෙහි යොදා සගමොක්ද ගෙනැ දෙනාහාහ රජුන් හිහි [නො රැකක මි]නිස් [ලො ති]රසේ වෙ

8 සි ඉහි රැකක දෙවුලොසේ වෙසී රජදරුවන්ට ගන්නා දුක් සුවයට වපුරන කිපුවටයැ එ එ ත .. .. බලා

9 තමා එ එ නුගුණයෙන් දුරුවිය යුතුයැ ලද සම්පත් රක්නවූ කුලාචාර රැක්ක යුතුයැ පි .. .. [උක්] දඩුසේ පක්‍ෂ

10 පාත රස වැහියැ යුතුයැ තනතුරෙන් පිරිහුණද නැටියෙන් ගිලිහුණු එලසේ රජ දරුව[න්ට] .. .. පවත්නේයැ

11 කැඳුවා වදාළ(දැයැයි) ඝිකල්හි නිවරද වූව මට කිම්දැයි නොබා යන නියායෙන් තමා .. .. කට [යුතුයැ රජු]න්ගේ රහස් දෙ

12 ඩිම් මරහු එන්නට මතුරන නියායැ රජුන්ට දිවි දෙනුයේ යශශ්ශරීරයෙන් බො(හො කලක් සි)ටිනේයැ දැනුම් න

13 ම් කෙළෙහිගුණ දැනුමැ වෙළඳහම් නම් ගොවිතැනැ හස්තසාර නම් දහමැ රැක්ක යුතු(යැ) .. .. මෙකී දෙය රජුන් නි

14 සා වත්නේයැ එහෙයින් රාජරක්‍ෂායෙහි නොපමාවියැ යුතුයැ රජදරුවෝ දපේපාඩනවනු(වන්) [නො රුස්නා]හ එහෙයින් උ

15 න්ගෙන් නම් තනතුරු සම්පත් ලදින් දපේපාඩන නොවියැ යුතෙත්යැ ඉදින් ගොවිකුලෙහි (සම)හ[ර] .. .. යෙක් තමා ලද න

16 ම් තනතුරු නො බලා දි .. .. (ම් කම)කට සිතානම් ලොවැස්සන් ඔහු හා නොහැණුණු මැනවැ ඔහු [එබඳු]වූ සිතත් සිතුවද රා

17 ජ හංස සිංහාදින්ගේ (චාරු) .. .. .. (වෙස් තැතු) කවුඩු කැණහිල් ආදීන්සේ මහ ජනයන්විසින් අපහා[ස] .. .. ලොසැපැත්හා එක්වැ මැ

18 කෙනෙත්යැ එබැවින් .. .. (ය යන) .. .. (ලොවැස්සන් එක්වැ ඔහු දු)රුකොටැ .. .. (යො .. පි) .. .. .. (කා) .. .. න්‍ය දශීනාත් යනු අ

19 පත වචන හෙයින් (බිජය) .. .. .. බ .. .. රාජයන්ගේ (දරු) ඈපා මහ පා(ව)න් බාලවූවද ලොකස්වාමි[හෙයින්] රාජ්‍යයට බලා ගෙනැ කුල

---

[1] 'වෙහෙර' වියයුතුයි

[2] 'සතත්වයො' වියයුතුයි

20 සිරිත් ද .. .. කටයුතු [ඔවු]නුදු නැත[හොත්] බිසොවරුන්ගේ
ආඥායෙහි පැවැතැ රක්ෂා කටයුතු උනුදු නැත මහරජු

21 න් පයැ ලූ වහන් මාත්‍රයකුදු රජතන්හි තබා රාජ්‍ය රැකක යුතු .. (ස) .. .. (ක) ..
.. .. විෂ ඕනාසේ කප්රුක් පිහිටි තැනැ විෂ රුක් හිඳුවන්නාසේ කා

22 ලිඟවංශයට හිමි ලක්දිවැ බුද්ධශාසනයට ප්‍රතිපක්ෂ අබෞද්ධ **චොඩ පාණ්ඩ්‍යාදි** රජුන්
නොපිහිටිවියැ යුත්තේයැ **විජය**රජකුමාරයන් කෙරෙ පට

23 න් ලක්දිව් හිමි කාලිඟවංශයෙහි රජදරුවන්ටයැ සොයා ගෙනැ(ත්) වීනම් උන්
ස්වාමිකොටැ ලොසසුන් රක්ෂා කරනු ආචාරයි දහම් නමෙ මේ මූ

24 එ ලො සඟන්නෙයැ[,] සිතා දෙලොසැපත් අඳරැති කරනෙයැ[,] මතු
වන රජවිරුන් මෙසේ අයදනෙයැ[,] **කලිඟු ලකිඳු නිසකරජ** ගුණ නඳ
නෙයැ

POSTSCRIPT.

1 ශ්‍රී **කාලිඟචක්‍රවර්ත්ති**
2 ස්වාමින්වහන්සේ
3 ඈති කළු නිශ්ශංක
4 හටයන් ලවා අඩි
5 **කාර තොට**[1](ද) නවු(මඤ්)
6 **නාවන්** සැගිරියෙන්
7 ගෙන්වූ ශිලාලෙඛ ගලයි

TRANSCRIPT.

A.

1 Śrī[!] Dharmas so 'yaṁ sarbba[2]-lok=aika-mānyaś=śreyo-dāyī sarbba[2]-dā rakṣaṇi-
-yaḥ [।] bhūpālendrān yācate kīrtti-hetor=bbhūyo bhūyo **Vīra-Niśśaṁka-
Mallaḥ** [॥]

2 Śrī-mat anat utum guṇa-geṇen hivi Okāvas-raja-parapurehi vū ākāśa-cārī
Kāliṅga-Cakravarttin-vahansē-kulen ā Vijaya-rājayan Budungē ni-

3 -yogayen deviyan-visin aragganā-laduvā Lak-divu bäsä yakṣa praḷaya-koṭä
manuṣy=āvāsa kaḷa ek-dahas sat-siyak havurudu giya-kalhi Budu Bosa-

4 -t Sakvittan upadanā utum Dambadivhi **Kaliṅgu-raṭä Siṁhapurayēhi**
memä raja-parapuraṭa tilakayak bañdu **Śrī-Jayagopa**-rājayan-vahansē
nisā **Pārbbatī**[3]

5 maha-devīnvahansē-kusen ipädä raja-peraharin väḍī taman yona-parapuren
himi Lakdivä rajakaranu-mänäväyi Lakdivä kula-je(ṭu) maha-rajun a-

6 -yadamen maha-peraharin me Lakaṭa bäsä āpā-himiyā tanaturu raja-isuru
vindimin śastra śāstr=āgama sakala kalā vidyāyēhi nipu[nu-se]vä raja-pi-

---

[1] 'කොට' යිද කියවියහැකියි

[2] Read *sarva*.

[3] Read *Pārvatī*.

7 -ḷiveḷin abhiṣēka ladin voṭunu päländä maha-raja-tan patvū voṭunu maṅgulehi ahas-kus puramin ā maha-mē-käla-da kipi bä[luva] pamaṇekin vi-
8 -suruvā bävi[1] lovässan äsaṭa tiyuṇu aṇasak äti krīḍā-vanayehi idiriyaṭa kakarā pinū kurūru säḍa väla-sinna divu käḍī siya (piḷu)nhā sämäṅgä
9 pāpiṭa heḷu mahā tada teda äti nir-udaka-katarehi-da pän vuva-mänäväyi sitū keṇehi-mä akāla meghayen maha-vaturu pavat-bävin kämäti täni-
10 -n pän-ūrana-siṁha-rāja-vikrama äti samudra-krīḍāvaṭa **Bāṇa**[2] väḍi tänä abhimukhayehi pänuṇu maha-poḷäṅgaku samīpa-vū-sē napuräyi paha-vä to-mä taṭa
11 tudussa danayi vadāḷa basaṭa tamā-mä tamā ḍähä divu pidū-bävin alaṁ-ghanīya ādeśa äti duṭu keṇehi-mä satuṭu-vä koñca-nāda-koṭā maṅgul-ätu tamā-mä piṭa du-
12 -n-bävin duṭu mahā-mahimā äti **Siri-Saṅgabo Kāliṅga Parākrama-Bāhu Vīrarāja Niśśaṁka-Malla Aprati-Malla** maha-rajapā-vahansē Udā-gal muṅdun pa-
13 -t hiruhu-sē satur-anduru duru-lā bahu-janayā muva-piyum pubudu-koṭā anat raja-sirin Śäkra-devendrayā-sē somi-guṇen [su]pun-sañdahu-sē dhīra-
14 -tāyen Meruva-sē gämburu-bävin sāgaraya-sē kṣānti-guṇen maha-poḷova-sē lo-vässan-pinin upan kap-rukak-sē väḍäsiṭā apage vaṁśayaṭa
15 parapuru mē Lakdivuhi bahu-janayā aturekä samahara rajakenekungē durnnīti-vaśayen kulācāra-dhanayen pirihuṇu(sē) [va]nayi mahā-karu-ṇāyen ovu-
16 -nṭa kulācāra tabā dī pas-havuruddekä aya härä ket-vat-aya gannā-kalä perä rajun davasä vaḍā gannā aya härä uttē amuṇaṭa ek-amuṇu tun-pāḷa hā ma-
17 -ṅḍa-ran sāka hā mände amuṇaṭa ek-amuṇu de-pāḷa hā maṅḍa-ran sataraka hā pässē amuṇaṭa ek-amuṇu pāḷa hā maṅḍa-ran tunaka bägin ganut-mut vaḍā no-gannā niyā-
18 -yen hā dukin karana sehen kaṭusara aya hämä-kalaṭa-mä no-gannā niyāyen hā vyavasthā koṭā kahavuṇu tamba loho ran ridī mutu mäṇik vastr-ābhara-
19 -ṇ-ādi aneka-dhana-varṣāyen diḷindu-gim nivā divel vahal sarak pamuṇu parapuru ran-ridī vaḷan gehila ādi boho sampat tabā dī amāty-ādīn äti-
20 koṭā tun-rajayehi boho kal apavat maha-vävu äḷa avuṇu bandavā e e raṭā subhikṣa-koṭā ehi satvayanaṭa[3] abhaya-dāna dī visamburu-[4]vata-da härä

[1] Perhaps for '*visuruvū bävin*'.
[2] Mt. *gona*.
[3] Read *sattvayanaṭa*.
[4] This may also be read *pisamburu-*.

21 no-ek janapadayehi dharmādhikaraṇa lavā anyāya nivāraṇa-koṭā sorunudu sorakam karannē dhan-āśāyen vedayi un un kämäti vastu dī cora-bhaya

22 duru-koṭā val-vässan päl-vässan hämä-täna-ma sādhā kaṇṭaka śodhanaya-koṭā Budu-sasnehi-da naya-vinayavū paridden duśśila-kaṇṭaka paha-koṭā lo-

23 -ka śāsana niṣkaṇṭaka-koṭā suśila maha-saṅganaṭa sivu-pasayen upasthāna-koṭā havurudu patā mahaṇuvam karavā kaṭhina-dāna dī deva-dāna daru-kusalān maṅga-kusalā-

24 -n pera paridden tabā dī sasnaṭa-da boho väḍa sādhā dī dharma-dhara śāstra-dharayanaṭa anurūpa vratti[1] dī dharmaśāstra-da pavatvā mesē lo sasun väḍa boho kal

B.

1 **pavatnē rāja-vaṁśaya** nisāyäyi Kaliṅgu-raṭa yavā Soma-Sūrya-vaṁśa boho **bisovarun** genvā urehidā yuvaraja-tan pat **Vīrabāhu** mahapāṇan-

2 **-vahansēṭa-da** rāja-kanyakāvan genvā rajakulaya mahat-koṭā aga mehesun **Kāliṅga Subhadrā Maha-devīn-vahansē** hā **Gaṅgavaṁśa Kalyāṇa Maha-**

3 **devīn-vahansē** hā saha-voṭunu-rajabaraṇin sä(dī) urehidā daru **Mahapāṇan-vahansē** hā dū **Sarbbāṅga-**[2]**sundarīn-vahansē** hā ekvä tulābhāra

4 näṅgī havurudupatā pas-tulābhārayak bägin dī navaratna-dāna-varṣā pavatvā no-ek digin räsvū mahaṇa bamuṇu kaṇa piḷu kuru kudun ādivū dī-

5 -nānātha janayan sanātha-koṭā mesē catussa(ṅgra)ha-vastuyen loka-śāsana sanahā sit gat bahu-janayā venä venä taman sitä äti sne-

6 -ha pakṣapāta-koṭā divi dī gevamhayi veḷa gannā paridden janānurañjana guṇayehi aga-tan-patvä davasä davasä dasa-pin-kiriya-vat purā

7 **Pulasti-pura** namäti **Kāliṅgaka-purayehi** väḍä vasana-seyek svamaṇḍaḷa paramaṇḍaḷaya cāra-cakṣusin satatayen dakutudu apa Lakdiva se-

8 -mehi tubū paridi pratyakṣa kaḷa(mänävä)yi si(vu)raṅga senaṅga pirivarā Tri-Siṁhaḷayehi gam niyam-gam rājadhāni jala-durgga giri-durgga vana-durgga paṁ-

9 -ka-durgga hā ek-koṭā krīḍā-bhavanayak-hi-men ävidä balā vadārā pra-tyanta-(vā)si bahu-janayan-da mahā-dāna-varṣāyen pinavā tun-rajayehi bä-

10 -lu bälu **Miyaṅguṇu Mahāvera**[3] (**Ma**)**hagama** [**Devunuvara**?] **Kä**(**lä**)**ṇi** ādivū jarā vihāravalä nava-karmmānta karavā **Dambulu-leṇā** hot hun siṭi piḷima dāgaba[4] ra-

---

[1] Read *vṛtti*.

[2] Read *Sarvāṅga-*.

[3] Probably for *Maha-vehera*.

[4] This may also be read *dāgäp*; Mt. *dāgap*.

11 -n gāvā lakṣayak dhana vi(yada)m-koṭā (mahā-)pūjā karavā **Anurādhapura-** **-ye Ruvanmäli**-mahasā-vahansēṭa satis-lakṣayak dhana viyadam-koṭā pūjā-kara-

12 -vā ē pūjāvaṭa satuṭu devatā(van) .. .. āśīrbbāda[1] kaḷa täna (ga)l-dāgabak karavā e e tanhi sadā-cāra śilā-lekha karavā mesē säravū budu-sasun pi-

13 -hiṭi Lakdiva pera davasä .. .. (sa) napuräyi dä(hä)vä Dambadivu (diniyaṭi)vä siyuraṅga senaṅga pirivarā tamanvahanse **Niśśaṁka-Malla** yana

14 virudu äti bävin kisi-tä(nakat) säkayak no-koṭā mahat rājānubhāvayen nilmiṇi a(sä)k-sē nisal vū maha-mūṅdu tärä Dambadivu väḍā dvanda[2]-yuddha sēnā-yuddha

15 ilvā dūtayan bhaṭayan naṅgā yavā yuddhayaṭa särahuṇu kal-hi **La[g-] Vijayasiṅgu Senevi Tāvurunāvan** Dambadivu sādhā dennaṭa mam-mä pamiṇimī danvā yu-

16 -ddhayaṭa nikmuṇu bava [däkä bhaya] patvū **Pāṇḍi**-rajjuruvan hā māṇiyan-visin apa jīvat-vana pamaṇa ga[m dī rā]jyaya taman-vahansē-mä genä vadāḷa mänävä-

17 -yi kiyā veḷa genä (evū ra)n-äṅgili hā rāja-kanyakāvan [hā hasty-aśvādi ?] no-ek paṇḍuru hā Soḷī-raṭin mesē-mä evū bohō paṇḍuru nämäti jaladhārāyen kopā(gni)

18 nivā **Karṇṇāṭa Nellūru Gauḍa Kaliṅga Ti**[**liṅga**] **Gu**[**rjjara** ādi] no-ek deśayē guṇa-kämäti raja-daruvan hā .. mitra santhāna-koṭā no-kämätta-vunṭa tamanvahansege

19 śauryyātiśayen bhaya eḷavā e e raṭin biso[varun hā] paṇḍuru genvā **Rāmeś-varayehi**-dī tulābhāra näṅgī no-ek deśavāsīnṭa ananta vastu tyāga-koṭā e-

20 -tan-hi boho kal pavatnā niyāyen jaya-stambha koṭā **Niśśaṁkēśvarayä** yana devālayak naṁvā pratimallayak-hu nätibävin apaṭa abhaya dī vadāḷa-

21 -mänäväyi Dambadivä rajun kaḷa ārādhanāyen (vahal) genä emä senaṅga pirivarā Lakdivu väḍā me lovä saturan näti bävin para-lovä saturan danamhayi

22 sitā svadeśa paradeśayehi no-ek tänä **Niśśaṁka-dāna-**[**sa**]**traya** ätuḷuvū no-ek dāna-satra karavā ran ridī vaḷan ādivū aneka anubhava vastu-

---

[1] *āśīrvāda.*

[2] Read *dvandva.*

23 -yen kap-ruk-se sarahā maha-dan pavatvā dan gat yācakayangē santoṣ-otsava balanu sandahā **Niśśaṁka-dāna-maṇḍapayä** yana maṇḍapayakudu ka-

24 -ravā daḷadā-pātra-dhātunvahansēṭa putaṇuvan-vahansē hā diyaṇiyan-vahanse hā pudā ghana-ran-dāgabak ätuḷuvū dhana pudā gaḷavā śilā-maya

C.

1 **Daḷadā-geya Vaṭa-geya Niśśaṁka-latā-maṇḍapaya** doraṭu pavuru bälū-vanṭa sit satuṭu-van svargga-mokṣa-vana niyāyen karavā **Ma-**

2 **-ha-vera**[1] dāgaba sā-koṭā upakāra-caityaya karavā rajageṭa uturu-digā asū at **Ruvanmäli-dāgab**-vahansē karavā sisārā doraṭu

3 pavuru saṁghārāma karavā loka-śāsanaya boho-kal pavatnā-sē koṭā tavada Laṁkā[-dvīpaya sasun] pihiṭi vū heyinudu uttama bhūmi-

4 -yä satvayo[2] utsīma guṇa ättāha avavāda kiyā rakṣā-kaḷa-mänāväyi karuṇāyen avavāda kiya(nu-seyek) [raja-]daruvan manuṣya-rūpaye-

5 -n siṭiyada nara-devatā heyin deviyan-sē däkkä yutuyä (mändahat) rajun läbīm budun läbīm sē [sälakiyä yutu]yä raja-daruvō varada-

6 -ṭa sudusu nigraha karannāhu śarīrayehi rogayakaṭa vedahu karana piḷiyamak-sē hita sitin kara[nnāha aka]ṭa yutten valakā

7 apāyehi no-hiya dennāha kaṭayuttehi yodā saga-mok-da genä dennāha rajun hiṅgi [no-räkka mi]nis[-lo ni]rā-sē ve-

8 -yi iṅgi räkka devu-lo-sē veyi raja-daruvanṭa gannā duk suvayaṭa vapurana bijuvaṭayä e e ta .. .. balā

9 tamā e e nuguṇayen duruviya yutuyä lada sampat raknavu kulācāra räkka yutuyä pi .. .. [uk-] daṇḍu-sē pakṣa-

10 -pāta rasa vähiyä yutuyä tanaturen pirihuṇada näṭiyen gilihuṇu phala-sē raja daruva[nṭa] .. .. pavatnēyä

11 käṅdavā vadāḷa-(däyäyi) kī-kal-hi nivarada vuva maṭa kimdäyi no-bā yana niyāyen tamā .. .. kaṭa [yutuyä raju]ngē rahas de-

12 -ḍīm marahu ennaṭa maturana niyāyä rajunṭa divi denuyē yaśaś-śarīrayen bo(ho kalak si)ṭinēyä dänum na-

13 -m keḷehi-guṇa dänumä veḷandaham nam govi-tänä hastasāra nam dahamā räkka yutu(yä) .. .. mekī deya rajun ni-

14 -sä vannēyä eheyin rāja-rakṣāyehi no-pamā-viyä yutuyä raja-daruvō dar-poddhatavanu(van) [no-rusnā]ha eheyin u-

[1] Probably for *Maha-vehera.* See B, l. 10, above.

[2] Read *sattvayo.*

15 -ngen nam tanaturu sampat ladin darpoddhata no-viyä yuttēyä idin govikulehi (sama)-ha[ra] .. .. -yek tamā lada na-

16 -m tanaturu no-balā di .. .. (-m kama-)kaṭa sitānam lo-vässan ohu hā no-häṇuṇu-mänavä ohu [ebandu]vū sitak situvada rā-

17 -ja-haṁsa siṁhādīngē (cäru) .. .. .. (ves tätu) kavuḍu käṇahil ādīn-sē mahajanayan-visin apahā[sa] .. .. lo-säpät-hā ekvä mä-

18 -kennēyä ebävin .. .. (ya yana) .. .. (lo-vässan ekvä ohu du)ru-koṭā .. .. (yo .. pi) .. .. .. (kā) .. .. -nyadarśanāt yanu ā-

19 -pta vacana heyin (bijaya)[1] .. .. .. ba .. .. rājayangē (daru) āpā **maha**pā(va)n bāla-vuvada lokasvāmi-[heyin] rājyayaṭa balā genä kula-

20 sirit-da .. .. kaṭayutu [ovu]nudu näta[hot] bisova**rungē** ājñāyehi pävätā rakṣā kaṭayutu unudu näta maharaju-

21 -n payä lū vahan mātrayakudu raja-tan-hi tabā rājya räkka yutu .. (sa) .. (ka) .. .. .. viṣa ōnā-sē kapruk pihiṭi tänä viṣa ruk hiṅduvannā-sē Kā-

22 -liṅga-vaṁśayaṭa himi Lakdivä Buddha-śāsanayaṭa pratipakṣa abauddha **Coḍa Pāṇḍyādi** rajun no-pihiṭi-viyä-yuttēyä **Vijaya**-rāja-kumārayan kere paṭa-

23 -n Lakdiv himi Kāliṅga-vaṁśayehi rajadaruvanṭayä soyā genä(t) vīnam un svāmi-koṭä lo-sasun rakṣā karanu äcārayi daham namē mē mu-

24 -ḷu lo saganneyä[,] sitā de-lo-säpat adar(ä)ti karaneyä[2][,] matuvana rajavirun mesē ayadaneyä[3][,] **Kaliṅgu-Lakindu-Nisaka-raja** guṇa **nanda**-neyä[4]

POSTSCRIPT.

1 Śrī **Kāliṅga-Cakravartti-**

2 svāmin-vahansē

3 äti kaḷa Niśśaṁka-

4 bhaṭayan lavā **Adhi-**

5 **-kāra Toṭa**[5](**da**)**navu**(**Mand-**)

6 **-nāvan** Sägiriyen

7 genvū śilā-lekha-galayi

[1] Probably for *Vijaya*; Mt. *bijaya.*

[2] *adarin rakneyä*, in the Häṭa-dā-gē Portico slab (ll. 22–23). See above, p. 89.

[3] *saganneyä*, ibid.

[4] *vindaneyä*, ibid.

[5] This may also be read *koḷa-*; Mt. *koṭa danvū mandi*, but see below, p. 123, note 2.

A

Scale 1¼ in. to 1 foot

Postscript on the south side of the slab

Scale 1¼ in. to 1 foot

C

TRANSLATION.

A.

[Line 1.] Hail! This *Dharma*, which gives happiness and which alone deserves to be honoured by the whole world, should always be preserved. **Vīra-Niśśaṅka-Malla** makes this appeal over and over again to the rulers of the earth in the name of [their] good fame [1].

[Lines 2-7.] King **Vijaya,** descended from the family of **Kāliṅga Cakravartin** who had the power of travelling through the air [2], and who belonged to the royal line of the Okkāka dynasty, exalted by [the possession of] an assemblage of auspicious and infinitely sublime qualities:—When one thousand seven hundred years had elapsed since this king, protected by the gods in accordance with the behest of the Buddha, arrived in the Island of Laṅkā, and destroying the *yakṣas* made it an abode for mankind [3], there was born the great king **Siri-Saṅgabo Kāliṅga Parākrama-Bāhu Vīrarāja Niśśaṅka-Malla Aprati-Malla** in **Siṁhapura** in the country of **Kaliṅga** in noble Dambadiva [4], the birth-place of Buddhas, Bodhisattas and Universal monarchs—[he was born] of the womb of the great queen **Pārvatī** unto king **Śrī-Jayagōpa** who was like unto a *tilaka* [5] ornament to this royal line [of the Okkāka dynasty]. He grew up in the midst of royal splendour, and being invited by the great king of the Island of Laṅkā, his senior kinsman [6], to rule over the Island of Laṅkā which is his by right of lineal succession of kings [7], he landed in Laṅkā in great state. Enjoying (thereafter) the regal dignities of governor and sub-king [8], and being proficient in the science of arms, in religion, and in all arts and sciences, he in due order of regal succession received the sacred unction and wearing the crown assumed supreme sovereignty.

[1] See Hāṭa-dā-gē Portico slab (lines 1-2), above, p. 89. Previous translators give no translation of this verse.

[2] See above, p. 89, note 3.

[3] This is a reference to the story given in *Dv*. ix. 1-31 and in *Mv*. vii. 1-45 and alluded to in other Ceylon historical works such as the *Rājāvaliya*, the *Pūjāvaliya*, &c.

[4] Skt. *Jambudvīpa*, India.

[5] See above, p. 80, note 8.

[6] *Kula-jeṭu* = Skt. *kula-jyēṣṭha* 'head of the family'.

[7] *Taman yona-parapuren himi* (line 5). Cf. *Lakdiv-polo-yen-parapuren himi* in this king's Dambulla record, line 2 (Vol. I, No. 9). See also Vol. I, p. 248, note 7.

[8] *Āpā himiyā tanaturu raja-isuru vindimin.* Cf. *āpā mahayā siri vindā*, Vol. I, p. 187, note 6.

[Lines 7–12.] His commanding personality is made dazzling to the eyes of the world through the fact that at his coronation festival he by a mere frown dispersed the clouds that gathered filling the vault of the firmament. His great majestic power is such that when hunting in the forest[1] a fierce savage she-bear sprang before him with a sharp growl, he laid her and her whelps dead[2] at his feet. He possesses the powers of a lion-king, which [can] extract water from any spot he likes, for [on one occasion] when [travelling] in a water-less desert, the moment he entertained the thought 'it would be well if there were water', [there fell a shower of rain] from an out-of-season cloud [and] produced an abundant stream. His power of command is such that it is not transgressible, for instance, when [once] on going to **Bāṇa**[3] to enjoy sea-sports[4], a huge *poloṅgā*[5] appeared in front of him, he said to it 'thy approach is unwelcome, be off and thyself prescribe what [punishment] is meet for thee'. The serpent then stung itself and sacrificed its life. He is endowed with a majestic personality, for the moment his state elephant saw him, the elephant was so delighted that he roared the shout of triumph and offered of his own accord his back [to ride on].

[Lines 12–18.] His Majesty drove away his enemies and gladdened the faces of the people just as the sun rising on the Orient Mount dispels darkness and expands the lotus blooms. Equalling Sakra, the Lord of the gods, in boundless regal splendour, the fu̥ll moon in gentleness, Mount Meru in firmness, the ocean in depth [of character], and the solid earth in patience, and flourishing like a 'wish-conferring' tree that has sprung up as a result of the merits of the world, [he thus thought to himself]:—'Many people in this Island of Laṅkā, which is the heritage of our dynasty, have through the unjust acts of some kings lost their family privileges and their wealth.' Then, [filled] with great compassion, he restored to them their family privileges[6]. He remitted taxes for five years, and enacted a law that in collecting revenue from lands and fields, the excessive taxes imposed by former kings should not be taken, that taxes should not exceed one *amuṇa* and three *päla* and six *maṇḍaran*[7] for an *amuṇa* [sowing extent of land]

---

[1] Lit. 'when in the sporting-forest' (*krīḍā-vanayehi*).

[2] *Divu käḍī*, lit. 'life being broken'. Cf. *divu pidū* 'sacrificed life' in line 11; *divu käḍī* may also mean 'the tongue being snapped' or 'the attack being frustrated'.

[3] *Bāṇa-samudra*, 'sea of Bāṇa', is the name of one of the immense tanks built by king Parākrama-Bāhu I (1153–1186 A.D.). See *Pūjāvaliya*, Extract, p. 30.

[4] *Samudra-krīḍā* 'sea-sports' may be either yachting, boating, or sports in the sea such as swimming, diving, &c. Some of the large tanks built by Parākrama-Bāhu I are designated 'seas'.

[5] A viper. [6] See this king's Dambulla record, lines 5–6 (Vol. I, pp. 132–133).

[7] See Vol. I, p. 133, note 2.

of the *uttē* (upper) tract, one *amuṇa* and two *pāla* and four *maṅḍaran* for an *amuṇa* of the *mändē* (middle) tract, and one *amuṇa* and one *pāla* and three *maṅḍaran* for an *amuṇa* of the *pässē* (lower) tract [1], and that for all times no tax should be collected from *chēna* cultivation [2] which is carried on with difficulty.

[Lines 18–24.] He quenched the fire of indigence with plenteous showers of wealth consisting of *kahavaṇu* [3] coins, copper, bell-metal, gold, silver, pearls, precious stones, clothes, and jewellery. He appointed ministers and other (officials) and provided them with 'livings' [4], serfs, cattle, permanent grants [5] and inheritances [6], gold and silver vessels [7], domestic utensils [8], and other riches in abundance. He repaired the great tanks, (irrigation) canals, and embankments [9] that had been long disused in the three kingdoms [10], and thus brought prosperity to every province, and security to the inhabitants thereof. He abolished the *visamburu-vata* [11]. With the aid of administrators of justice he put an end to injustice in various provinces. And thinking that robbers commit robbery on account of their desire for wealth [12], he gave them whatever things they liked and in this way he removed the fear of thieves. Everywhere amongst the dwellers in forests and dwellers in huts [13] he established order and cleansed

---

[1] The paddy land under a tank is divided into three tracts running parallel to the bund one below the other. The first which is nearest the tank is called *upayā-poṭa* or *mulpoṭa*, the one next to it, *härena-poṭa* or *peralā-poṭa*, and the third *kaṭṭakaḍuva*, *asväddum:a* or *koṭuvela*. These apparently correspond to *uttē*, *mändē* and *pässē* tracts of the present inscription. Each *poṭa* or tract is subdivided into two or three portions called *bāga*, namely, *ihala-bāge*, *mäda-bāge*, and *pahala-bāge*. They include the two strips, one at the tank end and the other at the opposite end, which are called *kurulu-pāḷu*, meaning an allowance of extra land as compensation for 'damage by birds'. Next to these, at each end are two larger strips called *älapat*, the property of the *gamarāla*, who is the hereditary chief cultivator of the village. For further particulars, see Ievers' *Manual of the North Central Province*, . 172.

[2] See above, p. 72, note 6.

[3] Skt. *kārṣāpaṇa*, P. Pkt. *kāhāpaṇa*, *kăhāvaṇa*. See Vol. I, pp. 209–210.

[4] *Divel.* See Vol. I, p. 105, note 4.

[5] *Pamuṇu* 'heritable lands' as distinct from *divel* lands held *ex officio*.

[6] See Vol. I, p. 133, notes 1 and 5.

[7] See above, p. 95, note 4.

[8] *Gehila.* This word is new to me. The above meaning is offered tentatively.

[9] See above, p. 69, note 10.

[10] See above, p. 90, note 4, and Vol. I, p. 181, note 3.

[11] Apparently a tax on fallow or barren land. See above, p. 69, note 6, and p. 96, where *pisamburu* should probably be read *visamburu*.

[12] Cf. Ruvanväli-dāgaba inscription of this king (lines 6–8), above, pp. 78–79.

[13] The phrase *val-vässan päl-vässan hämä-täna-ma ṣādhā kaṇṭaka śodhanaya koṭā* may also be rendered 'having stationed everywhere residents in forests and in huts [as overseers ?] he cleansed [the

[the country] of thorns [of disorder]. In accordance with the disciplinary rules he rid the Buddhist Church also of the thorns of irreligiousness, and thus rendered both the Church and the State free from evil. He provided the members of the Great Community who led pure lives with the four requisites, caused ordination ceremonies to be held every year, bestowed *kaṭhina*[1] gifts, and re-established offerings to gods, *daru-kusalān*[2] and *muṅga-kusalān*[2] as existed in the past. He rendered [in this way] great service to the cause of religion. He promoted [the interests of] religion and science by providing suitable means of subsistence for those versed in the *Dharma* and in the [various] branches of knowledge.

B.

Realizing that the long permanency of this kind of welfare of the world and of the religion [B, lines 1–5] depends on the royal dynasty, he sent [emissaries] to the country of **Kaliṅga** and caused many princesses of the Lunar and Solar dynasties to be brought over. And for his own son, the sub-king **Vīra-Bāhu Mahapā**, he secured royal maidens, and increased the royal family. Wearing the crown and other royal insignia, together with his chief queen **Kāliṅga Subhadrā Mahādēvī** and **Kalyāṇa Mahādēvī** of the **Gaṅgavaṁśa**, as well as his own son the sub-king and his daughter [the princess] **Sarvāṅga Sundarī**, His Majesty mounted the scale-pan and giving away every year wealth equal in weight to the five [royal personages][3], caused showers of *navaratna*[4] to fall, and afforded relief to the helpless and the distressed—such as monks, brahmans, the blind, the crippled, dwarfs, and hunchbacks, who had come from various quarters.

[Lines 5–10.] In this manner he conciliated the world and the church by the exercise of the 'four cardinal virtues[5]' and reached the very summit of

---

country] of thorns [of disorder]'. Cf. *ved-hal-vässan* 'hospital-residents' in Mäḍirigiriya pillar, side C, lines 9, 10 (above, No. 6), and *vel-vässan* 'field-dwellers' in Rajamäligäva pillar, side C, line 6 (above, No. 10).

[1] 'Robe made for a Buddhist monk in the course of a single day and night. This gift is considered highly meritorious.' Childers, *Pāli Dict.* s. v.

[2] Probably 'drinking vessels for children', and 'drinking vessels on the roadside for travellers'.

[3] See above, p. 73, and below, p. 133.

[4] Nine precious gems, namely, pearl, ruby, topaz, diamond, emerald, lapis lazuli, coral, sapphire, and *go-meda*. These are supposed to be related to the nine planets. M. W. *Dict.*

[5] *Catus-saṅgraha-vastu*. These are almsgiving, affability, promoting the prosperity of others, and loving others as ourselves. See *Dharma-pradīpikā* (Colombo, 1886), p. 189.

popularity, so much so that the people whose hearts he won protested their readiness to give their lives for him as a proof of the love and loyalty each entertained for him. Performing day after day the ten meritorious acts[1], he took his residence in the Kāliṅga city of **Pulastipura.** Though he constantly viewed with the eyes of spies his own kingdom and those of others as well, he thought that it would be well if he were to see with his own eyes how he had brought peace and order to the Island of Laṅkā (Ceylon). Accordingly escorted by his fourfold army, he went on a tour of inspection through the three kingdoms of Ceylon (*Tri-Siṁhala*), visiting the villages, towns, cities, and places difficult of access through water, hills, forests, and marshes, as if he were promenading in a house of amusements. He gladdened the dwellers in the border lands with great showers of gifts. In all the old vihāras in the three kingdoms which he visited—such as **Miyaguṇu**[2] **Maha-vehera, Mahagama**[3], **[Devunuvara?]**[4], and **Käläṇi**—he effected repairs.

[Lines 10–15.] **He caused the reclining, sitting, and standing images in the cave of Dambulla**[5] to be gilt, and made great offerings to the value of a *lac* [of *kārṣāpaṇa*]. He spent thirty-six *lacs* on making an offering to the **Ruvanmäli-maha-sä**[6] in **Anurādhapura**, and at the spot where the *dēvas* (gods) who were delighted with this offering uttered words of benediction, he caused a stone dāgaba to be raised. In all these places he had moral edicts inscribed on stone. Thinking it wicked that the Island of Laṅkā, the home of the excellent religion of the Buddha, should have been in times gone by .... and burning[7] [with indignation thereat] he made up his mind to conquer **Dambadiva** (India). So he set out in great royal state, surrounded by his fourfold army, and true to his title Niśśaṅka-Malla (dauntless warrior) he showed no hesitation anywhere, but crossed the great sea which was as calm as a blue sapphire eye[8] [set on an image of the Buddha] and landed in Dambadiva. There he dispatched heralds

---

[1] *Dasa-pin-kiriya-vata* = Skt. *daśa-puṇya-kriyā-vastu.* For an enumeration of them, see Childers' *Pāli Dict.* under *puñño.*

[2] P. *Mahiyaṅgaṇa-mahā-vihāra*, probably Bintenne-vehera. See Tennent, *Ceylon*, II, pp. 420–421; Geiger's *Mahāvaṁsa* (English tr.), p. 3, note 9, and p. 290, and Parker's *Ancient Ceylon*, pp. 315–316.

[3] See above, p. 59, and Parker's *Ancient Ceylon*, pp. 241, 386, and 394.

[4] Dondra Head. Cf. Forbes, *Eleven Years in Ceylon*, vol. ii, p. 176.

[5] See *E. Z.*, vol. i, No. 9.

[6] P. *Ratanamālika-mahā-cētiya*, the Ruvanväli Dāgaba in Anurādhapura. See above, No. 13.

[7] *Dāhävā*, from Skt. √*dah.* Cf. *danavā* 'to burn', pret. *dävā.*

[8] *Nil-miṇi-asäk-sē.* Cf. the expression *dā-raṅg-miṇin äs tabavā* (Vol. I, p. 222). Also Wijesiṇha's translation of the *Mahāvaṁsa*, p. 1, note 3.

and champions to demand single combats and army contests[1] and prepared for war.

[Lines 15–20.] Then the General **Lag-Vijayasiṅgu Senevi Tāvurunāvan,** intimating that he himself is going to be [at the battlefield] so as to secure the conquest of Dambadiva, set out to wage war. Whereupon the **Pāṇḍya** king and his mother, being filled with fear, made entreaties, saying 'be pleased to grant us lands enough for our maintenance and let Your Majesty take the kingdom', and sent [Niśśaṅka-Malla] 'golden fingers'[2], royal maidens, [elephants, horses], and various other gifts. By the copious streams of these and similar gifts from the country of the **Cōḷas** was quenched the flame of his indignation. He formed friendly alliances with such of the princes of **Karnāṭa, Nellūru, Gauḍa, Kaliṅga, Tiliṅgā, Gurjara,** and diverse other countries[3] as were desirous of his goodwill; but unto those who did not wish such friendship he struck terror by the very superiority of his own valour. He, moreover, exacted from such kingdoms princesses and tributes. Thereafter at **Rāmeśvara** he mounted the scale-pans and holding the *tulābhāra*[4] ceremony bestowed boundless wealth on inhabitants of many a land. He also had pillars of victory set up there as lasting monuments[5], and a temple (*dēvālaya*) built bearing the name *Niśśaṅkēśvara.*

[Lines 20–24.] Since there were no adversaries, he listened to the entreaties of the kings of Dambadiva to relieve them from fear. So (taking captives) he returned to the Island of Laṅkā escorted by the same [fourfold] army. Then reflecting that, as he had no enemies in this world, he would conquer the enemies of the next world, he caused many alms-houses, including the **Niśśaṅka-dāna-satra,** to be erected at many places in his own country as well as in other lands. He furnished these [houses] as 'wish-conferring trees'[6] with various objects for the enjoyment [of repasts, &c.], such as vessels of gold and silver[7] and the like, and held distributions of alms in abundance. For the purpose of witnessing the great rejoicings of the beggars who had received alms, he erected the pavilion

[1] For a repetition of this, see this king's Dambulla record, line 14 (Vol. I, p. 131), Häṭa-dā-gē Portico slab, line 13 (above, p. 88), Thūpārāma frieze, VIII, 2 (*A. I. C.*, No. 147), and Rankot-dāgaba inscriptions (*A. I. C.*, Nos. 150–151).

[2] *Ran-äṅgili.* See above, p. 90, note 7.

[3] See also the Dambulla slab (Vol. I, No. 9), and the Häṭa-dā-gē slabs (Nos. 14 and 15 above) for a repetition of this account.

[4] See above, pp. 73–74.

[5] Stated also in the Dambulla record.

[6] *Kap-ruk* = Skt. *kalpa-vṛkṣa* 'a tree of Indra's paradise fabled to fulfil all desires.

[7] See above, p. 95, note 4.

called **Niśśaṅka-dāna-maṇḍapaya**. To the Tooth and the Bowl relics he offered his son and daughter, and redeemed them by presenting in their stead [a model of] a dāgaba in solid gold together with other valuables.

C.

[Lines 1-5.] He built of stone the **Daḷadā-geya** (Tooth-relic house), **Vaṭa-geya** (the Rotunda), and the **Niśśaṅka-latā-maṇḍapaya** (Niśśaṅka flower-trail hall)[1], [all of them furnished] with gateways and walls so as to delight the hearts of beholders and be to them [as it were] heaven and *nirvāṇa*. He built also an *upakāra-caitya* (subsidiary dāgaba) adjoining the dāgaba at the **Mahā-vihāra** [in Poḷonnaruva], as well as the **Ruvanmäli** Dāgaba, eighty cubits [high ?] on the north side of the royal residence, with gateways, walls, and monks' residences surrounding it. [Thus] he ensured the long stability of the State and the religion. Moreover, considering that the Island of Laṅkā is a noble land because of the establishment of Buddhism there, that the living beings in it have lofty virtues, and that, therefore, they should receive advice and protection, he, out of compassion, proclaimed the [following] maxims of good counsel:

Though kings appear in human form, they are human divinities (*nara-dēvatā*) and must, therefore, be regarded as gods.

[Lines 5-10.] The appearance of an impartial king should be welcomed as the appearance of the Buddha. When kings inflict punishment commensurate with the offence [committed], they do so with good intentions, just as a physician applies a remedy for a bodily ailment. They restrain [their subjects] from evil and thus save them from falling into hell. They lead them to do good, thereby securing for them the [bliss of] heaven and release from re-births (*mōkṣa*). If the wishes of kings were not observed, the human world would be like hell; but if the wishes were respected, it would be like heaven. The trouble which one undergoes on behalf of kings is [like unto] the sowing of the seed of happiness. One must examine each . . . . and keep oneself aloof from all [such] evil ways. He who takes care of the wealth he has acquired should observe the duties incumbent on his family. Like sugar-cane [crushed in the press] one should [though . . . .] pour out sweetness of loyalty. Though one has fallen from office, one should be [loyal] to kings like a fruit fallen from the peduncle.

---

[1] See above, p. 85, note 2.

[Lines 11–18.] A subject should [so conduct] himself that when he is told that he has been summoned [to the presence of the king], he might go without fear, saying, 'Seeing I have done no wrong, what does it matter to me?' Talking about the secrets of kings is like invoking [the god of] Death by the repetition of charms. He who gives his life for the king will live long in the frame of glory. Real feeling is the feeling of gratefulness. The best occupation is the cultivation of land. The highest treasure is the *Dharma*. All these things ......, which should be cherished, exist through kings. Therefore one should not be remitting in the protection of the king. Kings do not like those who are puffed up with pride. So when one has received titles, offices, and wealth from them (i. e. kings), he should not become proud. If any one ..... belonging to the Govi caste, regardless of the titles and offices he has already received, were to think of .... the people should not associate themselves with him. Were he to entertain such an idea, he would be held by the public as an object of scorn—as crows, jackals, &c., that try to emulate the mien of swans, lions, and the like—and he himself would be wiped out with his worldly possessions. Therefore the people should unite and remove him ....

[Lines 18–24.] In accordance with the maxim '..............' they should elect for kingship the sons of .... kings, [namely, the princes holding the offices of] *āpā mahapā*, even though they be minors, for they are the lords of the world, and thus they should maintain family customs...... If there are no princes they should maintain [the kingdom] by submitting themselves to the sway of the queens. If there are no queens also, they should place in the position of king even a slipper worn on the feet of a great king and protect the kingdom. Just as pouring poison .... or planting poisonous trees where 'wish-conferring trees' stood, people should not establish in the Island of Laṅkā which belongs to the **Kāliṅga** dynasty, non-buddhistic kings of **Cōḷa, Pāṇḍya** [countries], &c., who are inimical to the religion of the Buddha. Since the time of prince **Vijaya**, it is to the princes of the Kāliṅga dynasty that the Island of Laṅka has belonged. Therefore, if there are any of them to be found, then it is the duty [of the people] to place them in the position of supremacy, and thus to protect the State and the religion.

It is indeed the *Dharma* that protects[1] this whole world. So reflecting, cherish love for the acquisition of happiness in both the worlds. Thus are future kings exhorted by king **Kaliṅgu Lakiṅdu Nisaka**[2] who loves virtue.

---

[1] 'Conquers' according to Mr. D. B. Jayatilaka. See, however, above, p. 90, note 8.

[2] = Kāliṅga Laṅkēndra Niśśaṅka [Malla].

POSTSCRIPT.

This stone for the lithic record[1] [given above] is the one which *Adhikāra*[2] **Toṭa-danavu Mand-nâvan** caused to be brought from **Sāgiri** by the Niśśaṅka[3], warriors maintained[4] by His Majesty the illustrious **Kāliṅga Cakravartin.**

No. 18. POḶONNARUVA: NIŚŚAṄKA-DĀNA-VINODA-MAṆḌAPA INSCRIPTION

AT the premises of the Archaeological Commissioner at Tōpaväva (Poḷonnaruva), there lies the upper portion of the shaft of a stone pillar with an inscription in twelve lines on two of its sides, six lines on each covering a smoothed surface of fifteen inches square. The letters are well incised between ruled lines[5] and are in size 1 to 1½ in.

The foregoing *galpota* record (section B, line 23) tells us that king **Niśśaṅka-Malla** had a pavilion called **Niśśaṅka-dāna-maṇḍapa** built for the express purpose of witnessing the great rejoicings of the beggars who had received alms. Now the present inscription indicates the *maṇḍapa* or pavilion so used. It is, therefore, quite obvious that the pillar containing this record originally stood somewhere at the entrance to it and served the same purpose as an inscribed tablet on the façade of a public building would do nowadays.

In his report upon the archaeological work done at Poḷonnaruva during

---

[1] *Śilā-lekha-gala* 'rock-record-stone' is a 'determinative' compound. Dr. Müller's translation 'this engraved stone' conveys the idea that the slab had already been engraved when it was brought to Poḷonnaruva from Sāgiri. This was apparently not the case.

[2] I am not sure that *adhikāra* is used here as a title, for if it be so, it should come after the name Toṭa-danavu Mand-nāvan. See, for example, the Gampola inscription of Vikrama-Bāhu, where occur the names Sivalkoḷu Lakdivu Adhikāra, Sēnālaṅkā[ra?] Adhikāra, and Parākrama Adhikāra, as those of some of his ministers (Bell's *Report on the Kegalla District*, p. 79). I am, therefore, inclined to read *adhikāra toṭa* as *adhikāra koṭa* and render the passage as follows:—'This slab for the lithic record is the one which Danavu-Mand-nāvan, exercising (his own) authority, caused to be brought from Sāgiri by the Niśśaṅka warriors maintained by His Majesty the illustrious Kāliṅga Cakravartin.' For the phrase *adhikāra koṭa* or *koṭā*, see the Ruvanväli slab of this king, line 30, above, p. 80. If, however, we still adhere to the first interpretation, we must then take the title *adhikāra* as standing for *Laṅkā adhikāra* and *Koṭa* or *Toṭa-danavu Mand-nāvan* as another title of the official. See above, pp. 100–101.

[3] Cf. 'Niśśaṅka Flower-trail hall', 'Niśśaṅka Tooth-relic house', above, p. 85.

[4] According to Dr. Müller 'in the time of the lord Çrī Kālinga Cakrawartti'.

[5] See accompanying facsimile (Plate 21).

the year ending March, 1886[1], Mr. S. M. Burrows makes mention of the discovery of this pillar-fragment at a site where he thought the whole pillar originally stood, namely, a ruined building, with massive pillars, abutting on the bund of Tōpa-väva tank[2] to the west of the road from Minnēriya, as shown in inset A of the plan of Poḷonnaruva facing page 84 above. Consequently he identified the ruin as that of *Niśśaṅka-dāna-vinoda-maṇḍapa*, 'the Pavilion for the past-time of Niśśaṅka-almsgiving'. Mr. H. C. P. Bell's excavations in 1902 fully confirmed this identification, for they revealed that the building which stood 'high at the centre of quadrangular terraced platforms' was in plan and style of architecture well suited for witnessing the distribution of alms[2].

A translation of the inscription is given by Mr. Burrows in *Ceylon Sessional Paper*, X, 1886, p. 13, as well as in *J. C. B. R. A. S.*, vol. x, 1887, pp. 70–71. Another version by Mr. Bell is to be found in his report for 1902, p. 11. The following is prepared independently of these.

TEXT.

A.		B.	
1	ශ්‍රී නිශශංකමල්ල	1	දෙශීන්ට (සව)
2	කාලිඟ පරාක්‍රමබා	2	දෙශීන්ට දි(වි තිළී)
3	හු චක්‍රවර්ත්ති සවා	3	වැඩැ හිඳ දන් දෙ
4	මින්වා[3]හන්සේ ද	4	වා වදාරන **නිශශං**
5	ඹදිවැ නො එක් ෙ[ද]	5	**[ක]දානවිනොද ම**
6	ශයෙන් ආ පර	6	**ඬපයයි**

TRANSCRIPT.

A.		B.	
1	Śrī **Niśśaṁka-Malla**	1	deśīnṭa (sva-)
2	**Kāliṅga-Parākrama-Bā-**	2	deśīnṭa di(vi tiḷī)[5]
3	**-hu Cakravartti-svā-**	3	väḍä hinda[6] dan de-
4	**-min-vāhansē**[4] Da-	4	-vā vadārana **Niśśaṁ-**
5	-mba-divä no-ek [d]e-	5	**[-ka-]dāna-vinoda-ma-**
6	-śayen ā para-	6	**-ňḍapayayi**

---

[1] *Ceylon Sessional Paper*, X, 1886, p. 10.

[2] For a detailed description of the ruin, see *A. S. C. Annual Report*, 1902, p. 10.

[3] 'වහන්සේ' වියයුතුයි.

[4] Read *vahansē*.

[5] Bell's transcript *dikṣilavä*.

[6] *hindina* in Bt.

TRANSLATION.

This is the Pavilion for taking pleasure in Niśśaṅka-almsgiving[1], wherein His Majesty **Śrī Niśśaṅka-Malla Kāliṅga-Parākrama-Bāhu Cakravarti-svāmī** is (graciously pleased)[2] to sit and cause the distribution of gifts among foreigners who have come from various parts of Dambadiva (India) and among his own countrymen.

No. 19. POḶONNARUVA: KĀLIṄGA FOREST GAL-ĀSANA INSCRIPTION

THIS granite seat or *āsana*, measuring 3 ft. 7 in. square, with moulded sides[3], stands 3 ft. above ground in the form of a pedestal a few feet off the south-east corner of the site (now identified as that of a *Piḷima-gē*[4], 'image-house') in the group of ruins on the Tōpa-väva quadrangle.

The inscription runs round all the four edges of the smoothed upper surface of the stone in four lines, the **letters**, 1 to 2 in. in size, being incised between ruled lines which are $2\frac{1}{2}$ in. apart, thus leaving a blank space of 22 in. square in the centre[5].

The record indicates the *āsana* as that on which king **Niśśaṅka-Malla** used to sit whenever he witnessed the dramatic and musical entertainments which were held in the **Kāliṅga-vana** after his return from his Ceylon tours and his Indian campaign. According to the inscription in the Häṭa-dā-gē vestibule (above, No. 15), this king began his journeys through the length and breadth of Ceylon in the second year of his reign, which was 1189 A.D. So the seat must have been set up at a later date, namely, between Sept. 1189 and Sept. 1196. The question as to whether it stands in its original place in the **Kāliṅga-vana**, 'Kāliṅga-forest', and whether this locality is identical with the **Kāliṅgodyāna**, 'the Kāliṅga-park', formed by Niśśaṅka-Malla[6] or not, must be left in abeyance until the publication of the other inscriptions discovered in this area.

---

1 *Niśśaṅka-dāna-vinoda-maṇḍapa* (B, lines 4–6).

2 *Divi tiḷi*, lit. 'granting or having compassion on their life'.

3 See *A. S. C. Annual Report*, 1903, p. 21, note †.

4 See shrine No. 11 in inset B of the plan of Poḷonnaruva, facing p. 84 above.

5 See accompanying facsimile (Plate 21).

6 See Häṭa-dā-gē Vestibule inscription (above, No. 15), line 8.

The following edition of the present record has been prepared from the two ink-impressions supplied by the Archaeological Commissioner.

TEXT.

1 [ශ්‍රී] **සිරිසඟබො වීරරාජ නිශ්ශංකමල්ල අප්‍රතිමල්ල කා[ලි]ඟ චක්‍රවර්ත්තින් වහන්සෙ** මුළු ලක්දිව නිෂ්කණ්ටක[කොටැ සත්] සෙත්කොටැ පෙරැ රජුන් නොබද අය ගෙනැ දු[ස්ථකළ ලංකාවාසීන්ට] පස් හවුරුද්දක අය හැරැ හවුරුදු පතා පස්

2 තුලාභාරයක් දී නම් ගම් වහල් සරක් **පමුණු** පරපුරු වස්ත්‍රාභරණාදි බොහො වස්තු දී සුවපත්කරවා කැති අඩ හැ(මැ කල)ටමැ හැරැ වල් මහවැ තැනැ ප්‍රාණීන්ට අභය දී (ස්වදෙශ) පරදෙශයෙහි බොහො සත්‍ර නංවා මහදන් පවත්වා තුන් රජ

3 ය පැදකුණුකොටැ සියලු ජලදුර්ග්ග ගිරිදුර්ග්ග වනදුර්ග්ග පංකදුර්ග්ග හා රට බිම් බලා ලොක ශාසන සම්‍රද්ධ[1]කොටැ යුද්ධාශායෙන් සියුරඟසෙනඟ පිරිවරා දඹදිවූ වැඩැ ද්වන්ද්ව යුද්ධ (ඉල්වා) නො ලදින් **චොඩ පාණ්ඩ්‍යාදි** රජදරුවන්

4 වෙලඟෙනැ එවූ රනැ ඇඟිලි හා රාජකන්‍යකාවන් හා පඬුරු දැකැ ජයස්තම්භ කරවා ලක්දිවූ වැඩැ දශරාජධර්මයෙන් රාජ්‍ය කෙරෙමින් **කාලිංගවනයෙහි** නෘත්‍ය[2]ගීත බලා වැඩගින්නා ශිලාසනයයි

TRANSCRIPT.

1 [Śrī] **Siri-Saṅgabo Vīra-rāja Niśśaṁka-Malla Aprati-Malla Kā**[li]**ṅga-Cakravarttin-vahanse** muḷu Lak-diva niṣkaṇṭaka-[koṭä sat] set-koṭä perä rajun no-bada aya genä du[stha-kaḷa Laṁkā-vāsīnṭa] pas havuruddaka aya härä havurudu patā pas

2 tulā-bhārayak dī nam gam vahal sarak pamuṇu parapuru vastrābharaṇādi boho vastu dī suva-pat-karavā käti-aḍa hä(mä kala)ṭa-mä härä val maha-vä tänä prāṇīnṭa abhaya dī (svadeśa) paradeśayehi boho satra naṁvā maha-dan pavatvā tun-raja-

3 -ya pädakuṇu-koṭä siyalu jala-durgga giri-durgga vana-durgga paṁka-durgga hā raṭa bim balā loka śāsana samraddha[3]-koṭä yuddhāśāyen siyuraṅga-senaṅga pirivarā Daṁba-divu väḍä dvandva yuddha(ilvā) no-ladin **Coḍa Pāṇḍyādi** raja-daruvan

---

[1] 'සමෘද්ධ' වියයුතුයි [2] 'නෘත්‍ය' වියයුතුයි

[3] Read *samṛddha*.

Kaliṅgu Forest Gal-āsana Inscription

Scale 2 inches to 1 foot.

Niśśaṅka-dāna-vinoda-maṇḍapa Inscription

A

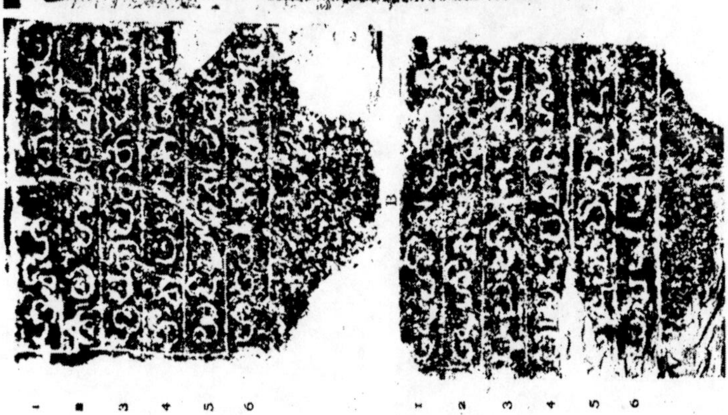

B

1 2 3 4 5 6

Scale 2 inches to 1 foot.

From ink-impressions supplied by the Archaeological Commissioner, Ceylon

4 veḷa-genā evū ranā ām̆gili hā rāja-kanyakāvan hā pam̆ḍuru dākā jaya-stambha karavā Lakdivu vāḍā daśa-rāja-dharmmayen rājya keremin **Kāliṁga-vana**yehi nratya[1]-gīta balā vāḍahindinā śilāsanayayi.

TRANSLATION.

[Prosperity!] His Majesty **Siri-Saṅgabo Vīra-rāja Niśśaṅka-Malla Aprati-Malla Kāliṅga-Cakravartī** freed the whole Island of Laṅkā from the thorns [of lawlessness] and restored peace to living beings[2]. He remitted taxation for five years for the benefit of the people of Laṅkā who had been distressed by the inordinate exactions of former kings[3]. And giving [to the people] five *tulābhāras*[4] every year, as well as bestowing [on them] titles, *divel*-lands[5], serfs, cattle, permanent grants, heritages, clothes, ornaments, and such [other kinds of] wealth in abundance, he made them prosperous. He abolished for all times taxes on *chēna*[6] cultivation and gave security to living beings in forests and large tanks. In his own country and in foreign lands he established many alms-houses and maintained the giving of abundant alms[7]. He made tours through the three kingdoms [of Ceylon] and inspected all lands in the country including those places difficult of access owing to water, mountains, forests, or marshes. [In this way] he promoted the welfare of the State and the Church.

Then being desirous of martial contests, he proceeded to India attended by his fourfold army and sought single combats. Finding none, and seeing [however] 'the golden fingers', the royal maidens, and other tribute that were sent by the suppliant kings of **Cōḍa, Pāṇḍya,** and other countries, he raised columns[7] of victory and returned to the Island of Laṅkā, where he is now ruling in accordance with the ten principles of regal duty[8]. And this stone-seat does His Majesty occupy for the purpose of witnessing dancing and singing in the **Kāliṅga Forest.**

[1] Read *nṛtya.*

[2] As in Häṭa-dā-gē Portico slab, lines 7–11 (above, No. 14).

[3] This is repeated in many of Niśśaṅka-Malla's inscriptions.

[4] See above, pp. 73 and 118, note 4.

[5] Here *gam* stands for *divel-gam*, lands granted by government in lieu of payment for services to be held whilst in service. Cf. the Dambulla inscription, line 5 (Vol. I, No. 9).

[6] See above, pp. 72, 90, and Vol. I, p. 133, note 4.

[7] Repeated in Häṭa-dā-gē Portico slab, lines 11–16, also in the Dambulla and the Galpota records.

[8] *Daśa-rāja-dharma.* See Vol. I, p. 181, note 7.

No. 20. POḶONNARUVA: KALĀ-KRĪḌĀ-VINODA-GAL-ĀSANA INSCRIPTION

THIS oblong stone-seat, measuring about 6 ft. by 3 ft., is now placed near the north-east angle of the *Piḷimagē*[1] ruin in the Tōpaväva quadrangle. According to Mr. Bell it was 'brought from the shrine of Thūpārāma[2] where it had been improperly utilized as a flower altar'[3]. We are, therefore, not sure of the exact spot where it originally stood.

The inscription in four lines runs round all the four edges of the smoothed upper surface of the slab, between ruled lines which are 3 in. apart, leaving thus a blank space of 4 ft. 6 in. by 1 ft. 9 in. in the centre[4]. The letters, in size 1–1½ in., are boldly engraved. Their type is the same as that of other inscriptions of king Niśśaṅka-Malla.

The record which begins with a Sanskrit stanza tells us that he sat on this seat to witness the entertainments of various artistes after he had returned from his campaign in India and had completed the restoration of Buddhist monuments in Ceylon. We know from his inscription at the Ruvanväli-dāgaba[5] that he undertook the reparation of the dāgabas in Anurādhapura in the fourth year of his reign (i.e. 1191–1192 A.D.). And if these were included (as they possibly were) in his reference to restorations effected by him, the date of placing this seat must obviously fall later, namely, between Sept. 1192 and 1196 A.D.

The following text and translation have been prepared from two ink-estampages supplied by the Archaeological Commissioner.

TEXT.

1 ශ්‍රී වීරනිශ්ශංකමල්ලෙන ශ්‍රීපරාක්‍රමබාහුනා । ඉදම්බාසිතම්භානුවශක්ෂිරාණ්ණවෙ
ඤුනා ॥ ඔකාවස් රජපරපුරෙන් ආ කාලිඟ ශ්‍රීපරාක්‍රමබාහු චක්‍රවර්ත්තීන්
වහන්සේ ලංකාවීපයට එක මඟලදීපයක්මෙන් පැනී ලංකාතංක ප්‍රශමය
කොටැ සමස්ත ලංකාවීපය අපවරක ගුහ[6]යක්සේ සම්බාධකොටැ සිතා වොඩ

[1] Shrine No. 11 in inset B of the plan of Poḷonnaruva, facing p. 84 above.

[2] *Ibid.*, No. 13.

[3] *A. S. C. Annual Report*, 1903, p. 21, note †.

[4] See accompanying facsimile (Plate 22).

[5] Above, No. 13.

[6] 'ගෘහ' වියයුතුයි

Kalā-krīḍā-vinoda-Gal-āsana Inscription

Scale 1½ inches to 1 foot.

2 **ගෞඩාදීන්** හා සඟ්‍රාමාර්ත්ථීවැ මහ**දඹදිවු** මහපිරිවරින් වැඩැ නංදෙසැ
රාජාදීන් රට්බිම් හැරැ වල් වදනවුන් බලා කුළුණින් අභය දී **දඹදිවැ** ද
ප්‍රතිමල්ලයක්හු නොදැකැ ජයස්තම්භ කරවා නැවැ[තැ] ලක්දිවු වැඩැ
බොහොකල් (නැ)සී (තුබූ) [වෙහෙර ම]හසෑ කර(වා) **දඹදිවැ ලක්දිවැ**
තන්

3 හි තන්හි සත්‍ර කරවා නංදෙසැ යාචකයනට් **අපමණ** වස්තු **විය**කොටැ එපමණෙ
කිනුදු සතුටු නොවැ හවුරුදු පතා සතර තුලාභාරයක් නැඟී [රන්] රුවන්
වස්ත්‍රාභරණාදීන් ලොවැ[ස්ස]ඳ දිළිඳු හැරැ ලොසසුන් වැඩකොටැ කලාක්‍රීඩා
විනොද(නපි)ණීසැ වැඩැ හි

4 ඳිනා ආසනයයි

TRANSCRIPT.

1 Śrī **Vīra-Niśśaṁka-Mallena Śrī-Parākrama-Bāhunā** | idam adhyāsitam
bhānu-vaṁśa-kṣīrārṇṇavendunā | Okāvas raja-parapuren ā
Kāliṅga-Śrī-Parākrama-Bāhu Cakravarttin-vahansē Laṁkā-dvīpa-
yaṭa eka maṅgala-dīpayakmen pänī Laṁkātaṁka praśamaya-koṭā samasta
Laṁkā-dvīpaya apavaraka grahayaksē[1] sambādha-koṭā siṭā **Coḍa-**

2 **Gauḍādīn** hā saṅgrāmārtthī-vä maha-**Dambadivu** maha-pirivarin väḍä
nan-desā rājādīn raṭ-bim härä **val** vadanavun balā kuḷuṇin abhaya dī
Dambadivä-da pratimallayak-hu no-däkä jaya-stambha karavā nävä[tä]
Lakdivu väḍä boho-kal(nä)sī (tubū)[vehera ma]ha-sā kara(vā) **Dambadivä**
Lakdivä tan-

3 -hi tan-hi satra karavā naṅ-desä yācakayanaṭ **apamaṇa** vastu viya-koṭä
epamaṇekinudu satuṭu novä havurudu patā satara tulā-bhārayak näṅgī
[ran-] ruvan-vastrābharaṇādīn lo-vä[ssa]n-da diḷindu härä lo-sasun väḍa-
koṭä kalā-krīḍā vinoda(na-pi)ṇisä väḍä hi-

4 -dinā āsanayayi

TRANSLATION.

Hail! The seat of[2] His Majesty **Vīra-Niśśaṅka-Malla Śrī-Parākrama-Bāhu** who is like unto a moon [that beams] on the milky ocean of the Solar race.

His Majesty **Kāliṅga-Śrī-Parākrama-Bāhu Cakravartī** descended from the royal line of the Okkāka dynasty, shining on the Island of Laṅkā like

[1] Read *gṛhayaksē*.

[2] Lit. 'This is sat upon by Vīra-Niśśaṁka-Malla', &c.

a unique and auspicious lamp, caused the afflictions of Laṅkā to cease and united[1] the whole Island of Laṅkā as it were a house with inner apartments. With the object of fighting with the **Coḍa, Gauḍa** and other nationalities he proceeded to the great [continent of] **Dambadiva** (India) with a large retinue; and there seeing that kings and other [personages] of various territories were leaving their homes and fleeing into the jungle, he out of compassion granted them security. Then, as he found no [equal] adversary in Dambadiva, he raised columns of victory and returned to the Island of Laṅkā. [Here] he restored the vihāras and great dāgabas which had long been in ruins.

In various places, both in Dambadiva and in Laṅkā, he established almshouses and expended countless wealth on beggars who came from divers lands. And, not contented with these [acts of generosity], he gave away every year four *tulābhāra*[2] weight of gold, jewels, clothes, and ornaments, and dispelled the poverty of the people. Thus he promoted the interests of the Church and the State. And this is the seat His Majesty occupies for the purpose of enjoying *kalā-krīḍā*[3].

No. 21. POḶONNARUVA: KĀLIṄGA PARK GAL-ĀSANA INSCRIPTION

THIS stone-seat, measuring 3 ft. 9 in. square, was unearthed outside the ruin, now identified as that of king Niśśaṅka-Malla's Council Chamber on the promontory[4] overlooking the Tōpa-väva tank in Poḷonnaruva.

The inscription, in eight lines, covers 3 ft. 6 in. square of the upper smoothed surface, and is engraved, as in other *āsanas* of the kind, between ruled lines, 2 in. apart, running parallel to each side of the square and leaving a blank space of 12 in. by 11 in. at the centre[5].

The letters are fairly well cut, averaging in size from 1 to 2 in., and represent the type of alphabet of the period. The contents form the usual panegyrical account of some of Niśśaṅka-Malla's acts and munificence as

---

[1] *Apavaraka-gṛhayak-sē sambādha-koṭā.*

[2] Five *tulābhāra* in other records. See above, pp. 73 and 118, note 4, and below, pp. 133 and 136.

[3] Entertainments connected with the sixty-four kinds of art, such as singing, dancing, &c.

[4] See the plan of Poḷonnaruva (inset C, ruin No. 1), facing p. 84 above.

[5] See accompanying facsimile (Plate 23).

given in his Dambulla record (Vol. I, No. 9) and in the Häṭa-dā-gē Portico slab (above, No. 14), followed by the statement that the 'lion-seat' is the one on which His Majesty sat whenever he witnessed the musical performances in the **Kāliṅga Park**, and that the stone itself was brought for this purpose from **Eṇḍera-galla**, which is most probably the village **Eṇḍēru-gala**, situated about five miles west of the famous rock-fortress of Sīgiri and half a mile from Inamalawa on the Dambulla-Trincomalee high road [1]. The exact locality of the **Kāliṅga Park**, which, we are told [2], was formed by this king Niśśaṅka-Malla, has as yet not been definitely fixed. But if the original site of the present 'lion-seat' is somewhere near the spot where it was unearthed, namely, just outside the ruin of the 'Council Chamber', then the Park must have occupied the open ground on the eastern side of it. Mr. Bell also admits the existence of a park here, for he says, 'The "Council Chamber" and "Audience Hall" each stood in its own enclosure, one wall pierced by two openings for mutual admission, sufficing to divide their premises north and south. The precincts of the "Audience Hall" were more spacious, allowing a width of some 15 ft. round the building on three sides, and in front running out east as a broad bay. Thence a flight of steps descended into the traditional "King's Garden" on the farther side of which, directly opposite, was one of the *doraṭu* (entrance porches) into the Citadel' [3]. But he identifies the garden with the **Nandana Park** formed by Parākrama-Bāhu I some few years before, because of the existence within this area of ruined buildings, stone baths, &c., similar to those described in the account of the Nandana Park in the *Mahāvaṁsa* [4]. The truth may be that Niśśaṅka-Malla made just a few trifling alterations and improvements and re-named the park as *Kāliṅgōdyāna* (Kāliṅga Park) after the name of the land of his birth.

The following edition and translation of the record have been prepared from two ink-estampages supplied by the Archaeological Commissioner.

TEXT.

1 ස්වස්ති ශ්‍රී සිරිසඟබො වීරරාජ නිශ්ශංක මල්ල අප්‍රතිමල්ල කාලිඟ චක්‍රවර්ත්තින්
වහන්සේ මුළු ලක්දිව නිෂ්කණ්ටක කොට සත් සෙත්කොට පෙරැ රජුන්
නොබඳ අය ගෙනැ දුසර කළ ලංකාවාසීන්ට පස්හවුරුද්දෙකැ අ

2 ය හැරැ හවුරුදු පතා පස් තුලාභාරයක් දී නම් ගම් වහල් සරක් පමුණු

[1] See *A. S. C. Annual Report*, 1894, p. 8.

[2] See Häṭa-dā-gē Vestibule inscription, line 8 (above, No. 15).

[3] *A. S. C. Annual Report*, 1900, p. 10.

[4] *Ibid.*, 1901, p. 13.

පරපුරු රන් රුවන් වස්ත්‍රාභරණාදි බොහො වස්තු දී සුවපත් කරවා කැති
අඩ හැමැ කලටමැ හැරැ වල් මහවැ තැනැ ප්‍රාණීන්ට අභය දී ස්වදෙශ

3 පරදෙශයේහි බොහො සත්‍ර නංවා මහදන් පවත්වා තුන්රජය පැදකුණුකොටැ
සියලු ජලදුර්ග්ග ගිරිදුර්ග්ග වනදුර්ග්ග පංකදුර්ග්ග හා රට බිම් බලා වදාරා යම්මැ
රජදරුකෙනකුන්ට දස්කම් කළවුන්ට

4 දෙන හිරසඳපමුණු වේයන් මීයන් කන පතැ ලියා දියෙහි ඈඳි හිරිසෙ
අස්ථිර නොකොටැ උන්ගේ වංශපරම්පරාවට බොහො කල් සිටුනා[1] පරිද්දෙන්
හා උන්ගෙ නමත් දුන් රජදරුවන්ගේ

5 නමත් පස්වාදහසට පවත්නා පරිද්දෙන් තාම්‍ර ශාසන ලංකායෙහි පවත්කොටැ
බොහො දස්කම්කළවුන්ට දී වදාරා ලොකශාසනය සම්‍රඬ[2]කොටැ යුඬාශායෙන්
සියු

6 රගසෙනඟ පිරිවරා **දඹදිවු** වැඩැ චත්වසුඬ සෙනාසුඬ ඉල්වා නොලදින් **චොඩ**
සඬාදි රජදරුවන් වෙළගෙනැ එවූ රනැ ඇඹිලි හා රා

7 ජ කන්‍යකාවන් හා පඬුරු දැකැ ජයස්තම්භ කරවා ලක්දිවු වැඩැ දශරාජ
ධර්ම්මයෙන් රාජ්‍ය කෙරෙමින් **කාලිංගොද්‍යානයෙ**

8 හි නෘ[3]ත්‍ය ගීතාදි කලා ක්‍රීඩාඃ පිණිසැ වැඩ හිඳිනා සිංහාසනයයි. මෙ ගල
එඬෙරගල්ලෙන් ගෙනා වදාළෙ.

TRANSCRIPT.

1 Svasti Śrī **Siri-Saṅgabo Vīra-rāja Niśśaṁka-Malla Aprati-Malla Kāliṅga-Cakravarttin-vahansē** muḷu Lakdiva niṣkaṇṭaka-koṭä sat set-koṭä perä rajun no-bada aya genä dustha-kaḷa Laṁkāvāsīnṭa pas-havuruddekā a-

2 -ya härä havurudu patā pas tulābhārayak dī nam gam vahal sarak pamuṇu parapuru ran ruvan vastrābharaṇādi boho vastu dī suvapat karavā käti-aḍa hämä kalaṭa-mä härä val maha-vā tänä prāṇīnṭa abhaya dī svadeśa

3 paradeśayēhi boho satra naṁvā maha-dan pavatvā tun-rajaya pädakuṇu-koṭä siyalu jala-durgga giri-durgga vana-durgga paṁka-durgga hā raṭa bim balā vadārā yam-mä rajadaru-kenakunṭa daskam kaḷavunṭa

4 dena hira-sanda-pamuṇu vēyan mīyan kana patā liyā diyehi ändi hiri-se asthira no-koṭä ungē vaṁśa-paramparāvaṭa boho kal siṭunā[4] paridden hā ungē namat dun rajadaruvangē

5 namat pasvādahasaṭa pavatnā paridden tāmbra-śāsana Laṁkāyehi pavat-koṭä boho daskam kaḷa-vunṭa dī vadārā lokaśāsanaya samraddha[5]-kotä yuddhāśāyen siyu-

---

[1] 'සිටිනා' වියයුතුයි [2] 'සමෘඬ' වියයුතුයි [3] 'නෘත්‍ය' වියයුතුයි

[4] Read *sitinā*. [5] Read *samṛddha*.

6 -raṅga-senaṅga pirivarā **Dambadivu** väḍä dvandva-yuddha senā-yuddha ilvā no-ladin **Coḍa Paṅḍyādi** rajadaruvan veḷa-genä evū ranä äṅgili hā rā-

7 -ja-kanyakāvan hā paṅḍuru däkä jaya-stambha karavā Lakdivu väḍä daśa-rāja-dharmmayen rājya keremin **Kāliṅgodyānaye-**

8 -hi nratya[1]-gītādi kalā-krīḍā-piṇisä väḍa hindinā siṁhāsanayayi. Me gala **Eṇḍeragallen** genvā vadāḷe.

TRANSLATION.

Hail! Prosperity! His Majesty **Siri-Saṅgabo Vīra-rāja Niśśaṅka-Malla Aprati-Malla Kāliṅga-Cakravartin-vahanse** freed the whole Island of Laṅkā from the thorns of disorder, and restored peace to living beings. By remitting taxation for five years, by giving away five *tulābhāras*[2] every year, and by bestowing titles, [*divel-*]lands, serfs, cattle, permanent grants, heritages, gold and gems, clothes and ornaments, and such other wealth in abundance, he relieved the people of Laṅkā who had been distressed by the inordinate exactions of former kings[3]. He abolished for all times the taxes on *chēna* cultivation[4], and gave security to living beings in forests and in great tanks. In his own country and in other lands he established many alms-houses and maintained the giving of abundant alms. He toured through the three kingdoms [of Ceylon], and having visited all places difficult of access owing to water, mountains, forests or marshes, he inspected the whole land.

With the object that perpetual grants[5] made to those who have performed loyal services to kings might not be made impermanent, like lines drawn on water, by being written on [palm] leaves which white ants and mice [as a rule] eat up; but in order that they might last a long time in the family lines of the donees, and that the donees' names as well as those of the kings who made the grants might remain for five thousand years, His Majesty introduced copper-plate grants into Laṅkā[6]. And he made many [such] grants to those who rendered loyal service.

Having [thus] promoted the interests of the Church and the State, he, longing for war, proceeded to Dambadiva, surrounded by his fourfold army.

---

[1] Read *nṛtya*.

[2] See above, pp. 73 and 130, note 2.

[3] See also Niśśaṅka-Malla's Dambulla inscription, lines 5–6 and 9 (Vol. I, No. 9) and the Häṭa-dā-gē Portico slab, lines 7–11 (above, No. 14).

[4] *Käti-aḍa*. See above, p. 72.

[5] *Hira-sanda-pamuṇu*, 'grants that are valid so long as the sun and moon endure'.

[6] See also the Dambulla record, lines 10–11 (Vol. I, No. 9).

There having in vain sought single combats and army contests, but seeing the presents consisting of 'golden fingers' and royal maidens sent by the **Cōḍa** and the **Pāṇḍya** kings[1] with their supplications, he raised columns of victory and returned to Ceylon, where he is now ruling in accordance with the ten principles of regal duty. And this 'lion-seat' does His Majesty occupy for the purpose of [witnessing] artistic performances, such as dancing, singing, &c., in the **Kāliṅga Park**. His Majesty was pleased to have this stone brought from **Eṇḍeragalla.**

No. 22. POḶONNARUVA: RANKOT-DĀGABA GAL-ĀSANA INSCRIPTION

THIS stone-seat with moulded sides[2], measuring about 3 ft. in height, 3 ft. square at the top and a little larger at the bottom, was discovered in the jungle some two hundred yards to the east of the ruin now known as **Ran-kot-vehera.**

The inscription which covers its upper surface is in six lines and is engraved between ruled lines, 2 in. apart, which run parallel to each side of the square, leaving a blank smooth space of 16 in. by 15½ in. at the centre[3].

The **letters** are fairly well preserved. They are in size 1 to 2 in., and resemble in type the script of other records of Niśśaṅka-Malla. There is also the usual lack of uniformity in writing consonantal groups, as, for example, Skt. නිෂ්කණ්ටක, instead of නිෂ්‍කණ්‍ටක ; Sinh. හවුරුදද, instead of හවුරුද්ද.

The **contents**, like those of the foregoing *gal-āsana* records, form but a repetition of some of Niśśaṅka-Malla's acts by way of introduction to the principal statement indicating the stone-seat which His Majesty occupied whilst watching the construction of the **Ruvanväli-dāgaba** at Poḷonnaruva.

The **date** of this record must be earlier than that of the Galpota inscription (above, No. 17), as the latter makes mention of the Ruvanväli-dāgaba, which was then already built on the north side of the palace to a height of eighty cubits, with gateways, walls, and monks' residences surrounding it[4].

---

[1] For a repetition of all this, see the Häṭa-dā-gē Portico slab, lines 21–15 (above, No. 14).

[2] For a wood-cut of this stone, see *J. R. A. S.* vii. 1875, p. 159.

[3] See accompanying facsimile (Plate 23).

[4] See section C, lines 2–3.

The *Pūjāvaliya* also refers to this dāgaba as one of Niśśaṅka-Malla's edifices[1], while the *Mahāvaṁsa* confirms the Galpota account in stating that Niśśaṅka-Malla built the **Ratanāvali**[2]**-cetiya** to an exceedingly great height and adorned it with a golden pinnacle[3]. It was evidently from this pinnacle that the dāgaba site got its present name **Ran-kot-vehera,** 'golden-spire-monastery'.

A transcript with a translation of the present record was first published by Professor Rhys Davids in *J.R.A.S.* for 1875 (pp. 166–167). Dr. Müller republished it with a lithographic plate as No. 150 of *A.I.C.* The present version is based on the two ink-estampages supplied by the Archaeological Commissioner.

TEXT.

1 ශ්‍රී **සිරිසඟබෝ වීරරාජ නිශ්ශංකමල්ල කාලිඟ චක්‍රවර්ත්තීන්වහන්සේ** ලක්දිව නිෂ්ක
ණ්ටක කොට සත් සෙත්කොට පෙර රජුන් නොබඳ අය ගෙනැ දුසථකළ
ලංකාවාසීන්ට පස්හවුරුද්දකට අය හැර හවුරු

2 දු පතා පස්තුලාභාරයක් දී නම් ගම් වහල් සරක් පමුණු පරපුරු රන් රුවන්
වස්ත්‍රාභරණාදි බොහො වස්තු දී සුවපත්කරවා කැතිඅඩ[4] හැමැ කලටමැ හැර
වල් මහවැ තැනැ ප්‍රාණීන්ට අභය

3 දී ස්වදෙශපරදෙශයෙහි බොහො සත්‍ර නංවා මහදන් පවතවා තුන්රජය
පැදකුණුකොට සියලු දුර්ග හා රට කිම් බලා ලොකශාසන සම්බ[5] කොට
පූඩාශායෙන් සිපූරගසෙ

4 නග පිරිවර දම්බදිවූ වැඩැ මඤ[6] පූඩාදි ඉල්වා නොලදින් චොඩ පාඩ්‍යාදි
රජදරුවන් වෙහෙළගෙනැ එවූ රනැඇතිලි හා රාජකනායකාවන් හා පඬුරු
දැකැ ජය

5 ස්තම්භ කරවා ලක්දිවූ වැඩැ දශරාජධර්මයෙන් රාජ්‍ය කෙරෙමින් **රුවන්වැලි
දගබා**[7] කරවා වදාරන සැලැ කර්මාන්ත බලා වදාරා

6 වැඩැ හුන් මුළුගලින් කළ ආසනයයි

---

[1] Kīrti-Niśśaṅka nam raja Poḷonnaruvē *Ruvanväli-dāgaba* baňdavā *kot* palaňdavā . . . (*Pūjāvaliya*, Extract, p. 30).

[2] This is the Pāli form of Sinh. *Ruvanväli.*

[3] Bandhāpetvā samuttuṅgaṁ *Ratanāvali-cetiyaṁ* | alaṅkarittha *sovaṇṇatthūpikāya* tam uttamaṁ || (*Mv.* lxxx. 20).

[4] 'අය' සිද කියවිය හැකියි

[5] 'සම්ඹ' වියයුතුයි

[6] 'මඬුව' වියයුතුයි

[7] 'දාගබ' වියයුතුයි

TRANSCRIPT.

1 Śrī **Siri-Saṅgabo Vīra-rāja Niśśaṁka-Malla Kāliṅga-Cakravarttīn**[1]-**vahansē** Lakdiva niṣkaṇṭaka-koṭa sat set-koṭa perä rajun no-bada aya genä dustha-kaḷa Laṁkā-vāsīnṭa pas-havuruddakaṭa aya härä havuru-

2 -du patā pas-tulā-bhārayak dī nam gam vahal sarak pamuṇu parapuru ran ruvan vastrābharaṇādi boho vastu dī suva-pat-karavā käti-aḍa[2] hämä kalaṭa-mä härä val maha-vā tänä prāṇīnṭa[3] abhaya

3 dī sva-deśa-para-deśayehi boho satra naṁvā maha-dan pavatvā tun-rajaya pädakuṇu-koṭa siyalu durgga hā raṭa[4] bim balā loka-śāsana samraddha[5]-koṭa yuddhāśāyen siyuraṅga-se-

4 -naṅga pirivarā Dambadivu väḍä dvanda[6]-yuddhādi ilvā no-ladin Coḍa Pāṇḍyādi rajadaruvan veheḷa[7]-genä evū ranä-äṅgili hā rāja-kanyakāvan hā paṅḍuru däkä jaya-

5 stambha karavā Lakdivu väḍä daśa-rāja-dharmmayen rājya keremin **Ruvanväli-dāgabā**[8] karavā vadārana kalä karmmānta balā vadārā

6 väḍä hun muḷu-galin kaḷa āsanayayi

TRANSLATION.

Prosperity! His Majesty **Siri-Saṅgabo Vīra-rāja Niśśaṁka-Malla Kāliṅga-Cakravartī** freed the Island of Laṅkā from the thorns [of lawlessness] and restored peace to living beings. He remitted taxes for five years for the benefit of the people of Laṅkā who had been distressed by the inordinate exactions of former kings. And giving [to the people] five *tulābhāras* every year, as well as bestowing [on them] titles, [*divel*-]lands[9], serfs, cattle, permanent grants, heritages, gold, jewels, clothes, ornaments, and such [other kinds of] wealth in abundance, he made them prosperous. He abolished for all times taxes on *chēna*[10] cultivation and gave security to living beings in forests and large tanks. In his own country and in foreign lands he established

[1] Read *-vartin.*

[2] This may also be read *aya.*

[3] Read *prāṇinṭa.*

[4] Mt. *durgga haraṭa bim.*

[5] Read *samṛddha.*

[6] Read *dvandva.*

[7] *veḷa* in other records of Niśśaṅka-Malla.

[8] Read *dāgaba.*

[9] See above, p. 127, n. 5.

[10] See above, p. 72, n. 6.

Kāliṅga Park Gal-āsana Inscription

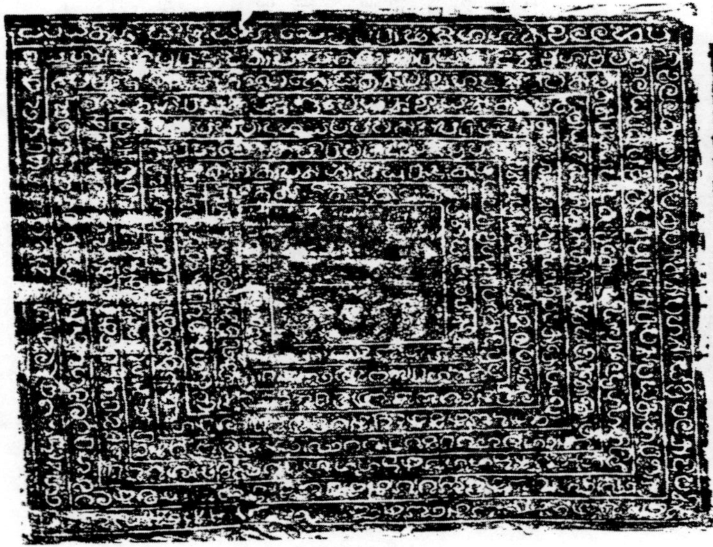

Scale $1\frac{5}{12}$ inches to 1 foot.

Rankot-dāgaba-Gal-āsana-Inscription

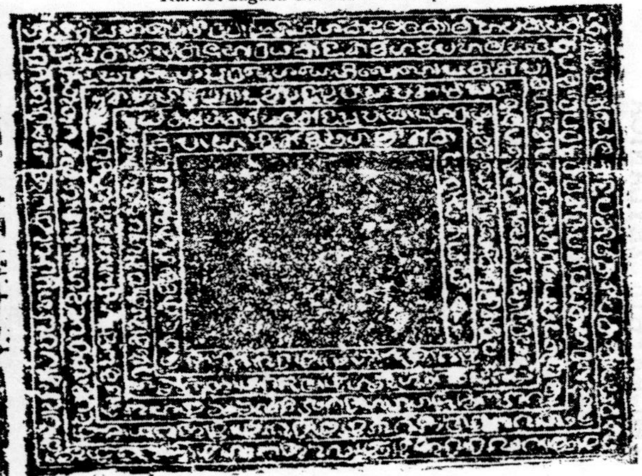

Scale $1\frac{3}{12}$ inches to 1 foot.

From ink-impressions supplied by the Archaeological Commissioner, Ceylon

many alms-houses and maintained the giving of abundant alms. He made tours through the three kingdoms [of Ceylon] and inspected lands and villages, including all places difficult of access. [In this way] he promoted the welfare of the State and the Church.

Then, being desirous of martial contests, he proceeded to Dambadiva (India), attended by his fourfold army, and sought single combats, &c. Finding none, but seeing 'the golden fingers', the royal maidens, and other tribute that were sent by the suppliant kings of Cōḍa, Pāṇḍya, and other countries, he raised columns of victory and returned to the Island of Laṅkā, where he is now ruling in accordance with the ten principles of regal duty. And as such, His Majesty was pleased to sit on this seat, carved out of a single stone, and watch the [progress of] work whilst superintending the building of **the Ruvanväli-dāgaba.**

No. 23. POḶONNARUVA: RANKOT-DĀGABA PILLAR-INSCRIPTION

THIS inscription is repeated on each of the four pillars which once supported the roof of an open pavilion on the southern terrace of the **Ruvanväli** or **Rankot-dāgaba**[1]. In the centre of the enclosed space which, according to Professor Rhys Davids, was about eight feet square, there must have been an *āsana*, a sort of *dais*, from which, as the inscription states, the king used to pay his adorations to the relics enshrined in the dāgaba.

The four pillars are now fallen, and two of them are broken. They are about 6 ft. long, 12½ in. square at top and bottom, and octagonal in the centre where the writing is in consequence narrower, being only about 5 in. wide.

The **letters** are engraved between ruled lines which are two inches apart and vary in size from 1 to 2 in. Their type is the same as that of the foregoing records of Niśśaṅka-Malla[2].

The **contents** are, as usual, a repetition of some of this king's acts as an introduction to the principal statement indicating the purpose for which the pavilion was built.

The **date** is not given, but it must be placed some time after the fourth

---

[1] For the exact situation of this ruin, see plan of Poḷonnaruva, facing p. 84 above.

[2] See accompanying facsimile (Plate 24).

year of Niśśaṅka-Malla's reign, that is to say between 1191 and 1196 A.D., because the record refers not only to his visit to Anurādhapura, which took place in his fourth regnal year, but also to the tours of inspection, some of which he made most probably at a still later period[1].

Of the four copies of the inscription on the four pillars, a lithographic plate of two of them, together with a transcript and a translation, was for the first time published by Professor Rhys Davids in the *R. A. S. Journal*, vol. viii for 1875[2]. A transcript and a translation of the third copy form No. 150 of *A. I. C.* The following is that on the fourth pillar. It differs from the other three in the number of lines on each side and also in the beginning and end of each line

TEXT.

A.

1 සිරි ලක පැදකු
2 ණුකොටැ සිසාරා
3 ගම් නියම්ගම් ප
4 ටුන්ගම් රා
5 ජධානී
6 ද දෙමු
7 නුවර කැ
8 ලැණි ද
9 ඔලු අ
10 නුරාධ
11 පුර නු
12 වර ඇ
13 තුළුවූ
14 තුන් ර
15 ජයෙ
16 හි නො
17 එක් ප්‍ර
18 සිඩ සථාන (ද) ජල
19 දුර්ග ගිරිදුර්ග
20 වනදුර්ග පංකදු
21 ර්ග අතඹුලුප
22 කක්සේ නිශෙෂ
23 කොටැ බලා වදාරා ර
24 න්තිසැ මිණ්හොරු
25 ශගනලා පදී (ඇතු)
26 එවූ තුන්රජයෙහි
27 නොඑක් මහවැතැ
28 නැ අශෙෂ ප්‍රාණීන්

B.

1 ට අභය දී නො
2 මරනනියායෙන්
3 සම්මත කොටැ වි[3]
4 සඹුරුවත
5 ද සෙ
6 හෙත්
7 කොටා
8 ගත් තෙ
9 නවද (හැ)
10 ම දව(ස)
11 ටමු කැ

---

[1] See above, p. 86.

[2] See p. 152 *et seq.*

[3] ‘ඍ’ සිදකියවියහැකිසි

12 තිඅ
13 ඞ හැ
14 ර පූවවී
15 රාජය
16 ත් දව
17 සැ අ
18 නෙක වඩබනධ
19 නතා(ඩ)නයෙන් හා
20 ගොමඟිෂාදී ස
21 වව්සඛ හරණයෙ
·22 න් ඉතා දූසථවැ
23 ඟිසාවූ ලොකවා
24 සීත්ට දඬනාදී
25 නොඑත් දෙය හැ
26 ර මුතු මැණික් ප
27 බළු ඇතුළු වූ
28 නො එක් රත්නද

C.

1 ගොමඟිෂ ධන
2 ධාන්‍ය දාසි දාස
3 යන් (හා) දිවෙල්
4 ගම් පමු
5 ණු [ඇ
6 තුළුවූ]
7 අනෙ
8 ක ප්‍රකා
9 ර වස්ත්‍රා
10 හරණ
11 (ද) ර(න්
12 වළත්) රි
1
14 දී සක)
15 ල ලොකවාසීන්
16 සවසථකොටැ
17 ලංකා(තල)ය නිඡ
18 ස.ණවකකොටැ
19 සෙමෙ(ශි ත)බා
20 වඤව(ූඩා)ශා
21 වෙන් හස්තය
22 ශ්වරථපදෘනි[1]
23 චතුරඟි(නී) මහ
24 සෙනඟ පිරිව

D.

1 රා මහදඹදී
2 වූඟි පාඬිර
3 ට වැඩැ සමා
4 න ප්‍රතිම
5 ල්ලය
6 ත් නො
7 දූකැ
8 වොළ
9 පාඬ්‍යා
10 දූනෙ
11 ක දෙ
12 ශයෙ
13 න් පඩු
14 රැ ගෙ
15 නැ වදා
16 රා දිකවී
17 ජය
18 කළ ශ්‍රී වීර කාලි
19 ඟ ලංකෙශව
20 ර අප්‍රතිමල්
21 ල නිශශංක
22 මල්ල පරාක්‍ර
23 මබාහු චක්‍ර
24 වර්ත්තිස්වාමී
25 න්වහන්සෙ
26 දා වැඤ වදා
27 ර (න කුඩ)මපි

---

[1] 'පදෘනි' වියයුතුයි

TRANSCRIPT.

A.

1 Siri Laka pädaku-
2 -ṇu-koṭä sisārā
3 gam niyam-gam pa-
4 -ṭun-gam rā-
5 -jadhānī-
6 da **Devu-**
7 **nuvara Kä-**
8 **-läṇi Da-**
9 **-m̆bulu A-**
10 **-nurādha-**
11 **pura**-nu-
12 -vara ä-
13 -tuḷu-vū
14 tun-ra-
15 -jaye-
16 -hi no-
17 ek pra-
18 -siddha sthāna (-da) jala-
19 durgga giri-durgga
20 vana-durgga paṁka-du-
21 -rgga at-aṁbulu-pa-
22 -kak-sē niśśeṣa-
23 koṭä balā vadārā **Ra-**
24 **-ntisä Miṇihoru**
25 **Gaṅgataḷā Padi** (ätu-)
26 -ḷu-vū tun-rajayehi
27 no-ek maha-vā̆-tä-
28 -nä aśeṣa prāṇīn-

B.

1 -ṭa abhaya dī no-
2 marana-niyāyen
3 sammata-koṭä vi-[1]
4 -saṁburu-vata-[2]
5 da se-
6 -hen
7 koṭä[3]
8 gat te-
9 -naṭa-da[4] (hä-)
10 -ma dava(sa-)
11 -ṭa-mä kä-
12 -ti-a-
13 -ḍa hä-
14 -ra pūrvva
15 rājaya-
16 -n dava-
17 -sä a-
18 -neka vadha-bandha-
19 -na-tā(ḍa)nayen hā
20 go-mahiṣādi sa-
21 -rvvasva haraṇaye-
22 -n itā dustha-vä
23 giyā-vū loka-vā-
24 -sīnṭa daṇḍanādi
25 no-ek deya hä-
26 -ra mutu mäṇik pa-
27 -baḷu ätuḷu-vū
28 no-ek ratna-da[5]

C.

1 go-mahiṣa dhana
2 dhānya dāsi dāsa-
3 -yan (hā) divel
4 gam pamu-
5 -ṇu [ä-

---

[1] This may also be read *pi-*.
[2] Mt. *-valu-*.
[3] Mt. *koṭā*
[4] Mt. *dī*.
[5] Mt. *dī*.

Rankot-dāgaba Pillar-Inscription

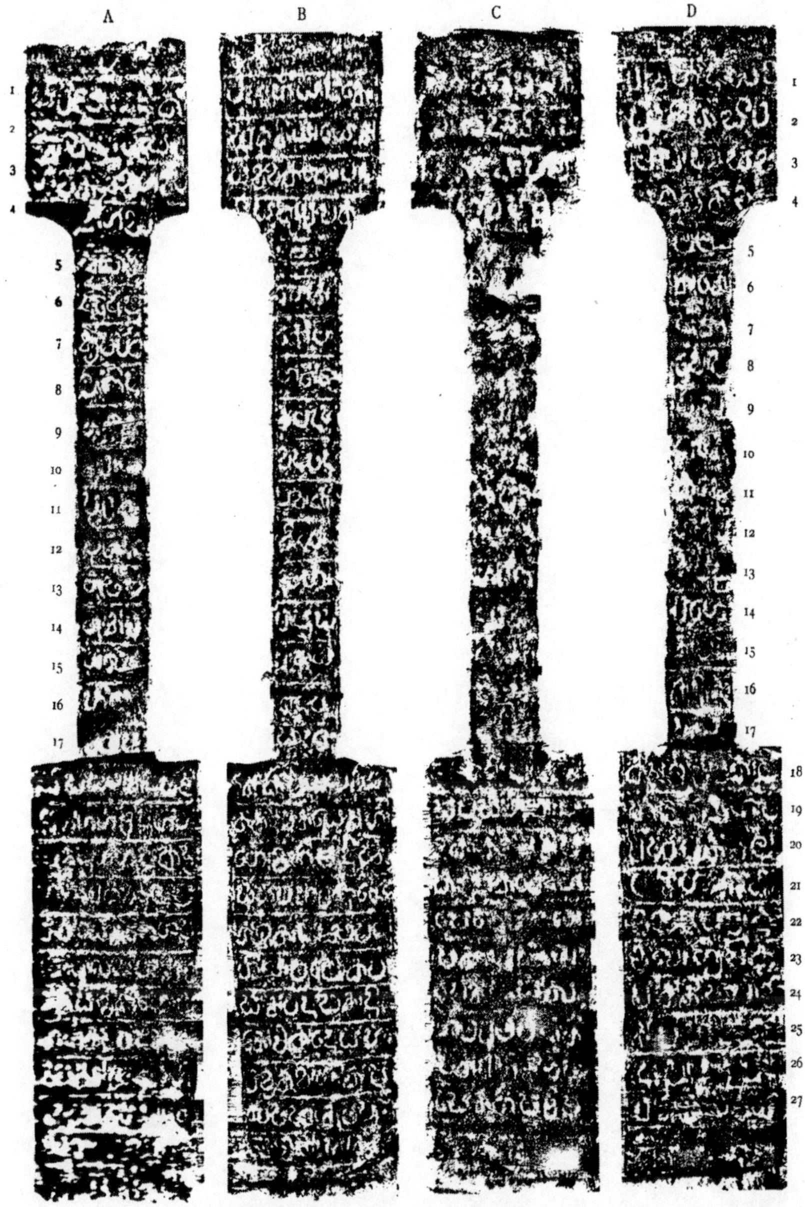

Scale $1\frac{7}{11}$ inches to 1 foot.

From an ink-impression supplied by the Archaeological Commissioner, Ceylon

6 -tuḷu-vū]
7 ane-
8 -ka prakā-
9 -ra vastrā-
10 -bharaṇa-
11 (da) ra(n-
12 vaḷan) ri-
13 -dī-(vaḷan-da[1]
14 dī saka-)
15 -la lokavāsīn
16 svastha-koṭā
17 Laṁkā(tala)ya niṣ-
18 -kaṇṭaka-koṭā
19 seme(hi ta)bā
20 dvandva-(yuddhā)śā-
21 -ven hastya-
22 -śva-ratha-padāti[2]
23 caturaṅgi(nī) maha-
24 senaṅga piriva-

D.

1 -rā maha-Daṁba-di-
2 -vuhi Pāṇḍi-ra-
3 -ṭa väḍā samā-
4 -na prati-ma-
5 -llaya-
6 -n no-
7 däkä
8 Coḷa
9 Pāṇḍyā-
10 -dy-ane-
11 -ka de-
12 -śaye-
13 -n paňḍu-
14 -ru ge-
15 -nä vadā-
16 -rā dik-vi-
17 -jaya
18 kaḷa **Śrī Vīra Kāli-**
19 **-ṅga Laṁkeśva-**
20 **-ra Aprati-Mal-**
21 **-la Niśśaṁka-**
22 **Malla Parākra-**
23 **-ma-Bāhu Cakra-**
24 **-vartti-svāmi-**
25 **-n-vahanse**
26 dā vända vadā-
27 -ra(na kūḍa)mayi[3]

TRANSLATION.

[Side A.] His Illustrious Majesty **Vīra Kāliṅga Laṅkeśvara Aprati-Malla Niśśaṅka-Malla Parākrama-Bāhu Cakravartī**[4] was pleased to tour round and throughout Laṅkā, inspecting completely, like a ripe *nelli* fruit in his hand[5], villages, market towns, seaport towns, cities, and many other localities of note in the three kingdoms[6] [of Ceylon], including **Devu-nuvara** (i. e. Dondra), **Käläṇi, Daṁbulu,** and **Anurādhapura,** as well as those places difficult of access either on account of water, mountains, forests, or marshes.

---

[1] Mt. *vaḷan dī*.
[2] Read *padāni*.
[3] Mt. *kuḍamayi*.
[4] Side D, lines 18–25.
[5] See *E. Z.*, vol. i, p. 134, note 1.
[6] Viz. Ruhuṇu, Māyā, and Pihiṭi.

He gave security to all animals in **Rantisä**[1], **Miṇihoru**[2], **Gaṅgataḷā**[3], **Padī**[4], and many other great tanks in the three kingdoms.

[Side B.] And he ordered that they should not be killed. He abolished for all times the *visaṁburu-vata*[5] and the dues on places under *chēna* cultivation. From punishments and the like he exempted the inhabitants who were reduced to straitened circumstances through various [kinds of] oppression, imprisonment, and chastisement, as well as through the seizure of entire personal property, such as cattle, buffaloes, &c., in the days of former kings. And he bestowed on them gifts of pearls, precious stones, corals, and such other jewellery in abundance.

[Side C.] He gave them also cattle, buffaloes, money, and grain, male and female serfs, *divel* villages and permanent grants, together with various sorts of clothes, ornaments, and gold and silver vessels[6]. Placing [in this manner] all the inhabitants in comfortable circumstances, he freed the land of Laṅkā from the thorns of lawlessness and kept it in a peaceful state.

[Thereafter] being desirous of single combats, he proceeded to the Pāṇḍyan country in the great [continent of] India, attended by his fourfold army of elephants, chariots, cavalry, and infantry.

[Side D.] Seeing [however] no opponent who would be his match [in a contest] he was pleased to exact tribute from the **Coḷa, the Pāṇḍya**, and various other countries.

And this is the pavilion[7] from which His Majesty, who has thus gained victories in all directions, is pleased to worship the relics [enshrined in the **Ruvanväli** dāgaba].

---

[1] Identical with the *Suvaṇṇa-Tissa* tank built by Mahāsēna in the third century A.D. and repaired by Parākrama-Bāhu I. See above, pp. 27–28.

[2] *Maṇihīra* tank constructed by Mahāsēna (*Mv.* xxxvii. 47), and repaired by Parākrama-Bāhu I. Same as modern *Minneriya*.

[3] The tank, now known as *Gantaḷā* or *Kantalāi*, formed by king Aggabodhi II in the seventh century A.D.

[4] The Padaviya tank, said to have been built by Mahāsēna (Parker's *Ancient Ceylon*, p. 212), and repaired by Parākrama-Bāhu I (*Mv.* lxxix. 34).

[5] See above, p. 117, note 11.

[6] *Ran vaḷan ridī vaḷan da.* See also above, p. 95, note 4.

[7] *Kūḍama.* Tamil *kūḍam*. Cf. Skt. *kuṭa*, *kūṭa*, and *kuṭī*.

No. 24. POḶONNARUVA: STONE BATH SLAB-INSCRIPTION

EXCAVATIONS of ruins on the 'Promontory' at Tōpaväva (Poḷonnaruva) during 1901 revealed the existence of a series of magnificently constructed baths which Mr. Bell has identified with those mentioned in the *Mahāvaṁsa* (lxxiii. 95–112) as the work of Parākrama-Bāhu I (1153–1186 A.D.) though manifestly repaired by some of his successors [1].

The slab on which the present record in 14 lines is cut, formed one of the flagstones of the rectangular bath [2]. It is now broken into several fragments, one of which was found in the Tōpaväva village: the others are missing. Nevertheless, we have been able to restore the text easily, as it is the same as that of the foregoing Rankot-dāgaba pillar-inscription, with the exception of the concluding sentence which states the purpose for which the cistern or *paläsa* was used by Niśśaṅka-Malla.

The date of the record may be placed between 1191 and 1196 A.D., for reasons given in connexion with that of the Rankot-dāgaba inscription. The letters vary in size from $1\frac{1}{4}$ to $2\frac{1}{2}$ in. They are well engraved between ruled lines $2\frac{1}{2}$ in. apart, and are of the same type as that of the script of the period.

TEXT.

1 ශ්‍රී සවසති සිරිලක පැදකුණුකොටැ සිසාරා ගම් නියම්ගම් පටුන්ගම් රාජ[ධානී
ද දෙවුනුවර]

2 කැලැණි දඹිදු අනුරාධපුරනුවර ඇතුළුවූ තුන්රජයෙහි නොඑක් ප්‍රසිඩ
සථාන[ද ජලදුර්ග ගි]

---

[1] For a full and accurate description of these ruins, see *A. S. C. Annual Report*, 1901, pp. 11–13.

[2] Site No. 6, in inset C of the plan of Poḷonnaruva facing p. 84 above. Mr. Bell describes this bath as follows:—

'From the middle of the wall of the Circular Bath on the south a drain conducted its water to a lower bath, rectangular in shape and sunk in the ground, its outer wall of brick and mortar, average 6 ft. in thickness, having to act as retaining walls to the well-like bath. Inside, the entire bath was paved and faced with smoothly laid slabs of stone. The back portion formed a recess nearly 6 ft. 2 in. square, flanked by delicately moulded pilasters now partly broken away......... The drain from the Circular Bath above and at back entered the Stone Bath over the abacus of this central pilaster at a height of 5 ft. 9 in. from the pavement....... The bath was covered in. Four stone pillars 10 in. square, embedded in the brick walls on either side, and 14 ft. 4 in. apart cross ways, held a roof, which was carried on to the edge of the *pokuṇa* by two additional pillar supports for this bayed vestibule to the bath.' *Op. cit.*, p. 12.

3 රිදුර්ග වනදුර්ග පංකදුර්ග අතඹුලු පකස්සේ නිශ්ශෙෂ කොටැ බලා වදාරා රන්[තිසැ මිණිහො]

4 රු ගඟතලා පදී ඇතුළුවූ තුන්රජයෙහි නොඑක් මහවැතැනැ අශෙෂ ප්‍රාණීන්ට අ[භය දී නොමරන නි]

5 යායෙන් සම්මතකොටැ විසඹුරු[1]වතද සෙහෙන් කොටා ගත් තැනවද හැමැ දවසට[මැ කැතිඅඩ හැර]

6 පූබ්බ[2] රජයන් දවසැ අනෙක වධබන්ධනතාඩනයෙන් හා ගොමහිෂාදි සබ්බසව[3] හ[රණයෙන් ඉතා දු]

7 සුවැ ගියාවූ ලොකවාසීන්ට දඩනාදි නොඑක් දෙය හැර මුතු මැණික් පබළු ඇතුළුවූ [නොඑක් රත්නද ගො]

8 මහිෂ ධන ධාන්‍ය දාසි දාසයන්ද දිවෙල්ගම් පමුණු ඇතුළුවූ අනෙක ප්‍රකාර වස්ත්‍රාභ[රණද රන්වළ]

9 න් රිදිවළන්ද දී සකල ලොකවාසීන් සුවසුවකොටැ ලංකාත]

10 ලය නිෂ්ක[ණ්ට]කකොටැ සෙ[මෙහි තබා මනු[4]ෂ්‍යඩාශාවෙන් හස්ත්‍යශ්ව රථ පදාති චතුරඞ්ගිනී මහ සෙ]

11 නහ පිරිවරා මහදඹදිවුහි පාඩිරම වැඩැ [සමාන පුහිමල්ලයන් නොදැකැ චොළ පාඩ්‍යාදානෙක]

12 දෙශයෙන් පඬුරු ගෙනැ වදාරා දිකවිජය [කළ **ශ්‍රී වීර කාලිග ලංකෙශ්වර අප්‍ර තිමල්ල** නි]

13 **ශ්ශංකමල්ල ශ්‍රී පරාක්‍රමබාහු ච[ක්‍රවර්තිස්වාමින්වහන්සේ** .. .. නි]

14 මවා වදාරහි පතැසයි

TRANSCRIPT.

1 Śrī svasti Siri-Laka pädakuṇu-koṭä sisārā gam niyam-gam paṭun-gam rāja[dhānī-da **Devunuvara**]

2 **Käläṇi Dam̐bulu Anurādhapura**-nuvara ätuḷuvū tun-rajayehi no-ek pra-siddha sthāna[-da jala-durgga gi-]

3 -ri-durgga vana-durgga pam̐ka-durgga at-am̐bulu-pakak-sē niśśeṣa-koṭä balā vadārā **Ran̐[tisä Miṇiho-]**

4 **-ru Gaṅgataḷā Padi** ätuḷu-vū tun-rajayehi no-ek maha-vä-tänä aśeṣa prāṇīnṭa a[bhaya dī no-marana ni-]

---

[1] 'පිසඹුරු' සීද කියවිය හැකියි

[2] 'පූර්ව' වියයුතුයි

[3] 'සර්වස්ව' වියයුතුයි

[4] 'මනුෂ්‍ය' වියයුතුයි

5 -yāyen sammata-koṭā visaṁburu[1]-vata-da sehen koṭā gat tänaṭa-da hämä davasaṭa-[mä käti-aḍa hära]

6 pūrbba[2] rājayan davasä aneka vadha-bandhana-tāḍanayen hā go-mahiṣādi sarbbasva[3] ha[raṇayen itā du-]

7 -sthavä giyā-vū lokavāsīnṭa daṅḍanādi no-ek deya hära mutu mäṇik pabaḷu ätuḷu-vū [no-ek ratna-da go-]

8 mahiṣa dhana dhānya dāsi dāsayan-da divel-gam pamuṇu ätuḷu-vū aneka prakāra vastrābha-[raṇa-da ran-vaḷa-

9 -n ridī-vaḷan-da dī sakala lokavāsīn svastha-koṭā Laṁkā-ta-]

10 -laya niṣka[ṇṭa]ka-koṭā se[mehi tabā dvanda[4]-yuddhāśāven hastyaśva-ratha-paḍāni caturaṅginī maha-se-]

11 -naṅga pirivarā maha-Daṁbadivuhi **Pāṅḍi-raṭa** väḍä [samāna prati-mallayan no-däkä Coḷa Pāṇḍyādy-aneka]

12 **deśayen** paṅḍuru genā vadārā dik-vijaya [kaḷa **Śrī Vīra Kāliṅga Laṁkeś-**
-vara Aprati-Malla Ni-]

13 **-śśaṁka-Malla** Śrī **Parākrama-Bāhu Ca[kravartti-svāmin-vahansē** .. .. ni-]

14 -mavā vadārana patäsayi

TRANSLATION.

[Lines 1–11. Same as the foregoing Rankot-dāgaba pillar-inscription sides A, B, and C.]

[Lines 11–14.] Seeing [however] no adversary equal to him, he was pleased to exact tribute from the **Coḷa**, the **Pāṇḍya**, and various other countries.

And this is the bathing-pond[5] in which His Majesty **Śrī Vīra Kāliṅga Laṅkeśvara Aprati-Malla Niśśaṅka-Malla Śrī Parākrama-Bāhu Cakravarti**, who has [thus] made conquests in all directions, is pleased to complete [the ceremony of bathing ?].

---

[1] This may also be read *pisaṁburu*.

[2] Read *pūrva*.

[3] Read *sarvasva*.

[4] Read *dvandva*.

[5] *Paṭäsa*, same as modern *paṭasa* or *paṭaha* 'a pit'. In the Neville Collection of Sinhalese manuscripts in the British Museum, there are two manuscripts of a poem entitled පටසේ පොත *Paṭasē pota* [Or. 6615 (167) and 6611 (104)], giving an account of a *paṭasa* or a pond constructed by order of a Pāṇḍyan king. I am indebted to Dr. Barnett for drawing my attention to this work.

No. 25. POḶONNARUVA: ŚIVA-DEVĀLAYE SLAB-INSCRIPTION

THIS inscription in five lines covers the upper smoothed surface of a quadrangular slab measuring 5 ft. 2 in. by 2 ft. 9 in., which once formed the top flagstone of a raised seat. Mr. Bell examined it some twelve years ago, between 1901 and 1905[1]. The slab was then lying inside the ruined shrine referred to by him as Śiva-Devālaya No. 1, and situated a little to the south of the main group of Buddhist ruins on the raised quadrangle near Tōpaväva tank[2].

The letters, from half an inch to one inch in size, are engraved, as in other *āsana* slab-inscriptions, between ruled lines, one inch apart, running parallel to each side of the rectangular slab and leaving a blank space of 3 ft. 8½ in. by 1 ft. 6 in. in the centre[3]. The type of the script is the same as that of the other records of Niśśaṅka-Malla.

The stone is much worn. Consequently a considerable portion of the inscription is totally illegible, but what remains readable clearly shows that the text agrees almost word for word with that of the foregoing stone-bath inscription, the only exception being the concluding sentence which indicates the present pedestal seat or *āsana* as the one which Niśśaṅka-Malla used to occupy when performing the function of lustral bathing (*nānu mē*[4]) at the ceremony of propitiating the nine planetary gods (*nava-graha-śānti*).

TEXT.

1 ශ්‍රී ස්වස්ති සිරිලක සිසාරා (එ)ක්වසින්[5] පැදැකුණුකොටැ ගම් නියම්ගම් පටුන්(ගම්
රාජධා)නිද **දෙවුනුවර කැලැණි දඹුලු අනුරාධපුරය** ඇතුළුවූ (තුන්)රජයෙහි
[නො]එක් [ප්‍රසිබ ස්ථානද ජලදුර්ග ගිරිදුර්ග වනදුර්ග පංකදුර්ග අනඹුලු
පකන්සේ නිශ්ශෙෂකොටැ බලා] වදුරු **රන්තිසැ මිණිහොරැ ගඟතලා පදි**
ඇතුළුවූ තුන්රජ

---

[1] See *A.S.C. Annual Report*, 1905, p. 40, No. 33.

[2] *Ibid.*, 1906, p. 17. See also plan of Poḷonnaruva, facing p. 84, above.

[3] See plate No. 25.

[4] *Nānu* = Skt. *snāna*, P. *nahāna* and *mē*, contraction of *mehe*, probably from Skt. *śrama*, P. *sama*, by metathesis. Cf. *nahana mehe* in Jayatilaka's *Elu Akārādiya* and in *Kavsiḷumiṇa*, verse 499. *Nānu* also means 'an ointment for anointing the heads of kings on great feast days'; perfumed powder scattered on the guests at feasts (Clough's *Sinh. Dict.*).

[5] 'හාත්පසින්' සීද කියවිය හැකිසි

Polonnaruva: Śiva-devālaye Slab-inscription

Scale about 1½ inches to 1 foot

Polonnaruva: Slab-inscription of Niśśaṅka-Malla

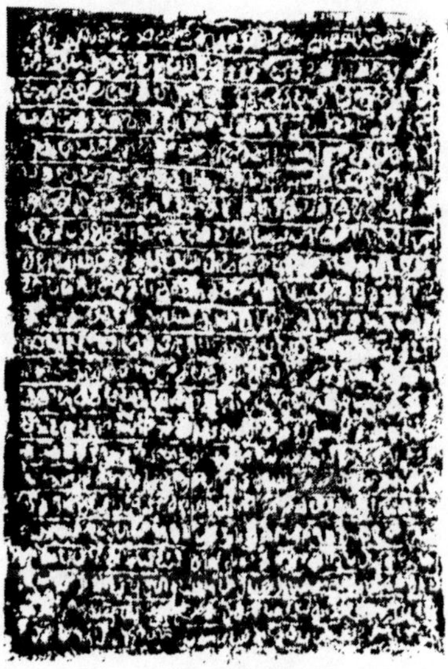

Scale about 1½ inches to 1 foot

From inked impressions supplied by the Archaeological Commissioner, Ceylon

2 යෙහි නොඑක් මහවෑ(තැනැ) අශෙෂ ප්‍රාණීන්ට අභය දී නොමරන නියායෙන් සම්මතකොටැ විසඹුරු(වතද සෙ)හෙන් කොටා ග(ත් තැනටද) හැමැ කලටමැ [කැතිඅඩ හැර පූර්බ්බරජයන් දවසැ අනෙක වධබන්‍ධනතාඩනයෙන් හා ගොමහිෂාදි සර්බ්බස්ව හරණයෙන්] ඉතා දුස්ථවැ ගියාවූ ලොකවාසීන්ට දඬනාදි නොඑක් දෙය

3 හැරැ මුතු මැණික් (පබළු ඈතුළුවූ) නොඑක් රත්නද (ගො)මහිෂ ධන ධාන්‍ය **දාසි** **දාසයන්ද** දිවෙල් පමුණු [ඈතුළුවූ අනෙක ප්‍රකාර වස්ත්‍රාභරණද රන් වළන් රිදීවළන්ද දී සකල ලොකවාසීන් ස්වස්ථකොටැ ලංකාතලය නිෂ්කණ්ටකකොටැ සෙමෙහි තබා ද්වන්ද්ව යුද්ධාශාවෙන් හස්ත්‍යශ්වරථ] පදනි චතුරඞ්ගිනී මහසෙනඟ පිරිවරා මහදඹ

4 දිව්හි **පාඬිරට** වැඩැ සමාන ප්‍රතිමල්ලයන් නොදැකැ **චොළ පාඬ්‍යාදී**නෙක දෙශයෙන් (පඬුරු) [ගෙනැ වදුරා දිග්විජය කළ **ශ්‍රී වීර කාලිඞ්ග ලංකෙශ්වර අප්‍රතිමල්ල නිශ්ශංකමල්ල ශ්‍රී පරාක්‍රමබාහු චක්‍රවර්ත්තිස්වාමීන්**]වහන්සෙ (නව ග්‍රහ)ශාන්තියෙහි වැඩැ හිඳැ නා

5 නුමේ නිමවා වදරන ආසනයයි 

TRANSCRIPT.

1 Śrī svasti Siri-Laka sisārā (e)kvasin[1] pädäkuṇu-koṭä[2] gam niyam-gam paṭun-(gam rājadhā)nī-da **Devunuvara Käläṇi Daṁbulu Anurādhapuraya** ätuḷuvū (tun-)rajayehi [no-]ek [prasiddha sthāna-da jala-durgga giri-durgga vana-durgga paṁka-durgga at-aṁbulu-pakak-sē niśśeṣa-koṭä balā] vadārā (**Rantisä**) **Miṇihoru Gaṅgataḷā Padī** ätuḷu-vū tun-raja-

2 -yehi no-ek maha-vä-(tänä) aśeṣa prāṇīnṭa abhaya dī no-marana niyāyen sammata-koṭä visaṁburu(-vata-da se)hen koṭā ga(t tänaṭa-da) hämä kalaṭa-mä [käti-aḍa hära pūrbba-rājayan davasä aneka vadha-bandhana-tāḍanayen hā go-mahiṣ-ādi sarbbasva haraṇayen] itā dustha-vä giyāvū loka-vāsīnṭa daṅḍan-ādi no-ek deya

3 härä mutu mäṇik (pabaḷu ätuḷu-vū) no-ek ratna-da (go-)mahiṣa dhana-dhānya dāsi-dāsayan-da divel pamuṇu [ätuḷu-vū aneka prakāra vastr-ābharaṇa-da ran-vaḷan ridī-vaḷan-da dī sakala loka-vāsīn svastha-koṭā Laṁkā-talaya niṣkaṇṭaka-koṭä semehi tabā dvandva-yuddh-āśāven hasty-aśva-ratha-] padāni catur-aṅginī maha-senaṅga pirivarā maha-Daṁba-

---

[1] This may also be read *hätpasin.*

[2] *Siri-Laka pädakuṇu-koṭä sisārā* in the foregoing two inscriptions.

4 divhi **Pāṇḍi-raṭa** väḍä samāna pratimallayan no-däkä **Coḷa-Pāṇḍy-ādy-** aneka-deśayen (paṇḍuru) [genä vadārā dig-vijaya kaḷa **Śrī Vīra Kāliṅga Laṁkeśvara Aprati-Malla Niśśaṁka-Malla Śrī Parākrama-Bāhu Cakravartti-svāmin]-vahanse** väḍä hindä nā-

5 -nu-mē nimavā vadārana āsanayayi

TRANSLATION.

[Lines 1–3] Hail! Prosperity! His Majesty **Śrī Vīra Kāliṅgā Laṅkeśvara Aprati-Malla Niśśaṅka-Malla Śrī Parākrama-Bāhu Cakravarti** having toured round and throughout Laṅka in one year[1] was pleased to inspect completely [&c., same as lines 1–11 of the foregoing stone-bath inscription, or sides A, B, C of Rankot-dāgaba pillar-inscription].

[Lines 4–5] Seeing [however] no adversary equal to him, he was pleased to exact tribute from the **Coḷa**, the **Pāṇḍya**, and various other countries.

And this is the seat on which His Majesty, who has [thus] made conquests in all directions, is pleased to complete the function of lustral bathing (when) attending[2] the ceremony of propitiating the nine planetary gods.

No. 26. POḶONNARUVA: KIRI-VEHERA SLAB-INSCRIPTION

THIS quadrangular slab, measuring 10 ft. by 5 ft. 3 in., lies on the *maḷuva* or terrace of the so-called 'Kiri-vehera' dāgaba in Poḷonnaruva[3], about eight or ten yards to the south-east of its south altar.

As will be seen from the accompanying facsimile[4], the slab has an ornamental border carved with swans (*haṁsas*) running in a single file from right to left along a fillet of foliaged creeper pattern which encloses a rectangular area of $9\frac{1}{2}$ ft. by $4\frac{1}{2}$ ft. Within this and at equal distance from its sides there is another

---

[1] Or *hätpasin* entirely.

[2] Lit. 'having come and sat down (*väḍä hindä*) at the *nava-graha-śānti*'.

[3] See plan of Poḷonnaruva, opposite p. 84, above.

[4] Plate No. 26.

rectangle also marked by a fillet engraved with what looks like a conventional crab and fish pattern. The smoothed space outside the inner rectangle is ruled with lines three inches apart, so as to receive between them three lines of the first inscription on each of the four sides. Similarly, the area within this rectangle is ruled so as to receive four lines of the second inscription on each side, leaving, thereby, a blank space of 6 ft. by 1 ft. 3 in. in the centre.

The **letters**, 1 to 2 in. in size, represent the type of the alphabet of the period, namely, the latter half of the twelfth century A.D. The text of the first or outer inscription is the same as that of No. 24 above[1], with the exception of the concluding clause which indicates the pavilion (*kūḍama*), as the one from which His Majesty Kīrti Niśśaṅka-Malla worshipped the (Buddhist) relics. The text of the second or inner inscription, of which a faulty and incomplete transcript and translation appear in *A. I. C.*, under No. 152, agrees word for word with the inscription at the **Niśśaṅka-latā-maṇḍapa**[2], the only exception being the final clause stating that the pavilion was built after His Majesty's return from the Indian campaign, and that it was used for worshipping the (Buddhist) relics.

It is obvious from both these records and from the few stumps of pillars still existing round the slab[3] that the *kūḍama* or pavilion in question was a structure similar in style to the one at Rankot-dāgaba[4] and that it was built about the same period, namely, between 1191 and 1196 A.D. The inscribed slab must have been the flagstone of a raised seat within it, from which the royalty was wont to worship the relics enshrined in the Kiri-vehera-dāgaba[5] opposite.

[1] Outer inscription—

Side A, three lines ending *giri-durgga paṁka* = lines 1–3 of No. 24.

Side B, three lines ending *vadha-bandhana-tāḍanayen* [*hā go-mahiṣ-ādi sarbbasva haraṇayen itā du-*] = lines 3–6 of No. 24.

Side C, the estampage is imperfect here. The three lines probably = lines 7–8 of No. 24.

Side D, the first two lines of this side ending *deśayen paṇḍuru genā* = lines 9–12 of No. 24; the third line runs (*vadārā dig-vijaya-kaḷa*) *Śrī Vīra Kāliṅga Laṁkeśvara Aprati-Malla Niśśaṁka-Malla Parākrama-Bāhu Cakravarttisvāmin-vahanse* (*dā*) *vandanā kūḍamayi.*

[2] See *A. S. C. Annual Report*, 1911–1912, p. 101.

[3] See plan of Kirivehera-dāgaba in *A. S. C. Annual Report*, 1910–1911.

[4] See p. 137, above.

[5] For a description of this ruin, see the last-mentioned Annual Report, p. 28 ff.

INNER INSCRIPTION

TEXT.

A.

1 **ශ්‍රී වීරරාජ නිශ්ශංකමල්ල අප්‍රතිමල්ල කා**

2 **ලිංග ලංකෙශ්වර පරාක්‍රමබාහු චක්‍රවර්ත්ති ස්වා**

3 මින්වහන්සේ නිශ්ශංකමල්ල යන විරුදු(වට සු)

4 (දුසුවැ) කිපිනෙනකැත් සැකයක් නැ(තිවැ) [සිවු]රඟ

B.

1 සෙන(ග) පිරිවර පාඩිරටැ දෙ(ව)රෙකැ වැඩැ තමන්වහන්සේගේ අ(සා)ධාරණ(වූ
පරාක්‍රම)යෙන් [චොළ පා

2 ඩ්‍යාද්‍යනෙක රාජයන් හා] යුධයට (සැ)රැහුණු (කල්)හි **ලඞ්විජයසිඟුසෙනෙවි නාවු
රුනාවන්** දඹදිවු සාධා දෙන්

3 නට මම්මැ (පමණිම්)දන්වා යුධයට නික්මුණු කල්(හි මේ) අසා භයපත්වූ පාඩි
රජ්ජුරුවන් හා (මැ)ණියන්වි

4 සින් අප ජීවත්වන පමණ ගමක් දී මෙ රාජ්‍යය තමන්වහන්සේම ගෙනැ වදාළ
මැනවැයි කියා එවූ (කිසොවරු)

C.

1 [න් හා ඇතුන් අසුන්ද සොළීරටින් එවූ නොඑක් පඬුරු

2 දැකැ කොපාග්නි සන්හිඳුවා කණ්ණාට නෙල්ලූරු ගෞඩ කලිඟ

3 තිලිඟ ගුර්ජර අරමණ කාම්බොජ] ඇතුළුවූ

4 (නොඑක්) දෙශයෙහි ගුණ කැමැති රජ[දරුව]

D.

1 න් හා ගුණෙන් මිත්‍රසන්ථාන කොටැ සන්ථාන නො(කැ)මැත්තවුන්ට තමන්
වහන්සේගේ ශෞර්‍ය්‍යාතිශයෙන්ම භය එළවා ඒ ඒ රට

2 න් කිසොවරුන් හා පඬුරු ගෙන්වා ප්‍රතිමල්ලවූ අන්‍ය රජයන් නැතිබැවින්
රාමෙශ්වරයෙහිදී තුලාභාර නැගී නොඑක්

3 දෙශ වාසීන්ට අනන්ත වස්තු ත්‍යාග කොටැ එතන්හි බොහො කලක් පවත්නා
පරිද්දෙන් ජයස්තම්භ කොටැ **නිශ්ශංකෙ**

4 (ශ්ව)ර යන දෙවාලයක් නංවා සිවුරඟසෙනඟ පිරිවර නැවැතැ ලංකාවට වැඩැ
කරවා වදාළ දෑ වන්‍දනා කුඩම්පි

Polonnaruva: Kiri-vehera Slab-inscription

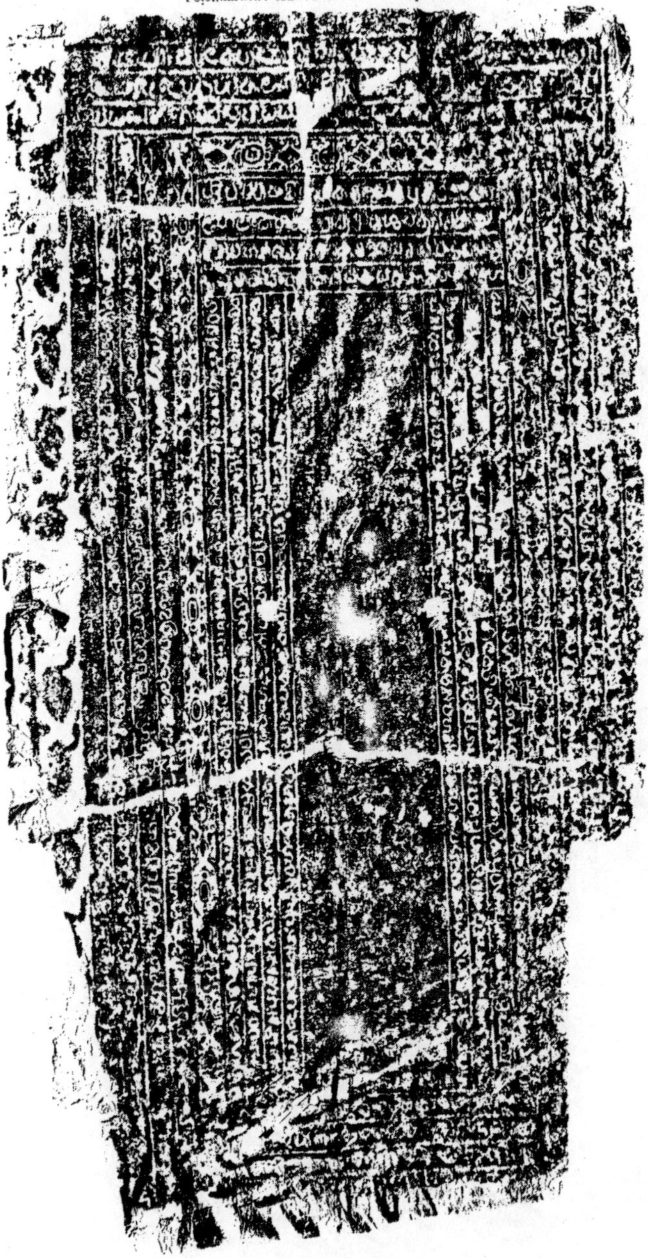

Scale about 1½ inches to 1 foot

TRANSCRIPT.

A.

1 **Srī Vīra-rāja Niśśaṁka-Malla Aprati-Malla Kā-**
2 **-liṅga Laṁkeśvara Parākrama-Bāhu Cakravartti**-svā-
3 -min-vahansē Niśśaṁka-Malla yana virudu(vaṭa su-)
4 (-dusu-vä) kisi-tenakät säkayak nä(ti-vä) [sivu]raṅga-

B.

1 sena(ṅga) pirivarā Pāṇḍī-raṭä de(va)rekä väḍā taman-vahansēgē a(sā)dhā- -raṇa(vū parākkrama)yen [Coḷa Pā-
2 -ṇḍy-ādy-aneka rājayan hā] yuddhayaṭa (sä)rähuṇu (kal)hi **Lak-Vijaya-siṅgu Senevi Tāvuru-nāvan** Dambadivu sādhā den-
3 -naṭa mammā (pamaṇimī) danvā yuddhayaṭa nikmuṇu kal(hi mē) asā bhaya-patvū Pāṇḍi-rajjuruvan hā (mā)ṇiyan-vi-
4 -sin apa jīvat-vana pamaṇa gamak dī me rājyaya taman-vahansē-ma genä vadāḷa mänaväyi kiyā evū (bisovaru-)

C.

1 [-n hā ätun asun-da Soḷī-raṭin evū no-ek paṇḍuru
2 däkä kop-āgni sanhinduvā Karṇṇāṭa Nellūru **Gauḍa Kaliṅga**
3 Tiliṅga Gurjjara Aramaṇa Kamboja] ätuḷuvū
4 (no-ek) deśayehi guṇa kämäti raja-[daruva-]

D.

1 (-n hā) guṇen mitra-santhāna koṭä santhāna no-(kä)mättavunṭa taman-vahansēgē śauryy-ātiśayen-ma bhaya eḷavā ē ē raṭi-
2 -n bisovarun hā paṇḍuru genvā pratimallavū anya rājayan näti-ḅavin **Rāmeśvarayehi**-dī tulābhāra nägī no-ek
3 deśa vāsīnṭa ananta vastu tyāga koṭä etanhi boho kalak pavatnā paridden jaya-stambha koṭä **Niśśaṁke-**
4 (-**śva**)**ra** yana devālayak **s**aṁvā sivu-raṅga-senaṅga pirivarā nävätä Laṁkā-vaṭa väḍā karavā vadāḷa dā vandanā kūḍamayi

TRANSLATION.

His Majesty **Śrī Vīra-rāja Niśśaṅka-Malla Aprati-Malla Kāliṅga Laṅkeśvara Parākrama-Bāhu Cakravartī,** consistently with the title *Niśśaṅka-Malla* (dauntless warrior), being without any misgiving [as to his might] at any place, twice proceeded to the Pāṇḍyan country, escorted by his fourfold army and prepared to wage war with his unsurpassed might [upon Coḷa, Pāṇḍya, and various other kings]. Then the general **Lak-Vijaya-siṅgu Senevi Tāvuru-nāvan,** declaring, 'I alone suffice[1] to secure the conquest of Dambadiva', started forth to the war. Hearing this, the Pāṇḍyan king and his (royal) mother, being filled with fear, made entreaties, saying, 'May Your Majesty be pleased to take possession of this kingdom, leaving to us only a village that will be enough for our maintenance', and sent [as peace-offerings] royal maidens together with [elephants and horses. Seeing these and various other gifts from the Coḷa country, His Majesty quenched the fire of his indignation]. And he formed friendly alliances with such of the princes of [Karnāṭa, Nellūru, Gauḍa, Kaliṅga, Tiliṅga, Gurjara, Aramaṇa, Kamboja] and divers other countries as were desirous of his goodwill, but into those who did not wish such friendship he struck terror by the very superiority of his own valour. He, moreover, exacted from such kingdoms royal maidens and tributes. Thereafter, as there were no hostile kings, he mounted the scale-pans at **Rāmeśvara** and (distributing *tulābhāra* alms) bestowed boundless wealth on the inhabitants of many a land. He also had pillars of victory set up there, as lasting monuments, and a temple (*devālaya*) built bearing the name **Niśśaṅkeśvara.** Then he returned to Laṅkā, escorted by his fourfold army, and had this pavilion (*kūḍama*) built for the purpose of worshipping the relics.

---

[1] *Mam-mă pamaṇimi.* With Mr. Bell, (*A.S.C. Annual Report*, 1911–1912, p. 10), we may take *pamaṇimi* as a denominative verb equivalent to *pamaṇemi* (Skt. *pramāṇayāmi*) and translate ***mammă*** *pamaṇimi* by 'I myself suffice', especially as we find the same sentiment expressed in *Mv.* lxxvi. 42. In Apabhraṁśa *pamāṇahu* = Skt. *pramāṇayata* (Pischel's Pkt. Gram., § 557). Regarding denominative verbs such as Sinh. *soremi*, 'I am a thief', Tamil *aḍiyeṉ*, 'I a servant', see Mendis Gunasekara's *Sinh. Gram.*, § 287; Geiger's *Litt. u. Spr. d. Sing.*, § 58, and Pope's *Tamil Grammar*, § 184 (*c*). In my translation of the Galpota inscription I took the view that *pamaṇimi* might be an older form of *pămiṇemi*, 'I arrive' (Skt. *pra* + √*āp*. *E. S.*, p. 59). I have now given up this derivation. My previous rendering should be altered accordingly.

No. 27. POḶONNARUVA: A SLAB-INSCRIPTION OF NIŚŚAṄKA-MALLA

THIS quadrangular slab, measuring 3 ft. by 2 ft. 7 in. and lying now at the premises of the Archaeological Commissioner at Poḷonnaruva, was brought there from the spot where the present rest-house is. Its original site is not known.

The first twenty-three lines of the inscription are engraved on the smoothed face of the slab between ruled lines, two inches apart[1]. The next four lines are cut, according to Mr. Bell[2], one on each of the four narrow sides. The rest of the inscription is wanting. It may possibly be found on the reverse side of the slab.

The **letters** vary in size from $\frac{1}{2}$ to $1\frac{1}{2}$ in. Their type is the same as that of other records of Niśśaṅka-Malla. The **subject** with which the inscription is really concerned is given only at the end of the text, now missing, if we may judge from the style of composition of other records of the kind. So the portion of the text appearing below is only the usual introduction to this subject, and contains nothing new. It agrees almost word for word with the inner inscription of the Kiri-vehera slab (above, No. 26) and with lines 10–12 of the Daṁbulla record (*E. Z.*, Vol. I, No. 9).

Variations in spelling such as *vānse* for *vahanse*, *rāmesvara* for *rāmeśvara* are not uncommon in other inscriptions of this period, namely, the latter half of the twelfth century A.D.

TEXT.

1 **ශ්‍රී වීරරාජ නිශ්ශංකමල්ල අප්‍රතිමල්ල කාලිඟ ලංකෙශ්**[3]
2 **වර සිරිපරාක්‍රමබාහු** (සවා)මීන්වාන්සේ තමන්වාන්සේ නි
3 ශ්ශංකමල්ල යන විරුදුවට සුදුසුවැ කිසි තෙනෙකැත්
4 සැකයක් නැතිවැ සිවුරඟසෙනඟ පිරිවරා පාඬිරට (දෙව)

---

[1] See plate No. 25.

[2] See *A. S. C. Annual Report*, 1911–1912, p. 102. This report came into my hands after I had made out the text from the two inked estampages in my possession. Nevertheless, Mr. Bell's edition has been of some value to me, especially as it contains four lines of the missing portion.

[3] 'ලංකෙශ්වර ශ්‍රීපරාක්‍රමබාහු' වියයුතුයි

5 රෙකැ වැඩැ තමන්වාන්සෙගෙ අ(නන්‍ය) සා(ධා)රණ බල පරාකුම
6 යෙන් චොඩ පාණ්ඩ්‍යාදීනෙක රජයන් හා යුද්ධය(ට) සැරහුණුකල්
7 හි **ලක්විජයසිඟු සෙනෙවි නාවුරුනාවන්** දඹදිව් සාධා
8 දන්නට මම්මැ පමණිමි දන්වා යුද්ධයට නික්(මුණු)කල්හි
9 එ අසා භයපත්වූ (පාණ්ඩි)රජයන් හා මැණියන්විසින්
10 අප ජීවත්වන පමණ (ග)මක් දී මෙ ර(ජ)යත් තමන්වා(න්සෙ)
11 මැ ගෙනැ වඩැළම්‍යැනැවැයි කියා එවූ කිසොවරුන් (හා ඇතුන්)
12 අශුන්ද සොලීරටින් එවූ නොඑක් පඬුරු දැකැ (කොපාග්නි) ස
13 න්හිඳුවා කණ්ණාට නෙල්ලූරු (ගුජ්ජර අ)රම්ණ (චොඩ ගෞඩ)
14 කලිඟු (කාම්බොජ) ඇතුළුවූ නොඑක් (දෙශයෙහි ගුණ කැමැති)
15 රජදරුවන් හා ගුණෙන් මිත්‍රස(න්ථාන) කොටැ ස(න්ථාන නොකැමැත්තවූ)
16 න්ට තමන්වහන්සෙගෙ (ශෞය්‍යාර්ජි)ශයෙන්මැ භය එළවා (එ එ රටින්)
17 කිසොවරුන් හා පඬුරු ගෙණ්වා ප්‍රතිමල්ලවූ අන්‍ය රජයන් නැති බැ
18 වින් රාමෙස්ව[1]රයෙදී තුලාභාර නැඟී අනෙකප්‍රකාරවූ වස්තු (සඬ)
19 යෙන් නා නා දෙශවාසීන් මනදොළ පුරා එතන්හි බොහො කලක් (ප)ව
20 ත්නා පරි(දෙදන්) ජයස්තම්භ කොටැ **නි(ශ්ශ)ංකෙශ්වර** යන දෙවා
21 ලයක් නංවා සිවුරඟසෙනඟ පිරිවරා නැවත ලංකාවට වැඩැ (තමන්ව)
22 (හන්සෙගෙ) අ(භි)ප්‍රායානුකූලවැ නොඑක්ලෙසැ දස්කම් කළවුන්(ට) .. ..
23 .. .. ද .. .. හිරසඳපවත්නාතෙක් පවත්වූව මැනැවැයි (සි)
24 [2]තා වදාරා ඉවසන් මියන් ඇතුළුවූවන් විසින් සොපද්‍රවවූ තල්පතැ
25 [2]නොලියවා ලක්දිව පෙරපවත් නුවූ තාම්‍රශාසන අකුරු කොටවා පවත් කොටැ ත
26 [2]මන්වහන්සෙ අසාධාරණ කරුණා ගුණයෙන් ප්‍රසන්නහෙයින් මහ(වැ)
27 [2]තැනැ ඇතුළුවූ නොඑක් වැතැනැ අශෙෂප්‍රාණීන්ට අභයදුන දී විස
28 [භූරුවන] .. ..

TRANSCRIPT.

1 **Śrī Vīra-rāja Niśśaṁka-Malla Apprati-Malla Kāliṅga-Laṁkes**[3]-
2 **-vara Siri**[4]**-Parākkrama-Bāhu-**(svā)mīn-vānsē taman-vānsē *Ni-*
3 *-śśaṁka-Malla* yana viruduvaṭa sudusu-vä kisi tenekä-t
4 säkayak näti-vä sivurañga-senañga pirivarā Pāṇḍi-raṭa (deva-)

---

[1] 'ශව' වියයුතුයි
[2] බැල්මහතාණේ 1911–1912 අබ්දික වාර්තාවේ 102 වෙනිපිටෙන් උපුටාගන්නාලදී
[3] Read *ś*.
[4] Read *Śrī*.

5 -rekä väḍä taman-vānsege a(nanya) sā(dhā)raṇa bala parākrama-
6 -yen Coḍa Pāṅḍy-ādy-aneka rājayan hā yuddhaya(ṭa) särahuṇu-kal-
7 -hi **Lak-Vijaya-siṅgu Senevi Tāvurunāvan** Daṁbadiv sādhā
8 dennaṭa mam-mä pamaṇimī danvā yuddhayaṭa nik(muṇu)-kalhi
9 e asā bhaya-pat-vū (Pāṅḍi-)rājayan hā māṇiyan-visin
10 apa jīvatvana pamaṇa (ga)mak dī me ra(ja)yat tamanvā(nse-)
11 mā genä vadāḷa-mänäväyi kiyā evū bisovarun (hā ätun)
12 asun-da Solī-raṭin evū no-ek paṅḍuru däkä (kop-āgni) sa-
13 -nhinduvā Karṇṇāṭa Nellūru (Gurjara A)ramaṇa (Coḍa Gauḍa)
14 Kaliṅgu (Kāmboja) ätuḷu-vū no-ek (deśayehi guṇa kämäti)
15 raja-daruvan hā guṇen mitra-sa(nthāna) koṭā sa(nthāna no-kämättavu-)
16 -nṭa tamanvahansege (śauryy-āti)śayen-mä bhaya eḷavā (e e raṭin)
17 bisovarun hā paṅḍuru genvā pratimallavū anya rājayan näti bä-
18 -vin Rāmes[1]varaye-dī Tulābhāra näṅgī anekapprakāra-vū vastu (sañca-)
19 -yen nā nā deśa-vāsin mana-doḷa purā etanhi boho kalak (pa)va-
20 -tnā pari(dden) jaya-stambha koṭä **Ni(śśa)ṁkeśvara** yana devā-
21 -layak naṁvā sivuraṅga-senaṅga pirivarā nävata Laṁkāvaṭa väḍā (taman-va-)
22 (-hansege) a(bhi)pprāy-ānukūla-vä no-ek-lesä das-kam kaḷavun(ṭa) .. ..
23 .. .. da .. .. hira-sanda-pavatnā-tek pavatvuva mänäväyi (si-)
24 [2]-tā vadārā veyan mīyan ätuḷuvūvan-visin sopadravavū tal-patā
25 [2]no-liyavā Lakdiva pera-pavat nuvū tāmbra-śāsana akuru koṭavā pavat-koṭā ta-
26 [2]-man-vahanse asādhāraṇa karuṇā guṇayen yukta-heyin maha-(vā-)
27 [2]-tänā ätuḷuvū no-ek vā-tänä aśeṣa-prāṇīṇṭa abhaya-dāna dī *visa-*
28 [*-ṁburu-vata*] .. ..

TRANSLATION.

[Lines 1–8] His Majesty **Śrī Vīra-rāja Niśśaṅka-Malla Apprati-Malla Kāliṅga Laṅkeśvara Śrī Parākrama-Bāhu** consistently with his title *Niśśaṅka-Malla* (dauntless warrior) being without any misgiving [as to his might] at any place, having twice proceeded to the Pāṇḍyan country escorted by his fourfold army, prepared to [go to] war against the rulers of Coḍa, Pāṇḍya, and various other kingdoms with the valour of his matchless and uncommon might. Then

---

[1] Read *śv*.
[2] From Mr. Bell's text in *A.S.C. Annual Report*, 1911–1912, p. 102.

the general **Lak-Vijaya-siṅgu Senevi Tāvuru-nāvan** declaring 'I alone suffice to secure the conquest of Dambadiva' set out for the war.

[Lines 9-17] On hearing this, the Pāṇḍyan king and his (royal) mother, being filled with fear, sent [as peace-offerings] royal maidens, elephants, and horses, and made entreaties, saying, 'May Your Majesty be pleased to take possession of this kingdom, granting us only a village that will suffice for our maintenance.' [The king] seeing [these presents], as well as diverse gifts sent from the Cōḷa country, quenched the fire of his wrath. He formed friendly alliances with such of the princes of Karṇāṭa, Nellūru, Gurjara, Aramaṇa, [Cōḍa, Gauḍa], Kaliṅga, (Kāmboja), and various other countries, as were desirous of his goodwill; but into those who did not wish such friendship he struck terror by the very superiority of his own valour. He, moreover, exacted from such kingdoms royal maidens and tributes.

[Lines 17-21] As he had now no other kings who were hostile to him, he mounted the scale-pans at **Rāmeśvara,** [had himself weighed against coin], and by [the bestowal of] hoards of various kinds of wealth satisfied the desires of inhabitants of divers lands. He also had pillars of victory set up there, as lasting monuments, and a temple (*devālaya*) built bearing the name **Niśśaṅkeśvara.** [Thereafter] he returned to Laṅkā accompanied by his fourfold army.

[Lines 21-28] Considering that grants in favour of those who rendered services in various capacities conformable to his wishes should last as long as Sun and Moon endure, he did not [as heretofore] have them written on *tal-pat* (palm-leaves) which were liable to be destroyed by white ants, rats, and the like, but had such grants engraved on copper (plates), and so established the practice which had not been in vogue aforetimes in Laṅkā. Moreover, being endowed with the virtuous qualities of an extraordinary sympathetic nature, he granted security to all living creatures in various tanks, including the large tanks as well. [He also abolished] the *Visaṁburuvata* [1] . . . .

---

[1] See above, p. 117, note 11.

No. 28. POḶONNARUVA: SLAB-INSCRIPTION AT THE NORTH-GATE OF THE CITADEL

THIS quadrangular slab, measuring about 6 ft. by 2 ft. 8 in., was found completely buried at the North-gate of the ruined citadel[1], where it was subsequently placed in an upright position. The inscription covers both its sides and is engraved, as is usual, between ruled lines two inches apart. The obverse, or side A, contains 37 lines and the reverse 36. The letters vary in size from one to two inches each. They agree with the form of script of the latter half of the twelfth century A.D. Another slab having the same shape and about the same dimension and containing a copy of the present record, similarly engraved, was discovered at the East-gate of the citadel. Both these copies and Dr. Müller's transcript[2] have been utilized in producing the text printed here for easy reference with a facsimile (pl. 27) of the former slab and an improved translation of the text.

The Sanskrit verse at the beginning and that at the end are in *śārdūla-vikrīḍita* metre. The rest of the inscription is written in Sinhalese in the usually bombastic style of the composer of Niśśaṅka-Malla's records with a repetition of his favourite phrases and expressions.

The subject-matter consists of a panegyrical account of Niśśaṅka-Malla's virtuous qualities and of his charitable acts, followed by an exhortation similar to that given in the Galpota record above, No. 17, in which he advises his subjects to choose for their sovereign a prince or princess of his own Kāliṅga dynasty. He denounces vehemently the aspiration of the Govi caste and of the non-buddhistic princes from Coḷa or from Kēraḷa to the throne of Ceylon, emphasizing these sentiments with the threat that all those who join them would be treated as traitors and would accordingly be extirpated together with their families and their worldly possessions. His policy, however, of consulting his subjects through the medium of a representative council[3] shows, as I stated at p. 101 above, that he did his best to popularize his rule.

---

[1] See plan of Poḷonnaruva, facing p. 84, above.

[2] See *A.I.C.*, No. 149. A transcript and a translation of this inscription by Professor T. W. Rhys Davids are also to be found in the *J.R.A.S.*, vol. vii.

[3] See *A.S.C. Annual Report*, 1900, p. 9.

TEXT.

A.

1 ලක්‍ෂ්මීං වර්ද්ධිතුම්ව්‍යාඝශමයිතුත් ත්‍රාතුං ස්ව
2 වංශස්ථිතිං [,] කෞලනධර්මමුපාසිතුං යදි මනසං
3 රක්‍ෂිතුංවාඤ්ඡිතාන් [।] ක්‍ෂාත්‍රෛණ්‍ය[1]ව කුලානි වො ග
4 මයත ස්වාමිත්වමන්‍යාන් පුන[,]ර්වර්ණ්‍යානෙන
5 හි නයානිමාන් භජත හොනීනි[2]ශ්ශංකමල්ලොදි
6 තාන් [॥] ඔකාවස්රජපරපුරෙහි සූර්‍ය්‍යවංශය
7 ට තිලකායස[3]මානවැ රජපිළිවෙළින් රාජ්‍ය ල
8 දින් වොටුනු පැලඳැ මහරජතන් පත්වූ නිශ්ශං
9 කමල්ල කාලිඟ ප්‍රා[4]ක්‍රමබාහු චක්‍රවර්ත්තීන්වහ
10 න්සෙ අනත් රජසිරින් ශක්‍රයාසේ විරාජමාන
11 වැ ත්‍යාග සත්‍ය ශෞර්‍ය්‍යාදි ගුණගණයෙන් අසාධ[ා]
12 රණවැ උදුගල් මුහුන් පත් හිරුසේ සතුරඳුරු
13 දුරුලා මුළු ලක්දිව සෙමෙහි තබා ලොවැස්සන් පි
14 නින් උපන් කල්පවෘක්‍ෂයක්සේ වැඩැ සිටැ
15 ලොවැඩ සසුන්වැඩ කොටැ දශරාජධම්මයෙන් රා
16 ජ්‍ය කෙරෙමින් පුලස්තිපුර නැමැති කාලිඟරාජපු
17 රයෙහි වැඩ වසනසෙයෙක් තමන්වහන්සේ රන්
18 රිදී කහවුණු මුතු මැණික් වස්ත්‍රාභරණාදී දුන ව
19 ෂ්ටියෙන් දිළිඳුන් ගිම් නිවූ මහාජනයන්ගෙ
20 සමුද්ධි[5] දැකැ සතුටුවැ අපගෙ කාලිඟවංශයැට
21 ස්වභාව ධම්මවූ ලොකොපකාර කළමහ කෘතඥ
22 ගයෙකැසෙ අප මෙ කොට ලූ සමුද්ධි[5]ය කල්
23 පාන්තයැ දක්වා කෙසෙ ස්ථිරකොටැ ගනි
24 ත්දෙහොයි මහාකරුණා ප්‍රාඥයෙන් ප
25 රීක්‍ෂාකොට(ැ) වදාරනසෙයෙක් ලොවට මවු
26 පියවැ නරදෙවතාවැ සිටි රජදරුවන්ගෙ
27 ගුණමහිමා නොදැනැ උන්ට අපරාධ කළ දු
28 ර්ජනයන්ගෙමැ වර්ග හා සම්පත් වනා නි
29 ර්මූල වන බව දැකැ එසෙද කිසිනෙනකුන්ට

---

1 'ක්‍ෂාත්‍රාණ්‍යව' වියයුතුයි
2 'හොනිශ්ශංක' වියයුතුයි
3 'තිලකායමාන' බොහෝ
4 'පරාක්‍රම' වියයුතුයි
5 'සමෘද්ධ' වියයුතුයි

30 විනාශ නුවූවමනා වෙදසි සිතා අඥානයෙන්
31 අනඬවූ ලොකයාහට ඇස් දෙනනාසෙ සතත
32 යෙන් බොහො අවවාද අනුශාසනා කොටැ රා
33 ජද්‍රොහනම් පචානනතර්‍ය්‍යකර්‍ම්මසෙ නොකට
34 යුතු දෙයෙකැයි ධර්‍ම්මනීති දක්වනසෙයෙක්
35 ප්‍රාණාතිපාතාදි දුශ්චරිත කළාහුද විෂ කැවොද
36 තුමූ මතු නසිති රාජද්‍රොහනම් කළවුන්ද උන්ගෙ
37 වර්‍ග්‍ගද උන් හා එක්වූවනනාසයි එහෙයින් රා

B.

1 ජද්‍රොහනම් සිතිනුත් නොසිතිය
2 යුතෙතයැ අරාජකවැද නොවිසි
3 ය යුතෙතයැ එහෙයින් මහරජුන
4 න් පත්වැ සිටියවුන් නැති තැනෙකැ
5 යුවරජවැ සිටියවුන් හො උනුදු
6 නැතහොත් රාජකුමාරවරුන් හො
7 උනුදු නැතහොත් බිසෝවරුන් හො
8 රාජ්‍යයට තැකිය යුතෙතයැ බුදුසසු
9 නට ශිම් ලක්දිවට අබෞධ චොළ කෙ
10 රළාදි රජදරුවොද නොතැකියැ යුතනාහ
11 උන් හා එක්වැ පෙරෙළිකළාහු රාජද්‍රො(හි)
12 නම් වෙති කාකයා හංස ගතියටද කොට
13 එවා සෙනඬවයන්ටද ගැඬනුලා නාග
14 රාජයන්ටද කණමැඩිරිය[ා] සූර්‍ය්‍යප්‍රභා
15 වයටද වටුව(ා) හසකින්ටද කැණහිලා
16 සිංහයන්ටද භාව කරනනාසේ ගොවිකුලෙ
17 හි ඇත්තන් රාජ ලීලාවට නොපැතුව[1] මැනැ
18 වැ කෙසෙ බලවත්වූවද ගොවිකුලෙහි
19 ඇතෙතා රාජ්‍යයට බලා නොගතයුතනාහ
20 තමා හා සමගැතතන් වැඳු පුදා රජසම්
21 භාවනා කළා[2]හුද උන්ගෙන් නම් තනතුරු ල
22 ද්දාහුද රාජද්‍රොහිනම්මැ වෙති මෙ කීවන් හා
23 වර්‍ග්‍ගසම්පත් රජදරුකෙනෙක් පැනුණු
24 විටැමැ නිර්‍ම්මූලකරන්නාහ එහෙයින් ලක්

---

[1] 'නොතැකුව' යිද කියවියහැකිපි

[2] 'කළහු' යිද කියවියහැකියි

25 දිව මනුෂ්‍යවාසකල විජයරාජයන්
26 පරම්පරායෙන් ආ ලක්දිවට හිමි ර
27 ජදරු කෙනෙකුන් සොයා ගෙනැති වී(න)
28 ම් ඇස රක්‍ෂාකරන්නාසෙ ලොවැසසන්
29 රක්‍ෂායෙහි යෙදී ස්වාමී පක්‍ෂවැ තමන්
30 වශීහ සම්පත් රක්‍ෂාකරනු මැනැවි
31 ධ්වා(ං)ක්‍ෂා හංසගතිං ඛරො හයවරං
32 ගණ්ඩුපද(ඃ) පන්නගං[,] ඛද්‍යොතො මිහිර
33 ම්මෘගෙන්ද්‍රල(ලි)තං ක්‍රොෂ්ටා විපං වඤ්ඡිත
34 කඃ[।] වර්ණ්‍යානෙන තුකරොති රාජචරි
35 තමන්‍යෙනාවාදෘතං කෙවලං [,] හාස්‍යස් සතු
36 දිනි වක්ති නීතිකුශලො **නිශ්ශංකමල්ලො** නෘපඃ [॥]

TRANSCRIPT.

A.

1 Lakṣmīṁ varddhayitum vyathāś śamayitun-trātuṁ sva-
2 -vaṁśa-sthitiṁ [,] kaulan-dharmmam upāsituṁ yadi manas saṁ-
3 -rakṣituñ-c-āśritān [।] kṣātreṇy[1]-eva kulāni vo ga-
4 -mayata svāmitvam anyān punar[,]vvarṇṇān n-e[2]-
5 -ti nayān imān bhajata bhorn[3] Niśśaṁka-Mall-odi-
6 -tān [॥] Okāvas-raja-parapurehi Sūryya-**vaṁśaya**-
7 -ṭa tilakāya-samāna-vä[4] raja-piḷiveḷin rājya la-
8 -din voṭunu pälandä maha-raja-tan patvū **Niśśaṁ-**
9 **-ka-Malla Kāliṅga Prākrama**[5]**-Bāhu Cakravarttin-vaha-**
10 **-nse** anat raja-sirin Śakrayā-sē virājamāna-
11 -vä tyāga[6] satya śauryy-ādi guṇa-gaṇayen asādh[ā-]
12 -raṇa-vä Udā-gal mundun pat hiru-sē satur-anduru
13 durulā muḷu Lakdiva semehi tabā lo-vässan pi-
14 -nin upan kalpa-vṛkṣayak-sē väḍā siṭā
15 lo-väḍa sasun-väḍa koṭā daśa-rāja-dharmmayen rā-
16 -jya keremin **Pulasti-pura** nämäti Kāliṅga-rāja-pu-
17 -rayehi väḍa vasana-seyek tamanvahansē ran

---

[1] Read *kṣātrāṇy*. [2] Mt. *vvarṇṇān ena*. [3] Read *bho Niśśaṁka*.
[4] Mt. *tilakāyayi mānavä*. Read *tilakāyamāna-vä*: the akṣara *sa* appears to be crossed out.
[5] Read *parākrama*. [6] Mt. *tyāgra*.

Poḷonnaruva : Slab-inscription at the North gate of the Citadel

A

B

Scale about 1½ inches to 1 foot

From an inked impression supplied by the Archaeological Commissioner, Ceylon

18 ridī kahavuṇu mutu mäṇik vastr•ābharaṇ•ādi dāna-va-
19 -rṣāyen diḷindun gim nivū mahā-janayange
20 samurddhi[1] däkä satuṭu-vä apage Kāliṅga-vaṁśayäṭa
21 svabhāva dharmma-vū lokopakāra kaḷamha kṛtayu-
22 -gayekä-se apa me koṭa lū samurddhi[1]ya kal-
23 -pāntayä dakvā kese sthira-koṭä gani-
24 -t-dohoyi mahā-karuṇā prājñayen pa-
25 -rīkṣā-koṭ(ä) vadārana-seyek lovaṭa mavu-
26 -piya-vä nara-devatā-vä siṭi raja-daruvan-ge
27 guṇa-mahimā no-dänä unṭa aparādha kaḷa du-
28 -rjjanayange-mä vargga hā sampat vahā[2] ni-
29 -rmmūla vana bava däkä ese-da kisikenakunṭa
30 vināśa nu-vuva-manā[3] ve-dayi sitā ajñānayen
31 andha-vū lokayāhaṭa[4] äs dennā-se satata-
32 -yen boho avavāda anuśāsanā koṭä rā-
33 -ja-droha-nam pañcānantaryya-karmma-se no-kaṭa
34 yutu deyekäyi dharmma-nīti dakvana-seyek
35 prāṇātipāt•ādi duścarita kaḷāhu-da viṣa kävo-da
36 tumū matu nasiti rājadroha-nam kaḷavun-da unge
37 vargga-da un hā ekvūvan nasayi eheyin rā-

B.

1 -jadroha-nam sitin-ut no-sitiya
2 yutteyä arājaka-vä-da no-visi-
3 -ya yutteyä eheyin maha-raja-ta-
4 -n patvä siṭiyavun näti tänekä
5 yuva-raja-vä siṭiyavun ho un-udu
6 näta-hot rāja-kumāravarun ho
7 un-udu näta-hot bisōvarun ho
8 rājyayaṭa täkiya yutteyä Budu-sasu-
9 -naṭa himi Lakdivaṭa abauddha Coḷa Ke-
10 -raḷ•ādi rajadaruvo-da no-täkiyä yuttāha
11 un hā ekvä pereḷikaḷāhu rājadro(hi)-
12 -nam veti kākayā haṁsa-gatiyaṭa-da koṭa-

---

[1] Read *samṛddhi*.
[2] Mt. *sampatvā hā*.
[3] Mt. *nu vu manā*.
[4] Mt. *lokayanaṭa*.

13 -ḷuvā saindhavayanṭa-da gäṅḍahulā nāga-
14 rājayanṭa-da kaṇamändiriy[ā] sūryya-prabhā-
15 -vayaṭa-da vaṭuv(ā) hastīnṭa-da käṇahilā
16 siṁhayanṭa-da bhāva karannā-sē govi-kule-
17 -hi ättan rāja-līlāvaṭa no-pätuva[1]-mänä-
18 -vä kese balavat-vuva-da govi-kulehi
19 ätto rājyayaṭa balā no-gata-yuttāha
20 tamā hā samagättan vända pudā rāja-sam-
21 -bhāvanā kaḷāhu[2]-da ungen nam tanaturu la-
22 -ddāhu-da rājadrohi-nam-mä veti me kīvan hā
23 vargga-sampat rajadaru-kenek pänuṇu
24 viṭā-mä nirmmūla-karannāha eheyin Lak-
25 diva manuṣyāvāsa-kaḷa Vijaya-rājayan
26 paramparāyen ā Lakdivaṭa himi ra-
27 -ja-daru-kenekun soyā genä-ti vī (na-)
28 -m äsa rakṣākarannā-se lo-vässan
29 rakṣāyehi yedī svāmī pakṣavä taman
30 vargga sampat rakṣā-karanu mänävi
31 Dhvā(ṁ)kṣo haṁsa-gatiṁ kharo haya-varaṁ
32 gaṇḍūpada(ḥ)[3] pannagaṁ [,] khadyoto mihira-
33 -m mṛgendra-la(li)taṁ kroṣṭā dvipaṁ vartta-
34 -kaḥ [।] varṇṇo 'nyo 'nukaroti rājacari-
35 -tan n-aiv-ādṛtaṁ kevalaṁ [,] hāsyas syā-
36 -d iti vakti nīti-kuśalo **Niśśaṁka-Mallo** nṛpaḥ [॥]

TRANSLATION.

Side A.

[Lines 1–6] If [it be] your desire to increase your prosperity, to allay your fears, to preserve the position of your own lineage, to respect the customs of your family and to protect your adherents, raise ye to kingship [a member of] your Kṣatriya families; not the other castes: embrace these precepts spoken by Niśśaṅka-Malla.

[Lines 6–17] His Majesty **Niśśaṅka-Malla Kāliṅga Parākrama-Bāhu Cakravartī**, who is like unto a *tilaka* [mark of adornment][4] of the Solar dynasty of the line of kings of the Okkāka family, receiving the kingdom by [right of]

---

[1] This may also be read *no-täkuva*.

[2] This may also be read *kaḷahu*.

[3] Mt. °*padaṁ*.

[4] See above, p. 80, note 8.

royal succession, wore the crown and assumed supreme sovereignty. [His Majesty] shining like Śakra in boundless regal splendour, and distinguished by the assemblage of virtuous qualities [he is endowed with], such as generosity, truthfulness, heroism, and the like, dispersed his enemies, even as the sun rising over the Orient Mount dispels darkness, and thus he kept the whole Island of Laṅkā in peace. Then flourishing like a 'wish-conferring' tree that has sprung up by reason of the merits of the world, he promoted the interests of the Church and the State; and ruling in accordance with the ten principles of regal duty he made his residence in the Kāliṅga royal city of **Pulastipura.**

[Lines 17–25] He quenched the fire of poverty with showers of gifts of gold, silver, *kahavuṇu*[1] pearls, precious stones, clothes, jewellery, &c. And being pleased when he beheld the prosperity of the people [so benefited], in great compassion and wisdom, he reflected, 'We have rendered help to the world, for such is the native disposition of our Kāliṅga dynasty; how can we maintain to the end of the present cycle (*kalpa*) the stability of this prosperity which we have secured as [it were] in the golden age (*kṛta-yuga*)?'

[Lines 25–37] Then perceiving that utter destruction forthwith befalls the wealth, nay the very tribe, of the wicked ones who work evil against kings in ignorance of the greatness of their virtues—kings who stand as gods in human form and as parents to the world, His Majesty determined that such destruction should not befall any one. So he constantly gave much advice and instruction as if bestowing eyes on the world blind through ignorance. [Further] declaring that treason, like the five unpardonable sins[2], is a thing which should not be committed, he was pleased to expound [as follows] the law and policy:—

Those who have committed evil acts such as destruction of life and the like and those who have taken poison destroy themselves alone, while on the other hand treason destroys those who have committed it, together with their families and their associates.

Side B.

Lines 1–19] Therefore even the thought of treason must not arise in the mind. Moreover, it is not right to live without a king. So whenever there is

---

[1] See above, p. 117, note 3, and Mr. Codrington's interesting article on 'the Poḷonnaruwa coin weight standard' in *The Ceylon Antiquary and Literary Register*, vol. i, pt. 4.

[2] *Pañcānantarya-karma* = murder of mother, murder of father, murder of a Buddhist saint, shedding the blood of Buddha, and causing dissension in the Order of Bhikṣus.

no one holding the position of king paramount, then either the heir-apparent, or, if there be no such personage, one of the princes, failing them, one of the princesses should be chosen for the kingdom. Over the Island of Ceylon, which belongs to the religion of the Buddha, non-buddhistic princes from Coḷa, Keraḷa, or other countries should not be chosen. Those who join them and cause disturbances shall be called traitors.

People of the Govi caste should never aspire to the dignity of kingship, [for this would be] like the crow aping[1] the swan, [or] the donkey the Saindhava[2] steed, [or] the worm the cobra-king, [or] the firefly the sunshine, [or] the snipe the elephant, [or] the jackal the lion. However powerful the people of the Govi caste may be, they should not be elected [to rule] the kingdom.

[Lines 20–30] Those who pay obeisance to persons of the same class as themselves and render them the honours due to kings, and those, too, who accept from them offices and titles shall indeed be called traitors. Such people with their families and their worldly possessions will be rooted out as soon as a royal prince appears [on the throne]. Therefore, if it so happen that a prince has been found, who has a right to the Island of Laṅkā, being descended from the lineage of King Vijaya who made Laṅkā an abode for mankind, be loyal to such a lord and join [with him] in protecting the inhabitants of the country, even as you care for your own eyes. In this way protect your own families and fortunes.

[Lines 31–36] As the crow may ape the mien of the swan, and the donkey the noble steed; as the worm may ape the cobra, and the firefly the sun; as the jackal may ape the lion, and the snipe the elephant; even so another caste may [try to] emulate the conduct of kings; yet [such an attempt] will assuredly meet not with respect, but only with derision. So says king **Niśśaṅka-Malla** who is skilled in the rules of statecraft.

---

[1] *Bhāva-karannā-sĕ.* Cf. *Bhāvam kṛ*, to have an affection for (M.-W. *Skt. Dict.*).

[2] The fame of the Indus horses goes back to the Upaniṣads (*Bṛhadāraṇyaka*, vi. 1–13); see also *Jātaka*, No 183, *Rasavāhinī*, tale No. 14 and Hopkins, *J.A.O.S.*, xiii. 256, 257 (Dr. A. B. Keith).

No. 29. POḶONNARUVA: PRĪTI-DĀNAKA-MAṆḌAPA ROCK-INSCRIPTION

THE construction of the new road from Minneriya to Poḷonnaruva in 1900 brought to light a group of 'Hindu ruins' about a mile to the north of Topaväva proper[1]. In September of the following year the Archaeological Commissioner (Mr. H. C. P. Bell) commenced a careful exploration of the site, with the result that among other finds he discovered the present inscription[2] on the western slope of the long hummock of granite rock which rises there to a height of about 60 ft., its length being 270 ft. or more, and its breadth (greatest at the centre) 90 ft.

The inscription is in forty-five lines, covering a smoothed surface (8 ft. by 8 ft. 3 in.) of the slope of the rock to the left or north of the flight of steps leading up to the building on the top. The **akṣaras** are in size 1½ to 2 in. They are well incised between ruled lines 2¼ in. apart, and are of the same type as those of Niśśaṅka-Malla's records described above. With the exception of portions of lines 1 and 2, and a number of letters in other parts, the whole inscription is quite legible. It begins with a Sanskrit verse in *sragdharā* metre and proceeds in the usual style of language of the period to give an account of Niśśaṅka-Malla's birth and parentage, his administrative and charitable acts, the religious edifices and alms-houses he built, his tours in Ceylon, the so-called invasion of Southern India, and finally the erection of **Prīti-dānaka-maṇḍapa**, 'joy-conferring pavilion', and its consecration as a sanctuary whereby every one entering its premises had the right of asylum. It was to commemorate this last act that the present record was inscribed.

All these details taken in conjunction with those given in the Galpota and other inscriptions of Niśśaṅka-Malla[3] yield the following facts:—He was born in Siṁhapura in Kaliṅga about the year 1157 A.D.[4]; he crossed over to Ceylon at the invitation of his senior kinsman (probably Vijaya-Bāhu II)[5], sometime between 1180 and 1186; he was sub-king[6] to Vijaya-Bāhu II in 1186–1187 and eventually ascended the throne in September 1187, in the thirtieth year of his age. The first two years of his rule (1187–1189) were marked by charitable acts and certain administrative reforms carried out most

---

[1] See plan of Poḷonnaruva (inset A), facing p. 84, above.

[2] See *A. S. C. Annual Report*, 1901, p. 13.

[3] For his full name and pedigree, see *E. Z.*, vol. i, p. 124, and above, pp. 91–92.

[4] See above, p. 103.

[5] See the Galpota record A, lines 5–6 (above, p. 115).

[6] See *Mv.*, lxxx. 18–19, and the genealogical table facing p. 59, above.

probably in consultation with his council of officials and representatives of various guilds [1]. He adjusted the taxation of land, abolishing for all time the **visamburu-vata** and the taxes on *chena* land, while remitting others for a number of years in consideration of the distressed condition of the people. He distributed **tulābhāra** gifts, and introduced the South Indian custom of recording grants on copper plates. He fixed the distance of a *gavu* [2], and, calling it a *Niśśaṅka-gavu*, set up inscribed milestones in their proper places. He repaired certain irrigation works and religious edifices, established courts of justice, and suppressed thereby many forms of injustice. By means of public inscriptions he proclaimed his policy of government and exhorted the people to be of good conduct [3]. In his second regnal year [4] (1189 A.D.) he started on his tours of Inspection. He seems to have made four tours in all, for when he visited Dambulla he had already been on three [5]. The first tour may have been a short one. The second was to **Anurādhapura** in 1191, when he made costly offerings to the **Ruvanväli-dāgaba** and effected repairs to it as well as to **Mirisaviṭi** and other vihāras in that city [6]. The third was probably the longest, as it must have comprised his visits to **Samanoḷa** (Adam's Peak), **Miyuṅguṇu** (in Bintenna), **Mahagama, Devunuvara** (on the southern coast) and **Käläṇi** (near Colombo). His fourth (probably the last) tour was to **Dambulla**, where, according to all the chronicles, he spent lavishly on the cave-temple and set up there seventy-three gilded statues of the Buddha. This tour, in which Niśśaṅka-Malla probably included **Mäḍiligiri** also, may have taken place about the end of 1194 A.D., that is to say subsequent to his so-called invasion of South India [7], but before the erection of the Vaṭa-dā-geya [8], the Niśśaṅka-Daḷadā-geya, the Niśśaṅka-latā-maṇḍapaya, the Upakāracaitya, and the Ruvanmäli-dāgaba in Poḷonnaruva, not to mention buildings of minor importance. It is, of course, more probable that all these edifices were under construction whilst he was away on circuit and in India.

---

[1] See *A. S. C. Annual Report*, 1900, p. 9.

[2] See Häṭa-dā-gē vestibule inscription, line 12 (above, No. 15).

[3] See above, Nos. 17 and 28, and also lines 15 and 16 of the present record.

[4] See above, No 15, lines 1–2.

[5] See the Dambulla inscription, line 12 (Vol. I, No. 9).

[6] See above, No. 13.

[7] The Indian expedition is mentioned in the Dambulla inscription. The present record is, therefore, not quite accurate in referring to it as if it took place after the visit to Dambulla.

[8] The present inscription places the building of the Vaṭa-dā-geya, the Upakāra-caitya and the Ratna-caitya or Ruvanmäli-dāgaba before Niśśaṅka-Malla's visit to Anurādhapura in 1191 A.D., but a reference to the Rankot-dāgaba pillar-inscription (above, No. 23) will show that this cannot be correct.

The account of the Indian campaign, so persistently mentioned in all his inscriptions as one of his great achievements, must not be taken as literally true. Niśśaṅka-Malla neither reigned long enough nor had the time (even if he had the ability and the men) to carry out successfully such a task and also to build the many edifices attributed to him. The truth may be that the composers of his inscriptions in their eagerness to please their vain-glorious monarch have magnified his visits to Rāmeśvara and probably to some of the South Indian courts, as if they were military expeditions, and credited him with the victories gained by Parākrama-Bāhu I, a decade or so before. That this is true in the case of several buildings is the opinion of Mr. Bell[1]. Besides, the historical works are absolutely silent as regards his Indian expedition. In fact they have dismissed his reign in a short paragraph without even telling us whether at the expiration of his nine years' rule in September 1196 A.D., he died a natural death in his thirty-ninth year of age or fell a victim to a party plot brewing at the time in spite of his conciliatory policy and his public exhortations[2].

Touching the different buildings mentioned in the present inscription, we see that the **Vaṭa-dā-geya** (circular relic-house), which is most probably identical with the Vaṭa-geya mentioned in the Häṭa-dā-gē[3] and Galpota records, was built under the supervision of General **Lak-vijaya-siṅgu Tāvuru-nāvan**[4] and that it received the name **Ratana-giri.** The **Upakāra-caitya** (subsidiary shrine), mentioned in line 24, is also referred to in the Galpota inscription (C, line 2), where it is stated that Niśśaṅka-Malla had it built adjoining the **Mahāvihāra** (of Poḷonnaruva), but we are not sure as to the exact situation of this monastery. Possibly the group of ruins in the Jetavanārāma area may be identified with it, and the Upakāra-caitya may accordingly be one of the ruined dāgabas close by, for example, the so-called **Kiri-vehera.**

Lines 34–37 give the names of cities where Niśśaṅka-Malla is stated to have established alms-halls. Some of them are not mentioned in any of his

---

[1] *A. S. C. Annual Report*, 1903, p. 13.

[2] See above, pp. 101–103 and Vol. I, pp. 124–126.

[3] This ruin has been identified with the *Niśśaṅka-daḷadā-geya* (above, p. 85). Its modern name, *Häṭa-dā-gē*, is supposed to mean a 'shrine of sixty relics' (*A. S. C. Annual Report*, 1903, p. 13), but the statement in the *Pūjāvaliya* that Niśśaṅka-Malla caused a Tooth-Relic Temple (evidently the present one) to be constructed of stone in sixty Sinhalese hours (*daḷadā-maḷuyehi śailamaya daḷadā-geya säṭa-päyakin karavā*) makes it possible to ascribe the origin of the name to this tradition. Accordingly *häṭa-dā-gē* may be paraphrased by *häṭa päyakin karana-lada dā-geya*, 'relic-house built in sixty hours'.

[4] Concerning this officer, see below, p. 191.

foregoing records, and their situation is uncertain, while the names such as **Brāhmaṇa-satra, Bauddha-satra,** and **Bahu-jana-satra** connote the class of people which some of these almshouses were intended to provide for. Finally we come to the **Prīti-dānaka-maṇḍapa.** We are told that Niśśaṅka-Malla had it built and made its premises a sanctuary in order that he might rest there in bliss, 'imparting the gift of religious doctrine (*dharma-dāna*) which is the noblest of all gifts' and also hear the joyous shouts of ***sādhu*** and the like from the people who had received alms from him.

The location of this *maṇḍapa* or pavilion is quite easy, for a flight of shallowly cut steps on the right leads up to a ruined building on the top of the rock[1]. This is no doubt the remains of the **Prīti-dānaka-maṇḍapa,** although in architectural details it does not seem to correspond with the *Niśśaṅka-dāna-vinoda-maṇḍapa* built for a similar purpose[2] about a dozen yards to the west.

The following text of the record is based upon two inked-impressions supplied by the Archaeological Commissioner in 1911[3].

TEXT.

1 ශ්‍රීඃ දෘප්‍යද්දුර්ද්ධර(කාග) (ප්‍ර)තිනෘපති කුලෙ වනවධූඩං[4]) විධිත්සුස්තාදෘක්ෂාණාම[5] ලාභාවිතර්ණවිධිනා දානවීර(ශ්‍රී –)।

2 [ශ්‍රී – – – ᴗ –] (භා[6]) න්‍යකෘත භුවි කෘති **ශ්‍රීපරාක්‍රාන්තිබාහුශ්‍රීමාන්නිශ්ශංකමල්ලස්සුචි** රමවිකලනතානි රක්ෂන්තු භූපාඃ ॥

---

[1] Mr. Bell's description of the building runs:—'Along the axis of this rock an elongated rectangular building was laid out, its longest faces being 125 ft. east and west, by only 40 ft. across. It was certainly pillared (as stumps prove) at its northern end, and in all probability divided into a range of rooms, about 30 ft. wide, in a straight line along their west face throughout. Mortice holes for pillars, and a "set" for wall foundation, show the southern termination. A gangway seems to have run outside the building; for there is a bare groove in the rock, and inside it parts of the thick vertical pebble and lime concrete facing of the walls remain.

Outhouses probably occupied the eastern slopes of the rock, which are the widest.

A flight of some twenty-five shallow steps cut in the rock leads down direct west.'—*A. S. C. Annual Report*, 1902, p. 8.

[2] See above, No. 18.

[3] Since writing the above I have received a copy of Mr. Bell's Archaeological report for 1911–1912 containing his text and translation as well as a photographic plate of the present inscription. These have now been utilized and all important variants have been duly added as footnotes to the present edition.

[4] 'ශ්‍රී දෘප්‍යද්දුර්ද්ධකුඩ්‍යං ප්‍රතිනෘපති කුලොත්තුඞ්ග සෞධං' යනු බැල්මහතාගේ පාඨයයි

[5] 'තාදෘක්ෂාන් ග්‍රාමලාභාවිතරණවිධිනා දානවීරාග්‍රපදමම්' යනු බැල්මහතාගේ පාඨයයි

[6] 'සපඩ්ලාභානපෙතානකෘත' යනුබැල්මහතාගේ පාඨයයි

3 ඔකාවස්රජපරපුරෙහි සූර්‍යවංශයට තිලකායමානවූ රජපිළිවෙළින් රාජ්‍ය ලදින්
වොටුනු පැලඳෑ මහරජනන් පත්වූ (සිරි)ස

4 **ඟබො නිශ්ශංකමල්ල කාලිංග පරාක්‍රමබාහු** චක්‍රවර්තින්වහන්සෙ **ශ්‍රී ජයගොප** මහාරා
ජයන්වහන්සෙ නිසා **සා(ඛ)ති** ම

5 හදෙවින්වහන්සෙ කුසෙන් උපන් කෙණෙහි(ම සැ)පත් [1] ලකුණු මනා නකත්
මොහොත් දැකැ කුලතිලකයක් ලත්මියි .. .. පියාණ

6 න්වහන්සෙ වදාළ බස සබා කෙරෙමින් උදගල් මුදුන් පත් හිරුහුසෙ සතුරු
(අඳු)රු දුරුලා අනත් රජසිරින් ශනුයාසේ

7 විරාජමානවූ ලොවැස්සන් පිනින් උපන් කල්පවෘක්ෂයක්සෙ වැඩී සිටැ ලොවැඩ
සසුන්වැඩ කොටැ දශරාජධම්මයෙ

8 න් රාජ්‍ය කෙරෙමින් පුලසතිපුර නෙ(මැති)[2] කාලිඟපුරයෙහි වැඩැවසනසෙයෙක්
. පෙරැ නොබඳ කරවූ වර දී මුළාවූ ලංකා

9 වාසීන්ට පස් හවුරුද්දකට (අය හැරැ) වදුරා දිවෙල් වහල් සරක් පමුණු පරපුරු
වස්ත්‍රාභරණාදි නෙ(ක) වස්තු දී මහාජනයා සමෘ

10 **ඩ කොටැ සොරුනුදු** ජීවිතාශා හැරැ සොරකම් කරනෙහ ධනාශාවෙන් වෙදැයි
(උත්කැමැති) වස්තු ගම් කිම් දී සොරකම් හරවා චොරභ

11 ය දුරුකොටැ අනමෙහෙසුන් සූර්‍යවංශ **කාලිඟ සුභද්‍රා** මහදෙවින්වහන්සෙ හා
ගඟවංශ **කල්‍යාණ** මහදෙවින්ව

12 හන්සෙ හා යුවරජවැ සිටි උරෙහිදු **වීරබාහු** මහපාණන්වහන්(සෙ) [හා ස]මැගැ
සහ වොටුනු රජඹරණී

13 න් සැදී පෙරැ රජදරුවන් නොකළ විරූ ලෙසැ හවුරුදු පතා තුලාභාර නැඟී
මහානවරතන දානවෂ්ටා පවත්

14 [වා] දිළිඳුභය දුරුකොටැ බොහො ඇළ අවුණු වැවූ බඳවා දුර්භික්ෂභය
දුරුකොටැ නොඑක් තැනැ ධම්මා

15 ධිකරණ ලවා අන්‍යායනිවාරණ කොටැ තමන්වහන්සෙ සමෘඩකොට ලූ ලො
වැසසන් අනාචාරකොටැ නොනස්නා

16 පිණිසැ රාජ[ධානියෙ]හි සදාචාර ශිලාලෙඛ කරවා මවුපියන්සෙ ලොසසුන් රක්නා
බොධිසත්ව[3] රාජගුණ

17 යට (මෙත් සිත් ඇති[4] ගුණන)හ පක්ෂපාත ශරීරයෙන්මැ පාමහයි තුන්රජයෙ
ඇතතවුන් වෙළුැගතතා දැකැ ඉමා

18 වුන්ට නෙසු රජදරුවන් හා සම සම්පත් දෙමිසි රන් රිදී වළන් මුතු මැණික් (ආදි)
නොඑක් සම්පත් දී නැමැදෙන සුව

---

[1] 'සක්වත්' යනු බැල්මනතාගේපාඨයයි

[2] 'නැමැති' වියයුතුයි

[3] 'සතතව' වියයුතුයි

[4] 'මෙත්සිතඇති' යිද කියවිය හැකියි

19 පත්කොටැ **චොඩ ගෞඩාදි** නොඑක් දෙශයෙහි රජදරුවන් කරා හච්වයන් යවා (මඬුව) ධූඛ ඉල්ලා දැ(ං) ප්‍රතිපක්‍ෂ රජකෙ

20 නොකුන් නැති හෙයින් පිටතැ සතුරන් නැත මිච්වැ දිනුවමනා කෙලෙස් සතුරන් (වෙ)දූසි දළදා පාත්‍ර ධාතූන්වහන්සෙ

21 ට උරෙහිදැ **වීරබාහු** මහපාණන්වහන්සෙ පුදා උන්වහන්සෙ ගලවන සඳහා අනැඟි රුවනින් විසිතුරු ඝනරන් දා

22 ගබක් කරවා දළදා වඩා බොහො පූජාකොටැ මළුවෙහි ද **ලක්විජයසිඟු සෙනෙවි තාවුරුනාවන්** කැඳුවා **රතනගිරි**

23 යැ යන නමින් අනැඟි චටදාගෙයක් කරවවා[1] ගම් කිම් වෙහෙරවැස්සන් ආදි මහපෙරහර තබා නැවතැ හවූ

24 රුදූකම ලක්දිවැ අය හැර ශිලාලෙඛ කරවා **උපකාරචෛත්‍යයයැ**[2] **රත්නචෛත්‍යයැ** යනාදි තුන්රජයෙහි

25 මහසෑ කරවා **අනුරාධපුරයම** වැඩැ සතලිස්ලක්‍ෂයක් (ධන වැයදම්) කොටැ කළ මහාපූජා බලා දෙවතා[ව]

26 න් ප්‍රත්‍යක්‍ෂවැ ලොවැඩ සසුන්වැඩ කළමනා මෙසෙ වෙදූයි සතුති[සොභාකල තැන්]හි දාගබක් බඳුවා ඊසිටැ මා(වතැ) ව

27 ධනා කලැ නැඟී වදාළ අසුගෙ ජව වෙගයෙන් සිඟාවෙන් .. .. (වැටුණා)[3] වොටුන්න සිඟාවෙහිමැ දෙවතාව

28 න් තබා කළ ආරක්‍ෂා දැකැ සුචරිත ඵල ප්‍රත්‍යක්‍ෂ කො[ටැ තුන්රජයෙහි] ගම් නියම්ගම් ආදි හැමැතැ(නට)

29 වැද බලා අනාථයන් සනාථකො[ටැ නට]බුන් වෙහෙර දා[ගබ් පවත්කරම්]යි සිතා වදාරා **දඹුලුලෙණම** (වැඩැ)

30 හොත් හුන් සිටි පිළිම (තෙ)සැත්තෑවක් හා දාගබ් වෙ(හෙර) [කරවා රන් ගාවා] සත්ලක්‍ෂයක් ධන වැයකොටැ ම

31 හා පූජා කරවා **මැඬිලිගිරි වෙලගම්වෙහෙර මහගම (දෙවුනුවර) [කැ]ලැණි** ආදිවූ නොඑක් ප්‍රසිඬ විහාරය(න්)ට වැ

32 ඩැ අනන්‍ය වස්තු පරිත්‍යාග කොටැ මහාපූජා කොටැ (වදාරා සුපිළිපන්) මහා සංඝයාට සිවුපසයෙන් උපසථා

33 න කොටැ ධම්මධර ශාස්ත්‍රධර පණ්ඩිතවරුන්ට අනුරූපවෘත්ති දී වදාරා තෙසු රජ දරුවන් අනුභවකරන (ලෙස)

34 (මා) දවසැ යාව(ත)යත් සම්පත්වූව මැනැවැයි සිතා **අනුරාධපුරයැ ශ්‍රීපුරයැ ශ්‍රීවා(ස)පුරයැ නිශ්ශංකපුරයැ**

---

1 'කරවා' වියයුතුයි

2 'චෛත්‍යයැ' වියයුතුයි

3 'උඩපැනැනැඟි වොටුන්න' යනු බැල්මහතාගේ පාඨයයි

35 **(කා)ලිඟවිජය(පු)රයයෑ මහපුවුපයෑ** [1] **ශොනයයෑ (කාලි)ඟයයෑ රාමෙශවරයයෑ** යනාදි නොඑක් සවදෙශ පරදෙශයෙ

36 හි දනසත්‍ර කරවා මහාදනවඨ්‍යා පවත්වා වැඩැවසන **පුලස්තිපුර** නැමැති **කාලිඟ පුරයෙහි (ද ත්‍රිගු)වනසත්‍ර(ය)යෑ**

37 **නිශශංකාසත්‍රයයෑ බ්‍රාහමණසත්‍රයයෑ බෞඩසත්‍රයයෑ බහුජනසත්‍රයයෑ** යනාදි නොඑක් දනශාලා කරවා

38 (අනු)භවයට (සු)දුසු සියලු විසතුයෙන් කප්රුක්සේ සරහා (නොඑක්) සවදෙශ පරදෙශයෙන් ආ යා(චක)

39 (යන් පිළිගන්)වා (නොඑක් ඉච්ඡිත) භො(ජන මනාවූ පාන) වඟීග පුපජාති ඵලජාති අනුභවකොටැ රන්(විලැ) රිදී(විලැ)රන්

40 [කෙණ්ඩියෙන් රිදීකෙණ්ඩි]යෙන් මුව ශොධා සුවඳකල්කයෙන් අත් මැඩැ පස්පලව නි[ත්]යුන් බුලත් කා (සි)

41 තුසෙ භ) .. .. (ව) .. .. සුවඳවිලවුන්ගෙන් සම්පන්න (ප)රිවා(ර)යන්ගෙන් අ(ව) .. .. .. (භ)විඤ්ඤිමින් අන

42 හි ශයනාසනයෙහි සැතැපී මහත්වූ ප්‍රීතීන් අනන්ත දනාදි(ක) සාධු යනාදීන් [නෙක ප්‍රීති]ඝොෂා (අස) අසා (දන)

43 ප්‍රීතිසුව අනුභවකොටැ වැඩැහිඤිනටද සියලු දනයට උත්තමවූ බම් (දනය) පවත්වන්නටද **ප්‍රීතිදන(ක)**

44 **මඩපයක්** කරවා මහාපරව කළවුනුදු මෙය වන් කල අභයයැයි අභය දී වදෑරා කරවා වදාළ මෙ ශිලා

45 ලෙව බලා මතුවන රජදරුවනුදු (ත)බා වදාළ (දනධම්) පවත්වා (සව)ගීග මො(ක්‍ෂ) සම්පත් අත්පත් කරනු මැනැවි

TRANSCRIPT.

1 Śrī: dṛpyad-dor-ddaṇḍa(k-āṅga-pra)ti-nṛpati-(kule dvandva-yuddhaṁ)[2] vi--dhitsus[,] tādṛkṣāṇām alābhād-[3]vitaraṇa-vidhinā dāna-vīr-ā(nujī –) ।

2 [śrī – – – ◡ –] (bhā)ny-akṛta[4] bhuvi kṛtī **Śrī-Parākrānti-Bāhuś**[,] **śrīmān Niśśaṁka-Mallas** suciram avikalan tāni rakṣantu bhūpāḥ ॥

3 Okā-vas-raja-parapurehi Sūryya-vaṁśayaṭa tilakāyamāna-vä **raja-piḷiveḷin** rājya ladin voṭunu päländä maha-raja-tan patvū (**Siri**) **Sa-**

---

[1] 'වුවු(පු)යැ' සිද කියවිය හැකිපි

[2] *Śrī dṛpyad-dor-ddaṇḍa-kuḍyaṁ prati-nṛpati-kul-ottuṅga-saudhaṁ* in Mr. Bell's text. The letters are almost illegible at this point in both the estampages.

[3] Bt. *tādṛkṣān grāma-lābhād-vitaraṇa-vidhinā dāna-vīrāgra-padmam.*

[4] Bt. *sparddhālābhān apetān akṛta.*

4 -ñga-bo **Niśśaṁka-Malla Kāliṅga Parākrama-Bāhu** cakravarttīn-vahanse **Śrī Jayagopa** māhārājayan-vahanse nisā **Pā(rbba)tī** ma-

5 -ha-devīn-vahanse-kusen upan keṇehi-(ma sä)pat[1] lakuṇu manā nakat mohot däkä kula-tilakayak latmi-yi .. .. piyāṇa-

6 -n-vahanse vadāḷa basa sabā-keremin udā-gal-mundun pat hiruhu-se saturu (andu)ru duru-lā anat raja-sirin Śakrayā-sē

7 virājamāna-vä lo-vässan pinin upan kalpa-vṛkṣayak-se väḍä siṭä lo-väḍa sasun-väḍa koṭä daśa-rāja-dharmmaye-

8 -n rājya keremin Pulastipura ne(mäti[2]) Kāliṅga-purayehi väḍä vasana-seyek perä no-bada karavū vara dī muḷāvū Laṁkā-

9 vāsīnṭa pas havuruddakaṭa (aya hārä) vadārā divel vahal sarak pamuṇu parapuru vastr-ābharaṇ-ādi ne(ka) vastu dī mahājanayā samṛ-

10 -ddha koṭä sorunudu jīvit-āśā hārä sorakam karanne dhan-āśāven vedäyi (un kämäti) vastu gam bim dī sorakam haravā cora-bha-

11 -ya duru-koṭä aga-mehesun Sūryyavaṁśa **Kāliṅga Subhadrā** maha-devīn-vahanse hā Gaṅgavaṁśa **Kalyāṇa** maha-devīn-va-

12 -hanse hā yuva-raja-vä siṭi urehidā **Vīra-Bāhu** maha-pāṇan-vahan(se) [hā sa]mäṅgä saha voṭunu rajaṁbaraṇi-

13 -n sädī perä rajadaruvan no-kaḷa virū lesä havurudu-patā tulābhāra näṅgī mahā-navaratna-dāna-varṣā pavat-

14 [-vā] diḷindu-bhaya duru-koṭä boho äḷa avuṇu[3] vävu bandavā durbbhikṣa-bhaya duru-koṭä no-ek tänä dharmm-ā-

15 -dhikaraṇa lavā anyāyan nivāraṇa koṭä taman-vahanse samṛddha-koṭa lū lo-vässan anācāra-koṭä no-nasnā-

16 -piṇisä rāja[dhāniye]hi sadācāra śilā-lekha karavā mavu-piyan-se lo-sasun raknā bodhi-satva[4]-rāja-guṇa-

17 -yaṭa (met sit äti[5] sne)ha pakṣa-pāta śarīrayen-mä pāmhayi Tun-rajaye ättavun veḷä-gattä[6] däkä mo-

18 -vunṭa tesu rajadaruvan hā sama sampat demi-yi ran ridī vaḷan mutu mäṇik (ādi) no-ek sampat dī hämä-dena suva-

19 -pat-koṭä **Coḍa Gauḍ**-ādi no-ek deśayehi rajadaruvan karā bhaṭṭayan yavā (dvandva) yuddha illā dä(ṁ) prati-pakṣa raja-ke-

---

[1] Bt. *sakvat.*
[2] Read *nämäti.*
[3] Bt. *amuṇu.*
[4] Read *sattva.*
[5] This may also be read *met sita äti*; Bt. *apa sita äti.*
[6] Bt. *veḷagannā.*

Poḷonnaruva: Prīti-dānaka-maṇḍapa Rock-inscription

Scale about $\frac{11}{12}$ inch to 1 foot

From an inked impression supplied by the Archaeological Commissioner, Ceylon

20 -nekun näti heyin piṭatä saturan näta miviṭä dinuvamanā keles saturan (ve)däyi[1] daḷadā-pātra-dhātun-vahanse-

21 -ṭa urehidā **Vīra-Bāhu** mahapāṇan-vahanse pudā unvahanse gaḷavana sandahā anäňgi ruvanin visituru ghana-ran dā-

22 -gabak karavā daḷadā vaḍā boho pūjā-koṭā maḷuvehi-da **Lak-vijaya-siňgu Senevi Tāvurunāvan** kändavā **Ratana-giri-**

23 -yä yana namin anäňgi vaṭa-dā-geyak karavavā[2] gam-bim vehera-vässan ādi maha-perahara tabā nävatā havu-

24 -ruddakaṭa Lak-divä aya härä śilā-lekha karavā **Upakāra-caityayayä**[3] **Ratna-caityayä** yanādi Tun-rajayehi[4]

25 maha-sā karavā **Anurādhapurayaṭa** väḍä satalis-lakṣayak (dhana väyadam-) koṭä kaḷa mahā-pūjā balā devatā-[va-]

26 -n pratyakṣa-vä lo-väḍa sasun-väḍa kaḷamanā mese vedäyi stuti-[ghoṣā-kaḷa tän]hi dāgabak bandavā ī-siṭä mā(vatä) va-

27 -ḍanā kalā näňgī vadāḷa asuge java-vegayen siňgāven .. .. (väṭuṇa)[5] voṭunna siňgāvehi-mä devatāva-

28 -n tabā kaḷa ārakṣā däkä sucarita phala pratyakṣa ko[ṭä Tun-rajayehi] gam niyamgam-ādi hämä-tä(naṭa)

29 väda balā anāthayan sanātha-ko[ṭä naṭa]bun vehera dā[gab pavat-karami-]yi sitā vadārā **Dambulu-leṇaṭa** (väḍä)

30 hot hun siṭi piḷima (te)sättävak hā dāgab ve(hera) [karavā ran gāvā] sat-lakṣayak dhana väya-koṭä ma-

31 -hā pūjā karavā **Mäňḍili-giri Velagam**[6]**vehera Mahagama (Devuṇuvara) [Kä]läṇi** ādivū no-ek prasiddha vihāraya(n)ṭa vä-

32 -ḍā ananta vastu parityāga koṭä mahā-pūjā koṭä (vadārā supiḷipan[7]) mahā-saṁghayāṭa sivu-pasayen upasthā-

33 -na koṭä dharmma-dhara śāstra)dhara paṇḍita-varunṭa anurūpa-vṛtti dī vadārā tesu raja-daruvan anubhava-karana (lesa)

34 (mā) davasä yāca(ka)yan sampat-vuva mänäväyi sitā **Anurādhapurayayä Śrīpurayayä Śrīvā(sa)purayayä Niśśaṁkapurayayä**

35 **(Kā)liňga-Vijaya(pu)rayayä Mahapuṭupayä**[8] **Śonayayä (Kāli)ňgayayä Rāmeśvarayayä** yanādi no-ek svadeśa-paradeśaye-

---

[1] Bt. *kelesa saturan biňda siňda.*

[2] Read *karavā.*

[3] Read *caitya-yä.*

[4] Bt. *tun vargayehi.*

[5] Bt. *uḍapänä näňgi voḷunna.*

[6] Bt. *veragam.*

[7] Bt. *me piḷipan.*

[8] This may also be read *Mahavuṭupayä* or *Mahapuṭuvayä*, or *Mahavuṭuvayä*; Bt. *Mahapuṭuvayä.*

36 -hi dāna-satrạ karavā mahā-dāna-**varṣā** pavatvā väḍä-vasana **Pulastipura** nämäti **Kāliṅga-purayehi** (-da **Tribhu)vana-satra(ya)yä**

37 **Niśśaṁka-satrayayä Brāhmaṇa-satrayayä Bauddha-satrayayä Bahu-jana-satrayayä** yanādi no-ek dāna-śālā karavā

38 (anu)bhavayaṭa (su)dusu siyalu vastuyen kap-ruk-sē sarahā (no-ek) svadeśa-paradeśayen ā yā(caka-)

39 (-yan piḷigan)vā[1] (no-ek icchita) bho(jana manthavū pāna-)vargga pūpa-jāti phala-jāti anubhava-koṭā ran-(vilä) ridī-(vilä) ran-

40 [keṇḍiyen[2] ridī-keṇḍi]yen mukha śodhā suvanda-kalkayen at mäḍä paspala-vati[n] yut bulat kā (si-)

41 (-tu se ha- .. .. (va) .. .. suvanda-vilavungen sampanna (pa)rivā(ra)-yangen a(va) .. .. .. (ha) vindimin ana-

42 -ṅgi śayanāsanayehi sätāpī mahatvū prītin anna-dān-ādi(ka) sādhu yan-ādīn [neka prīti-] ghoṣā (asa) asā (dāna-)

43 prīti-sukha anubhava-koṭā väḍähindinaṭa-da siyalu dānayaṭa uttama-vū dharmma-(dānaya) pavatvannaṭa-da **Prīti-dāna(ka-)**[3]

44 **maṇḍapayak** karavā mahāparādha kaḷavunu-du meya van kala abhayayäyi abhaya dī vadārā karavā vadāḷa me śilā-

45 lekha balā matuvana rajadaruvanu-du (ta)bā vadāḷa (dāna-dharmma) pavatvā (sva)rgga-mo(kṣa)-sampat atpat-karanu mänävi

TRANSLATION.

[Lines 1–2] Hail! His Majesty **Śrī Parākrama-Bāhu Niśśaṅka-Malla** [ever] active in the world, desiring to establish single combat in the community of kings, proud and long-armed, ... a hero of liberality in the exercise of bounty on account of the losses of such kings[4] made . . . . [benefactions]. Let kings long preserve them unimpaired.

[Lines 3–8] His Majesty **Siri Saṅgabo Niśśaṅka-Malla Kāliṅga Parā-krama-Bāhu Cakravartī**, being like unto the *tilāka*[5] [mark] of the Solar dynasty

---

[1] Bt. *pin karava.*

[2] Bt. *kot ridī-kot . . . . niyāyen mukha sodhā.*

[3] Bt. *prīti dānana mama pasak karavā.*

[4] Several words of this Sanskrit stanza in *sragdharā* metre not being clear on both the estampages before me, their reading is not at all certain. So the above translation can only be offered tentatively.

[5] Cf. *Rāṣṭrakūṭa-kula-tilaka* (Ep. Ind., vii, p. 217), and above, p. 32, note 1.

of the royal line of the Okkāka race received the kingdom [of Ceylon] in due order of royal succession and wearing the crown assumed supreme sovereignty.

As soon as His Majesty was born of the womb of the great queen **Pārvatī,** his father, the great king **Śrī-Jayagopa,** observing the lucky marks [on his body] and the auspiciousness of the stars and of the hour [when he was born] made the announcement, 'I have received a *tilaka* to [adorn] my race'. And His Majesty [on coming to the throne] made good this assertion in that he scattered his enemies even as the sun, rising on the Orient Mount, scatters the darkness[1]. Shining like Śakra in boundless royal splendour, he flourished like a 'wish-conferring' tree that has sprung up by reason of the merits of the inhabitants of the world[2] and promoted the welfare of the world and the (Buddist) religion. [Thus] ruling the kingdom with the ten regal virtues, he made his residence in the Kāliṅga city of **Pulastipura.**

[Lines 8–14] He relinquished the revenue for five years in favour of those inhabitants of Laṅkā who had become destitute by the payment of inordinate imposts in former times. By gifts of divers property, such as *divel*-lands, serfs, cattle, permanent and heritable grants, clothes, and ornaments, he enriched the people[3]. Reflecting that thieves steal, even at the risk of their lives, through their desire for wealth, he bestowed on them village lands and property as much as they desire and made them desist from stealing. Thus did he dispel fear of theft[4]. [Again] His Majesty wearing the crown and other royal insignia, together with his chief queen **Kāliṅga Subhadrā Mahādevī** of the Solar race, and **Kalyāṇa Mahādevī** of the Gaṅga race, as well as his own son, the sub-king **Vīra-Bāhu Mahapāṇan-vahanse,** mounted the scale-pan and giving away every year wealth equal in weight to themselves, caused showers of *navaratna*[5] gifts to fall as kings had never done before. Thus did he dispel the fear of poverty. He dispelled also the fear of famine by the construction of many [irrigation] canals, embankments, and tanks.

[Lines 14–19] Through courts of justice he suppressed injustices in many places[4]. And with the object that the people whom he had thus made

---

[1] Cf. Galpota record, Section A, lines 12–13 (above, No. 17), and the Daṁbulla inscription, line 4 (Vol. I, No. 9).

[2] Cf. Galpota, A, line 14.

[3] This is found repeated in many other records of Niśśaṅka-Malla.

[4] See also Galpota A, lines 21–22 (above, No. 17), and the Ruvanväli-dāgaba slab, lines 6–8 (above, No. 13).

[5] See above, p. 118, note 4.

prosperous might not be ruined by wrong conduct, he set up in his capital moral edicts engraved on stone. [Moreover] thinking, 'I will show myself in my [true] body[1] which is endowed with benevolent regard for and attachment to the virtuous qualities of a Bodhi-satta king[2] who, like a parent, protects the world and the religion'; and seeing that the inhabitants of the threefold kingdom [of Ceylon] were in distress[3], His Majesty decided, 'I will give them wealth equal to that of kings', and bestowing on them gold and silver vessels, pearls, precious stones, and various other wealth made every one happy.

[Lines 19-25] He dispatched champions to the princes of Coḍa, Gauḍa, and many other countries demanding single combat. There being now no hostile king, he pondered: 'I have no enemies without, [therefore] it is now meet [for me] to conquer the enemies [within me, namely] the evil passions.' So he dedicated his own son, the sub-king **Vīra-Bāhu**, to the venerated 'Tooth-relic' and the 'Bowl-relic,' and for the purpose of redeeming him, His Majesty had [a model of] a dāgaba made in solid gold, ornamented with priceless gems. He exhibited [therein] the 'Tooth-relic' and made offerings in profusion[4]. Then summoning [to his presence] the general **Lak-Vijaya-siṅgu Senevi Tävurunāvan,** he caused him to build on the *maluva* (terrace) a priceless circular relic-house called **Ratanagiri** and amply endowed it with landed property, monastic staff, and the like. Further, he remitted the taxes in the Island of Laṅkā for one year and had stone inscriptions set up [to that effect]. In the threefold kingdom [of the Island] he erected great sacred shrines, such as the **Upakāra-caitya,** the **Ratna-caitya,** &c.

[Lines 25-31] Thereafter His Majesty visited **Anurādhapura** and made magnificent offerings with an outlay of wealth amounting to forty *lacs* [of *masuran* coins][5]. The divine beings (*devatās*) observing this, manifested themselves [in bodily form], and uttered shouts of praise, saying, 'thus indeed should duties

---

[1] Lit. 'with (my) body itself'.

[2] Cf. the expression *Siri-Lak-hi no bosat-hu no raj vanhayi*, 'that none but the *Bodhi-sattas* would become kings of prosperous Laṅkā' in the Jetavanārāma slab (No. 2), line 52; *E. Z.*, vol. i, No. 20.

[3] *Veḷä* same as *veḷa* in Galpota, B, line 17 (above, No. 17) and *veheḷa* in Rankot-dāgaba Galāsana, line 4 (above, No. 22) = Skt. *viheṭha*.

[4] Cf. Galpota, B, lines 23-24 (above, No. 17), and Häṭa-dāge Portico slab, lines 17-20 (above, No. 14), according to which Niśśaṅka-Malla's daughter also was dedicated to the Tooth and Bowl relics.

[5] See Ruvanväli-dāgaba slab, line 25 (above, No. 13).

for the benefit of the world and the religion be performed'. At that spot he built a dāgaba [1]. As he was proceeding thence along the road, it happened that his crown was jerked off the *siṅgā* [2] through the speed of the horse he was riding; but the *devatās* [soon] replaced it on the selfsame *siṅgā*. His Majesty observing the [divine] protection thus vouchsafed to him, reflected, 'I have made manifest the reward of virtuous actions. I will [now] visit and inspect the villages, towns, and all other places in the threefold kingdom [of Ceylon], afford relief to the helpless, and restore the vihāras and the dāgabas that have fallen into dilapidation.' Accordingly he visited the cave of Daṁbulla and caused the erection of a vihāra and a dāgaba and [the setting up of] seventy-three recumbent, sitting, and standing statues [of the Buddha]. He [had them gilded and] caused great offerings to be made with an expenditure of seven *lacs* of money [3].

[Lines 31–36] Further, he visited many celebrated vihāras, such as those at **Mäṇḍili-giri, Velagama, Mahagama,** (**Devunuvara**), and **Käläṇi,** and giving away boundless wealth made great offerings to them. He served the well-conducted community of Buddhist monks with the four priestly requisites

---

[1] See also Galpota, B, lines 11–12.

[2] *Siṅgā*, 'a topknot, a peacock's crest' (see Jayatilaka's *Elu Akārādiya*), apparently from a Skt. form *śṛṅgaka*. Here it may refer either to the knot of hair on the crown of the king's head or to his head-dress, probably conical in shape. The statement that the gods replaced the crown on the *siṅgā* itself seems to lend colour to the last meaning. Compare the following quatrain in *Kāvya-śekhara*, III. 25, where, according to the commentator, *siṅgā* is equivalent to Skt. *śikhā*:—

bäñdalā *siṅgā*-suṅga
lelavā dāta manaraṅga
kumaru maga yana raṅga
balā äda gata häkida netyuga.

'When one beholds how the handsome youth with crest bedecked and arms swinging gracefully, moves along the road, can one withdraw one's eyes from (gazing at) him?'

As regards the shape of the Sinhalese crown of the twelfth century A.D., the following description of the crown of the last Kandyan king may perhaps enable the reader to form a general idea:—'The king of Kandy's Crown, of a very singular, but tasteful form, gold, with projecting angles, from which are suspended ornaments of table diamonds, small rubies, &c.; round the circle, which embraces the forehead, are fifteen ornaments of gold, set with rose diamonds, and rubies, which screw on; on the top is an ornamental tuft of gold and pearls, and in front attaches an enamelled gold ornament of great beauty, in the form of a plume, covered with table diamonds, emeralds, and rubies, the centre ruby of a very large size, forming altogether a singularly splendid, and costly mark of royalty.' See *Catalogue of the Regalia of the King of Kandy*. Printed by W. Smith, King Street [London], 1820.

[3] See also the Daṁbulla record, lines 24–25 (*E. Z.*, Vol. I, No. 9) and Galpota, B, lines 10–11. (above, No. 17).

and bestowed suitable means of subsistence on learned men versed in law and science. Then reflecting, 'in my days let beggars have wealth wherewith they may also enjoy themselves as do the royal personages', he built almshouses in **Anurādhapura, Śrī-pura, Śrīvāsa-pura, Niśśaṅka-pura, Kāliṅga-vijaya-pura, Mahapuṭupa, Śonaya, Kaliṅga, Rāmeśvara,** and in many other places both in this country and in other lands, and caused great showers of gifts to fall.

[Lines 36–39] Also in the Kāliṅga city called **Pulastipura,** where he resides, he built many alms-halls, such as **Tribhuvana-satra** (the three-world almshouse) **Niśśaṅka-satra, Brāhmaṇa-satra, Bauddha-satra, Bahu-jana-satra** (public almshouse), and the like, and furnished them as 'wish-conferring trees' with everything fit for enjoyment. Here he entertained the beggars who had come from many places in this country and in foreign lands.

[Lines 39–45] That His Majesty after partaking such food as he desired, drinking divers mixed beverages, eating various kinds of cake and fruit, rinsing his mouth [with water out of gold and silver ewers filled] at 'the golden pond' and at 'the silver pond'; and after rubbing on his hands sweet-smelling unguent, chewing betel with the five ingredients . . . . . . and sleeping on a priceless sleeping-couch, (waited upon) by attendants with fragrant ointment, may remain there in the enjoyment of the bliss (of almsgiving), ever hearing the joyous shouts of *sādhu* and the like in response to the distribution of food; and that His Majesty may inaugurate the impartation of the gift of religious knowledge, which is the highest of all gifts, he caused to be erected a **Prīti-dānaka-maṇḍapa,** 'joy-conferring pavilion', and enacted that whosoever enters its premises shall have the right of asylum even though he has committed a serious crime.

To this effect this rock-edict has been inscribed. May future princes read it and continue the virtuous practice of almsgiving which has thus been established, and so attain the realization of heaven and release from re-birth, (*mōkṣa*).

No. 30. POḶONNARUVA: SLAB-INSCRIPTION OF VIJAYA-BĀHU II (1186–1187 A.D.)

THIS slab stands near the ancient irrigation canal at Poḷonnaruva. Both sides of it are smoothed so as to receive the inscription between ruled lines, two inches apart. Side A has 37 lines, covering an area of 5 ft. 8 in. by 1 ft. 7 in.: side B, 28 lines, occupying 4 ft. 5 in. by 1 ft. 7 in. of the surface. With the exception of a few words and letters here and there, lines 3 to 7 of side A and the whole of side B are illegible. So at least it appears from the two inked estampages before me [1].

The **letters**, which vary in size from $\frac{3}{4}$ to $1\frac{3}{4}$ in., agree in type with the **alphabet** of the latter half of the twelfth century A.D. The **style** of the **language too** points to the same period.

After the usual auspicious word *svasti* and a Sanskrit verse of which only the first line is partially legible, the record goes on to state that Vijaya, the eldest son of Siṁha-Bāhu of the Kāliṅga-Cakravarti dynasty came over to Ceylon, defeated the Yakṣas, and became king; that a descendant of his was **Parākrama-Bāhu**, who brought the Island of Laṅkā under one canopy of dominion; and that this king, desiring the continuation of his dynasty, invited his sister's son (*bāna*) over from Siṁhapura, invested him with royal dignity, and in course of time died. The nephew was thereafter duly anointed king **Vijaya-Bāhu**, but the day after his accession to the throne some treacherous ministers rose against him. A chieftain named **Vijayāyān-tän-nāvan** [2], however, protected the king and, quelling the rebellion, restored peace to the country. In recognition of these distinguished services, king Vijaya-Bāhu granted him heritable lands with certain privileges described on side B, lines 1 to 22, and ending with the usual clause to the effect that the regulations so enacted should be preserved. The remaining six lines contain an illegible Sanskrit stanza in Tamil character of the type in use during the twelfth century A. D.

Such are the **contents** of the present inscription. The historical facts

---

[1] See plate 29.

[2] *Yāna* = *yahana* and *yahan-tän* = Skt. *śayana-sthāna* (*Kavsilumiṇa*, vv. 598 and 741). So *Vijayā-yān-tän-nāvan* may mean 'Vijaya, the lord of the bed-chamber.' I am indebted to Mr. D. B. Jayatilaka for this suggestion.

therein alluded to not only corroborate the account in the *Mahāvaṁsa* but also throw additional light on the short reign of that unhappy monarch **Vijaya-Bāhu II** (1186–1187 A. D.). We are now absolutely certain that he was a son of a sister[1] of Parākrama-Bāhu I; and, as is shown in the genealogical table facing p. 59 above, this sister could be no other than **Bhaddavatī**, the spouse[2] of king Gaja-Bāhu II (1132–1153 A. D.), for Parākrama-Bāhu had only two other sisters who were married to his hostile cousin Māṇābharaṇa, son of Siri Vallabha. Their issues were Siri Vallabha and Kitti-Siri-Megha, and they all belonged to the party which opposed the political ascendancy of the Kāliṅga dynasty. It is true, however, that in the course of the war both these princes were taken captive[3] and were brought before Parākrama-Bāhu, but nothing is known as to their fate and we have no grounds to presume that Parākrama-Bāhu took pity on them and adopted one of them as his heir. It is also true that there is the statement of certain Buddhist monks in *Mv.* lxx. 333 that Gaja-Bāhu II had neither a son nor any brothers, but this may mean, judging from the circumstances under which the statement was made, that he had no son or brother near him at the time to continue the war and eventually to succeed him on the throne. In the absence of any reference to a fourth sister of Parākrama-Bāhu I, it is probable that his *bāna* or nephew was Bhaddavatī's son either by Gajā-Bāhu II or by a second marriage, unless, of course, the word *bāna* is applied loosely, as is often done, to indicate a more distant relative. As to where the nephew was when Parākrama-Bāhu sent for him, the chronicles are silent. The inscription alone tells us quite definitely that he was then living in Siṁhapura, the capital of Kaliṅga. We must, therefore, assume that when war broke out between Gaja-Bāhu II and Parākrama-Bāhu I, Bhaddavatī, queen of the former and sister of the latter, fled to India with her son for safety as many a royal personage had done so before. Some years later the Buddhist monks brought about a reconciliation[4] between the two monarchs. This, and the continuation of the war with Māṇābharaṇa may have paved the way for Parākrama-Bāhu to look on Bhaddavatī's son with favour. So, when he found towards the close of his reign that he was still childless and the question of a successor had to be settled, he rightly chose this prince in preference to the sons of his other sisters by Māṇābharaṇa. That there was much opposition to this election is clear both from the insurrection that took place on the day after the accession of this

---

[1] P. *bhāgineyya*; Sinh. *bāna*.

[2] *Mv.* lxvi. 149.

[3] *Mv.* lxxii. 324, 333–344.

[4] *Mv.* lxx. 326–335 and lxxi. 1–6.

prince to the throne as Vijaya-Bāhu II and from his tragic death a year later at the hands of Mahinda and Dīpanī[1]. The *Mahāvaṁsa* speaks of him both as a renowned poet of great learning and as a just and benevolent ruler deeply attached to the Buddhist religion. He is stated to have written with his own hand a letter in Pāli to the Burmese king of Arimaddana[2], and thus established friendly intercourse with that monarch.

As to the general **Vijayāyān-tän-nāvan**, whose loyal services are recognized by the present grant, there is every probability that he was the same personage as **Baṇḍārapota Pirivatu-bim Vijayāyān-nāvan**, who was, according to Kalyāṇavatī's inscription at Ruvanväli Dāgaba, a powerful minister even at the time of Parākrama-Bāhu I (1153–1186 A.D.)[3]. This Ruvanväli inscription, gives an account of a festival he held together with his mother **Sumedhā-devī** and his nephew (*bāna*) **Laṅkādhikāra Koṭadanavu Deval-nāvan** in making offerings to the dāgaba.

TEXT.

Side A.

1 (ස්වස්ති)
2 ශ්‍රී කාලිඟනාථඃ පරාක්‍රමබාහු(ජො)
3 .. ..
4 .. ..
5 .. ..
6 .. ..
7 .. ..
8 ශ්‍රීමත්වූ මහත් (එඩි සිංහවංශැති කා
9 ලිඟ)චක්‍රවර්තීන්වහන්සෙගෙ ව
10 ශයෙහි උපන් **සිංහබාහු** රජපාව
11 හන්සෙට ජේෂ්ඨ[4] පුත්‍රවූ කාලිඟයෙන්
12 ලංකාවට බැසැ යක්‍ෂ ප්‍රලයකොට මනුෂ්‍ය
13 වාසකොට එකාතපත්‍රරාජ්‍ය කළ **විජයරා**
14 ජයන්වහන්සෙගෙ වංශපරම්පරායෙන්

---

[1] *Mv.* lxxx. 15.

[2] This was a town in Rāmañña, and was the capital of Burma about this period

[3] See *J. C. B. R. A. S.*, 1882, pp. 181–182.

[4] 'ජ්‍යෙෂ්ඨ' වියයුතු.

15 ආ ලක්දිව ඒකරා(ජ්ජ)[1] කළ **පරාක්‍රමබා**
16 **හු** වත්හිමියන්වහන්සේ සවවශය
17 මත්තටද පවත්නා කැමැතිවැ පූර්වරාජ
18 යන් කොට ආ පරිද්දෙන්මැ **සිංහපුරයට**
19 යවා බෑනණුවන් වහන්සේ ගෙන්වා තම
20 න්වහන්සේ (නමුලා) හිමියා පටබැඳුවා
21 ශස්ත්‍ර ශාස්ත්‍රයෙහි නිපුණ කරවා ඇති
22 කොට වදාරා රාජ්‍යය සනාථකොට කලතුරෙ
23 න් ස්වර්ගසථවූ කල්හි (ඉපට) ක්‍රමයෙන්
24 අභිෂිකතවූ **විජයබාහු** වහන්සේට (ප)
25 (නදා) දුෂ්ටාමාත්‍යයන් රාජද්‍රොහීවැ ලංකාව(ට ක)
26 (ළ විලුපත) සාධා **විජයාශාන්තැන්නාව**
27 **න්** සෙ(මෙ)හි තබා දුන් රාජ්‍යයෙහි හිමියා(ණ)
28 න්වහන්සෙ අභිෂිකතව සහවොටුනු (අ)
29 බරණින් සැදි සිංහාසනාරූඪව දස්කම් කළ
30 වුන්ට අභිවෘද්ධිවූව මැනැවයි සිතා වදාරා
31 **විජයාශාන්තැන්නාවන් රූවන්දඹුයෙහි**
32 පටන් ශ්‍රීශරීරරක්ෂයෙහි සිටිහෙයිනුත්
33 පෙරළ පරිද්දෙන්මැ කාලිඟ පරම්පරාවටම රා
34 ජ්‍යයයි සාධා දුන් සෙයිනුත් මෙතුන්ගෙ වංශ
35 පරම්පරාවද විජයරාජයන්වහන්සෙ
36 කෙරෙ පටන් කාලිඟවංශයටමැ දස්කම්
37 කොට ආ හෙයිනුත් මෙ කළ දස්කමට (හි)

TRANSCRIPT.

Side A.

1 (Svasti)
2 Śrī Kāliṅga-nṛpaḥ Parākrama-bhu(jo)
3 .. ..
4 .. ..
5 .. ..
6 .. ..
7 .. ..
8 Śrīmat-vū mahat (eḍi Siṁha-vaṁśāti Kā-
9 -liṅga-)cakravarttin-vahansege va-

[1] 'ඒකරාජ්‍ය' වියයුතුයි

Polonnaruva: Slab-inscription of Vijaya-Bāhu II

Side A

Scale about 1⅜ inches to 1 foot

From an inked impression supplied by the Archaeological Commissioner, Ceylon

-ṁśayehi upan **Siṁha-Bāhu**-rajapā-va- -hanseṭa jeṣṭha [1] putravū Kāliṅgayen Laṁkāvaṭa bäsä yakṣa praḷaya-koṭa manuṣya- vāsa-koṭa ekātapatra-rājya kaḷa **Vijaya**-rā- -jayan-vahansege vaṁśa-paramparāyen ā Lak-diva ēkarā(jja [2]) kaḷa **Parākrama-Bā-** **-hu**-vat-himiyan-vahansē sva-vaṁśaya mattaṭa-da pavatnā kämäti-vä pūrvva-rāja- -yan koṭa ā paridden-mä **Siṁha-purayaṭa** yavā bānaṇuvan-vahansē genvā tama- -n-vahansē (namulā) himiyā paṭbandavā śastra-śāstrayehi nipuṇa-karavā äti- koṭa vadārā rājyaya sanātha-koṭa kalature- -n svarggasthavū kalhi (iṣṭa) kramayen abhiṣiktavū **Vijaya-bāhu**-vahansēṭa (pa-) (-nadā) duṣṭ•āmātyayan rājadrohīvä Laṁkāva(ṭa ka-) (-ḷa vilupta) sädhā **Vijayāyāntän-näva-** **-n** se(me)hi tabā dun rājyayehi himiyā(ṇa)- -n-vahanse abhiṣiktava sahavoṭunu (a-) -baraṇin sädi siṁh•āsan•ārūḍhava daskam kaḷa- -vunṭa abhivṛddhi-vuva mänävayi sitā vadārā **Vijayāyāntän-nävan Ruvandaṁbuyehi** paṭan śrī-śarīra-rakṣayehi siṭiheyinut perä paridden-mä Kāliṅga-paramparāvaṭa-ma rā- -jyaya sädhā dun seyinut mekunge vaṁśa- paramparāva-da Vijaya-rājayan-vahanse- -kere paṭan Kāliṅga-vaṁśayaṭa-mä das-kam- koṭa ā heyinut me kaḷa das-kamaṭa (ti-)

TRANSLATION.

Side A.

[Lines 8–16] His Majesty king **Siṁha-Bāhu** was born of the Kāliṅga Cakravarti family of the illustrious and very (proud Siṁha race). His eldest son, king **Vijaya,** came to Laṅkā from the Kāliṅga country, destroyed the Yakṣas,

[1] Read *jyeṣṭha*.

[2] Read *ēka-rājya*.

and making [the Island] habitable for men ruled it under one canopy of dominion. From his lineage was descended His Majesty **Parākrama-Bāhu,** the Lord of the soil [1], who also brought the Island of Laṅkā under [his] single sovereignty.

[Lines 16–27] [This king,] desiring the continuance of his dynasty in the future, sent [emissaries] to Siṁhapura as previous kings had done, and had his *bāna* brought over [to Ceylon]. (Without delay [2]) he had the prince invested with royal rank and brought him up, making him skilful in the science of arms. [Parākrama-Bāhu] having thus made the kingdom possessed of a [future] ruler, attained to heaven in course of time. Then, in accordance with his wishes, **Vijaya-Bāhu** was anointed [king]. On the following day, however, certain treacherous ministers became traitors and caused (disturbances) in Laṅkā. But the chief **Vijayāyān-tän-nāvan** suppressed them and, restoring peace, delivered the kingdom to His Majesty.

[Lines 27–37] His Majesty having been enthroned [again], arrayed himself in his crown and [other royal] attire, and mounting the lion-throne thought that those who had rendered loyal services should become prosperous. And as **Vijayāyān-tän-nāvan** was engaged in guarding the person of the royalty from **Ruvandaṁbu**, as he subdued the country and delivered it to the Kāliṅga dynasty just as before, and as [members of] his family from the time of king Vijaya have been rendering loyal services to this same Kālinga dynasty, in recognition of these loyal services . . . . . .

No. 31. DIṀBULĀ-GALA: MĀRĀ-VĪDIYE ROCK-INSCRIPTION

DIṀBULĀ-GALA ('Gunner Quoin' Hill), called in the present record **Duṁbulā-gala**, is a range of hills about ten miles to the south-east of Poḷonnaruva or sixty miles from Anurādhapura in the same direction.

The Archaeological Commissioner (Mr. H. C. P. Bell) who made a thorough exploration of the whole locality in September 1897, tells us that 'at the back the cliff towers slightly concave (recalling the east face of Sīgiriya, but steeper) with many *bambara wada* (rock-bee hives) hanging hundreds of feet up. Further east the range rises still higher with two more rocky scarps well marked.

[1] *Vat-himiyan-vahanse* (line 16). See *E. Z.*, vol. i, p. 199, note 1.

[2] *Namulā* probably for *numuḷā*.

Directly behind Kuḍā Uḷpota is a slight dip in the range (*degala*) at no mean height. North-west by north, nestling high near the summit, can be seen some caves with white plastered walls, like the Sīgiriya "gallery". At the east end of Diṁbulā-gala lies Kosgaha Uḷpota, another Vädda hamlet; and round opposite its west face Mannampiṭiya, the largest and most thriving village in Tamankaḍuwa, two miles this side of the Mahaväli-gaṅga across the Mahagantoṭa ferry . . . . All the west, north-westerly side of Diṁbulā-gala is known as **Mārā-vīdiya** from the ancient road which passed round its base to Mannampiṭiya. The highest point is immediately west of the dip and above the caves. Thence the hill gradually falls away round to northwards with two rocky buffs breaking the outline. The approach to the caves is along a spur and very gradual until nearing the cliff under which the caves lie. These were natural caverns in the scarp near its summit. Cave No. 1 is the best preserved: its plastered walls are nearly perfect, and paintings which adorned them may be faintly traced. This cave has an arched doorway and another entrance. High up on the overhanging rock beyond the reach of ladder is an inscription of very large letters. Passing to the left a rock pool of clearest water, a gradual rise by a ledge, two to three feet only in width, leads towards the second cave, No. 3, thirty yards or more east. A few yards' crawl along the ledge, a dip through a natural rock tunnel, more creeping across a further ledge equally narrow, then descent to a broader passage, culminates in a second tunnel. This emerges on to cave No. 2. A fine view is obtained of the Kandyan hills from this cave. It is larger than No. 1, and was centuries ago a *gal vihāre*. The rock floor being wider here than at any other point, provided a fair-sized natural terrace in front. Portions of the walls still stand, and there are remains of drawings mostly in black and white.

On the rock roof are two inscriptions—the older in a few cave letters, the second dated in the twenty-seventh year of "Jaya Bāhu" (Wijaya Bāhu I, 1065–1120 A. D.). This latter record of seven lines is cut on a smooth raised panel, and is of great interest. It proves the occupation in the eleventh century by monks, for whom the caves were prepared by Queen Sundari, wife of Wikrama Bāhu I 1121–1142 A. D.) and mother of Gaja Bāhu I, the cousin and chief rival of Parākrama Bāhu the Great.'

Such is Mr. Bell's lucid description of the locality. The inscription with which we are concerned here is that engraved on the raised panel between ruled lines two inches apart in Sinhalese characters of the twelfth century A. D., varying from one to one and a half inches in size[1]. The record seems to be complete, though the unusual ending suggests the possibility of it being continued on other panels on the rock roof which might have escaped even the long trained eye of an indefatigable explorer like Mr. Bell.

The **contents** tell us that **Sundara-Mahā-devī**, the chief queen of **Vikrama-Bāhu** and the mother of **Gaja-Bāhu**, caused the construction of a road at **Duṁbulā-gala** between **Sanda-maha-leṇa** (the great Moon-cave) and **Hiru-maha-leṇa** (the great Sun-cave); that she had it paved with stone and had also cave temples built with statues, dāgabas, and sacred bodhi trees; and that she further testifies to a certain benefaction which she had made to **Demaḷā-pähä** in the 27th year of the reign of **Vijaya-Bāhu**[2].

It is clear from these historical references that the inscription belongs neither to Vijaya-Bāhu I nor to his brother Jaya-Bāhu I, but to **Sundara-Mahā-devī**. It is the only record by her so far known to us, and was set up in her capacity as the chief queen of **Vikrama-Bāhu I** (1111–1132 A.D.)[3]. That this view must be correct we see first from the form of the script and the phraseology which debar us from giving the inscription a date later than the third quarter of the twelfth century A.D., secondly from the reference to Gaja-Bāhu II (1132–1153 A.D.) by the title *deva* which suggests that he had not yet come to the throne, and, thirdly, from Sundara-devī's confirmation of the benefaction which she had made to Demaḷā-pähä in the reign of her father-in-law, Vijaya-Bāhu I (1055–1110 A.D.). Her object was obvously to make in her present official position a legal record of the gift. It seems that as the chief queen of the reigning monarch she had the right to make such permanent grants to public institutions—a right which she apparently did not enjoy when her husband Vikrama-Bāhu was only a viceroy[4] of Vijaya-Bāhu I.

Attention may be drawn to the name **Sundara-Mahā-devī**. In the printed edition as well as in manuscripts of the second part of the *Mahāvaṁsa* Vikrama-Bāhu's queen is called **Sunārī**, but there is no doubt that the former is her correct name. And it is confirmed by the Sinhalese rendering of *Mv.* lix, v. 49 by *ovu[hu] suḷu buhun* **Sundarīn** *Vikrama-Bāhu-haṭa saraṇapāvā dī mesē bandhu vardhanaya keḷeyi* in the British Museum MS. Or. 6606 (61) of the

---

[1] See plate 30.

[2] This clause may also be interpreted as Sundara-devī's confirmation of Vijaya-Bāhu's grant, not of her own; but the above rendering seems to be the right one.

[3] More correctly Vikrama-Bāhu II. See the Genealogical Table facing p. 59 above.

[4] See *Mv.* lx. 88–90.

Narendracaritāvalokaṇa-pradīpikā[1]. The form *Sunārī* probably originated from a copyist's mistake some centuries ago. He evidently misread the Sinhalese combined *akṣara* ඬ *ṇda* as ණා *ṇā* owing to the close resemblance of the two signs to each other in early manuscripts. Later copyists and editors unconsciously perpetuated the error, possibly because the reading *su-nārī* like *sundarī* happened to give an appropriate meaning and was, therefore, not jarring to their ears; while Yaṭanvala Thera, the author of the *Narendracaritāvalokaṇa-pradīpikā*, did not fall into the error probably because he happened to base his version on MSS. of the *Mahāvaṁsa* derived from a different archetype.

As regards the other proper names in our record, **Gaja-Bāhu Deva** is no doubt identical, as mentioned above, with **Gaja-Bāhu II** (1132–1153 A.D.), although the word at the end of the second line which tells us his relationship to Queen Sundarī is hardly legible. **Vijaya-Bāhu Vat-himi** is obviously **Vijaya-Bāhu I** (1055–1110 A.D.), the syllable *vi* being fairly clear in one of the estampages before me. Mr. Bell's original identification[2] is, therefore, correct; but the later suggestion[3] that Vijaya-Bāhu of our record might be Jaya-Bāhu I is inadmissible.

The monastery **Demaḷā-pähä**[4] might at first sight be identified with the ruin now known as **Demaḷa-maha-sāya**[5] in Poḷonnaruva but this is not so. The context makes it almost clear that the Demaḷā-pähä was a distinct building erected at Dum̆bulā-gala, probably by Vijaya-Bāhu I. Demaḷa-maha-sāya, on the other hand, might be the great *thūpa*, which, according to the *Mahāvaṁsa*, lxxviii, v. 81, Parākrama-Bāhu I built and gave the name **Damila-thūpa** because the Tamils who were brought from the Paṇḍu country as prisoners of war were employed in the building of it.

In the *Nampota* and other Sinhalese works we find **Dim̆bulā-gala** mentioned as an important seat of the Buddhist priesthood. The *Nikāyasaṅgraha* speaks of two celebrated monks, namely, the Mahāthera Buddhavaṁsa Vanaratana and his chief pupil, the Mahāthera Āranyaka Medhankara, both of the **Dim̆bulā-gala** fraternity. They lived in the first half of the thirteenth century and assisted

[1] See fol. ඩි *b*.

[2] *A. S. C. Annual Report*, 1897, p. 9.

[3] *Ibid.*, 1909, p. 27.

[4] P. *Damiḷa-pāsāda*.

[5] P. *Damiḷa-mahā-cetiya*. For a complete description of this important ruin, see *A. S. C. Annual Report*, 1909, pp. 9–16.

both Vijaya-Bāhu III and his son Parākrama-Bāhu II in the purification of the Buddhist Order. Again, it is a common belief that the Thera Mahā Kāśyapa of **Udumbara-** or **Audumbara-giri** who presided over the Buddhist synod[1] held at Poḷonnaruva under the patronage of Parākrama-Bāhu I, some ninety years before, also belonged to the same fraternity, and that **Dim̆bulā-gala** or **Dum̆bulā-gala** is only a Sinhalese form of **Udumbara-giri**[2]. But definite proof is still wanting to regard that these names refer to one and the same place, namely, the **Dum̆bulā-gala** of the present inscription.

The **Sanda-maha-leṇa** and the **Hiru-maha-leṇa,** as well as the road made by the order of Queen Sundarī, may be identified with the two caves and the ancient street mentioned in Mr. Bell's report quoted above.

TEXT.

1 ඔකාවස්රජකුලෙන් නිපන් සුදොනාපරපුරෙන් ආ හිරුගොත්කුලෙන් (අභින්නවූ රූසිරින් සිරි)

2 දිනූ ලදවොටුනු මැ .. .. .. න් **විකුම්බා** නිරිඳුහට අගමෙහෙසුන්වූ **ගජබාහු** දෙවයන් (වැදූ)

3 **සුන්දරමහදෙවින්වහන්සෙ** පන්සියක් මහසඟනට ආවාසවූ අප මුනිරජහු සිරුරු

4 දා පිහිටි **දුඹුලාගලැ සඳමහලෙණ්**(න්) **හි**(රු)**මහලෙණ** දෙඅතුරෙහි මග(දුණ්ණු එවූ අ .. .. රෙඹු)

5 න්(යෙදූ) කැබලිගල් (හසවා) මග පවත්කොට ලෙණ පිළිම දාගැබ් මහ(බො) පිහිටුවා (කලිඟුලෙ)

6 **ණ** යා (දානවන් වි)**ජයබාහු වත්හිමියන්වහන්සෙ** සත්විසිවන හවුරුදු පොසොනැ පුර පො

7 හොයැ **දෙ**(**මළුසැහැ** සිරිකුසලාන්) කරවා යාබත් පුදනුකොට (ලොව්) පවත්නා තාක් කලට දුන් බවට **සුන්දරමහදෙවි** (මැ)

TRANSCRIPT.

1 Okā-vas-raja-kulen nipan Sudonā-parapuren ā Hiru-got-kulen (abhinnavū rū-sirin siri)

2 dinū lada-voṭunu mä .. .. n) **Vikumbā**-nirindu-haṭa aga-mehesun-vū **Gaja-Bāhu** Devayan (vädū)

---

[1] See the Galvihāra inscription (*A. I. C.*, No 137), the *Sāsanavaṁsa*, p. 26, and the *Nikāyasaṅgraha*.

[2] See the *Catalogue of Sinhalese MSS. in the British Museum*, Introd., p xv.

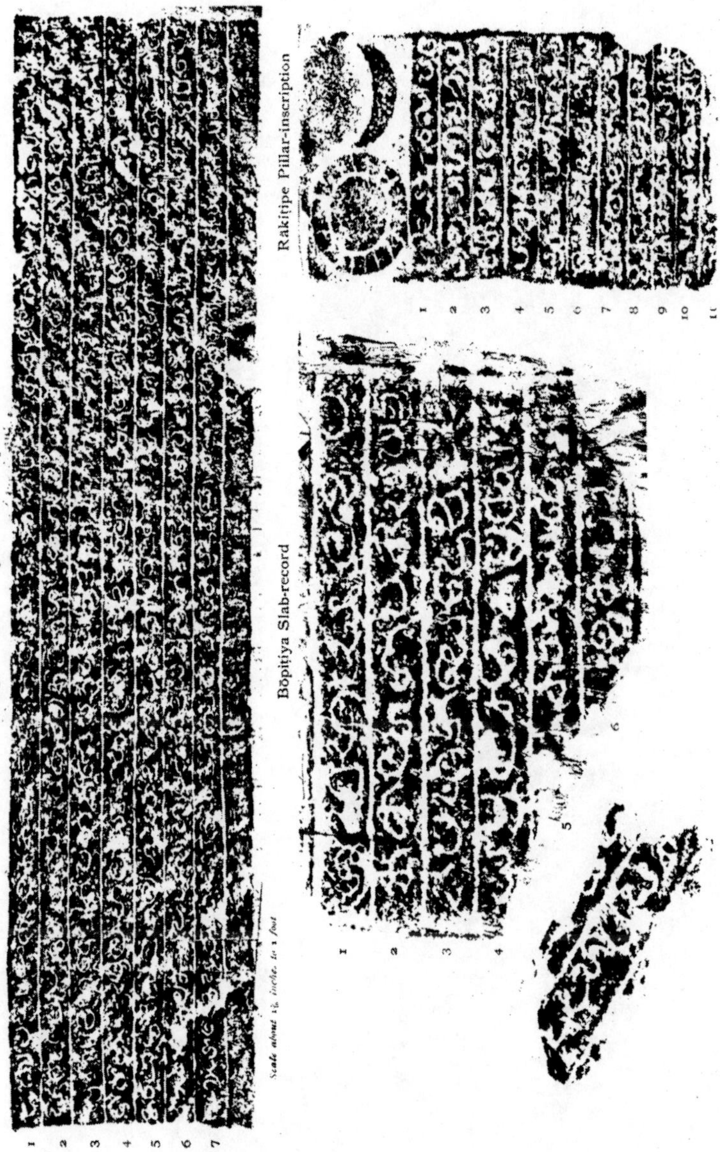

Diṁbulāgala : Mārā-vidiye Rock-inscription

Scale about 1⅜ inches to 1 foot

Rakiṭipe Pillar-inscription

Bōpiṭiya Slab-record

Scale about 1⅜ inches to 1 foot

3 **Sundara-maha-devīn-vahanse** pansiyak maha-saṅganaṭa āvāsavū apa muni-rajahu siruru

4 dā pihiṭi **Dumbulā-galä Sanda-maha-leṇi(n) Hi(ru)-maha-leṇa** de-aturehi maṅga (duṇu evu a .. .. rembu-)

5 -n (yedū) käbaligal (hasvā) maṅga pavat-koṭa leṇa piḷima dāgab maha-(bo) pihiṭuvā (**Kaliṅgu-le-**)

6 **-ṅa** yā (dānavat **Vi**)**jaya-Bāhu Vat-himiyan-vahanse** sat-visi-vana havu-rudu Posonā pura po-

7 -hoyā **De**(**malā-pähä** siri-kusalān) karavā yā-bat pudanu-koṭa (lov)pavatnā-tāk kalaṭa dun bavaṭa **Sundara-maha-devī**-(mä)

TRANSLATION.

Her Majesty **Sundara-Mahā-devī,** chief queen of king **Vikumbā** who .. .. the crown[1] which he had received and mother[2] of **Gaja-Bāhu Deva,** who surpasses the goddess Śrī in her beauty and is directly descended from the Solar dynasty, which belongs to the lineage of Sudonā[3] that has sprung from the Okkāka royal race—[this queen] caused the construction of a road between **Sanda-maha-leṇa** (the great moon-cave) and **Hiru-maha-leṇa** (the great sun-cave) at **Dumbulā-gala,** where 500 members of the 'Great Community' reside and where relics of the body of our Lord Buddha also exist, and had the street paved with flagstones[4] . . . . Then she had caves established with statues, dāgabas and sacred *bodhi* trees. Adjoining **Kaliṅgu-leṇa** (Kāliṅga-cave) also, on the *uposatha* day of the bright half of (the lunar month) Poson [May–June], in the twenty-seventh year of [the reign of] the munificent king **Vijaya-Bāhu Vat-himi,** she caused the construction of sacred *kusalān* (vessels ?) for the **Demaḷā-pähä** (monastery), and, after making an offering of gruel [in them], dedicated them [to it] so long as the world exists. To this effect **Sundara-Mahā-devī** herself[5] [testifies].

---

[1] This may possibly be a reference to the fact that he was still not properly anointed as king though he had got the crown. Cf. *Mv.* lxi. 30.

[2] Lit. who brought forth.

[3] P. *Suddhodana.*

[4] *Käbali-gal hasvā.* The greater part of the text here is hardly legible.

[5] If the last syllable be *mha*, the translation should be 'To this effect I am [lit. we are] Sundara-Mahā-devī'.

No. 32. BŌPIṬIYA SLAB-INSCRIPTION OF KALYĀṆAVATĪ

THIS stone was discovered between the years 1906 and 1912 in Bōpiṭiya, a village in Hevāvissa Kōrale in the Central Province of Ceylon. As the facsimile (plate 30) shows, it is in two fragments. The first piece is the top portion of a slab about 2½ ft. wide. It contains the first six lines of the inscription. The second piece evidently belongs to the lower end, as we see on it the words *hira sanda*, 'sun and moon', which usually occur at the end of a grant.

The **letters**, measuring 1½ to 2½ inches in size, are boldly engraved between ruled lines three inches apart. Their type is practically the same as that of other records of the last quarter of the twelfth and the first of the thirteenth century A.D.

Of the inscriptions of Niśśaṅka-Malla's queen, **Kalyāṇavatī,** who, like Līlāvatī, bore the title Abhā Salamevan, only two are so far known. The first is the one on the pavement of Ruvanväli dāgaba[1] at Anurādhapura, dated in her second regnal year, and the second is the present record. Though we have here only a fragment of the latter, yet what little information its contents give throws some light on the final events of her reign. As stated in the article No. 14 of Volume I on the slab-inscription of Līlāvatī, nothing is known regarding the fate of Sāhasa-Malla whom Lag-Vijaya-siṅgu Ābōnā or Āyasmanta installed on the throne on Wednesday August 23, 1200 A.D., and deposed after he had reigned two years, which would be up to September 1202. Thereafter the latter administered the government for six years through Queen Kalyāṇavatī of the present record, and for one year subsequently by placing on the throne a three-months-old prince named Dhammāsoka. Then a governor called Anikaṅga, with a large army from the Coḷa country, invaded the Island, put both Āyasmanta and Dhammāsoka to death, and took up the reins of government. The chronicles are silent as to what became of Kalyāṇavatī. That she disappeared from the scene is certain. Otherwise Āyasmanta, her champion, would surely not have placed somebody else on the throne. The mystery is to some extent cleared up by the present record. The Tamil insurrection which it speaks of, is probably Anikaṅga's invasion about 1208 A.D. The destruction of Kalyāṇavatī's stronghold by the Tamils might be interpreted as the defeat of Āyasmanta in a battle, when Kalyāṇavatī had to seek safety in flight across the river Mahaväli-

---

[1] *A.I.C.*, 158, and *J.C.B.R.A.S.*, 1882, p. 181.

gaṅga into the mountainous districts of Kandy. Here she may have lived more or less in concealment, while Āyasmanta, regaining his lost ground, held Poḷonnaruva against the invaders, and nominally ruled the country for nearly a year by placing on the throne an infant-prince named Dhammāsoka until both were put to death by Anikaṅga. Such being the probable sequence of events, Kalyāṇavatī's present grant may have been made in 1208 or 1209 while she was living in retirement possibly somewhere near Bopiṭiya.

As to the general **Āyasmanta,** he has already been identified with **Elaḷu Ābō Senevirat** of the *Pūjāvaliya* and **Lag-Vijayasiṅgu Senevi Ābō-nāvan** or **Tāvuru-nāvan** of the Galpota and Sāhasa-Malla inscriptions [1]. According to the chronicles he seems to have been quite a different person from **Lag-Vijaya-siṅgu Kit Senevi** of the Abhayavāva pillar [2], who, in 1197 A.D., put Queen Līlāvatī on the throne. But the following arguments may be urged in support of the theory that these names refer to one and the same person:—

(*a*) *Āyasmanta* (Skt. *āyuṣmat*, Sinh. *ābō*) is not a proper name. It is an honorific title applied to Buddhist monks and elderly persons in high positions. At the time of Queen Kalyāṇavatī (1202–1208 A.D.) Lag-Vijayasiṅgu Kit Senevi might have been popularly spoken of as *Senevi Ābō-nāvan*, in Pāli *Āyasmanta-camūpati*, 'the venerable general', owing to his seniority in age and rank, just as a king might be referred to by a popular title such as *mahallaka-rājā* (Sinh. *mahalu raja*), 'the old king', more than by his proper name.

(*b*) The close similarity of the two names *Lag Vijayasiṅgu Kit Senevi* and *Lag Vijayasiṅgu Senevi Ābō-nāvan*, the last word being only an honorific.

(*c*) The contemporaneity of the bearers of these names and the similarity of the rôle they played in politics within a period of only twelve years.

TEXT.

1 ශ්‍රී අභා සලමෙව
2 න් කල්‍යාණවතී ස්වාමි
3 න්වහන්සෙ දෙමළ වි
4 යවුලින් කඳවුර බිඳී
5 .. .. .. නෑ (කර) ගිහුවා ගෙන
6 .. .. .. මත (පඩි)
[?] වුළු ගිර සඳ

---

[1] See above, p. 101. For an account of his administration, see *Mv.*, lxxx, 35–43.
[2] *A.I.C.*, 157.

TRANSCRIPT.

1 **Śrī Abhā Salameva-**
2 **-n Kalyāṇavatī** svāmi-
3 -n-vahanse Demaḷa vi-
4 -yavulin kandavura bindī
5 .. .. .. nā (kara) hinduvā gena
6 .. .. .. mata (paḍi)
[?] vuḷa hira sanda

TRANSLATION.

Her Majesty **Śrī Abhā Salamevan Kalyāṇavatī**—her stronghold having been broken-up through the Tamil insurrection—was carried away on the shoulder . . . . sun and moon.

No. 33. RÄKIṬIPE PILLAR-INSCRIPTION OF LĪLĀVATĪ

RÄKIṬIPE[1] is a village in Unantänna-vasam, Diyatilaka kōrale in the Nuvara Eliya District. The inscribed stone shown in the accompanying facsimile (plate 30) was found in this village between the years 1906 and 1912[2], but no details are available as to its discovery. The abrupt ending of the inscription as well as the sun and moon emblems carved above it show that the stone is only the top fragment of a pillar about 13½ inches square. The letters, varying from one to two inches in size, are incised as usual between ruled lines two inches apart. Their type is the same as that of Līlāvatī's slab-inscription forming No. 14 of the first volume of the present work, though the letters *m* and *r* show a shade more modern.

---

[1] As to the origin of the name, 'the tradition is that a king having gone out hunting was watching for game for an hour at a place in this village, hence the name "Räkahiṭiyapäya" (the hour that was watching), corrupted into Räkiṭipe' (Lawrie's *Gazetteer of the Central Province of Ceylon*, p. 785).

[2] See *A. S. C. Annual Report*, 1911–1912, p. 122.

As we have here only the first ten lines of the inscription we are unable to say what its subject-matter is; but that it records a grant of land or some other benefaction in the reign of **Līlāvatī,** the Queen-dowager of Parakkama-Bāhu I, is apparent from the first clause. The date of the record we can only guess on palaeographic considerations to be 1211 A.D., when Parakkama of the Kāḷanāgara race installed Līlāvatī on the throne for the third time and administered the government for seven months until deposed by the Pāṇḍyan King Parakkama. From Līlāvatī's Anurādhapura inscriptions[1] we see that she had the *biruda* title Abhā Salamevan, and the present record refers to her as belonging to the Solar race. Her pedigree and details connected with her intermittent rule are given in the genealogical table facing p. 59 above and in *E.Z.*, Vol. I, pp. 177-178.

TEXT.

1 **ශ්‍රී සඟබො පරා**
2 **ක්‍රමබාහා**[2] චක්‍රව
3 ර්ත්තීන්වහන්සේ
4 ට අගමෙහෙසුවූ
5 සූරියවංශාභිජාත **ලී**
6 **ලාවතීන්වහන්සෙ**
7 රජ පැමිණැ ස (මා)
8 (චූ)නුවණ .. .. (රක්‍ෂා)
9 (කරන) සම්යෙ (ලො තරු වැ)
10 .. .. (වය) .. .. .. ට .. ..
11 .. ..

TRANSCRIPT.

1 **Śrī Saṅgabo Parā-**
2 **-krama-Bāhā**[3] Cakra-va-
3 -rttīn-vahansē-
4 -ṭa aga-mehesu-vū
5 Sūriya-vaṁś-ābhijāta **Lī-**

---

[1] *E.Z.* Vol. I, No. 14, and *A.I.C.*, No. 157.

[2] 'හු' විය යුතුයි

[3] Read *bāhu*.

6 **-lāvatīn-vahanse**
7 raja pämiṇä sa (mā)
8 (vū) nuvaṇa .. .. (rakṣā)
9 (-karana) samaye (Lo-taru-vä)
10 .. .. (ṭaya) .. .. .. ṭa .. ..
11 .. ..

TRANSLATION.

At the time when Her Majesty **Līlāvatī,** nobly born in the Solar race, chief Queen-dowager of His Majesty **Śrī Saṅgabo Parākrama-Bāhu** Cakravarti, having assumed sovereignty, was ruling . . . . with wisdom . . .

34.* DIMBULĀGALA: MĀRĀ-VIDIYE ROCK-INSCRIPTION

THE fresh material which Mr. H. C. P. Bell has brought to light in his scholarly review in the *Ceylon Antiquary* of July, 1917 (pp. 4–12) of my article on the above record makes it desirable to publish a new edition and translation of the text and revise my account thereon, both in the interest of Ceylon epigraphy and particularly in order to pave the way for a fuller discussion of events during the reigns of Vijaya-Bāhu I and his successors.

REVISED TEXT.

1 ඔකාවස්රජකුලෙන් නිපන් **සුදෙනා** පරපුරෙන් අ **සිරුගොණ්** කුලෙන් අභින් නවූ රුසිරින් **සිරි**
2 දිනූ (දෙ)වොටුනු මැ(ඇ උප)ත් **විකුඹා** නිරිඳුහට අග මෙහෙසුන්වැ [1] **ගජබාහුදෙවයන්** වැදූ
3 **සුභද්‍රමහදෙවින්වහන්සෙ** පන්සියක් මහසඟනට ආවාසවූ අප මුනිරජහු සිරුරු
4 දා පිහිටි **දුඹුලාගලැ සඳමහලෙණින් සි(රි)මහලෙණ** දෙඅතුරෙහි මඟ දුණු එවූ [2] (දුම එළි යන මිනිසු
5 න්ගෙ දුක බලා) ගල් හස්වා මඟ පවත් කොට ලෙ(ණැ) පිළිම දාගබ් මහබො පිහිටුවා **කලිඟුලෙ**

---

* 31 revised

[1] 'වූ' සිද කියවියගැකිසි [2] 'වි' සිද කියවියගැකිසි

6 ණ (යැය් නම් තබා **ජය)බාහුවත්හිමියන්වහන්සෙ** සත්විසිවන හවුරුදු පොසො නැ පුර පො

7 හොයැ **දෙමළැපැහැ** සිරිකුසලාන් කරවා යාබත් පුදනුකොට ලොව් පවත්නා තාක් කලට දුන් බවට **සුඳරමහදෙවිමු**[1]

TRANSCRIPT.[2]

1 Okā-vas-raja-kulen nipan **Sudonā**-parapuren ā **Hiru-got**-kulen abhinna-vū rū-sirin **Siri**

2 dinū (de-)voṭunu mä(ndä upa)n **Vikum̆bā**-nirindu-haṭa aga mehesun-vä[3] **Gaja-Bāhu-devayan** vädū,

3 **Sundara-mahadevīn-vahanse** pansiyak maha-sañganaṭa āvāsa-vū apa muni-rajahu siruru-

4 dā pihiṭi **Dum̆bulā**[4]**-galä Sanda-maha-leṇin Hi(ri**[5]**)-maha-leṇa** de-aturehi mañga duṇu evu[6] (dama elī yana minisu-)

5 (-nge duka balā) gal hasvā mañga pavat koṭa le(ṇā) piḷima dāgab maha-bo pihiṭuvā **Kaliñgu-le-**

6 **-ṇa** (yäy nam tabā **Jaya-)Bāhu-vat-himiyan-vahanse** sat-visi-vana havurudu Posonä pura po-

7 **-hoya Demaḷā-pähä** siri-kusalān karavā yā-bat pudanu-koṭa lov pavatnā tāk kalaṭa dun bavaṭa **Sundara-mahadevīmu**[7].

TRANSLATION.

Her Majesty Sundara-mahādevī[8] who surpasses[9] (the goddess) **Śrī** in beauty and gracefulness[10], who is directly descended from the **Solar dynasty**

---

[1] ' මහ ' සිඳ කියවියහැකිසි.

[2] The portions of the text within parentheses are either different from or entirely wanting in my original edition on p. 188, above. The notes which follow the translation here will show where Mr. Bell's reading differs from mine.

[3] Or *vū*.

[4] Or *-lä*.

[5] Read *hiru*.

[6] Or *ev*.

[7] Or *mha*.

[8] The principal sentence of this record is *Sundara-mahadevīn-vahanse Demaḷā-pähä kusalān-karavā dun bavaṭa Sundara-mahadevīmu*, ' To the effect that Her Majesty Sundara-mahadevī having had *kusalāns* built at the Tamil monastery dedicated the same [to the monastery], We are Sundara-mahadevī '. This last phrase is more or less similar to the final sentence of a modern royal or legal announcement. I prefer, therefore, to close the translation with it rather than put it at the beginning as Mr. Bell has done.

[9] Or ' transcends ' as Mr. Bell renders.

[10] *Rū-siri.* Cf. P. *Kisāgotamī Bodhisattassa rūpa-sirim̆ disvā.* Anderson (*Pāli Reader*, p. 220)

which belongs[1] to the lineage of **Suddhodanā** that has sprung from the royal race of Okkāka[2], who became the chief queen of king **Vikkama-Bāhu** born of crowned parents[3], and gave birth[4] to **Gaja-Bāhu-deva**: [this queen] seeing the hardship of people who, like old folk, hang on[5] to chains and tread the path between the **Sanda-maha-leṇa** (the great Moon-cave) and **Hiru-maha-leṇa** the great Sun-cave) at **Dumbulāgala**[6], where 500 members of the 'Great Community' reside and where also relics of the body of our Lord Buddha are enshrined, caused the stones to be cut[7] and the path (thus) improved.

Then at the Cave[8] she had statues, dāgabas, and great bodhi-trees established and gave to it (i. e. the cave) the name **Kāliṅga-leṇa.**[9] And on the *uposatha* day of the bright half of (the lunar month) Poson[10] (May – June) in the twenty-seventh [regnal] year of **Jaya-Bāhu-Vat-himiyan-vahanse**[11], she caused the construction of sacred *kusalān*[12] (vessels?) at **Demalā-paha**[13], and for the

---

takes *rūpa-siri* as a dvandva compound, 'beauty and majesty', but it can very well be a tatpuruṣa compound and be rendered simply by 'loveliness' or 'beauty', as Mr. Bell has done.

[1] *Parapuren ā*, 'which has come down from the lineage'.

[2] Mr. Bell has *Ikhwaka*. I do not know where he got this form from. Possibly it is a misprint for *Ikṣvāku*.

[3] *De-voṭunu mändä upan*. See notes below. [4] *Vädū*. See notes below.

[5] *Dunu evu dama eli*. See notes below. *Dama* (Skt. P. *dāma*) may also mean 'a rope'.

[6] Mr. Bell omits this in his translation and makes the Sun-cave the residence of 500 Buddhist monks!

[7] *Hasvā*, 'having caused to cut', causative of *hasinavā* or *hahinavā*, 'to cut with an adze, to chip, to smooth the sides of a bank' (Clough's *Sinhalese Dictionary*). Possibly the meaning of this is that steps were cut in the rock.

[8] Possibly at the *Hiru-maha-leṇa* (the great Sun-cave). Mr. Bell's rendering of this passage is '(further) that having established cave (shelters) dāgabas and great bō-trees, (I) gave (to this cave temple) the appellation "Kalinga Leṇa".'

[9] Evidently in honour of her Kāliṅga nationality, she had the name *Hiru-maha-leṇa* changed to *Kaliṅgu-leṇa*.

[10] *Posonä pura pohoyä*. Cf. *Poson pura pasaḷos-vaka*, 'on the fifteenth day of the bright fortnight of Poson' (*E. Z.*, Vol. I, p. 75, n. 4); *Väp pura poho davas* 'on the full moon day of Väp' (Ib., p. 158); *Hilä pura mändi poho davas*, 'on the middle *poho* day of the waxing moon (i. e. the full moon day) of *Hil*' (Ib., p. 174). There are, as every Indologist knows, four *uposatha* days (two in the bright half and two in the dark half) in every lunar month. Of these, the second in the bright fortnight, namely, the full-moon day is apparently the one meant here as in the foregoing quotations.

[11] After *Jaya-Bāhu-Vat-himiyan-vahanse*, the words *sat längū*, as found in other inscriptions must be supplied (e.g. *E. Z.*, Vol. I, Nos. 8, 15, 19, and 20). Otherwise the grammatical relationship of *vahanse* to the rest of the sentence is difficult to be explained. See also *E. Z.*, Vol. I, p. 52, n. 16. Mr. Bell's translation 'in the 27th year (of the reign) of Jaya-Bāhu Vat-himiya' seems to me to convey the idea that the king was alive at the time. That this was not the case, the reader will presently see.

[12] *Siri kusalān*. See notes below. [13] P. *Damiḷa-pāsāda*.

purpose of offering[1] (therein) gruel and boiled rice[2] granted them (to the Monastery) so long as the world[3] exists. To this effect we[4] are **Sundara-mahādevī.**

NOTES.

Line 1. Mr. Bell has *ahinnavū*. Obviously *hi* is a misprint for *bhi*, the word being *abhinnavū* as in my text.

Line 2. *Dinū* (not *dinu*) is quite clear on my estampage.

Line 2. *Devoṭunu mändä upan*, as read by Mr. Bell, must be accepted, for the present at least, as correct. His eye-copy as well as the photographic facsimile of the record show the akṣaras more or less distinctly. Besides, in the printed proof I submitted to the Government, the reading I gave was *devoṭunu mänduruvan*, and this was before I was aware of Mr. Bell's better reading *devoṭunu mändä upan*.

As to the meaning, I agree with Mr. Bell. The expression does seem to cover both the father and the mother (of Vikkama-Bāhu) as equally crowned sovereigns. And this is corroborated by the *Mahāvaṁsa*, for according to it Vijaya-Bāhu I held his coronation ceremony in the eighteenth year of his reign (lix. 9) after he had wrested the northern districts of Ceylon from the Coḷa domination, while Tiloka-Sundarī (the mother), besides being of royal blood, was a duly anointed queen (lix. 29–32).

Line 2. Mr. Bell has *Gaja-Bāhu-devayan lada*. If this reading is accepted, *devayan* must be in the accusative case governed by *lada*, in spite of the fact that *lada* is derived from P. *laddha*, the past passive participle of √*labh* and that it qualifies *Sundara-mahadevīn-vahanse* in the nominative case. This active use of the past passive participle is not uncommon in Sinhalese. Still I prefer the reading *vädū* for two reasons. First my estampage supports it, and secondly it agrees with the Pāli expression *putta vijātā*, 'she who has brought forth a son', *vijātā* (Sinh. *vädū*) being here used in an active sense.

Line 4. Mr. Bell gives *Dum̐bulu-galä*. A careful comparison of the akṣaras *lu* and *lä* with *lā* in *balā* (l. 5), and in *kusalān* (l. 7) will make it clear

---

[1] *Yā-bat pudanu koṭa dun.* Cf. the similar phrase *sivur denu koṭ dun vissak*, 'the twenty (kaḷan̄das weight of gold) granted for the purpose of providing robes', in the Vessagiri slab-inscription (*E. Z.*, Vol. I., p. 25.

[2-3] See notes below.

[4] Honorific plural for the singular.

that *lu* must be read either as *lā* or *lä*. I would, therefore, adhere to my reading *Dum̆bulā-galä* and give *Dum̆bulä-galä* as an alternative.

Line 4. As Mr. Bell is quite certain of the reading *hiri*, I now alter mine, namely *hiru* to *hiri*, although the latter is not the form usually found in compounds. Cf. *hiru-got* in line 1.

Lines 4–5. Mr. Bell gives *mañga daṇa eva dama valī yana minisunge duka balā*. Here my estampage being very faint, I was not able to make out a satisfactory reading. But with the aid of Mr. Bell's eye-copy and facsimile of the record, I think, I have succeeded in improving upon Mr. Bell's text. I would read the passage as *mañga* (or *mañgä*) *duṇu ev* (or *evu*) *dama elī yana minisunge duka balā* and render it 'seeing the hardship of persons who, hanging on to chains like old[1] folk, tread the path'. It is true that one is tempted to read *daṇa eva* instead of *duṇu evu*, as the former seems to correspond with the familiar expression *daṇa gā* 'crawling on knees', but the estampages and facsimiles of the record I possess do not support this reading.

Line 5. Mr. Bell has *gal-gasvā*, but there is some difference between the *ga* in *gal* and the *ga* in *gasvā*. The latter seems to me to be more like *ha* than *ga*. So I prefer to retain my reading *gal-hasvā*, which most probably means 'having had steps cut in the rock to facilitate climbing'.

Line 5. Mr. Bell gives *leṇa*, but *leṇä*, the locative form, is quite legible and suits the construction of the sentence better.

Lines 5–6. Mr. Bell reads *Kaliñga leṇa yäy nam tabā Jaya-Bāhu-Vat-himiyan-vahanse*. Here again my estampage is most unfortunately indistinct, while Mr. Bell's eye-copy and the facsimile support his reading. The only suggestion I can make is *Kaliñgu* as given in my text for *Kaliñga*. Although the *u* vowel sign is not quite clear here, yet the former is the form usually employed in forming compounds, e.g. *Kaliñgu-raṭa* (*E. Z.*, Vol. II, p. 109) *Kaliñgu-lakiñdu-nisaka-raja* (Ibid., p. 114). That Jaya-Bāhu is the name of the King, there is not the slightest doubt now, and as regards his date, I shall presently show that, after all, there is nothing very remarkable.

Line 7. Mr. Bell has *Demaḷā vähäsara kusalān karavā*, but I still adhere to my reading for the following reasons:—

I have as yet not come across the word *vähäsara* in inscriptions or in Sinhalese literature. Mr. Bell seems to connect it with *vä-sar* or *väsara* (*E. Z.*, Vol. I, pp. 49 and 93) but *vä* stands there for *vavi* (P. *vāpi*) and *vähä* can

---

[1] *Duṇu* = P. *jiṇṇa*.

hardly be an intermediate form. Further, in the sentence *Mahendra-Laṅkā-Adhikāra-piriveṇä kusalānayi*, '(this) is the *kusalāna* of (lit. at) Mahendra-Laṅkā-Adhikāra Pariveṇa,' the word *piriveṇä* is in the locative case. There is no such construction in *demaḷā-vähäsara-kusalān karavā*. On the other hand, the reading I have made out from my estampage, namely, *Demaḷā-pähä siri-kusalān karavā*, 'having had auspicious *kusalāns* made at Damiḷa-pāsāda' is grammatically correct. *Pähä* is the locative case of *paha* (P. *pāsāda*) and stands in the same relationship to *kusalān* as *piriveṇä* to *kusalāna* in the foregoing quotation. *Siri* is, of course, Skt. *śrī*, 'auspicious, sacred or royal', but as to what a *kusalāna* is I am still uncertain. According to Clough's *Sinhalese Dictionary*, it means a drinking-vessel [1]. Mr. Bell thinks that it is a *pin-gama* (Skt. *puṇya-grāma*) a village dedicated for the sake of acquiring religious merit, but he gives no authority for his interpretation. His quotation *kusalānaṭa pidi*, 'offered to (or for) the *kusalāna*,' gives him no help but supports my interpretation. Besides, if Mr. Bell's view is accepted, the clause *daru-kusalān, maṅga-kusalān pera paridden tabā* in the Galpota record (*E. Z.*, Vol. II, p. 111) would be difficult of explanation.

Line 7. Mr. Bell reads *pā-bat* as against mine *yā-bat*. The compound *pā-bat* (P. *patta-bhatta*) is rather a novel expression. Until another example is cited, I prefer to retain my reading *yā-bat* (P. *yāgu-bhatta*) a dvandva compound meaning 'gruel and boiled rice'. Cf. *yāku ca bata ca* in Maharatmale rock-inscription (*E. Z.*, Vol. I, No. 5, l. 3).

Line 7. Mr. Bell reads *leṇa*, but *lov* is clear on the estampage and it sounds more in keeping with the idiom of the language of inscriptions to say in connexion with a perpetual grant *lov pavatnā tāk kalaṭa*, 'as long as the world endures', than to say *leṇa pavatnā tāk kalaṭa*, 'as long as the cave exists' [2].

Line 7. Mr. Bell has *Sundara-mahadevīma*. The last syllable in this compound obviously represents the ending of the first person singular or plural (honorifically). So it would be either *-m* (*devīm*) or *-mi* (*devīmi*) or more likely plural *-mu* (*devīmu*), if not *-mō* (*devīmō*) or *-mha* (*devīmha*) but not *ma* (*devīma*). Mr. Bell's observation that *-ma* is an older form of *-mha* requires proof I would, therefore, suggest *-mu* (*devīmu*) with *-mha* as an alternative reading.

---

[1] Cf. also *kusalāna*, 'a drinking-vessel,' in the *Piyummala*, p. 62.

[2] Cf. the expression *hira sanda pavatnā tek*, 'so long as the sun and the moon endure,' in the Devanagala and other inscriptions. Besides, no document has yet come to light recording a grant subject to the existence of a cave-temple or the like.

In the foregoing notes I have, I think, met all the important points raised by Mr. Bell in respect of the record under discussion, with the exception of the question as to its date.

I have already admitted that Mr. Bell's eye-copy and the photographic facsimile of the inscription distinctly give the date as the twenty-seventh year (after the coronation) of Jaya-Bāhu I. Nevertheless, the record belongs to Queen Sundara-mahādevī and *not* to the reign of Jaya-Bāhu as Mr. Bell contends, for the simple reason that Jaya-Bāhu was no longer living at the time when the inscription was indited.

This anomaly of dating from the coronation of a deceased king, the first of its kind yet known in Sinhalese chronology, requires explanation, as it raises the important question of the use of the coronation of deceased kings in dating records [1]. That this is true in the case of Jaya-Bāhu I is obvious from the following facts :—

Vijaya-Bāhu I and his successor Jaya-Bāhu I being uterine brothers, it is not altogether unreasonable to suppose that the difference of age between them was not more than fifteen years. Vijaya-Bāhu I died after keeping his seventy-third birthday festivities [2], that is to say, he died in his seventy-fourth year. Jaya-Bāhu I succeeded him immediately. So Jaya-Bāhu's age at the time of his coronation must have been at least fifty-nine. Now a Tamil pillar-inscription [3] in Poḷonnaruva is dated in the thirty-eighth year of Jaya-Bāhu who is correctly identified with Jaya-Bāhu I of our inscription. Thus, if this King was alive at the time, he would have been over ninety-seven years of age. He would also have been over eighty-six years of age when our record was composed. Such longevity is not very probable. The shorter the difference of age between the two brothers, the stronger becomes my argument on this point.

Moreover, if we follow the sequence of events as narrated in the *Mahāvaṁsa* (ch. lxi and lxii), we are bound to come to the conclusion that Jaya-Bāhu's death took place in Rohaṇa during the lifetime of Vikkama-Bāhu (lxii, 1–2) and long before the birth of Parakkama-Bāhu I, whom Vikkama-Bāhu

---

[1] Dr. Fotheringham, a well-known authority on dates, tells me that Papyrus B in Aramaic papyri discovered at Asman, edited by Sayce and Cowley (1906), is dated in the twenty-first year of Xerxes, though it really belongs to a time when Xerxes was dead and Artaxerxes had been proclaimed King. The exact date of the papyrus is 2nd January, 464 B.C.

[2] Poḷonnaruva Tamil slab-inscription (*A.S.C.*, *Annual Report*, 1911–1912).

[3] *A.S.C.*, *Annual Report*, 1909.

offered to adopt as his successor (*Mv.*, lxii, 52-62). Vikkama-Bāhu died in the twenty-second year of his Poḷonnaruva rule and was succeeded by his son Gaja-Bāhu II, who held the sceptre for twenty-two years (*Mv.*, lxiii, 18-19, and lxxi, 1-5. Thus the information we have regarding the period that elapsed between the death of Vijaya-Bāhu I and that of Gaja-Bāhu II may be expressed as follows:—

(*a*) The length of Jaya-Bāhu's rule at Poḷonnaruva up to his enforced retirement to Rohaṇa on Vikkama-Bāhu's wresting the sceptre from him . . . = x

(*b*) Vikkama-Bāhu's Poḷonnaruva rule . . . . = 21 years

(*c*) His son Gaja-Bāhu's rule . . . . . . = 22 years

(*d*) The Tamil pillar-inscription makes the fifteenth year of Gaja-Bāhu = the thirty-eighth year of Jaya-Bāhu.

If we reduce this to an equation we get

$$x + 21 + 15 = 38$$
$$x = 2 \text{ years.}$$

This result practically agrees with the Sinhalese chronicles. Jaya-Bāhu I was not allowed to rule long at Poḷonnaruva. Vikkama-Bāhu ousted him in his third year, as confirmed by the three years' reign allotted to him in the *Rājāvaliya.* But the most important bit of information which throws light on the Jaya-Bāhu riddle is to be found in the *Pūjāvaliya.* It is stated there that he reigned for fourteen years. I take this to mean that he ruled about two years in Poḷonnaruva and lived for about twelve years in retirement as *de jure* King of Ceylon, exactly agreeing with what one can gather from the account in the *Mahāvaṁsa* as stated above. Jaya-Bāhu's death must, therefore, have taken place in the thirteenth year of Vikkama-Bāhu's reign and he was at the time about seventy-three years old. Thus the date thirty-eight years of Jaya-Bāhu in the Tamil inscription is composed of fourteen years (2 + 12) of his lifetime and twenty-four years after his death. Similarly, our Diṁbulāgala inscription, dated in the twenty-seventh year after his coronation, was actually incised in the thirteenth (expired) year after his death, which, according to the *Mahāvaṁsa*, would also be the fourth year after the death of Vikkama-Bāhu or the fourth year of Gaja-Bāhu's Poḷonnaruva rule.

Finally, as to why the inscriptions in question were dated in the years reckoned from the coronation of the deceased monarch Jaya-Bāhu I, two reasons might be urged. First, his successors Vikkama-Bāhu and Gaja-Bāhu were not crowned, and so the documents had to be dated from the last crowned king, in conformity perhaps with general usage in such matters. Secondly, Vikkama-Bāhu, as Mr. Bell has already pointed out, was no friend of the Buddhist church. His son, Gaja-Bāhu, too, was not thought of highly (*Mv.*, lxii, 58–59), nor was he at any time firmly established on the throne[1], whereas Jaya-Bāhu was a monarch fully recognized and favoured by the priesthood.

In these circumstances, it was quite natural and reasonable on the part of Sundara-mahādevī, the queen-dowager, to allow the composer of the inscription to follow the usual form of expression and make mention of her late royal spouse Vikkama-Bāhu I and her royal son Gaja-Bāhu II (then ruling at Poḷonnaruva) and yet to have the record dated from the coronation of Jaya-Bāhu either by way of pleasing the pious monks then residing at Dim̆bulāgala or at their special request, or to make the grant perfect in the eye of the law.

No. 35. AM̆BAGAMUVA ROCK-INSCRIPTION OF VIJAYA-BĀHU I (1058–1114 A.D.)

MR. H. C. P. BELL, to whom we owe so much for his services to the cause of Ceylon archaeology, examined this inscription some twelve or fifteen years ago;[2] ink-estampages were in due course taken and sent to England to be dealt with. The present Archaeological Commissioner (Mr. A. M. Hocart) also has been good enough to supply the epigraphist with all the particulars necessary for its publication in addition to an eye-copy and another ink-estampage. All these have been utilized in the following account of the record.

Am̆bagamuva, where the inscription is, is a small village of about 500 inhabitants situated among the tea estates of Upper or Uḍa Bulatgama, 5·65 miles from Nāwalapiṭiya on the main road from Kandy to Hatton and to Colombo via Ginigat-hēna, the road passing through the village fields.

---

[1] He is altogether omitted both in the *Pūjāvaliya* and in the *Rājāvaliya*.

[2] See *A. S. C. Annual Report*, 1911–12, p. 121.

Dr. Davy, in his description of a tour in 1819, speaks of the village as follows:—

'The next day's journey brought us to Ambigammmuwe [*sic*] in Upper Boulatgamme. From the highest mountain ridge which we crossed and which I conjecture was about 3,000 ft. above the level of the sea, the prospects in every direction were particularly fine. One way we looked down upon Ambigammuwa in the midst of cultivated green paddy fields surrounded by hills, many of them bare and green, like those of Upper Ouvah. . . . Ambigammuwa, though elevated between fifteen and sixteen hundred feet above the sea, is in every direction surrounded by mountains. . . . The Mahawiliganga flows by the old post at Ambigammuwa . . . . it is here an inconsiderable stream and, except when flooded, hardly knee deep.'

'In and around this village there are about ten hills, one of which is called **Akuru-keṭū-gala-kanda,** "inscribed rock hill". It stands to the east of the hill called Hasti-gala, "elephant rock".' According to Mr. Jayasekara's description, the record seems to be engraved on two boulders which lie on the summit of the hill 'in a depression facing south-east and north-west and are surrounded by about a score of similar boulders of various dimensions.'

The letters, two to three inches in size, are unevenly incised between ruled lines about four inches apart. They cover an area of 12′ 3″ by 9′ 3″ of the rough surface of one boulder and 9′ 3″ by 9′ 7″ of that of the other. They, moreover, exhibit a remarkable mixture of old and more advanced types as well as some forms hitherto not found in Sinhalese inscriptions. The following are some of the types, but an examination of the accompanying facsimile will give the reader a better idea of the peculiar character of the alphabet.

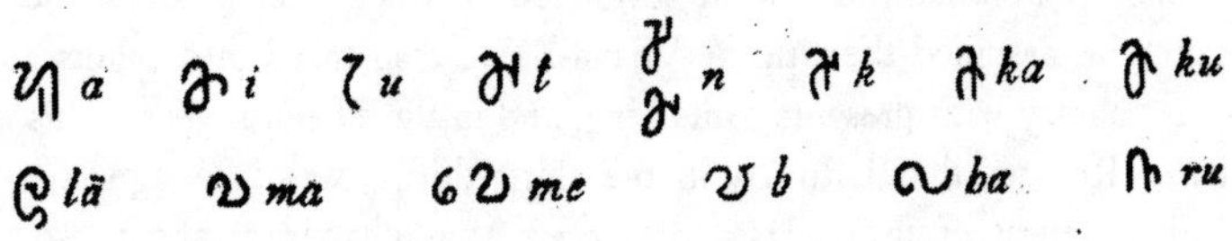

As is noticeable here, the difference between *i*, *ta*, and *na* is hardly distinguishable; so, too, between *pa*, *va*, and *ṭa*. The akṣara *lā* with the long vowel mark attached to the tail of the letter as in inscriptions of Niśśaṅka-Malla and others of the twelfth and thirteenth centuries A.D. betrays more than others the real age of the record, which on palaeographical grounds can hardly be earlier than the eleventh century A.D.

As regards **orthography**, attention may be drawn to the clerical errors *ta-ṭikak* (l. 9) for *talā-ṭikak*, *kap* (l. 13) for *kandap*, *kuluṇu-rin* (l. 13) for *kuluṇu sarin*, *bhāhu* (l. 21) for *bāhu*, *mändin-ndina* (ll. 23–24) for *mändin-dina*, *pihiṭi* (l. 26) written twice, obviously by mistake, and *kiri-gairi* (l. 47) for *kiri-geri*.

Note also the punctuation marks not found in any other inscription known to us.

The **style** of the record is more or less antique, the minister who composed it having adopted the phraseology of some of the inscriptions of Mahinda IV, notably that of the Jetavanārāma[1] slab.

The writer of the Devanagala inscription[2] of Parakkama-Bāhu I also followed the same practice and made good use of our inscription for the introductory part of his. But what will puzzle the reader is the appearance of the names of the parents of Mahinda IV, namely **Abhā Salamevan** and Queen **Dev Gon** as those of Vijaya-Bāhu I. This must either be a mistake or these names were intentionally retained because they were mere epithets or *birudas* and could, therefore, be applied to any one of royal descent. That the king dealt with in our record is Vijaya-Bāhu I, there is not the slightest doubt. But his parentage, his early career, and the exact period in which he lived need investigation.

A reference to the genealogical tree, facing page 59 above, will give all the information regarding his parentage and family connexions. As for his early career, we gather from the *Mahāvaṁsa* that his name during his boyhood was Kitti, at the age of thirteen he was 'full of wisdom and valour and possessed great skill as an archer', and he dwelt in the village Mūlasāla, at fifteen he took the title of *ādipāda* (governor), at sixteen he attacked and killed Kesadhātu who held Rohaṇa for six months, and at seventeen he freed Rohaṇa from enemies.[3] Thereafter he assumed the title of Vijaya-Bāhu, dispatched messengers to the Rāmañña country with presents to its king, and in the fifteenth year of his reign as ruler of Rohaṇa, that is to say in the thirty-third year of his age[4] he completed his conquest of the Coḷas and entered Anurādhapura;[5] about two years later, in the thirty-fifth year of his age, he was crowned King of all Ceylon.

These are some of the salient events of his early career. He ruled at Poḷonnaruva for forty years, and died in the forty-first year of his Poḷonnaruva

---

[1] *E. Z.*, Vol. I, No. 19. [2] *A. S. C.*, *Kegalle Report*, p. 75. [3] See *Mv.*, ch. lvii., 43–76.

[4] He had most probably completed his seventeenth year of age when he assumed the title of Vijaya-Bāhu (*Mv.*, ch. lviii., 1).

[5] *Mv.*, ch. lviii., 59.

rule, or the fifty-sixth year of his Rohaṇa and Poḷonnaruva reign, after he had kept his seventy-third birthday festival[1].

It will be seen from the *Mahāvaṁsa* account that the gift to the worshippers of the so-called Buddha's footprint on Adam's Peak was one of Vijaya-Bāhu's last acts, and this is confirmed by the present Aṁbagamuva record which dates the event in the thirty-eighth year after his coronation (line 23), that is to say, in the fifty-fifth year (38 + 17) of his Rohaṇa-Poḷonnaruva rule, or the seventy-third year of his age, probably just before his death.

We will now proceed to find out the exact dates according to the Buddhist and the Christian eras in which the foregoing events took place. To enable us to do so, we have to settle first the date of Parakkama-Bāhu I.

The *Mahāvaṁsa* describes three coronations of this king; the first, when he was appointed to the office of Mahādipāda (chief governor) in succession to his uncle Kitti-Sirimegha (lxvii., 91–94); the second, after the death of Gaja-Bāhu (lxxi., 27–32); and the third, two years later, after the death of Mānābharaṇa, when he became paramount lord of the Island (lxxii., 361–362). Therefore the fact that he was thrice crowned probably accounts for the diversity of dates given as the year of his accession by various writers.

The *Nikāyasaṅgraha*[2] states that Parakkama-Bāhu came to hear of the decline of the Buddhist religion during the 1254 years intervening between the fifteenth year of King Vaḷagam Abhā (Vaṭṭagāmanī Abhaya) and the fourth year of his own reign. It was then (in the fourth year) that he set about to purify the religion. The same work also mentions that Vaḷagam Abhā succeeded to the throne 439 years, 9 months, and 10 days A.B., so that the fifteenth year of his reign must correspond to the current year 455 A.B. Between this year and the fourth year of Parakkama-Bāhu's reign was an interval of 1254 years. Therefore, the fourth year of his reign was 1709 A.B. or 1165 A.D. according to the present Buddhist era, and, consequently, the commencement was in 1705 A.B. or 1161 A.D. This date is supported by the Galvihāra record[3] as well as by the Kalyāṇi inscriptions of Dhammaceti[4] in Pegu.

---

[1] Poḷonnaruva Tamil slab-inscription (*A. S. C., Annual Report*, 1911–1912).

[2] Printed edition, p. 21.

[3] *A. I. C.*, No. 137.

[4] *Ind. Ant.*, Vol. xxii., pp. 151 and 206, It is true that in the second reference to the Buddhist Convocation held in 1708 A.B. expired, the Kalyāṇi inscription adds that this was the eighteenth year of the reign of Parakkama-Bāhu (*Siri-Saṅghabodhi-Parakkama-Bāhu-mahā-rājassa Laṅkādipe rajjābhiseka-pattato aṭṭhārasame vasse*). This is probably either a miscalculation or an error for *aṭṭhame vasse*, as the reader will presently see.

Again, in the *Nikāyasaṅgraha* and the *Rājaratnākara*, it is stated that Parakkama-Bāhu became king over Laṅkā after the lapse of 1696 years from the death of the Buddha, which would be equivalent to 1153 A.D.[1] This is confirmed by the Sāhasa-Malla's inscription[2] at Poḷonnaruva, which gives 1743-3-27 A.B. as the date of his accession. If we deduct from this forty-seven years, which, according to the *Mahāvaṁsa*, form the total of the reigns of his predecessors up to the commencement of the reign of Parakkama-Bāhu I, we get 1696 A.B. expired or 1153 A.D. The two Ārppākkam inscriptions of Rājādhirāja II also go to support this date of Parakkama-Bāhu's accession as pointed out by Dr. Hultzsch[3] and Mr. Codrington[4] for whose constructive criticisms the present writer is greatly indebted.

Further, the *Daḷadāpūjāvaliya* says that the 1254th year after the fifteenth year of Vaḷagam Abhā was also the seventh year of Parakkama-Bāhu's coronation. This gives 1702 A.B. expired or 1159 A.D. current.

The Sinhalese and Pāli works, as well as inscriptions, thus point to three coronations of Parakkama-Bāhu I, the first in 1153 A.D., the second in 1159 A.D., and the third in 1161 A.D. As stated above, his first coronation took place immediately after the death of his uncle or foster-father Kitti-Sirimegha[5], and as the latter was styled 'king', Parakkama-Bāhu was also called 'king'[6], although he was only *mahādipāda*. The second coronation was held soon after the death of Gaja-Bāhu[7]. That there was an interval of six years between the first festival in 1153 and the second in 1159 is clear from the *Mahāvaṁsa* itself, because it places the many improvements to the Rohaṇa kingdom effected by Parakkama-Bāhu, his preparation for war and his campaign against Gaja-Bāhu between these two events. Moreover, we know from the authorities quoted above, that a coronation took place in 1161 A.D., and, as this seems to be the last or the third according to our calculation, and as there was another within an interval of two years[8], the latter must be the one referred to in the *Daḷadā-pūjāvaliya*.

Having thus fixed the dates of Parakkama-Bāhu's three coronations, we will proceed with our calculation backwards. If we follow the *Mahāvaṁsa* and the inscriptions and take the first coronation in 1153 A.D. as our starting-point,

---

[1] 1696-543 A.B. = 1153 A.D.

[2] *A.I.C.*, No. 156. 5 and below No. 36.

[3] *J.R.A.S.*, 1913, pp. 518-519.

[4] *Ceylon Antiquary*, 1918, p. 35.

[5] *Mv.*, lxvii., 92-93.

[6] *Mv.*, lxviii., 29.

[7] *Ib.*, lxxi., 19-32.

[8] *Ib.*, lxxii., 342.

we shall see that the thirty-three years' length of reign allotted to Parakkama-Bāhu consists of six years of war against Gaja-Bāhu II, two years against Mānābharaṇa, and twenty-five years as paramount king of all Ceylon. This will oblige us to reduce either Gaja-Bāhu's reign from twenty-two to sixteen years (1137 to 1153 A.D.) or Parakkama-Bāhu's reign from thirty-three to twenty-seven (1159–1186 A.D.) the total length of the two reigns being forty-nine instead of fifty-five of the *Mahāvaṁsa.* Gaja-Bāhu's predecessors Vikkama-Bāhu I and Jaya-Bāhu I reigned twenty-three years (1114–1137 A.D.).[1] So the death of Jaya-Bāhu's predecessor Vijaya-Bāhu I was in 1114 A.D.[2] With the aid of this result, the dates of the principal events of Vijaya-Bāhu's career may be fixed as follows:

(*a*) Vijaya-Bāhu's birth in	1040 A.D.	current.
(*b*) He became *ādipāda* in the fifteenth year of his age	1055 A.D.	„
(*c*) He freed Rohaṇa of enemies and assumed the title of Vijaya-Bāhu when he was seventeen years old	1058 A.D.	„
(*d*) In the fifteenth year of his Rohaṇa rule, that is in the thirty-third year of his age, he entered Anurādhapura and became ruler of all Ceylon	1073 A.D.	„
(*e*) His coronation at Anurādhapura about two years later	1075 A.D.	„
(*f*) Thirty-seven years after his raising the canopy of dominion, his grant to Adam's Peak pilgrims as recorded in the present Aṁbagamuva inscription	1111 or 1113 A.D.	„
(*g*) His death, soon after the seventy-third birthday which was the fifty-sixth year of his Rohaṇa-Poḷonnaruva rule or the forty-first year of Poḷonnaruva rule	1114 A.D.	„

---

[1] See p. 201, above.

[2] The Devanagala inscription states that Parakkama-Bāhu intending to promote the Buddhist religion and the interests of the people, which had been neglected for forty-two years since the death of his grandfather, King Vijaya-[Bāhu] made war with the two princes Gaja-Bāhu [and Mānābharaṇa] and brought Laṅkā under one canopy of dominion' (*A. S. C.*, *Kegalle Report*, p. 75). But this statement does not signify precisely that Parakkama-Bāhu made the resolution in 1153 A.D., as Mr. Codrington seems to think (*Ceylon Antiquary*, 1918, p. 33). What it implies is simply that sometime after his coronation in 1153 A.D., when he found he was strong enough to carry out his original intention of conquering the King's country, which he had formed even before his visit to the Court of Gaja-Bāhu during the lifetime of his foster-father Kitti-Sirimegha, he commenced his campaign against Gaja-Bāhu and Mānābharaṇa with the avowed object of restoring the Buddhist church. The total of forty-two years of the Devanagala record seems at first sight to be made up of fourteen years of Jaya-Bāhu I and

The author of the Sinhalese *Narendra-caritāvalokanapradīpikā* calculating the lengths of reigns of Ceylon kings from the earliest times forward fixes the accession of Vijaya-Bāhu I in 1550 A.B.[1] Here is some confirmation of the fact that the Buddhist era of 483 B.C. prevailed in Ceylon before the time of Vijaya-Bāhu I for 1550 483 gives 1067 A.D. expired, and this is only five years earlier than the date which we have arrived at by reckoning back and using the present Buddhist era of 543 or 544 B.C. It must, of course, be borne in mind that this date was probably equivalent to the fifteenth year of Vijaya-Bāhu's Rohaṇa rule, although it is not so stated in the *Narendra-caritāvalokanapradīpikā.*

Taking 1073 A.D. as the probable date of Vijaya-Bāhu's victorious entry into Anurādhapura, we may continue our chronological investigations further back as follows:—

Vijaya-Bāhu's campaign against the Coḷas .	15 years
The sum of the reigns of General Kitti to Lokissara (Wijesinha's Nos. 117 to 122) .	16 „
Prince Kassapa or Vikkama-Bāhu's rule . .	12 „
Interregnum during Mahinda's captivity . .	12 „

The total of these four periods is fifty-five years, and if we deduct it from 1073 we get 1018 as the probable year when Mahinda V was taken captive by the Coḷas, and this agrees with what is recorded in the inscriptions of the sixth year of Rājendra Coḷa I, dated 1017–1018 A.D.[2] The author of the *Narendra-caritāvalokanapradīpikā*, on the other hand, makes out that after the capture of Mahinda V by the Coḷas, the latter held sway in the king's country (Rāja- or Pihiṭi-raṭa) for only sixteen years. During this time Vikkama-Bāhu and others down to Lokissara (Nos. 116 to 122 of Wijesinha's list), including Vijaya-Bāhu I,

---

twenty-eight years of Vikkama-Bāhu I, totally ignoring Gaja-Bāhu, as in the *Pūjāvaliya* and the *Rājāvaliya.* But this cannot be right. The period in question should consist of

2 years of Jaya-Bāhu's reign.
12 „ „ „ „ in enforced retirement.
9 „ Vikkama-Bāhu's reign.
16 „ Gaja-Bāhu's reign (not yet at war with Parakkama-Bāhu).
In the sixteenth year of the former, the latter was crowned king of Rohaṇa.
3 or 4 years Parakkama-Bāhu's preparation for war.

Thereafter in 1156 A.D., at the expiration of about forty-two years since the death of Vijaya-Bāhu I, he set his army in motion as described in the 70th chapter of the *Mahāvaṁsa.*

[1] *Jinendra-varṣayen ekvādahas pansiya ekun panas avurudu pas masak ikutva giya pasu Mahaḷu Vijaya-Bāhu nam rajek,* &c.

[2] See Hultzsch in *J. R. A. S.*, 1913, p. 523.

ruled in different parts of Rohaṇa, more or less contemporaneously fighting sometimes among themselves, but most of the time with the Colas. Thereafter Vijaya-Bāhu I, having eventually defeated them, entered Anurādhapura in the fifteenth year of his Rohaṇa rule. So according to this authority the date of the captivity of Mahinda V would fall in 1057 (i.e. 1073–16) A.D., or 1052 (1068–16) A.D. Thus we have three dates for the accession of Mahinda V, thirty-six years earlier, namely 982 (i.e. 1018–36)[1] A.D., 1016 (1052–36)[2] A.D., and 1021 (1057–36)[2] A.D. Calculations based on the date 1016 A.D. (1499 A.B., i.e. 1016+483 the Buddhist era before Vijaya-Bāhu I) give approximately 881 A.D. (1363 A.B. expired)[3] as the date of the accession of Sena II, but *not* that of Sena I, as in the *Nikāyasaṅgraha*.

Reverting to the subject of the present inscription, we see that the date of the benefaction is given in lines 23–24 as the seventh day of the waxing moon in the month of Mäṅdindina (February–March) in the thirty-eighth year of the reign of Vijaya-Bāhu I, which would be either in 1111 (1073+38) A.D., or in 1113 (1075+38) A.D.. The date of the incision of the inscription, however, is not given, but it may be presumed that, as Aṁbagamuva was one of the villages affected by the grant, no time was lost in proclaiming this fact.

The contents of the record inform us (*a*) of Vijaya-Bāhu's parentage dealt with above; (*b*) of his intrinsic qualities both as a war lord and as a benevolent ruler; (*c*) of his victory over the Tamil forces that dominated the northern half of the Island; (*d*) of the offerings made to the sacred foot-print[4] on Adam's Peak; (*e*) of the many improvements effected at the shrine; and (*f*) of the charitable institutions and endowments made for the convenience of pilgrims. These are followed by the usual statement of 'sanctions' in respect of the villages dedicated to the shrine and the names of ministers who carried out the order of the King in Council.

As pointed out above, the present grant is one of the last charitable acts of Vijaya-Bāhu I. The *Mahāvaṁsa* (lx., 64–65) refers to it as follows:—'Saying, "Let no man endure hardship who goeth along the difficult pathway to make obeisance at the foot-print[4] of the Chief of Sages on the Samanta-kūṭa rock",

[1] According to the dates in the *Mahāvaṁsa*. If, however, we regard Prince Kassapa's rule of 12 years as identical with the 12 years' Interregnum, the accession of Mahinda V would fall 12 years later, namely in 994 A.D. instead of 982 A.D.

[2] According to the dates in the *Narendra-caritāvalokanapradīpikā*.

[3] That is A.D. 1016–135, or A.B. 1499–135, the sum of the regnal years from Sena II to Mahinda V.

[4] The legend connected with the mark resembling a gigantic foot-print on Adam's Peak is that

he (Vijaya-Bāhu) caused the village of Gilīmalaya[1], that abounded in rice-fields and other land, to be granted, wherewith to supply them [i.e. the pilgrims] with food. And on the Kadalīgāma[2] highway and Hūva[3] pathway he built resting-places (sālā), and gave lands unto each one of them separately and caused it to be inscribed on a stone pillar, saying, "Let no lord of the land that cometh hereafter take them away".'

This account of the benefaction agrees more or less with that given in our record, the lands named in both being situated in the Central and the Uva Provinces.

Regarding the four ministers who carried out the King's order, nothing is known, although the names Kitu and Kitḷi-deṭu, as well as the official titles Mekāppara-vädärum and Kuḍasalā, and also the places Koḷom̆ba-galu[4] and Kaḷunnaru[5] are familiar to us from other inscriptions.

TEXT.

A.

1 සිරිවත් අපිරියත් ලෙව්
2 ඉතුත්[6] ගුණමුළින් උතුරත් මුව් ද
3 ඔදවුහි අත් කැත්කුල පාමිලි කළ
4 රිවුනු අන්වයැ ඕ(කාව)ස් (රජ්)පරපුරෙන් බව්
5 කැත්(උසබ **අභා සලමෙවන්**) මහරජපාහ(ට එ)ම
6 කුලෙන් සමදැ (**දෙමුගො**)**න්** රැජනැ කුසි(නි)පිදැ ඇපා ම
7 හයා සිරි විදැ පිළිවෙළසෙ රජවැ මිණිවුටුනෙන් පැහැ

during the Buddha's third visit to Ceylon in the eighth year of his attainment to Buddhahood, he made an impression of his left foot at the request of Sumana, the presiding deity of Adam's Peak, so that people may be enabled to make their obeisance to the Buddha and thereby acquire merit. The story is given in full in the Pāli poem *Samantakūṭa-vaṇṇanā*, the two verses (Nos. 779–780) which refer specially to the foot-print run:—

Sutvāna nātho giram etam assā
passaṁ mahābhūtim anāgatesu,
lokassa lokehi mahīyamāno
akāsi vāmena padena lañchaṁ.

Sambodhito aṭṭhamasāradasmiṁ
vesākha-māse muni puṇṇamāyaṁ
pādassa 'bhiññāṇaṁ akā 'paraṇhe
sadevake sassamaṇe mahente.

For a complete description of this sacred mountain, see Lawrie's *Gazetteer of the Central Province of Ceylon* as well as Skeen's *Adam's Peak* and Cave's *Nuwara Eliya and Adam's Peak.*

[1] 'Gilīmalē, a fine large village on the bank of the Kaluganga and intersected by it and its tributaries.' Minor road: Ratnapura to Gilīmalē (seven miles) and to Adam's Peak (sixteen miles further). See Fyers' *Itinerary*, Pt. II, p. 21.

[2] Modern Kehelgamuva in Kandy district where the old pilgrims' path is to be seen.

[3] Modern Ūva.

[4] Probably identical with Kolomgalu (*E. Z.*, I, p. 68, note 3).

[5] P. Kāḷa-nāgara (*Ib.*, p. 178, and *Mv.*, lxxx, 49).

[6] 'ඉතස්' පීදකියවියහැකිවි

8 යූ ලොව්තුරා බිසෙස්නෙන් බිසෙස්(වූ ලක්දි)වූ පොළො මෙහෙසු
9 රුත් පරපුරට තටිකත්[1] (බ)සුවූ තුමා ස(ර)ණ නියරසින් නන්
10 රජ මුහුනු බිසෙස්වූ ස(ා)හනෙදින් ගිරු පැළකෙව්[2]න් මෙහෙසු
11 රු දළදැපි[3]න් උව්හු රජව්රිහින් සූරිඥු (පබඥු) දෙනෙන් දිනිසුර
12 න් සත්(සෙනින් කිනි)සුරු පැනැඵ(රි)න් සුරගුරු සොම්ගුණෙණන් නි[ස]
13 පුරු රුසරින් ක[ඥ]ප් කුලුණු[ස](රින් බොසත් දුනු) සහවූටුනු රජබරණ කිර
14 ණ වූ(පු) රුදුරු (තුලනල) අ(රා) තුමා තු(නු) කප්තරුමින් නොමින් නන් රුවින් දුන් (ව)
15 තුරෙන් නන් දෙසෙන් ප(තළෙ) මුළු දිළිඥු (සි)ත්සපුරා පුරමින් මුළු ලෙව්හු ප
16 තළෙ යස පබඥ ඇති තුමා සිරින් (ලක්දිවූ පහයා) නන් නය් දෙසෙනි ර
17 (පු)න් වටන අසිරි (පඩුරු) සිරින් දවහ පිරෙනු **රජගෙදෙරගි** දසතා
18 වන් පැරැකුම් සිරින් සිරිලකට (යසෙ එළ)වූ (තුනුරුවනට පුද ඇපරන)
19 (ව උවටන්) පුත්නට ගැවුරු වියත්(නට) සසිරි සියනට නුගුරු මිතුරනට වි
20 යම්[4] සතුරනට (ද)පැ සවු[සත්නට] කුලුණුවත් සබවට නුවණ
21 තුමහට එකත්සරු කල **සිරිසඟබො විජයබා**[5]හු රජපාවගාය්
22 සෙ තුමා සියවින්මෙන් දෙමෙළබලන් මුළු අසුරු දුරුලා මුළු ලක්දිවූ එක් සෙසත්
23 කැරැ රජ වලනුමින් සත්තිස් හවුරුද්දන් ඉකුත් සත් ලැගු අටූහිස් වනුයෙහි මැ
24 ඤින්ඥින[6] සඥ (පුර මස්)හි (පුර සතවක්) දවසැ (මෙ කැපැ) බුදුවූ කකුසඥ කොණාග
25 මන කාස්සපෙ[7] ගොනම යැ සිවූ බුදුන් සරණ තඹුරු ද මුහුනෙන් ඉසිලූ ස
26 **මනොලකුලෙහි** පිහිටි පදලස් ද පිහිටි විසිතුරු සත්රුවනින් සැදුණු නන් බර
27 ණින් පුද කරපි නොඑක් පට වැරැලි වියන් දද (කො)ඩි නගයි සිවූ දැ ගඥන් අ
28 ලෙවූකොට තුමා මිණි වූටුනෙන් පදලස් ද සඳ වැඩැසිවැ පදලස්
29 ද පිහිටි **සමනොලකුලෙහි** කම්නවාම් පුද සිතියම් වැට දලවනු ව
30 වහා මෙහි දවඥනට සිවු දෙ(ස)න් වැඩි මහසඞුන්වහන්සෙ
31 ව වටනා පිඩු පසයට හා සෙසු ද වඥනට රැස්වන ආගත
32 (දුබබා)ගතයනට දෙන දන්වට(ට හා රජ)රට මැ(ගැ) අ(ෙග) පස්
33 ගවුයෙහි අප නැමින් ගවුයෙකැ දන්හලක් බැවින් කරවා

B.

34 දනොපකරණ ඇතිකොට දන් දෙනු කොට හා පදලස් ද පිහිටි මළු(යෙ)න් පා
35 (තැ මළු)වක් කරවා සෙසු (අඩමජානින් දුග්)ද වඥනුකොට හා පෙරමළු

---

[1] 'තලාටිකන්' වියයුතුයි [2] පැළකෙමින්? [3] 'දමින්' සිදකියවියහැකියි

[4] මෙය 'විසඹ' (මිතුඹය) වෙනුවට වැරදියෙදුමකැයිහැණේ

[5] 'බාහු' වියයුතු යි [6] 'මැඥින්දින පුරමස්හි' වියයුතුයි

[7] 'කැස්සැබැ' සිදකියවියහැකියි

36 යෙහි මහවුරු බඳුවා දෙමැගැ දෙදෙරොටුවක් කරවා කෙසිමුඤු ඇති
37 කොට රක්‍ෂා යොදැවියැයුත්තන් ඉඟි ද වඤනුකොට හා පදලසැ දැ
38 ල ඇතිකොට (අවටැ)කෙත් කරවනු කොට හා විල්බාගෙ (ඇපසක්[1] බෙද)
39 ඉමහි බිඳ කෙලගමුව් පුවක් අරඹි එකක් නිනියගල් කොට
40 වැලි එකත් (සො)රගොඩ කොටවැලි එකක් ලියවළ කොටවැලි
41 එකක් බදුලුවනැ කොටවැලි එකක් උඩුහො කොටවැල්ලෙ (පුවක්)
42 කළුග[2] වෙලැ බද මකුළුමුල් අඹගමුව් (වැලි)ගම්(පො)ළ් උල
43 පනා ඇතුළුවැ මෙතුවාක් තැන් කුසලාන් බො(පා)
44 කොට මෙයට (තුඩිනාළා) රජ්කොල් කැමියන් නොවද්නා
45 කොට් දෙරුවනැ දෙකම්නැන් නොවද්නාකොට් මගිව් පියගි
46 ච් කුළී මෙලාසි වි(ඩෙ)වි(ඩෙ)[3] දුත් පඬුරු නොගන්නා කො[ට]
47 ගැල්ගොන් (කිරිගෙ)රි[4] අදනා වැරියන් නොගන්නා කොට්
48 පස්මාදෙසින් ඇතුළත් වරදක් කොට ගම් වත්න[වුන්]
49 ඇත ගම්හිම් පත්වා දුන්මුන් ගම් වැදැ නොගන්නා
50 කොට අටතිස් (ව)න්න (මතු) හවුරුදු පටන්කොට එක්තැන්
51 සමුයෙන් පා වැඳැ ආ මෙකාප්පරවැදෑරුම්[5] **කළුග්න**
52 **රුහිම් අ(යනනාන)වන්**[6] **වරැ හසකගම් කිතු කොලො**
53 **ඹගලු දෙවු මහකිලිංගම් කි(ත්)ළිදෙවු රමු**
54 **ක්කඩු** (අ)**ගා**[7] **රක්ඛමණින් වරැ කුඩසලා කිතු** ඇ
55 තුළුවැ මෙතුවාක් සම්දරුවන්විසින් මෙ අතනාණ්
56 කණු පෙරැහැර දෙනු ලදි .. .. (යෙ බඳ) .. ..
57 .. .. (නවාම්කැම්නාවන්) .. .. (යලු ගම් ගො)
58 .. .. වහන්සෙ කරවනු (ලදි)

TRANSCRIPT.

A.

1 Sirivat-apiriyat-lev-
2 ikut[8]-guṇa-muḷin uturat muḷu Da-
3 -mbadivuhi an Kät-kula pāmili kaḷa
4 rivuhu anvayä O(kāva)s-(raj-)parapuren baṭ

---

[1] 'අයසක්' නොහොත් 'ඇටස(ක්/න්)' සිදැකියවියහැකිසි

[2] 'කළුන' සිදැකියවියහැකිසි

[3] 'විසෙ පිසෙ' සිදැකියවියහැකිසි

[4] 'කිරිගෙරි' වියයුතුයි

[5] වැදෑරුම්' සිදැකියවියහැකිසි

[6] අයනනානවන්' සිදැකියවියහැකිසි

[7] 'අනා' වියයුතුයි

[8] This can also be read *naḷak*.

5 Kät (-usaba **Abhā Salamevan**) Maharajapā-ha(ṭa e)ma
6 kuḷen sama-dā (**Devu Go**)n-räjanä kusi(n-i)pidä äpā ma-
7 -hayā siri vindä piḷiveḷase raja-vä miṇi-vuṭunen pähä-
8 -yū lovturā-bisesnen bises(-vū Lak-di-)vu poḷo-mehesu-
9 -run parapuraṭa taṭikak[1] (ba)ndu-vū tumā sa(r)aṇa-niya-rasin nan
10 raja mundunä bises-vū s(ā)ha-tedin hiru päḷakev[2]in mehesu-
11 -ru daḷa-däpin[3] uvindu raja-viritin surindu (pabanda) denen dinisura-
12 -n sat(setin kiti)suru pänä-sa(ri)n suraguru somi-guṇen ni[sa-]
13 -yuru rū-sarin ka[nda]p kuluṇu-[sa-](rin Bo-sat dunu) saha-vuṭunu raja-barana kira-
14 -ṇa vu(ju) ruduru-(tulatala) a(rā) tumā tu(nu) kap-tarumin nomin nan ruvin dun (va-)
15 -turen nan desen pa(taḷe) muḷu diḷindu (si)t-sayurä puramin muḷu levhu pa-
16 -taḷe yasa pabaṇda äti tumā sirin (Lak-divu pahayā) nan nan desehi ra-
17 (-ju)n vaṭana asiri-(pañḍuru-) sirin davaha pirenä raja-ge-dorahi dasa-nā-
18 -van pärākum-sirin siri-Lakaṭa (yase eḷa-)vū (tunu-ruvanaṭa puda äjarana-)
19 (-ṭa uvaṭan) yutnaṭa gävuru viyat(naṭa) sasiri siyanaṭa nugurā mituranaṭa vi-
20 -yami[4] saturanaṭa (da)pä savu [satnaṭa] kuluṇu-vat sabavaṭa nuvaṇa
21 tumahaṭa ekatsaru kaḷa **Siri Saṅgabo Vijaya-Bhāhu**[5] raja-pā-vahan-
22 -se tumā siyavikmen Demeḷa-baḷan-muḷu-anduru duru-lā muḷu Lak-divu ek sesat
23 kärä raja vaḷandamin sat-tis havuruddak **ikut sat** läṅgū aṭa-tis vanu-yehi Mä-
24 -ndinndina[6] sanda (pura-mas)hi (pura-satavak) davasä (me käpä) budu-vū Kakusanda Koṇäga-
25 -mana Kāssape[7] Gotama yä sivu budun saraṇa-tamburu-dā mundunen isilū **Sa-**
26 **-manoḷa-kuḷehi** pihiṭi padalas-ḍā pihiṭi visituru sat-ruvanin säduṇu nan bara-
27 -ṇin puda karayi no-ek paṭa väräli viyan dada (ko)ḍi naṅgayi sivu-dā-gandin a-

[1] Read *talāṭikak.*
[2] Probably for *päḷakemin*, but see Devanagala record, line 5 (Bell's *Kegalle Report*, p. 75).
[3] This can also be read *-dävin.*
[4] Possibly in error for *visam̃ba.*
[5] Read *Bāhu.*
[6] Read *Mändindina pura-mas-hi.*
[7] This can also be read *kässäbä.*

28 -levu-koṭa tumā miṇi-vuṭunen padalas-dā sadā väḍä-siṭä padalas-
29 dā pihiṭi **Samanoḷa-kuḷehi** kam-navām puda sitiyam väṭa dalavanu va-
30 -ṭahā mehi dā vandanaṭa sivu-de(s)en väḍi maha-saṅgun-vahanse-
31 -ṭa vaṭanā piḍu pasayaṭa hā sesu dā vandanaṭa räsvana āgata
32 (dubbā)gatayanaṭa dena danvaṭa(ṭa hā raja-) raṭa mä(ṅgä) a(g)e pas
33 gavuyehi apa nämin gavuyekä dan-halak bävin karavā

B.

34 dānopakaraṇa äti-koṭa dan denu-koṭa hā padalas-dā pihiṭi maḷu(ye)n pā-
35 (-tä maḷu)vak karavā sesu (adhama-jātin ihi)-dā vandanu-koṭa hā pera-maḷu-
36 -yehi mahavuru bandavā de-mäṅgä de-doroṭuvak karavā kesi-mundu äti-
37 koṭa rakṣā yodäviyä-yuttan ihi-dā vandanu-koṭa hā padalasä dä-
38 -la äti-koṭa (avaṭä) ket karavanu-koṭa hā Vilbāye (äpasak[1] bedā)
39 mehi bada Kelagamuva® puvak aräb ekak® Tiniyagal koṭa-
40 -väli ekak® (So)ra-goḍa koṭaväli ekak® Liyavaḷa koṭaväli
41 ekak® Badulu-vanä koṭaväli ekak® Uḍu-ho koṭavälle (puvak)®
42 Kaḷaṅga[2]-velä bada Makuḷu-mula® Aṁbagamuva® (Väli)gam(po)ḷa® Ula-
43 -panā ätuḷuvä metuvāk tän kusalān bo(pā)
44 koṭa meyaṭa (tuḍināḷä raj-kol kämiyan no-vadnā-
45 koṭa® deṙuvanä de-kamtän no-vadnā-koṭa® magiv piyagi-
46 -v kulī melāsi vi(ḍe) vi(ḍe)[3] dun paṇḍuru no-gannā-ko(ṭa)®
47 gäl-gon (kiri-gai)ri[4] adanā väriyan no-gannā-koṭa®
48 pas-mā-dosin ätuḷat varadak koṭa gam vanna[vun]
49 äta gam-him panvā dun-mut gam vädä no-gannā
50 -koṭa aṭa-tis vanna (matu) havurudu paṭan-koṭa ektän
51 samuyen pā vändā ā mekāppara-vädärum[5] **Kaḷunna-**
52 **-ru-bim A(yannāta)van**[6] varä **Hakkagam Kitu**®, **Koḷo-**
53 **-ṁbagalu Dovu**®, **Mahakiliṁgam Ki(t)ḷi-deṭu**®, **Ramu-**
54 **-kkaḍu (A)gā**[7] **Rakkamaṇan** varä **Kuḍasalā Kitu** ä-
55 -tuḷuvä me-tuvāk samdaruvan-visin me attāṇi-
56 kaṇu perähära denu ladi .. .. (-ye bada) .. ..
57 .. .. (navām-käm-nāvan) .. .. (yalu gam go-)
58 .. .. vahanse karavanu (ladi)

---

[1] This can also be read *ayasak* or *äṭasak* or *-san*.

[2] This can also be read *kaḷahä*.

[3] This can also be read *vise pise*.

[4] Read *-geri*.

[5] This can also be read *vädärum*.

[6] This can also be read *Ayatnālavan*

[7] Read *Abhā*.

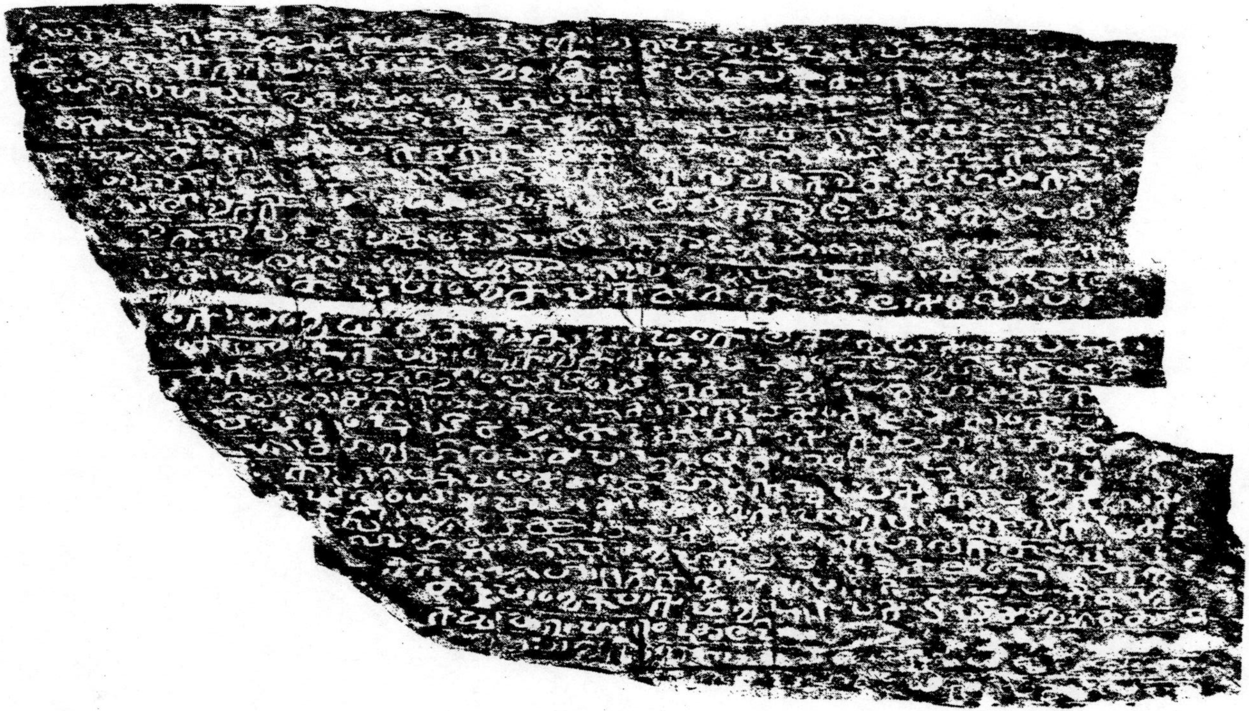

Scale 1 inch to 1 foot.

ecological Survey, Ceylon.

TRANSLATION.

[Lines 1-6] His Majesty, King **Siri Saṅgabo Vijaya-Bāhu**[1], was born[2] unto the great King **Abhā Salamevan**[3], the Kṣatriya Lord[4] descended from the Royal line of the Okkāka dynasty, [a branch] of the Solar race[5], which, abounding in a multitude of benignant, boundless and transcendental virtues[6], has caused other Kṣatriya dynasties of the whole of Jambudvīpa (India) to render it homage[7]. [He was born] in the womb of Queen[8] (**Dev Gon**) of equal birth and descent[9].

[Lines 6-10] After enjoying the dignities of Governor and Chief Governor, he, in due course, became King, and was anointed on his head, resplendent with the bejewelled crown, with the unction of world supremacy. He is [thus] like unto a *tilaka* mark (of adornment) to the lineage of great lords[10] of the soil of Laṅkā, anointing the heads of other Kings with the effulgence of the nails of his feet.

[Lines 10-15] He has surpassed[11] the Sun in the majesty inherent in him, Maheśvara (Śiva) in prowess, Viṣṇu in haughty spirit, the Chief of the Gods (Indra) in kingly state, the Lord of riches (Kuvera) in inexhaustible[12] wealth, Kitisuru[13] in (bestowing) happiness to living beings, the Preceptor of the Gods (Bṛhaspati) in the fertility of his wisdom, the Moon in gentleness,

---

[1] See line 21.

[2] *Ipidä*, 'having been born'. Other forms of this adverbial participle or gerund are '*upada, ipädä*, and *ipäjä*'. See Vol. I, p. 224, note 2.

[3] This is a *biruda* adopted by several kings. (See Vol. I, p. 165.) According to the Sinhalese *Atvanagalu-vaṁśaya* (p. 4 of edition 1914), King Siri Saṅghabodhi's father was a Kṣatriya potentate, a contemporary of King Vohārika-Tissa (A.D. 263-285) and he bore the title Abhā Salamevan.

[4] *Käl-usab* : P. *khattiya-usabho*.

[5] *Rivuhu anvayä*. Cf. *rivi-anvayen* in the slab inscription of Kassapa V, line 12 (Vol. I, No. 4).

[6-7] See Vol. I, p. 224, notes 3-4.

[8] *Devu Gon räjanä*. In other instances *Dev Gon biso* (or *bisev*) *räjna*. See Vol. I, p. 49, note 7.

[9] See Vol. I, p. 225, note 2.

[10] *Lak-divu-poḷo-mehesurun*. Cf. *Lak-poḷo mehesanaṭ* (Vol. I, p. 232). The substitution of *mehesuru* (Skt. *maheśvara*) for *mehesana* in other records confirms our derivation of *mehesana* from Skt. *maheśāna* (Vol. I, p. 26, note 10).

[11] *Dunu*. For other meanings, see Vol. I, p. 190, note 3.

[12] The Devanagala record also has *pabaňda denen*. See *Kegalle Report*, p. 75.

[13] *Kitisuru* : Skt. *kīrtīśvara*. Cf. *kiti-sara* (*kīrti-sāra*) in the Devanagala inscription.

Kandarpa in the richness of his beauty and the Bodhisatta in the fullness of his benevolence. Glittering[1] in the resplendence of his crown and royal apparel and mounting the massive scale pan[2], he fills the ocean of hearts of all poor folk that have migrated from various countries with the waters poured out without measure in [the shape of] gems of various sorts, as if his person itself were the wish-conferring tree[3].

[Lines 15–21] (His Majesty) who has [thereby acquired] an unbroken fame which was spread by the people of the whole world[4] illumines[5] the Island of Laṅkā with his glory. With the prowess of governors of districts[6] displayed at the gate of the Palace[7] which is constantly filled with the wonderful[8] presents that are being offered[9] by kings of various lands, His Majesty brought fame upon prosperous Laṅkā. Veneration for the Triple Gem, hospitable attention to preceptors, homage to the righteous, prosperous conditions to the learned, assistance[10] to kinsmen, intimacy[11] to friends, haughtiness towards foes, compassion for all living beings, wisdom in council—(all these qualities) he made completely secure[12] for himself.

[Lines 22–27] With his own valour he drove away wholly the darkness of Tamil forces and brought the whole Island of Laṅkā under one canopy (of dominion). He passed thirty-seven years in the enjoyment of his kingdom and in the thirty-eighth year of his raising the canopy (of dominion), in the first half of the lunar month Mäṅdindina (February–March), on the seventh

---

[1] *Vuju* (line 14) or *vudu*, a participial form like *dunu* in line 13, probably derived from Skt. *vidyut*. Cf. P. *vijjotati*, and *vijju*.

[2] *Ruduru tula tala arā*. Skt. *raudra-tulā-talam āruhya*. The Devanagala record uses *rudu* instead of *ruduru* and *rudu* in Sinhalese means 'big'. For *arā*, see Vol. I, p. 50, note 10.

[3] *Tumā tunu kap-taru-min*. The reading *tulakala aritu itunu kapturamen* in the Devanagala record seems to admit of improvement.

[4] *Muḷu levhu pataḷe yasa pabaňda äti*. Cf. *muḷu lohi pataḷa* in the Devanagala rock.

[5] *Pahayā*, lit. 'having illumined'. See Vol. I, p. 221, line 4.

[6] *Dasa-nävān* (lines 17–18) = Skt. *diśānāthānām* or *diśā-nāyakānām*. *Dasa-nā* may also be the title of the chief administrative officer of a *dasa-gam* 'group of ten villages'. See the article on the Vēvälkäṭiya slab (Vol. I, pp. 243–244). The reading *diyanāvan* in the Jetavanārāma slab, line 4 (Vol. I, pp. 221 and 225, note 4) may also be read *disa-nāvan*.

[7] *Raja-gedorahi*. See Vol. I, p. 225, note 5.

[8] *Asiri*: Skt. *āścarya*.

[9] *Vaḷana* from Skt. $\sqrt{}$*vṛt*. Cf. the two Pāli forms *vaṭṭati* and *vattati*. The Sinhalese verbal stem *vaḷa* seems to be a derivative of the former with the meaning of the latter.

[10] *Nugurā*, probably from Skt. *anugraha*.

[11] *Viyami*, probably in error for *visaṁba*, Skt. *viśrambha*. So Mr. D. B. Jayatilaka suggests. A possible derivation of *viyami* is from Skt. *vyāyāma*, 'bodily exertion', but this hardly suits the context.

[12] *Tumahaḷa ekatsaru kaḷa* (line 21). Cf. *mok maňga tumahaṭ ekatsaru koṭ* in line 4 of the Vessagiri slab (Vol. I, p. 31).

day of the waxing moon, (His Majesty) made offerings of various adornments studded with beautiful gems of seven kinds to the Sacred Footprint[1] impressed on the summit of Samanoḷa rock (Adam's Peak) which sustained the Sacred lotus-like feet of the four Buddhas that attained Buddhahood in the present cycle, namely, Kakusandha, Koṇāgamana, Kassapa, and Gotama. He raised also various canopies, flags and banners made of silk cloth (over the footprint) and, anointing it with the four kinds of unguents, he decked it with his own bejewelled crown.

[Lines 28–38] Thereafter, he instituted the maintenance of repairs, offerings, paintings, lighting of lamps on Samanoḷa rock (Adam's Peak) which bears the sacred footprint (of the Buddha); and for providing the great community of Buddhist monks who arrive from the four quarters to worship the (foot-)relic here, with suitable food and other necessary things, and also for keeping up the alms given to those other travel-worn pilgrims who come together to worship the relic, he had almonries (dāna-śālā) established in his name, one at each of the last five *gows* of Rāja-raṭa road[2] and endowed them with means for almsgiving. He had a terrace constructed below the terrace where the sacred footprint is, and [thus gave facility] for low caste people to worship the relic of the Sage[3]. He had the first terrace enclosed by a great wall with two gateways at the two roads [leading in and out], which are fitted with locks and keys. [Thus] did he give those worthy of his protection facility to worship the relic of the Sage. He had a net also put over the sacred footprint, and in the neighbourhood all round it he caused the formation of paddy fields.

[Lines 38–50] He moreover made [a partition of] Vilbā and dedicated (to the sacred footprint) all the [following] properties (situated) therein, namely, one garden[4] of areca-nut trees in Kelagamuva, one *koṭaväli* in Tiniyagal, one *koṭaväli* in Soragoda, one *koṭaväli* in Liyavaḷa, one *koṭaväli* in the forest of Badulla, the areca-nuts of the *koṭavälla* at the Uḍu-hō (upper stream), as well as Makuḷumula, Aṁbagamuva, Väligampoḷa and Ulapanā in Kaḷaṅgavela. In

---

[1] *Pada-las-dā* = Skt. *pāda-lāñchana-dhātu*, 'foot-print-relic'.

[2] This apparently refers to the ancient road which ran from north to south, connecting Anurādhapura and Poḷonnaruva with Māgama the capital of the southern kingdom of Ruhuṇa.

[3] *Ihi* = P. *isi*.

[4] Arăb. = P. *ārāma*. See *arab* in the slab-inscription of Mahinda IV (Vol. I, p. 221, line 13).

all these places he set up *kusalān*[1] and *bō-pā*[2] and made the order that into none of these there shall enter (tuḍināḷā) employés of the Royal family, or *deruvanä-de-kamtän*[3]; that wayfarers, tramps[4], coolies, and melāsī[5] shall not take away the offerings made (from time to time); that cart-oxen[6], milch cows[7], and hauling labourers[8] shall not be taken away; that, should persons after committing a crime that comes within the [purview of] the 'five great crimes' enter (these) villages [for refuge], they can be delivered over [to the authorities] only after they have been made to get outside the boundary line of the [respective] village, but no arrest can be made by entering the village. [And this decree is in force] from the thirty-eighth (regnal) year for future years[9].

[Lines 50–58] **Hakka-gam Kitu, Koḷom̆ba-galu Dovu** and **Mahakilim̆-gam Kitḷi-deṭu** (all) of the family of **Mekāppara-vädārum**[10] **Kaḷunnaru-bim Ayannātavan,** as well as **Kuḍasalā Kitu** of the family of **Ramukkaḍu Abhā-rakkamaṇan**—by all these lords who have come from the King's Council[11] after taking leave of him by prostrating at his feet[12], this Council Warrant of immunity (inscribed) on the pillar is granted .. .. the superintendent of repairs .. .. was caused to be done.

---

[1] The exact meaning of this word is still uncertain. Cf. *daru kusalān* and *mañga kusalān* above p. 118. Note also the name Kusalāna-kanda, near Rūgama, in the Eastern Province (Parker's *Ancient Ceylon*, p. 445) where there is an ancient pond cut in the rock.

[2] *Bō-pā* may be a derivative of P. *bodhi-pāda*, 'the sacred Bodhi tree', or more likely *bodhi-patta*, 'bowl for the Bodhi tree'. Cf. *maha-pā* (*mahā-patta*) in the Mihintale inscription (Vol. I, p. 106, note 16).

[3] The meaning of this expression which occurs frequently in inscriptions of the tenth and eleventh centuries is still obscure. See, however, Vol. I, p, 207, note 3, and the index for other references.

[4] *Magiv, piya-giv.* See above, p. 33, note 7.

[5] See above, p. 5, note 6.

[6] *Gäl-gon.* See above, p. 33, note 3.

[7] *Kiri-geri.* See Ätavīragollāva pillar, side C, line 8 (above, p. 48).

[8] *Adanā väriyan.* The meaning of this is not clear. *Adanā* is the present relative participle of *adinavā*, 'to pull or haul', *väriyan* is a word of common occurrence. See index for references.

[9] *Aṭa-tis vanna matu havurudu paṭan* (line 50). This phrase can also be rendered 'from the year after the thirty-eighth year', but I do not see why the decree should be post-dated.

[10] See Vol. I, p. 193, for an explanation of this and other official titles.

[11] *Ektän-samuyen* more commonly *eklän samiyen.* We find this word replaced by *sabhāyen* in Kukurumahan-damana pillar (side A, line 22, above, p. 23), thus confirming our interpretation of this expression in Vol. I, p. 206, note 2. See also Vol. I, p. 35, note 12.

[12] *Pā-vända* (line 51) = *Pādam̆ vanditvā.*

No. 36. POḶONNARUVA: SLAB-INSCRIPTION OF SĀHASA-MALLA

THOUGH kings of old Ceylon, like those of Southern India, have left behind a very large number of inscriptions recording their charitable acts, yet, with the exception of a few of a comparatively late period, all followed the ancient method of dating by regnal years of kings. This, however, does not help us much in the task of arranging the chronology of Ceylon kings. So the present record of Sāhasa-Malla with its definite date in the Buddha-varṣa, the earliest yet come to light, is of great historical interest.

It was found more than half a century ago incised on a quadrangular slab (about 6¼′ × 2¾′) standing upright at a spot north of the Hāṭadāgē on the present footpath to Rankot-vehera in Poḷonnaruva. Both the sides of the stone are made smooth and are ruled horizontally with lines two inches apart to receive between them the inscription boldly engraved in 69 lines (32 on side A and 37 on side B).

The type of the **akṣaras** agrees with that of the alphabet of the twelfth and thirteenth centuries. There is as usual no noticeable difference between the *ṛ* vowel sign and *ra* when affixed to a consonant. The medial long *ā* vowel sign (*älapilla*) is attached to the lower end of *l*, ල, as in the records of this period, though in a few inscriptions we find it detached as ලො in side B, line 3. The *visarga* is indicated by the usual vertical stroke convexed to the left (꞉), sometimes by double curves ꞉ as in *nṛpāḥ* (side B, line 37).

The **orthography** is correct with few exceptions such as *se* which is sometimes written *sē*, the doubling of consonants in conjunction with a preceding *r* so common in manuscripts and, in one instance only, the unnecessary use of the *virāma* in consonantal groups of Sanskrit and Pāli words, instead of the combined letters, e.g. *vighna* (B, line 5).

The **grammar** also is satisfactory, although we should prefer the addition of *vū* after *urehi-dā* (A, lines 7–8) and of the genitive suffix *gē* after *mahadevīn-vahanse* (A, line 8).

The **language** is Sanskritic Sinhalese and agrees in style with that of the inscriptions of Niśśaṅka-Malla. The first five lines of side A and the last five lines of side B contain two Sanskrit stanzas in *śārdūlavikrīḍita* metre separated from the Sinhalese text by a fish emblem as shown in the facsimile.

The **date** given in the inscription is 1743 years, 3 months and 27 days of the Buddhavarṣa, Wednesday[1], the twelfth day of the bright fortnight of the lunar month of *Binera* (*Bhādrapada*, Aug.–Sept.). It is not that of the record itself or of the grant, but that of the anointment of Sāhasa-Malla as king of Ceylon and, as already stated, it is the earliest known instance of the use of the Buddhist era in a public document. Dr. Fleet, in his article on this subject[2], says that the year 1743 treated as the completed year in accordance with the general practice, takes us, for the given month, to 1200 A. D. or 1201 according as it is counted from an initial point in 544 or in 543 B. C. The given details, *Bhādrapada śukla* 12, Wednesday are correct for Wednesday, 23rd August, 1200 A. D. So we have the date of the anointment of Sāhasa-Malla (alias Siri Saṅgabo Kāliṅga Vijaya-Bāhu) as a definitely fixed point in the later chronology. Further, this result shows that when the reckoning was set going, it was made to run from an initial point in 544 B. C. (not 543). As to how far back this reckoning of the Buddha-varṣa from 544 B. C. was in vogue in preference to, or rather in ignorance of, the earlier one reckoned from 483 B. C., the reader is referred to pages 208–209 above where the question has been threshed out to some extent.

The **contents** of the record tell us that **Siri Saṅgabo Kāliṅga Vijaya-Bāhu** bore the *biruda* epithet **Sāhasa-Malla,** that he was born in Siṁhapura as a legitimate son of **Śrī-Gopa** of the Kāliṅga Cakravarti dynasty by Queen **Loka-mahādevī,** that he was a brother of Niśśaṅka-Malla who was king of Ceylon before him, that after the latter's death, one **Lolupälā-kuḷu Dūttäṭi Ābonävan,** an adhigār of Ceylon, in association with his friend and colleague **Lolupälā-kuḷu Budal-nāvan,** also an adhigār of Ceylon, determined to reinstate the Kāliṅga dynasty on the throne and so sent a Kāliṅga noble called **Mallikārjunā** to Siṁhapura with an invitation to Sāhasa-Malla to come over and take up the sovereignty of Ceylon, that after two years, when the two adhigārs had completed the subjugation of their antagonists, he was raised to the throne and was anointed on the above-mentioned date, that in recognition of these services, the king raised the first adhigār to the rank of **Senevirat** and his mother to that of **Laṅkātilaka-mahādevī** with the decoration of the waist-band of gold and that he further appointed the Senevirat called also **Lak-Vijaya-Siṅgu-Senevi Ābonāvan** as his prime minister and granted him much wealth in the shape of *pamunu* lands, escorts, &c.

---

[1] Müller erroneously translates 'Tuesday'.

[2] *J. R. A. S.*, 1909, p. 331.

The information we can gather from Niśśaṅka-Malla's records coupled with what is given here enables us to construct the following genealogical tree of the Ceylon members of the Kāliṅga dynasty, from which it will be seen that Sāhasa-Malla was only a half-brother of Niśśaṅka-Malla :—

Pārvatī Mahādevī = { Śrī Jaya-Gopa-rāja or Śrī Gopa-rāja of the Kāliṅga Cakravarti dynasty, Siṁhapura } = Loka-Mahādevī

- (by Loka-Mahādevī) Sāhasa-Malla called also Śrī Saṅghabodhi Kāliṅga Vijaya-Bāhu 1200–1202 A.D.
- (by Pārvatī Mahādevī):
  - Sister
    - Coḍa-Gaṅga 1197 A.D.
  - Vikrama-Bāhu 1196 A.D.
  - Kāliṅga Subhadrā Mahādevī } = { Kīrti Niśśaṅka-Malla called also Śrī Saṅghabodhi Kāliṅga Parākrama-Bāhu Vīra-rāja, Aprati-Malla, Cakravarti, Siṁhapurēśvara and Laṅkeśvara 1187–1196 A.D. } = Gaṅgāvaṁśa Kalyāṇa or Kalyāṇavatī who held the sceptre of Ceylon for six years 1202–1208 A.D.
    - Son Vīra-Bāhu 1196 A.D.
    - Daughter Sarvāṅga-Sundarī

As regards the ministers, we see that **Āyuṣmat-pṛtanāpati** mentioned in the Sanskrit verse both at the beginning and at the end of the inscription is identical with **Lak-Vijaya-Siṅgu Senevi Ābonāvan** and most probably with **Laṅkādhikāra Lolupālā-kuḷu Dūttāṭi Ābonāvan** in the Sinhalese portion[1], for it was this general that was instrumental in placing Sāhasa-Malla on the throne and it was he who received gifts and honours for his loyal services to the king. It is true that owing to the political intrigues that were going on at the time between the contending parties at the Court, as explained above (pp. 101–103), Sāhasa-Malla's reign did not last long. What happened to him is not stated anywhere, but we read in the *Mahāvaṁsa*, (ch. lxxx., 32–44) that after the second year of this king's reign, this Āyuṣmat general, 'a bold and resolute man', took the power into his own hands and ruled the country

1 For further information about this minister, see above, pp. 100–101.

according to law and justice for six years with the help of Kalyāṇavatī, the dowager-queen of Kīrti Niśśaṅka-Malla. Thereafter he placed on the throne an infant prince of three months old called Dharmāśoka and continued to wield the sceptre for one year more, when Aṇikaṅga came over with a large army from the Coḷa country and put to death both the prince and the general at Poḷonnaruva, in his turn to be slain by his own general after seventeen days' rule.

There have been several editions and translations of this inscription, the last being *A.I.C.*, No. 156. But they are not quite satisfactory, and the late Dr. Fleet in discussing the question of the Buddhist era expressed the hope that a more critical text and translation would appear before long in the *Epigraphia Zeylanica*. The present edition has been prepared independently and is based upon the two ink-estampages supplied by Mr. H. C. P. Bell when Archaeological Commissioner of Ceylon.

TEXT.

A.

1 ශ්‍රීමත් **සාහසමල්ල** සිංහළපති(ඃ) කාලිඞ්ගවංශා
2 ග්‍රණීරානීයාත්‍ර කලිඞ්ගතො ජීවිතවතෙ ලංකාධිරා
3 ජ්‍යශ්‍රියාම්[।]ආපන්නමත්පාතනාධිපාය මහතීං ග්‍රාමා
4 දිකාං සම්පදමද්‍රෙවෛවං කෘතවාන් ස්වයං කෘතවිද
5 මෙකාධිරාජ්‍ය පදම්[॥]  සිරිසර ඔකාවස් පරපු
6 රෙහි මුළු සක්වළ එක්සත් කළ කාලිඟචක්‍රවර්ති
7 පරම්පරායාත **ශ්‍රීඝොෂ** රාජයන්වහන්(සෙ උරෙ)
8 හිද **ලොකමහදෙවින්** වහන්සෙ කුසින් **සිංහපුරෙ**
9 **හි** ප්‍රසූතවූ අසම සාහසයෙන් **සාහසමල්ල** යැයි
10 විරුදු ලද **සිරිසඟබො කාලිඟ විජයබාහු** රජපා
11 වහන්සෙ පළමු ලංකායෙහි රජසිරි පැමිණ සිටි **නි**
12 **ශ්ශංකමල්ල** නම් බෑණන්වහන්සෙ ස්වර්ගස්ථවූ
13 පසු හිරු අස්තයට ගිය තෙනැ තරුගණනක්සෙ
14 ඛිප රජකෙනකුන් ගිලි ගිය තන්හි ලංකාව අස්වා
15 මිකවැ සඳ උද නොලත් රැයක්සෙ අඳුරුවැ තුබූ ස
16 ඳ **ලංකාධිකාර ලොලුපැලැකුළු දූන්නැම් අබොනාව**
17 **ණ්** තමන් ශෘත[1] ශීලකුලාචාරාදි මනාගුණෙණන් යෙ

[1] 'ශ්‍රුත' වියයුතුයි

18 දී නීති පරවැවනහෙයින් තමන්ට පරමමිත්‍රවූ ලං
19 **කාධිකාර ලොලුපැලැකුළු බුදල් නාවන්** හා එක්වැ ර
20 ජගු නැති රජය නම් තියමුවා නැති නැවක්සෙ නො ප
21 වත්නෙයැ ගිරු නැති දවසසෙ නොහොබනෙයැ බුඩශා
22 සනයද අණසක් නැතිවැ නිරාලම්බ වත්නෙයැ තවද
23 ලක්දිව නම් විජයරාජයන් යක්‍ෂ ප්‍රලය කොටැ ක
24 ණු මුල් බා තැනූ වියළක්සෙ පවත් කළ හෙයින්
25 එමැ වංශයෙහි රජුන් බොහොසේ රක්‍ෂාකළ තෙනැයැ
26 එබැවින් මෙහි රජකළ නිශ්ශංකමල්ල ස්වාමින්
27 ගෙ මලණුවන් වහන්සෙ කලිඟුරට යවා වඩා
28 අවූත් ලොසසුන් රකුම්හයි බැණැ නිශ්චය
29 කොටැ ස්වාමි පක්‍ෂපාත ධීර සාර ගුණෙන් යුක්ත
30 එරට වැසි **මල්ලිකාර්ජුනා** නම් ප්‍රධානී කලිඟුරට
31 යවා ආරාධනා කොටැ මහ පෙරහරින් ගෙන්වා සො
32 ළී රටැ **කහකොඩ** [1] පට්ටණමැ වඩා හිඳුවා රත්නාභ

B.

1 රණ වස්ත්‍රාදින් මිනුවන රාජ්‍යශ්‍රීයට අනු
2 රූප ශ්‍රීන් සත්කාර කරන කල්හි එබව අසා
3 අනුග්‍රහාපග්‍රහ දෙකට පොහොසත් ලොස
4 සුන් රක්නා රාජවරයන් නොකැමැතිවැ තමතමා
5 ගේමැ ආධිපත්‍යය පතා විස්නකරන දුම්බි
6 නත්‍රීන් දෙ හවුරුද්දෙකින් සාධා පුන්සඳ නැගැ
7 පානාසේ ශුභ නකත් මොහොත්හි මුහුනු පිටැ
8 මග පෙතැ නිරුපද්‍රව කොටැ වඩා අවූත් ත්‍රිසිං
9 හළය ඒකාතපත්‍ර කොටැ බුඩවර්ෂ එකදහස්
10 සත්සිය තෙසාලිස් හවුරුදු තුන්මස් සත්
11 විසි දවසක් ගිය තෙනැ බිනෙර පුර දොළොස්
12 වක් ලද බදා දවස් ශුභ නකත් මොහොතින් අ
13 භිෂෙක කැරැවූ මෙ අනන්‍යසාධාරණ දස්කමට
14 තමන්වහන්සෙට පළමුවන්නෙහි **සෙනෙවිරත්**
15 පට බඳුවා අග්‍ර මන්ත්‍රී කොටැ සිටුවා මෙවැනි දරු
16 වන් ලද මවූන්ට වැඩි සත්කාර කළමනා වෙදයි

---

[1] 'තහකොඩ' සිදැකියවියනැකිසි

17 මොවුන් මැණියන්ට **ලංකාතිලකමහදෙවී** යැයි
18 නම් දී බඩැ රත්පට බඳුවා බොහො සම්මාන දී
19 ගිර සඳ පමුණු කොටැ **ලක්විජයසිඟු සෙනෙ**
20 **වි අබොනාවන්ට** දී වදාළ ගම්වර හා පර්වාර
21 හා සියලු සම්පත්තියට මතුවන රජදරුව
22 නුදු තමන්තමන්ට දස්කම් කළවුන් රක්‍ෂා
23 කිරීම රාජධර්‍මමහෙයින් විලොපයක් නොකො
24 ටැ මෙමැ පරිද්දෙන් තබා දී ඔවුන් වශ රක්‍ෂාක
25 රනු මැනැවැයි ශිලාලෙඛ කරවා වදාළසෙයෙ
26 කැ මෙ බලබලා රාජවල්ලභවැ සිටි අමාත්‍යාදී
27 හු ද බලාත්කාරයෙන් මේ කී දෙය ගත්හුනම්
28 වෙවයි රජස්‍ය කළානු නම් වෙවයි රාජාඥ මැකු
29 වා නම් වෙති කුලෙන් හීනයන් හා ද කවුඩු බලුන්
30 හා ද සමනම් වෙති එ හෙයින් ස්වාමිපක්‍ෂපාත
31 රක්‍ෂාකරන්නා කැමැත්තවුන්විසින් මොවුන්ට දු
32 න් හැමැ සම්පත් රක්‍ෂාකරනුමැනැවි දෙව
33 ස්සාහසමල්ල එෂ ජගතාම්මාන්‍යස්ස්වයං යා
34 චතෙ භූපාලානාං යදෑප්‍රපක්‍ෂප(ා)තධූරීණාං ක්‍ෂාත්‍රො හි
35 ධර්‍මඃ පරම් [।] ආයුෂ්මත්ප්‍රෘතනාපතෙඃ කෘතවතඃ
36 කාලිඞ්ගවංශොදයම් ලංකාවර්ධිසම්පද ස
37 හ තතො රක්‍ෂන්තු වශ්‍යාන්නෘපාඃ [॥]

TRANSCRIPT.

1 Śrīmat **Sāhasa-Malla**-Siṁhaḷa-pati(ḥ) Kāliṅga-vaṁśā-
2 -graṇīr, āṇīyā-tra Kaliṅgato rppitavate Laṁkādhirā-
3 -jya-śriyām [।] Āyuṣmat-pṛtanādhipāya mahatīṁ grāmā-
4 -dikāṁ sampadam, datvaivaṁ kṛtavān svayaṁ kṛta-vidā-
5 -m ekādhirājye padam [॥] sirisara Okāvas parapu-
6 -rehi muḷu sakvaḷa ek-sat kaḷa Kāliṅga-Cakravartti-
7 paramparāyāta **Śrī Gopa**-rājayan-vahan(se ure [1]-)
8 -hidā **Loka-mahadevīn**-vahanse kusin **Siṁhapure-**
9 **-hi** [2] prasūta-vū asama sāhasayen **Sāhasa-Malla** yäyi
10 virudu lada **Siri Saṅgabo Kāliṅga Vijaya-Bāhu** raja-pā-
11 vahanse paḷamu Laṁkāyehi raja-siri pämiṇa siṭi **Ni-**

---

[1] Mt. *Bahidāloka.*

[2] Mt. *Siṁhapurhi.*

12 **-śśaṁka-Malla**-nam bāṇan-vahanse svarggastha-vū
13 pasu hiru astayaṭa giya tenä[1] taru-gaṇanak-se
14 kīpa raja-kenakun gili giya tanhi Laṁkāva a-svā-
15 -mika-vä sanda udā no-lat räyak-se anduru-vä tubū sa-
16 -nda **Laṁkādhikāra Lolupälā-kuḷu Dūttäṭi**[2] **Ābonā-va-**
17 **-n** taman śṛta[3] śīla-kulā-cārā-di mantrī-guṇen ye-
18 -dī nīti paravävana-heyin tamanṭa parama-mitra-vū **Laṁ-**
19 **-kādhikāra Lolupälā-kuḷu Budal-nāvan** hā ek-vä ra-
20 -jahu näti rajaya nam niya-muvā näti nävak-se no-pa-
21 -vatne-yä hiru näti davasa-se no-hobaneyä Buddha-śā-
22 -sanaya-da aṇasak näti-vä nir-ālamba-vanne-yä tavada
23 Lak-diva nam Vijaya-rājayan yakṣa praḷaya koṭä ka-
24 ṇu-mul bā tänū viyaḷak-se pavat kaḷa heyin
25 emä vaṁśayehi rajun boho-sē rakṣākaḷa tenäyä
26 e-bävin mehi raja-kaḷa Niśśaṁka-Malla-svāmin-
27 -ge malaṇuvan-vahanse Kaliṅgu-raṭa yavā vaḍā
28 avut lo-sasun rakumha-yi bäṇä niścaya
29 koṭä svāmi pakṣapāta dhīra-sāra-guṇen yukta
30 e-raṭa väsi **Mallikārjjunā** nam pradhānī Kaliṅgu-raṭa
31 yavā ārādhanā koṭä mahaperaharin genvā So-
32 -ḷī-raṭä **Kahakoṇḍa**-[4]paṭṭaṇamä vaḍā hinduvā ratnābha-

B.

1 -raṇa vastrādīn matu-vana rājya-śrīyaṭa anu-
2 -rūpa śrīn sat-kāra karana kalhi e-bava asā
3 anugrahā-pagraha[5] dekaṭa pohosat lo-sa-
4 -sun raknā rājavarayan no-kämäti-vä tama-tamā-
5 -gē-mä ādhipatyaya[6] patā vighna-karana durmma-
6 -ntrīn de havuruddekin sādhā pun-sanda näṅgā
7 pānā-sē śubha nakat mohot-hi muhundu piṭä
8 maṅga petä nir-upadrava koṭä vaḍā avut Tri-Siṁ-
9 -haḷaya ekātapatra koṭä Buddha-varṣa ek-dahas
10 sat-siya te-sālis havurudu tun-mas sat-
11 visi davasak giya tenä Binera pura doḷos

---

[1] Mt. *emä*. [2] Mt. *dūttävi*. [3] Read *śruta*.
[4] This may also be read *Taṅgakoṇḍa*. [5] Mt. *parigraha*.
[6] Mt. *adhipatyaya*.

12 vak lada Badā davas śubha nakat mohotin a-
13 -bhiṣeka kärä-vū me ananya-sādhāraṇa das-kamaṭa
14 taman-vahanseṭa paḷamu-vannehi **Senevirat**
15 paṭa bandavā agra mantrī koṭä siṭuvā me väni daru-
16 -van lada mavunṭa väḍi satkāra kaḷamanā vedayi
17 movun māṇiyanṭa **Laṁkātilaka-mahadevī**-yäyi
18 nam dī baḍä ran-paṭa bandavā boho sammāna dī
19 hira sanda pamuṇu koṭä **Lak-Vijaya-Siṅgu Sene-**
20 **-vi Ābonāvanṭa** dī vadāḷa gamvara hā parivāra
21 hā siyalu sampattiyaṭa matu-vana rajadaruva-
22 -nudu taman-tamanṭa das-kam kaḷavun rakṣā-
23 kirīma rāja-dharmma-heyin vilopayak no-ko-
24 -ṭä memä pariḍḍen tabā dī ovun vaṁśa rakṣā-ka-
25 -ranu mänäväyī śilā-lekha karavā vadāḷaseye-
26 -kä me bala-balā rāja-vallabha-vä siṭi amātyādi-
27 -hu da balātkārayen mē kī deya gat-hu nam
28 vevayi rajasya[1] kaḷāhu nam vevayi rājājñā mäku-
29 -vā nam veti kulen hīnayan hā da kavuḍu balun
30 hā da samanam veti e-heyin svāmi-pakṣapāta
31 rakṣā-karannā kämättavun-visin movunṭa du-
32 -n hämä sampat rakṣā-karanu mänävi Deva-
33 -s Sāhasa-Malla eṣa jagatām mānyas svayaṁ yā-
34 -cate, trāṇaṁ yad-dṛḍha-pakṣa-p(ā)ta-dhuriṇāṁ kṣātro hi
35 dharmmaḥ param [।] Āyuṣmat-pṛtanāpateḥ kṛtavataḥ
36 Kāliṅga-vaṁśodayañ, candrārkkā-vadhi[2] sampadā sa-
37 -ha tato rakṣantu vaṁśyān nṛpāḥ [॥]

TRANSLATION.

A.

[Lines 1–5] The illustrious **Sāhasa-Malla**, lord of the Siṁhaḷas and head of the Kāliṅga dynasty, gave[3] to the venerable[4] general who brought[5] (him) here from Kaliṅga and established (him) in the splendour of sovereignty over Laṅkā, great wealth, such as villages, &c.; and so he established himself in the

[1] Mt. *rajastha-laḷāhu.*

[2] Mt. *candrārkaḥ vadhi.*

[3] *Datvā*, 'having given'.

[4] *Āyuṣmat* here used more or less as a *biruda* title.

[5] *Āniya* (gerund of *ān*) + *atra.*

A

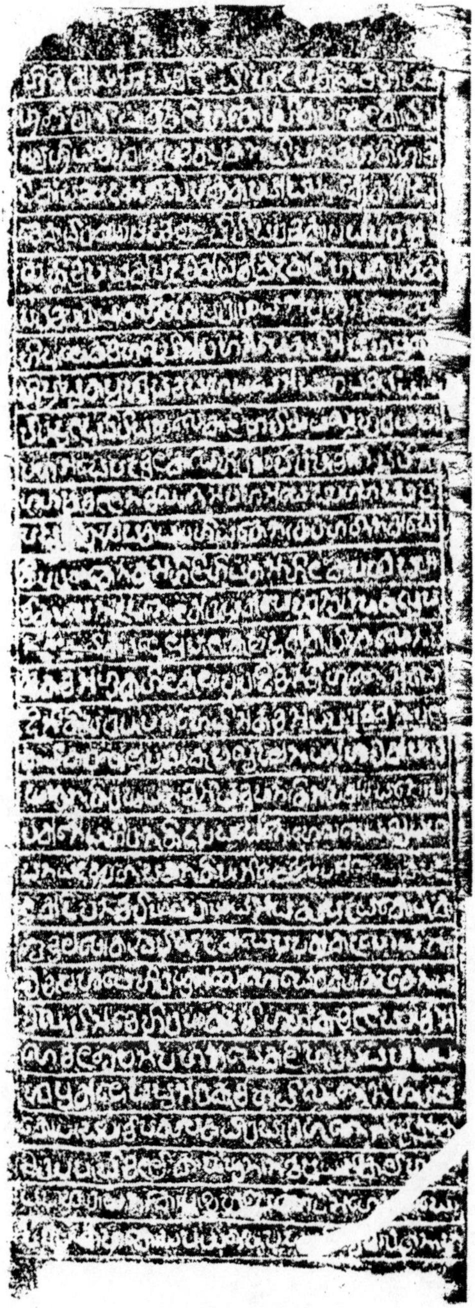

Scale 1⅓ inches to 1 foot.

From ink-impressions supplied by the A

Scale 1½ inches to 1 foot.

From ink-impressions supplied by the Archaeological Survey, Ceylon

kingship of grateful men. [i.e. displayed himself as the most grateful person possible].

[Lines 5–11] His Majesty, King **Siri Saṅgabo Kāliṅga Vijaya-Bāhu** who has received the epithet (*biruda*) **Sāhasa-Malla** on account of his incomparable valour, was born in **Siṁhapura** of the womb of the great queen **Lokā**[1] as a legitimate issue[2] of His Majesty King **Śrī Gopa** of the lineage of Kāliṅga-Cakravarti (emperors) who, in the illustrious line of the Okkāka dynasty, had brought the whole universe under one canopy of dominion.

[Lines 11–15] Since the attainment to heaven (*svarga*) of his Majesty's exalted brother[3] **Niśśaṅka-Malla** who had before (him) risen to kingly power in Ceylon, several kings passed away like so many stars (that rise) after sunset[4] and Laṅkā became kingless and darkness, like (that of) a moonless[5] night, prevailed over it.

[Lines 16–22] Then **Laṅkādhikāra**[6] **Lolupālā-kuḷu Dūttāṭi Ābonāvan,** being himself imbued with ministerial qualities such as learning, virtuous conduct, family (or caste) propriety, and the like, and being one adhering to justice[7], associated himself with his intimate friend **Laṅkādhikāra Lolupālā-kuḷu Budal-nāvan** and deliberated [as follows] :—'A kingdom without a king, like a ship without a steersman, would not endure; like a day without the sun, it would be lustreless, and the Buddhist religion without the "wheel of the law" would be devoid of support.'

[Lines 22–32] 'Moreover, King Vijaya preserved the Island of Laṅkā by destroying the yakṣas, like a tract of land[8] which he had prepared by removing stumps and roots, and on this account the Island has been a place much protected by kings of the same dynasty (as Vijaya). In these circumstances we should dispatch (an embassy) to the country of Kaliṅga and, having had the younger brother of our late king Niśśaṅka-Malla brought over here,

---

[1] *Loka-maha-devī.* [2] *Urehi-dā* : P. *orasa-jāla.*

[3] *Bāṇan-vahanse.* At first sight one may be inclined to connect *bāṇan* with P. *bhāgineyya*, Sinh. *bāṇā*, 'nephew', but the presence of the cerebral *ṇ* shows that it is made up of Sinh. *bā* (P. *bhātā*), 'brother', and the honorific suffix *-āṇa.* So Müller is correct here.

[4] The sunset being the death of Niśśaṅka-Malla.

[5] *Saňda-udā no lat räyak se,* lit. 'like a night which has not received the rising of the moon'.

[6] The *adhikāra* of Laṅkā, now corrupted to *adigār*, seems in the present case to be a mere *biruda* title.

[7] *Nīti paravā vana heyin.* The meaning of this clause is not quite clear. The above is offered tentatively though one may suggest 'since justice is on the wane' as an alternative translation.

[8] *Viyaḷak.* See Vol. I, p. 119, n. 1.

should (through him) protect the people and the religion.' So they (the two ministers) decided and sent to the country of Kaliṅga, the chieftain **Mallikārjunā,** a resident of that country, who was endowed with the virtue of profound and steadfast loyalty to (one's) lord. They (thus) invited (the prince) and had him brought in great pomp to the (sea-port) town of **Kahakoṇḍa**[1] in the Coḷa country.

B.

[Lines 1–8] And he was being entertained here with (gifts of) bejewelled ornaments, wearing apparel, &c., in such splendour as befits the dignity of the prospective king. (The two ministers) heard of this fact. So, in the course of two years, they subdued the evil ministers who were causing obstruction with the object of gaining personal power for themselves and so were not desiring to have kings that would be powerful enough both for (granting) rewards and (for inflicting) punishments, and that would protect the people and the religion. Thereafter, they caused the prince to resume the journey by sea at an auspicious moment, just as the full moon rises and shows herself.

Lines 8–13) The prince having been thus escorted (to Ceylon) in safety, brought the Trī-Siṁhaḷa[2] under one canopy of dominion and was crowned at a lucky moment on Wednesday, the twelfth day of the waxing moon in (the lunar month of) Binera[3] after the expiration of 1743 years, 3 months, and 27 days of the Buddhist era.[4]

[Lines 13–18] For this unique[5] act of loyal service [on the part of the first named minister],[6] His Majesty, in the first year of his reign, invested him with the rank of **Senevirat** and appointed him as his prime minister. Then thinking that it is but right to do high honour to mothers who have given birth to[7] children such as this [minister], he conferred on the minister's mother the title of **Laṅkātilaka-mahādevī,** and decorating her with the waist-band of gold, granted her many privileges.

---

1 Or Taṅga-koṇḍa.

2 The three divisions of the island of Ceylon, viz. Ruhuṇa, Māyā, and Pihiṭi.

3 *Binera* = Skt. *Bhādra-pada,* August—September.

4 *Buddha-varṣa.*

5 *Ananya-sādhāraṇa,* lit. 'not common to any one else'.

6 The text is somewhat vague here, but there is no doubt that the minister meant was Laṅkādhikāra Lolupālā kuḷu Dūttāṭi Ābonāvan.

7 Lit. 'who have obtained children'.

[Lines 19–25] His Majesty, moreover, bestowed on [this minister] **Lak-Vijaya-Siṅgu Senevi Ābonāvan** perpetual grants[1] of lands, as well as escorts and all (kinds of other) riches. Then he made the declaration: 'since it is the duty of kings to protect those who have rendered them loyal services, let future kings not cause harm but [continue to] maintain these gifts as they are now maintained and thus preserve the families of these (loyal men)' and thereafter caused this declaration to be inscribed on stone.

[Lines 26–32] With this continually before their eyes,[2] should any ministers or others in royal favour [at the time] forcibly appropriate the above-mentioned gifts or should they utterly destroy them[3], they would be as though they have obliterated the Royal Order and would be on a level with those degraded from caste as well as with crows and dogs. Therefore, let those who desire to foster loyalty to kings protect all the riches bestowed on this (minister).

[Lines 32–37][4] This King Sāhasa-Malla (who is) honoured by the world makes (this) prayer personally:—'As the protection of strongly loyal adherents is in the highest degree a duty incumbent on kings, so let (future) kings protect, as long as the sun and moon endure, the lineal descendants of this venerable general who caused the ascendancy of the Kāliṅga dynasty, together with their possessions.'

No. 37. ALUTVÄVA PILLAR-INSCRIPTION.

ALUTVÄVA is a hamlet in Eppāvala Korale, North Central Province. The inscribed pillar here is one of those examined by Mr. H. C. P. Bell[5] in 1895. It is quadrangular and measures about 4 ft. by 9½ in. square.

The **akṣaras**, each about an inch in size, are clearly incised between ruled lines two inches apart. They cover three sides of the pillar, sides A and B containing 21 lines in each, and side C 12 lines, terminating with the usual emblems of the sun, the moon, the crow, and the dog, one above the other in succession, as

---

[1] *Hira-sañda-pamuṇu*, 'grants which are in force so long as the sun and moon exist'.

[2] *Me bala balā*, 'continually looking at this'.

[3] Lit. 'reduce to powder'.

[4] The Sanskrit verse.

[5] In his *Annual Report* (p. 8) we find the following reference to it:—'Alutveva—a pillar-inscription in fine preservation which served as one of the supports to a modern vihâré of Kandyan plan. This is another record of "Siri Saṅg Bo" and is dated in his twentieth year. Substituted other stones as underpinning and had the inscribed pillar set up in front of the vihâré.'

may be seen from the accompanying facsimile. Generally speaking, the letters resemble the alphabet of the tenth century A.D. A comparison, however, of the akṣaras *i*, *ka*, *ma*, *ya*, and *ra* in the present record with those in the pillar-inscriptions of Īripinniyāva[1] Rambāva, Kirigallāva, and Noccipotāna, ascribed to Udaya I (*circa* 952-963 A.D.) will make it obvious that palaeographically our inscription belongs to a date later than these. The same reasons compel us to consider our record to be even later than the pillar-inscriptions at Timbirivāva[2] and Nāgama[2] of the first and the seventh year respectively of Kassapa IV (*circa* 963-980 A.D.). On the other hand, the script both of Kukurumahan-damana[2] pillar of the eleventh year of Kassapa IV and of the Mäḍirigiriya pillar of the third year of Kassapa V (*circa* 980-990 A.D.) resembles that of the present record in every respect.

Further, at page 9 above, we have pointed out that many of the ninth- and tenth-century kings, such as Sena I and his successors down to Dappula V, appear to have adopted the *biruda* titles Salamevan and Siri Saṅgbo alternately. Accordingly Sena II was a Siri Saṅgbo, his successor Udaya I, a Salamevan, and the next king, Kassapa IV, a Siri Saṅgbo. The king mentioned in our record of about the same period was also a Siri Saṅgbo. This fact makes us identify him either with Sena II or Kassapa IV. The form of script, as stated before, is decidedly against the former identification, while the regnal year, if taken as the twentieth, supports it, for Sena II was the only king about this time who held the sceptre for more than twenty years. If, however, we accept the alternative reading *päs vanne*, 'fifth year', as the correct one instead of *väs vanne*[3], there will be no difficulty in classing the record as one of Kassapa IV.

There are two dates in our inscription, both in the same month of Uňd-vap and in the same regnal year. The first is *ava viseni davas* (A, lines 5-6), 'the fifth day of the waning moon', and is apparently the day on which the decree was passed by the King in Council. The second is *pun mashi dasa pak davas* (C, lines 5-6) 'the tenth day of the bright half of the month'. It is the date on which the *attāṇi perahära* or the Council Warrant was proclaimed. But both these dates being in one and the same month of Uňd-vap and if the month was an *amānta* Uňd-vap, the second date referring to a subsequent event should also be in the *apara pakṣa* like the first date, otherwise it would fall in *amānta* Durutu, the month after Uňd-vap. We are, therefore, compelled to think

[1] See Vol. I, Nos. 11 and 13, and Vol. II, Nos. 1 and 2.

[2] See Vol. II, Nos. 3-6.

[3] See note to the translation below.

that the month in question was a *pūrṇimānta* Uňd-vap, which is calculated to begin on the first day of the waning moon (*ava pāḷaviya*) of the solar month *vṛścika* and end on the full moon day (*pura pa°aḷos-vaka*) of *dhanus* and that the promulgation of the decree took place twenty days after its passage through the Council.[1]

Owing to the illegibility of certain words in the text, we are unable to say what the exact purport of the Council Warrant is. The readable portion enumerates certain properties in Mahademeṭi-kuḷiya, which were at the time under the management of one **Tinḍī Kitu,** but whether they were gifted to this man or whether he only received certain privileges in connexion therewith, we are unable to gather from the present imperfect text.

The two officials who carried out the order of the King in Council were (a) Mekāppar **Mahanavagam-kaḍayim Kelā Mihindim** of the family of **Maňgul-rad Senu** and (b) **Kuňḍasalā**[2] **Viset-devu** of the family of **Mahāle Kasbā Raksamaṇan.** Neither of them is mentioned in any of the records yet known to us, but Kuṇḍasalā Viset-devu may have been closely related to **Kuṇḍasalā Kit** of the Mäḍiligiri pillar of Kassapa V and to Kuṇḍasalā Siňgim of the Äṭavīra-golläva pillar of Dappula V and also to Kavasilāňg Gavayim of Kirigalläva pillar of Udaya I, because they were kinsmen of the Chief Secretary Kasbā Raksamaṇan.

The **language** of our record is similar in style to that employed in other pillar-inscriptions of the tenth and eleventh centuries. There are, however, a few agricultural terms that need elucidation. They are (a) *hevitiya* probably for *hōviṭiya*, modern *ōviṭiya*, possibly a derivative of Skt. *śrotas* (P. *sota*, Pkt. *soa*) + *pṛṣṭha* (or **pṛṣṭhika*, P. and Pkt. *piṭṭhī*), 'the lowland by a riverside'; (b) *kärärtasā* or *kärärsā* probably land under certain form of tenure, (c) *kiri*, *pā*, and *massa*. These are no doubt names of measures of capacity. When applied to land measure they mean the extent of land which they will normally cover in sowing. *Kiri* is the same as *kiriya* or *karīsa*[3] and is equivalent to four *amuṇu* (P. *ammaṇa*). *Pā* or *paya* (Skt. *pāda*) is a quarter of a *kiri*, i.e. an *amuṇa*[4], while a *massa*, a term known to us only as the name of a coin[5], seems from the context to indicate that it is equal to a quarter of a *pā* in which case it is another name for a *payala* or *pāla*[6].

The following edition of the record is based on a single estampage supplied by the Ceylon Archaeological Department.

---

[1] I am indebted to Professor Keith for drawing my attention to this possibility.

[2] See above, p. 28. [3] See Vol. I, p. 3, n. 4. [4] *Ibid.*, p. 36, n. 7.

[5] *Massa* or *māsa*. See Rhys Davids' *Ancient Coins and Measures of Ceylon*, pp. 27, 28.

[6] See Vol. I, p. 55, n. 3.

TEXT.

A.

1 ලක්දිව් පොළො
2 යොන පර්පුරෙන් හි
3 මි වූ සිරි සග්බො
4 මහරද්නු (වැ[1])ස්වන්
5 නෙය් උඤ්වැපැ අව
6 විසෙනි දවස් (වැඳ)
7 වදෘළෙසින් ආ ම
8 ඟුල්රද් සෙනු වරැ මෙ
9 කාප්පර් මහන(ඩ)ග
10 මිකඩසිම් කෙලැ
11 මිගිඤ්දිම් ඉසා ම
12 හාලෙ කස්බා රක්
13 සමණින් වරැ කු
14 ඩසලා විසෙන්දෙ
15 වූ ඇතුළ්වැ මෙතුවා
16 ක් ඉදනමො එක්සෙ
17 වැ ම(හ)[2]දෙමෙපිකු
18 ළිසෙණි අයවූ (හෙ)
19 විපියෙන් කැරැ(ර්)
20 (සා) දෙ කිරි එක් පා
21 තුන් මස්සක් (ජි)

B.

1 වැල් කරැ තුන් පා
2 තුන් මස්සක් ඇ
3 තුළ් වැ සා කිරියක්
4 ඉසා රට් සිවු කිම්
5 .. ..
6 ඇතුළ් කොට් ස ගෙ
7 කිම්කට් ගබ් ගෙ
8 වතු පැල[3] දෘර් ඉසා
9 කැරැර්(තසා)[4] තල්
10 .. .. .. ඉසා ගොවි
11 .. .. .. (ඇ)රුබ් ඉසා
12 .. .. (රැ) මී ගජ් අට
13 කි ගොවින් නැමැ (පි)
14 පියෙන් සතර් අ
15 මූණක් හමුයන
16 පිපිහා දෙ අමු
17 ණකට් උඤ්බිම් ඇ
18 තුළ්වැ මෙතුවාක්
19 තැන් අයවූ සෙ ඇ
20 තුළ් රක්වල් කර
21 න කිඬිකිතු නමා[5]

C.

1 .. ..
2 (රැ)ග දෙන්ව [නූ ඉ]
3 සා දෙනු කොට් (වැ[1])
4 ·ස් වන්නෙ උඤ්වජ්
5 සඤ් පූත් මස්හි ද
6 ස පක් දවස් මෙ
7 අත්තාණි පැරැහ
8 ර් දෙනු ලදි මෙය
9 වි අනියා කළහු
10 කවුඩු බලු වෙත්
11 වා එළු මැරුවා කළ
12 අකුසල් ගත්තහ

---

[1] ‘පැ’ සීද කියවිය හැකිසි
[2] ‘ග’ සීද කියවිය හැකිසි
[3] ‘පැළි’ සීද කියවිය හැකිසි
[4] ‘කසා’ සීද කියවිය හැකිසි
[5] ‘තුමා’ සීද කියවිය හැකිසි

TRANSCRIPT.

A.

1 Lak-div poḷo-
2 -yona parpuren hi-
3 -mi-vū **Siri Saṅg-bo**
4 maha-rad-hu (vä[1])s-van-
5 -ney Und-väpä ava
6 viseni davas (vända)
7 vadāḷeyin ā **Ma-**
8 **-ṅgul-rad Senu** varä me-
9 -kāppar **Maha-na(va)-ga-**
10 **-m-kaḍayim Kelā**
11 **Mihindim** isā ma-
12 -hā-le **Kasbā Rak-**
13 **-samaṇan** varä **Ku-**
14 **-ṇḍasalā (Viset)-de-**
15 **-vu** ätuḷ-vä metuvā-
16 -k denamo ek-se-
17 vä **Ma(ha)[2]demeṭi-ku-**
18 **-ḷiyehi** aya-vū (He-)
19 -viṭiyen kärä(r-)
20 (-sā) de kiri ek pā
21 tun massak (ji-)

B.

1 -väl karä tun pā
2 tun massak ä-
3 -tuḷ-vä sā kiriyak
4 isā raṭ sivu bim
5 .. ..
6 ätuḷ koṭ sa ge-
7 bimakaṭ gab ge-
8 vatu pāḷa[3] dor isā
9 kärär(tasā)[4] tal
10 .. .. .. isā govi
11 .. .. (a)rub isā
12 .. (rä) mī gas aṭa-
13 -ki govīn-nämä (pi-)
14 -ṭiyen satar a-
15 -muṇak hamu-yana
16 piṭihā de amu-
17 -ṇakaṭ und-bim ä-
18 -tuḷ-vä metuvāk
19 tän aya-vū se ä-
20 -tuḷ rakval kara-
21 -na **Tiṇḍī Kitu** tamā[5]

C.

1 .. ..
2 (rä)ga denva[nu i-]
3 -sā denu koṭ (vä-[1])
4 -s vanne Undvap
5 sand pun mas-hi da-
6 -sa pak davas me
7 attāṇi päräha-
8 -r denu ladi meya-
9 -ṭ aniyā kaḷahu
10 kavuḍu balu vet-
11 -vā eḷu mä16ruvā kaḷa
12 akusal gattaha

---

[1] This may also be read as *pä*.
[2] This may also be read as *maṅga*.
[3] This may also be read as *pāḷi*.
[4] This may also be read as *kasā*.
[5] This may also be read as *tumā*.

TRANSLATION.

Whereas, on the fifth day of the waning moon of (the lunar month of) Und-väp (Nov.–Dec.) in the twentieth[1] regnal year of the great king **Siri Sañg-bo**, lord by lineal succession of the lords[2] of the soil of the Island of Laṅkā, it was graciously (so) decreed,[3] Mekāppar **Mahanavagam-kaḍayim Kelā Mihindim** of the family[4] of **Mañgul-rad-Senu**[5] as well as **Kuṇḍasalā Viset-devu** of the family of the chief secretary[6] **Kasbā Raksamaṇan**—these ministers have come and in full accord have on this tenth day of the waxing[7] moon of the month of Und-väp in the twentieth[1] regnal year granted this Warrant of His Majesty in Council (to the following effect).

Six *kiri*[8] [sowing extent of land] inclusive of [an additional] three *pā* and three *massa*, after converting to *jivel* land two *kiri*, one *pā* and three *massa* of *kärär-tasā* land from the *heviḷiya*[9] in **Mahademeṭi-kuḷiya**[10]; rooms[11], house-gardens[12], and western doorways[13] for six building sites[14] including . . . . the four (kinds of) lands in the country; the palmyna trees of *kärärtasā* . . . . . cultivation . . . . groves[15] . . . . eight *mī*[16] trees; four *amuṇa* sowing

---

[1] *Väs* (l. 4), 'twentieth', or *päs*, 'fifth'. Here and on side C, lines 3–4, the two akṣaras give the reading *väs* better than *päs*, but both *väs* for P. *vīsati* or *vīsaṁ*, Pkt. *vīsaï* or *vīsa*, Sinh. *visi* and *päs* for P. *pañca*, Sinh. *pas* are forms hitherto not met with in Sinhalese documents. Cf. also remarks on p. 230 above.

[2] See Vol. I, p. 248. note 7.

[3] *Väňda vadāleyin.* See above, pp. 39 and 43, note 7.

[4] *Varä.* For an explanation of this word, see Vol. I, pp. 193–194, and above, p. 28.

[5] P. *Maṅgala-rāja-senaka.*

[6] *Mahā-le* = P. *mahā-lekhaka.*

[7] *Undväp-sand pun-mashi dasa-pak davas.* This must be the date of the promulgation of the decree passed by the king in Council twenty days before, namely, on the *ava viseni davas.* See remarks on pp. 230–231 above

[8] For comments on the technical names of land measures, &c., appearing here, see above, p. 231.

[9] Probably for *höviḷiya*, modern *öviḷiya*, 'low ground bordering a river'.

[10] *Kuḷiya.* This appears to be a name for a subdivision of land like the term *tālukkā* in India. Cf. *Pan-kuḷiya*, a hamlet near Anurādhapura, *Padonnaru-kuḷiya*, Vol. I, p. 206. *Amgam-kuḷiya*, I, p. 246, and above, p. 2, and *Loholuvilä-kuḷiya*, above, p. 38.

[11] *Gab.* = P. *gabbha.*

[12] *Ge-vatu.*

[13] *Pāḷa-dora*, 'door opening to the west, backdoor' (Clough).

[14] *Ge-bim.* See Vol I, p. 198, n. 8.

[15] *Arub*, 'groves' or 'orchards' (Clough).

[16] See Vol. I, p. 106, n. 3.

extent of lowland from **Govīn-nämäpiṭiya** including *unḍu* sowing land to the extent of two *amuṇas*. [Unto] **Tinḍī Kitu** who looks after all within these properties, there shall be given . . . .

Whoever that do injustice to this [decree], may they become crows and dogs [in their future births]. They would (moreover) incur [such] sins as those committed by a slaughterer of goats.

No. 38. POḶONNARUVA: ĀNAULUNDĀVA SLAB-INSCRIPTION (REG. No. 1)

THIS inscription was discovered in July 1921 at a spot 'about 92 feet east of 0 mile 60 chains on the Poḷonnaruva section of the railway trace to Batticaloe' in or near the village called Ānaulundāva, north of Poḷonnaruva [1].

It consists of three lines of writing engraved between ruled lines $1\frac{1}{2}$ in. apart and covering an area of only $4\frac{1}{2}$ in. by 3 ft. $5\frac{1}{2}$ in. at the upper end of the prepared surface of a stone slab measuring 6 ft. 10 in. × 3 ft. $5\frac{1}{2}$ × 10 in. The top part is obviously intended to remain above ground and is, therefore, ornamented with ogee moulding on its sides.

The **script** is Sinhalese, the size of each letter being about $1\frac{1}{4}$ in. on the average. The type is that of the alphabet of the twelfth and thirteenth centuries.

As to the **language**, we cannot say that it is wholly Sanskrit owing to the total illegibility of the third line, but what is readable consists only of a number of high sounding titles of honour in Sanskrit. It will be seen from the notes following the translation that these titles are practically identical with those applied to certain members of a guild of merchants called **Vīra-Baṇañju** or **Vīra-Vaḷañjiyar** [2] who are referred to as prominent donors in several of the Kanarese inscriptions of the twelfth century A.D., for example those from Kolhāpūr, Miraj, and Mamdāpūr. I am indebted to Dr. Barnett not only for drawing my attention to the similarity of the titles but also for kindly giving me all the references to the Vīra-Vaḷañjiyar. His edition of the Kanarese

---

[1] See *A. S. C., Annual Report*, 1920–1921, p. 8.

[2] *Vaṇañju* or *vaḷañja* = Sinh. *veṇaňda* or *veḷaňda*, 'merchant'. References to them are to be found in *Epigr. Carnat.* VII. Sk. 94, 118, 119; *Mysore Inscr.*, pp. 73, 120, 123; *Madras Epig. Report*, 1905–6, pp. 11, 17, 1912–13, pp. 99–102, 1914–15, p. 102; *Mysore Ann. Arch. Report*, 1920, p. 31.

records will appear in due course in the *Epigraphia Indica.* The presence of these merchants in Ceylon in the twelfth century leads us to infer the possibility of their having acquired important trading and other concessions during the time of Kīrti Niśśaṅka-Malla. Following their practice in Mysore and elsewhere in India they may have set up the present slab recording one of their pious gifts to a Hindu temple.

TEXT.

1 ශ්‍රී සමසථ[1] භුවනාග්‍ර පඤ්චශතවීර ශාසනම්(ආලිඞ්ගිත ලක්‍ෂ්මි)

2 (යා)[2] ලක්‍ෂණ[3] (වක්‍ෂ)[4] සථල භුවනපරාක්‍රම ශ්‍රීවාසුදෙව කණ්ඩළී[5] මූල (පූර්ත්ති භ)

3 .. ..

TRANSCRIPT.

1 Śrī samastha[6]-bhuvanāgra-pañca-śata-vīra-śāsanam-āli(ṅgita Lakṣmi-)

2 (-yā)[7] lakṣaṇa-(vakṣa-)[8] sthala bhuvana-parākrama Śrī-Vāsudeva-Kaṇḍaḷī[9] Mūla-(pūrtti-[10]bha-)

3 .. ..

TRANSLATION.

1 Hail! [They who have[11]] embraced the decree of the five hundred heroes foremost in the whole world;

2 [who possess] breasts with the characteristics of Lakṣmī; [who are] powerful on earth; [who are born in the races of] the illustrious Vāsudeva, Khaṇḍalī, Mūla-pūrtti[10]-bha-[dra].

3 .. ..

NOTES.

In certain Kanarese inscriptions of 1094 and 1150 A.D.,[12] as well as in those from Kolhāpūr, Miraj, and Mamdāpūr, dated 1135, 1142, and 1250 A.D. respectively, we find the foregoing titles expressed as follows:—

---

1 'සමස්ත' වියයුතුයි

2 'ලක්‍ෂ්මයා' වියයුතුයි

3 'ලක්‍ෂණාලක්‍ෂණ' යිදකියවියහැකියි

4 'වක්‍ෂස්' වියයුතුයි

5 'ඛණ්ඩළී' වියයුතුයි. 'කුණ්ඩළී' යිද කියවියහැකියි

6 Read *samasta.*

7 Read *lakṣmyā.* This may also be read *lakṣaṇālakṣaṇa,*

8 Read *vakṣas.*

9 Read *khaṇḍaḷī.* This can also be read *kuṇḍaḷī.*

10 This can also be read *pūrṇṇa.*

11 Lit. 'by whom the decree is embraced.

12 See *Ep. Carnat.* VII. 1. Sk. 94 and 118

A B C

Ânaulundâva Slab-Inscription.

Scale 2 inches to 1 foot.

From ink-impressions supplied by the Archaeological Survey, Ceylon.

Svasti samasta-bhuvana-vikhyāta-paṁca-śata-vīra-śāsana-labdhānēka-guṇa-gaṇālaṁkṛta satya-śaucācāra-cāru-cāritra-naya-vinaya-vijñāna Vīra-Baṇaṁja-dharmma-pratipāḷana-viśuddha guḍḍa-dhvaja-virājitānūna-sāhas-ōttuṁga kīrtty-aṁgan-āliṁgita nija-bhuja-vijaya-lakṣmī-nivāsa-vakṣa[s-]sthaḷa bhuvana-parākram-ōnnata Vāsudēva-Khaṇḍaḷī-Mūḷabhadra-vaṁśōdbhavaruṁ, &c. Dr. Barnett's translation runs:—

Hail! they who are adorned by a series of many virtues obtained by the decrees of the Five-hundred men renowned over the whole earth, possessing truthfulness, pure conduct, agreeable behaviour, policy, courtesy, and intelligence, pure in maintenance of the Vīra-Baṇañja religion, splendid with the banner (bearing the device) of a hill, exalted in abundant boldness, embraced by the lady Fame, having their breasts a home for the goddess of victory (won) by their own arms, lofty in prowess (extending) over the world, scions of the races of Vāsudeva, Khaṇḍaḷī, and Mūḷabhadra,' &c.

It is apparent from this that, according to Dr. Barnett, each of the titles in the above passage ends respectively in *guṇa-gaṇālaṅkṛta*, *vijñāna*, *viśuddha*, *virājita*, *sāhasōttuṅga*, *āliṅgita*, *vakṣas-sthaḷa*, *parākram-ōnnata*, and *vaṁśōdbha-varuṁ*. Mr. Rice's grouping of the words of each epithet is different, for example, the first ends in *vikhyāta*, 'famed in all the world'; the second in *labdha*, 'obtainers of five hundred *vīra-śāsanas*; the third in *alaṅkṛta*, 'adorned with clusters of many good qualities,' &c.

In our record we find *bhuvanāgra* in the place of *bhuvana-vikhyāta* and *śāsanam āliṅgita* in that of *śāsana-labdha*. The expression *śāsanam āliṅgita* points to the use of the past passive participle with an active meaning, which is not uncommon both in Sinhalese and in Dravidian languages. As *śāsanam* is in the singular number, *pañca-śata* seems to refer to *vīra*, although in Dravidian vernaculars the neuter singular may be used for the plural and Mr. Rice may, therefore, be correct in translating *pañca-śata-vīra-śāsana* by 'five-hundred vīra-śāsanas' instead of by the 'śāsana of the five-hundred heroes'. If he is right, we should follow him and treat *samasta-bhuvanāgra* as the first epithet, rendering it by '[they who are] foremost in the whole world'. The phrase *lakṣmyā lakṣaṇa-vakṣa*[*s-*]*sthala* corresponds to *lakṣmī-nivāsa-vakṣa*[*s-*] *sthaḷa* in the Mysore records, while the remaining titles in our record agree almost word for-word with the Indian ones.[1]

---

[1] These records are being edited by Dr. Barnett for the *Epigraphia Indica*.

39. POḶONNARUVA. POT-GUL VEHERA INSCRIPTION

THE so-called 'Pot-Gul Vehera' is the central shrine of a group of ruined buildings erected on raised sites within a quadrangular mound once held up by a brick rampart faced with elephant head decorations. It lies about a mile to the south of the ancient city of Poḷonnaruva, not far from the southern end of the Tōpa-väva bund[1]. In his annual report for 1906 (pp. 10–17), the late Archaeological Commissioner (Mr. H. C. P. Bell) has given a detailed and exhaustive description, as well as a plan, of the whole site. In order to make the contents of the present inscription more intelligible to our readers, we give here a reproduction of the plan[2] and quote the following passages from his account:—

'The sole means of access to the raised site upon which stand the structure, now styled "Pot-gul Vehera", and its annexes was up a perron stairway, with plain faced wing walls, footed by rough pavement.'

'On mounting to the precincts of the shrines it is seen that the temenos was slightly oblong, measuring 130 ft. from east to west by 112 ft. across north and south. It rose 7 ft. above the level of the inner quadrangle, which contains the *piriven* lying below.'

'Within the sacred temenos the same symmetry is again noticeable as in the arrangement of the flanking *piriven.*'

'Here are situated a central shrine "supported" by four diminutive *stúpas* at each corner of the quadrangular *peribole*, following the exact disposition of those quincunx coteries of a viháré and its four appurtenant *piriven* so familiar amid the ruins at Anurádhapura.'

'The four small ruined dágabas are of one size, 18 ft. in diameter, and were probably mere cenotaphs, added to appropriately balance, and set off, the important shrine located in the middle of the temenos.'

'And that shrine, unidentified but obviously mistermed "Pot-gul Vehera" was well worthy of such special honour. For this structure is perhaps unique in the ancient Buddhist architecture of Ceylon. Certainly no other ruin at all like it has been yet discovered in the Island.'

---

[1] See plan of Poḷonnaruva facing p. 84 above.

[2] See plate facing p. 240, below.

'Whatever uncertainty may exist as to the identification of the "Pot-gul Vehera" itself, there can hardly be any regarding the source of inspiration for the laying out of the Monastery as a whole on lines unique even at Poḷonaruwa, and markedly divergent from the nearest approximation discovered at Anurádhapura: viz. the Monasteries at Puliyamkuḷam (ancient "*Puvaram Vehera*" and Vijáyaráma.'

'The "Sat-mahal Prásádaya" is a standing witness to the adoption of modified Kambodian architecture for at least one structure at Poḷonnaruva.'

'Lithic record points to the "Kambodian quarter" of the old City probably lying to the south. What more natural than to find further evidence of Khmer influence in the isolated Monastery established a mile or more distant from the City enciente on this side.'

'The French savant Monsr. Tissandier has figured and described a Kambodian Monastery at *Mi Baume* in Siamese Kambodia, the design of which may be said to have been transplanted to Ceylon and reproduced, *mutatis mutandis*, on humbler lines in the "Pot-gul Vehera" monastery at Poḷonnaruwa.'

'Succinctly described, the edifice was in plan a rotunda, with an oblong vestibule attached on the east, from which was thrown out still further to the front a *maṇḍapaya*.'

'The *maṇḍapaya* (23 ft. by 21 ft. 4 in.), of which only the wall outline (2 ft. 9 in. thick) survives, was a *pergula*—an addition of later construction than the rest of the structure.'

'If we may hope to identify the so-called "Potgul Vehera" from the *Mahávaṇsa* record, it may not improbably have been that "delightful circular house" which, as the chronicle relates, Parákrama Báhu the Great (1164-1197 A.D.)[1] had constructed "wherein he might listen to the Játakas of the Great Sage, read by the learned priest, who dwelt there".'[2]

'Nameless though it be, it can be definitely classed among the *chef d'œuvres* of that monarch. For an inscribed door jamb of the *maṇḍapaya*, falling and lying *perdu*, sheds valuable light on the history of this Monastery.'

'In twenty-six[3] lines of clear-cut letters of the twelfth century[4] is a record in **Páli** of its original construction by Parákrama-Báhu I, and its rebuilding and improvement by his two queens.'

After this clear account, it remains for us only to give here a revised text

---

[1] More correctly 1153-1186 A.D. See above, p. 207.

[2] *Mv.* lxxiii. 72.

[3] More correctly twenty-five.

[4] See Plate 34.

and translation of the inscription published for the first time in Mr. Bell's report for 1906.

There are twenty-five lines, each consisting of four to five **akṣaras** about an inch in size engraved within ruled lines two inches apart. The **language** is Pāli as stated above and the composition is metrical, the whole inscription being framed in three *ślokas* or *gāthās*, each consisting of two sixteen-syllable lines. The end of the first *śloka* is shown by the mark ⸸ and that of the second by □.

As regards the **subject-matter,** we see from the expression *jinānattiṁ visodhayi* a definite allusion to the Buddhist Convocation held by Parakkama-Bāhu I in his fourth regnal year, namely in 1165 A.D.[1] So the **date** of our record must be later than this year and indeed it should be placed after Parakkama-Bāhu's death, in or shortly after the first reign of his queen-dowager **Lilāvatī** (1197–1200 A.D.)[2]. The expression *rajje ṭhitā* makes this quite clear[3]. Further, there is the statement that **Candavatī,** the second chief queen of the late king, caused the erection of the *Maṇḍapa* mentioned above. From the context it seems that this work was done after the rebuilding of the vihāra by Līlāvatī. Thus the *maṇḍapa* was a later addition, and as the inscription is on a pillar which formed one of the door jambs of this structure, it may have been put up there by order of Candavatī. We agree with Mr. Bell in identifying her with Parakkama-Bāhu's second queen **Rūpavatī,** who 'was adorned with the ornament of many virtues, as faith, piety, and such like, who was skilled in dancing and music and was richly endued with a mind as keen as the point of the blade of a Kusa grass.' It was she who 'caused the great golden Thūpa to be built in the midst of the City.'[4]

TEXT.

1	ලංකාධිනා	9	පරකකම
2	ථො සො ධීරො	10	නරිඥසස
3	ජිනාණතති[ං]	11	මහෙසි ත
4	විසොධයි	12	සස ඪිම
5	පඨමං කාරි	13	තො රජෙජ
6	තානෙතත	14	ඨිතා සා කා
7	විහාරං සක	15	රෙසි විහා
8	ලං ඉමං ⸸	16	රං සකල

[1] See above, p. 205. [2] See *E. Z.*, Vol. I, p. 178.

[3] The Archaeological Commissioner (Mr. Hocart) inclines to think that *dutiyaṁ aggataṁ* may mean 'second sovereignty' or 'the sovereignty for a second time' and may refer to Līlāvatī as ruling queen for the second time in 1209 A.D.

[4] For a panygyric on this lady, see *Mv.* lxxiii, 136–147.

Potgul-vehera inscription.

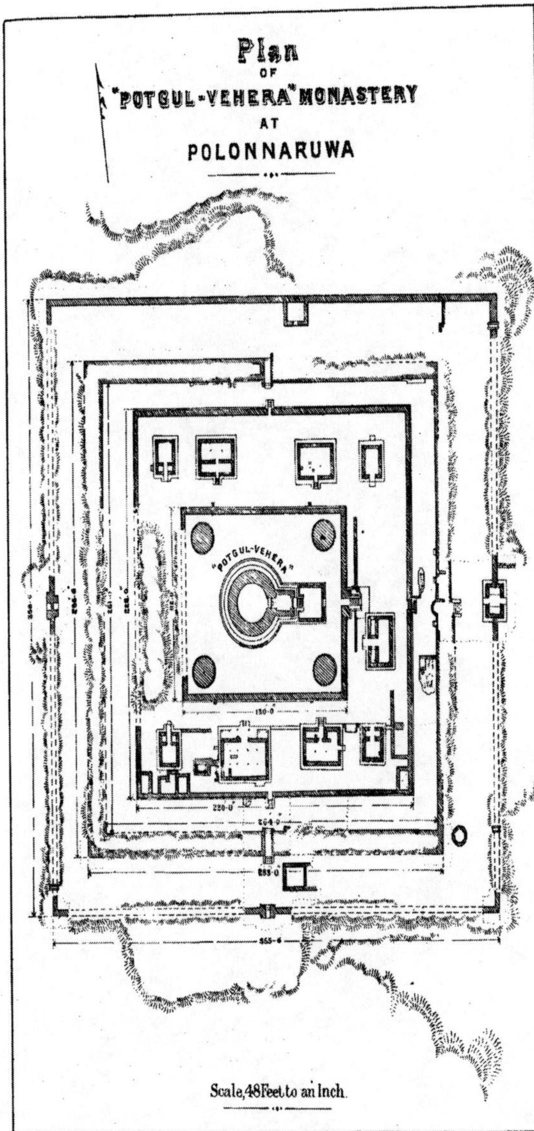

17 ම්පුන □

18 තසෙස

19 ව නරදෙව

20 ස්ස දුති

21 යං යා අග්ග

22 තං ගතා සා රා

23 ජිනී චන්ද

24 වතී තාය කා

25 රිතමඩපො[1]

TRANSCRIPT.

1 Laṁkā-dhinā-

2 -tho so dhīro

3 Jināṇatti[ṁ]

4 visōdhayi [।]

5 paṭhamaṁ kāri-

6 -tan tena

7 vihāraṁ saka-

8 -laṁ imaṁ ✻ [॥]

9 **Parakkama-**

10 **narindassa**

11 mahesī ta-

12 -ssa dhīma-

13 -to rajje

14 ṭhitā sā kā-

15 -resi vihā-

16 -raṁ sakala-

17 -m puna □ [॥]

18 tass' e-

19 -va ñara-deva-

20 -ssa duti-

21 -yaṁ yā agga-

22 -taṁ gatā sā rā-

23 -jinī **Canda-**

24 **-vatī** tāya kā-

25 -rita-maṇḍapo [2]

TRANSLATION.

[Lines 1–4] The doughty over-lord of Laṅkā purified the [vinaya] precepts of the Victorious One (the Buddha).

[Lines 5–8] By him this entire vihāra was first caused to be built.

[Lines 9–17] The Queen (**Mahesī**) of that wise king **Parakkama,** having been installed in the kingdom, caused the entire vihāra to be rebuilt.

[Lines 18–25] She who has attained to the position of second head [queen] of that very king [is] **Rājinī** [3] **Candavatī.** By her the **maṇḍapa** was caused to be built.

---

[1] 'කාරිතො මඩපො' වියයුතුයි. [2] For *kārito maṇḍapo.*

[3] This is the title of the sub-queen, that of the chief queen being *mahesī.* See *E.Z.*, Vol. I, p. 26, note 9, and p. 49, note 7.

No. 40. (Reg. No. 2.) POḶONNARUVA: SLAB-INSCRIPTION OF THE VĒḶĀIKKĀṞAS (*circa* 1137–1153 A.D.)

THE present inscription was, we believe, brought to public notice for the first time by Mr. H. C. P. Bell in his Annual Report of the Ceylon Archaeological Survey for 1903 (p. 11). His words are: 'To the west of Viháre No. 2[1], close to its basement is lying prone a fine slab of granite (9ft. 6 in. by 2 ft. 9 in.), on which are cut, inside beaded framing, forty-four lines of writing in Tamil and Grantha characters, besides five more lines at the head. Below are carved a pair of vases in *messo relievo.* But this inscription has no connection whatever with the present viháre.' The appendix to this report contains a provisional translation of the record by Mudaliyar R. C. Kailāsa Piḷḷäi with Mr. Bell's historical introduction. His Annual Report for 1911–1912 (appendix, E), furnishes us with a complete text and an improved translation with explanatory notes contributed by Rao Sahib H. Krishṇa Śāstri Avargaḷ. We have, moreover, before us two fairly good ink-estampages supplied by the Archaeological Commissioner (Mr. Hocart), and a photographic plate published in Mr. Bell's report. These form the material utilized in the preparation of the present edition and translation of the record which has now been framed with cement and plăced *in situ* near vihāra No. 1 in Poḷonnaruva Quadrangle.

As Mr. Bell says, the inscription consists of forty-nine lines clearly incised between ruled lines, two inches apart, and covering an area of 2 ft. 9 in. by 8 ft. of the smoothed surface of the slab. Its characters are one to two inches in size each, and belong to a mixed alphabet of a period between the tenth and the fourteenth centuries A.D. The following table, which we have prepared for easy reference and for the benefit of Ceylon students, will show the form of character and the particular alphabet to which each letter belongs; T. being the abbreviation for Tamil, G. for Grantha, and S. for Sinhalese. Owing to this mixed nature of the script we are obliged to adopt a slight modification in the transliteration of the sibilant letters as indicated below, which will be adhered to in the future.

T. அ a (ll. 7, 10, 18, 33, 37), ஆ ā (l. 21).
T. அ a̤ (ll. 9, 22, 28, 35).
G. 𑌅 a (l. 18).
T. இ i (l. 13), இ i (ll. 34, 39, 44).

---

[1] See plan of Poḷonnaruva, facing p. 84 above.

G. ഇ i (l. 6).
T. உ u (ll. 19, 24, 26), ஊ ū (l. 35).
T. எ e (ll. 14, 17, 27, 28, 29, 32).
T. ஐ ai (l. 13).
T. ஒ o (ll. 13, 33, 34).
S. க் k (l. 3), க ka (l. 25), கா kā (l. 2), கி ki (l. 18), கு ku (ll. 6, 24).
T. க் k (l. 8), க ka (ll. 7, 10, 20, 21, 28, 29), கா kā (l. 12), கு ku (ll. 8, 12, 19),
கூ kū (ll. 29, 30), கை kai (ll. 13, 41), கொ ko (l. 15).
G. S. ഗ ga (ll. 24, 27) ഗി gi (l. 18), ഗു gu (l. 26), ഗൃ gṛ (l. 21).
G. ഘ gha (ll. 9, 11, 15).
T. ங் ṅ (ll. 10, 13, 21, 28).
G. ച ca (l. 15), ചാ cā (l. 26).
T. ச śa, see after ça.
G. ജ ja (ll. 2, 7, 16, 17, 26), ജാ jā (l. 27).
T. ஞ ñ ஞ் (ll. 13, 14, 15, 19, 23, 29), ஞா ñā (l. 38).
G. ടി ṭi (l. 24).
T. ட ḍa (l. 27), டா ḍā (l. 35) டி ḍi (ll. 8, 9, 30), டு ḍu (ll. 12, 13, 17, 21, 25),
டை ḍai (l. 13).
T. ண் ṇ (l. 7, 14), ண ṇa (l. 9), ணா ṇā (l. 23), ணி ṇi (l. 7), ணீ ṇī (l. 26),
ணு ṇu (l. 11).
G. S. T. த் t (ll. 6, 10, 11, 12, 14), த ta (ll. 16, 18, 19, 28), தா tā (ll. 9,
12), தி ti (ll. 9, 22), து tu (ll. 1, 21, 26, 28), தெ te (ll. 16, 20),
தை tai (l. 29), தொ to (l. 19).
G. ഥ tha (l. 21).
G. S. ദ da (ll. 1, 12, 20), ദാ dā (ll. 20, 24), ദി di (l. 2) ദെ de (ll. 16, 24).
G. S. ധ dha (l. 8), ധാ dhā (ll. 1, 20), ധി dhi (ll. 2, 15).
G. S. T. ന് n (ll. 22, 27), ന na (ll. 14, 17, 18), നാ nā (l. 32), നി ni (ll. 9,
10, 12, 13, 20, 22), നെ ne (l. 7).
T. நு nu (ll. 7, 16).
G. പ pa (ll. 5, 6), പാ pā (l. 20), പു pu (l. 3), പൊ po (l. 2).
T. ப் p (ll. 10, 17, 24), ப pa (l. 7), பி pi (ll. 10, 18), பெ pe (l. 24).
G. ബാ bā (l. 16), ബു bu (ll. 23, 48), ബൊ bo (l. 15).
G. ഭ bha (ll. 1, 18, 20), ഭാ bhā (l. 11), ഭി bhi (l. 21).
G. S. മ ma (ll. 3, 18, 27), മാ mā (ll. 21, 27), മി mi (l. 20).

T. ம் m (l. 24), ம ma (l. 9), மா mā (ll. 21, 45), மு mu (ll. 13, 26), மூ mū, (ll. 11, 14, 18, 19, 26, 29), மை mai (l. 28).

G. ய் y (ll. 13, 23, 31), ய ya (ll. 7, 16, 18, 22, 23), யா yā (l. 13, 20, 25), யி yi (ll. 19, 26), யு yu (ll. 23, 29), யொ yo (l. 9).

G. S. ர ra (ll. 8, 26), ரா rā (ll. 2, 12, 26, 27), ரி ri (l. 18), ரூ rū (l. 26), ரெ re (l. 3), ரை rai (ll. 10, 29).

T. ர் r (ll. 16, 20, 24), ரி ri (l. 26), ரு ru (ll. 9, 14, 19, 22, 24, 26, 28), ரொ ro (l. 27).

T. ற் ṟ (l. 14), ற ṟa (l. 3), றி ṟi (l. 14), று ṟu (ll. 11, 12, 22, 25).

G. ல la (ll. 1, 3, 23, 25), லா lā (ll. 23, 25).

T. ல் l (ll. 9, 12, 16, 19, 28), ல la (ll. 13, 18, 19, 21, 23, 27), லு lu (l. 15).

G. T. வ va (ll. 6, 16, 20), வி vi (ll. 11, 18, 27), வெ ve (l. 4, 25).

G. ça (ll. 6, 7, 12), çā (ll. 8, 25), çi (l. 23), çī (l. 25).

T. ஶ் ś (l. 28), ஶ śa (ll. 10, 22), ஶி śi (l. 19), ஶெ śe (ll. 14, 15, 16, 28, 29), ஶூ śū (l. 9).

G. ṣe (l. 21).

G. sa (ll. 25, 26), sū (l. 6).

G. ha (l. 21), hā (ll. 18, 23, 27) hu (l. 16).

G. ḷa (l. 20, 31), ḷai (l. 3).

T. ள் ḷ (ll. 16, 24, 29), ள ḷa (ll. 19, 26, 29), ளா ḷā (l. 29), ளி ḷi (ll. 14, 24, 27, 28), ளு ḷu (ll. 20, 29), ளை ḷai (ll. 19, 26, 28, 31), ளொ ḷo (l. 30).

T. ழ ḻa (l. 13), ழி ḻi (l. 7), ழு ḻu (ll. 13, 14, 27), ழை ḻai (ll. 10, 28).

T. ன் ṉ (ll. 10, 11, 12, 25), ன ṉa (ll. 15, 16, 17, 19, 21, 22, 26), னை ṉai (l. 38).

G. ஃ ḥ (visarga).

G. ௦ ṁ (anusvāra) vaṁ (l. 6), naṁ (l. 1), saṁ (ll. 11, 15), maṁ (l. 23).

Combined consonants.

G. S. க்ஷ kṣa (ll. 15, 22, 25), க்ஷி kṣi (l. 8), kṣvā (l. 6).

G. grā (l. 18).

G. jya (l. 14), ñca (l. 46).

T. ட்டா ḍḍā (l. 21).

G. S. T. த்த tta (ll. 13, 18), த்தா ttā (l. 10), த்தி tti (l. 15) tya (l. 20), tra (l. 15).

G. 𑌦𑍍𑌧 ddha (l. 23), 𑌦𑍍𑌧𑌾 ddhā (l. 5), 𑌦𑍍𑌧𑌿 ddhi (l. 11), 𑌨𑍍𑌧 ndha (l. 24), 𑌨𑍍𑌧𑍇 ndhe (l. 5).

G. 𑌨𑍍𑌤 nta (l. 7).

G. 𑌰𑍍𑌭𑍁 rbhu (l. 5).

G. 𑌮𑍍𑌪 mpa (l. 26), 𑌰𑍍𑌮𑍍𑌮 rmma (l. 12), 𑌰𑍍𑌮 rma (l. 15).

G. 𑌰𑍍𑌯𑍍𑌯 ryya (l. 6).

G. 𑌵𑍍𑌯𑌾 vyā (l. 26).

G. 𑌶𑍍𑌰𑍀 çrī (ll. 1, 2).

G. 𑌰𑍍𑌷𑍀 rṣī (l. 2).

G. 𑌸𑍍𑌵𑌾 svā (l. 20), 𑌸𑍍𑌤𑍍𑌰𑌾 strā (l. 25), 𑌸𑍍𑌤𑌿 sti (l. 1), 𑌸𑍍𑌥 stha (l. 27), 𑌸𑍍𑌥𑌾 sthā (l. 18).

The **types** shown in the foregoing list are, it is true, not unknown to South-Indian inscriptions. The *virāma* is represented by a short vertical stroke over the letters as in the Tamil portion of the Kūram Pallava grant[1] and in the pillar inscription of Rājasiṁha-varmeçvara shrine[2], where the later sign, the *puḷḷi* or the dot over the consonant, also occurs five times. Here the vertical *virāma* has a close resemblance to the initial *r* in ligatures, which in Indian inscriptions is shown by a wedge[3] or by an angle or curve open to the right. The medial *ai* is indicated by 𑍈 and ை: the former follows the Grantha form in having the two signs placed one above the other, instead of one behind the other as in Rājarāja's Tañjāvūr inscription[4], while the latter is probably an advanced form. We find, however, all these four varieties in South-Indian inscriptions from the tenth to the twelfth centuries[5], A.D. Attention may also be drawn to the close similarity between *gṛ* and *gra*, *ṅa* and *nu*, *bha* and *ha*, as well as between *mu* and *ḻu*. The anusvāra is engraved on the right side of the akṣara except in the case of the syllable *saṁ*, where the older method of marking it above the letter is retained. No distinction is shown between the short and long forms of *e* and *o*.

As regards **orthography**, it is more or less a peculiarity of Tamil inscriptions to use indiscriminately Grantha letters side by side with those of Tamil. We

---

[1] *S. I. I.* vol. i, p. 147.

[2] *Ibid.* p. 113. Sometimes the vertical *virāma* assumes a zigzag shape (Vēlūrpālaiyam plate, *S. I. I.*, vol. ii, No. 78.)

[3] See also the Jetavanārāma Sanskrit inscription (*E. Z.*, Vol. I, No. 1).

[4] *S. I. I.*, vol. iii, No. 1.

[5] *Ibid.*, Nos. 12 and 18.

find Sanskrit words and even pure Tamil words written in a mixture of Grantha and Tamil characters: for example, in our inscription the words *maṅgala*, *dēvar*, and *saṁgha* follow in some places (ll. 10, 20, and 21) the Tamil spelling and in other places the Grantha spelling. *Kuḍuttu* (ll. 12 and 34), is for *koḍuttu*, a spelling more often found in Kanarese and Malayāḷam languages. *Arumaṇa* (l. 9), for Sinh. *Aramaṇa*, P. *Rāmañña*; *aiñpattayyāṇḍu* (l. 13), for *aimpattayyāṇḍu*; *Nuvara-kal* (l. 16), probably for Sinh. *Nuvara-gala*, P. *Nagara-giri*; *daḷadā* (l. 20) Sinh. for P. *dāṭhādhātu*; *vyāriṇī* (l. 26), probably a Sinh. derivative from a Sanskrit form *vyākaraṇin*[1] (or *-ṇika* or *-ṇiya*); *Mugalan* (ll. 26–27), Sinh. for P. *Moggallāna*.

The **language** is Tamil with an introductory Sanskrit verse in *Çārdūla-vikrīḍita* metre usually employed in records of this class both in South India[2] and in Ceylon. Its **style,** however, cannot be called *maṇippiravāḷam*, for it is devoid of those bombastic expressions replete with Sanskrit *tatsamas* that are found in some of the Kanarese records of about this period, namely the twelfth century A. D. The reason why our record is written in Tamil, though with traces of the influence of Sanskritic construction, is quite obvious from the fact that it is an agreement entered into with the Tamil speaking Vēḷaikkāṟa community.

As regards the **contents,** the inscription may be divided into two parts. The first part is the introduction. It gives us the information that King **Çrī Saṅgha-Bodhi Varmar** *alias* Emperor **Çrī Vijaya-Bāhu-Devar** was a descendant of the Ikṣvāku family; that he overcame many enemies and entered Anurādhapura; that, at the request of the Buddhist clergy to protect the Buddhist church, he put on the crown; that he invited Buddhist monks from Aramaṇa and had the three nikāyas of the Buddhist church purified; that he made *tulā-bhāra* gifts to the three nikāyas, reigned over the whole of Ceylon for fifty-five years and celebrated seventy-three birthday festivals; that under his orders **Nuvarakal Deva-Senevirattar**[3] built the great temple of the Tooth-relic[4] in **Vijayarāja-puram,** otherwise called **Pulanari**[5], as a permanent repository for the Tooth and the Bowl-relics of the Buddha which were originally at Uttoruḷa-mūḷa[6], the chief fane of the Abhayagiri Mahāvihāra; that this Tooth-relic temple was also the auspicious house for the first anointment ceremony and that it is [now

---

[1] Cf. Skt. *vyākaraṇa*, Sinh. *viyaraṇa*.

[2] See *S. I. I.*, vol. i, Nos. 75 and 76.

[3] P. *Nagaragiri Deva-Senāpati.*

[4] *Daḷadāy-p-perum-paḷḷi.*

[5] *Poḷonnaruva* or *Pulastipura.*

[6] See *Mv.* xxxvii. 46, 47.

utilized also as] the Hall of Fragrance[1] for the auspicious and colossal stone statue of the Buddha, in which is held every year the ceremony of loosening the sacred eyes (of the statue) and of applying collyrian to them.

The charitable acts of Vijaya-Bāhu I dealt with here are related in detail in the *Mahāvaṁsa*[2] also, although the minister **Nagaragiri Deva Senāpati** who built the Tooth-relic temple is not mentioned by name.

The second part, or inscription proper, contains no date or any expression indicating that the compact set forth therein was entered into in pursuance of royal command. In fact we may infer from the context that owing to the disturbed state of the country Moggallāna Mahāthera in association with certain ministers of the State, whose names are not given, entrusted the Vēḷäikkāṟa community, who were then in the zenith of their power, with the entire custody of the Sacred Tooth-relic Temple, built (probably some twenty or thirty years before) by Deva Senāpati under the orders of Vijaya-Bāhu I (1058–1114 A.D.). The independent spirit of the Vēḷäikkāṟas may be gauged by the fact that on undertaking the control of the shrine they called it 'the great temple of the Tooth-relic, belonging to the illustrious Vēḷäikkāṟa (army) of the three divisions'[3] and regarded it as their own charitable institution under their entire support. So they assigned to it lands, guards, &c., for its maintenance. They further declared that any act conducive to an infringement of this contract would be held as an offence against the Vēḷäikkāṟas and the Mahā-Tantra as well as against the Buddhist church.

In this connexion we must bear in mind that since the capture of Mahinda V in 1017–1018 A. D.[4], the expeditionary forces of Rājēndra Coḷa I, among whom were Vēḷäikkāṟas[5], held sway in the northern half of Ceylon. Even before Mahinda's capture, Anurādhapura was overrun by people of divers races[6], among whom the Keraḷas (i. e. the Maläiyāḷar of the present record) and the Kaṇṇāṭas who were no doubt the Vaḷañjiyar and the Nagarattār (leading sects of the Vēḷäikkāṟa community), 'exercised full authority at that time in other parts of the Island'[7]. It was only after fifty-five years[8], namely in 1073 A. D., that they were brought to some sort of subjection by Vijaya-Bāhu I.

---

[1] *Gandhakuṭi* (line 24).
[2] See ch. lx. 4–8, and 16–23, and above, pp. 208 ff.
[3] *Mūṉṟu-kai*, for an explanation of this term, see below p. 251.
[4] See above, p. 208.
[5] *Annual Report on South-Indian Epigraphy* 1913, p. 102.
[6] *Mv.* lv. 2.
[7] *Mv.* lv. 12.
[8] See above, p. 208.

Nevertheless, the Vēḷāikkāṟas remained a powerful and wealthy community for a long time after. In the thirtieth year of Vijaya-Bāhu's reign, when they were asked to go to war against their kinsmen, the Coḷas, they 'rebelled like unto furious elephants . . . . took the city of Pulatthi; they also took the king's sister captive with her three sons, and burnt the king's palace'[1]. The rebellion was, however, immediately quelled by the king's forces. Still they continued to be a power to be reckoned with, for we read in the *Mahāvaṁsa* that about thirty-five years later in the reign of Gaja-Bāhu II (1137–1153 A.D.), they were bribed to rise against the King[2]. Even during the powerful rule of his successor Parakkama-Bāhu I (1153–1186 A.D.), they raised a rebellion in which they lost many of their leaders and much of their landed property[3]. That they possessed wealth and made benefactions to temples about this period may be inferred from the Ānaulundāva slab-inscription dealt with above[4], as well as from the contents of the present record.

In addition to all these facts supporting our opinion that the **date** of this inscription should be placed in the reign either of Vikkama-Bāhu (1116–1137 A.D.) or of his son Gaja-Bāhu II (1137–1153), about twenty to thirty years after the death of Vijaya-Bāhu I in 1114, there is the name **Moggallāna Mahā-thera** of **Uturuḷa-mūḷāi**[5] as the dignitary who represented the Buddhist church in the compact. He is described there as a Rāja-guru and grammarian, well known for his profound learning and saintly conduct. Among the elders of the Buddhist church who lived about this period (twelfth century A.D.), and to whom the foregoing description may be applicable, four bearing the name Moggallāna are known to the literary history of Ceylon, namely:

(1) Moggallāna Mahā-thera, author of the Pāli grammar *Moggallāna Vyākaraṇa* (Sinh. *Mugalan-viyaraṇa*), with its *vutti* and *pañcikā* (or *pañjikā*). The late Dhammārāma Thera in his introduction[6] to the printed edition of the Moggallāna Pañcikā-pradīpa says that this Moggallāna Thera took part in

---

[1] *Mv.* lx. 36–39. [2] *Ibid.*, lxiii. 24–30. [3] *Ibid.*, lxxiv. 44–50. [4] No. 38.

[5] *Sakala çāstrāgama çīlācāra-sampannar-āṉa rāja-guru Uturuḷa-mūḷāiyil vyāriṇī Mugalan-mahā-sthavirar.* We take *vyāriṇī* as a derivative of a Sanskrit form *vyākaraṇin* (or *-ṇika*, or *-ṇiya*), equivalent to *veyyākaraṇa* grammarian, just as Skt. *vyākaraṇa* > Sinh. *viyaraṇa*. *Mugalan* is, of course, the Sinh. form of P. *Moggallāna*. The syntax, though somewhat loose, yet agrees with that of the phrase *Abhayagiri Mahāvihāra.tu agrāyatanam-āṉa Uttoruḷa-Mūḷāiyil mū-v-ulakukkuñ śikāmaṇi-y-ākiya*, &c. The Uttoruḷa monastery might have been the one built by king Mānavamma (670–705 A.D.) at Abhayagiri for the use of his brother (*Mv.* lvii. 20).

[6] P. xiv.

upholding the Buddhist church either as a pupil or as a colleague of Dimbulāgala (Udumbaragiri) Mahā-Kassapa Saṅgharāja, who presided over the Buddhist synod held at Poḷonnaruva in 1165 A. D., the fourth[1] regnal year of Parakkama-Bāhu I, and that he might have written his Pāli grammar when he was residing in the Thūpārāma monastery at Anurādhapura.

(2) Moggallāna-Thera, the author of the Vinaya-gaṇṭhipadam who lived in the time of king Parakkama-Bāhu[2].

(3) Moggallāna-Thera who compiled the Abhidhānappadīpikā under the patronage of Parakkama-Bāhu I, dwelling amongst the Sirogāma (Vilgam-mūḷa) fraternity in the Jetavana-vihāra built by this king[3].

(4) Moggallāna-Thera, who, according to the *Mahāvaṁsa*[4], attended the Buddhist Council from the country of the Yuva-rāja.

Of these we are inclined to identify No. 1 with the Rāja-guru Mugalan Mahāsthavira of our record, for both were grammarians and were profoundly learned. At one time, we are told, they lived in Anurādhapura, one in the Uturuḷamūḷa monastery of the Abhayagiri, and the other in the Thūpārāma, probably then allied to the Abhayagiri fraternity. Further, Moggallāna No. 1 seems to have been at the time of the synod an elderly dignitary well versed in the Vinaya or he could not have been an assistant to Mahā Kassapa, the President. He may most probably have written the Pāli grammar at Anurādhapura before he came to Poḷonnaruva. Let us then suppose that our Moggallāna was one of those young sāmaṇeras whom Vijaya-Bāhu I patronized during the last days of his reign (1058–1114 A.D.). He need not have been more than thirty-five years old when Vikkama-Bāhu I died in 1137 and may have by that time already become an author. So when Parakkama-Bāhu I held the Buddhist Council twenty-eight years later in 1165, Moggallāna might have been a venerable monk of high reputation. It was, therefore, not surprising that he was elected to assist Mahā-Kassapa who was perhaps slightly his senior.

If these facts and inferences establish the identity of Moggallāna of the present inscription with Moggallāna No. 1, we can go a step further and identify with this personage the Moggallāna (No. 4) who attended the Council

---

[1] See above, pp. 205–206.

[2] Atha mahātherehi saṁgharājapamukhehi tasmiṁ gandhe pi dassite Vinayagaṇṭhipadaṁ Sīhaḷadīpe Parakkamabāhu-rañño kāle Moggallāna-thero akāsī ti āgataṁ, na Cūlagaṇṭhipadaṁ Sīhaḷadīpe Anurādhapurassa dakkhiṇadisābhāge Pokkantigāme arahā Moggallāna-thero akāsī ti. Bode's ed. of *Sāsanavaṁsa* p. 136.

[3] See the colophon to the *Abhidhānappadīpikā*.

[4] *Mv.* lxxviii. 9.

from the Yuvarāja's country. It is conceivable that between 1137 and 1153 A. D., that is to say, either at the end of Vikkama-Bāhu's reign, or at the beginning of that of his son Gaja-Bāhu, both of whom were no friends of the Buddhist church, Moggallāna, fearing that the king might lay his devastating hands on the rich Tooth-relic temple, then containing the Tooth- and Bowl-relics that were originally at Moggallāna's own Uttaroḷa Vihāra, at Abhayagiri, prevailed upon the powerful Vēḷāikkāṟas to take over the full custody of the temple and fled southward to Rohaṇa or the Yuvarāja's country. The *Mahāvaṁsa* also lends colour to this view, for we gather from it that the Paṁsukūlika brethren took away the relics to Rohaṇa, and that they were there until recovered by Parakkama-Bāhu I[1]. Moggallāna may have returned to Poḷonnaruva on the invitation of this king to take part in the purification of the Buddhist religion.

There now remain two Moggallānas, No. 2, the author of the Vinaya-gaṇṭhipada, and No. 3, the compiler of the Abhidhānappadīpikā, to be accounted for. They were contemporaries, and seem to us to refer to one and the same person; while there is so far no evidence to establish their identity either with No. 1 or with the Mugalan of the inscription, although they all lived during the reign of Parakkama-Bāhu I (1153–1186 A. D.)

The present record has hitherto been taken as one of Vijaya-Bāhu I (1058–1114 A. D.), but the foregoing discussion compels us to call it an inscription of the Vēḷāikkāṟa community and to assign to it a date between 1137 and 1153 A.D., this being fully supported by palaeographic evidence.

As regards the Vēḷāikkāṟas, it is, of course, incorrect to call them a 'community of working classes'[2]; besides, the word is spelt வேளைக்காறர் (with the lingual ḷ and the hard ṟ), and not வேலைக்காரர் (labourers). Although the etymology of the term is still obscure, proof is not wanting as to the power and social position of this clan. Fourteen regiments of the army of Rājendra Coḷa I were composed of these Vēḷāikkāṟas of the right-hand (*valaṅ-kai*) sect[3]. We see from the present record that there were also Vēḷāikkāṟas of the left-hand (*iḍaṅ-kai*) division[4]. Their leaders were the Nagarattār and the Valañjiyar

---

[1] See *Mv.* lxi. 54–62, and lxxiv. 160–162, 185–186.

[2] *South-Indian Epigraphy, Annual Report*, 1913, p. 102.

[3] See *S. I. I.*, vol. ii, Introd., pp. 9–10.

[4] For detailed information on these two sects, see *Madras Manual of Administration*, vol. iii, p. 1036 ff. Thurston's *Ethnographic Notes on Southern India*, p. 48. In the Sinhalese semi-religious game of 'horn-pulling' (*aṁ-ädīma*), there are two parties, the *uḍu-pila* and the *yaṭi-pila*. Families

who figure also in the Ānaulundāva record. Their present representatives are the Nagartta and the Baṇajiga communities of the Kanarese country.

At the time of our record the Vēḷāikāṟas were adherents of the *Mahātantra* which was not a Buddhist sect as has been suggested, but a form of Çaiva-darçana [1]. Whether the term *mūṉṟu-kai* refers to the triple principle, namely, *Çiva-Çakti-Aṇu* or *Pati-pāça-paçu* corresponding to *trika* of Cashmere Çaivaism [2], or it is only an epithet of the Vēḷāikkāṟas [3] due possibly to their army being composed of three wings, we are unable at present to say. In the inscription, however, more than three classes of Vēḷāikkāṟas are mentioned with Valañceyar and Nagarattār as leaders. They are:—(*a*) Valaṅ-kai, (*b*) Iḍaṅ-kai, (*c*) Śiṟu-taṉam, (*d*) Piḷḷäikaḷ-taṉam, (*e*) Vaḍukar, (*f*) Maläiyāḷar, (*g*) Parivāra-k-kontam, and (*h*) Palakalaṉäi. Of these *a* and *b* may be taken as attributes of the names that follow, while *c* and *d*, as well as the term Peruntaṉam occurring in Tanjore records, might probably be only honorary titles [4] as suggested by Rao Sāhib Krishṇa Śāstri Avargaḷ [5]. Similarly, the others, too, might be distinctive names of regiments [6] that once composed the expeditionary forces of the Coḷa kings.

for generations belong either to the one or to the other. Can this be a survival of the South-Indian *valaṅ-kai* and *iḍaṅ-kai* divisions, both these distinctions being observed, more or less, in ceremonies connected with Durgā worship?

[1] Sarvadarçana-saṅgraha defines it as follows:

Tripadārthaṁ catuṣpādaṁ **Mahātantraṁ** *jagad-guruḥ* |
sūtreṇaikena saṁkṣipya prāha vistarataḥ punaḥ ||

[2] See Chatterji's *Kashmir Shaivaism*, and Schomerus' *Der Çaiva-Siddhānta*, pp. 104–143.

[3] Since writing the above, I have been favoured with a copy of Mudaliyar Rasanayagam's article (unpublished, I believe), on the present record. Touching the Vēḷāikkāṟas, he says: 'The late Mr. T. A. Gopinath Row has, in a learned article contributed to the Sen Tamil (vol. xvi, pp. 134–143), cleared the ground for the elucidation of the term. From time immemorial it was a custom in India, and perhaps in Ceylon too, for loyal and faithful servants who failed to carry out the orders of their king or of their master, to kill themselves, and it was not uncommon for kings to have soldiers who took the oath (*vañciṉam*) that they would do away with their lives if any misfortune befell the king. . . . These were called Vēḷāikkāṟas. The acts of self-sacrifice committed by these Vēḷaikkāṟas are known not only from Tamil classics but also from inscriptions and sculptures.'

[4] Cf. *Śiṟu-taṉattu Vaḍukakkālavar* and *Peruntaṉattu Valaṅkai Vēḷāikkāṟappaḍäikaḷ*, these being names of two of the regiments of Rājendra Coḷa I. (*S. I. I.*, vol. ii, Introd. p. 9).

[5] Cf. *S. I. E.*, *Annual Report*, 1913, p. 97.

[6] Cf. *Parivārameykāpparkaḷ* and *Palavakai-Paṟam-paḍaikaḷilār*, *S. I. I.*, vol. ii, Introd. p. 9).

TRANSCRIPT.

1 Ṣvasti Çrīḥ | Laṁkāyāṁ Jina-danta-dhātu-bhavanaṁ yad **Deva-**
2 **Senādhipo** 'kārṣīt **Çrī Vijayādi-Bāhu**-nṛvarādeç[ā-]
3 -t Pulasteḥ pure [1] **Veḷaikkāṟa**-samā(hitā)n tad api ta-
4 -t-paryyanta-devālayān Veḷaikkāṟa-balāni pā-[1]
5 -ntu nitarām[2] ākalpa-sandher bhuvi [||] Namo Buddhāya
6 Çrī Laṁkādvīpattu Sūryya-vaṁçattu Ikṣvākuvi-
7 -n vaḷi vanta aneka çatrūn vijayam paṇṇi Anurā-
8 -dha-puram pukku Buddha-çāsanaṁ rakṣikka veṇḍi sa-
9 -ṁgha-niyogattāl tiru-muḍi śūḍi **Arumaṇattil** ni-
10 -ṉṟum śaṅkattārai aḷaippittu mūṉṟu nikāya-
11 -ttu saṁgha çuddhi paṇṇuvittu mūṉṟu tulābhāram
12 mūṉṟu nikāyattukku kuḍuttu daça-rāja-dharmmattāl
13 aiñpattayyāṇḍu Ilaṅkāi muḻutum oru kuḍāi niḻa-
14 -ṟṟi-t-tiru-virājyañ śeyt 'aruḷi eḻupattu mū-v-āṇḍu tiru na-
15 -kṣattrañ śeluttiṉa ko **Çrī Saṁgha-Bodhi-varmar**-āṉa cakravartti-
16 -kaḷ **Çrī Vijaya-Bāhu-Devar Nuvarakal Te[va]śeṉavirattar-**
17 **-kku** niyokittu-p-Pulanari-y-āṉa Vijayarāja-purattu eḍup-
18 -pitta mūla-sthānam-ākiya Abhayagiri Mahā-vihārattu Agrā=
19 =yatanam-āṉa Uttoruḷa-mūḷaiyil mū-v-ulakukkuñ śikāmaṇi-
20 -y-ākiya Daḷadā-Pātra-dhātu-svāmi-tevarkaḷukku nitya vāsa-bhavana-
21 -m-āṉa pratham=ābhiṣekattukku maṅkala-gṛham-āṉa āḍḍāṇḍu-
22 toṟun tiru-nayana-mokṣam paṇṇi añśaṉa niṟukkum
23 kaṇṇālañ śeyyum maṁgala-mahā-çilāmaya-Buddha-
24 devarkku gandha-kuṭi-y-āṉa **Daḷadāy-p-perum-paḷḷi**[3] uṅka-
25 -ḷ rakṣa-y-āka veṇḍum eṉṟu sakala çastrāgama çīlā=
26 =cāra-sampannar-āṉa rāja-guru Uturuḷa-mūḷaiyil (vyāriṇi) **Mu-**
27 **-galan-mahā-sthavirar** rājāmātyaroḍuṅ kūḍa eḻunt' aruḷi-y-i-
28 -runtu eṅkaḷai aḷaittu aruḷi-ś-śeytamaiyil **Mātantirat-**
29 **-toṅ** kūḍi eṅkaḷukku mūtātaikaḷāy-uḷḷa Vaḷañśeyarai-y-um e-
30 -ṅkaḷoḍu kūḍi varun Nakarattāruḷḷiḍḍāraiyuṅ kūḍḍi **Mūṉ(ru-)**
31 **kai-t-tiru-Veḷaikkāṟan Daḷadāy-p-perum-paḷḷi**-y-eṉṟu

---

[1] This may also be read *sā*.
[2] This may also be read *nityām*.
[3] This may also be read *piḷḷi*.

Slab-inscription of the Vēḷaikkāṟas

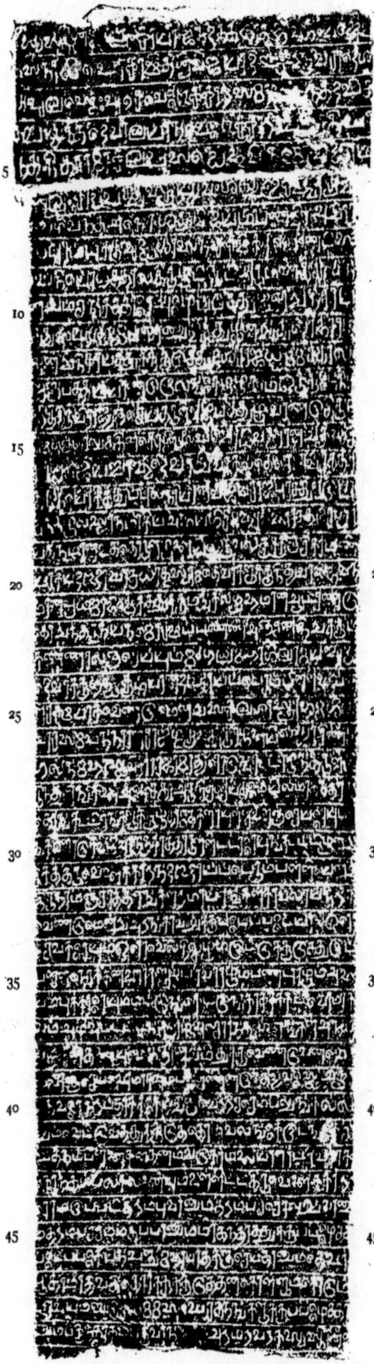

32 tiru-nāmañ śātti eṅkaḷ aṟam-āy eṅkaḷ kāvalāy niṟka
33 veṇḍum eṉṟu aṟaṅ-kāvalukku paḍai-p-paḍaiyāl oro
34 śevakarai-y-um oro veli nilam-um iḍḍu-k-kuḍuttu ip-
35 -paḷḷi nokkiṉa ūrkaḷ-um parivāram-um paṇḍāram-um abha-
36 -yam pukkāraiy-um paḍḍuṅ keḍḍuṅ kākka-k-kaḍavom āka
37 -v-um aḷivu paḍḍaḍaṅkaḷ aḷivu śorntum eṅkal anva-
38 -yam-uḷḷataṉai-y-um eññāṉṟum itukku veṇḍuvaṉa-v-e
39 -llāñ śeyvom āka-v-um paṉṉiṉa inta vyavasthai candrā-
40 -ditya-varai niṟpatāka-k-kaiyvi(ḷu) veṟṟi-ś-śempil-uṅ kalli-
41 -l-um veḍḍuvittu-k-kuḍuttom valaṅ-kai iḍaṅ-kai śi-
42 ṟu-tanam[1] piḷḷaikaḷ-taṉam Vaḍukar Malaiyāḷar Parivāra-k-
43 kontam Palakalaṉai-y-um uḷḷiḍḍa tiru **Velaikkāṟa-**
44 **-rom** ippaḍi tiṟampuvāṉ-um tiṟampa-ś-śolluvāṉ-u-
45 -m tirampa-ś-śammatippāṉ-um **Mātantirattukku**-p-piḷaitta
46 paḍai-p-pakaiyan[2] pañca mahā-pātakañ śeytāṉ-um tevar
47 pūtar mā-tavattorkku-k-kuḍuttaṉa koḷḷum koḍum
48 pāvi-y-um Buddha-Dharmma-Saṁgha-ratnaṅkaḷukku-p-piḷaittā-
49 -ṉ-um pukun narakam pukuvān[3] .. .. .. aṟa-maṟavaṟaka[4] svasti çrīḥ.

TRANSLATION.

[Lines 1–5] Hail! Prosperity! May the **Veḷaikkāṟa** forces protect that Temple of the Buddha's Tooth-relic which the Chief **Deva-Senādhipa**[5] has built in the city of **Pulasti** in Laṅkā by order of the King, **Çrī Vijayādi-Bāhu,** as well as the shrines around it founded by the Veḷaikkāras, throughout (the whole period) unto the dissolution of the world[6].

[Lines 5–11] Obeisance to the Buddha! In the prosperous Island of Laṅkā, the Emperor **Çrī Vijaya-Bāhu Devar** *alias* **Çrī Saṅghabodhi-varmar,** a scion of the lineage of Ikṣvāku of the Solar race, gaining victory over many an enemy, entered Anurādhapura and, at the request of the Buddhist priesthood, put on the sacred crown in order to look after the Buddhist religion. So, His Majesty had Buddhist priests invited from **Aramaṇa**[7] [to Ceylon], and [with

---

[1] Read *taṉam.* [2] Read *pakaiyaṉ.* [3] Read *pukuvāṉ.* [4] Read *-maṟavaṟka.*

[5] *Devasenādhipo = Devasenāpati* = Sinh. *Deva-Senavi* (see line 16).

[6] *Nitarām ā-kalpa-sandher bhuvi.* Here *sandhi* means the period of transition between two kalpas.

[7] On the extent of the kingdom of Rāmaññadesa, see Taw Sein Ko's notes on the Kalyāṇi inscription. (*Ind. Antiq.*, 1894, pp. 100 and 224).

their aid], effected the purification of the Buddhist Order of the three Nikāyas [fraternities].

[Lines 11–15] He, moreover, bestowed thrice his own weight (of coins) upon the three Nikāyas and having brought the whole of Laṅkā under a single canopy of dominion was graciously pleased to rule the kingdom for fifty-five years by practising the ten regal virtues. He also celebrated seventy-three sacred birthdays.

[Lines 16–21] His Majesty gave directions to **Nuvarakal Deva Sena-virattar** and through him had the **great Temple of the Tooth-relic**[1] built at **Vijayarājapuram,** otherwise called **Pulanari;** and it became the permanent repository for the Tooth and the Bowl-relics of the Buddha [which are like unto] the crest gems of the Three Worlds (and which were) at **Uttoruḷa-mūḷa,** the chief fane at the **Abhayagiri Mahāvihāra,** the original place of deposit [of the relics][2].

[Lines 21-24] It became also the auspicious house for [holding] the first anointment ceremony and the Hall of Fragrance[3] for the auspicious and colossal stone statue of the Holy Buddha, in which is held annually the ceremony of unloosening the sacred eyes (of the image) and applying collyrium to them.

[Lines 25–30] The royal preceptor[4] and (grammarian) **Mugalan**[5] **Mahāthera** of Uturuḷa-mūḷa who is endowed with piety and virtuous conduct and with (a knowledge) of all the Çāstras and Āgamas, associating himself with ministers of the state[6], was pleased to come to the spot, send for us and say '(this) Tooth-relic Temple should be under your custody'. Thereupon, we, the members of the **Mātantra** met together and convened a meeting of the Vaḷañśeyar who are our elders[7] and of the kinsmen, the Nagarattār[8], who usually associate with us [in our deliberations].

---

[1] *Daḷadāy-p-perum-paḷḷi* (line 24).

[2] See *Mv.* xxxvii, 96–97.

[3] *Gandha-kuṭi*, Sinh. *Gaṅda-kiḷi*, the name applied by the Buddhists to the chamber, occupied either by the Buddha himself during his lifetime or by a statue of him after his demise.

[4] *Rājaguru*, here probably only an honorary title.

[5] *Vyāriṇi Mugalan*, see above, p. 246. Between the locative *Uturuḷa-mūḷaiyil* and *Mugalan*, one would expect a word connoting the sense of residing, but as pointed out above (p. 248, n. 5), the phrase *Uturuḷa-mūḷaiyil vyāriṇi* 'the grammarian at Uturuḷa-mūḷai' is similar in construction to that in l. 19 *Uttoruḷa-mūḷaiyil mū-v-ulakkuñ śikāmaṇi* 'the three-world crest gems at Uttoruḷa-mūlai,' the word 'existing' or 'existed' being understood in both cases.

[6] *Rājāmātyar.* This does not necessarily imply ministers of the present king.

[7] Or 'whom we regard as our leaders'.

[8] Or 'of those belonging to the community of Nagarattār'

[Lines 30–38] [In this assembly] we (all of us) invested (the Tooth-relic Temple) with the sacred name of **Mūnṟu-kai**[1]**-t-tiru-Veḷaikkāṟan Daḷadāy-p-perum-paḷḷi** 'the great temple of the Tooth-relic belonging to the illustrious Veḷaikkāṟa (army) of the three divisions' and made the declaration[2] that it shall remain[3] as our charitable institution under our own custody, that by assigning[4] for the protection of this charity one servitor from each regiment (of our army) together with one *veli* of land (for his maintenance), we shall protect the villages, the retainers, and the property belonging to this shrine, as well as those who enter it for refuge, even though (thereby) we may suffer loss or ruin, and that we shall always do everything necessary for this (shrine) as long as our lineage exists even though everything that has already suffered ruin may fall deeper into ruin.

[Lines 39–44] To this effect we, the illustrious **Veḷaikkāṟas,** among whom are included the communities of Valaṅ-kai (the right-hand), Iḍaṅ-kai (the left-hand), Śiṟu-tanam (the minor class ?), Piḷḷaikaḷ-tanam (Vellāḷar class ?), Vaḍukar (the Telugus), Malaiyāḷar (the Malayālese), Parivāra-k-kontam (the retinue of spearmen ?), and Palakalanai (the army of Kalanai-men ?), have set (our) hand-attestations [to this agreement] and have delivered it over, having had it engraved both on copper (plates) and on stone, so that it may last as long as the sun and the moon endure.

[Lines 44–49] Accordingly, whoever that infringes (this contract) or that tells [another] to infringe it or that consents to the infringement of it becomes an enemy of the [Veḷaikkāṟa] army, who has committed an offence against the **Mātantra,** or [he becomes] one who has committed the five great sins, or [he becomes] the wicked sinner who has appropriated what had been offered to gods or to spirits or to great ascetics, or (he becomes) one who has committed an offence against the [three] gems [namely] the Buddha, his Doctrine, and his Order, or [he becomes] one who will enter the hell into which [such sinners] usually go. Forget not charity! Hail! Prosperity!

---

[1] See above, p. 251 for explanation of this term.

[2] *Paṇṇiṇa inta vyavasthai* (line 39), lit. the declaration which was made. For the use of the word *vyavasthā* in this sense, see *South Indian Inscriptions*, vol. ii, pp. 507 and 514.

[3] *Niṟka veṇḍum enṟu* (lines 32–33).

[4] *Iḍḍu-k-kuḍuttu* 'having assigned'.

No. 41 (Reg. No. 278). POḶONNARUVA [1], GAL-VIHĀRA: ROCK-INSCRIPTION OF PARAKKAMA-BĀHU I (1153–1186 A.D.)

ONE of the monasteries built by Parakkama-Bāhu I was the **Uttarārāma** [2] (North Park) of Poḷonnaruva with its rock-cut temple, now popularly called **Gal-vihāra,** its Buddhist figures and the inscription on the vertical face of the rock. These have been known to the public for a long time. Pilgrims, sightseers, and government officials, who have, from time to time, visited the spot, have expressed in writing and otherwise their profound admiration of these ruins which bear witness to the religious enthusiasm and the artistic taste of the twelfth century A.D.

A graphic description of the site appears from the pen of Mr. H. C. P. Bell, in his *Annual Report of the Archaeological Survey* for 1907. For the benefit of the readers of the *Epigraphia Zeylanica*, however, we need quote only an extract with a photograph [3] of the temple indicating the exact position of the inscription.

Mr. Bell says: 'This rock-hewn shrine stands unrivalled as, *in its special features*, the most impressive antiquity *par excellence* to be seen in the Island of Ceylon, and possibly not rivalled throughout the Continent of India.

The line of gigantic figures carved from the gray rock which forms their background, calm, immovable, majestic, amid the hush of the surrounding forest, gazing ever fixedly into space with the pensiveness of profound meditation, or wrapped in eternal slumber, must inspire in the thoughtful beholder wonder and admiration, mingled with an instinctive sense of silent awe.

The irresistible charm and sublimity of the "Gal Viháré" could not but appeal forcibly to the few observant visitors who, for the last century, have chanced to view it in its peaceful wooded seclusion untouched by axe and spade.

The limited outcrop of rock from which the "Gal Viháré" was formed lies about 1½ miles north of the Promontory [4] situated between Tópávewa lake, which once washed it, and the Citadel. It is less than a quarter of a mile from the extensive oblong site, artificially banked up, whereon are located "Kiri Vehera" Dágaba, "Jétawanáráma" Viháré and other connected ruined buildings.

---

[1] In G. 22 of the Index map of Ceylon, see *Ceylon Journal of Science*, Vol. I, Pt. 2.

[2] See *Mv.* lxxviii. 76–78.

[3] Kindly supplied by the present Archaeological Commissioner of Ceylon.

[4] See plan facing p. 84, above.

Poḷonnaruva : Gal-vihāra

From a photograph supplied by the Archaeological Survey, Ceylon

The *galpota* stretches from south-west to north-east, broadly speaking; nowhere does it reach to more than 30 ft. above the level ground.

It was the south-east face of this rock-reach, rising most abruptly before it trends eastwards, which was selected by the stone-masons as best adapted for this purpose.

This portion of the rock, 56 yards in length, falls away gradually at each end, but most to north-east; and it was this physical conformation which doubtless decided the distribution of the several images.

The tall standing figure, therefore, and the shrine pierced into the rock, occupy the middle, with the colossal recumbent Buddha and a gigantic sedent image to right and left respectively.

The rock face had to be cut back nearly 15 ft. for the sculpturing of the three great images, and scooped out as much as 17 ft. to provide the cave shrine and its pronaos.

The sloping rock face immediately to the right of the cave was chiselled smooth for a space (13 ft. 3 in. by 9 ft. 9 in.) to receive a long Sinhalese inscription in 51 lines, now much weathered by exposure. This record is a *kathikáwa* [*sic*] or ordinance for the guidance of Buddhist clergy, cut in stone by Parákrama Báhu (1164–1197 A.D.)[1], the Great Monarch of Sinhalese history and tradition.

To that ruler's credit is known to belong beyond question the construction of the "Gal Viháré", whatever doubt may exist as to the many other shrines at which the bombastic Nissaṇka Malla, his near successor, has showered his records.

For the *Maháwaṇsa*[2] chronicler alludes to the execution of the work with direct blunt brevity too definite to admit of dispute, however wanting in due appreciation of the grandeur of the most impressive sculptures existing in Laṇká.

"And this ruler of men built likewise the *Uttaráráma*, nigh unto the *Mahá Thúpa*, after that he had caused the rock that was there to be hewn out. And when he had finished all the work he caused cunning workmen to make three caves in the rock, namely the *Vijjádhara Guhá* ("the cave of the spirits of knowledge"), the *Nisinna-paṭimá Leṇa* ("the cave of the sitting image"), and the *Nipanna-paṭimá Guhá* ("the cave of the sleeping image"[3])".

Their semi-brick, semi-rock shelters no longer enshrine the colossal *Nisinna-paṭimá* and *Nipanna-paṭimá*. But Brahma and Vishṇu still hover over the Buddha as guardian angels (*Vidyádharas*) in his cave temple.'

---

[1] More correctly 1153–1186 A.D. [2] Chap. lxxviii. 76–78. [3] Wijesinha's translation.

Such is the general description of the site. The photograph reproduced here shows exactly the spot where the inscription is on the rock-face between the central cave shrine and the recumbent figure of the Buddha.

It will also be seen from the accompanying (plate 37) facsimile of the record that its **letters**, $1\frac{1}{2}$ in. to 2 in. each in size, are, as usual, engraved between ruled lines $2\frac{1}{2}$ in. apart, and that in type they may be assigned to a **date** between the Aṁbagamuva record of Vijaya-Bāhu I (1058–1114 A.D.)[1], and the Poḷonnaruva slab of Vijaya-Bāhu II (1186–1187 A.D.)[2]. A comparison of the akṣaras *ka*, *ta*, *na*, *ra*, and *ma* in these inscriptions will make this apparent. There is hardly any difference between the medial *u*, *ṛ*, and *ra*. See, for example, the akṣaras *pu*, *pra*, and *hṛ* in line 9. There is also a tendency to avoid compound letters even in words borrowed from Sanskrit and Pāli.

As Müller has already stated[3], the **language** of our record is very much the same as that of the Sinhalese commentaries of the beginning of the thirteenth century and of works such as the *Amāvatura*, the *Thūpavaṁsa*, &c. There is a good sprinkling of Sanskrit words, more than in the earlier inscriptions[4], but not so much as in the later ones[5].

As regards the **contents**, the inscription may be divided into two parts: (*a*) the historical introduction (ll. 1–18), and (*b*) the disciplinary injunctions (ll. 18–51), the end of each section being indicated by a fish symbol.

The historical material embodied in the introduction, when compared with the statement in the *Mahāvaṁsa*[6], gives us the information that the Buddha died in the Sāla grove of the Malla princes after a religious career of 45 years since his 'Enlightenment'. Thereafter, when 454 years had elapsed, there reigned in Ceylon **Vaḷagam Abhā**[7], and from thence for a period of 1254 years, the Buddhist Church or *sāsana* continued her course of disintegration[8]. Then Çrī Saṅghabodhi Parakkama-Bāhu I was already holding the reins of government. No sooner had he brought the Island under his sway, than he turned his attention to reform and revivify the *sāsana* which, he declared, as had Duṭṭhagāmaṇi more than twelve and a half centuries before, was his object in assuming sovereignty.

[1] See No. 35 above. [2] No. 30 above. [3] *A.I.C.*, p. 62.

[4] See, for example, the Mihintale Tablets of Mahinda IV (*E. Z.*, Vol. I, No. 7).

[5] See the records of Niśśaṅka Malla above, pp. 104 ff. [6] Ch. lxxiii–22 and lxxviii.

[7] Vaṭṭagāmaṇi Abhaya, 439 and 454–466 A. B. (44 and 29–17 B.C.).

[8] See also *Epigraphia Birmanica*, Vol. III, Pt. 2, p. 217.

Mahā-Kassapa Thera, the abbot of **Udumbaragiri**[1] monastery, and his community of theras were at the time celebrated for their knowledge of the Buddhist scriptures, especially the Vinaya section. His Majesty enlisted their services, and through them convened a synod of Elders representing the various schools of thought in the Order.

At this assembly the scriptures were rehearsed and the debatable points were solved. This is what is meant by the statement in line 13 that 'by bringing about a reconciliation of the three *nikāyas*, His Majesty made them [united] into one *nikāya*'. Those who did not consent to be so united had, of course, to leave the *Theriya* or orthodox church. The *Mahāvaṁsa* mentions further the names and particulars of some of the Elders who took part in the rehearsal of the scriptures.

Mahā-Kassapa Thera presided over the meeting. He is supposed to be the author of the Sanskrit Grammar *Bālāvabodhana* and of a Sinhalese *sanne* to the *Samantapāsādikā*. The others present were **Ñānapāla Thera** with his disciples from Anurādhapura; some Theras from Saphara (Saparagamuva?); **Nāgundapalliya Thera, Moggallāna Thera** and others from the sub-king's country, as well as representatives of the three *nikāyas* from Rohaṇa led by **Nanda Thera** of the Selāntarāyatana Vihāra. **Sāriputta Thera,** the pious author of seven important works[2], was also living at the time in Poḷonnaruva in a mansion of great splendour built by the King. As he belonged to Mahā Kassapa's Udumbaragiri fraternity[3], he may have taken part in the deliberations of the ecclesiastical board, though he is not mentioned by name. Regarding Moggallāna Thera, see above pages 248–250.

The **date** of this convocation, as explained on p. 205 above, was in 1165 A.D. As soon as the reconciliation was effected, there arose the question regarding the precautionary measures to be adopted for the due maintenance of discipline, harmony, and purity of the Order in the future.

Now, **Parakkama-Bāhu I** must have learnt the tradition as regards the procedure observed in bygone days by the Indian Emperor **Asoka** as well as by some Ceylon kings under similar circumstances. So, Parakkama-Bāhu emulated the example of Asoka and using almost the same sort of expressions which the

---

1 Called in Sinhalese Duṁbulāgala, now corrupted to Diṁbulāgala. See Nos. 31 and 34 above.

2 See *B.M. Catalogue of Sinhalese MSS.*, Introd., p. xv.

3 See Dhammārāma Thera's Introd. to his edition of the *Moggallāna-pañcikā-pradīpa*, p. xiv.

latter is stated to have employed in his appeal to Moggaliputta Tissa[1] (*circa* 246 B.C.), he asked Mahā Kassapa Thera and his Board of Elders to issue the ecclesiastical rescript which forms the second part of the present inscription. It is to be noted that, strictly speaking, the king has no authority to issue orders to the monks. The Church has to do that, but the king can enforce their obedience to the laws of the church.

According to Buddhaghosa, the reputed author of the Commentary on the *Kathāvatthu*, one of the results of the third Rehearsal of the Buddhist Canon under Asoka's patronage was the production of the *Kathāvatthu* by Moggaliputta-Tissa 'to avert all bases of heresy that had arisen, and that might in the future arise'[2]. We venture to suggest another compilation for the same purpose, namely, the *Vinaya-samukasa* mentioned in the Calcutta-Bairāṭ rock-inscription addressed by Asoka to the Saṅgha.

Our reasons for this assertion are: (*a*) Though we have as yet no reliable material to accept as true the traditions of Asoka's actual conversion to Buddhism in the fourth year after his coronation, or of his building thousands of monasteries during the following three years, yet there is sufficient evidence to infer that he was in touch with Buddhism and was attracted by its tenets; (*b*) After experiencing the horrors of the Kāliṅga war, in the ninth year of his reign, he became a Buddhist *upāsaka* and seems to have studied Buddhist texts, notably the *Dhammapada*, for it is its teachings that he has promulgated by means of his edicts; namely, the principles of *mettā*, *karuṇā*, and *muditā*, including *ahiṁsā* and *dāna*—all of which covered more or less common ground with the doctrines of other contemporary schools[3]; (*c*) Like Parakkama-Bāhu of our record, Asoka also paid visits to the Buddhist saṅgha[4] and presumably made himself acquainted with the Pātimokkha and other Vinaya treatises; (*d*) As a result he may have himself noticed the existence of heresies in the Saṅgha, and, possibly at the request of the Elders of the Theriya sect, determined to purge the religion of its impurities; (*e*) So, the Rehearsal of the Buddhist Canon may have taken place, for the third or second time, in the seventeenth regnal

---

[1] See *Kathāvatthu Aṭṭhakathā* (Introd. tr. in Aung's and Rhys Davids' *Points of Controversy*, pp. 5–7). See also the Kalyāṇī Inscription (*Ind. Antiq.*, Vol. xxii, 1893, p. 16).

[2] *Ibid.*, p. 7. Contrast, however, Keith, *Buddhist Philosophy* (1923), pp. 16–19.

[3] See also Hultzsch, *Inscriptions of Aśoka*, Introd. p. xlix.

[4] Cf. *sagha upete*, *saghe upayāte*, and *saṁghaṁ upagate* in Rupnāth, Bairat, and Maski rock-inscriptions. We still think that M. Senart's interpretation of this phrase is the more correct one. Professor D. R. Bhandarkar infers that Asoka became a *bhikṣu-gatika*, a co-resident with the bhikṣus of a vihāra. See his *Asoka*, pp. 78–81.

year of Asoka, and for the future guidance of monks Moggaliputta Tissa, the President of the Board of Elders (probably identical with Upagupta), the Buddhist patriarch of Mathurā, wrote the *Kathāvatthu* and he or the Board may have compiled the *Vinaya-samukasa*, an abstract of the Vinaya precepts; (*f*) Thereafter, we think, Asoka addressed his Calcutta-Bairat rescript to the Saṅgha [1] and with the knowledge of the Buddhist writings he now possessed, advised both the clergy and the laity to act according to the rules of conduct prescribed in the *Vinaya-samukasa* and the other treatises mentioned in the record; (*g*) In the later inscriptions of Asoka, as for example, the pillar edicts, we notice a slight change of tone. They do not contain merely the pious wishes of Asoka as in earlier records, but they assume the character of injunctions culminating in the threat that breakers of the union of the Saṅgha shall be expelled from the Community [2].

This is exactly what has happened in Ceylon. Whenever a pious king noticed corruptions or dissensions in the Buddhist church, he had the Canon rehearsed and a *Katikā-vatta* (Sin. *katikā-vata*) issued. The *Vinaya-samukasa* [3] of the Calcutta-Bairat rock-inscription is no doubt a compilation either of this description, or of that of the *Sikkhāpada-valañjana*, containing a summary of Vinaya precepts both for the bhikkhus and the sāmaṇeras, the observance of which Buddhist kings used to enforce by means of a decree called *dhamma kamma* [4] which may have included a list of punishable offences as in the *katikā-vatas*.

The lithic records such as the Jetavanārāma Sanskrit inscription [5], Anurādhapura slab-inscription of Kassapa V [6], and the Mihintale tablets of Mahinda IV [7] afford us glimpses of the administration of monastic institutions in Ceylon and incidentally of the strict rules which the monks had to observe under pain of expulsion, but we have so far not come across a complete copy of a *dhamma kamma* or of a *katikā-vata* anterior to the present one [8] on the Gal-vihāra rock.

---

[1] Hultzsch places this inscription in the twelfth year of Asoka's reign (*Ins. of Asoka*, p. xlvii); while Barua's calculations bring its date down to the thirty-seventh year (*The Mahābodhi*, June 1926, p. 302). The latter date agrees with the views of V. A. Smith in his *History of India*, p. 101.

[2] See the pillar edicts of Kausambi, Sānchi, and Sarnāth.

[3] For divergent opinions of scholars regarding this treatise, see Senart's *Inscriptions of Piyadasi*, Edmunds' *Buddhist Bibliography* (San Francisco, 1904), *J. R. A. S.*, 1915, pp. 808–809. Bhandarkar's *Asoka*, pp. 86–88.

[4] *Mv.* xliv. 46–47, 77; xlviii. 71; lii. 10, 44. Cf. also Wijesinha's note to *Mv.* xliv. 46.

[5] *E. Z.*, Vol. I, No. 1. [6] *Ibid.*, No. 4. [7] *Ibid.*, No. 7.

[8] Mr. D. B. Jayatilaka, the learned editor of the *Katikāvat-saṅgarā*, says in his introduction that he received three copies of a *katikā-vata* supposed to have been that of Vohārika Tissa (269–291 A.D.). but on examination he found that they were later compilations of no authority.

Of the later *katikā-vatas*, we see in the Häṭadāge wall-inscription[1] a fragment of the one issued by Kitti Niśśaṅka Malla (1187–1196 A.D.). During the reign of Vijaya-Bāhu III (*circa* 1227–1231 A.D.) Saṅgharakkhita Thera, a pupil of the celebrated author, Sāriputta Thera of Poḷonnaruva, with the co-operation of another eminent Elder, Duṁbulāgala Medhankara, held an ecclesiastical court at which the sacred text was revised and a new code of disciplinary rules was promulgated. Thereafter his distinguished son Parakkama-Bāhu II (1231–1265 A.D.) had the *Daṁbadeṇi Katikā-vata* issued by an assembly of Elders presided over by Āraṇyaka Medhaṅkara of the Duṁbulāgala fraternity[2]. In this, the authors have included practically the whole of the contents of Parakkama-Bāhu's Gal-vihāra *katikā-vata*. Evidently taking this as a precedent, Välivița Piṇḍapātika Saraṇaṅkara, when he and his collaborators issued a *katikā-vata* under the patronage of King Kīrti Çrī Rājasiṁha (1746–1780 A.D.), incorporated the contents of the Daṁbadeṇi-katikā-vata. His successor Rājādhi Rājasiṁha (1780–1797 A.D.), also had a disciplinary rescript promulgated. More particulars regarding all these and a few others more or less fragmentary are given in the *Katikāvat-saṅgarā* to which we are indebted for much useful information.

As stated above, the present inscription has been known to the public for a long time. But no one published it until Dr. Müller included an edition and an English translation of it in his *Ancient Inscriptions in Ceylon* (London, 1883). Since then an improved edition appeared in the *Katikāvat-saṅgarā* (Colombo, 1922).

The edition given below is based on the two ink-estampages supplied by Mr. A. M. Hocart, the present Archaeological Commissioner of Ceylon. A perusal of the second part of the record and of the notes accompanying the translation will give the reader a fair idea of the strict character of the disciplinary rules and the scriptural authorities they are based on.

---

[1] *E. Z.*, Vol. II, No. 16.

[2] MS. copies of this work are to be found in the British Museum. For a printed edition, see *Katikāvat-saṅgarā*, No. 2.

TEXT.[1]

1 අප බුදුන් කල්ප ශතසහස්‍රාධික ච(තු)රසංඛ්‍ය පරිමිත කාලය(ක්) සමතිස් පැරුම් පුරා මාරසංග්‍රාම භූමිවූ මහාබොධි පර්‍ය්‍යංකාරූඪවැ දුර්වාර සප

2 රිවාර මාර පරාජය කොටැ සර්වඥපද ප්‍රාප්තවැ පන්සාලිස් හවුරුද්දක් දිවස්[2] චාතුර්ද්වීපක මහාමෙඝයක්සෙයින් වැඩැ සිටැ අනෙ

3 ක කල්ප කොටි ශතසහස්‍රයෙහි[3] කෙලශාග්නීන් දග්ධවෙමින් සිටි ස(ත්ව)යන් ධර්මාමෘතවර්ෂායෙන් නිවමින් සකලබුද්ධකෘත්‍ය නිමවා කුසිනාරානුවරැ අභි යෙස්හි ම

4 ල්ලරජයන්ගෙ සාලවනොද්‍යානයෙහි නිරුපධිශෙෂ[4] නිර්වාණ ධාතුවෙන් (පිරි)නිවි සාරසිය සූපනැස් හවුරුද්දක් ගිය කලැ **වලගම් අභා මහරජු** දවසැ පටන් එක්වාදහස් දෙසිය සූ

5 පනැස් හවුරුද්දක් භින්න නිකායවැ ශාසනය පිරි(ය)මින්[5] සිටි කල්හි මහා සම්මතාදි පරම්පරායාත[6] සූර්‍ය්‍යව(ං)ශොද්භූත රාජාධිරාජ නෛකදිග්භිව්‍යාප්ත[7] යශොමරීචීන් විරාජමා

6 න **ශ්‍රීස(ං)ඝබොධි පරාක්‍රමබාහු[8] මහරජාණන්** සකල ලංකාතෙලෙහි එක රාජ්‍යාභි ෂෙකයෙන් අභිෂික්තවැ විජෘම්භිත පුණ්‍යර්ධී ඇතිවැ රාජ්‍යසුඛානුභව කොටැ වසනුවන්

7 අඥාන දුර්ඥාන මූලක අප්‍රතිපත්ති දුෂ්ප්‍රතිපත්ති විපවෙග විහතවැ අපායා න්නවන[9] ශාසනාවචර කුලපුත්‍රයන් දැකැ සුපරිශුද්ධ බුද්ධශාසනයෙහි මාවැනි ආඥාවූව

8 ක්‍ෂත්‍රියක්හු මෙවැනි කිලුටක් දැකැ දැකැ උදාසීන වූවහොත් බුදුසස්න නස්සි බොහො සත්නුදු අපායභාග් වෙති. පස්වාදහසක් පවත්නා බුදුසස්නට මා වහල්වූව මැනැවැයි

---

[1] දඹදෙණි කතිකාවතටද (දැ. කති.) කීර්තිශ්‍රීරාජසිංහ කතිකාවතටද (කී. කති.) ඇතුළත් කරනලද කොටස් සසඳනකොට පාඨප්‍රභෙද දැනගත හැකිය. මෙයින් සමහරක් මෙහි පහත දක්වමු.

[2] 'දිවස්'—කතිකාවත්දෙකෙහිම ඌනයි.

[3] 'අනවරාග්‍රසංසාරවෘත්තයෙහි'—කතිකාවත් දෙකෙහිම.

[4] 'නිරුපධිශෙෂ' වියයුතුයි

[5] 'පිරිහෙමින් '—කති. දෙකෙහිම.

[6] 'පරම්පරානුයාත'—කති. දෙකෙහිම.

[7] 'නෛකදික්හි ව්‍යාප්ත'—කති. දෙකෙහිම.

[8] 'ශ්‍රී පරාක්‍රමබාහු'—කති. දෙ.

[9] අපාය ව්‍යසනාපන්නාවන'—කති. දෙ.

9 ප්‍රඥාපුරස්සර කරුණායෙන් සංචොදිත හෘදය ඇතිව මෙසෙ නට සසුන් කවුරුත් වහල්කොට අපගතකලංකව[1] පස්වාදහසක් පවත්නා පරිද්දෙන් කෙරෙම් දෙහොයි සිතා අඛඩාච්ඡිද්‍රතාදි විවි

10 ධ ගුණගණාග සගහ කොට රක්ෂිත වර්ධිත පොෂිත ශීලස්කන්ධාදි ලෞකික ගුණරත්නාලංකාරයෙන් සමලංකෘතවූ **උදුම්බරගිරි** නිවාසී **මහාකාශ්‍යප මහාස්ථවිර** ප්‍රමුඛ **මහාවිහාරාධිවාසී**

11 භික්ෂුසංඝයා දූත ඔවුන් වහල් කොට බුදුන්විසින් අනුජ්ඥත බුධකල්ප[2] **මොග්ගලිපුත් තිස් මහතෙරුන්** වහල්කොට පාපභික්ෂු[3] නිම්මථනය කොට දුල්ලබ්ධි මැඩ ශාසනම

12 ල විශොධා තෘතීය ධර්මසංගායනා කැරවූ **ධර්මාශොක** මහරජනුවෙන් අනෙක ශත පාපභික්ෂූන් ශාස්තෘශාසනයෙන් අපගත කොට **ෂඩභිඥාද්‍යනෙක** ගුණගණොපෙත මහා **ක්ෂීණා**

13 ශ්‍රවයන් ඇතිකල්හි පවා පූර්වරාජයන්විසින් මහොත්සාහයෙනුදු සමග නො කොට ගත හුණු[4] තුන්නකා සමගකිරීමෙන් එක්නකා කොට **ජෙතවනමහා විහාරාදි** නොඑක් මහඇගි වි

14 හාර ලක්දිව තන්හි තන්හි කරවා එහි සහස්‍ර සංඛ්‍යාතික්‍රාන්ත[5] මහාසංඝයා වාසකරවා නිරන්තර ප්‍රවෘත්ත ධර්මාමිෂදානයෙන් උපස්ථාන කෙරෙමින් සංඝ දර්ශන ප්‍රභව ප්‍රීතිප්‍රාමොද්‍ය රසා

15 ස්වාදයෙහි ලොලව කාලානුකාලයෙහි පොෂථාග[6] ශීලස(මු)පෙතව විහාරයට එළඹ සන්නිපතිත[7] සංඝමධ්‍යගත ව තද් දර්ශන ප්‍රසූත ප්‍රීතිප්‍රාමොද්‍යරසාස්වාද කොට මාවිසින් මහොත්සා

16 හයෙන් සාධිතවූ මෙ සංඝ[සා]මග්‍රිය පස්වාදහසක් අභින්නව පවත්නා පරිද්දෙන් මතුවන සංඝයාද අප්‍රමාදව ග්‍රන්ථවිදර්ශනාධූරවයෙහි යෙදී අලෙප විජතාදි ගුණෙන් යුක්තව වසනා ප

17 රිද්දෙන් අවවාදානුශාසන කොට ශාසනය රක්ෂාකළමැනවැයි යුක්ත ව්‍යක්ත ගුණොපෙතව කරන[8] ආරාධනාද අසා **මහාකාශ්‍යප මහාස්ථවිර** ප්‍රමුඛස්ථවිර වරයන්මැවිසි

---

1 'වහල්කොටවවා පස්වාදහසක්'—කති. දෙ.

2 කති. දෙකෙහිම ඌනයි.

3 'අනෙක සහස්‍ර පාපභික්ෂූන්'—කති. දෙ.

4 'සමගකොට ගත හුහුණු'—කති. දෙ.

5 'අනෙක සහස්‍ර සංඛ්‍යා ඇති'—කති. දෙ.

6 'පොෂධාග' හෝ 'පොසථාග.—වියයුතුයි

7 කති. දෙකෙහිම ඌනයි.

8 'කරනලද'—කති. දෙ.

18 න් ප්‍රමාදවිහාරීන් අවකාශ නොලබන සඳහා බම්මිවින[ය] සසඳනකොටැ ඇඳුරොල්ද[1] නොවිහිදැ කළ කතිකාවති[2]  ගණදෙටු තෙරවරුන් විසින් තම තමා නිසා වන අතෙතුවාසික සඩිවි

19 හාරිකයන් අතුරෙහි නිස දෙන්නට නිසයෙන් මිඳෙන්නට යොග්‍යවැ වසන්නවුන් පමා නොවියැදී[3] ග්‍රන්ථධුරයෙහි යොදා යැටත්පිරිසෙසින් **විනයෙන් කුදුසිබ** හා **පාමොක් ද සූතනින් දසධම් සූත්‍රානුස අනුමාන**

20 **සූත්‍රස** ද වනපොත්[4] පිරිහෙළියැ නොදී ගණසංගණිකාදීන් දුරුකොටැ ග්‍රන්ථ ධුරයෙහි යෙහි[5] යෙදෙන්නවුන්විසිනුදු සතතයෙන් විවෙකවත් පිරුව මැනැවැයි වදාළබැවින් තුන්වෙලෙහි ඉ

21 රියව් (සුමනා)සිල් පිරිසුදුකොටැ කාගියාසි ආදිවූ කමටහනෙක්හි යෙදී දෙතුන් පලගක් හුණුගන්වා දවස කඩ නොකොට විවෙකවත් පූරවා අත්තානමෙව පඨමං පතිරූපෙ නිවෙසයෙ[6] යි වදාළබැවින් තම

22 **තමාද මෙ(ත්)** ගුණගයෙහි වෙසෙසින් යෙදී අත්වැඩ පරවැඩ සාධමින් නී (වදාළෙන්)[7] ග්‍රන්ථධුරයෙන් වැඩියක් කොටැ ගත නොහෙන අතෙතුවාසික සඩිවිහාරිකයන් ලවා **මුල්සිඛ සෙඛියා** වන

23 පොත් කරවා **සිඛවළඳවිනිස** අස්වා සමසින් සමසැ ආඥාත්ත තොටැ සුමනා විචාළ තැනැක කියන්නට පොහොසත් කරවා **දසධම්** සතතයෙන් මෙනෙ හිකරවා යැටකී විවෙකවතුදු

24 පූරවා ශක්තිපමණක් හදැරා නිමිකලැ චරිතානුකූල කමටහනක් උගන්වා විදර්ශනා ධුරයෙහිමැ යොදා චතුසම්පජංඤ කථායෙහි වදාළ පරිද්දෙන් දවස් යවනු කොටැ පැවැත්වියැ යුතු

25 හෙරණනුදු **හෙරණසිඛ සෙඛිය(ා) දසධම් සූනහ්** වනපොත් කොටැ අසා නො පිරිහෙළා පරිහරණකරනුකොටැ යොදා විවෙකවතුදු පූරවා හික්මැවියැ යුතු මෙවුන් හැමැදෙනාමැගෙ නොහැම්මෙන වැ

26 දූ මව්පිය දෙදෙනා හා මෙසෙමැ එක්කුසහොත් කණවැඳුම් නනුන් බූනුන් හා සබ්‍රම්සරුන් හා මෙහෙකරුවන් පිණිසැ අහර සිගා යන ගමනක් හා මෙකීවවුන්මැ රොගී වූව බෙහෙදක් හා සබ්‍රම්

---

[1] ‘ඇජරොල්’—කති. දෙ.

[2] මීට මතු ශාසනකථාප්‍රවෘත්තිය දඹ. කතිකාවතේද, කී. කතිකාවතේද ප්‍රස්තාවනා බලා දැනගත හැකිය.

[3] කති. දෙකෙහිම ඌනයි.

[4] ‘යටත්පිරිසෙසින් යට කී උභය ප්‍රාතිමොක්ෂාදිය පිරිහෙළිය නො දී’—දඹ. කති.

[5] මෙය පුනරුක්ත්‍ය

[6] ධම්මපද : අත්තවග්ගයෙහි.

[7] ‘පරිද්දෙන්’—දඹ. කති.

27 සරුන්ට බෙහෙත් පස් සිගා යන ගමනක් හා (පැවැරූ තැනකට) පිරිතට යන ගමනක් මුත් මෙසින් පිටත් කටයුත්තකට කාලවිකාලයෙහි ඇත්ගමට් සමු නොදියැ යුතු ගිලානාදි කෘත්‍යයෙ

28 න් පිටතට යන්නවුන්ට සමු දෙත්හොත් අව්‍යක්තයන්ට සමු දෙන උපාධ්‍යායන්ට දුකුළා අයැත් වදාළබැවින් හුදු අව්‍යක්තයන්ටමැ සමු නොදි පොහොපවරුණුනා ආප(ත්තා)නාපත්ති (මාතෘ)

29 යක් දන්නා ව්‍යක්ත සඟකෙනකුන් මුල්කොටැ සමු දියැ යුතු නන් ගණයෙකින් ආ සඟකෙනකුන් තමා සමීපයෙහි වසවත හුන් තැනැ ගණ(තෙ)රුන්ගෙන් පතක්

30 හො පැවිදිකෙනකුන් දූකැ මුත් නොවැසැවියැ යුතු සථවිර නව මධ්‍යම හැම සංඝයාවිසින්මැ මැඳින් යැමැ සිහිසති සම්පජංඤයෙන් යුත් නිඳි .. සෙවුම්ත් සිරුරු

31 සතපා අලුයැමැ නැගී කමටහන්හි යෙදි හිඳැ සිටැ සක්මන් කිරීමෙන් දවස් ගෙවා පුහුණු ගත් පිරිවහා සිවුරු සකසා හැඳ පෙරවැ දැහැටිකිස

32 නිමවා දහගබ් මාඹො අඟණවතුදු ඈඳුරුවත් තෙරවත් ගිලන්වත් සෙනසුන් වත් ඈ කඬුවතුදු සපයා උවනහොත් බොජුන්හල් එළැබැ කැඳිනි වළඳා

33 බොජුන්හලැ වතාවත් නිමවා එක්බිත්තෙහි පත්පොත් බලනුවන් ගෙත්තම් රජන්නම් කරනුවන් පස බෙදනුවන් ඈ ඉක්මන් කටයුතු ඇතියවුන් මුත් සෙස්ස

34 වුන් කැඳිනි වැළැඳූ ඉක්බිත්තෙහි කමටහන්හි යෙදි දවස් යවා පස්බත්හිදු කී නියායෙන් ග්‍රන්ථවිදශීනා ධූරයෙහි යෙදි හිගිම්නිස් පැවිජියන් හා සංසඩ

35 නොවැ වත්වෙලා දක්වා දවස් යවා ඉරියව් නොපොහොනා කරුණක් ඇතමුත් වත්පිරිතට ලැබී රැස්වූවන්විසිනුදු සන්නිපතිතානං වො භික්ඛවෙ වයං කරණීයං ධම්මී වා ක

36 ථා අරියො වා තුණ්හීභාවො [1] සි වදාළ බැවින් ධම්මකථා මනස්කාර දෙකින් පිටත් තිරශ්චීන කථා හා කාම විතක්කාදි පාප විතක්කයෙන් නොයෙදි පෙරැ යැමැද බණ කියනු කියවනු අස

37 නු ධරනු ධම්මකථා කිරීම් ඈ නොසිස් පියෙවින් හා විදශීනා ධූරයෙන් ගෙවා මැඳින් යැමැ සපත් සඳැ සති සම්පජංඤයෙන් යුත් නිඳි සෙවියැ යුතු පිටතවියැ යුතු කටයුත්තෙකින් එළ

38 බෙන මඟි පැවිජියන්විසින් පසිලිපැල් පිළිමගෙ ඈ කැපතැනෙක්හි ලැගුම් ගතයුතු හැමැ වෙලෙහිමැ කිපිසිතින් වත් කෙළිසිතින් වත් නොසරුප් තෙපුල කිසිවක්හු හා නොබිණියැ යු

[1] මජ්ඣිම නිකාය—3 වග්ග, අරියපරියෙසන සුත්ත.

39 තු මවුනුදු වූව වි(ෂ)භාගයන් හාද මලකුදු වූව ළදරු බාලයකු හාද (රහස්හි) නොබිණියැ යුතු වැඩිමහල්ලවුන් නොදන්ව මෙහෙකරුවන්ට දූහැවිලි නො වියැ යුතු තමා අයැතියකුදු මහල්ලන් අනුනොදන්ව අන්

40 නට නොදියැ යුතු ග(ම)න් යන්නක්හුවිසින් මහලු සඟුන්ගෙ තෙම් නස්නට සුදුසු පිරිකරක් තමා අත්හි ඇත මුත් අතුරෙහි වැසි අවද පියවි ගමනින් මැ නොතෙමෙන තැන් එළැකියැ යුතු එබඳු පි

41 රිකරක් ඇත සරුප් (.. වෙලෙ)වියෙකින්මැ යැ යුතු (න හි එතං .. .. න .. තුවෙච .. .. ත .. වත්තසමා හසනං යස්මිං විහිත මත්තනො තං වට්ටති)[1] යි වදාළබැවින් සිනාවට නිසි කරුණෙක්

42 හිදු හඬ නොවිහිදූ මුව වසා සතුටුපමණක් දක්වියැ යුතු තමා වන වෙහෙර සත්හිඳෙන අධිකරණ බැහැර නොපනළ කට යුතු අන් වෙහෙර සත්හිඳෙන අධිකරණ තමා නො ඉසිලියැ යුතු ස

43 ල්ලෙඛං අච්චජන්තෙන අප්පමත්තෙන භික්ඛුනා කප්පියෙපි න කාතබ්බා ආමිසාදීසු ලොලතා[2] යි වදාළබැවින් කැපපසයෙහිදු ලොල්බව් නොකට යුතු දහගබ් මහබො ඈ වඳුම්

44 න් ගඳ දු(ම්මල්) ඈ පුදමින් දූවුවු වලඳමින් පා කස්සෙහි ලමින් නොබිණියැ යුතු ඇත්ගම්හි ගිහිමිනිසුන් හා පසපිළිබඳ කථාද විසභාග කථාද නො කට යුතු ඉධෙකච්චො සංඝ ග

45 තොපි අචිත්තීකාරකතො ථෙරෙ භික්ඛු ඝට්ටයන්තො පි තිට්ඨති ඝට්ටයන්තොපි නිසීදති ඨිතකොපි භණති බාහා වික්ඛෙපකොපි භණති කුමාරස්සපි සිරං පරාමසති[3] යි අනාචා

46 රනිද්දේශ[යෙ]හි වදාළබැවින් සඟමැඳුට එළකියහුවිසිනුදු වෙරින් එව් සිවුරෙන් එව් නොසැපියැ යුතු මහළු සඟුන් හා බිණුවමනා කරුණක් ඇත ආදර දක්වා ඉතා නොළංවැ නැමී සිටැ අ

47 ත් නොවනා බිණියැ යුතු කිසිතැනෙක්හිදු කොමරුන් වෙරළ අත්ලා නො සැනැවියැ යුතු පධන්සෙරෙහි වසනුවනට විබෙවූ නොකොටැ හැදෑරියැ යුතු පබ්බාජෙන්තා සොධෙත්වා පබ්බාජෙ

48 න්ති සොධෙත්වා උපසම්පාදෙන්ති සොධෙත්වා නිස්සයං දෙන්ති එකො පි හි කුලපුත්තො පබ්බජ්ජඤ්ච උපසම්පදඤ්ච ලභිත්වා ස[ක]ලම්පි සාසනං පතිට්ඨාපෙති[4] යු බැවින් පිරික්සා පැවිජි කට යුතු පිරික්

---

[1] මෙපාලිපාඨයේ බොහෝතැන් ශිලාලිපියෙහි මැකීගොස්තිබෙන නිසා කිය වාගන්ට උගහටයි.

[2] සමන්තපාසාදිකා—කඨිනවග්ග, සික්ඛාපදවණ්ණනා.

[3] විසුද්ධිමග්ග—සීලනිද්දෙස—කායික අනාචාරවණ්ණනා.

[4] සමන්තපාසාදිකා—චුල්ලවග්ග—සෙනාසනග්ගාහවිනිච්ඡය වණ්ණනා.

49 සා උපසම්පත්ති කට යුතු පිරික්සා නිස දියැ යුතු තමා යගන පමණ
සමාදන් වියැ යුතු මෙ කීතාක් වතැ නොරිසින් පවතුකුදු අප්‍රඥ නො:
යම් කෙනෙක් මේ කළ කතිකා

50 වත්හි නොහික්මැ වරද(වා) පවතිත්නම් තුන් යැලක් දක්වා වරදට නිඃ
කරවා අවවාදකොටැ නැවැතැද එසෙමැ පවතිත්නම් නිස නො
දක්වා හිඳුවා විනයානුකූල පැවැ

51 ත්මක් නැතහොත් උත්කෙරෙහි නොබැඳි හැරැවියැ යුතු ගණදෙටු තෙ
විසිනුදු තමන් තමාත්ට යෙදූ ධුරයෙහි පමාවැ සංඝයා හික්මවා නෙ.
හොත් මහතෙරවරුන් යෙදූ දඬුවම් කට යුතු

TRANSCRIPT.[1]

1 Apa Budun kalpa çatasahasrā⸗dhika ca(tu)r-asaṁkhya parimita k
samatis-pärum purā Māra-saṅgrāma-bhūmi-vū Mahābodhi pary
⸗rūḍha-vä durvvāra sa-pa-

2 -rivāra Māra parājaya koṭä sarvvajña-pada prāpta-vä pansālis havı
divas[2] cātur-dvīpaka mahāmeghayak-seyin väḍä siṭä ane-

3 -ka kalpa koṭi çata-sahasrayehi[3] kleçāgnīn dagdha-vemin siṭi sa(
dharmmāmṛta-varṣāyen nivamin sakala-buddha-kṛtya nimavā Kı
nuvarä abiyes-hi Ma-

4 -lla-rājayange sālavanodyānayehi nirūpadhiçeṣa[4] nirvvāṇa dhātuven
sārasiya sū-panäs havuruddak giya kalä **Vaḷagam Abhā Ma**
davasä paṭan ekvādahas desiya sū-

5 -panäs havuruddak bhinna nikāya-vä çāsanaya piri(y)emin[5] siṭi kalhi
sammatā⸗di paramparāyāta[6] Sūryya-va(ṁ)çodbhūta rājādhirāja na
abhivyāpta[7] yaçomarīcīn virājamā-

6 -na **Çrī-Sa(ṁ)ghabodhi Parākrama-Bāhu**[8] **Maharajāṇan** sakala I
telehi eka rājyābhiṣekayen abhiṣikta-vä vijṛmbhita puṇyardhi
rājya-sukhā⸗nubhava koṭä vasanuvan

---

[1] For certain textual differences, collate with this the portions included in the Daṁbadeṇ vata (*Damb. K.*) and in the Kīrtti-Çrī-Rājasiṁha-katikāvata (*Ki. K.*). See Jayatilaka's *Katikāvat-*

[2] Omitted in both the *Katikāvatas*.

[3] *Anavarāgra-saṁsāra-vṛttayehi* in both the *Katikāvatas*.

[4] Read *nirupadhiçeṣa*.

[5] *pirihemin* in both *K.*

[6] *paramparānuyāta* in both *K.*

[7] *naika-dik-hi vyāpta* in both *K.*

[8] *Çrī Parākrama-Bāhu* in both *K.*

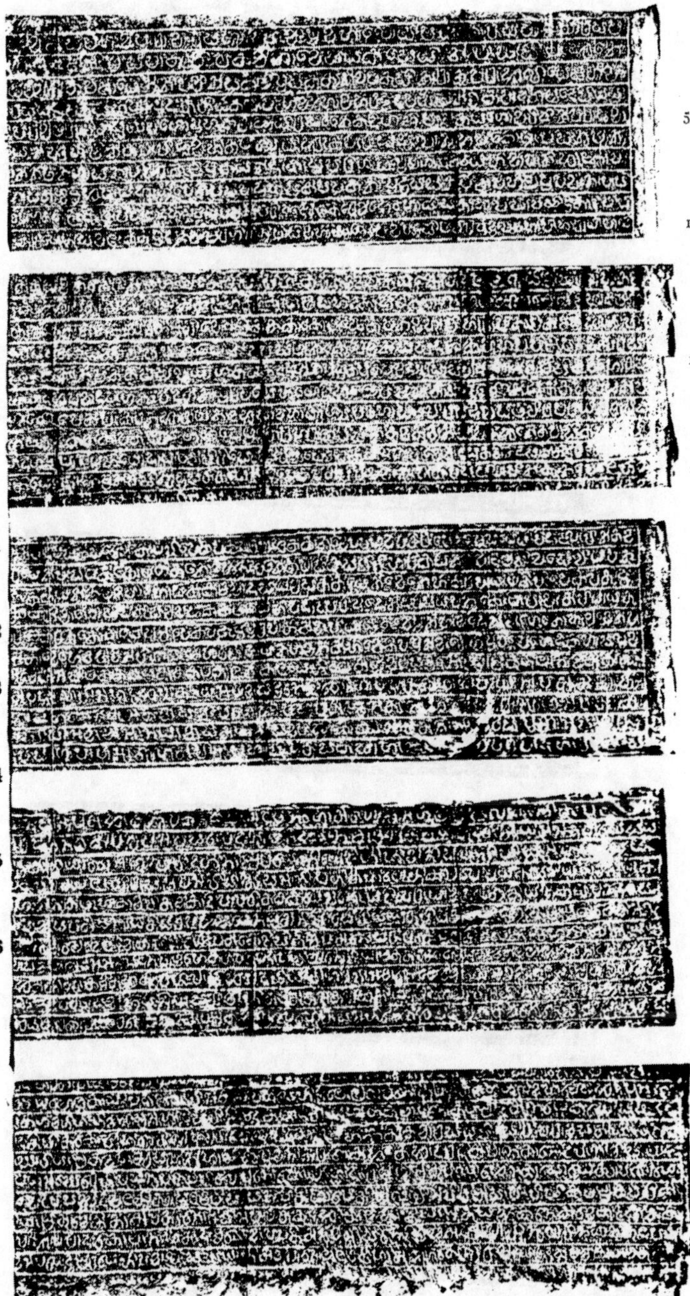

about 1½ inches to a foot

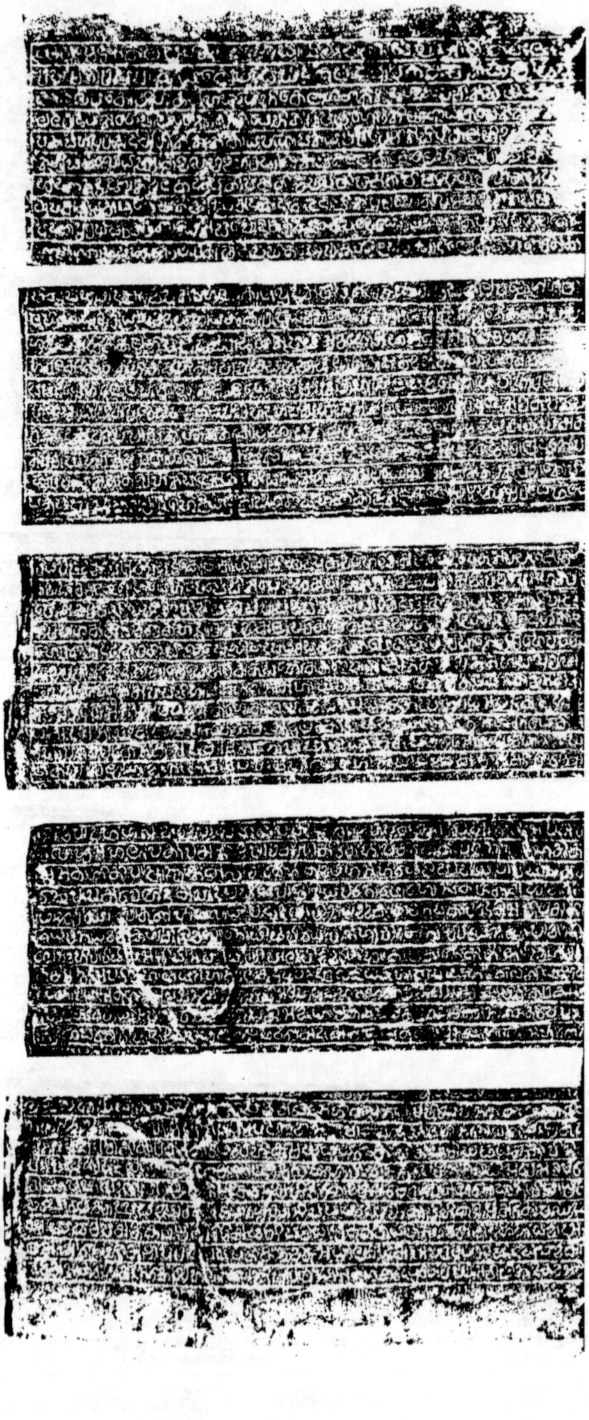

7 ajñāna durjñāna mūlaka apratipatti duṣpratipatti viṣa-vega vihata-vä apāyā-
-nnavana [1] çāsanāvácara kula-putrayan däkä supariçuddha Buddha-çāsa-
-nayehi mā-väni ājñā-ca-
8 -kravarttiyak-hu me väni kiluṭak däkä däkä udāsīna-vuvahot Budu-sasna
nassi boho sat-hu-du apāyabhāg-veti pasvā-dahasak pavatnā Budu-sasnaṭa
mā vahal-vuva-mānäväyi
9 prajñā-purassara karuṇāyen saṁcodita hṛdaya-äti-vä mese naṭa sasun
kavurun vahal-koṭā apagata-kalaṁka-vä [2] pasvā-dahasak pavatnā
paridden kerem-dohoyi sitā akhaṇḍācchidratā-di vivi-
10 -dha guṇagaṇāṅga saṅgata-koṭā rakṣita vardhita poṣita çīla-skandhā-di
laukika guṇaratnālaṁkārayen samalaṁkṛta-vū **Udumbaragiri** nivāsī
Mahā-Kāçyapa Mahā-sthavira pramukha **Mahāvihārā-dhivāsi-**
11 bhikṣu-saṁghayā däkä ovun vahal-koṭā Budun-visin anujñāta Buddha-kalpa [3]
Moggaliput-Tis-Maha-terun vahal-koṭā pāpa-bhikṣu [4] nirmmathanaya-
koṭā durllabdhi mäḍā çāsana-ma-
12 -la viçodhā tṛtīya dharmma-saṁgāyanā kärävū **Dharmmāçoka**-maha-rajahu-
men aneka çata pāpa-bhikṣūn çāstṛ-çāsanayen apagata-koṭā ṣaḍ-abhijñā-
-dyaneka guṇa-gaṇopeta mahā-kṣīṇā-
13 -çravayan äti-kalhi pavā pūrvva-rājayan-visin mahotsāhayen-udu samaṅga
no-koṭā gata huṇu [5] Tun-nakā samaṅga-kirīmen ek-nakā koṭā **Jetavana-
mahā-vihārādi** no-ek maha-ägi vi-
14 -hāra Lak-divä tanhi tanhi karavā ehi sahasra saṁkhyā-tikrānta [6] mahā-sa(ṁ)-
-ghayā vāsa-karavā nirantara pravṛtta dharmmāmiṣa-dānayen upasthāna-
keremin saṁgha-darçana prabhava prīti-prāmodya-rasā-
15 -svādayehi lola-vä kālānukālayehi pauṣathāṅga [7]-çīla-sa(mu)petā-vä vihārayaṭa
eḷabā sannipatita [8] saṁgha-madhya-gata-vä tad darçana prasūta prīti-
prāmodya-rasā-svāda-koṭā mā-visin maho-tsā-
16 -hayen sādhita-vū me saṁgha-[sā]magriya pasvādahasak abhinna-vä pavatnā
paridden matu-vana saṁghayā-da apramāda-vä grantha-vidarçanā-dhura-
dvayehi yedī alpe-cchatā-di-guṇen yukta-vä vasanā-pa-

---

[1] *apāya vyasanāpanna-vana* in both *K.*

[2] *vahal-koṭavavā pasvā-dahasak* in both *K.*

[3] Omitted in both *K.*

[4] *aneka sahasra pāpabhikṣūn* in both *K.*

[5] *samaga-koṭa gata nu huṇu* in both *K.*

[6] *aneka sahasra saṁkhyā äti* in both *K.*

[7] Read *pauṣadhāṅga* or *posathāṅga.*

[8] Omitted in both *K.*

17 -ridden avavādānuçāsana-koṭā çāsanaya rakṣā-kaḷa-mänäväyi yukta vyakta guṇopeta-vä karana[1] ārādhanā-da asā **Mahā-Kāçyapa-Mahā-sthavira**-pramukha-sthaviravarayan-mä-visi-

18 -n .pramāda-vihārīn avakāça no-labana sandahā dharmma-vina[ya] sasandana-koṭā ädurol[2]-da no-vihidā kaḷa katikāvati[3]  gaṇa-deṭu teravarun-visin tama tamā nisā vana antevāsika saddhi-vi-

19 -hārikayan aturehi nisa dennaṭa nisayen mindennaṭa yogya-vä vasannavun pamā no-viyädī[4] grantha-dhurayehi yodā yäṭat-piriseyin **Vinayen Kudusikha** hā **Pāmok**-da **Sutatin Dasadham-sūtratraya Anumāna-**

20 **sūtraya**-da vana-pot[5] piriheḷiyā no-dī gaṇa-saṁgaṇikādīn duru-koṭā grantha-dhurayehi yehi[6] yedennavun-visin-udu satatayen viveka-vat piruva-mänä-väyi vadāḷa-bävin tun-velehi i-

21 -riyav (sumanā)sil pirisudu-koṭā kā-giyā-sī-ādi-vū kamaṭahanek-hi yedī detun palagak huṇu-ganvā davasa kaḍa no-koṭa viveka-vat puravā 'attānam-eva paṭhamaṁ patirūpe nivesaye[7] 'yi vadāḷa-bävin tama

22 tamā-da me(kī) guṇāṅgayehi vesesin yedī at-väḍa para-väḍa sādhamin kī (vadāḷen)[8] grantha-dhurayen väḍiyak-koṭā gata-no-hena antevāsika saddhi-vihārikayan lavā **Mulsikha Sekhiyā** vana-

23 -pot karavā **Sikhavaḷaṅdavinisa** asvā samasin samasä ādyanta-koṭā sumanā vicāla tänäka kiyannaṭa pohosat karavā **Dasa-dham** satatayen menehi-karavā yäṭakī viveka-vatu-du

24 puravā çakti-pamaṇak hadārā nimi-kalä caritānukūla kamaṭahanak uganvā vidarçanā dhurayehi-mä yodā catu-sampajaṁña kathāyehi vadāḷa paridden davas yavanu koṭā pävätviyā yutu

25 heraṇanu-du **Heraṇa-sikha Sekhiy**(ā) **Dasadham sutat** vanapot-koṭā asā no-piriheḷā parihараṇa-karanu-koṭā yodā viveka-vat-udu puravā hikmäviyā yutu mevun hämā-denā-mä-ge no-hämmena vä-

26 -du mav-piya dedenā hā mese-mä ek-kusa-hot kaṇavändaṁbu naṅgun būnun hā sa-bramsarun hā mehekaruvan piṇisā ahara siṅgā yana gamanak hā mekīvavun-mä rogī-vuva behedak hā sa-bram-

---

[1] *karana lada* in both *K.*

[2] *äjarol* in both *K.*

[3] This historical introduction is to be found repeated and brought down to their respective dates in the two *Katikāvatas.*

[4] Omitted in both *K.*

[5] *Yaṭatpiriseyin yaṭa kī ubhaya prātimokṣādiya piriheḷiya no-dī* in *Damb. K.*

[6] Repeated in error.

[7] See *Dhammapada: attavagga*, v. 2.

[8] *paridden* in *Damb. K.*

7 -saruṇṭa behet pas siṅgā yana gamanak hā (pävärū tänakaṭa) piritaṭa yana gamanak mut meyin piṭat kaṭayuttakaṭa kāla-vikālayehi ät-gamaṭ samu no-diyä yutu gilānādi-kṛtyaye-

8 -n piṭataṭa yannavunṭa samu det-hot avyaktayanṭa samu dena upādhyāyanṭa dukuḷā ayät vadāḷa-bävin hudu avyaktayanṭa-mä samu no-dī poho-pavaru-ṇu hā āpa(ttya)nāpatti (māttra-)

9 -yak dannā vyakta saṅga-kenakun mul-koṭä samu diyä yutu nan gaṇayekin ā saṅga-kenakun tamā samīpayehi vasavata hun tänä gaṇa-(te)rungen patak

0 ho pävidi-kenakun däkä mut no-väsäviyä yutu sthavira nava madhyama häma saṁghayāvisin-mä mändin yämä siti-sati-sampajaṁñayen yut nindi .. sevumin siruru

1 satapā aluyämä nägī kamaṭahanhi yedī hindä siṭä sakman-kirīmen davas gevā puhuṇu gat pirīvahā sivuru sakasā händä peravä dähäṭi-kisa

2 nimavā dahagab māṁbo aṅgaṇa-vatu-du äduru-vat tera-vat gilan-vat senasun-vat ā kandu-vatu-du sapayā uvanahot bojun-hal eḷäbā känditi vaḷandā

3 bojun-halä vatāvat nimavā ekbittehi patpot balanuvan gettam rajannam karanuvan pasa bedanuvan ā ikman kaṭayutu ätiyavun mut sessa-

4 -vun känditi väḷändū ikbittehi kamaṭahanhi yedī davas yavā pas-bat-hi-du kī niyāyen grantha-vidarçanā-dhurayehi yedī gihi-minis pävijiyan hā saṁsaṭṭha

5 no-vä vat-velā dakvā davas yavā iriyav no-pohonā karuṇak äta mut vat-piritaṭa läbī räsvūvan-visin-udu 'sannipatitānaṁ vo bhikkhave dvayaṁ karaṇīyaṁ dhammī vā ka-

6 -thā ariyo vā tuṇhī-bhāvo'[1] yi vadāḷa-bävin dharmma-kathā manaskāra dekin piṭat tiraçcīna kathā hā kāma-vitarkkā-dī pāpa-vitarkkayen no-yedī perä yämä-da baṇa kiyanu kiyavanu asa-

7 -nu dharanu dharmma-kathā kirīm ā no-sis-piyevin hā vidarçanā-dhurayen gevā mändin yämä sapat sandā sati sampajaṁñayen yut nindi seviyä yutu piṭataviyä yutu kaṭayuttekin eḷa-

8 -bena maṅgī pävijiyan-visin pasili-päl piḷima-ge ā käpa-tänek-hi lägum gata yutu hämä velehi-mä kipi-sitin vat keḷi-sitin vat no-sarup tepul kisivak-hu hā no-biṇiyä yu-

---

[1] See *Majjhima-nikāya, vagga* iii. *ariyapariyesana-sutta.*

39 -tu mavun-udu vuva vi(ṣa)bhāgayan hā-da malak-udu vuva ḷadaru bālayaku hā-da (rahas-hi) no-biṇiyä yutu väḍimahallavun no-danva mehe-ka--ruvanṭa dähävili no-viyä yutu tamā ayatiyak-udu mahallan anu-no-danva an-

40 -naṭa no-diyä yutu ga(ma)n yannak-hu-visin mahalu-saṅgunge temī nasnaṭa sudusu pirikarak tamā at-hi äta mut aturehi väsi avada piyavi gamanin-mä no-temena tän eḷäbiyä yutu ebandu pi-

41 -rikarak äta sarup (.. vele)viyekin-mä yā yutu (na hi etaṁ .. .. na .. tu .. veva .. .. ta .. vattasmā hasanaṁ yasmiṁ vihita-mattan taṁ vaṭṭatī)[1] yi vadāḷa-bävin sināvaṭa nisi karuṇek-

42 -hi-du haṅḍa no-vihidä muva vasā satuṭu-pamaṇak däkviyä yutu tamā vana veherä sanhindena adhikaraṇa bähära no-pahaḷa kaṭa yutu an veherä sanhindena adhikaraṇa tamā no-isiliyä-yutu 'sa-

43 -llekhaṁ accajantena appamattena bhikkhunā kappiyepi na kātabbā āmisatthāya lolatā'[2] yi vadāḷa-bävin käpa-pasayehi-du lolbav no-kaṭa yutu dahagab mahaṁbo ā vandimi-

44 -n ganda du(m mal) ā pudamin dävūṭu vaḷandamin pā kassehi lamin no-biṇiyä yutu ät-gamhi gihi-minisun hā pasa-piḷibada kathā-da visabhāga kathā-da no-kaṭa yutu 'idhekacco saṁgha-ga-

45 -to'pi acittikārakato there bhikkhū ghaṭṭayanto'pi tiṭṭhati ghaṭṭayanto 'pi nisīdati ṭhitako'pi bhaṇati bāhā vikkhepako'pi bhaṇati kumārassa 'pi siraṁ parāmasati'[3] yī anācā-

46 -ra nirdeça[ye]hi vadāḷa-bävin saṅga-mändaṭa eḷabiyahuvisin-udu verin ev sivuren ev no-ghäṭiyä yutu mahaḷu saṅgun hā biṇuvamanā karuṇak äta ādara dakvā itā no-ḷaṁ-vä nämī siṭä a-

47 -t no-vanā biṇiyä yutu kisitänek-hi-du komarun verä at-lā no-sänāviyä yutu padhan-gherehi vasanuvanaṭa vikhevu no-koṭā hädāriyä yutu 'pabbājentā sodhetvā pabbāje-

48 -tha sodhetvā upasampādetha sodhetvā nissayaṁ detha eko'pi hi kulaputto pabbajjañ-ca upasampadañ-ca labhitvā sa[ka]lam-pi sāsanaṁ patiṭṭhāpeti'[4] yū-bävin piriksā päviji kaṭa yutu pirik-

---

[1] The Pāli quotation is too faint to be made cut.

[2] *Samantapāsādikā: Kaṭhinavagga, Sikkhāpadavaṇṇanā.*

[3] *Visuddhi-magga.—Sīlaniddesa-Kāyika-anācāra-vaṇṇanā.*

[4] *Samantapāsādikā—Cullavagga—Senāsanaggāha-vinicchaya-vaṇṇanā.*

49 -sā upasampatti kaṭa yutu piriksā nisa diyä yutu tamā yahana pamaṇak duhaṅga samādan viyä yutu me kī-täk vatä no-risin pavatuk-udu ayuṇu no-kiyä yutu yam kenek mē kaḷa katikā-

50 vat-hi no-hikmä varada(vā) pavatit-nam tun yälak dakvā varadaṭa nisi daṅḍuvam karavā avavāda-koṭä nävätä-da ese-mä pavatit-nam nisa no-dī masak dakvā hinduvā vinayā-nukūla pävä-

51 -tmak nätahot un-kerehi no-bändi häräviyä yutu gaṇa-deṭu teravarun-visin-udu taman tamanṭa yedū dhurayehi pamā-vä saṁghayā hikmavā no-lālat--hot mahateravarun yedū daṅḍuvam kaṭa yutu

TRANSLATION.

[Lines 1–4] Our Buddha having fulfilled the exercise of all the thirty pre-eminent virtues[1] over a period of four *asaṅkhyas* and one hundred thousand cycles of years (*kalpas*), mounted on the dais at [the foot] of the great Bodhi[2] tree, which formed [as it were] the field of battle with Māra, vanquished this [well-nigh] irresistible Māra together with his host, and attained to the state of omniscience. Thereafter, for forty-five years he manifested himself like a great rain-cloud over the four continents,[3] and so, with showers of nectar-like Dhamma[4], he assuaged [the torments of] the living beings who were being burnt by the kleça[5] fire of many *kalpa* cycles old, numbering hundreds of thousands of kōṭis. Having thus accomplished all the duties of a Buddha, he passed away into the *nirupadhi-çeṣa*[6] *nirvāṇa* state in the grove of sāla trees of the Malla princes in the neighbourhood of the city of Kusinārā.

[Lines 4–9] At the expiration of 454 years [from this event], there reigned the great King **Vaḷagam Abhā**[7]. Thereafter, for 1254 years the Buddhist Fraternity remained disintegrated, and the religion also continued its course of decadence. At this juncture, there came to the throne the mighty king of

---

[1] *Pärum* (line 1) spelt also *perum*, P. *pāramī* or *pāramitā*. See Rhys Davids's *Pāli Dict.* for an explanation of this term.

[2] *Mahā-bodhi-paryaṅka* 'the divan of thorough enlightenment' (Müller).

[3] Namely, *Uttarakuru* on the north, *Jambudvīpa* on the south, *Pūrvavideha* on the east, and *Aparagodāna* on the west of the *Mahā Meru* mountain which is supposed to stand on three other mountains (*Trikūṭa*) at the centre of the basin-like earth encircled by the Cakkavāḷa range.

[4] Referring to the Sermons of the Buddha.

[5] For a Buddhistic definition of this word as applied to hereditary desires of a vicious nature, see Rhys Davids's *Pāli Dict.*

[6] The state which leaves no substratum of being behind, that is to say, entirely free from rebirth.

[7] Vaṭṭa-Gāmaṇi Abhaya, 439 A.B. and 454–466 A.B. (44 and 29–17 B.C.).

kings[1], **Çrī Saṁghabodhi Parākrama-Bāhu,** a scion of the lineage of Mahā-sammata, born of the Solar race and resplendent with the rays of [kingly] glory that diffused themselves through many a region [of the globe]. His Majesty was anointed with the unction of paramount dominion over the whole land of Laṅkā. And, whilst he was enjoying the delight of kingship with a display of abundant virtues, he witnessed sons of noble families of the Buddhist persuasion on the road to the *apāya*[2], having succumbed to the evil effects[3] of non-perception or ill-perception through ignorance or imperfect knowledge. Now, His Majesty reasoned[4] thus:—'Seeing over and over again a blot such as this on the immaculate Buddhist religion, if a mighty emperor like myself were to remain indifferent, the Buddhist religion would perish, and many living beings will be destined to the *apāya*[2]. Let me serve the Buddhist religion which should last five thousand years.' So, with a heart animated by forethought and sympathy[5], [he argued further:] 'whose services should I enlist to restore[6] the religion which has thus been ruined, so that I may make it endure for five thousand years?'

[Lines 9–18] Then, noting the congregation of Buddhist monks resident in the **Udumbaragiri** monastery with **Mahā-Kāçyapa Mahā-sthavira** as their chief—all of whom sparkled with the brilliancy of gems of virtues highest in the world, such as the body of moral piety which has been preserved, increased and cherished by the consolidation of various groups of good qualities that have no flaws or hiatuses; (His Majesty pondered that in days gone by) the great king **Dharma Açoka,** enlisting the services of **Moggaliputta Tissa,** the Great Elder of the Buddha Cycle acknowledged by the Buddha himself[7], crushed out the sinful

---

[1] *Rājādhirāja* (line 5).

[2] *Apāya* 'purgatory'. According to Buddhist writings, there are four *apāyas* or transitory states of suffering after death.

[3] *Viṣa-vega*, lit. 'poison-impetus'.

[4] See line 9.

[5] *Prajñā-purassara karuṇāyen.*

[6] *Apagata-kalaṅka-vä*, 'having become freed of stain.' Cf. *apagata-vyādhi.*

[7] *Budun-visin anujñāta Buddha-kalpa Moggali-put-Tis.* In the later recensions of this portion of the *Katikāvata*, the word *Buddhakalpa* is omitted. See Jayatilaka's *Katikāvat-saṅgarā*, Nos. 2 and 3. We are indebted to Mrs. Rhys Davids for the suggestion that this phrase alludes to the belief of a prophetic utterance by the Buddha to the effect that when in the future the turn for setting forth the *Kathāvatthu* shall have arrived, his disciple the greatly-wise Elder, Moggaliputta Tissa will purge the blemishes that have arisen in the religion. (*Points of Controversy*, p. 2.) Cf. also the statement *apagē Buduhu Sävät-nuvaradī yamā maha peḷahara-koṭa tīrtthakayangē man bin̆dalā tripāda vikramayen Tavutisā dev-lovaṭa vāḍa paṇḍu-im̆bul sal-hasnehi vāḍa hin̆da māṭr-divya-putra pramukha deviyanṭa Vijam-piṭakaya desanāgamanē 'mama Damsaṅgunu, Vibhaṅga, Dhatūkathā, Puggalaprajnapti, Yamaka, Paṭ-ṭhāna desimi. Mā pirinivī kala Dharmāçoka rajjuruvan sahāya koṭa gena . . . māgē Moggaliputta-Tissa-maha-terahu . . . Kathāvastu desati' yamsē vaddāḷasēk-da* etc., in *Saddharmaratnāvaliya: Nāgasena-kathā.*

Bhikkhus; suppressed the heretics; purged the religion of its impurities and brought about the holding of the Third Rehearsal of the *Dhamma*. In like manner, His Majesty [Parakkama-Bāhu] also enlisted the services of those (Udumbara-giri) bhikkhus and, removing from the Master's religion many hundreds of sinful monks, brought about a *rapprochement* of the three fraternities[1] and a coalition of them into one single fraternity (*nikāya*)—a reconciliation which former kings, despite their great efforts, were not able to effect, even though there were at the time eminently holy personages[2] endowed with aggregates of divers faculties such as the six psychic powers[3], &c. At various spots in the Island of Laṅkā, His Majesty caused costly monasteries to be built, such as the Jetavana-mahā-vihāra[4], &c. In these he provided lodgings for members of the Order over a thousand in number, and treated them to a constant flow of spiritual and material gifts[5].

Being desirous of enjoying the sensation of joyous thrills arising from seeing the priesthood, His Majesty, from time to time, had recourse to the observance of the Uposatha-sīla precepts[6]. [On these occasions], he used to enter the monastery and go[7] amongst the assembled priesthood. Then, moved by the sensation of thrills of joy emanating from the spectacle of the reverend monks, [he was wont to say] 'in order that this union of the Buddhist priesthood, which I have effected with great effort, may last unbroken for five thousand years and also that future members of the Order may prosper, endowed with virtues such as contentment and the like, devoting themselves diligently to the two tasks of scriptural study and contemplation, may the reverend Sirs preserve the religion by the administration of exhortations and instructions'.

---

[1] Namely, the Mahāvihara, the Abhayagiri and the Jetavana fraternities. In a MS. copy of the *Daṁbadeṇi-katikāvata* (British Museum, Or. 6603(133), it is, however, pointed out that the three fraternities in question were the three heretical sects called Dhammaruci-nikāya, Sāgaliya-nikāya and Vetulya-vāda-nikāya.

[2] *Kṣiṇāçravayan* 'those whose *āsavas* are destroyed'. See the *Pāli Dict.*, s.vv., *āsava* and *khīṇāsava*.

[3] *Ṣaḍ-abhijñā*. For particulars, see the *Pāli Dict.*, s.v., *Abhiññā*.

[4] In the B. M. MS. mentioned above, there is the interesting information that this Jetavana monastery is the place where the Pāli *nighaṇṭu* was produced (*Pāli nighaṇḍuḥppatti Jetavana-mahā-vihāra*), obviously referring to the *Abhidhānappadīpikā* of Moggallāna Thera. For a discussion on the identity of this author, see above, pp. 249–250.

[5] *Dharmāmiṣa-dāna* (line 14).

[6] *Uposathaṅgasīla* = *aṭṭhaṅga-samannāgata uposatha*, 'the Sabbath with the eightfold ethical injunctions'. *Sam-upetä-vä* (l. 15) 'having had recourse to'.

[7] Cf. *sagha upele* in Rupnāth rock-inscription. Asoka's visits to the Saṁgha, see Hultzsch's *Asoka Inscr.*, Introd., p. xiv., Bhandarkar's *Asoka* pp. 78–81.

Having hearkened unto these [repeated] appeals made with manifestations of appropriate decorum, the Community of Theras, headed by the great Thera Mahā Kassapa, formulated the [following] code of disciplinary injunctions without deviating from the customary formalities observed in the lineage of preceptors, and after due consultation of the *Dhamma* (doctrine) and the *Vinaya* (disciplinary regulations), in order that those of negligent conduct may not find an opening [for transgression].

[Lines 18–24] The head Theras[1] of chapters of monks should not permit any negligence on the part of those among their respective co-resident *saddhivihārikas* and *antevāsikas*,[2] who are eligible either to be vouchsafed the *nissaya*[3] or to be released from it, but should set them to the task of studying the scriptures.

They should not be allowed to neglect the learning at least of the **Kudusikha**[4] and the **Pāmok**[5] from the Vinaya literature] and the three **Dasadhamma-sutta** and the **Anumāna-sutta** from the **Suttanta** [Piṭaka].

They should also be dissuaded from [unbecoming conduct such as] taking delight in company[6], &c.

Since it is stated that those engaged in the study of the scriptures should

---

[1] Viz. *Upajjhāyas* 'spiritual preceptors' and *Ācariyas*, 'teachers'.

[2] A *saddhivihārika* is a spiritual disciple of the *upajjhāya* while an *antevāsika* is a pupil of the *ācariya*. A *sāmaṇera* or novice can, therefore, have an *upajjhāya* who stands in the capacity of a father to him, as well as an *ācariya* from whom he learns the prescribed religious texts. Sometimes the two offices are combined in one Elder. For further particulars, see *Mahāvagga*, i. 25–37, *Cullavagga*, viii. 11–14, and *S.B.E.*, xiii, Pt. I, p. 178 n. 2.

The note 4 on p. 31 of Geiger's translation of the *Mahāvaṁsa* is misleading.

[3] *Nissaya* is the protection given by a senior monk to a co-resident novice who becomes then in *statu pupillari*. After a certain period, as in the case of a University student, he receives his absolution on passing the prescribed tests as regards his geneneral conduct and his knowlege of the scriptures. See also *S.B.E.*, xiii, Pt. I, p. 179, n. 1, *E.Z.*, Vol. I, p. 7 n. 5.

[4] *Khudda Sikkhā*—a summary of Vinaya precepts composed in 467 Pāli stanzas by Dhammasiri Thera. The date of this work has not been yet ascertained, but there are two *Ṭīkās* to it, an old one (*porāṇa ṭīkā*) by an anonymous author and a new one (*abhinava ṭīkā*) by Saṅgharakkita Thera, a pupil of Sāriputta Thera who took part in the Buddhist Council dealt with in the present record (See B.M. Cat. of Sinh. MSS., Introd. p. xvi). There exist two more scholia on this work, a *Porāṇa Padayojanā* by Vicittālaṅkāra Thera of Burma and an *Abhinava Padayojanā* also by a Burmese monk, as well as a Sinhalese interverbal translation *Kudusika-sanne* by Diṁbulāgala Medhaṅkara (13th century).

[5] *Pātimokkha*, see *S.B.E.*, xiii, Pt. I.

[6] *Gaṇa-saṁgaṇikā* 'coming into contact with one another' *Dh.A.*, I. 162. 'Delighting in society' is sinful for a Buddhist monk.

always cultivate concentration of thought in seclusion [1], they [namely the saddhi-vihārikas, &c.], all throughout the three divisions of the day, should mould their ways of deportment [2] perfectly, and their character absolutely without blemish.

Engrossed in meditation on subjects such as the consciousness of the [impermanency of the] body [3] and rehearsing [the prescribed texts] in two or three ways [4], they should day by day cultivate without interruption concentration of mind in seclusion.

Since it is stated [5] 'one should set himself at first in the right', each one should establish for himself these (afore)said attributes of virtue and promote one's own welfare as well as that of others.

Those *antevāsikas* and *saddhivihārikas* [6] who are unable to master a great portion of the [prescribed] course of study, should [at least] be made to learn by heart **Mul-sikha** [7] and **Sekhiyā** [8] and to rehearse the **Sikhavalaṅda-vinisa** [9].

---

[1] This is apparently the idea conveyed here by the expression *viveka-vat piruva mänävä* (should fulfil the functions of solitude).

[2] *Iriyav sumanā sil pirisudu koṭā* (lines 20-21). There are four *iriyāpathas* or postures, viz. walking, standing, sitting, and lying down.

[3] *Kā-giyāsī* = P. *kāya-gatāsati.*

[4] *De tun palagak huṇu ganvā.* The meaning is not quite clear. *Palaṅga* or *palak*, P. *pallaṅka*, Skt. *paryaṅka, palyaṅka*, 'sitting cross-legged,' a couch, a seat or divan as in *saraba palaṅgak sädū denelā* (*Kāvyaçekhara*, viii. 24). But the word here is *palaga*, given in *Piyummala* as a synonym of *ayuru* (Skt. *ākāra*) 'form, shape, manner'. Cf. *pälaṅgin* (*Sasadāvata*, v. 57), *palaṅga* (*Siyabaslakara*, v. 81 and *Nāmāvaliya*, v. 220), 'way, manner'. *Huṇamin*=*çravaṇaya karamin* (*Sidatsaṅgarā*, pp. 41-42).

[5] In *Dhammapada*, xii. 2.

Attānam eva paṭhamam patirūpe nivesaye,
Ath' aññam anusāseyya, na kilisseyya paṇḍito.
One should set himself first in the right,
Then should he teach another, the wise man [who acts so]
should receive no blame.

[6] See above, p. 276, n. 2.

[7] *Mūlasikkhā.* There are two *Ṭīkās* and a Sinhalese *sanne* to this work. For Müller's edition, see *P. T. S. Journal*, 1883.

[8] Evidently the *Sekhiyā* portion of the *Pātimokkha*. See *S. B. E.*, xiii. Pt. I. pp. 59-67.

[9] *Sikhavalaṅda* and its commentary *Sikhavalaṅda-vinisa* are two of the oldest Sinhalese treatises extant. The colophon to the latter tells us that they are the works of one author but does not give his name or the time he lived. In the Mihintale-rock record of Mahinda IV (954-970 A.D.), however, reference is made to the *Sikakaraṇī* (*E. Z.*, Vol. I. p. 99) dealing with the *Sekhiyā* rules of the *Pātimokkha*. As this is only a chapter of the *Sikhavalaṅda-vinisa*, the latter work must have been in existence at the time. About forty years before this period Kassapa V (908-918 A.D.) wrote the *Dampiyā-aṭuvā gäṭapada*, the language of which is practically the same as that of the *Sikhavalaṅda* and the *Sikhavalaṅda-vinisa*. Hence the date of both these works may be assigned to the first half of the tenth century A.D. An edition of these two treatises by Mr. D. B. Jayatilaka appeared in Colombo, 1924. This, as well as his edition of the *Katikāvatas*, has been of great use to us in the interpretation of the present record.

They should thus be rendered capable of repeating correctly any portion of the text from beginning to end on being questioned every six months.

They should be made always to remember the *dasa-dhamma*[1] and cultivate the aforementioned concentration of thought in seclusion.

After they have finished committing to memory as much as they can [of the prescribed texts], they should be taught a subject of meditation conformable to the custom [in vogue] and be set to the task of contemplation[2] thereon.

Thereafter, they should be made to spend the day in the manner related in the discourse on the fourfold circumspection[3].

[Lines 25–30] Novices should also learn and rehearse the **Heraṇasikha,** the **Sekhiyā** and the **Dasadhamma-sutta.** They should be made to practise this [rehearsal] without abatement and to cultivate concentration of thought in seclusion. This should be their training.

No permission to enter the village at wrong times[4] shall be given to any of these [monks and novices] on any business whatsoever, save on account of a journey for begging food in order to succour[5] their unsupported[6] parents who had given birth to them, likewise their consanguineous[7] and widowed elder and younger sisters, as well as the co-followers of the religious life[8] or, in case of illness, on account of a journey to procure medicine [for parents and sisters] or to beg for medicine and other requirements of the co-followers of the religious life, or [finally], on account of a journey to recite the Paritta[9] at an appointed place.

---

[1] Probably the *dasadhamma-sutta* is meant here. The ten objects, are, the four *maggas*, the four *phalas*, *nirvāṇa*, and the scriptures. See Hardy's *Eastern Monachism.*

[2] *Vidarçanā-dhura* 'obligation of introspection' (Rhys Davids's *Pāli Dictionary.*)

[3] *Catu-sampajañña-kathā.* See Rhys Davids's *Pāli Dictionary*, s.v. *sampajañña.*

[4] *Kāla-vikālayehi* 'when the time is wrong time', i.e. from sunset to sunrise. See *Pātimokkha: Pacittiyā Dhammā* and *S.B.E.*, xiii. Pt. I, p. 53, note 2.

[5] *Mehekaruvan piṇisä.*

[6] *No hämmena.* The meaning is not clear. Cf., however, *hammana* 'depending' (*Meghadūtasanne*, v. 4.)

[7] *Ek kusa hot* 'reposed in the same womb'.

[8] *Sa-bram-sarun*; *P. sa-brahmacārin* 'a fellow student' referring here to the junior monks and novices. See *Khuddasikkhā*, vv. 279–281, *Sikhavalaňda* (Jayatilaka's edition, 1924), p. 5 and pp. 58–59 and *Visuddhimagga*, pp. 337–340.

[9] *Paritta*, the ceremony of chanting certain texts of the Buddhist canon in order to exorcize evil spirits and make a person or place freed and protected from evil influence by means of talismans or charmed amulets.

As it is declared that if permission be given to those [bhikkhus] who have to go out [into the village] on duties due to sickness, &c., those preceptors who grant such permission to those not versed [1] [in the Buddhist regulations] shall be guilty of *dukhaṭa* [2] offence; so, no permission shall be given to unlearned (bhikkhus) unaccompanied. Permission, however, should be given [to them] on the responsibility of a learned bhikkhu who at least knows [the procedure of] the Uposatha and Pavāranā services [3] and is cognizant of what constitutes a fall and what not.

Should a bhikkhu who has come from one monastic community (wish to) take up his residence with another, no lodging ought to be given to him except after seeing either a letter [of recommendation] or a bhikkhu [emissary] from the Head Thera of the monastic establishment where he had (before) lived.

[Lines 30–35] The [Senior] Theras, the junior bhikkhus and those of the middle grade [4]—[in fact] every member of the Buddhist Order should seek sleep at midnight, engrossed in thoughts on the fourfold discriminations [5] and (thereby) should give repose to the body.

They should rise at dawn and should pass the morning [6] perambulating and immersed in meditation [7].

They should then rehearse a text which they had learnt.

They should, thereafter, don the yellow robe, covering themselves properly with it, and, after they have finished cleansing the teeth [8], and have attended to the duties specified in the Khandaka [9], such as those rules of conduct in respect of the Dāgabas, the Sacred Bodhi tree, the Temple terrace, the preceptors, the

---

[1] *Vyakta* is explained in the *Kudusika-sanne* as one who has heard and learnt that portion of the Buddhist scriptures, which is appropriate for one's redemption from *nissaya*, the probationary period when he is *in statu pupillari*. See *Kudusika-sanne* (Colombo edition of 1894, p. 79), also *S. B. E.*, xvii. p. 337, note 3.

[2] See *S. B. E.*, xiii. Pt. I, pp, xxiv–xxvi. For enumerations of *dukkaṭa* offences, see *Cullavagga* v., *Mūlasikkhā* and *Khuddasikkhā* as well as *Sikhavaḷaňda* and *Sikhavaḷaňda-vinisa*.

[3] See *Mahāvagga* ii and iv.

[4] *Sthavira nava madhyama häma saṁghayā.* Cf. *bahū bhikkhū therā ca navā ca majjhimā ca*, 'many bhikkhus, old and middle-aged and young' (*Cullavagga* vi, 1.)

[5] *Sati-sampajañña.* For a detailed explanation, see *Sumaṅgala-vilāsinī: Sāmaññaphala-sutta-vaṇṇanā.*

[6] *Davas gevā*, lit. 'passing the day'.

[7] *Kamaṭahan.* See the *Pāli Dict.*, s.v. *kammaṭṭhānam.*

[8] *Dähäṭi-kisa.* See *E. Z.*, Vol. I., p. 99, note 4. For the use of tooth-sticks, see *Cullavagga* v. 31 (*S. B. E.*, xx. pp. 146–148).

[9] *Kandu-vatu.* P. *khandaka-vatta.* See *Cullavagga*, viii. and *Visuddhimagga*, 12, 101.

theras, the sick and the lodging places[1], should, if need arise, enter the refectory, partake of the gruel and finish attending to the requirements of the refectory.

Then, with the exception of those (bhikkhus) who have pressing duties to perform, such as the consultation of books and documents, sewing (robes, &c.), dyeing, distribution of priestly requisites, &c.; all the rest, soon after they had partaken of the gruel, should pass the time deep in meditation[2].

After the midday meal[3] too, they should be occupied in obligatory study and introspective meditation[4] as already stated.

They should thus pass the time without consorting with lay or priestly society[5] until the time arrives for [the performance of] obligatory duties.

[Lines 35–40] As it is declared[6] 'Oh Bhikkhus! There are two things [one of] which should be observed by the assembled [monks, namely] religious conversation or noble silence', so, those [bhikkhus] also, who have congregated for [holding] a Paritta ceremony, should not dwell upon worldly[7] talk or sinful thoughts, sensual and the like, which are outside [the sphere of] the two subjects, religious talk and meditation, unless indeed there exists a cause which precludes one from observing the correct deportment[8].

Moreover they should spend the first watch of the night in a manner void of emptiness, such as in preaching (the doctrine), reading (the scriptures), hearing or learning (the same) by heart, conversing on religious topics, &c., and in the task of introspective meditation; and when the middle watch has come, they should seek sleep engrossed in discriminative thoughts[9].

The bhikkhu-wayfarers who arrive from some business which had to be transacted outside [monastery precincts] should take up their lodgings at an appropriate[10] place, such as the hermits' hut[11], the image house and the like.

---

[1] *Senāsana*, lit. 'sleeping and sitting' bed and chair. See *Cullavagga*, viii. 7. Cf. *äduru-vat*, *tera-vat*, *āgantuka-vat*, *gamika-vat*, *senasun-vat*, and *gilan-vat* in *Sikhavaḷaňda* and *Sikhavaḷaňda-vinisa* (Jayatilaka's edition, pp. 9 and 83).

[2] *Kamaṭahan-hiyedī* connotes, more the idea of concentrating their minds on the instruments of meditation.

[3] *Pas-bat*. P. *pacchābhatta*.

[4] *Grantha-vidarçanā-dhura*.

[5] Cf. *Cullavagga*, iv. 1–2.

[6] In *Majjhima-nikāya*, *Vagga* iii. *Ariyapariyesana-sutta*.

[7] *Tiraççina-kathā* 'animal talk' i.e. wrong or childish talk in general. Cf. *Mahāvagga*, v. 6.

[8] *Iriyav*, see above, p. 277, n. 2.

[9] *Sati sampajaññayen yut*.

[10] *Käpa* = P. *kappiya* 'allowable' according to Vinaya rules.

[11] Or 'the backyard shed'. Cf. *päsulu dora*.

At all times, bhikkhus should refrain from uttering inappropriate words with any one either in anger or in fun [1].

They should not hold conversation in secret either with the opposite sex [2], even though she be (one's own) mother, or with a youth, even though he be (one's own) younger brother.

They should not be angry with servants without [first] complaining to the elders [regarding the servants' misdeeds].

Articles whatsoever belonging to oneself should not be given away to another without the permission of the elders.

[Lines 40–45] If rain fall while the bhikkhus are on a journey, they should continue their natural walking gait, and arrive at a place where they will not get wet, provided that they do not carry in their hands any articles of equipment [robes, &c.] belonging to the elder monks, that are liable to be damaged by the wet [3]. If there be such an equipment, they should indeed go in appropriate haste.

As it is stated [4] '.. .. .. that is only proper', so, even if there be a just cause for laughter, the bhikkhus should only show their mirth with mouths closed and with no sound allowed to escape [5].

The disputes which are being settled in a monastery which one has entered, should not be made known outside, nor should one take upon himself the disputes of another monastery which are also being settled [6].

As it is stated [7] 'a bhikkhu who does not give up even a little of the religious life ought not to exercise desire for material enjoyment, even in respect of things permissable to him [according to the Vinaya code]', therefore bhikkhus should not be coveteous even in respect of requisites allowed [by the Vinaya rules].

They should not talk whilst in the act either of worshipping the dāgabas, the Sacred Bodhi tree, &c., or in the act of making offerings of frankincense,

---

[1] Lit. 'with angry mind or with playful mind.

[2] *Visabhāga.*

[3] Cf. *Sace maggaṁ gacchantena buddhatarānaṁ parikkhāro gahito hoti deve vassante magga-majjhe ṭhitaṁ sālaṁ pavisituṁ vaṭṭati, sace na kiñci gahitaṁ hoti sālāyaṁ ṭhassāmiti vegena gantum na vaṭṭati pakati gatiyā gantvā paviṭṭhena pana yāva vassuparamā ṭhatvā gantabbaṁ.* (*Visuddhimagga*, Colombo edition, 1890, p. 273.)

[4] The Pāli quotation is illegible on the estampages we possess.

[5] Cf. *Pātimokkha*: *Sēkhiyā* rule 12 and *Sikhavaḷaňdā-vinisa.*

[6] The exact meaning of this passage is not clear. *Adhikaraṇa* means also 'management of affairs', 'administration', and *san-hiňdena* 'being cut, destroyed, alloyed or appeased'.

[7] *Samantapāsādikā: Kaṭhina-vagga, Navama sikkhāpada-vaṇṇanā.*

flowers, &c., or of using the tooth-stick[1], or of slipping the begging-bowl into its case.

They should not converse with the lay persons of the village on matters touching the priestly requisites or on unorthodox subjects[2].

As it is stated in the *Anācāra-nirdeça*[3] (Definition of misconduct), 'whatsoever person[4] enters a congregation of bhikkhus and with no respect for them, stands or sits knocking against the senior bhikkhus[5] or speaks standing [in close proximity to them] or swaying his arms to and fro or strokes the head of a boy [he commits a misdemeanour]'. Therefore those [bhikkhus] who move amongst the members of the Buddhist Order, should not brush against them (the senior monks) either with their bodies or with their robes.

[Lines 46–51] If there be a matter which needs talking over with a senior bhikkhu, the junior should converse with him with a show of regard for him and with his body bent forward (respectfully). He should not stand too near or sway his arms.

He should never at any place put his arms round a boy's body and console him.

He should recite [and learn the scriptures] without disturbing those in the Hall of meditation.

As it is stated[6] 'when admitting [persons] into the priesthood, admit them after examination, ordain them after examination, give them (your) protection after examination. For, when even one son of a respectable family receives admission into the priesthood and (subsequently) the *upasampadā* ordination, he is instrumental in the establishment of even the whole Buddhist church'. Therefore, admission into the Buddhist Order should be made after examination. Likewise the *upasampadā* ordination as well as the *nissaya* protection ought to be conferred after examination. One should cultivate the Dhūtaṅga[7] ascetic practices as much as one can.

No ill shall be spoken [of any one] for unwillingly observing these aforesaid duties.

---

[1] *Dävuṭu*, spelt also *däviṭu*, and *däviṭi* as *däviṭi-daṇḍu* (*Visuddhimagga-sanne*, p. 360).

[2] Cf. *Vusuddhimagga-Sīlaniddeso-Vācasika-anācāra-vagga* (pp. 14–15 of edition, Colombo, 1920).

[3] *Ibid.*, *Kāyika-anācāra-vaṇṇanā.*

[4] Referring most probably to a junior bhikkhu.

[5] The Sinhalese *sanne* adds 'either with his robes or with his body'.

[6] In *Samantapāsādikā : Cullavagga*, *Senāsanaggāha-vinicchaya-vaṇṇanā.*

[7] For explanation and scriptural references, see Rhys Davids's *Pali Dictionary* s.v. *Dhūta.*

Whosoever conducts himself in disobedience to and in violation of the disciplinary injunctions which have thus been enacted, shall receive the punishment due to the offence committed and be warned.

When this has been done three times successively and the bhikkhu still continues his misbehaviour in the selfsame manner, he shall not be given *nissaya* protection, but, after letting him remain (in the monastery) a month, if his demeanour be not in accordance with the Vinaya precepts, he should be expelled, and no one should hold communion with him.

Likewise, if the Theras who are heads of chapters of monks should neglect their respective duties and [as a result] fail to bring their community of bhikkhus under discipline, they should receive the punishments determined by the Senior Theras.

No. 42 (Reg. No. 3). KANTALÄI GAL-ĀSANA INSCRIPTION OF KITTI NISSAṄKA-MALLA (1187–1196 A.D.).

THIS stone seat (*gal-āsana*) was discovered in 1921 in the village of Kantalāi[1] on the Trincomalee Railway trace at a spot in 'section 2, mile 14, chains 77 and 78'. It has since been removed to Anurādhapura where it now lies among others brought together from various localities.

As shown in the illustration on this page the seat has a moulded base three feet in height surmounted by a slab measuring 3 ft. $5\frac{1}{2}$ in. square. The surface of this top piece is made smooth. Like other *āsanas* of the kind, this too is engraved with an inscription between ruled lines, 2 in. apart, running parallel to each side of the square and leaving a blank space of $6\frac{1}{2}$ in. square at the centre[2].

The **letters** are fairly well cut, averaging in size from 1 to 2 in., and represent the type of the Sinhalese alphabet in use in the twelfth and thirteenth centuries[3].

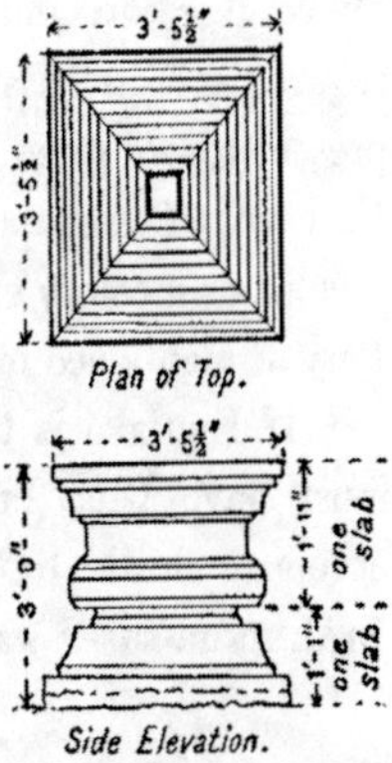

No. 3 'Āsana' Slab at Kantalāi on the Trincomalee railway trace. Now in Anurādhapura.

The **orthography** is correct with the exception of those points noted below.

---

[1] Kantalāi is Tamil for *Gaṁ-* or *Gaṅga-taḷā*, see above, pp. 140, 142, 144, and 147.

[2] See Plate 38.

[3] See *E.Z.*, Vol. I, No. 9; and II, Nos. 13–16.

The **language** is in keeping with the style of **Kitti Nissaṅka-Malla's** other records; the phraseology of the first line like that of the first three lines of his Daṁbulla inscription being copied from earlier epitaphs either of Vijaya-Bāhu I or of Parakkama-Bāhu I [1].

The **contents** are practically the same as those of many other *gal-āsana* records of Nissaṅka-Malla, forming as they do, only the oft-repeated bombastic account of his military achievements and charitable acts by way of an introduction to the principal statement, indicating that the stone seat on which the present epitaph is engraved, was the one that His Majesty Kitti Nissaṅka-Malla, after his return from the Indian campaign, used to occupy whilst witnessing the various diversions such as alms-giving, dancing, singing, &c., in the **Pārvatī-satra** erected at this king's request in **Caturveda-Brahmapura,** 'the city of the Four-Vedic Brahmans'.

The inscription is not **dated,** but from the references to his tours of inspection and his alleged expedition to India, we may class it among those records indited at about the end of his short but eventful reign of nine years (1187–1196).

In the articles on the Prītidānaka-maṇḍapa and on Sāhasamalla's slab, above Nos. 29 and 36, we put together all the information then available regarding Kitti Nissaṅka-Malla's lineage, his *biruda* titles, and his career. The present record gives nothing fresh, save the reference to a Pārvatī-satra built in Caturveda-Brahmapura. The former was probably an alms-hall established in honour or memory either of his mother Pārvatī Mahādevī [2] or of Her Highness Pārvatī mentioned in the Hāṭadāgē wall-inscription [3].

If Kantalāi is the original site of the present *gal-āsana,* then this locality must have been once the town called **Caturveda-Brahmapura,** probably occupied mostly by Brahman families for whose benefit an almshouse called **Brāhmaṇa-satra** was also established by this King Nissaṅka-Malla [4].

TEXT.

1 A. සිරිවත් අපිරියත් (ලො ඉ)කුත් ගුණ මුළිනුතුරත් මුළු දඹදිවුහි (අන්) කැත් කුල පාමිලි (කළ)

B. (ය)ක්‍ෂ ප්‍රළය කොට‍ැ ලංකාව මනුෂ්‍යවාස කළ විජයරාංජයන්වහන්සේගෙ පරම්පරාංවෙන් අ ලක්

[1] See above, p. 204.
[2] See above, p. 221.
[3] See above, p. 92. This lady might possibly be identical with the King's mother.
[4] See above, p. 178.

C. දිවූ පොළො(යො)න් පරපුරෙන් හිමි නොමින් ගුණ ගැඹර තෙද නිසල
සොමිගුණ(වත් දිනිස)[1]

D. රූ රජසිරිත (දත්) මහ(වතුරු) සත් සෙත් කුලුණු යස සිරින් පුන් **කලිඟු
පෙරකුඹා මහර**

2 A. **ජයාවහන්සේ** සිරිලක පැදකුණු කොටැ අතඹුලු පකක් සෙ බලා නිෂ්ක
ණ්ට ක

B. රවා මහවැතැනැ ප්‍රාණීනට අභය දී පිසඹුරුවත ද කැතිඅඩ ද හැමැ
කලට

C. මැ ගැරැ උත්තෙ අමුණට අය එකමුණු තුන් පැළ හා මඩරන් සක හා
මැදෙඬු අ

D. මුණට එකමුණු දෙපැළ හා මඩරන් සතරක් හා පස්සෙ අමුණට එකමුණු
පැළ හා ම

3 A. ඩරන් තුනක් බැගින් ගනුත් මුත් වඩා නො ගන්නා නියායෙන් ව්‍යවස්ථා
කොටැ ග

B. වුරුදුපතා පස්තුලාභාරයක්බැගින් තැගී අනෙක ප්‍රකාර වස්ත්‍රාභරණ

C. නවරත්න දානයෙන් ලොසතුන් සනහා දස්කම් කළවුනට පමුණු දෙන
කලැ

D. දුන් රජදරුවන් මඩ ගත්තවුන් නම ද බොහො කලක් පවත්නා පරිද්

4 A. දෙන් තාම්‍රශාසන දී **කලිඟු** වෙග **කණ්ණට නෙල්ලූර** ආ

B. දිවූ නො එක් දෙශයෙන් ඇත් අස් බොහො පරිවාර සහිත

C. වූ බිසොවරුඤ ගෙන්වා **නිශ්ශංකමල්ල** යන විරුදුවට සුදු

D. සුවැ නො එක් රජ්දරුවන් කරා හට්ටයන් යවා තනි අඟිමු

5 A. (ද[2]) ඉල්වා නො ලදින් පූඩාශාවෙන් සිවුරගසෙන

B. ග පිරිවරා සමුද්‍රොල්ලසනය කොටැ දෙවන වාරෙහි

C. **සොළී පඬි** දෙරට් ම(ඩ)යට්[3] ගොස් වනතැනැ දෙරටැ

D. ඇත්තවුන් භයින් රට් තබා පලායිය හෙයින් **සා**

6 A. **ඕරමැ** තුන් මසක් ගිනැ සමාන ප්‍රතිමල්ලයන්

B. නැතිහෙයින් තුලාභාර නැඟී නානා ප්‍රකාර ව

C. සතු දානයෙන් නත් දෙසෙනොසල මුළු දිළිඳුන්

D. සිත් පූරා එතන්හි ජයස්තම්භ කොටැ

7 A. **නිශ්ශංකෙශ්වරය** යන දෙවාලයක් ද ක[ර]වා

B. මෙසෙ කළ නො එක් වික්‍රමයෙන් භය ප

---

[1] දිනිසුරු? [2] 'අඹිමදී' වියයුතුයි. [3] 'මධ්‍යයට්' වියයුතුයි.

C. ත්වූ **සාඩ්‍ය** රාජයන්ගෙන් ඇත් අස්

D. බොහො පරිවාර සහිතවූ තිසොවරුන්

8 A. හා සත්‍රුයට ගම්වරක් ආදිවූ අයද

B. **සොළීරටින්** එවූ පඬුරු ද ගෙනැ ගු

C. ණ කැමැති රජදරුවන් හා මිත්‍ර

D. සැඳෑන කොටැ ගුණ නො කැමැ

9 A. ති රජදරුවන්ගේ දප්පය මැඩැ

B. උන් උන්ගෙන් එවූ බොහො පඬුරු

C. ද ගෙනැ ලක්දිවට වැඩැ **වත්‍ර**

D. **වේවද බ්‍රහ්මපුරයෙහි** නැං

10 A. වූ **පාවීවතීසත්‍රයෙහි**

B. දත් බලා වදාරන පිණි

C. සැ (පසැදන) නෘත්‍ය ගී

D. තාද්‍යනෙක ක්‍රීඩා

11 A. වෙ නිපූත්තවැ වැ

B. ඩැ ගිඳිනා

C. **ශිලාසනයයි** 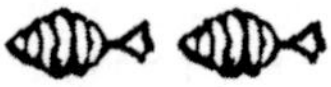

TRANSCRIPT.

1 A. Sirivat apiriyat (lo i)kut guṇa muḷin-uturat muḷu Daṁbadivuhi (an) kät-kula pāmili (kaḷa)

B. (y)akṣa praḷaya koṭä Laṁkāva manuṣya-vāsa kaḷa Vijaya-rājayan-vahansēge paramparāven ā Lak-

C. divu poḷo(yo)n parapuren himi nomin guṇa gäṁbara teda nisala somi-guṇa(vat dinisa-)[1]

D. -ru rajavirita (dan) maha (vaturu) sat set kuluṇu yasa sirin yut **Kaliṅgu Perakuṁbā Mahara-**

2 A. **japā-vahansē** siri-Laka pädakuṇu koṭä at-aṁbulu pakak se balā niṣkanṭa ka-

B. -ravā mahavā-tänä prāṇīnṭa abhaya dī pisaṁburu-vata da käti-aḍa da hämä kalaṭa-

C. -mä härä utte amuṇaṭa aya ek-amuṇu tun pāḷa hā maňḍa-ran saka hā mände a-

D. -muṇaṭa ek-amuṇu de-pāḷa hā maňḍa-ran satarak hā passe amuṇaṭa ek amuṇu pāḷa hā ma-

[1] *Dinisuru?*

Scale about 2⅛ inches to 1 foot

From an ink-impression supplied by the Archaeological Survey, Ceylon.

3 A. -ṅda-ran tunak bägin ganut mut vaḍā no gannā niyāyen vyavasthā koṭā ha-
B. -vurudu-patāpas- tulābhārayak-bägin tāgī aneka prakāra vastrābharaṇa
C. nava-ratna-dānayen lo-sasun sanahā das-kam kaḷavunṭa pamuṇu dena kalä
D. dun rajadaruvan maṅḍa gattavun nama da boho kalak pavatnā parid-

4 A. -den tāṁbra-çāsana dī **Kaliṅgu Veṅga Karṇṇāṭa Nellūra** ā-
B. -divū no ek deçayen ät as boho parivāra sahita-
C. vū bisovarun-da genvā **Niççaṁka-Malla** yana viruduvaṭa sudu-
D. -su-vä no ek rajadaruvan karā bhaṭṭayan yavā tani abhi-mu-

5 A. (-dra [1]) ilvā no ladin yuddhā-çāven sivuraṅga-sena-
B. -ṅga pirivarā sumudrollasanaya koṭā devana vārehi
C. **Soḷī Paṅḍī** de-raṭ ma(ddha)yaṭ [2] gos van-tänä de-raṭā
D. ättavun bhayin raṭ tabā palāgiya heyin **Pā-**

6 A. **-ṅḍi-raṭä** tun masak hindä samāna pratimallayaṁ
B. näti-heyin tulā-bhāra näṅgī nānā prakāra va-
C. -stu dānayen nan deseno saḷa muḷu diḷṅdun
D. sit purā etanhi jaya-stambha koṭā

7 A. **Nīççaṁkeçvaraya** yana devālayak da ka[ra]vā
B. mese kaḷa no ek vikramayen bhaya pa-
C. -tvū **Pāṅḍya**-rājayangen ät as
D. boho parivāra sahita-vū bisovarun

8 A. hā satrayaṭa gam-varak ādivū aya-da
B. **Soḷī-raṭin** evu paṅḍuru-da genä gu-
C. -ṇa kämäti rajadaruvan hā mitra
D. sandhāna koṭā guṇa no kämä-

9 A. -ti rajadaruvangē darppaya mäḍä
B. un ungen evū boho paṅḍuru-
C. da genä Lak-divaṭa vädä **Catu-**
D. **-rvveda-Brahma-purayehi** näṁ-

---

[1] Read *abhimarda*.

[2] Read *madhyayaṭ*.

10 A. -vū **Pārvvatī-satrayehi**
B. dan balā vadārana piṇi-
C. -sä (pasädana) nṛtya gī-
D. -tādy=aneka krīḍā

11 A. -ve niyukta-vä vä-
B. -ḍä hindinā
C. **çilāsanayayi**

TRANSLATION.

[Lines 1–4] The illustrious monarch **Kaliṅgu Perakumbā**[1], abounding in a multitude of virtuous qualities which are pre-eminent in the boundless world; lord by (right of his) lineal descent from the lords[2] of the soil of the Island of Laṅkā, who were descended from the race of King Vijaya, that threw into shade the other Kṣatriya races of Daṁbadiva[3], and that made Laṅkā a habitation for man by extirpating the yakṣas; [His Majesty] who is gloriously endowed with qualities which are manifold, deep, majestic, unchangeable and gentle, [rich as] the Lord of wealth[4] (Kubera), of kingly mien, floodlike in gifts[5] and sympathetic for the happiness of living beings,[6] was pleased to make tours[7] throughout prosperous Laṅkā, inspect it thoroughly as if it were a ripe *nelli* fruit on the palm of his hand[8] and free it from the thorns of lawlessness.

[His Majesty, moreover], gave security to animal life[9] in great tanks, remitted for all times the taxes *pisaṁburu-vata*[10] and *käti-ada*[11] and enacted that taxes should not be levied exceeding one *amuṇa*[12] and three *pāḷa*[12] [in grain]

---

[1] For his full name, see *E.Z.*, Vol. I, p. 124, and II, p. 91.

[2] See *E.Z.*, Vol. I, p. 26, n. 10, and p. 248, n. 7.

[3] Skt. *Jambudvīpa*, India.

[4] *Dinisaru* = *dinisuru*, Skt. *dhaneçvara*. Cf. *denen dinisuran* 'the Lord of Riches in wealth' in the Aṁbagamuva rock, line 11 (above p. 213).

[5] *Dan maha vatura*. Cf. *dan-vaturen levan upulvay* 'having made the people float on the flood of his gifts' in the slab-inscription of Mahinda IV (*E.Z.*, Vol. I, p. 235), and *dāna pravāha* in No. 13, line 19 above, p. 79.

[6] *Sat-set-kuluṇu*. Cf. *E.Z.*, Vol. I, No. 9, line 3, and II, No. 35, line 12.

[7] *Pādakuṇu koḷā* = Skt. *pradakṣiṇā-kṛtvā* 'circumambulating from left to right of a person or object.

[8] See *E.Z.*, Vol. I, p. 134, note 1.

[9] See also No. 21 above, l. 2.

[10] See above p. 117, n. 11.

[11] See above, pp. 72 and 117.

[12] See *E. Z.*, Vol. I., p. 3, n. 4, p. 55, n. 3, and p. 103, n. 11.

and six *maṅḍa-ran*[1] (in coin) for an *amuṇa* [sowing extent of land] of the *utte* (uppermost) tract, one *amuṇa* and two *pāḷa* and four *maṅḍa-ran* for an *amuṇa* of the *mände* (middle) tract, and one *amuṇa* and one *pāḷa* and three *maṅḍa-ran* for an *amuṇa* of the *passe* (lowermost) tract[2].

His Majesty presented also five *tulābhāras*[3] every year [to the people] and with the bestowal of gifts of the nine precious gems[4] and of divers kinds of clothes and ornaments, he conciliated the Church and the State.

Further, when bestowing perpetual grants (*pamuṇu*) to those who have performed loyal services, His Majesty gave these grants [engraved] on copper plates in order that both the royal donor's name and the donee's name may last for a long time[5].

[Lines 4–7] From various countries **Kaliṅga, Veṅga, Karṇṇāṭa, Nellūru**[6], &c., His Majesty had queens brought to him, together with large retinues of elephants and cavalry. True to his title **Niççaṅka-Malla** (dauntless warrior), he dispatched champions to [the Courts of] various kings and sought single combats[7]. Finding none, and yet being desirous of martial contests, he crossed over the sea[8], accompanied by his fourfold army. When on the second occasion he entered the Coḷa and the Pāṇḍya countries with intent to conquer them, the owners of the two countries gave up their territories through fear and took to flight. So, His Majesty remained three months in the Pāṇḍyan kingdom, and, not finding an adversary that would be his match [in a contest], he mounted the scale-pan and, giving away his weight of various kinds of wealth, filled [with satisfaction] the hearts of the poor that thronged from various quarters[9]. Moreover, he had pillars of victory set up there and caused also a temple (*dēvālaya*) named **Niççaṅkēçvara** to be built.

---

[1] *Ibid.*, p. 133, n. 2. See also Codrington's *Ceylon Coins and Currency*, pp. 80, 199.

[2] See above, p. 117, n. 1. [3] See above, p. 73. [4] See above, p. 118, n. 4.

[5] Cf. *Das-kam kaḷavunṭa dena hira-sanda-pamuṇu vēyan mīyan kana patä liyā diyehi ändi hiri-se asthira no koṭā ungē vaṁça-paramparāvaṭa boho kal siṭinā paridden hā ungē namat dun rajadaruvangē namat pasvādahasaṭa pavatnā paridden tāmbra çāsana Laṁkāyehi pavai-koṭā* in Kāliṅga Park Gal-āsana, above, No. 21, lines 3–5.

[6] See also Häṭa-dā-gē Vestibule Inscription, above, No. 15, line 8.

[7] *Tani abhimarda ilvā.* The phrase usually employed to express this idea in other records of this king is *dvandva-yuddha senā-yuddha ilvā.*

[8] *Samudrollasanaya koṭä* 'having effected a jump over the sea'.

[9] Cf. *Anurādhapurehi nan desen osaḷa muḷu diḷindun sit purā* in Līlāvatī's Inscription (*E.Z.*, Vol. I., No. 14, lines 12–14). Nissaṅka-Malla's Daṁbulla Record (*ibid.*, No. 9), line 18 should, therefore, read *tulābhāra vastu dānayen nan desen osaḷa muḷu diḷiṅdun*, &c.

[Lines 7–11] From the Pāṇḍyan king who was frightened by the heroic deeds thus performed, His Majesty accepted [tributes of] elephants, horses, queens with large escorts, endowments of a village income [1] and the like to alms-houses, as well as the [peace] offerings sent from the Coḷa country. He established friendly alliances also with such of the princes as were desirous of his goodwill; but crushed the arrogance of those princes who did not wish such friendship. Then, accepting the many peace offerings sent from each of them, he returned to the Island of Laṅkā.

Thereafter, he proceeded to witness [the distribution of] alms in the **Pārvatī** alms-hall erected in [the town called] **Caturveda-Brahmapura.** And this stone seat does His Majesty occupy whilst engaged in witnessing the various diversions [that take place therein], such as dancing, singing [2], and the like.

---

[1] *Gam-varak.* This may be a derivative of either Skt. *grāma-kara* (*gam-kara* > *gam-vara* as *sil-karu* > *sil-varu*), or, as Dr. Barnett suggests, of Sinh. *gam* + Tamil *vāra.* Cf. T. *mēl-vāra* and *kīḻ-vāra.*

[2] Or 'theatrical plays and concerts' (*nṛtya-gītā*).

INDEX

The following is a complete index of words and proper names occurring in the first and second volumes of the Epigraphia Zeylanica.